THE

WILLARD J. GRAHAM SERIES

IN ACCOUNTING

BOOKS IN
THE WILLARD J. GRAHAM SERIES
IN ACCOUNTING

COST ACCOUNTING

Principles and Practice

COST ACCOUNTING

Principles and Practice

The First Phase of Managerial Control

for Attaining the Profit Objective

of Business Operations

JOHN J. W. NEUNER, Ph.D.

Certified Public Accountant (New York)
Professor of Accounting
Bernard M. Baruch School of Business and Public Administration
The City University of New York

SAMUEL FRUMER, D.B.A.

Certified Public Accountant (Indiana)
Professor of Accounting
Graduate School of Business
Indiana University

Corrected Seventh Edition · 1967
RICHARD D. IRWIN, INC.
Homewood, Illinois

Seventh Edition

First Printing, May, 1967
Second Printing, March, 1968
Third Printing, August, 1968
Fourth Printing, June, 1969
Fifth Printing, July, 1970

Printed in the United States of America

Library of Congress Catalog Card No. 67–15837

Preface

This seventh edition has been prepared to update cost accounting methods and procedures in a rapidly changing business world, and to improve the teachability of the already most teachable collegiate cost accounting textbook.

To bring the subject matter of the text up to date, a chapter on the planning budget has been added early in the text (Chapter IV). This has been found desirable because of the importance of budgetary procedures in modern management and because of its importance in accumulating the costs of manufacturing overhead, and analyzing manufacturing cost operations.

The subject matter of the learning curve and PERT-Cost have been included in the discussion of estimated cost accounting. Later in the text, the more intricate problems of budgeting in its relation to cost accounting are discussed as precedent to a study of the managerial aspects of standard costs, cost-volume, break-even, direct costing and distribution cost accounting. A section has been added, because of numerous requests, on how to install a cost accounting system.

To improve the teachability and accelerate the study of cost accounting, the discussion of the basic principles and practices of cost accounting in the first nine chapters has been revised, condensed, and supplemented with new questions and problem material. As in the past editions, alternate sets of problems have been provided. All problems contain an introductory statement of the educational purpose involved. The three practice sets—Job Order, Process Costing, and Standard Costs—have been revised, and, where possible, shortened. The initial transactions in each set have been worked out as an illustrative guide for the student, thus facilitating the teaching and learning of the subject matter, and at the same time serving as a comprehensive review of the principles and practices previously learned. New and revised objective tests have been prepared to use with the text.

To obtain a better balance of the entire subject matter of cost accounting, the basic principles and practices applicable to job order and process cost accounting have been reduced from seventeen to fourteen chapters, thus permitting a greater emphasis on the managerial use of cost data. Since the majority of manufacturing firms in the United States are engaged in some form of process or departmental manufacturing operations, the most comprehensive discussion of this phase of costing has been retained in the six chapters devoted to these principles and practices. Eleven chapters are devoted to the managerial use of cost data through an improved presentation of the comprehensive budget, standard costs, managerial reports, cost system installation, profit planning through direct costing, cost-volume-profit analyses, distribution costs and nonmanufacturing costs.

For his excellent critical review of the revised manuscript, the authors are indebted to Professor Dennis Gordon of the University of Akron. Since no revision of an established textbook is ever the sole work of its authors, grateful acknowledgment is made to the many unnamed students and professors, who have over the years offered valuable suggestions for improvements and changes for this Seventh Edition.

Finally, but not least in the author's acknowledgments must be noted the colleagues and administrators of the Bernard M. Baruch School of Business and Civic Administration of the City University of New York, and the Graduate School of Business, Indiana University, for their constant interest and encouragement in the preparation of this revision. Among these must be included, Dr. Emanuel Saxe, dean, and Dr. Nathan Seitelman, chairman of the Accountancy Department of the Baruch School, and D. Lyle Dieterle, chairman of the Department of Accounting, Indiana University.

May, 1967

JOHN J. W. NEUNER
SAMUEL FRUMER

Table of Contents

SECTION III
PRINCIPLES AND PRACTICES OF PROCESS COST ACCOUNTING

SECTION IV

MANAGERIAL CONTROL THROUGH THE USE OF COST ACCOUNTING DATA AND PROCEDURES

SECTION I

Managerial Implications,

Definitions, and Basic Procedures

Cost accounting provides quantitative information that helps in evaluating performance, making decisions, and controlling the activities of both profit and nonprofit-making organizations. It is concerned with such goals as improving efficiency, ascertaining unit costs, and gathering information needed to help set selling prices.

Cost accounting is not limited to manufacturing operations; it is equally useful in controlling distribution and administrative costs. Banks, hospitals, railroads, retailing organizations, and governmental units are among the institutions which can benefit from cost analysis.

The basic principles of cost accounting are introduced in this section. Emphasis is placed on the three elements which enter into the cost flow of a manufacturing operation: materials, labor, and overhead. Three introductory phases of cost accounting are discussed:

1. Managerial and organizational aspects of cost accounting.

2. Forms and entries in the manufacturing cost accounting cycle.

3. Accounting records of the cost accounting cycle.

CHAPTER

1 | Organizational and Managerial Aspects of Cost Accounting

The Nature of Cost Accounting

Cost accounting is an expanded phase of the financial accounting of a business concern which provides management promptly with the cost of producing or selling an article, or the cost of rendering a particular service. To be most effective cost accounting should provide for a comparison of these costs with predetermined or standard costs as a measure of the effectiveness of managerial control and administration. Special cost compilations and analyses may at times provide management with data useful in making decisions in such matters of whether to buy or make a product; whether a new machine should be purchased to replace an older one; and whether selling prices should be raised or lowered.

Cost accounting frequently involves much clerical work known as cost bookkeeping. Cost accounting data may be incorporated directly into the financial accounting records or may be compiled separately as statistical data. With the advent of electronic computers, it is now possible to collect more detailed information promptly and at lower costs. Action can then be taken in time to correct the inefficiencies.

Cost accounting work is influenced by a number of variable factors such as (1) the size of the firm; (2) the number of products being manufactured; (3) whether the products are standardized or made to order; (4) the complexity of the manufacturing or distribution operations; (5) the attitude of management toward the compilation and use of cost accounting data for managerial control; and finally, (6) the expense to be incurred in compiling effective cost information.

3

Managerial Implications in Cost Accounting   Business management's function is to plan business operations with certain definite objectives in mind. Although the basic objective is usually the realization of a profit, this objective is often realized through a variety of supplementary decisions such as making a better product at a lower price, making a new product, using newer materials or methods in production, and many others. Management accomplishes its basic objective by organizing the business activities and controlling the operations. Controlling business operations involves placing responsibility, which means that certain administrative personnel must be held accountable for the operating results of the business. Accountability is usually evidenced by accounting reports and data. Accounting reports include the customary historical financial statements, budgetary statements and comparisons, and detailed costs of production and distribution both on a historical and a predetermined basis. Without appropriate and detailed accounting data, management would not be able to control operations, nor be able to make the large number of decisions inherent in successful business operations. One of the important phases of managerial control through accounting data and reports revolves around costs and their compilation.

Cost Classifications and Concepts   Costs may be variously classified under the following headings:

1. Function of business activity.
2. Nature of manufacturing operations.
3. Time factor of cost determination.
4. Type of business activity.
5. Elements of the cost of production.
6. Relation to the volume of production.
7. Costs for planning and decision making.

1. *Costs classified according to the function of business activity.* For example:

a) *Manufacturing costs* deal with the cost of producing or manufacturing a definite product.

b) *Distribution or marketing costs* are incurred in selling a finished product and the sale of parts and services.

c) *Administrative costs* are incurred in administering and setting policies for all the activities of a business.

While all three types of costs are important to management, this text is primarily concerned with those relating to manufacturing.

2. *Costs classified according to the nature of manufacturing operations.*

a) *Job order costs* which refer to the material, labor, and manufacturing overhead necessary to complete a *specific* order or lot of finished goods. These goods may be manufactured for a specific customer or for the stock room. In this type of costs, a *definite quantity* is to be manufactured on a specific order. All material, labor, and overhead costs are accumulated and recorded on the basis of the amount used or assigned to this particular job or order. Since each job or order is given a number, the accumulations are recorded on a form known as the *job order cost sheet,* to which an identifying number has been assigned.

b) *Process* or *departmental costs* are used by firms manufacturing products on a more or less continuous or regular basis, and they include the production of such items as gas, electricity, chemicals, petroleum products, coal, minerals, etc. In such firms, costs are accumulated not on a job order basis but by *departments* or *processes,* for a *definite period of time.* Costs are recorded on *departmental cost sheets* and summarized on *cost of production reports.*

c) *Class costs* are a form of job order costs in which a number of jobs may be combined into a single production cycle, providing that they include a number of products of similar sizes or classes. The best illustration of this method is found in gray iron foundries where costs are determined by classes such as:

> Group I—a number of job orders calling for castings weighing from 1 to 10 pounds.
> Group II—refers to castings weighing from 11 to 25 pounds.
> Group III—refers to castings from 26 to 50 pounds, etc.

To compute the cost per pound of castings, costs must be apportioned on the basis of the amount of labor involved in each group or class of products.

d) *Assembly costs* are a form of job order costs used by firms which manufacture or purchase finished parts to be used in assembling a salable product. Many firms manufacturing such products as oil burners, washing machines, or vacuum cleaners use this method of assembling parts into a salable product. Assembly costs involve primarily labor and manufacturing overhead, since the costs of materials were determined when the parts were manufactured or purchased. The summary sheets used for compiling these costs are known as *assembly* or *subassembly cost sheets.*

3. *Costs classified according to time factor of cost determination* would include the following:

a) *Postmortem* or *historical costs* which may be job order, process, assembly, or class costs determined during the manufacturing operations but not available until some time *after* the completion of the manufacturing operations.

b) *Estimated, standard,* or *predetermined costs* which also may refer to job order, process, assembly, or class costs computed or ascertained *before* manufacturing operations begin. In other words, it is frequently necessary to compute beforehand the *expected* costs of manufacturing a product—

either to fix selling prices or to measure the effectiveness of the historical costs.

c) *Daily, weekly,* or *monthly costs* which refer essentially to continuous process work and merely indicate the period of time for which the summaries are prepared.

4. *Costs classified according to type of business activity.* Costs may also be classified according to type of business not engaged in manufacturing. This phase of cost accounting, though simpler than that of manufacturing costs, has been receiving increased attention in recent years. In this classification are found such cost analyses as:

a) *Cost accounting for banks,* whereby it is possible to determine, for example, the cost of maintaining a checking account, rendering a trust service, or making a loan.

b) *Cost accounting for municipalities,* whereby it is possible to compute the cost of police protection, fire protection, schools and education, water and sanitation services, etc.

c) *Cost accounting for retail or department stores,* which is a form of departmentalized distribution cost analysis.

d) *Cost accounting for large service organizations,* such as insurance companies, public utility firms, etc. This type is mainly an analysis of the costs of the various types of office work.

5. *Classifying costs by elements which make up the finished product.* Costs incurred in converting materials into a product ready for sale include:

a) *Direct material*—costs of the substances which can be identified with a specific unit of production or can be identified with a department or process.

b) *Direct labor*—wages paid for work done on a specific unit of production or performed in a specific department.

c) *Manufacturing overhead costs,* sometimes known as manufacturing expenses, are the variety of indirect manufacturing costs which cannot be identified and allocated, or which it is inexpedient to attempt to allocate, to specific units of production.

6. *Costs classified on the basis of volume of production.* Costs sometimes have a definite relationship to the volume of production. As such, they are described as *fixed* or *variable,* and sometimes further delineated as *semivariable.*

a) *Fixed costs* remain fairly constant and do not fluctuate with the volume of production, such as fire insurance on the buildings, depreciation of buildings and machinery, real estate taxes, and rent.

b) *Variable costs* fluctuate in the same manner as the volume of production. Among these are direct materials, direct labor, and such manufacturing overhead costs as supplies, electric power, compensation insurance, payroll taxes, royalties, and spoilage.

When such costs do not fluctuate consistently with production but by steps and degrees, a more precise description terms these costs as *semifixed* when certain costs arise because of plant expansion or *semivariable* as in the case of supervision and inspection. As volume increases, the per unit cost of the fixed costs decreases, whereas the per unit cost of the variable costs remains more or less constant.

These costs have been further characterized as *controllable* and *noncontrollable*. In the long run, all costs are controllable. However, in cost accounting, management is primarily concerned with the short-run controllable costs because these offer the greatest opportunities for cost reduction. Variable costs are the controllable costs because these are under the direction of intermediate management and supervisors who will be held accountable for operating results.

7. *Decision making and planning through costs.* These are costs compiled for use in making managerial decisions when there are alternatives. They are special situation costs and are sometimes termed economic costs. Such compilation of costs would provide the answers to these questions:

Should the firm buy or make all or part of its product?
Should the firm buy a new machine to replace an old one?
Should a firm take an order for a job at less than the total cost to manufacture?
What effect will raising or lowering the selling price have on the break-even point and earnings of the firm?

Cost Accounting's Contribution to More Effective Management Cost accounting must ultimately contribute either directly or indirectly to the maintenance of or increase in the profit of the firm. This goal is accomplished by furnishing management with important figures which can be used in making decisions which will either reduce the costs of production or increase the sales volume. Among the reasons why a business firm should have a cost accounting system which will contribute to the success of the business operations are the following:

1. *The determination of the costs* of the material, labor, and manufacturing overhead incurred on a specific job—or in a specific manufacturing department or for a specific process—in the manufacture of a single unit or a group of units for managerial control and reports. This work is known as cost finding or *cost keeping* and is essentially a routine bookkeeping or clerical operation.

2. Having determined these unit costs, management is able to study and analyze them *with the view of reducing them.* Reductions in cost may be effected by managerial decisions such as using substitute materials, changing the design of the product so that less material or fewer labor operations will be

required, changing wage systems to reduce idle labor or overtime labor costs, installing more modern and efficient machinery, and revising the procedures involved in purchasing and issuing materials to reduce waste. This analysis is known as *cost control* and becomes more effective when budgets and predetermined costs are used for comparative purposes.

3. Unit costs of production provide a guide for *testing the adequacy of selling prices.* Selling prices are influenced by competition, supply and demand, governmental regulations, and trade association practices, as well as by the costs of production. By means of a cost accounting system, the unit costs can be ascertained promptly so that any changes in selling prices may be made without delay, provided that competition and other outside influences permit it. Furthermore, a comparative study of unit costs of the same product over a long period of time may enable a manufacturer to decide whether the economies of production can be passed along to the buyers to increase the volume of sales.

4. An effective cost accounting system facilitates the preparation of a series of reports for *managerial decisions.* The essential purposes of some of these reports are:

a) Periodic comparisons of materials, labor, and manufacturing overhead costs by products or departments will enable management to exercise more specific and more prompt cost reduction control to eliminate inefficiencies. These comparisons may enable management to decide whether *to manufacture certain units* or *to purchase them,* and also, whether *to add new products* or *to drop unprofitable items now being produced.*

b) Specific reports on spoilage, scrap, defective work, idle time, efficiency of specific workmen, and inefficient or idle equipment help to localize specific areas of cost reduction and to place responsibility for inefficiencies.

c) Reports on the cost of plant and equipment operations will indicate whether to increase plant capacity or to use several shifts, or whether there is too much idle equipment which might be sold or used in producing new products. Sometimes this report will result in the acceptance of orders at less than full cost (but in excess of variable costs) so that some of the fixed manufacturing overhead costs can be absorbed by the additional production.

d) Reports on distribution costs may be used to determine what products should be emphasized by the sales force because of their larger margin of profit, what products are unprofitable and might be eliminated, what territories are not producing a sufficient volume of business and should either be further developed or eliminated, and finally what methods of distribution are most profitable for the firm.

The cost information supplied by these reports will be of direct value in making managerial decisions. In other cases, the cost data will be used to supplement or substantiate decisions made by the engineering or marketing divisions of a firm.

The Cost Accounting System

Although some firms compile their costs in the form of statistical data independent of the financial accounting records, the more effective method is the accumulation of cost data in the accounting records which are controlled by and subsidiary to those of the general financial accounting. Under the latter conditions, the cost accounting system is made up of a series of *forms, journals, ledgers, accounting entries, and management reports* integrated into an efficient series of procedures so that unit costs can be determined promptly and used in managerial decisions.

Among the forms that are commonly used in a cost accounting system are:

1. *Production orders* instructing the factory superintendent what to manufacture.
2. *Material requisitions* indicating the quantity and cost of materials used on the specific jobs or in the various producing departments.
3. *Job time tickets* indicating the quantity and cost of labor used on the specific jobs.
4. *Job order cost sheets* or *departmental cost of production reports* on which the material, labor, and overhead costs are accumulated.

Among the journals and ledgers which make up the cost accounting system are the following. These will be discussed and illustrated in more detail in Chapter 3.

1. *Factory journals* to record and summarize cost data.
2. *Stores, work-in-process,* and *finished goods* subsidiary ledgers.
3. Special subsidiary or departmentalized *manufacturing overhead ledgers.*

The journal entries used to record and summarize the cost accounting data shown on the various forms will be explained in detail in Chapter 2. Since a large variety of reports can be prepared to help management, a discussion of them is presented in Chapter 20 after the study of the basic mechanics of collecting and recording cost data has been given. These reports either summarize the results of manufacturing or measure the efficiency of men, materials, and machines used.

Functional Organization of the Cost Accounting Department Since cost accounting is an expansion of the financial accounting work, it is necessary to understand the function and importance of the accountant's role in modern business organization and management. The chief accounting officer in modern business is titled the *controller.* It is his job to organize the system, verify its operations, and present top management with the facts relating to the business operations. In many concerns today, the controller's department will cover the following: (*a*) general and financial accounting, (*b*) cost accounting, (*c*) budgeting, (*d*) systems and procedures, (*e*) internal auditing, (*f*) data processing, and (*g*) taxes and reports. Among the cost accounting activities are the records for inventory control, payroll accounting, preparing the manufacturing overhead budgets, determining the budgeted manufacturing overhead rates, compiling the costs by jobs or by departments, studying the

Illustration 1–1. Organization Chart of a Manufacturing Company

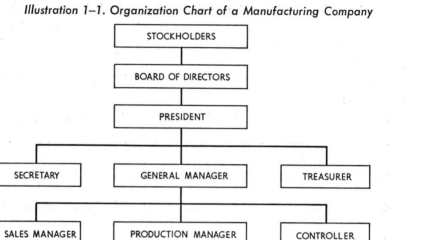

variations in costs, and preparing a number of special cost analyses and reports or summaries.

Illustration 1–1 indicates the functional organization of a manufacturing concern in which the chief accounting officer is the controller.

Illustration 1–2 shows the functional organization within the accounting department. In examining this chart, the place of the cost accounting department should be noted. This chart emphasizes the fact that the purpose of the cost accounting department is to record, compile, and analyze cost information and present it in administrative reports for managerial use.

Illustration 1–2. Organization of the Controller's Department

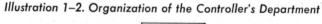

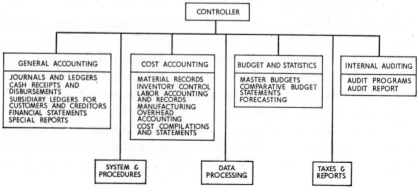

Governmental Influence
on Cost Accounting
At the present time, government interest in cost accounting operates through a number of regulatory agencies. The Internal Revenue Service is interested in cost accounting because the methods of computing costs have an effect on the income of a business concern and hence on the income tax report prepared for the government. The Federal Trade Commission is interested in cost accounting because the cost of manufacture and the cost of distribution are factors in determining compliance with the Robinson-Patman Act. The operation and enforcement of the Social Security Act comes under the control of the Internal Revenue Service. The Wages and Hours Law operates through the Labor Department. Either directly or indirectly, all of these agencies affect cost accounting.

For income tax purposes the government is particularly interested in the following four items because of their effect on costs and profits:

1. The valuation of inventories.
2. Rates of depreciation of plant equipment.
3. Valuation bases on which depreciation is computed.
4. Treatment of interest on investment as an element of cost.

The government's position on inventory valuation as reflected by the Internal Revenue Service is that the method used must conform, as nearly as possible, to the best accounting practice in the trade or industry in which the concern operates; and that, in addition, the inventory valuation practice must be consistent from year to year. Specific reference to income tax regulations affecting inventories is made in Chapter 5.

Items to be included in the cost of goods manufactured are specified by the Internal Revenue Service. Such regulations are necessary because the items used in the computation of costs affect the final figure on which income taxes are calculated. The general regulations require the inclusion of:

1. The cost of materials and supplies entering into or consumed in producing the article.
2. The cost of the direct labor used in manufacturing the article.
3. Indirect costs incident to and necessary for the production of the article. However, these indirect costs do *not* include the cost of selling, interest on capital, or estimated profit.

Depreciation of plant and equipment is included in the indirect costs. This item has given governmental tax bureaus a great deal of difficulty. Differences in the depreciation allowance may increase or decrease the cost of goods manufactured and, ultimately, the inventories and net income. The desire for correct operating statements, therefore, has caused governmental authorities, through the Internal Revenue Service, to specify methods and tentative depreciation rates to be used in preparing income tax returns.

The Robinson-Patman Act, enforced through the agency of the Federal Trade Commission, has stimulated and extended the interest of government in cost accounting. The purpose of the act is to prohibit price discrimination by the seller between purchasers of large and small quantities of the same goods. Unless a manufacturer can prove that the cost of selling (*distribution* or *marketing cost*) is less when sales are made in large quantities, he is prohibited from setting different unit prices for large and for small quantity orders.

The present defense program of the United States has brought the government into the market as a purchaser of huge quantities of naval and military materials. Most of these supplies are purchased through agreements with private contractors to manufacture according to government specifications. For these contracts the price is set in relation to the cost of production. In some instances, the price paid by the government is *cost plus a fixed fee.* Therefore, the government agents in making price agreements and the government accountants in examining a manufacturer's records to determine prices to be paid on contracts must be thoroughly familiar with cost accounting practices and procedures. These government officials must be able to distinguish between legitimate and incorrect charges to the cost of manufacturing; they need to know what items are to be omitted and what items included. They must be able to protect the interests of the government and yet allow the manufacturers fair prices. This interest of the government in cost accounting is of primary importance.

Because of laws such as the Federal Insurance Contribution Act, the federal and state unemployment insurance laws, and the Fair Employment and the wages and hours laws, accounting requirements for labor costs have been materially increased. Complete records must be kept of the time spent in employment, the hourly wages, and the total earnings. These governmental requirements for financial accounting have aided cost accounting in that the keeping of such records makes easier the task of compiling labor costs.

Managerial Expansion of Cost Accounting and Analysis   For many years cost accounting work has been concentrated in the field of manufacturing because in this area the greatest economies and reductions were possible since the cost of manufacturing constituted such a large part of the sales price. More recently cost analysis has been extended into the field of distribution because selling and distribution costs have increased proportionately so much that management has been forced competitively to give this area of cost control more attention. This expansion into the field of distribution costs has also been stimulated by the Robinson-Patman Act which requires proof of the lower distribution costs to justify giving some customers lower prices. Similarly, clerical and office costs have also risen greatly in recent years. Business firms such as banks, life insurance companies, public utilities, and even some industrial firms have large office staffs. To reduce the cost of office work in these instances has required a careful analysis of the procedures involved. Minimum wage and hour laws and the numerous governmental reports which must be prepared by business firms have caused management to take a second look at the office costs to simplify, reduce, and eliminate all unnecessary office work. State and local governmental organizations which have had difficulty in increasing their revenues through taxation have also been forced to apply cost control to their work. Department stores, chain stores, and wholesalers have studied their distribution and office costs in order to increase their profit margins. All of these cost controls and analyses follow the plans, principles, and procedures used in cost control of the manufacturing operations.

QUESTIONS FOR REVIEW

1. Future management must have better and cheaper cost accounting data than ever before. Explain how this will be possible and why it will be necessary.
2. Costs have a variety of classifications. Of these, which is considered basic or fundamental for all business concerns? Why?
3. What is the significance of the expression "costs for planning and decision making"? Be specific in its application.
4. Costs are frequently classified as fixed, variable, semivariable, and semifixed. What is the significance of this classification managerially?
5. What elements constitute a cost accounting system? Modern technology has changed the form of these elements but not the necessity for them. Explain.
6. In the functional organization of the cost accounting department, what relationship does the addition of a data processing department have on the cost accounting work?
7. In the future of American business, the government will have an even greater influence on cost accounting. Explain.
8. Why will the modern and progressive cost accounting system have a greater influence on decision making by management than ever before?
9. The executive of one of the largest corporations in the United States has stated that the major objective of business management is not necessarily

to increase sales or to develop new markets unless these result in a profit or an increase in profits for the firm. The main objective of business corporations today is to make or increase the profits. Assuming the accuracy of this statement, explain the cost accounting implications.

10. Cost accounting may be in the form of a statistical compilation of figures or may be integrated with the financial accounting records of the firm. What financial, managerial, or accounting advantages result from the integrated system? Do you feel that the additional cost of an integrated system is justified by its results? Explain.

PROBLEMS—GROUP A

Problem 1–1. Purpose: *Cost Computations and an Income Statement*

A combination home-appliance machine is produced and sold by the Johnson Corporation. The selling price of the machine in 1968 was $300, and 4,000 machines were sold. Cost of goods sold was $210 of which 50 percent was material cost, 20 percent was labor cost, and 30 percent was overhead of the factory. Selling and expenses of administration were $30 per unit.

During 1969, material costs are expected to increase 10 percent and labor costs are expected to increase 40 percent. It is expected that a 15 percent increase in selling price will result in a 30 percent decrease in sales. Selling and administrative expenses are not expected to change in 1969.

Required:

a) Prepare a projected income statement for 1969.

b) Prepare a projected income statement for 1969 under an additional assumption that $20 of the factory overhead consists of *fixed* costs and do not change as production changes.

Problem 1–2. Purpose: *Cost Computations and an Income Statement*

Jelson Industries manufactures a stamping machine which retails for $600. During the coming year, it plans to sell 700 of these machines. The projected net income is 15 percent on sales before taxes. Jelson purchases all of the parts for the machine on the outside and assembles them. The cost of all of the purchased parts is expected to be $140. Laborers are paid on a piece-rate basis at a cost of $150 per machine. As a result, to ensure a net income of 15 percent, the main controllable cost of the factory operations is the manufacturing overhead.

Selling expenses for the coming year are estimated at $35,000, and administrative expenses are estimated at $21,000.

Required:

a) Compute the maximum manufacturing overhead cost that can be incurred to realize the planned profit.

b) Prepare an income statement under the assumption that 750 machines were produced and 700 were sold.

Problem 1–3. Purpose: *Problem on Cost Computations*

The Jacques Boat Company produces and sells an outboard fiber glass boat for $500. The company is negotiating on an order for 600 boats with a large chain of department stores. The Jacques Company wants to bid on the order at a selling price so that in anticipation of certain changing costs it will realize the same ratio of *gross profit* as in the past.

Currently, material costs make up 20 percent of the cost of goods sold, labor costs are 40 percent, and manufacturing overhead 40 percent of cost of goods sold.

The expectation is that material costs will increase 10 percent and labor costs will increase 40 percent. The increased costs would cause a 40 percent decrease in the amount of gross profit on the present sales price of $500.

Required:

a) What price should the Jacques Boat Company quote for the order to obtain the same percentage of gross profit as before the price increases?

b) Prepare a projected schedule showing expected revenue, cost of goods sold, and gross profit from the order.

Problem 1–4. Purpose: *Relationships between Sales and Profits*

Management of the Joliet Company is contemplating adding a line of ash trays to its present line of candy dishes. The ash trays' addition would require an increase in the fixed costs of $54,000 per year. The variable costs are expected to be $2.10 per ash tray. The sales department estimates that the selling price would be $3 per ash tray.

Required:

a) At what point will the Joliet Company "break even" on the ash tray operation? (That is, at what point will there be no profit or loss?)

b) What will the profit be if 50,000 ash trays are sold? 70,000? 90,000?

c) How many ash trays must be sold if the company wants to earn a profit of $30,000 on its ash tray operation?

Problem 1–5. Purpose: *Relationships between Production and Profits*

During the month of August, the Jenkins Company manufactured 1,000 units of its one product and sold 900 of these. No inventories were on hand at the beginning of the month. The variable costs of production amounted to $8.10 per unit produced. Fixed costs of the factory were $60,000. Selling price was $15 per unit. Variable selling and administrative expenses were $2 per unit sold, and fixed costs were $20,000.

Required:

a) Compute the net income and the ending inventory for the Jenkins Company for August.

b) Compute the unit cost of the product.

c) Assume that 1,200 units had been made in August and that 900 had been sold. Compute the unit cost of the product. Compute the net income and the ending inventory for August.

d) Explain the reason for the difference in unit costs between (b) and (c).

Problem 1–6. Purpose: *Cost Computations and a Statement of Cost of Goods Sold*

The Jensen Manufacturing Corporation manufactures a single product. It does not use a detailed cost accounting system. Instead, at the end of each month it prepares a statement of cost of goods sold and computes therefrom the unit costs of manufacturing.

For the two months ending March 31, 19—, the manufacturing and sales data are as follows:

	February	*March*
Finished machines on hand at beginning of month:		
(200 in February and 500 in March)..............$18,400	$18,400	?
Work-in-process at beginning of month:		
Materials..	18,000	?
Direct labor.....................................	28,400	?
Manufacturing overhead...........................	12,100	?
Materials used during the month....................	50,000	$60,900
Direct labor......................................	24,000	27,600
Manufacturing overhead.............................	6,000	6,700
Work-in-process at end of month:		
Materials..	14,000	None
Direct labor.....................................	14,400	
Manufacturing overhead...........................	3,100	
Number of units completed...........................	1,500	1,400
Number of units sold, including 200 on hand February 1....	1,200	1,300

From the above information, prepare (*a*) a statement of your own design, including each element of cost and a computation of the unit costs for material, direct labor, and manufacturing overhead for each month; and (*b*) a statement of the cost of goods sold for the two-month period.

PROBLEMS—GROUP B

Problem 1–7. Purpose: *Cost Computations and Income Statement*

The Trufreeze Company manufactures refrigerators. The refrigerators are sold under the Trufreeze name, and in addition, the Trufreeze Company manufactures refrigerators that are sold by a chain of department stores under the store's own label. During 1969, Trufreeze plans to produce 20,000 refrigerators for department stores and 3,000 for its own sales. The present plan is to earn $35 of net profit for each unit sold to the stores and $50 for each of its own sales.

The Trufreeze Company purchases all of the parts used in the refrigerators from outside sources and has contracted to purchase parts for 23,000 refrigerators at a cost of $70 per refrigerator.

Other costs are as follows:

Manufacturing overhead.....................$40 per refrigerator
Administrative expense...................... 34 per refrigerator sold
Selling expense............................. 46 per refrigerator sold
(own trade name, only)

The selling price of a refrigerator to the department store is $249 per unit.

Required:

a) Compute the maximum that can be paid per machine for direct labor.

b) Compute the unit cost to make and sell one refrigerator to the department store chain.

c) Compute the unit cost to make and sell one refrigerator under the Trufreeze name.

d) Prepare an income statement assuming 20,000 machines are produced and sold to the department stores, and if 3,500 machines are produced but only 3,000 are sold under the Trufreeze name.

Problem 1–8. Purpose: *Cost Computations*

The Trumbull Equipment Company sold 200 air-conditioning units to the Olympia House for $400 each. The materials cost $100 per unit, and direct labor amounted to $35 per unit. Manufacturing overhead amounted to 100 percent of direct labor cost, or $35. Each of the above costs were in effect at the time the order for the air-conditioning units was received.

Before the units for the Olympia House were manufactured, some cost changes became effective. Material costs decreased 10 percent, and labor costs increased 20 percent.

Required:

a) Compute the gross profit to be realized from the order under the assumption that the costs did not change.

b) Compute the gross profit to be realized from the order under the assumption that the costs did change and that there was no change in the rate of manufacturing overhead.

c) Compute the gross profit to be realized from the order under the assumption that $30 of the manufacturing overhead consists of fixed costs and will not increase if the labor rates or the volume of production changes.

Problem 1–9. Purpose: *Relationships between Sales and Profits*

Trendex Industries is planning to open a new plant to manufacture "trex" which is a new fiber. The new plant would increase fixed costs by $108,000, while the variable cost would be 50 cents per yard of "trex."

Preliminary estimates indicate a potential selling price of $1.20 per yard.

Required:

a) Compute the number of yards Trendex must sell in order to cover all costs but no profit.

b) What will the profit be if 200,000 yards are sold? 250,000? 300,000?

c) The company wants to earn $25,000 on its "trex" production. How many yards must be sold?

Problem 1–10. Purpose: *Relationships between Production and Profits*

Timpson Manufacturers, Inc., produces a chemical compound known as "Timpex" at the following cost:

```
Materials............................$6 per cwt.
Labor............................. 4 per cwt.
Other variable costs................. 2 per cwt.
```

In addition the company incurs $80,000 of fixed costs each month. During the month of September, 20,000 cwt. are produced and 15,000 cwt. are sold at $25 per cwt.

Required:

a) Compute the net income and the ending inventory for the Timpson Company for September.

b) Compute the unit cost of the product.

c) Compute the net income and the ending inventory for September under the assumption that 30,000 units had been made and 15,000 units sold. Compute the unit cost of the product.

d) Explain the differences in unit costs between (*b*) and (*c*).

Problem 1–11. Purpose: *Cost Computations and an Income Statement*

Tiempo, Inc., manufactures an electric clock that retails for $6. The budget for the coming year calls for sales of 7,000 clocks, and the company desires to earn 12½ percent on sales as net income before income taxes.

The cost of the parts that are purchased on the outside is $2, and the labor is expected to cost $1.60 per clock. The main item of concern to management is factory overhead cost, since selling and administrative costs of $7,000 are relatively fixed.

Required:

a) Compute the maximum overhead cost that can be incurred to realize the anticipated profit.

b) Prepare an income statement under the assumption that 7,500 clocks were manufactured and 7,000 were sold.

Problem 1–12. Purpose: *Statements: Cost of Goods Sold and Income Statement*

The following information was taken from the records of The Tempest Manufacturing Corporation for the year ending June 30, 19—:

1. During the year, 1,180 units of the single product manufactured were completed.
2. One thousand units were sold at a unit of price of $350.
3. Material costs showed an initial inventory of $6,000, purchases of materials during the year of $80,000, and a final inventory of $11,000.
4. Direct labor costs were $25,000; manufacturing overhead amounted to $30,000.
5. There was no work-in-process inventory at the beginning of the year.
6. The work-in-process inventory at the end of the fiscal year included material costs of $5,500, direct labor of $3,800, and manufacturing overhead of $2,700.
7. The finished goods inventory at the beginning of the year (July 1) amounted to 100 units costing $130 each.
8. Selling expenses were 20 percent, and administrative expenses 10 percent of the selling price.

Required:

a) Schedule of cost of goods sold. (Goods moved on a first-in, first-out basis.)

b) Condensed statement of income.

CHAPTER

2 | The Cost Accounting Cycle—
| Business Forms and Entries

The Cost Accounting Cycle   In compiling unit costs for a manufacturing business, either of two systems may be used: (1) the *job order cost system* in which costs are ascertained by jobs or lots, and (2) the *process or departmental cost system* whereby costs are accumulated departmentally for a definite period of time. In either case, material, labor, and manufacturing overhead costs are first recorded in separate accounts. As they are applied to production, they are recorded in an inventory account called *work-in-process.* Goods completed flow into the *finished goods* account. When sold they are transferred into the *cost of goods sold* account. This represents the cost accounting cycle and may be further described as the conversion of raw materials to a finished or salable product.

To complete this cycle, a variety of business forms and papers must be used to fix responsibility, reduce the possibility of error, and provide a smoothly functioning system for prompt and accurate recording in the accounts.

The Summary of the Cost of Manufacturing Operations   To record and summarize the cost incurred in the manufacturing operations, two different forms are used:

a) The *job order cost sheets* summarizing the results when costs are compiled for a specific job or lot being manufactured.

b) The *cost of production report* used when costs are accumulated more or less continuously on a departmental basis for a definite period of time.

Although job order costs may also be accumulated departmentally, the basic characteristic is the *job* not the department; whereas in the cost of production report, it is the department and the time basis which are emphasized in computing the unit costs. The following presentation will be shown in two sections: job order costing and process costing.

Job Order Cost
Accounting Procedures
Manufacturing operations are started when a *production order* is issued to the plant manager authorizing the manufacture of a specific job or lot of goods either for a named customer or for replenishment of the finished goods inventory. When this order has been issued, the cost accounting department prepares a summary form known as a *job order sheet* on which will be recorded the material, the labor, and the manufacturing overhead costs incurred in producing this lot of goods. For control purposes each job order cost sheet is numbered and has separate columns in which to record the cost of the *direct materials* used, the *labor,* and the *manufacturing overhead.* Illustration 2–1 is a nondepartmentalized job order cost sheet. If more detailed control is desired, the labor and manufacturing overhead costs may be divided departmentally as shown in Illustration 2–2. These forms also provide a section for summarizing the costs by elements and departments. Provision may also be made for managerial use of the estimated selling and administrative expenses and the estimated profit on the production. Sometimes the job order sheet is redesigned to provide management with greater detail such as the kinds of materials used and the various labor operation costs. In a few firms, this cost sheet is printed on the outside of a large manila envelope into which will be placed the material requisitions and the labor cost tickets applicable to the specific job.

Recording Material Costs
Materials are variously described as *direct materials, raw materials, indirect materials, factory supplies, finished parts, stores.*

Direct materials, generally speaking, are materials the costs of which are readily identifiable with or are traceable to the cost of the product being manufactured. *Raw materials* are a form of direct materials which usually undergo a rather thorough change in the manufacturing operations. The term *direct materials,* however, is more acceptable in the preparation of cost reports and statements, since it more accurately covers most materials which become part of the finished product. There are some materials which become part of the finished product but their costs are not readily identifiable with specific production, nor is it practicable to attempt to trace their costs to specific lots or jobs. These are treated as part of the indirect materials.

These last-mentioned materials and others not part of the product but

Illustration 2–1. Nondepartmentalized Job Order Cost Sheet

FOR F. & M. Supply Co.   JOB ORDER NO.: 136

DESCRIPTION: Five Maple Kitchen Cabinets

From Blueprint Supplied

DATE STARTED: 3/3/—   DATE COMPLETED: 3/15/—

MATERIAL COSTS		LABOR COSTS		FACTORY OVERHEAD COSTS	
19—		19—		19—	
3/3	$60.00	3/10	$130.00	3/10	$195.00
3/10	15.00	3/15	200.00	3/15	300.00
3/12	10.00				
Total	$85.00		$330.00		$495.00

COST ANALYSIS

	ESTIMATED COST	ACTUAL COSTS	DIFFERENCE
Materials..........................	$ 95.00	$ 85.00	
Labor.............................	300.00	330.00	
Factory overhead..................	450.00	495.00	
	$ 845.00	$ 910.00	+$65.00
Selling price......................	$1,250.00	$1,250.00	
Manufacturing cost................	845.00	910.00	
Selling and administrative expenses, estimated 10% of sales price.......	125.00	125.00	
Profit............................	$ 280.00	$ 215.00	−$65.00

used to facilitate the manufacturing operation are the *indirect materials,* sometimes called *factory supplies,* and are included in the manufacturing overhead costs. Technically speaking, some accountants differentiate between these terms and classify materials used for the maintenance of machines and plant in operating condition as factory supplies, limiting the term *indirect materials* to miscellaneous items used in production.

Finished parts may represent the finished products ready for sale, in which case they would be called *finished goods,* or they may represent a manufactured product which will be used subsequently in manufacturing a larger product. In the latter instance, the finished parts would be direct materials for the second product.

Although the above definitions are of interest and importance at times, most manufacturing firms use the term *Stores* as the title of a ledger account which includes direct and indirect materials purchased. All materials of both classifications are usually placed in the same

Illustration 2–2. Departmentalized Job Order Cost Sheet

PRODUCTION ORDER & JOB ORDER COST SHEET

FOR _Ward & Co._ JOB NUMBER _178_

ADDRESS _Toledo, Ohio_ DATE _December 22, 19—_

DESCRIPTION _20 Special Machines_ CUSTOMER'S NUMBER _____

DATE COMPLETED _1/10/——_ SELLING PRICE $ _20,000.00_ TOTAL COST $ _13,979.60_ UNIT COST $ _698.98_

DATE	DIRECT LABOR COSTS								MATERIAL COSTS		
	MACH. DEPT. #1		MACH. DEPT. #2		ASSEMBLING		FINISHING				
	Mach. Hrs.	Amount	Mach. Hrs.	Amount	Labor Hrs.	Amount		Amount	Date	Req. No.	Amount
Jan 2		2,000.00		1,400.00		1,000.00		400.00	Jan 2		3,200.00
10	206	328.60	38	68.40					10	605	110.00
Totals		2,328.60		1,468.40		1,000.00		400.00			3,310.00

DATE	APPLIED MANUFACTURING OVERHEAD COSTS										SUMMARY	
	MACH. DEPT. #1			MACH. DEPT. #2			ASSEMBLING			FINISHING		
	Hrs.	R.	Amt.	Hrs.	R.	Amount	Hrs.	R.	Amount	Cost	%	Amt.

											Cost Element	Amount
Jan 2			2,400.00			1,620.00			850.00			600.00	MATERIAL	3,310.00
10	206	2.20	453.20	38	1.30	49.40							LABOR #1	2,328.60
												LABOR #2	1,468.40
												LABOR #3	1,000.00
												LABOR #4	400.00
												O.H. #1	2,853.20
												O.H. #2	1,169.40
												O.H. #3	850.00
												O.H. #4	600.00
Total			2,853.20			1,169.40			850.00			600.00	TOTAL COST	13,979.60

storeroom, and their ultimate classification is determined at the time of use.

Most manufacturing plants maintain a subsidiary book inventory record for each kind of material used. This record will show the receipts, the issuances, and the balance on hand for each kind of material. When goods are purchased, the entry in the voucher register is:

Stores Control..20,000.00
    Accounts Payable.....................................   20,000.00
      To record the purchases.

Illustration 2–3. Materials Purchased

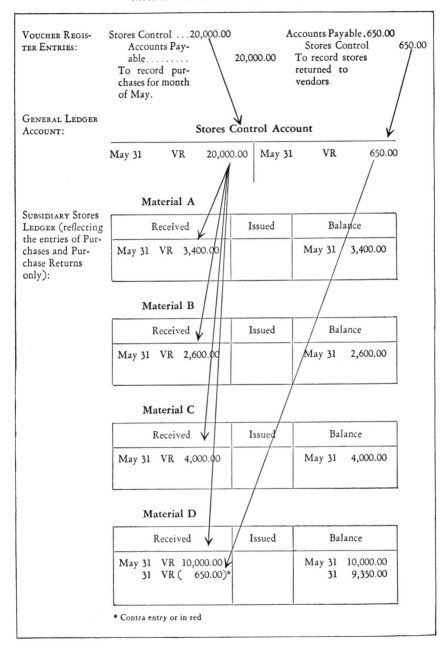

VOUCHER REGIS- TER ENTRIES:	Stores Control ...20,000.00 Accounts Pay- able......... 20,000.00 To record pur- chases for month of May.	Accounts Payable.650.00 Stores Control 650.00 To record stores returned to vendors

GENERAL LEDGER ACCOUNT:

Stores Control Account

| May 31 | VR | 20,000.00 | May 31 | VR | 650.00 |

SUBSIDIARY Stores LEDGER (reflecting the entries of Pur- chases and Pur- chase Returns only):

Material A

Received	Issued	Balance
May 31 VR 3,400.00		May 31 3,400.00

Material B

Received	Issued	Balance
May 31 VR 2,600.00		May 31 2,600.00

Material C

Received	Issued	Balance
May 31 VR 4,000.00		May 31 4,000.00

Material D

Received	Issued	Balance
May 31 VR 10,000.00 31 VR (650.00)*		May 31 10,000.00 31 9,350.00

* Contra entry or in red

Diagrammatically the accounting for materials purchased would be as shown in Illustration 2–3.

The accounting procedures for materials used in a job order cost system differ slightly from that of the continuous process system. In the job order cost system, the accounting department prepares a job order cost sheet which is assigned an identification number and which contains a statement of the quantity and description of the goods to be manufactured and any other necessary supplementary information. All material requisitions will use this *job order number* so that later they may be properly sorted and charged to the job on which they were used.

Illustration 2–4. Material Requisition Job Order Cost System

	MATERIAL OR SUPPLY REQUISITION Storeroom Copy		No. 11017
A 201			

BRADFORD WORKS

CHARGE			CHECK ONE ▼	
DATE	USED FOR		MATERIAL REQ.	✓
Apr. 4,19--	JOB ORDER NO. 762		SUPPLY REQ.	
DEPT. NO.	ACCT. NO. CHARGED		INVENTORY ACCT. CR.	
14-A	401		4-801 Steel Bars	

QUANTITY	CODE NO.	DESCRIPTION——SIZE	UNIT PRICE	AMOUNT
300	801	¼" Stainless 48"	1.20	360.00

REQUISITIONED OR APPROVED BY	RECEIVED BY	$
G X Mascare	*C. M. Olson*	

COPY 2 TO COST ACCOUNTING DEPARTMENT

Standard Register Co.

In addition to the job number, the requisition will indicate the date, quantity of materials used, description of materials issued, the unit and total costs, and signatures authorizing the issuance (Illustration 2–4).

In a job order cost system, the costs of materials, labor, and manufacturing overhead applicable to the various jobs must be recorded on the job order cost sheets and summarized in the work-in-process accounts. The detailed postings to the job order costs sheets can be made daily or weekly, but the summary postings to the work-in-process and finished goods control accounts can be made weekly or monthly. Since there are separate columns on the job cost sheets for the materials, labor, and manufacturing overhead entries, the work-in-process *account* is usually subdivided into the three parts: *work-in-process—materials, work-in-process—labor,* and *work-in-process—manufacturing overhead.* Thus errors in posting to the cost sheets can be traced more readily if there are three control accounts instead of one. For example, if a detailed listing of the three sections of the subsidiary cost sheets shows that the materials in process does not agree with the related control account and everything else is in balance, then only the materials section of the cost sheets need be checked.

The materials used are separated into *direct materials* which become part of the finished product and into the *indirect materials or supplies* used to facilitate the manufacturing operations but which do not become part of the finished product and hence are part of the manufacturing overhead. On Illustration 2–4, the nature of the materials used is indicated by a check mark in the upper right-hand corner.

Entries made weekly or daily to summarize the material requisitions would be:

```
Work-in-Process—Materials..............................10,000.00
Manufacturing Overhead—(Indirect Materials Used)..........  1,500.00
    Stores Control.........................................             11,500.00
    To record the materials used.
```

Illustration 2–5 presents diagrammatically the accounting procedure for materials issued.

Forms and Procedures in Cost Accounting for Labor. Labor terminology in cost accounting includes: *payroll, direct labor, indirect labor, superintendence, idle time, overtime bonus.* Payroll and sometimes the payroll clearing account represent the total of wages paid. It is subsequently analyzed into factory payroll, administrative salaries, and sales and distribution salaries. Factory payrolls are further analyzed into that which represents direct labor, indirect labor, superintendence, idle time, and overtime bonus. *Direct labor* is that part of the factory payroll which can be identified with specific jobs, whereas *indirect labor* is the remainder of the factory payroll and is part of the manufacturing overhead costs.

In job order cost accounting, the direct labor costs must be allocated to the specific jobs. The simplest method of doing this is by means of *job time tickets.* Each worker completes a ticket for each different job on which he works, showing as illustrated (2–6) the name of employee, date, job number on which work was performed, operation, time started

Illustration 2–5. Materials Issued

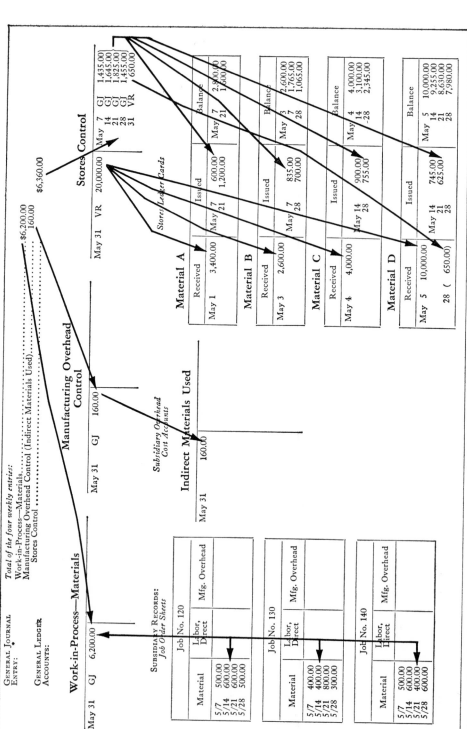

* Although the illustration shows the entry on a monthly basis, it would be practical to make these entries weekly or even daily.

and time finished, and earnings for that elapsed time. Weekly, and on rare occasions daily, these time tickets are sorted by jobs, totaled on the adding machine, and totals entered on the respective job order cost sheets.

Instead of having a separate job time ticket for each job on which the employee worked, modern business practice makes use of a single time

Illustration 2–6. Individual Job Time Ticket

Hours	Pieces	Hourly Rate	Piecework Rate
4		$1.80	

JOB TIME TICKET			
Employee's Name	J. Robinson	Date	April 2
Clock No.	547	Department	Bending
Operation	Bending	Time Finished	12:00
Job No.	762	Time Started	8:00

Hours	Pieces	Hourly Work	Piecework
4		$7.20	

Approved   Y. Lorde

Adding Machine Tape

```
        Job #762
           *
         7.20
         5.00
         4.00
         6.40
         3.60
         2.40
         3.20
         3.20
         6.23
        _____

        41.23 *
```

Illustration 2–7. Daily Job Time Ticket

WORKMAN'S	TIME TICKET AND			RECORD	
CUSTOMER NAME	ABC COMPANY			QUIT	12:00
JOB NO. 762	OPERATION	REG.	OVT.		
DATE Apr. 2-	BENDING	4		BEGAN	8:00
WORK NO. 547					
CUSTOMER NAME	M-N Corporation			QUIT	5:00
JOB NO. 780	OPERATION	REG.	OVT.		
DATE Apr. 2	Bending	4		BEGAN	1:00
WORK NO. 547 £					
CUSTOMER NAME				QUIT	
JOB NO.	OPERATION	REG.	OVT.		
DATE				BEGAN	
WORK NO.					
CUSTOMER NAME				QUIT	
JOB NO.	OPERATION	REG.	OVT.		
DATE				BEGAN	
WORK NO.					
CUSTOMER NAME				QUIT	
JOB NO.	OPERATION	REG.	OVT.		
DATE				BEGAN	
WORK NO.					
CUSTOMER NAME				QUIT	
JOB NO.	OPERATION	REG.	OVT.		
DATE				BEGAN	
WORK NO.					

CUSTOMER WORK		COMPANY WORK			FOREMAN AND CLERKS	COME BACK	SHOP & UNAS-SIGNED	TRNG. PROG.		TOTAL	
		TRADE &REPOS	A & H	ALL OTHER						REG.	OVT.
REG.	OVT.										
8										8	
APPROVED *C J Collins*					SIGNED *J Robinson*						
										WORKMAN NO.	

Moore's Business Forms

ticket for the entire day, with spaces provided for each job, as shown in Illustration 2–7. The earnings must be computed in the payroll department, with a carbon copy being sent to the cost accounting department.

In job order cost accounting, two sets of entries are required: (*a*) the financial accounting representing the computation of the earnings with deductions required by law or authorized by the employee, and (*b*) the distribution of the factory payroll to the various jobs or to the manufacturing overhead control account, viz:

a) Computing the earnings (diagrammatically shown in Illustration 2–8):

```
Payroll.................................................12,000.00
    F.I.C.A. Taxes Payable (4.4%)........................          528.00
    Federal Withholding Taxes Payable...................        1,800.00
    State Withholding Taxes Payable.....................          300.00
    Accounts (Vouchers) Payable.........................        9,372.00
    To record payroll for the week.
```

b) Distributing the payroll to the various jobs, daily, weekly, or monthly (Illustration 2–9):

```
Work-in-Process—Labor................................10,000.00
Manufacturing Overhead (Indirect Labor)................ 2,000.00
    Payroll.........................................          12,000.00
    To close out the factory payroll account.
```

Manufacturing Overhead Costs

Manufacturing overhead refers to those manufacturing costs which in a job order cost system cannot be identified with a specific job or lot of production; such as heat, light and power costs, factory insurance of all types, factory repairs, factory rent or taxes, superintendence, and depreciation charges for plant and equipment. In a job order plant, indirect materials and supplies and indirect labor costs are part of the manufacturing overhead, but in a process or departmental accounting system, direct and indirect materials and direct and indirect labor are not separated.

The total amount of these indirect manufacturing overhead costs does not become known until the last one of them has been recorded some time late in the accounting period. In the meantime, goods must be costed out of production as finished, and most of them will be finished *before* the total of manufacturing overhead is finally known. It becomes expedient, therefore, to estimate in advance the manufacturing overhead of a period in order to allocate part of it to each of the products leaving the factory. It will also be necessary to estimate in advance the volume of production in terms such as units, direct labor hours, machine-hours, direct labor cost, or some other base.

Illustration 2–8. Financial Accounting for Payrolls in Factory

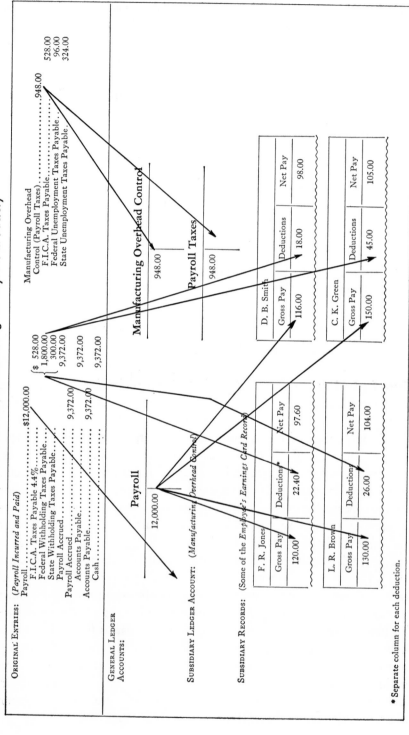

ORIGINAL ENTRIES: *(Payroll Incurred and Paid)*

Payroll..$12,000.00
    F.I.C.A. Taxes Payable 4.4%........... $ 528.00
    Federal Withholding Taxes Payable....   1,800.00
    State Withholding Taxes Payable......   300.00
    Payroll Accrued......................   9,372.00
Payroll Accrued...........................   9,372.00
    Accounts Payable.....................   9,372.00
Accounts Payable..........................   9,372.00
    Cash.................................   9,372.00

Manufacturing Overhead
  Control (Payroll Taxes).................948.00
    F.I.C.A. Taxes Payable.............   528.00
    Federal Unemployment Taxes Payable.   96.00
    State Unemployment Taxes Payable...   324.00

GENERAL LEDGER ACCOUNTS:

Payroll

12,000.00

Manufacturing Overhead Control

948.00

Payroll Taxes

948.00

SUBSIDIARY LEDGER ACCOUNT: *(Manufacturing Overhead Control)*

SUBSIDIARY RECORDS: *(Some of the Employee's Earnings Card Records)*

F. R. Jones		
Gross Pay	Deductions*	Net Pay
120.00	22.40	97.60

L. R. Brown		
Gross Pay	Deductions	Net Pay
130.00	26.00	104.00

D. B. Smith		
Gross Pay	Deductions	Net Pay
116.00	18.00	98.00

C. K. Green		
Gross Pay	Deductions	Net Pay
150.00	45.00	105.00

* Separate column for each deduction.

Illustration 2-9. Distribution of Payroll Costs in Job Order Cost Accounting Cycle

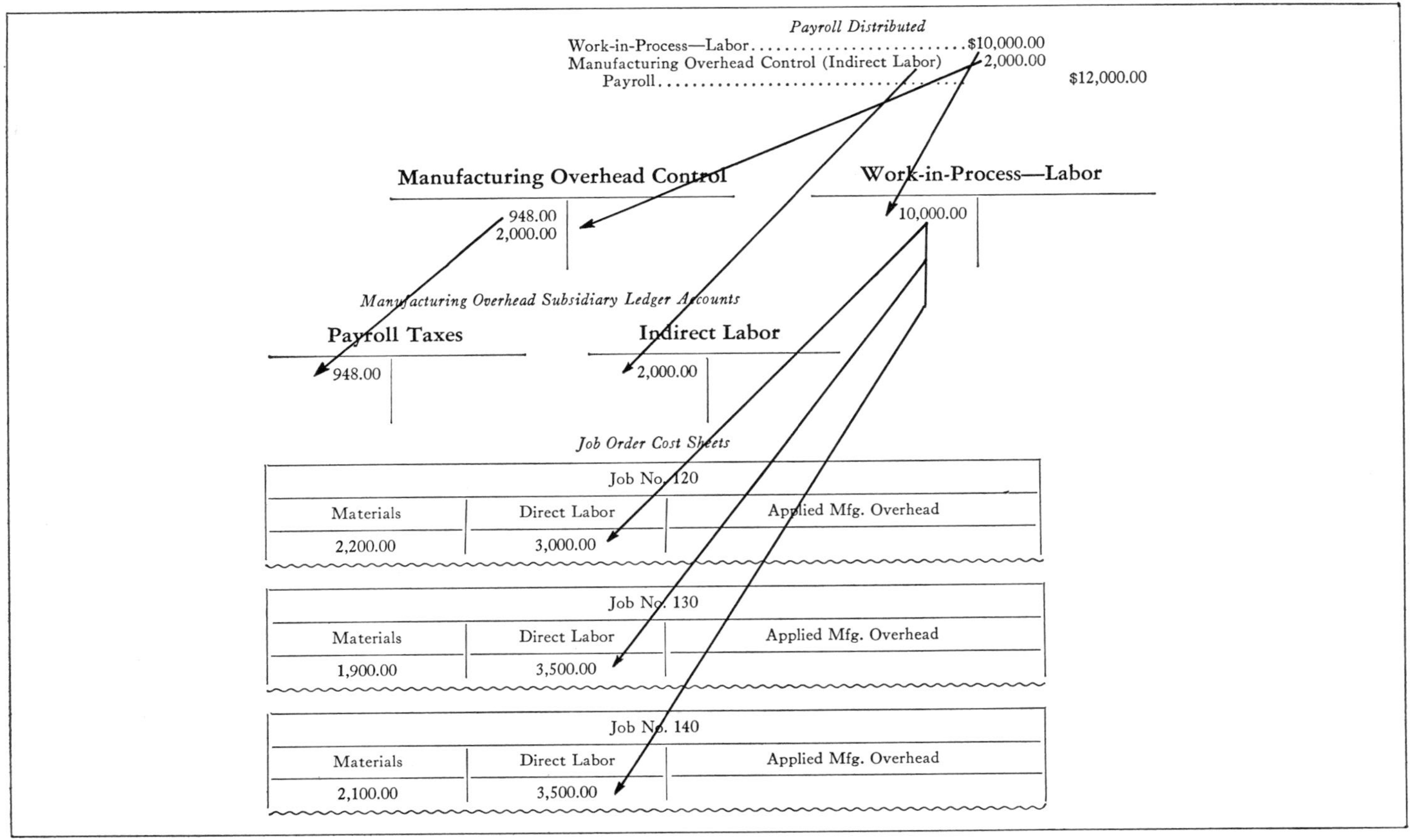

Payroll Distributed

Work-in-Process—Labor		$10,000.00
Manufacturing Overhead Control (Indirect Labor)		2,000.00
Payroll		$12,000.00

Work-in-Process—Labor

10,000.00

Manufacturing Overhead Control

948.00
2,000.00

Manufacturing Overhead Subsidiary Ledger Accounts

Indirect Labor

2,000.00

Payroll Taxes

948.00

Job Order Cost Sheets

Job No. 120

Direct Labor	Applied Mfg. Overhead
3,000.00	

Materials	
2,200.00	

Job No. 130

Direct Labor	Applied Mfg. Overhead
3,500.00	

Materials	
1,900.00	

Job No. 140

Direct Labor	Applied Mfg. Overhead
3,500.00	

Materials	
2,100.00	

The relationship between this estimated manufacturing overhead and estimated volume of production must be established in order to allocate a proportionate part of the overhead cost to each unit of product. This relationship (estimated manufacturing overhead divided by estimated volume of production) is known as the *predetermined manufacturing overhead rate*. When this rate is applied to the base selected for this purpose to measure volume produced, estimated (or applied) manufacturing overhead is available to complete the cost of production. When direct material costs and direct labor costs are recorded on the job order cost sheets, usually weekly, the job costing is completed by the addition of estimated manufacturing overhead as the third element of cost. (See Illustrations 2–1 and 2–2.)

When the various jobs have been completed, the cost sheets are summarized to ascertain the total cost and the unit cost of the goods manufactured. These goods are then either transferred to the finished goods stock room or are shipped to a customer. The cost of the shipments becomes the cost of the goods sold.

Entries to accumulate the actual manufacturing overhead in a job order cost system usually involve indirect materials and supplies, various indirect labor costs, those expenses which involve the payment of cash, and those which are valuation charges. These are summarized in a Manufacturing Overhead Control account supplemented by a subsidiary ledger for the detailed accounts. The entries made to record the various types of overhead charges would be:

For indirect materials used:

Work-in-Process—Materials	6,200.00	
Manufacturing Overhead Control (Indirect Materials)	340.00	
Stores		6,540.00
To record the materials used.		

For indirect labor costs:

Work-in-Process—Labor	10,000.00	
Manufacturing Overhead Control (Indirect Labor)	300.00	
Payroll		10,300.00
To close out the factory payroll account.		

For cash disbursement entries:

Manufacturing Overhead Control (Rent of Factory)	650.00	
Accounts (Vouchers) Payable		650.00
To record voucher for rent for month.		

For valuation entries:

Manufacturing Overhead Control (Depreciation of Equipment)	200.00	
Allowance for Depreciation Machinery		200.00
To record the depreciation of factory machinery.		

As previously indicated in a process type of cost accounting, no charge would be made to the Manufacturing Overhead Control account for indirect materials or indirect labor, since these items are already included in the total materials used and total factory payroll. The amount of manufacturing overhead allocated to the various jobs may be credited either to the *Manufacturing Overhead Control* account or to a separate *Applied Manufacturing Overhead* account. If the latter account is used, it is closed into the Manufacturing Overhead Control account at the end of the fiscal accounting period to ascertain the amount of the over- or underapplied overhead. This amount may be closed out into the *cost of sales account* or may be closed into the work-in-process, finished goods, and cost of sales accounts on a pro rata basis.

The entry to record the charge for manufacturing overhead on a job order cost system would be:

```
Work-in-Process—Manufacturing Overhead.................. 2,100.00
    Applied Manufacturing Overhead......................            2,100.00
    To summarize the overhead charged to jobs during the month
    at a rate of $1.50 per direct labor hour.
```

Diagrammatically, the actual and applied manufacturing overhead accounting for a *job order* firm is as shown in Illustration 2–10.

Accounting for Finished Goods and Cost of Sales   To complete the job order accounting cycle, the cost of goods completed and the cost of goods sold are recorded as follows:

```
Finished Goods.........................................16,500.00
    Work-in-Process—Materials...........................            6,000.00
    Work-in-Process—Labor...............................            8,800.00
    Work-in-Process—Manufacturing Overhead..............            1,700.00
    To record the cost of jobs completed.
```

The entry for the cost of goods sold would be recorded as:

```
Cost of Sales..........................................12,000.00
    Finished Goods......................................           12,000.00
    To record the cost of goods sold during the month.
```

The complete cost accounting cycle for a *job order manufacturing firm* can best be shown by the diagram in Illustration 2–11.

Process or Departmental Cost Accounting   For those firms whose manufacturing operations result in a more or less continuous flow of production from one department to another, costs are summarized on a form called the *cost of production report*. (See Illustration 2–12.) This form is characterized by

Illustration 2–10. Manufacturing Overhead Accounting in Job Order Cost Cycle

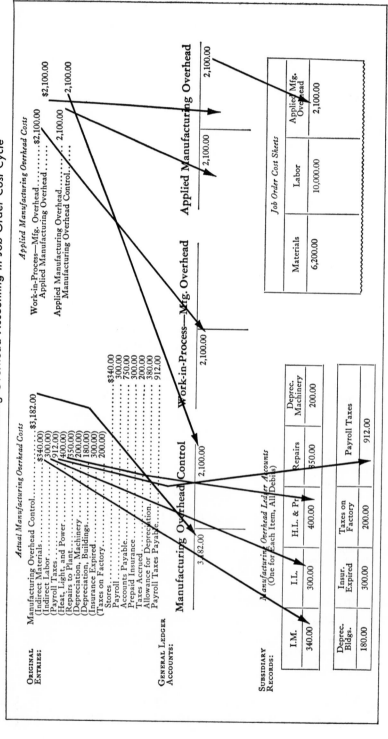

ORIGINAL ENTRIES:

Actual Manufacturing Overhead Costs

Manufacturing Overhead Control.........$3,182.00
  (Indirect Materials..........$340.00
  (Indirect Labor...............300.00
  (Payroll Taxes.................912.00
  (Heat, Light, and Power........400.00
  (Repairs to Plant..............350.00
  (Depreciation, Machinery.......200.00
  (Depreciation, Buildings.......180.00
  (Insurance Expired.............300.00
  (Taxes on Factory..............200.00
    Stores.......................$340.00
    Payroll.......................300.00
    Accounts Payable..............750.00
    Prepaid Insurance.............300.00
    Taxes Accrued.................200.00
    Allowance for Depreciation....380.00
    Payroll Taxes Payable.........912.00

Applied Manufacturing Overhead Costs

Work-in-Process—Mfg. Overhead.......$2,100.00
    Applied Manufacturing Overhead.......$2,100.00

Applied Manufacturing Overhead.........2,100.00
    Manufacturing Overhead Control.......2,100.00

GENERAL LEDGER ACCOUNTS:

Manufacturing Overhead Control

3,182.00 | 2,100.00

Work-in-Process—Mfg. Overhead

2,100.00 |

Applied Manufacturing Overhead

2,100.00 | 2,100.00

SUBSIDIARY RECORDS:

Manufacturing Overhead Ledger Accounts
(One for Each Item, All Debits)

I.M.	I.L.	H.L. & Pr	Repairs	Deprec. Machinery
340.00	300.00	400.00	350.00	200.00

Deprec. Bldgs.	Insur. Expired	Taxes on Factory	Payroll Taxes
180.00	300.00	200.00	912.00

Job Order Cost Sheets

Materials	Labor	Applied Mfg. Overhead
6,200.00	10,000.00	2,100.00

Illustration 2–11. Diagrammatic Summary of the Job Order Cost Cycle

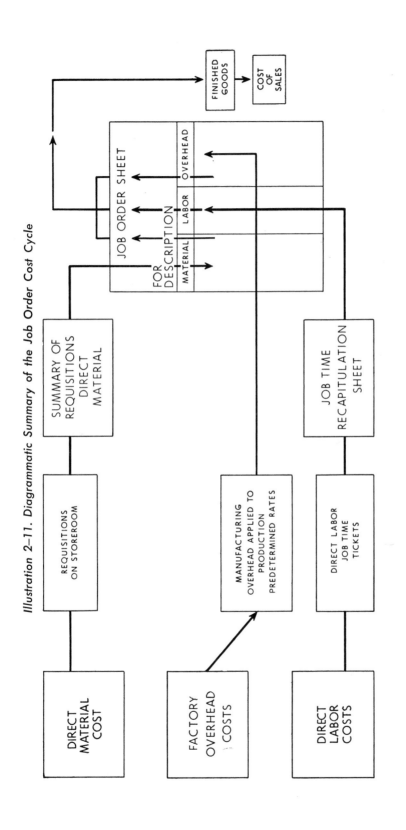

showing material, labor, and overhead costs on a departmental basis for a definite period of time such as a week or a month. Also, since production is on a more or less continuous basis, unit costs cannot be computed unless a record is maintained showing the quantity of units produced in each department. Unit costs are computed by elements of cost in each department. A simple illustration of such a production report is given. The quantity of production statistics by departments for the week of March 26 were as follows: (It is assumed that all work was completed at the end of each week.)

	Department I	Department II	Department III
Started in production	60,000 gals.		
Received from preceding department		55,000 gals.	50,000 gals.
Added in the department		10,000	20,000
Total to be accounted for	60,000 gals.	65,000 gals.	70,000 gals.
Transferred to next department	55,000 gals.	50,000 gals.	60,000 gals.
Lost due to spillage or evaporation	5,000	15,000	10,000
Total accounted for	60,000 gals.	65,000 gals.	70,000 gals.

Illustration 2–12

COST OF PRODUCTION REPORT*
For the Week Ending March 26, 19—

	DEPARTMENT I		DEPARTMENT II		DEPARTMENT III	
	Total Costs	Unit Costs	Total Costs	Unit Costs	Total Costs	Unit Costs
Costs during Week:						
Material added...	$ 82,500		$ 10,000		$ 11,250	
Material received from previous department.....			123,750		168,750	
Total material....	$ 82,500	$1.50	$133,750	$2.675	$180,000	$3.00
Labor costs.........	27,500	0.50	25,000	0.50	18,000	0.30
Manufacturing over- head costs......	13,750	0.25	10,000	0.20	6,000	0.10
Total..........	$123,750	$2.25	$168,750	$3.375	$204,000	$3.40
Amount transferred out of depart- ment.........	$123,750	$2.25	$168,750	$3.375	$204,000	$3.40
Quantity produced..	55,000 gals.		50,000 gals.		60,000 gals.	

* A more detailed discussion of process or departmental costs is given in Chapters 9 through 14.

In a continuous process cost system, there is less emphasis on the distinction between direct and indirect materials. It is customary to debit the work-in-process account for the department using materials and supplies as illustrated in the following entries:

```
Work-in-Process—Department I...........................82,500.00
  Stores...............................................          82,500.00
  To record the materials used in Department I during the week.
```

and

```
Work-in-Process—Department II..........................10,000.00
Work-in-Process—Department III.........................11,250.00
  Stores...............................................          21,250.00
  To record weekly issuance of materials.
```

Similar procedures are used in the treatment of direct and indirect labor costs in a process cost system. The financial accounting for the payroll will remain the same as for a job order system. Closing the Payroll account may be illustrated as follows without a distinction between the direct and indirect labor costs:

```
Work-in-Process—Department I...........................27,500.00
Work-in-Process—Department II..........................25,000.00
Work-in-Process—Department III.........................18,000.00
  Payroll..............................................          70,500.00
  To close out the Payroll account.
```

The applied manufacturing overhead for a process plant would be recorded as follows:

```
Work-in-Process—Department I...........................13,750.00
Work-in-Process—Department II..........................10,000.00
Work-in-Process—Department III......................... 6,000.00
  Applied Manufacturing Overhead......................          29,750.00
  To record the applied manufacturing overhead on the prede-
  termined rates.
```

For work completed and the cost of goods sold the entries would be:

```
Finished Goods.........................................204,000.00
  Work-in-Process—Department I........................          123,750.00
  Work-in-Process—Department II.......................          45,000.00
  Work-in-Process—Department III......................          35,250,00
  To record the cost of work completed.
```

```
Cost of Sales..........................................170,000.00
  Finished Goods......................................          170,000.00
  To record the cost of goods sold during the week.
```

The cost accounting cycle for a *departmental or process type* of control operations is illustrated in the chart in Illustration 2–13. For the

Illustration 2–13. Diagrammatic Illustration of Cost Accounting Cycle for a Process Type of Plant

Material Costs → REQUISITIONS ON STOREROOM → Departmental Summary of Materials Used

Departmental Transfers out of Department

Departmental Payrolls

Manufacturing Overhead on a Predetermined Rate Basis

Finished Goods

COST OF PRODUCTION REPORT
For Week Ending January 14, 19——

	Department I		Department II		Department III	
	Total	Unit	Total	Unit	Total	Unit
Cost from preceding department...	...	...	42,000	6.00	72,100	10.30
Material costs...	21,000	3.00	11,200	1.60	4,200	0.60
Labor costs...	14,000	2.00	14,000	2.00	2,800	0.40
Overhead costs...	7,000	1.00	4,900	0.70	1,400	0.20
Total Cost...	42,000	6.00	72,100	10.30	80,500	11.50
Transferred out...	42,000	6.00	72,100	10.30	80,500	11.50
Work-in-process...	0	...	0	0	0	0
Total...	42,000	...	72,100	10.30	80,500	11.50

sake of simplicity, all work put into production in each department is completed and transferred out. A study of the more complicated and advanced problems and procedures of process cost accounting is presented in Chapters 9 through 14.

Financial Statements of the Cost Accounting Cycle. Operating results for a manufacturing concern are shown in two statements: (1) *Exhibit B*—a condensed statement of income—supported by (2) *Schedule B-1*—a statement of the cost of goods sold. Although there are several different forms of the Schedule B-1, the main differences arise in the sequence or arrangement of the various elements of cost: some statements start with the work-in-process inventories; others with the finished goods or with the stores accounts. Furthermore, it should be noted that since most firms use a predetermined rate for the overhead applied to production, there will be an adjustment at the end of the accounting period for the over- or underapplied manufacturing overhead before the actual cost of goods sold can be determined. The cost of goods sold before this adjustment is known as the cost of goods sold *at normal*—the term *at normal* signifying what the cost of goods sold would normally have been if the predetermined rate had been 100 percent correct.

For illustrative purposes, the following Schedule B-1 are shown:

1. Schedule B-1—cost of goods sold statement starting with the initial work-in-process inventory when a single work-in-process account is used. (See Illustration 2–14.)
2. Schedule B-1—cost of goods sold statement starting with the initial work-in-process inventories when three work-in-process accounts are used. (See Illustration 2–15.)
3. Schedule B-1—cost of goods sold statement starting with the initial finished goods inventory. (See Illustration 2–16.)
4. Schedule B-1—cost of goods sold statement starting with the material costs without the details of the materials inventories. (See Illustration 2–17.)

In each illustration, the cost of the goods sold at actual is the same.

Since the details of the cost of goods sold are shown in a separate schedule, the income statement will appear in condensed form, further supported by detailed schedules of the selling and administrative expenses, as shown in Illustration 2–18.

Illustration 2–14. Cost of Goods Sold Statement Starting with the Initial Work-in-Process Inventory—One Work-in-Process Account

Schedule B-1

BRENNER MANUFACTURING COMPANY
New York, New York

STATEMENT OF COST OF GOODS MANUFACTURED AND SOLD
For the Year Ended December 31, 19—

Work-in-Process Inventory, 1/1/—..........................		$ 10,000.00
Direct Materials: *		
Inventory, 1/1/—.......................................	$ 75,000.00	
Purchases...	100,000.00	
Freight-In..	3,000.00	
Total..	$178,000.00	
Less: Inventory, 12/31/—...............................	85,000.00	93,000.00
Direct Labor...		98,000.00
Applied Manufacturing Overhead............................		60,000.00
Total..		$261,000.00
Less: Work-in-Process Inventory, 12/31/—....................		72,000.00
Cost of Goods Manufactured at Normal......................		$189,000.00
Deduct: Increase in Finished Goods Inventory:		
Finished Goods Inventory, 12/31/—......................	$102,000.00	
Finished Goods Inventory, 1/1/—.........................	100,000.00	2,000.00
Cost of Goods Sold *at Normal*............................		$187,000.00
Add: Underapplied Manufacturing Overhead..................		3,000.00
Cost of Goods Sold at Actual to Exhibit B...................		$190,000.00

* In many statements, instead of showing the purchases, inventories, and resulting figure of materials used, only one figure is shown for the materials used. (See Illustration 2–17.)

Illustration 2–15. Cost of Goods Sold Statement Starting with the Initial Work-in-Process Inventories When Three Work-in-Process Accounts Are Used

Schedule B-1

BRENNER MANUFACTURING COMPANY
New York, New York

STATEMENT OF THE COST OF GOODS MANUFACTURED AND SOLD
For the Year Ended December 31, 19—

Direct Material Costs:		
Work-in-Process, 1/1/—................................	$ 3,500.00	
Applied during the Year................................	93,000.00	
Total..	$ 96,500.00	
Less: Work-in-Process, 12/31/—..........................	20,000.00	$ 76,500.00
Direct Labor Costs:		
Work-in-Process, 1/1/—................................	$ 4,000.00	
Applied during the Year................................	98,000.00	
Total..	$102,000.00	
Less: Work-in-Process, 12/31/—..........................	35,000.00	67,000.00
Manufacturing Overhead Costs:		
Work-in-Process, 1/1/—................................	$ 2,500.00	
Applied during Year...................................	60,000.00	
Total..	$ 62,500.00	
Less: Work-in-Process, 12/31/—..........................	17,000.00	45,500.00
Cost of Goods Manufactured at Normal......................		$189,000.00
Less: Increase in Finished Goods Inventory:		
Finished Goods, 12/31/—...............................	$102,000.00	
Finished Goods, 1/1/—.................................	100,000.00	2,000.00
Cost of Goods Sold at Normal.............................		$187,000.00
Add: Underapplied Manufacturing Overhead Costs.............		3,000.00
Cost of Goods Sold at Actual to Exhibit B...................		$190,000.00

Illustration 2–16. *Cost of Goods Sold Statement Starting with the Initial Finished Goods Inventory*

Schedule B-1

BRENNER MANUFACTURING COMPANY
New York, New York

STATEMENT OF COST OF GOODS MANUFACTURED AND SOLD
For Year Ended December 31, 19—

Finished Goods Inventory, 1/1/—..............			$100,000.00
Work-in-Process Inventory, 1/1/—.............		$ 10,000.00	
Direct Materials:*			
Inventory, 1/1/—........................	$ 75,000.00		
Purchases...............................	100,000.00		
Freight-In..............................	3,000.00		
Total...............................	$178,000.00		
Less: Inventory, 12/31/—..................	85,000.00	93,000.00	
Direct Labor..............................		98,000.00	
Applied Manufacturing Overhead.............		60,000.00	
Total..............................		$261,000.00	
Less: Work-in-Process Inventory, 12/31/—......		72,000.00	
Cost of Goods Manufactured at Normal........			189,000.00
Total..............................			$289,000.00
Less: Finished Goods Inventory, 12/31/—.......			102,000.00
Cost of Goods Sold at Normal................			$187,000.00
Add: Underapplied Manufacturing Overhead.....			3,000.00
Cost of Goods Sold at Actual to Exhibit B......			$190,000.00

* In many statements, instead of showing the purchases, inventories, and resulting figure for materials used, only one figure is shown for the *materials used.*

Illustration 2–17. *Cost of Goods Sold Statement Starting with the Material Costs without the Details of the Materials Inventory and Purchases*

Schedule B-1

BRENNER MANUFACTURING COMPANY
New York, New York

STATEMENT OF COST OF GOODS MANUFACTURED AND SOLD
For Year Ended December 31, 19—

Direct Materials Used......................................		$ 93,000.00
Direct Labor Costs...		98,000.00
Applied Manufacturing Overhead Costs......................		60,000.00
Total Costs of Manufacturing...........................		$251,000.00
Deduct: Increase in Work-in-Process Inventories:		
Work-in-Process Inventory, 12/31/—.......................	$ 72,000.00	
Work-in-Process Inventory, 1/1/—........................	10,000.00	62,000.00
Cost of Goods Manufactured at Normal......................		$189,000.00
Deduct: Increase in Finished Goods Inventories:		
Finished Goods Inventory, 12/31/—.......................	$102,000.00	
Finished Goods Inventory, 1/1/—........................	100,000.00	2,000.00
Cost of Goods Sold at Normal............................		$187,000.00
Add: Underapplied Manufacturing Overhead...................		3,000.00
Cost of Goods Sold at Actual to Exhibit B...................		$190,000.00

Illustration 2–18. Condensed Statement of Income

Exhibit B

BRENNER MANUFACTURING COMPANY
New York, New York

CONDENSED STATEMENT OF INCOME
For Year Ended December 31, 19—

Sales..		$295,000.00
Sales Returns...		2,000.00
Net Sales...		$293,000.00
Cost of Sales (Schedule B-1).............................		190,000.00
Gross Profit on Sales...................................		$103,000.00
Selling Expenses (Schedule B-2)........................	$46,000.00	
Administrative Expenses (Schedule B-3).................	14,000.00	
Total Selling and Administrative Expenses..............		60,000.00
Net Operating Profit....................................		$ 43,000.00
Financial Management Income............................	$ 4,200.00	
Financial Management Expense...........................	3,000.00	
Net Financial Management Income....................		1,200.00
Net Income...		$ 44,200.00

QUESTIONS FOR REVIEW

1. There are two different basic types of manufacturing operations which are used to characterize the cost accounting systems used. What are these?
2. What are the distinguishing characteristics of the two types of cost accounting systems? Which is more prevalent in modern business operations? Why?
3. What is meant by the "cost accounting cycle"? Why is it important to understand that there is a cycle and what it is?
4. The cost accounting cycle may be expressed in three different forms. What are the characteristics of each of these cycles?
5. The cost accounting cycle is merely the picture of the cost accounting system, expressed as forms, accounting entries, and statements. Which of these is the more comprehensive picture? Explain.
6. What are the three elements of the cost of goods manufactured? How does the accounting for these differ in the job order and the continuous process cost accounting cycles?
7. Outline the forms and procedures used in accounting for the materials used in the cost accounting cycle for job order costs. How does this procedure differ from that used when process cost accounting is used?
8. What is the main difference in the cost accounting procedures for payroll costs in a job order system as compared with the process cost system?
9. Manufacturing overhead costs may be classified as fixed, variable, semivariable, and semifixed. What is the managerial significance of this classification?
10. In what respect are the financial statements of a corporation representative of the cost accounting cycle? In what respect does the financial and cost

accounting presentation of these statements differ? For income tax purposes, how are these statements influenced by the governmental regulations?

PROBLEMS—GROUP A

Problem 2–1. Purpose: *Process Cost Computation*

Korman Industries' Plant No. 1 manufactures a chemical known as KORM in a continuous process operation. KORM passes through three departments, and in a typical month it experienced the following costs when 40,000 gallons were produced:

	Material	Labor
Department 1...............	$6,000	$3,000
Department 2...............	2,000	1,000
Department 3...............	–0–	4,000
	$8,000	$8,000

Overhead was incurred as follows:

	Dept. No. 1.	Dept. No. 2.	Dept. No. 3.
Incurred by department...............	$1,800	$2,000	$1,000
Rent apportioned to department........	400	500	400
Other apportioned items..............	1,000	700	1,600

Prepare a report showing total and unit costs in each department and at the end of each stage of the productive process.

Problem 2–2. Purpose: *Job Order Cost Computation*

Kingman Manufacturing Company makes machines as per customer orders. The manufacturing operations take place in three departments.

On February 10 an order is received for 30 machines. The job is started the next day and is completed on March 15. The machines are shipped to the customer on March 16 at a sales price of ___?___

The following costs were incurred:

	Dept. A.	Dept. B.	Dept. C.
Material........................	$6,000	–0–	–0–
Labor hours.....................	700	800	300
Labor rate per hour..............	$3.25	$3.00	$4.00
Machine-hours...................	–0–	500	–0–
Applied overhead................	$3.00 per labor hour	$2.00 per machine-hour	60% of labor cost

Required:

a) Prepare a cost sheet for the job.

b) What should the unit sales price be if Kingman desires to earn a gross profit of 40 percent of cost?

Problem 2-3. Purpose: *Cost of Manufacture; Cost Comparisons*

Kling Textile Mills manufactures wool comforters. Production for the month of August was 2,000 dozen comforters. A synthetic fiber used in making the tops and bottoms costs 30 cents a yard, and each comforter requires 10 yards. The wool filling material costs $2 a pound, and each comforter requires two pounds. There were no goods in process at the beginning or the end of the month, and no material was wasted.

During August, $98,000 of wool was consumed and $74,000 of tops and bottoms was consumed. Other data includes:

```
Direct labor........................$6,000
Manufacturing overhead............ 4,000
Tops and bottoms:
   Beginning inventory..............165,000 yards
   Ending inventory................190,000
   Purchases.......................272,000
```

There was no wool inventory at the beginning or end of the month.

Required:

a) Prepare a statement of the cost of manufacture.

b) Are there any differences between what was done and what should have been done? Comment on what the facts apparently show. Make the assumption that prices remained stable during the month.

Problem 2-4. Purpose: *Statement of Cost of Goods Sold*

The King Corporation produces a product in a continuous process type of operation. During July, 19—, when 10,000 units were produced, the following costs were incurred:

```
Materials purchased............................$180,000
Factory supplies purchased......................  4,000
Direct labor....................................  70,000
Supervision.....................................   6,000
Indirect labor..................................   5,000
Payroll taxes applicable to factory.............   6,000
Heat, light, and power..........................   5,000
Rent of factory building........................   4,000
Insurance.......................................   2,000
Depreciation of machinery.......................  15,000
Tools and dies expense..........................   2,000
Miscellaneous manufacturing expenses............   2,000
```

The inventories were as follows:

	June 30	July 31
Materials	$ 80,000	$60,000
Work-in-process	45,000	30,000
Finished goods	100,000	50,000
Factory supplies	3,000	2,000

Required:
 a) Prepare a cost of goods sold statement for July.
 b) Compute the unit cost of goods completed during July.

Problem 2–5. Purpose: *Gross Profit Analysis*

The Kent Corporation, a manufacturer of a line of houseware products, performs its manufacturing in two plants. Data pertaining to the two plants show the following:

PLANT NO. 1

	1968	1967
Sales......................	$200,000	$300,000
Cost of sales................	160,000	210,000
Gross profit................	$ 40,000	$ 90,000

PLANT NO. 2

(One Product Is Produced at This Plant)

	1968		1967	
	Amount	Per Unit	Amount	Per Unit
Sales................	$112,200	$10.20	$100,000	$10.00
Cost of sales.........	64,240	5.84	60,000	6.00
Gross profit..........	$ 47,960	$ 4.36	$ 40,000	$ 4.00

Prepare a detailed analysis of the causes for the decline in gross profit for each of the plants. Assume no changes in selling prices of the several products produced in Plant No. 1.

PROBLEMS—GROUP B

Problem 2–6. Purpose: *Statement of Cost of Goods Sold*

The United Company had the following inventories on hand at the beginning and end of September:

	September 1	September 30
Materials........................	$40,000	$50,000
Factory supplies..................	4,000	6,000
Goods-in-process.................	30,000	45,000
Finished goods...................	70,000	90,000

Twenty thousand units of the product "Unee" were produced with the result that the following costs were incurred:

Direct labor.....................................$100,000
Superintendence.................................   8,000
Other indirect labor..   6,000
Payroll taxes—factory...........................   9,000
Depreciation of machinery......................   17,000
Light and power................................   4,000
Tools, dies, and patterns.......................   7,000
Rent—factory building.........................   5,000
Insurance......................................   2,000
Sundry factory expenses........................   1,000

The following items were purchased:

Materials.......................................$220,000
Factory supplies..............................   8,000

Required:

  a) Prepare a cost of goods sold statement for September.

  b) Compute the unit cost of goods completed during the month.

Problem 2–7. Purpose: *Cost of Manufacture; Cost Comparisons*

During the month of January, the *U-Need Sleep* Corporation manufactured 8,000 pillows—its only product. Cotton cloth is used for the outside covering, and a special material is used as filling. One pound of filling and one yard of material are needed for each pillow. Covering material costs 80 cents a yard, and filling is $3 a pound. No pillows were in process either at the beginning or the end of the month.

The filling consumed during the month amounted to $26,000, and $6,800 of covering was used. Direct labor amounted to $6,000, and $6,000 was the amount of overhead incurred.

The beginning inventory of covering was 7,500 yards, and the ending inventory was 9,000 yards. Ten thousand yards were purchased. There was no inventory of filling material either at the beginning or the end of the period.

Required:

  a) Prepare a schedule showing the cost to manufacture.

  b) Are there any differences between what happened and what should have happened? Comment. You may assume that prices remained stable during the period.

Problem 2–8. Purpose: *Job Order Cost Computation*

The Univess Manufacturing Company maintains a machine shop where tools are manufactured to specification. Job No. 225 was started on April 1 and completed on April 19 and consisted of the manufacture of 800 special tools for the Bigelow Manufacturers. The following data is available for the three-week period:

	Week of April 5	Week of April 12	Week of April 19
Materials purchased...............	$12,000	–0–	$4,000
Materials used—Job No. 225.......	$800	$400	$600
Direct labor used this job..........	200 hours	150 hours	300 hours
Labor rate per hour...............	$3.00	$3.50	$3.40
Actual overhead incurred.........	$7,000	$5,000	$8,000

Factory overhead is applied at a rate of 110 percent of direct labor cost.

Required:

a) Prepare a cost sheet for the job.

b) What should the unit sales price be if Univess wants to earn 25 percent of cost as gross profit?

Problem 2–9. Purpose: *Process Cost Computation*

Untrell Industries manufactures a single product that is produced in the fabricating, assembly, and finishing departments. Forty thousand units were manufactured during the month of February. There were no goods in process at the beginning or at the end of the month.

All of the material is introduced in the fabricating department and amounted to $60,000 in February. Monthly labor cost amounted to $20,000 in fabricating, $50,000 in assembly, and $30,000 in finishing. Factory overhead is applied at the rate of 80 percent of labor cost.

Prepare a report showing total and unit cost in each department and at the end of each stage of the productive process.

Problem 2–10. Purpose: *Profit Analysis*

The Union Company management has become concerned over a decline in profits after examining the following statements. Profits declined even after sales prices were increased 10 percent on January 1, 1968.

	1968	1967
Sales...............................	$840,000	$940,000
Cost of goods sold...................	540,000	620,000
Gross profit.........................	$300,000	$320,000
Selling and administrative costs.......	70,000	75,000
Net income.........................	$230,000	$245,000

Prepare an analysis explaining the change in net profits.

CHAPTER

3 Accounting Records of the Cost Accounting System

Controlling Accounts and Subsidiary Ledgers in a Cost Accounting System

As the volume of transactions increases in a business, the need for summary or control accounts becomes more urgent. In a cost accounting system the following controlling accounts are especially useful:

1. Stores Control.
2. Manufacturing Overhead Control.
3. Work-in-Process Control.
4. Finished Goods Control.
5. Plant and Equipment Control.

The *Stores Control* account summarizes the detailed information recorded in a large number of subsidiary inventory ledger accounts, each representing a single kind of material. The entries in the control account summarize in a few figures the details recorded in the subsidiary accounts representing the receipt of materials in the storeroom either by purchase or as a return from the factory as excess issues, and the issuance of materials for use in the factory or as a return to the vendor. In the subsidiary accounts, a running balance is usually maintained. The following accounts and entries illustrate the stores control and the subsidiary records:

Stores Control

Mar.	1	Inventory at beginning	1,900	00	Mar.	31	Materials issued during the month	3,000	00
	31	Purchases for month	3,150	00					

The subsidiary ledger accounts (one for each kind of material) show the following information:

Material A

Receipts			Amounts Issued			Balance	
			Mar. 3	500.00	Mar. 1		800.00
Mar. 4	400.00				3		300.00
			10	300.00	4		700.00
20	700.00				10		400.00
			24	400.00	20		1,100.00
					24		700.00

Material B

Receipts			Amounts Issued			Balance	
			Mar. 4	350.00	Mar. 1		600.00
Mar. 5	800.00				4		250.00
			10	450.00	5		1,050.00
					10		600.00

Material C

Receipts			Amounts Issued			Balance	
			Mar. 5	250.00	Mar. 1		500.00
Mar. 12	550.00				5		250.00
			15	600.00	12		800.00
26	700.00				15		200.00
			27	150.00	26		900.00
					27		750.00

The balance in the Stores Control account on March 31 is $2,050. The sum of the balances in the accounts in the subsidiary ledger equals this amount, viz:

```
Material A........................$  700
Material B........................    600
Material C........................    750
    Total........................ $2,050
```

A similar arrangement of controlling accounts and the subsidiary ledger is usually established for the Finished Goods. However, the debits to the Finished Goods Control account will represent the balance on hand at the beginning of the period and the *cost of the goods manufactured and placed in the stock room* during the period.

A *Manufacturing Overhead Control* account is used to summarize a variety of indirect manufacturing costs. Since there are a large number of indirect costs, it becomes a practical matter to summarize these in a controlling account. The relation of the controlling account to the individual indirect cost account parallels that of the Accounts Receivable Control account to the individual customer accounts. The *Work-in-Process Control* is peculiar to cost accounting. It summarizes the costs incurred in manufacturing until the product is completed. The *subsidiary records* of the Work-in-Process Control account are the various job order cost sheets or the departmental cost of production reports. For a job order cost system instead of a single account, the Work-in-Process Control is usually presented in three accounts, each representing one of the elements of costs, namely, Work-in-Process—Materials, Work-in-Process—Labor, the Work-in-Process—Manufacturing Overhead. This subdivision may be illustrated with its subsidiary cost sheets as follows:

Work-in-Process—Materials

Mar.	1	Balance	1,000	00	Mar.	31	Orders completed	7,500	00
	31	Requisitions for month	8,000	00					

Work-in-Process—Labor

Mar.	1	Balance	3,000	00	Mar.	31	Orders completed	12,000	00
	31	Job time tickets for month	13,000	00					

Work-in-Process—Manufacturing Overhead

Mar.	1	Balance	900	00	Mar.	31	Orders completed	3,600	00
	31	Applied to production during month (30% of labor)	3,900	00					

At the end of the month three uncompleted job orders were still in the factory; they contain the detail shown in Illustration 3–1.

At the end of the month the balances in the three control accounts for the work-in-process were:

Work-in-Process—Materials...............................$1,500
Work-in-Process—Labor.................................. 4,000
Work-in-Process—Manufacturing Overhead................. 1,200

The subsidiary records (job order sheets) showed the following balances:

	Material	Labor	Overhead
Job Order No. 172........................$	600	$1,800	$ 540
Job Order No. 178........................	400	1,000	300
Job Order No. 179........................	500	1,200	360
Total............................$	1,500	$4,000	$1,200

Illustration 3–1

Manufactured for: Stock	Job Order No. 172 Date started: March 2, 19—
30 Model XX Machines	Date completed:———————

Material Charges	Labor Charges	Manufacturing Overhead Applied
Mar. 31 600.00	Mar. 31 1,800.00	Mar. 31 540.00

Manufactured for: Mullins Mfg. Co. Detroit, Michigan	Job. Order No. 178 Date started: March 5, 19—
25 Model XBR Special Machines	

Material Charges	Labor Charges	Manufacturing Overhead Applied
Mar. 31 400.00	Mar. 31 1,000.00	Mar. 31 300.00

Manufactured for: Stock	Job Order No. 179 Date started: March 6, 19—
20 Model 2XR Machines	

Material Charges	Labor Charges	Manufacturing Overhead Applied
Mar. 31 500.00	Mar. 31 1,200.00	Mar. 31 360.00

Plant and Equipment Control Account   Because of the ever increasing investment in plant and equipment in modern manufacturing operations and because of certain income tax regulations affecting depreciation, investment credit, and profit and loss on equipment replacements, it is a modern accounting necessity to keep detailed records of plants and equipment. The total of the investment may be recorded in a Plant and Equipment Control account, with subsidiary records for each plant on type of equipment maintained in a subsidiary *plant and equipment ledger.*

The Payroll Journal   The payroll journal or payroll book is not exclusively a cost accounting record. However, its importance is magnified somewhat when a cost accounting system is in use because of the large number of factory workers. Separate payroll books may be used for the factory workers and the office and sales employees. Modern payroll journals contain the following minimum information:

> Name of employee
> Social security number
> Time clock number
> Withholding tax status
> Total hours worked
> Rate of pay per hour
> Regular earnings
> Overtime earnings
> Total earnings
> The various deductions which include:
>> Federal Insurance Contribution Act tax
>> Withholding tax (federal, state, and city)
>> Insurance—life, hospital, medical, pension
>> Government bonds
> Net pay

The more specific accounting applications and use of payroll records will be given in Chapter 7. However, an illustration of the factory payroll journal is given in Illustration 3–2 to complete the discussion of the accounting records of a cost accounting system.

Adapting the Voucher Register to Cost Accounting Work   Most manufacturing concerns use a voucher system because it provides better internal control and also expedites the accounting work. However, since the transactions of a manufacturer differ somewhat from those in a mercantile firm, the columnar headings in the voucher register will also differ. For

Illustration 3–2
FACTORY PAYROLL JOURNAL

Week Ended March 14, 19—

Name of Employee	W.H. Status	Clock No.	Regular			Overtime		Gross Pay	Deductions					Net Pay	Check No.
			Hours	Amount	Rate Hourly	Hours	Amount		Fed. W.H.	State W.H.	F.I.C.A. 4.4%	Union Dues	Total		
A. G. Brown 543-01-4509	2	44	42	$ 84.00	2.00	1	$ 2.00	$ 86.00	$ 11.00	$ 1.00	$ 3.78	$ 3.00	$ 18.78	$ 67.22	61-101
V. E. Kelly 769-07-9632	3	45	46	92.00	2.00	3	6.00	98.00	8.60	0.90	4.31	3.00	16.81	81.19	61-102
J. C. Marbery 176-03-4816	1	46	40	80.00	2.00	0	—	80.00	12.30	1.20	3.52	3.00	20.02	59.98	61-103
			2,600	$5,200.00		80	$160.00	$5,360.00	$480.00	$56.20	$235.84	$165.00	$937.04	$4,422.96	
													=		

Summary of postings made weekly from this record:

Dr. Payroll.................................$5,360.00
   Cr. Federal Withholding Taxes Payable....... $ 480.00
   Cr. State Withholding Taxes Payable......... 56.20
   Cr. F.I.C.A. Taxes Payable 4.4%*............ 235.84
   Cr. Union Dues Payable...................... 165.00
   Cr. Payroll Accrued......................... 4,422.96

* At rate in effect when illustration was prepared.

example, a column must be provided for *Stores,* in place of the *Merchandise Purchases.* Provision must also be made for the factory payroll and for the variety of items falling under the heading of manufacturing overhead. For a manufacturing concern which does not maintain a separate factory ledger and yet whose cost accounting system is tied in with the regular financial accounting records, the voucher register should have columns for the following:

Accounts Payable, Credit	Stores, Debit
	Payroll Accrued, Debit
	Manufacturing Overhead Control, Debit
	Selling Expense Control, Debit
	Administrative Expense Control, Debit
	Sundry Accounts, Debit
	Sundry Accounts, Credit

These columns, however, require further consideration. Since the payroll journal is usually a book of original entry, the liability recorded in this journal after deductions is Payroll Accrued. The summary of the payroll journal previously illustrated results in the following debit and credits (see p. 53):

Payroll	5,360.00	
Federal Withholding Taxes Payable		480.00
State Withholding Taxes Payable		56.20
F.I.C.A. Taxes Payable 4.4%		235.84
Union Dues Payable		165.00
Payroll Accrued		4,422.96

The entry made in the voucher register for this payroll would be:

Payroll Accrued	4,422.96	
Accounts Payable		4,422.96

Since this payroll entry in the voucher register will occur regularly, a special column, headed Payroll Accrued, Dr., will reduce the posting work.

The Manufacturing Overhead Control account will be posted in total to the control, the individual items being posted to the subsidiary ledger accounts. To facilitate the posting to the subsidiary ledger accounts, most voucher registers have a special column next to the money column for the Manufacturing Overhead Control. This column is called the Code column; and in it, by means of numbers or letters, the subsidiary ledger accounts are indicated. This procedure facilitates posting to the subsidiary ledger. A similar procedure is used for the Selling Expense Control and the Administrative Expense Control columns.

Because some special entries may require adjustments, the Sundry column is sometimes provided with a *credit,* as well as a *debit,* money column. An illustration of such a voucher register is given in Illustration 3–8, page 65.

The Use of the Factory Journal and Factory Ledger
Many companies use a factory ledger which is separate from the general ledger. This system permits the detailed cost accounting work to be kept independently of the general accounting records and still interlock with it. This system also permits companies with factories in various parts of the country to maintain control over each plant, and at the same time each factory can retain all the records it needs for day-to-day operations. Companies which have factories in the same location as the general offices also use the factory ledger system to gain the subdivision of the clerical work. The same concepts used with a factory ledger system have found application in some nonmanufacturing firms such as chain stores which wish to prepare separate income reports for each store or branch sales organizations.

Separate records are kept at the factory. These include a *factory journal* (comparable to the columnar general journal); *factory ledger* (comparable to the general ledger); subsidiary inventory, payroll, manufacturing overhead, and cost accounting records are also maintained at the factory. The basic idea of the system is that the *Factory Ledger* account is kept in the general ledger in place of the accounts which control the cost accounting system—Stores, Work-in-Process, Finished Goods, Payroll, Manufacturing Overhead. And on the factory office books, a reciprocal account—*General Ledger*—is maintained corresponding to the Factory Ledger account on the general office books.

Accounting Procedures When Factory Ledger Is Used
When a factory journal is used to supplement the general (financial) accounting record, the general office will charge the factory office for the following:

1. Materials sent to it.
2. Money transferred for the payrolls.
3. Various overhead costs incurred by or recorded by the main office. These include items for which cash has been spent, the valuation charges for depreciation, and the accrual or deferral of factory expenses at the end of the accounting period.
4. Cost of goods shipped to customers.

To illustrate the cost accounting cycle affecting the factory office and the general office for these entries, the parallel example in Illustration 3–3 is given.

Illustration 3–3

Nature of Entry	General Office Books			Factory Office Books		

1. Materials shipped to factory.	Factory Office.............................2,500.00
	  Accounts (Vouchers) Payable.........
			2,500.00	Stores..............................2,500.00
				  General Office............
						2,500.00

	To record the voucher for materials purchased.			Materials received.		

2. Payroll remitted by the general office to factory.	Factory Office.............................8,000.00
	  F.I.C.A. Taxes Payable............
	  Federal Withholding Taxes Payable...
	  State Withholding Taxes Payable......
	  Accounts Payable..................
			356.00
			1,744.00
			600.00
			5,300.00
				Payroll..............................8,000.00
				  General Office............
						8,000.00

	To record voucher for weekly factory payroll.			To record weekly factory payroll sent to the general office.		

3. Manufacturing overhead costs involving the payment of cash.	Factory Office.............................. 800.00
	  Insurance Expense...................
	  Heat, Light, and Power..............
	  Office Supplies, etc.................
			300.00
			400.00
			100.00
				Manufacturing Overhead Control......... 800.00
				  General Office............
						800.00

	To transfer charges applicable to the factory.			To record factory overhead costs paid for by general office.		
4. Shipped to customers.	Accounts Receivable........................4,600.00 Sales...............................		4,600.00	No entry.		
	Selling prices of orders.					

	Cost of Sales.............................3,250.00
	  Factory Office......................
			3,250.00	General Office............................3,250.00
				  Finished Goods..............
						3,250.00

	Cost of sales shipped.			Cost of goods shipped to customers.		

These four entries are representative of the transactions affecting both the general office and factory office so that reciprocal entries must be made. On the basis of these entries, the Factory Office Control account on the general office books and the General Office account on the factory books are as shown below. It should be noted that the debit balance in the Factory Office account on the general office books is offset by the credit balance in the General Office account on the factory ledger.

Factory Office (Ledger) Account

(1) Purchases	2,500.00	(4) Cost of sales	3,250.00
(2) Payrolls	8,000.00		
(3) Manufacturing overhead	800.00		

General Office (Ledger) Accounts

(4) Cost of sales	3,250.00	(1) Materials received	2,500.00
		(2) Factory payrolls	8,000.00
		(3) Manufacturing overhead charges incurred by general office	800.00

The balance of each of these accounts is as follows: On the general office books, the *debit* balance of the Factory Office account is $8,050, and on the factory office books, the *credit* balance of the General Office account is $8,050. When the trial balances of the general office and the factory office are combined, these debit and credit items cancel each other, making the trial balance as though it were of a single location firm.

Form of the Factory Journal   There are two forms of the factory journal that can be used:

1. *A condensed summary type* in which entries are made less often in summary form, and
2. *The multicolumn form* in which the entries are made more frequently.

These forms are shown in Illustrations 3–4 and 3–5. In small plants entries may be made each week in summary form for the materials received, materials used, the factory payrolls, and factory overhead. For such a firm the *condensed summary* type may be used. For other firms requiring more detailed cost information, the *multicolumn* factory journal may be used. Each of these forms is illustrated.

The special features of the *condensed* summary form are:

Illustration 3–4

FACTORY JOURNAL—CONDENSED FORM

DEBIT General Ledger Control Amount	DEBIT Factory Operating Accounts — Account	DEBIT Factory Operating Accounts — Amount	L.F.	Date	Explanation	L.F.	CREDIT Factory Operating Accounts — Account	CREDIT Factory Operating Accounts — Amount	CREDIT General Ledger Control Amount
	Stores	2,300.00	11	Sept. 7	Stores Received during Week	√			2,300.00
	Payroll	3,000.00	12	7	Payroll for Week	√			3,000.00
	Manufacturing Overhead Control	1,260.00	13	7	Journal Voucher No. 12	√			1,260.00
	Work-in-Process—Material	1,410.00	14	7	Requisitions for Week	11	Stores Control	1,600.00	
	Manufacturing Overhead Control	190.00	13	7	Supplies Used				
	Work-in-Process—Labor	2,750.00	14	7	Payroll Analysis for Week	√			
	Manufacturing Overhead Control	250.00	13	7	Indirect Labor Costs	12	Payroll	3,000.00	
	Work-in-Process—Manufacturing Overhead	1,375.00	14	7	Applied Manufacturing Overhead	17	Applied Manufacturing Overhead	1,375.00	
	Finished Goods	4,000.00	15	7	Job Orders Completed	14	Work-in-Process—Material	1,300.00	
						14	Work-in-Process—Labor	1,800.00	
						14	Work-in-Process—Overhead	900.00	
3,600.00	General Ledger		√	7	Cost of Goods Shipped	15	Finished Goods	3,600.00	
37,000.00 (4)		40,000.00 (√)						55,000.00 (√)	22,000.00 (4)

MULTICOLUMN FACTORY JOURNAL

Date	Explanation	General Ledger Cr.	Stores Dr.*	Pay-roll Dr.	Manu-facturing Overhead Control Dr.	Work-in-Process Dr.*†	Finished Goods Dr.*	General Ledger Dr.	Miscel-laneous Dr.	Miscel-laneous Cr.	L. F.	Miscellaneous Accounts
Sept. 1	Stores from Brown & Co.	700 00	700 00									
2	Stores Summary					510 00				510 00	11	Stores
3	Supplies Received	120 00	120 00									
4	Payroll for Week‡	380 00		380 00								
5	Depreciation of Machines	178 00			178 00							
6	Taxes on Factory	82 00			82 00							
8	Supplies Used				61 00					61 00	11	Stores
9	Sundry Factory Charges	102 00			102 00							
10	Labor in Process				80 00	300 00				380 00	12	Payroll
11	Overhead in Process					320 00				320 00	13	Manufacturing Overhead
12	Goods Finished						1,021 00			1,021 00	14	Work-in-Process
13	Goods Shipped							768 00		768 00	15	Finished Goods
		1,562 00	820 00	380 00	503 00	1,130 00	1,021 00	768 00	(√)	3,060 00	√	
		(4)	(11)	(12)	(13)	(14)	(15)	(4)				

* It is possible to have separate columns for Stores, Cr., Work-in-Process, Cr., and Finished Goods, Cr., thus reducing the number of entries in the Miscellaneous Accounts section.

† Often there are three work-in-process accounts—one each for Materials, Labor, and Manufacturing Overhead.

‡ Payroll and withholding taxes recorded on general office books only. Payroll Book is used as memorandum record.

1. The total purchases received during a week are lumped together into a single entry which summarizes the journal vouchers or duplicate invoices received from the general office or shippers.
2. A similar procedure is followed for the manufacturing overhead items charged to the factory from memoranda received from the general office.
3. Materials used, labor costs applicable to production, the applied manufacturing overhead, and the cost of work completed *during the week* are each recorded in a single summary entry.
4. The total cost of all goods shipped to customers *during the week* is entered in a single entry.

Interoffice Accounting Forms

No matter which journal form is used, there must be some method whereby the factory is informed by the general office as to what entries must be made and vice versa. Otherwise, the reciprocal accounts will not check each other. In order that each office may know what the other is doing so that each office may make corresponding entries, *interoffice* vouchers are used. These are known as *journal* or *transfer* vouchers. Sometimes vouchers are kept in a binder and used as the book of original entry from which postings are made directly to the ledgers affected.

The main office may purchase material and have it sent directly to the factory. The invoice is sent to the main office to be recorded in the voucher register. But how does the factory bookkeeper know the cost of the goods when they are entered on perpetual inventory cards? One method is to have a duplicate invoice sent directly to the factory. Another method is to use a factory journal voucher (a specially printed form prepared by the main office) on which is recorded the data and information to be used by the factory bookkeeper in making entries in the factory books.

When this form is used to transfer part of an account already in the general office books, it is sometimes known as a *transfer voucher* (see Illustration 3–6). For example, at the end of a fiscal period the main office opens a depreciation account for plant and equipment and credits the allowance for depreciation account. That portion of the depreciation which is a factory cost and which must be recorded on the factory books is entered on a transfer voucher which is sent to the factory office. The transfer voucher is the equivalent of a letter from the main office stating that the factory account has been charged or credited with the information, and in the amount of the voucher. The reverse procedure is used if the factory office wishes to notify the general office that the general office has been charged or credited with a certain amount.

The purposes of the factory journal voucher and the transfer voucher

Illustration 3–6. Journal and Transfer Voucher

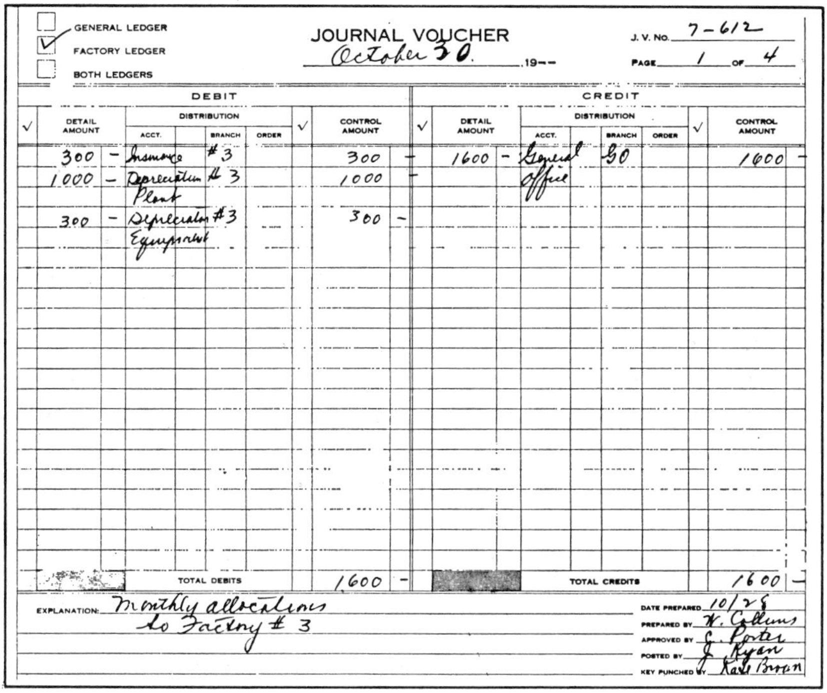

☐ GENERAL LEDGER
☑ FACTORY LEDGER
☐ BOTH LEDGERS

JOURNAL VOUCHER

October 30, 19--

J. V. No. 7-612

PAGE 1 OF 4

DEBIT							CREDIT						
√	DETAIL AMOUNT	DISTRIBUTION ACCT.	BRANCH	ORDER	√	CONTROL AMOUNT	√	DETAIL AMOUNT	DISTRIBUTION ACCT.	BRANCH	ORDER	√	CONTROL AMOUNT
	300 –	Insurance	#3			300 –		1600 –	General Office	GO			1600 –
	1000 –	Depreciation Plant	#3			1000 –							
	300 –	Depreciation Equipment	#3			300 –							
		TOTAL DEBITS				1600 –			TOTAL CREDITS				1600 –

EXPLANATION: Monthly allocations to Factory # 3

DATE PREPARED 10/28
PREPARED BY W. Collins
APPROVED BY G. Porter
POSTED BY J. Ryan
KEY PUNCHED BY Kate Brown

are identical, i.e., to provide the basis for entries in the factory journal or in the general journal.

Illustrative Entries When a Factory Journal Is Used

On the factory books, entries must be made for the receipt and use of materials; for the incurrence of the payroll liability and its payment; for the manufacturing overhead and its application to the finished product; and for the shipment of the finished product. Although conditions in the various firms may differ, in order to understand the entries given in Illustration 3–7, the following assumptions are made:

1. All cash receipts and disbursements are handled and recorded through the general office. Therefore, all accounts payable, accounts receivable, purchase books (or voucher registers), cash disbursements, and cash receipts journals are kept in the general office.
2. All plant accounts, such as Factory Buildings, Machinery, Tools, and Patterns, as well as their respective valuation allowances for depreciation, are kept in the general ledger.
3. Such accounts as Prepaid Taxes and Prepaid Insurance, as well as Estimated Income Taxes Payable, are kept in the general ledger.

4. All manufacturing or cost accounts are kept in the factory ledger. By the use of carbon copies of the purchase vouchers and journal vouchers, the general office informs the factory office what entries are to be made on the factory books; by means of duplicate shipping reports, the factory informs the general office what customers are to be billed for the goods sold.

Illustrative entries made in journal form are given for the general and factory office records in Illustration 3–7.

When a process or departmental cost system is used, the entries would be the same as those illustrated except that instead of using a Work-in-Process—Materials, Work-in-Process—Labor, and a Work-in-Process—Manufacturing Overhead account, the Work-in-Process—Department I and the Work-in-Process—Department II, etc., would be used for the respective charges of materials, labor, and manufacturing overhead. In this latter instant, when goods are completed, the debit to finished goods would be by credits to the departmental work-in-process accounts.

Adapting the Voucher Register to the Factory Journal System
The use of the factory journal may modify the form and use of the voucher register. When a factory ledger is used, it should be noted that a *Factory Ledger* column and control is used in place of the usual Stores and Manufacturing Overhead accounts. Two illustrations are given: Illustration 3–8—voucher register when a factory journal is not used; Illustration 3–9—when a factory journal is used.

Mechanizing the Cost Accounting Work
Cost accounting has always involved a large amount of repetitive or routine clerical work in assigning the various costs either to the jobs or to the departments. Many forms must be prepared, sorted, computed, and summarized. The discussion in this text relates to the manual operation of the cost accounting system. However, cognizance must be taken of the fact that what is done manually can usually be done better and more cheaply mechanically.

Three objectives are achieved by these newer mechanical devices: (1) better, quicker, and lower cost *recording of cost data;* (2) quicker *transmission* at lower cost of cost data detail; and (3) more detailed, quicker, and less costly *summaries* for managerial control.

To speed the *recording of labor cost data,* as well as *transmission of* it, some firms make use of telephones scattered throughout the factory so that cost information can be transmitted directly to the cost accounting or control department, where it may be recorded on a tape recorder or

Illustration 3–7. Entries of the Cost Accounting Cycle

Transaction	General Office Entry	Factory Office Entry
1. Materials or supplies purchased and sent to factory.	Dr. Factory Ledger Cr. Accounts Payable This entry is made in voucher register upon receipt of invoice from vendor and notification that goods have been received and approved by factory.	Dr. Stores Cr. General Ledger This entry is made in factory journal upon receipt of goods. The cost of the goods may be determined from duplicate invoices from vendor, duplicate copy of purchase order from general office, or by duplicate copy of voucher. When this entry has been made, detailed entries are also made on stores ledger cards.
2. Materials requisitioned from storeroom for use in factory.	No entry	Dr. Work-in-Process—Materials Dr. Mfg. Overhead Control (Indirect Materials) Cr. Stores This entry is a summary entry made in the factory journal either daily, weekly, or monthly from a summary of material requisitions. The material requisitions are also deducted on the individual perpetual inventory cards.

3. Factory payroll for the week.	(3b) Dr. Factory Ledger
	      Cr. Accounts Payable
	This entry is made in the voucher register to record voucher check for payroll.
	(3c) Dr. Accounts Payable
	      Cr. Cash
	To record the issuance of payroll check in check register.
	
	(3h) Dr. Factory Ledger
	      Cr. F.I.C.A. Taxes Payable
	      Cr. Federal Withholding
	         Taxes Payable
	      Cr. State Withholding
	         Taxes Payable
	To record the liability for payroll taxes and withholding taxes prior to payment.
		(3a) Dr. Payroll*
		      Cr. Payroll Accrued
		      Cr. F.I.C.A. Taxes Payable
		      Cr. Federal Withholding
		         Taxes Payable
		      Cr. State Withholding
		         Taxes Payable
		This entry is made in the factory payroll book.
		(3d) Dr. Payroll Fund*
		      Cr. General Ledger
		To record the receipt of check for payroll.
		(3e) Dr. Payroll Accrued*
		      Cr. Payroll Fund
		To record disbursement of fund.
		(3f) Dr. Work-in-Process—Labor
		      Dr. Mfg. Overhead Control
		         (Indirect Labor)
		      Cr. Payroll
		Summary entry in factory journal to record the analysis of job time tickets and indirect labor costs.
		(3g) Dr. F.I.C.A. Taxes Payable*
		      Dr. Federal Withholding
		         Taxes Payable
		      Dr. State Withholding
		         Taxes Payable
		      Cr. General Ledger
		To transfer the payroll and withholding tax liability to the general office for payment.

* If no Payroll Fund account is to be used and payroll taxes are to be shown in general office books only, then entry (3a) would be Dr. Payroll and Cr. General Ledger, and entries (3d), (3e), and (3g) are omitted.

Illustration 3-7—Continued

Transaction	General Office Entry	Factory Office Entry
4. To record factory expenses entered in general office books originally but now being transferred to factory ledger.	Dr. Factory Ledger Cr. Allowance for Depreciation of Factory Buildings Cr. Allowance for Depreciation of Machinery <small>To set up and charge factory with depreciation. This entry is made in general journal usually at the time of closing or summarizing of books.</small>	Dr. Mfg. Overhead Control (Depreciation of Factory Buildings and Depreciation of Machinery) Cr. General Ledger <small>This entry is recorded in factory journal upon receipt of a debit memorandum from general office.</small>
5. Vouchering of taxes or any other factory expense involving the payment of cash.	Dr. Factory Ledger Cr. Accounts Payable <small>This entry is made in voucher register.</small>	Dr. Mfg. Overhead Control (Taxes, etc.) Cr. General Ledger <small>This entry is made in factory journal.</small>
6. To set up accrual for compensation insurance.	Dr. Factory Ledger Cr. Compensation Insurance Payable <small>This entry is made in general journal.</small>	Dr. Mfg. Overhead Control (Compensation Insurance) Cr. General Ledger <small>This entry is made in factory journal.</small>
7. To record overhead charged to production.	No entry	Dr. Work-in-Process—Mfg. Overhead Cr. Applied Mfg. Overhead <small>This entry is made weekly or monthly in factory journal.</small>
8. To close the Applied Manufacturing Overhead into the actual Manufacturing Overhead Control account.	No entry	Dr. Applied Mfg. Overhead Cr. Mfg. Overhead Control <small>This entry is made at end of fiscal period in factory journal.</small>
9. To record cost of work completed in factory.	No entry	Dr. Finished Goods Cr. Work-in-Process—Materials Cr. Work-in-Process—Labor Cr. Work-in-Process—Mfg. Overhead <small>This entry is made periodically in factory journal.</small>
10. Sale of goods.	(10a) Dr. Accounts Receivable or Cash Cr. Sales <small>This entry is made at selling price in sales register.</small> (10b) Dr. Cost of Goods Sold Cr. Factory Ledger <small>This entry may be made in sales register or general journal.</small>	No entry for sales price of goods sold (10b) Dr. General Ledger Cr. Finished Goods <small>This entry is made in factory journal for cost price of goods shipped.</small>
11. To close out the over- or underapplied manufacturing overhead at the end of the accounting period.	Dr. Cost of Goods Sold Cr. Factory Ledger (assuming that the applied overhead is less than the actual) <small>This entry is made in general journal at the close of the accounting period.</small>	Dr. General Ledger Cr. Mfg. Overhead Control <small>This represents the balance in the account after entry 8 has been posted. It is usually not closed out until the end of the accounting period.</small>

Illustration 3–8. Voucher Register for Manufacturing Concern NOT Using a Factory Ledger

Date	Payable to	Voucher No.	Paid Date	Check No.	Accounts Payable, Cr.	F.I.C.A. Taxes Payable, Cr. 4.4%*	Federal Withholding Taxes Payable, Cr.	Stores, Dr.	Payroll Accrued, Dr.	Mfg. Overhead Control, Dr. L.F.	Code	Amount	Selling Expense, Dr. L.F.	Code	Amount	Administrative Expense, Dr. L.F.	Code	Amount	Sundry Accounts — Account	L.F.	Amount, Dr.	Amount, Cr.
Oct. 1	Service Realty Co.	815	10/2	732	400 00					✓	403	400 00										
2	Butler Harris & Co.	816			125 00					✓	401	125 00										
4	Knox Manufacturing Co.	817	10/10	736	622 52			622 52														
8	Payroll of Factory†	818	10/9	733	1,087 00	6 60	20 00		1,087 00													
8	Office Salaries	819	10/9	734	123 40	8 80	25 00									✓	602	150 00				
8	Salesmen's Salaries	820	10/9	735	166 20								✓	502	200 00							
10	A. N. Stewart & Co.	821			725 00			725 00														
12	A. C. Collins	822			200 00					✓	406	200 00										
15	Payroll of Factory	823	10/16	737	1,482 00				1,482 00													
18	Brown & Sharpe	824			3,000 00														Machinery	71	3,000 00	
24	Payroll of Factory	825	10/25	738	1,008 00				1,008 00													
25	Tower Supply Co.	826			50 00											✓	604	50 00				
27	National Fuel Co.	827			100 00					✓	405	100 00										
31	Payroll of Factory	828	10/31	739	1,531 00				1,531 00													
31	Office Salaries	829	10/31	740	390 20	19 80	40 00									✓	602	450 00				
31	Salesmen's Salaries	830	10/31	741	483 60	26 40	90 00						✓	502	600 00							
31	Internal Revenue Service	831	10/31	742	1,410 49														F.I.C.A. Tax Pay.	72	410 49	
																			Fed. W.H. Tax Pay.	73	1,000 00	
31	A. N. Stewart & Co.	821																		Accounts Pay.	42	120 00	
																			Stores	44		120 00
					12,904 41	61 60	175 00	1,347 52	5,108 00	✓		825 00	✓		800 00	✓		650 00		✓	4,530 49	120 00
					(42)	(72)	(73)	(44)	(48)	(50)			(55)			(56)						

* Assumes rate in effect when text was written.

† Assumes use of payroll journal as book of original entry.

Illustration 3–9. Voucher Register for Manufacturing Concern Using Factory Ledger

Date	Payable to	Voucher No.	Paid Date	Check No.	Accounts Payable, Cr.	F.I.C.A. Taxes Payable, Cr. 4.4%*	Withholding Taxes Payable, Cr.	Factory Ledger, Dr.	Selling Expense, Dr. L.F.	Code	Amount	Admin. Expense, Dr. L.F.	Code	Amount	Sundry Account	L.F.	Amount, Dr.	Amount, Cr.
Oct. 1	Service Realty Co.	815	10/2	732	400 00			400 00										
2	Butler, Harris & Co.	816	10/10	736	125 00			125 00										
4	Knox Mfg. Co.	817	10/9	733	622 52			622 52										
8	Payroll for Factory†	818	10/9	734	1,087 00			1,087 00										
8	Office Salaries	819	10/9	735	123 40	6 60	Fed. 15 00 State 5 00					✓	602	150 00				
8	Salesmen's Salaries	820	10/9	735	166 20	8 80	Fed. 20 00 State 5 00		✓	502	200 00							
10	A. N. Stewart & Co.	821			725 00			725 00										
12	A. C. Collins	822			200 00			200 00										
15	Payroll for Factory†	823	10/16	737	1,482 00			1,482 00										
18	Brown & Sharpe	824			3,000 00										Machinery	71	3,000 00	
24	Payroll for Factory†	825	10/25	738	1,008 00			1,008 00										
25	Tower Supply Co.	826			50 00							✓	604	50 00				
27	National Fuel Co.	827			100 00			100 00										
31	Payroll for Factory	828	10/31	739	1,531 00			1,531 00										
31	Office Salaries	829	10/31	740	390 20	19 80	Fed. 30 00 State10 00					✓	602	450 00				
31	Salesmen's Salaries	830	10/31	741	483 60	26 40	Fed. 75 00 State15 00		✓	502	600 00							
31	Internal Revenue Service	831	10/31	742	1,410 49										F.I.C.A. Taxes Payable	72	410 49	
															Federal With-holding Taxes Payable	73	1,000 00	
					12,904 41	61 60	175 00	7,280 52	✓		800 00	✓		650 00		✓	4,530 49	120 00
					(42)	(72)	(73)	(45)	55			56						
31	A. N. Stewart & Co.	821													Accounts Payable	42	120 00	
															Factory Ledger	45		120 00

* Assumes rate in effect when text was written.

† Payroll tax deductions for factory payroll are made in payroll book at factory.

entered on a punch card by a telephone operator. Such information is then ready for *automatic* processing with practically no delay.

By the use of telegraphic handwritten records inserted in machines such as the Tel-Autograph or the Electrowriter (Comptometer Company), it is possible to record in the cost accounting department and in the stores inventory department, facsimiles of job time tickets, or material requisitions. It is also possible by using the *common-language-tape punching device* connected with adding machines, time-clock records, or bookkeeping machines to prepare tapes which will automatically analyze or summarize cost detail at very high speeds; or if necessary, *convert* the accounting information to punch cards or magnetic tapes for processing in electronic computers.

Summaries are provided also by punched-card tabulating (accounting) machines and some of the smaller electronic computers.

QUESTIONS FOR REVIEW

1. Why has the use of punched-card accounting equipment been so useful in modern cost accounting work?
2. Why is it desirable to segregate the accounting record of costs from the financial records? Explain and illustrate.
3. In what way does the use of such modern mechanical devices as the electronic computers affect the segregation of cost and financial accounting recordings?
4. Under what conditions would you recommend the use of a multicolumned factory journal and a condensed factory journal?
5. What interoffice accounting forms are used when the cost accounting records are segregated from the financial accounting records? Why are these necessary?
6. What alterations should be made in the voucher register when a separate factory journal and factory ledger are used? Explain why this is necessary.
7. Should the payroll journal be used as a memorandum record? Explain.
8. What controlling accounts are usually associated with the factory journal and factory ledger? Why are these necessary?
9. What is the purpose of a plant and equipment subsidiary ledger? Is such a ledger necessary or desirable under the modern federal income tax law? Explain.
10. The budget is an important phase of managerial cost accounting procedure. Explain and illustrate why this is so.

PROBLEMS—GROUP A

Problem 3–1. Purpose: *Journal Entries Covering Cost Accounting Cycle*

The following amounts appeared in the inventory accounts of the L & I Company on October 1:

Stores.................$80,000
Work-in-process......... 60,000
Finished goods......... 50,000

The following transactions were completed during the month:

1. Materials in the amount of $40,000 were purchased on account.
2. Requisitions representing issues of direct material amounted to $60,000.
3. Indirect materials in the amount of $6,000 were issued.
4. October's payroll amounted to $70,000. Income taxes withheld amounted to $7,000, and F.I.C.A. taxes deducted were $2,200.
5. The employer's share of F.I.C.A. taxes amounted to $2,200. Other payroll taxes were $2,000 for the month.
6. The $70,000 payroll was distributed as follows:

Direct labor....................$50,000
Indirect labor................... 10,000
Sales salaries.................... 6,000
Office salaries................... 4,000

7. Factory overhead is applied to production on the basis of 50 percent of direct labor cost.
8. Overhead costs in addition to those listed above amounted to $6,000.
9. $125,000 worth of goods were completed and transferred to the stock room.
10. Billings to customers amounted to $200,000; the cost of these goods was $140,000.

Required:

a) Prepare journal entries to record the above information.
b) Prepare any necessary closing entries.

Problem 3–2. Purpose: *Journal Entries Covering Cost Accounting Cycle Using General Office and Factory Journals*

The Lyle Manufacturing Company maintains both a general office journal and a factory journal for cost accounting transactions. The factory ledger contains the following accounts:

Stores	Work-in-Process—Materials
Factory Payroll	Work-in-Process—Labor
Manufacturing Overhead	Work-in-Process—Manufacturing Overhead
Applied Manufacturing Overhead	Finished Goods

The following transactions took place during December:

1. Purchased $80,000 materials on account.
2. Paid freight on purchases of $1,100. Treat this as a manufacturing overhead.
3. Issued $20,000 of direct material; $2,000 of indirect materials.
4. Returned defective materials for credit to vendor in the amount of $3,000.
5. Payroll records are maintained in the payroll department and are recorded here in summary form only. Direct labor amounted to $29,000, and indirect labor was $6,000. The following amounts were withheld from the payroll:

```
F.I.C.A................................................$1,100
Federal withholding taxes................................ 3,500
State withholding taxes.................................. 1,000
```

6. Manufacturing overhead is applied to production at the rate of 90 percent of direct labor cost.
7. Vouchers received from the general office by the factory were:

```
Depreciation—plant and equipment.......................$8,000
Heat, light, and power.................................. 5,000
Factory share of property taxes......................... 2,000
Factory share of insurance.............................. 1,000
```

8. The employer's share of F.I.C.A. was $1,100. The factory share of unemployment taxes was $800.
9. Cost of the work completed during the month:

```
Material.......................$11,500
Direct labor.................... 25,000
```

10. Sale price of goods shipped was $60,000; cost was $42,000. Goods sold for $1,500 that cost $1,100 were returned by customers for credit.

Prepare journal entries to record the above transactions: Use the following columnar headings: Transaction, General Office Entries, and Factory Office Entries.

Problem 3–3. Purpose: *Journal Entries for the Cost Accounting Cycle Prepared from the Schedule of Cost of Goods Sold*

The following schedule represents the cost of goods manufactured and sold by the Little Manufacturing Company for three months ended June 30, 19—:

Schedule B-1

LITTLE MANUFACTURING COMPANY

Cost of Goods Manufactured and Sold
For Three Months Ended June 30, 19—

Cost of Manufacturing:

Stores Inventory, 4/1/—...............................			$15,000.00
Stores Purchased..			75,000.00
Total..			$90,000.00
Less: Stores Inventory, 6/30/—...............		$10,000.00	
Indirect Materials Used..................		6,000.00	16,000.00
Direct Materials Used........................			$ 74,000.00
Direct Labor..			90,000.00
Manufacturing Overhead Applied, 50% of Direct Labor			
Costs..			45,000.00
Total..			$209,000.00

Less: Increase in Work-in-Process Inventory:

	June 30	April 1	
Work-in-Process—Material....................	$10,500.00	$ 8,500.00	
Work-in-Process—Labor......................	12,500.00	10,000.00	
Work-in-Process—Overhead..................	6,250.00	5,000.00	
Total..	$29,250.00	$23,500.00	5,750.00

Cost of Goods Manufactured at Normal.....................			$203,250.00
Add: Decrease in Finished Goods Inventory:			
Finished Goods, 4/1/—................................		$40,000.00	
Finished Goods, 6/30/—..............................		34,250.00	5,750.00
Cost of Goods Sold at Normal............................			$209,000.00
Less: Overapplied Manufacturing Overhead................			3,000.00
Cost of Goods Sold at Actual...........................			$206,000.00

From this schedule, prepare in journal form, entries which will summarize in logical sequence the transactions representing the cost accounting cycle for the three-month period. Use three work-in-process accounts.

Problem 3–4.   Purpose: *Journal Entries and T-Ledger Accounts for Cost Accounting*

The A. B. Lincoln Company manufactures furniture on a job order cost basis, making items according to customer specifications. The following data is available for the month of March:

Stores..	$ 15,000
Work-in-process—materials...................................	7,000
Work-in-process—labor..	6,000
Work-in-process—overhead....................................	6,000
Finished goods...	30,000

Overhead is applied to production on the basis of 100 percent of labor cost.

Material purchases during the month...........................	$ 83,000
Stores used:	
Direct materials...	65,000
Indirect materials..	7,000
Payroll data:	
Total payroll..	80,000
Indirect labor..	10,000
Payroll deductions:	
Federal withholding taxes................................	9,000
State withholding taxes..................................	1,500
F.I.C.A. taxes..	3,000
Payroll taxes...	5,500
Depreciation of plant and equipment...........................	9,000
Factory overhead requiring cash outlays........................	40,000
Cost of work completed during March:	
Materials...	60,000
Labor...	72,000
Cost of goods sold...	210,000
Sales..	290,000

Required:

a) Prepare in journal form entries to record the cost accounting cycle.

b) Prepare a T-ledger account for Stores, three work-in-process accounts, Finished Goods, Payroll, Manufacturing Overhead, Manufacturing Overhead Applied, Cost of Goods Sold. Record any beginning balances in the accounts.

c) Post to the selected accounts and determine ending balances in the inventory accounts.

Problem 3–5.   Purpose: *Preparation of Cost of Goods Sold Statement from Ledger*

The Long Manufacturing Company ledger contained among others the following ledger accounts as of January 31:

Stores

Jan. 1	Balance	30,000.00	Jan. 31		40,000.00
31		70,000.00			

Payroll

Jan.31	60,000.00	Jan. 31	60,000.00

Manufacturing Overhead Control

Jan. 31	4,000.00		
31	3,000.00		
31	48,000.00		

Work-in-Process

Jan. 1	Balance	10,000.00	Jan. 31	135,000.00
31		36,000.00		
31		57,000.00		
31		50,000.00		

Manufacturing Overhead Applied

	Jan. 31	50,000.00

Finished Goods

Jan. 1	Balance	16,000.00	Jan. 31	140,000.00
31		135,000.00		

Prepare a cost of goods sold statement for the month of January.

Problem 3–6. Purpose: *Journal Entries for an Integrated Job Order Cost System When One Set of Books Is Used; Income Statement*

The following accounts represent a part of the ledger of the Lammermans Manufacturing Company for the first calendar month of the fiscal year. The cost accounts are integrated with the financial accounting into a single set of books (no factory journal).

Stores Control

June 1	Balance	20,000.00	June 30	Returns to vendors	3,000.00
30	Purchases	40,000.00	30	Requisitions	27,000.00
30	Returns to stock	500.00			

Payroll

June 30	Factory	31,500.00	June 30	Into production	31,500.00

Manufacturing Overhead Control

June 30	Indirect materials	6,000.00	June 30	Applied	17,400.00
30	Indirect labor	2,500.00			
30	Taxes	350.00			
30	Depreciation	2,650.00			
30	Insurance	200.00			
30	Sundry (payables)	4,000.00			

Work-in-Process—Materials

June 1	Balance	2,100.00	June 30	Returns	500.00
30	Stores	21,000.00	30	Finished goods	18,000.00

Work-in-Process—Labor

June 1	Balance	2,600.00	June 30	Finished goods	28,000.00
30	Direct labor	29,000.00			

Work-in-Process—Manufacturing Overhead

June 1	Balance	1,560.00	June 30	Finished goods	16,800.00
30	Applied	17,400.00			

Finished Goods

June 1	Balance	5,000.00	June 30	Cost of sales	58,800.00
30	Jobs completed	62,800.00			

Cost of Goods Sold

June 30	Goods shipped	58,800.00	June 30	Profit and loss	58,800.00

Sales

June 30	Profit and loss	78,000.00	June 30	For month	78,000.00

Selling Expense Control

June 30,	Sundry charges	5,600.00	June 30	Profit and loss	5,600.00

Administrative Expense Control

June 30	Sundry charges	4,000.00	June 30	Profit and loss	4,000.00

Profit and Loss

June 30	Cost of sales	58,800.00	June 30	Sales	78,000.00
30	Selling expenses	5,600.00			
30	Administrative	4,000.00			

From these ledger accounts, prepare:

a) Entries in journal form for the cost accounting cycle.
b) Condensed income statement for the month of June, 19— (Exhibit B).
c) Schedule of cost of goods sold (Schedule B-1).
d) Schedule of manufacturing overhead (Schedule B-2).

PROBLEMS—GROUP B

Problem 3–7. Purpose: *Journal Entries Covering Cost Accounting Cycle*

The Vincent Company engaged in the following transactions during the month of November:

1. Purchases of materials net of discounts amounted to $70,000.
2. $7,000 of supplies were issued from the storeroom, along with $53,000 of direct materials.
3. The November payroll amounted to $65,000. Of this, $40,000 was direct labor and $8,000 was indirect labor. Sales salaries were $9,000, and office salaries made up the balance.
4. Income taxes withheld amounted to $7,000, and the F.I.C.A. tax deduction was $1,800. The employer's share of F.I.C.A. taxes was also $1,800, and the other payroll taxes amounted to $1,500.
5. Factory overhead is applied to production on the basis of $2 per machine-hour. Records indicate 21,000 machine-hours in November.
6. Actual factory overhead costs in addition to those listed above amounted to $21,000.
7. Goods costing $110,000 were completed and put in stock.
8. Sales for the month amounted to $160,000; the cost of goods represented in the customer billings was $94,000.

Required:

a) Prepare journal entries to record the above information.
b) Prepare any necessary closing entries.

Problem 3–8. Purpose: *Journal Entries Covering Cost Accounting Cycle Using General Office and Factory Journals*

The following is a summary of transactions that took place during July:

1. Stores in the amount of $105,000 were purchased on account.
2. Paid a freight charge of $2,000 on incoming stores. This item should be treated as an overhead item.
3. Requisitions representing issues of direct materials amounted to $120,000.
4. Indirect materials of $12,000 were issued.
5. The monthly payroll amounted to $140,000. Income tax withholding amounted to $16,000, and $4,500 of F.I.C.A. taxes were deducted. The

employer's share of F.I.C.A. was the same amount. Other payroll taxes amounted to $4,000. The payroll records are maintained in the payroll department and are recorded here in summary form only.

6. The burden rate for applying overhead to production is 80 percent of direct labor cost.

7. Of the $140,000 payroll, direct labor amounted to $110,000. Indirect labor made up the balance.

8. The general office transfer vouchers received by the factory showed:

```
Depreciation.............................................$20,000
Heat, light, power.......................................  9,000
Factory share of insurance and property taxes............  8,000
```

9. Cost of goods completed during the month:

```
Materials................................................$80,000
Labor....................................................  95,000
Manufacturing overhead...................................  80% of direct
                                                           labor cost
```

10. Finished goods inventory July 1, $30,000.

11. Sales amounted to $325,000; cost of goods sold were $270,000. Goods that cost $6,000 and sold for $9,000 were returned by customers for credit.

The Victor Company maintains both a general office and a factory office journal for cost accounting transactions. The following accounts are found in the factory ledger: Stores, Payroll, Manufacturing Overhead, Manufacturing Overhead Applied, three work-in-process accounts, Finished Goods.

Prepare journal entries to record the above transactions. Use the following columnar headings: Transaction, General Office Entries, Factory Office Entries.

Problem 3-9. Purpose: *Preparation of Cost of Goods Sold Statement from Ledger Accounts*

The following accounts are found among those in the general ledger of the Ventor Company:

Payroll

Mar. 31	5,000.00	Mar. 31	5,000.00

Stores

Mar. 1	Balance	4,000.00	Mar. 31	3,000.00
31		6,000.00		

Goods-in-Process

Mar. 1	Balance	2,000.00	Mar. 31	9,000.00
31		3,500.00		
31		2,500.00		
31		4,200.00		

Manufacturing Overhead Control

Mar. 31	1,500.00		
31	500.00		
31	3,800.00		

Manufacturing Overhead Applied

		Mar. 31	4,200.00

Finished Goods

Mar. 1	Balance	2,100.00	Mar. 31	10,100.00
31		9,000.00		

Prepare a cost of goods sold statement for the month of March.

Problem 3–10. Purpose: *Journal Entries for the Cost Accounting Cycle, Prepared from the Cost of Goods Sold Schedule*

The cost of goods sold schedule of the Vellman Manufacturing Company for the three months ended September 30, 19—, is given below.

From this data, prepare journal entries, in logical sequence, to summarize the transactions of the cost accounting cycle for the three months, using one work-in-process account.

VELLMAN MANUFACTURING COMPANY
Cost of Goods Manufactured and Sold
For the Three Months Ended September 30, 19—

Cost of Manufacturing:

Work-in-Process, 7/1/—..........................			$ 50,000.00
Direct Material Used:			
Stores Inventory, 7/1/—.......................	$ 18,000.00		
Stores Purchases, Net.........................	82,000.00		
Total.....................................	$100,000.00		
Less: Stores Inventory, 9/30/—.........$15,000.00			
Indirect Materials Used........... 2,000.00	17,000.00		
Direct Materials Used...................		83,000.00	
Direct Labor..		87,000.00	
Manufacturing Overhead Applied, 30% of Direct Labor			
Costs...		26,100.00	
Total Cost of Manufacturing.................		$246,100.00	
Less: Work-in-Process, 9/30/—......................		46,100.00	
Cost of Goods Manufactured at Normal................		$200,000.00	
Add: Decrease in Finished Goods Inventory:			
Finished Goods, 7/1/—..........................	$ 52,500.00		
Finished Goods, 9/30/—.........................	22,500.00	30,000.00	
Cost of Goods Sold at Normal.......................		$230,000.00	
Add: Underapplied Manufacturing Overhead...........		4,200.00	
Cost of Goods Sold at Actual.......................		$234,200.00	

Problem 3–11.   Purpose: *Journal Entries and T-Ledger Accounts for Cost Accounting Cycle*

The Victory Chemical Company produces a chemical known as "vit" in a continuous process operation. Following is the data covering the month of May:

Work-in-process	$180,000
Stores	140,000
Finished goods	290,000
Stores purchased	172,000
Requisitions processed by the storeroom:	
Direct materials	220,000
Supplies	11,000
Direct labor	209,000
Superintendence	12,000
Indirect labor	39,000
Federal withholding tax	31,000
State withholding tax	9,000
F.I.C.A. taxes deducted from employees	10,000
Payroll taxes (does not include F.I.C.A.)	8,000
Depreciation and amortization	32,000
Other factory overhead items	80,000
Transfer to finished goods	580,000
Sold to customers	800,000
Cost of goods sold	620,000

Overhead is applied to production at the rate of 90 percent of labor cost.

Required:

a) Prepare T-ledger accounts for Stores, Work-in-Process, Payroll, Manufacturing Overhead, Manufacturing Overhead Applied, Finished Goods, Cost of Goods Sold. Record beginning balances.

b) Prepare in journal form entries to record the cost accounting cycle.

c) Post to the selected accounts and determine the ending balances in the inventory accounts.

SECTION II

Managerial Control of the
Elements of Costs

In view of the fact that planning and budgetary procedures are part of the efficient operations of a manufacturing plant and because budgetary procedures are an important part of cost accounting, an introductory chapter on budget planning is the starting point of this discussion of managerial cost control. This is followed by discussions of managerial control of material acquisitions; cost control of materials used; cost accounting for factory payrolls; manufacturing overhead applied to production; and the accumulation of the actual manufacturing overhead costs. Emphasis is primarily on the principles and practices of these elements of cost when applied to the job order cost system, with occasional comparisons with the process or departmental cost procedure. Detailed applications to the process or departmental cost accounting are given in Chapters 9 through 14.

CHAPTER

4 ⁝ The Planning Budget:

Basic Considerations

Introduction   The preceding chapters might leave the impression that cost accounting is only historical in nature and that the cost accountant does nothing more than report the transactions after they have taken place. Although the cost accountant does accumulate historical data and although this cost accumulation is an important part of the management information system, another important segment of cost accounting has to do with providing data that may be used by management as aids in *planning for the future*. In this manner cost accounting is not only historical but becomes *forward-looking*.

Planning for the future may be in terms of *period planning* and/or in terms of *project planning*. For example, a forecast of direct labor needs for the coming year would constitute an element of period planning while a plan for the construction of a new plant would be in terms of project planning. In recent years new techniques such as PERT and PERT/COST have been used by some business firms as aids in the project planning process. These techniques set out in a logical manner the steps necessary to accomplish a given project and could be considered as the starting point in the planning process.

All of the financial plans of the business organization whether they are period plans or project plans constitute the budget. A *budget* is thus the *financial plan* for the organization and is important as it places in financial form the objectives of the organization. As a result, top management can use the budget as a guide to action.

The use of a budget by an organization not only helps in placing the objectives of the business firm into financial terms but permits comparison of actual with forecasted data. The budget is a useful instrument in the *control* function. Later discussions will point out that budgets should be constructed around people so that performance may be evaluated. In addition, the idea of having to prepare a financial plan may be rewarding in that personnel from the various departments and areas of the organization have to work together. By its nature, budgeting encourages *coordination.*

The following paragraphs examine the basic considerations of budgeting. Detailed examination of budgets is deferred until Chapters 15 and 16.

Nature of Budgets   A budget is a carefully prepared estimate of future business conditions that can be used by management as a guide to action in the operation of the business organization. Ideally, a budget for a business firm should be all-inclusive and encompass revenue, costs, expenses, and funds flow.

Budgets are designed to assist management in the planning, coordination, and control of the various business functions of sales, production, and administration. Since conditions in businesses vary, the budgets prepared will also vary. The basic principles, however, will be the same for any size business and for almost any type of industry.

Budgets are classified under two categories: (1) *static* or *fixed* and (2) *variable* or *flexible.* The fixed budget is based upon a single (estimated as probable) volume of business activity, while the flexible budget is based on a *series* of possible volumes, all considered within the range of probability. The fixed budget, therefore, will be prepared from a relatively constant set of figures, using figures for the sales and expenses for a single definite estimated volume. Of course, these figures will be presented in great detail for each period (usually a month) so that maximum managerial control may be exerted by making comparisons with the actual operating figures.

The *flexible* or *sliding scale* budgets are a series of comparable budgets prepared for a *series* of volumes, one of which is the standard volume and represents the 100 percent figure. Budget figures will then be prepared for 90 percent volume of sales or production, and for the 80 percent, 70 percent, as well as 110 percent and 120 percent. Thus a flexible budget can readily be used for making comparisons with the actual operating conditions without preparing a completely new budget. Whether a budget is static or flexible, it is always desirable to have all manufacturing overhead costs and selling and administrative expenses grouped into fixed, variable, and semivariable classifications, so that when making comparisons of the budgeted with the actual figures, management can evaluate to what extent the variations in costs or income were controllable.

Advantages in Using Budgets   The use of budgets by the business firm may be advantageous for the following reasons:

1. The preparation of budgets forces management personnel to engage in *planning;* management must become forward-looking. In addition, the objectives of the firm have to be defined and stated in financial terms.

2. The use of budgets lends itself to *coordinating* the activities of the various segments of the business. For example, the use of budgets may have the effect of coordinating distribution effort with the sales effort as well as with the production effort.

3. The implementation of budgets may provide an instrument for *control.* Deviations from a prescribed course of action may be determined, and management may take steps to eliminate the reasons for the deviations.

4. The techniques used in budgeting force management to examine carefully the uses of labor and capital with the result that a more efficient use of resources may result.

5. The use of budgets results in a management team that is *"cost conscious"* before funds are committed. The emphasis in budgeting is not in cost reduction per se but rather in the maximization of long-run profit. Additional costs will be incurred if these costs can be expected to produce additional profits.

6. The use of budgets provides the machinery to aid in choosing among *alternative courses of action.* Better decisions may be reached when such problems as make or buy, lease or build, etc., are being considered.

Limitations of Budgets   The limitations of the use of budgets must be understood if the advantages of budgets discussed in the preceding paragraphs are to be achieved.

First and foremost, one must remember that at best a budget is a sophisticated estimate; no one knows what will happen in the future. That does not mean budgets are useless; on the contrary, they can be very useful if one doesn't lose sight of the fact that they are estimates.

Second, the budgetary system should not be a device that would take the place of management. A budget cannot be a substitute for management but should be used by management.

Third, the benefits to be derived from the use of budgets will only be as good as the effort expended to establish the budget. Even though a budget is an estimate, there are various degrees of reliability of the estimation.

Fourth, a budgetary system will provide desired results only if the system is reviewed continuously and amended as needs and activities change. An antiquated system provides little benefit.

The Budget Period   The *budget period* is an important factor in developing a complete budgetary plan. For the most effective results, all three of the following time plans should be used:

1. A *long-range* planning period covering several years. Such a program would affect company expansion policy regarding new products and the matter of investing in new plant and equipment.

2. Overall planning for the *fiscal accounting period.* Usually this covers a period of one year and refers to the master budget, since it sets forth the operating plans and profit objective for the next fiscal period. This budget phase includes all areas of the business and coordinates the sales, production, distribution, and finance functions.

3. A *month-to-month basis budget* gives the detail, by months, of the overall planning budget for the fiscal accounting period. This plan will be the most effective in controlling costs, sales, and expenses because of the shortness of the period. The month-to-month budget is used as a major guide to action by the businessman.

Most budgets are prepared on both long-term and short-term bases. A total budget for the year gives a complete picture of estimated conditions; and a short-period budget is prepared in greater detail to cover the requirements of the immediate period. Some companies engage in continuous budgeting. For example, each month a budget is prepared for the same month of the following year. Thus, at any one time, the company has an operating budget for a full year. Obviously, the businessman that has this is at a considerable advantage; the plan for an entire year is always there.

Requirements of a   For a budget program to achieve the
Successful Budget   desired results, the firm's responsibility
Program   organization must be carefully planned. Each person in a supervisory capacity from the foreman to the president must have his duties defined. The firm's organization chart serves as the center of focus for a well-defined organization. The chart should be accompanied by a manual of job classifications.

The budgets that are prepared must be realistically attainable. A budget that is not realistic affects employee morale and disrupts the efforts toward coordination. Budgets have to be implemented by *people*. Therefore, budgets will produce desired results only when people are motivated properly; realistically attainable budgets help.

The chief executive of the firm must give his complete support to the budget program if it is to achieve success. The need for using budgetary control must originate with top management.

Organization for Budgetary Control   Generally, the direction and execution of the budget is delegated to a budget committee which reports directly to top management. The actual preparation of the budget, however, should be started as far down the line as possible. One member of the budget committee is the *budget director* who is in charge of preparing a budget manual of instruction and the accumulation of the budgeted and actual figures and reports. Customarily, other members of the budget committee are the functional department heads and include the sales manager, the production manager, the treasurer, and the controller. The controller or an assistant is frequently appointed to serve as the budget director. The duties of the budget committee under the leadership of the director would include:

1. Receiving from the various executives, department heads, and supervisors, estimates for the long- and short-term periods, and where necessary to supply the previously used figures to these employees;
2. Assembling this budget data in accordance with a previously organized master plan;
3. Evaluating and revising, where necessary, the data thus collected before preparing the final budget; and
4. Issuing periodically—daily, weekly, monthly, quarterly—reports showing the comparisons of the actual with the budgeted figures.

A Manufacturer's Complete Budget Plan   A complete budgetary control system in a manufacturing concern should cover the following types of budgets, each of which can be broken down into smaller units:

    I. Selling function: Sales or income budget.
    II. Production function:
        a) Cost of production budget:
            1. Materials budget.
            2. Labor budget.
            3. Manufacturing overhead cost budgets.
        b) Inventory budget.
        c) Purchases budget.

III. Operating expense functions:
    a) Distribution cost budget.
    b) General and administrative expense budget.
    c) Financial expense budget.
IV. Financial budgets:
    a) Cash receipts budget.
    b) Cash expenditures budget.
V. Capital expenditures budget:
    a) Plant and equipment proposals.
    b) Other proposals.

A complete budgetary system is shown diagrammatically in Illustration 4–1.

The Sales Budget

The most important budget upon which all others are contingent is the *sales budget* —the forecast of goods to be sold. Four classes of information are usually considered in preparing the sales estimates:

1. Quantity and value of past sales, usually by products and territories.
2. General business and market conditions.
3. Conditions within the particular industry.
4. Plans and policies of the company.

The detailed method used in preparing sales budgets varies with each individual company. For example, one very successful machine manufacturer has been able to forecast, in August, and based almost entirely upon the orders received in August, the probable sales for the following February. In February the actual orders received are used to predict sales for the next August. Some companies have the sales personnel submit budgets of expected sales in each of their territories. The success of this forecast over a period of years has been surprising.

Ideally, a firm should combine all three techniques. Sales personnel who are in contact with the customers should aid in the preparation of sales budgets. Top management, although not as close to the customers as the salespeople, might have a better overall view of the market and competition and would be in a position to evaluate the sales picture. Economic indicators must also be examined and considered in the formation of the sales budget.

The Production Budget

Supplementing the sales budget, and subsidiary to it, is the *production budget*. When it is estimated how many units of each product will probably be sold, provision must be made for their production. This involves budgeting the figures for the manufacturing department. The completed

Illustration 4–1. Complete Budgetary System

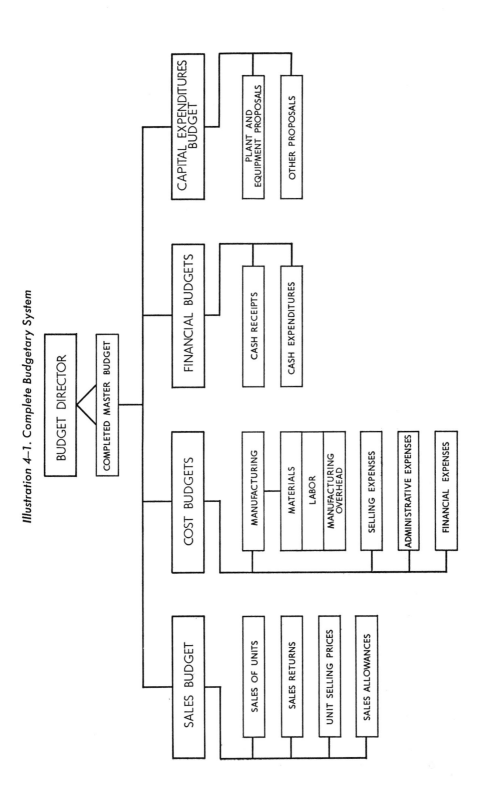

budget of this department is known as the *production budget.* Studying the actual and the budgeted production figures is one of the most important tasks of managerial control because by analyzing the unfavorable variations and their causes it should be possible to correct inefficient production costs and even reduce costs. The production budget starts with a weekly or monthly estimate of the number of units to be produced, as indicated by the sales budget and by the most efficient number of units that can be produced at one time. This could be followed by a *standard cost sheet* for each product, although a production budget may be used in an organization that does not employ a standard cost system. On this would be shown the estimated amount of material, labor, and manufacturing overhead for each product. Considering the predetermined costs for each product and the quantity of each product to be produced, it is possible to prepare budgets showing the materials requirements, the labor budgets, and the manufacturing overhead budgets for the entire plant and by departments.

Although the foregoing are listed as separate budgets, they are all closely interrelated. From the sales budget and the inventories of finished goods, it is possible to determine the quantity of each product that must be produced. When the number of units to be produced has been established, the materials, labor, and overhead costs can be determined. Purchases budgets may also be prepared. In certain instances, it will be necessary to study and prepare a plant and equipment budget showing to what extent the plant will or will not be used on the basis of budgeted production figures. Upon the completion of the sales and the production budgets, that portion of an estimated income statement which will indicate the estimated gross profit on sales may be prepared.

To illustrate how the sales budget may be converted into a production budget, Illustration 4–2 gives the estimated plant load in direct labor hours—a production budget for the year. This budget must take into consideration (1) the quantity in finished goods inventory, (2) the quantity on order and in process, and (3) the quantity to be manufactured in each of the next four quarters of the fiscal year. These production statistics can then be converted into labor hours per week, material requirements, and the flexible manufacturing overhead cost budget.

A complete illustration of the operating budget is deferred until Chapter 16.

Flexible Budgeting. A basic consideration in the preparation of a budget is the expected level of operations. In the case of a manufacturing situation, production might be the major consideration whereas the level of sales might be the major consideration in budgeting distribution costs.

Illustration 4–2

COMPUTATION OF ESTIMATED DIRECT LABOR HOUR PLANT LOAD FOR YEAR 19—
BASED ON SALES FORECAST AND INVENTORY ANALYSIS

(Prepared in November for Next Year)

	On Order and in Process at Time Budget Is Prepared	To Be Manufactured in 19— (Budgeted)		
		First Quarter	Second Quarter	Last Half of Year
Total amount to be produced per inventory analysis as at November, 19—.................	$750,000.00	$400,000.00	$370,000.00	$700,000.00
Less: Work-in-process inventory, November, 19—..............	400,000.00	....	....	....
Balance to be manufactured.......	$350,000.00	$400,000.00	$370,000.00	$700,000.00
Total estimated direct labor hours required.....................	76,000	91,000	84,500	169,000
Direct labor hours required per week.......................	9,500 (8 weeks)	7,000 (13 weeks)	6,500 (13 weeks)	6,500 (26 weeks)
Plant capacity in direct labor hours per week, November, 19—:				
First shift.................	8,200	8,200	8,200	8,200
Second shift...............	1,300	1,300	1,300	1,300
Total capacity...........	9,500	9,500	9,500	9,500
Percent of plant capacity to produce budgeted sales:				
Two-shift basis.............	100%	73.7%	68.4%	68.4%
One-shift basis.............	116%	85.4%	79%	79%

The level of operations would not be a serious problem in the budgeting process if one of the following two conditions were present:

1. The level of operations was always the same; no fluctuations in production or sales occurred, or
2. All costs and expenses behaved in the same manner.

Obviously, these conditions do not exist in the majority of companies. Not only does the level of operations vary from one year to the next but variations within the year may also occur. To complicate matters, not all costs behave in the same manner. Generally, an assumption is made that direct material and direct labor costs are *variable,* i.e., these costs vary in direct proportion with production.

Although the *total* costs of direct material and direct labor are considered variable, the *unit* costs would be constant or fixed especially if proper controls for the quality of materials purchased have been used and if, as is so frequently the case, the volume of work per hour is controlled by the speed of the machines. However, with the long list of items making up the *manufacturing overhead* or *indirect manufacturing costs,* the cost per unit may or may not vary as the volume for a given period changes, i.e., not all these costs behave in the same manner. It is with these manufacturing overhead costs that management is primarily concerned. Management has, therefore, grouped these manufacturing overhead items into *fixed* and *variable* and then attempted to indicate their effect on the budget at different operating volumes. For example, if a firm rents its buildings, then the rental cost will be fixed regardless of the volume of production. At all capacities of production, the budget will show the same figure. The same would probably be true if the firm owned the buildings and included the charge for real estate taxes in place of the rental cost. However, as the volume of production increases, the *per unit cost* for rent or taxes will decrease, and vice versa.

There are, however, many manufacturing overhead costs which will fluctuate as the volume of production increases or decreases. The rate or degree of variability is not the same for each of these. Some, variable costs, will fluctuate consistently and at the same rate as production increases or decreases; others, semivariable, will fluctuate intermittently or only when the change has reached a certain volume. Most of the costs which are characterized as having variability are of the semivariable nature.

To avoid the problem, many firms prepare annually a *flexible budget* which is nothing more than a series of alternative budgets prepared at various operating (volume) capacities such as 60, 80, 100, and 120 percent of capacity. A brief illustration of a flexible budget for factory overhead costs follows:

	Capacity Used		
	Theoretical	Practical	Normal
Percentage of productive capacity...........	100%	80%	60%
Capacity expressed in terms of direct labor hours..............................	1,500 hrs.	1,200 hrs.	900 hrs.
Budgeted overhead costs:			
Fixed costs...........................	$3,000	$3,000	$3,00C
Variable costs........................	3,000	2,400	1,800
Total.............................	$6,000	$5,400	$4,800
Budgeted manufacturing overhead rate based on direct labor hours.................	$4.00	$4.50	$5.33

Advantages of   A company president once remarked, "I
Flexible Budgets   don't understand flexible budgets; it seems
                        to me that a budget is fixed and that for
any one given time period there can be but one budget." If what the
president says is true, what, if any, are the advantages of using flexible
budgets?

Three main advantages may be attributed to the use of flexible
budgets. The first has to do with the budgetary process. The use of flexible budgets simplifies the task of preparing a budget for a particular
period. For example, Department A has established a monthly flexible
overhead budget in the amount of $10,000 in fixed costs plus 50 cents
per machine-hour of variable costs. If the budget estimate is that 50,000
machine-hours will be the level of operations for a particular period, the
preparation of the overhead budget is a mechanical operation. The
budgeted amount for overhead for Department A for the time period
would total $35,000.

Second, the use of flexible budgets may result in the preparation of
more accurate budgets. Flexible budgeting techniques require that consideration be given to the volume factor in budget preparation. The
basic idea underlying flexibility is that budgets are established for
various levels of activity. Since all costs do not behave in the same
manner as some costs rise faster than others when production increases,
a budget giving consideration to the volume factor is bound to be more
accurate than one where volume is not considered.

Third, the use of flexible budgeting techniques results in a more
meaningful comparison between actual and budgeted data as *comparable* data are compared. An illustration will aid in pointing out the
advantage.

A monthly overhead budget of 50 cents per machine-hour plus
$10,000 for fixed costs had been established. Fifty thousand machine-
hours had been budgeted for a particular period resulting in a dollar
budget of $35,000 (50¢ × 50,000 + $10,000). The actual costs
incurred by the department amounted to $33,000. An immediate reac-
tion would be that efficient procedures resulted in a cost saving of
$2,000. If flexible budgeting techniques had not been utilized, the
analysis would have ended at this point.

To continue the illustration, suppose that 42,500 were the actual
number of machine-hours worked in the department. A budget
adjusted to the actual number of hours worked showed that
42,500 × 50¢ + $10,000 or $31,250 was the amount allowable. A
comparison of the $33,000 costs incurred with the $31,250 allowable

shows that $1,750 more was incurred than should have been. Thus, flexible budgeting techniques provide the machinery to achieve better control over overhead costs.

Control through the Use of Flexible Budgets   By the preparation of reports showing the actual versus the budgeted standard figures and analyzing these as to volume and price causes, it is possible to make available a management control that will help reduce losses and permit the business operations to be conducted more efficiently. The preparation of periodic (monthly) comparisons of the budgeted (standard) total and unit costs with the actual total and unit costs is desirable. These comparison reports must follow the same plan as the original budget preparation. Therefore, the comparisons in this instance, adequately supported by detailed schedules analyzing each important fact, will cover the following:

1. Budget report of sales.
2. Budget report of cost of production, supported by:
    a) Budget report of material costs.
    b) Budget report of labor costs.
    c) Budget report of manufacturing overhead costs.
3. Budget reports of the operating expenses:
    a) Distribution costs, supported by:
        (1) Selling expense reports.
        (2) Administrative expense reports.
        (3) Financial expense reports.

Two illustrations are given—a budget report of monthly sales (Illustration 4–3) and a budget report of the cost of production (Illustration 4–4).

Illustration 4–3

BUDGET REPORT OF MONTHLY SALES

Territory 1   Month of March   Operating Rate 60%

Product	Quantities		Values		Increase or Decrease*	Remarks
	Budget	Actual	Budget	Actual		
A..........	1,000	1,100	$16,500.00	$18,150.00	$1,650.00	Increased quantity
B..........	800	800	16,500.00	18,000.00	1,500.00	Increased price
C..........	800	700	7,000.00	5,250.00	1,750.00*	Smaller quantity higher price
Total....	2,600	2,600	$40,000.00	$41,400.00	$1,400.00	

Illustration 4-4

BUDGET REPORT OF THE COST OF PRODUCTION

Month of March

Operating Capacity: 60%

Cost Element	Product A Budget	Product A Actual	Product A Increase Decrease*	Product B Budget	Product B Actual	Product B Increase Decrease*	Product C Budget	Product C Actual	Product C Increase Decrease*
Material—Cutting Department.........	$ 3,600.00	$ 4,000.00	$ 400.00	$ 3,000.00	$ 2,900.00	$100.00*	$ 900.00	$ 675.00	$ 225.00*
Material—Finishing Department.......	240.00	260.00	20.00	600.00	610.00	10.00	300.00	200.00	100.00*
Labor—Cutting Department..........	2,400.00	2,600.00	200.00	2,000.00	2,000.00	....	1,600.00	1,280.00	320.00*
Labor—Stamping Department.........	1,200.00	1,300.00	100.00	1,000.00	1,200.00	200.00	400.00	320.00	80.00*
Labor—Finishing Department........	2,160.00	2,340.00	180.00	1,800.00	1,700.00	100.00*	800.00	640.00	160.00*
Manufacturing Overhead—Cutting Department........................	692.64	975.00	282.36	577.20	577.20	....	461.76	460.00	1.76*
Manufacturing Overhead—Stamping Department........................	432.00	468.00	36.00	360.00	432.00	72.00	144.00	115.20	28.80*
Manufacturing Overhead—Finishing Department........................	756.00	819.00	63.00	630.00	567.00	63.00*	280.00	224.00	56.00*
Total Costs.........	$11,480.64	$12,762.00	$1,281.36	$9,967.20	$9,986.20	$ 19.00	$4,885.76	$3,914.20	$971.56*
Number of Units.........	1,200	1,300	100	1,000	1,000	0	1,000	800	200*

The combined cost of production report comparing budgeted with actual figures will probably be quite voluminous. It therefore becomes necessary to subdivide it into separate sections for materials, labor, and manufacturing overhead, and subsequently to consolidate these into a single summary report. These variations, it should be noted, are the same as those that will be presented in the discussion under standard costs, and therefore they can be recorded on the books as operating data. The consolidated report for the end of any month would appear as shown in Illustration 4–4.

QUESTIONS FOR REVIEW

1. Is the concept of the budget compatible with the principle of *management by exception?* Explain.
2. "If a budget has been properly prepared, it can take the place of management as a control device." Do you agree with this statement? Explain.
3. What are the requirements for a successful budget program?
4. The Thomas Company operates several dairies in medium-sized midwestern cities. The products are distributed by trucks to supermarkets. In addition, the company operates house-to-house sales routes. Management is considering adding a frozen juice line. How would you budget the sales of this new product if you are convinced management will add the line?
5. What is the function of the accountant in the development of the production budget?
6. "It is useless to budget; no one can tell what the future holds." Comment.
7. "We could never come out exactly as we had budgeted, so we gave up budgeting." Comment.
8. What kinds of variances from budget are determinable? Whom would you hold responsible for these variances?
9. What are the limitations of budgets? Why do you think the advantages of using budgets outweigh the disadvantages?
10. How can PERT be used as a managerial cost control device? Explain.

PROBLEMS—GROUP A

Problem 4–1. Purpose: *Comparison of Actual and Budgeted Costs*

The budget for the second quarter of 1968 for the Able Company contained the following data:

	Budget No. of Functional Units	Budget Unit Costs	Total Budget
Mailing samples..............................	8,250	$0.20	$ 1,650
Assembling stock for orders...................	120,000	0.07	8,400
Issuing promotional literature................	17,000	0.16	2,720
Salesmen's calls on prospects.................	12,000	8.00	96,000

The actual results for the second quarter were as follows:

	Actual No. of Functional Units	Total Cost
Mailing samples..	9,300	$ 2,046
Assembling stock for orders.............................	119,000	9,520
Issuing promotional literature..........................	18,000	2,880
Salesmen's calls on prospects..........................	12,500	96,500

A comparison of budgeted and actual costs disclosed that in every case the actual was greater. Management was concerned over this and called you in as a consultant.

Required:

  a) What factors caused the differences in each case between actual and budgeted costs and what was the dollar effect of each of the factors?

  b) Was management justified in being concerned? Why or why not? Explain fully.

Problem 4–2. Purpose: *Analysis of Budgeted and Actual Costs*

  The Abercrombie Manufacturing Company's budgeted and actual performance for February, 1968, is shown below:

	Budget	Actual
Sales (units)...	400,000	380,000
Sales (dollars).......................................	$320,000	$319,200
Production (units)....................................	400,000	380,000
Direct materials used (lbs.)...........................	300,000	290,000
Direct materials cost per pound........................	$0.20	$0.21
Direct labor hours used...............................	100,000	100,000
Direct labor cost per hour.............................	$1.50	$1.53
Factory burden incurred..............................	...	$ 79,600
Burden budgeted—fixed...............................	$ 40,000	...
Burden budgeted—variable............................	$ 40,000	...

Prepare a report for the company president commenting on the results of the month. Be concrete in your answer and give as much quantitative support as possible.

Problem 4–3.   Purpose: *Budgetary Comparison of Costs; Budgeted versus Actual Costs*

  The Atlas Manufacturing Corporation uses a budgetary system in an attempt to achieve better control over costs. Atlas manufactures several products, but for cost purposes groups these under one product line since studies have shown that cost differences among the products are negligible.

  Two raw materials are used in the manufacture of the products: "Avon" which is purchased by the pound and "Bavon" which is purchased by the foot. The first-in, first-out method of issuing raw material is used. The nature of the products is such that all goods are completed on the day started, and as a result, there are no beginning or ending work-in-process inventories.

Materials purchased during the year:

Avon:
Budgeted.............................100,000 lbs. @ $1.10 per lb.
Actual................................ 70,000 lbs. @ 1.20 per lb. *and*
                                       60,000 lbs. @ 1.30 per lb.
Bavon:
Budgeted............................. 25,000 ft. @ $1.90 per ft.
Actual............................... 12,000 ft. @ 1.80 per ft. *and*
                                      15,000 ft. @ 1.60 per ft.

Materials on hand at beginning of the year:

Avon.................................. 35,000 lbs. @ $1.10 per lb.
Bavon................................ 6,000 ft. @ 1.90 per ft.

Finished units on hand at beginning of year: 4,000 units costing $18.

The estimated production for the year was 12,000 units, and actual production was 15,000 units.

The budgeted and actual cost and expense figures for the year were as follows:

	Budgeted	Actual
Avon...	80,000 lbs.	90,000 lbs.
Bavon..	18,000 ft.	20,000 ft.
Labor costs..................................	$72,000	$84,000
Manufacturing overhead.......................	42,000	43,000
Selling expenses.............................	48,000	50,000
Administrative expenses......................	30,000	28,000
Financial expenses...........................	8,000	5,000

The sales figures for the year were:

12,500 units @ $40.00
15,000 units @ 45.00

Required:

a) Prepare a schedule showing the budgeted and actual inventories at year-end.

b) Prepare a schedule comparing actual and budgeted cost of goods manufactured and sold.

c) Prepare a schedule comparing actual and budgeted net profit for the year.

Problem 4–4. Purpose: *Budget Preparation*

The Andrews Manufacturing Company makes two products, X and Y. X sells for $10 per unit, and Y sells for $25 per unit. Production of one unit of X requires two units of material A and one unit of material B. Production of one unit of Y requires two units of material B and three units of material C. Inventories on November 1 are estimated to be as follows:

Product X..........................20,000 units
Product Y..........................20,000
Material A.........................20,000
Material B.........................20,000
Material C.........................20,000

Sales estimated for November: Product X—100,000 units; Product Y—45,000 units.

Desired ending inventory: Product X—10,000 units; Product Y—5,000 units; Material A—20,000 units; Material B—10,000 units; Material C—15,000 units.

The purchasing department estimates that during November A will cost $1 a unit, B will cost $2 per unit, and C will cost $3 per unit. Labor costs are anticipated at $1 per unit for making X and $2 per unit for making Y. Overhead is applied at 100 percent of labor cost. Estimates indicate that selling and administrative expenses will run about 10 percent of sales.

Required:

a) Compute the quantity of materials that will have to be purchased to meet the November requirements.

b) Compute the budgeted cost of goods manufactured and sold for the month.

c) Prepare a budgeted income statement for November.

PROBLEMS—GROUP B

Problem 4–5. Purpose: *Comparison of Actual and Budgeted Costs*

A comparison of budgeted and actual costs for the King Company disclosed that the actual costs were greater than the budgeted costs. The president was concerned over this and asked for your advice.

The budget for the month of January follows:

	Budget No. of Functional Units	Standard Unit Costs	Total Budget
Salesmen's calls on prospects..................	10,000	$5.00	$50,000
Mailing samples............................	9,375	0.10	938
Assembling stock for orders..................	100,000	0.05	5,000
Issuing promotional literature................	6,000	0.11	660

The actual results were:

	Actual No. of Functional Units	Total Actual Cost	Actual Unit Cost
Salesmen's calls on prospects...............	12,000	$61,200	$5.10
Mailing samples...........................	9,300	1,023	0.11
Assembling stock for orders................	95,000	4,750	0.05
Issuing promotional literature..............	5,000	500	0.10

Required:

a) Why were the actual costs greater than the budgeted costs? Support your reasons with data.

b) Do you think the president was justified in being concerned? Explain fully.

Problem 4–6. Purpose: *Analysis of Budgeted and Actual Costs*

The Keller Manufacturing Company's actual performance for July, 1969, is shown below:

> 395,000 units were sold @ $2 each.
> 396,000 units were produced using the following:
> 200,000 lbs. of Q @ 30¢ per lb.
> 200,800 direct labor hours @ $2.55 per hour.
> $95,000 of overhead.

The budget for July had shown the following:

> Expected sales of 400,000 units @ $2.05.
> Expected production 400,000 units utilizing the following:
> 200,000 lbs. of Q @ 32¢ per lb.
> 200,000 direct labor hours @ $2.52 per hour.
> $50,000 fixed overhead cost.
> $50,000 variable overhead cost.

Analyze the differences between budget and actual costs. Be as detailed as possible.

Problem 4–7. Purpose: *Budgetary Comparison of Costs; Budgeted versus Actual Costs*

The Klever Manufacturing Company manufactures one product known as Kleve. Following is the budgeted cost for one unit of Kleve:

Materials:
A, 10 lbs. @ $1.50......................................$15.00
B, 8 gal. @ 2.50....................................... 20.00 $ 35.00
Direct labor:
Dept. No. 1, 8 hrs. @ $2.10.............................$16.80
Dept. No. 2, 5 hrs. @ 2.00............................. 10.00   26.80
Manufacturing overhead:
13 hrs. @ $3.00..   39.00
Total... $100.80

	Budget	Actual
Finished units:		
Sold.....	10,000	9,000
Inventory, 1/1/—.....	2,000	2,200
Inventory, 3/31/—.....	4,000	3,000
Materials:		
A:		
Inventory, 1/1/—.....	$20,000	$18,000
Inventory, 3/31/—.....	$18,000	$15,000
Price per pound:		
Inventory, 1/1/—.....	$1.50	$1.60
Current purchases.....	$1.50	$1.70
B:		
Inventory, 1/1/—.....	$8,000	$7,500
Inventory, 3/31/—.....	$6,000	$6,000
Price per gallon:		
Inventory, 1/1/—.....	$2.50	$2.50
Current purchases.....	$2.50	$2.80

Additional information:

1. The company uses FIFO in costing all inventories. There was no work-in-process inventory at the beginning or end of the period.
2. Actual materials used exceeded budget by 5 percent.
3. Actual direct labor costs were:

> Department No. 1.............................100,000 hrs. @ $2.10
> Department No. 2............................. 50,000 hrs. @ 2.05

4. Actual manufacturing expenses amounted to $344,000.
5. Budgeted finished inventory on January 1 had a unit cost of $95; the actual was $100.

Required:

a) Prepare a comparative statement of cost of sales, actual and budget.

b) Analyze the differences between budgeted and actual amounts.

Problem 4–8. Purpose: *Budget Preparation*

The Kitchen Products Company manufactures three products: namely, stools, chairs, and tables. In 1968, sales of stools amounted to $100,000; chair sales were $200,000; table sales amounted to $400,000.

Salesmen's estimates for 1969 indicate that stool sales are expected to increase 10 percent. Chair sales are expected to remain constant, and table sales should increase 30 percent. The above salesmen's estimates were reviewed and adopted as the 1969 sales forecast.

Cost of goods sold amounted to the following in 1968:

Chairs—50 percent of sales. Of this amount 80 percent represented materials, labor, and variable overhead. The other 20 percent represented fixed overhead.

Tables—60 percent of sales. Of this amount 70 percent represented materials, labor, and variable overhead. The other 30 percent represented fixed overhead.

Stools—the same relationship existed for stools as did for tables.

Selling and administrative costs amounted to 15 percent of sales for each of the products. Of these amounts, half were variable costs and half were fixed costs.

Required:

a) Compute the budgeted costs of goods sold for each of the products for 1969.

b) Prepare a budgeted income statement for 1969.

CHAPTER

5 | Managerial Control of

Material Acquisition Costs—

Purchasing, Receiving, and Storing

Nature of Material Acquisition Cost Control

Material cost control covers two procedures: (1) the managerial and accounting problems of the purchase, receipt, and storage of the materials required in manufacturing; and (2) the managerial and accounting problems relating to the issue and use of the materials in manufacturing operations. In this chapter, attention is focused on the first of these procedures—*the acquisition and storage of the materials.*

The managerial objectives of the material acquisition cost control are:

1. *Procurement* of a sufficient quantity of the required materials at the lowest prices so that manufacturing operations will be performed smoothly and uninterruptedly.
2. *Storage* of the materials in the plant so that the material handling costs, both receiving and issuing, will be kept at a minimum, and at the same time the materials will be properly protected against loss by theft, damage, or deterioration.
3. *Elimination* of all inactive, obsolete, and defective materials from the regular storeroom areas.
4. *Investment* in inventories at a minimum, consistent with smooth factory operations, the delivery time of purchases, storage facilities, and market-price forecasts.

To achieve the maximum managerial control over material costs in a manufacturing firm, the following organizational and operating procedures should be followed:

1. *Budgeting* of the sales, finished goods inventory, and production schedules on both a long- and short-term basis so that a *centralized* purchasing department will have guidelines for its operations.

2. *Routinizing and systematizing* the ordering, purchasing, receiving, storing, and issuing of all materials.
3. Using a well-integrated series of *printed forms* to prevent errors and fix responsibility.
4. Protecting the inventory investment by an adequate *system of internal checks* to insure accurate accounting and the prevention of fraud and theft.
5. *Maintaining* efficient inventory records of the quantities received, issued, and balance on hand of all materials, together with the costs thereof. In many large business firms these records are maintained mechanically by the use of punched cards, punched tapes, and magnetic tapes used with computers.
6. *Pricing* all requisitions and inventories on a basis to insure reliable costs of manufacturing and effective income tax planning.
7. *Controlling* and *summarizing* the accounting for the acquisition and use of materials by means of control accounts, subsidiary ledgers, and reports of material usage, returns, and spoilage.
8. *Organizing* the administrative and supervisory staff of the material cost control so that decisions can be made promptly and effectively.

Functional Cycle of
Materials Control

There are five activities associated with materials procedures:

1. Engineering, planning, and routing of factory production.
2. Purchase of materials.
3. Receipt and inspection of materials.
4. Storage and issuance of materials.
5. Accounting for materials transactions, including book inventory records.

The *engineering, planning, and routing departments* of an organization have an important role in business management, in addition to that of controlling the flow of production through the plant. First, they must design the product and prepare material specifications before much of the materials can be purchased. They must further study the effects of the use of various materials and their substitutes and make recommendations. In addition, these departments must make up bills of materials to be issued for the various kinds of production orders. The work of these departments will be discussed in detail later in the chapter. Here it serves as an introduction to materials control.

The *purchasing department* performs the following business activities: (1) receives or prepares purchase requisitions for all materials and equipment to be used in the factory; (2) requests price quotations from the vendors; (3) prepares and places purchase orders; (4) approves vendors' invoices; and (5) sends approved invoices to the general accounting department for entry. The purchasing department may operate either as a service department of the factory organization or as a part of the central administrative staff of the business, whereas the receiving and storeroom departments are essentially factory service departments.

The *receiving department* performs the following functions: (1) receives the goods from truckmen, railroads, or other carriers and signs the authorized receipts; (2) counts, weighs, or otherwise verifies the quantity of goods received; (3) inspects quality of goods and reports breakage; (4) moves the goods to the storeroom; and (5) sends copies of the receiving report to the purchasing department and to the storeroom department.

The *storeroom department* (1) receives and acknowledges the goods from the receiving department; (2) verifies the quantity received; (3) places the goods in the proper bins, shelves, or yards; (4) issues materials on properly authorized requisitions; (5) enters receipts and issuances on the bin cards; and (6) sometimes summarizes the requisitions for the *cost accounting department*.

Entries must be made to record the purchase of materials, the return of materials purchased to the vendors, the use of materials, the return of excess materials to the storeroom, and spoilage or defective production. Subsidiary inventory records must also be maintained. Each of these operations will be described later in the chapter.

Functional Organization and Personnel of Materials Control

The organization and personnel of materials control varies somewhat with the size of the organization and the extent to which materials costs are a part of the total cost of a product. In the larger firms, the huge investment in inventories necessitates more detailed control and greater supervision. As previously indicated, the three functional activities for adequate materials control are (1) planning, budgeting, and accounting; (2) purchasing; and (3) receiving, storing, and issuing. These must be properly coordinated into a single management function responsible to the top management, as shown in Illustration 5–1.

Controlling the Investment in Materials Inventory

In Chapter 4, emphasis was placed on the need of a budget for efficient business management. This budget affects the purchasing and inventory practices of a business firm. Ordinarily, the inventory investment should be kept at a minimum. After planning and forecasting the sales and production for the coming year, management must consider:

Illustration 5–1. Organization Chart of the Materials Control Function

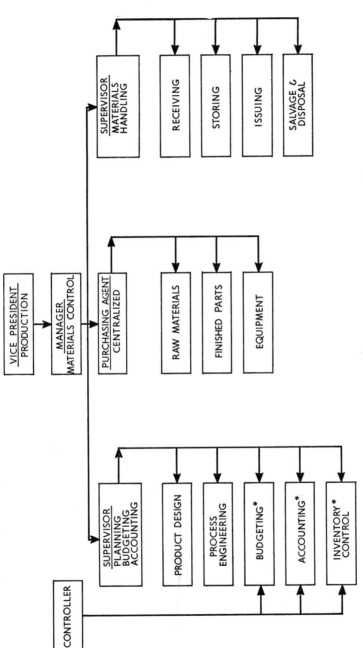

* These functions must be coordinated by the manager—materials control and the controller.

a) Quantity of material now on hand.

b) Expected requirements during the budgeted period—on a monthly, quarterly, semiannual, and annual basis.

c) Length of time required for delivery of any newly ordered material.

d) Material presently on order.

e) Amount of material to be maintained as a safety or base-stock requirement.

f) Forecasted conditions which might require higher or lower commitments.

g) Most economic quantity that should be purchased.

By studying the above factors in connection with its purchases of raw materials and parts, one large industrial concern was able to reduce its average investment in inventory from $30,000,000 to $20,000,000—a saving of more than $10,000,000 in invested funds. These savings were achieved by specifying different and quicker delivery methods, obtaining supplies closer to the manufacturing plants, and rescheduling the delivery dates and quantities to be delivered.

When a firm sets selling prices based upon the estimated or predetermined costs, it may be necessary to make long-term purchase commitment contracts with the suppliers and then schedule deliveries of these contracted materials as required.

In recent years, the materials control department has given greater attention to the most economical quantity to be ordered because of the resulting savings in invested funds, interest on borrowed funds, and reduction in storage, maintenance, and accounting costs. It has been estimated that the cost of storing and issuing materials averages 30 percent of the average inventory on hand. It may be desirable to order more often, if this does not interfere with the smooth operations in the factory. The amount to be ordered will establish the maximum size of the materials inventory. Two methods may be used in determining this inventory: (*a*) the inventory turnover rates, and (*b*) the cost of maintaining and carrying the inventory.

To ascertain the inventory turnover, the total inventory on hand, $40,000, divided into the amount used during the year, $120,000, would result in an inventory turnover of three and an inventory of four months' supply on hand. This, however, ignores the economy resulting from the carrying costs of the inventory. If it is assumed that this figure is 30 percent of the average inventory, then a charge of $12,000 should be taken into account in determining whether or not to order more frequently or having speedier deliveries by such means as airfreight, thus reducing the average inventory on hand.

By preparing a table showing the number of orders, the average inventory, and the carrying charges, it will be possible to determine the most economic quantity to be ordered. For example, in the following table it becomes quite evident because of the high carrying costs that the more frequent the order the lower the inventory cost, provided it does not interfere with the smoothly functioning manufacturing operations:

No. of Orders	Units per Order	Average Inventory (One-half Purchases)	Average Inventory Invest-ment @ $10 per Unit	Inventory Carrying Charge (30%)	Clerical Cost per Purchasing Order ($15 per Order)	Total Cost of Inventory and Purchasing
1.........1,200	600	$6,000	$1,800	$ 15	$1,815
2......... 600	300	3,000	900	30	930
3......... 400	200	2,000	600	45	645
4......... 300	150	1,500	450	60	510
5......... 240	120	1,200	360	75	435
6......... 200	100	1,000	300	90	390
7......... 172	86	860	258	105	363

Assuming that the total units to be ordered in a given period such as a year, with an average inventory of one half the purchase, an inventory carrying charge of 30 percent and clerical costs per order of $15, it is evident that ordering a smaller quantity more often (in this instance seven times a year) results in an inventory carrying cost of $363 compared with a carrying cost when only a single order is placed for the entire year's supply.

A somewhat simpler formula has been developed for determining the most economical quantity to purchase on a single order by using the following formula:

$$\text{Economical quantity to order} = \sqrt{\frac{2GS}{Ci+ B}}$$

in which the following data are used:

G = Cost of placing and following up an order (assumed).........$16.00
S = Number of units required in a year (assumed)............... 900
C = Purchase price net, plus freight and receiving (assumed).....$25.00
i = Interest rate per annum (assumed)......................... 6%
B = Annual cost of storage per unit of material (assumed).......$15.50

Solving this equation results in the following:

$$\text{Quantity} = \sqrt{\frac{2 \times \$16 \times 900 \text{ units}}{\$25 \times 6\% + \$15.50}}.$$

This will result in the most economical quantity to order of 41 units.

Forms and Reports Used in Materials Acquisition

Behind the principle of internal control in business is the use of printed forms. Printed forms represent a method of placing responsibility for business activities and serve as a means of internal check. One basic principle in the use of forms is that one copy is always retained in the department preparing it.

The forms most frequently found in controlling the purchase and the receipt of materials are:

1. Purchase requisition.   4. Returned purchases report.
2. Purchase order.   5. Stores ledger card.
3. Receiving report.   6. Bin card.

1. The *purchase requisition* (see Illustration 5–2) is a request to the purchasing department to buy certain materials, either to replenish present stocks on hand or to acquire original stock. If it is a replenishment of stock, the requisition is prepared by the storeroom clerk; if it is for new or experimental stock, the requisition is made or authorized by a member of the engineering or factory staff. Two copies of the requisition are prepared—one kept as a memorandum in the storeroom department and the other sent to the purchasing department.

2. The *purchase order* (see Illustration 5–3) is the form prepared by the purchasing department authorizing the shipment of the goods by the vendor. In addition to the original, which is sent to the vendor,

Illustration 5–2. Purchase Requisition

PURCHASE REQUISITION		
No. 24		*Date* Jan. 15, 19—
Quantity	*Description*	*Ordered from*
5 tons	Tempered Blade Steel	*Name* United States Steel Corp.
		Address Gary, Indiana
		Price $200.00
		Terms 2/10/N/30
		Delivery—How Railroad, F.O.B.
		Delivery—When Jan. 20, 19—.
		Remarks

Above Quantity Will Last for   Three months

Present Stock Will Last for   Six months

Quot. from Loraine	Quot. from Duluth	Quot. from Joliet	Quot. from Gary
Price $197.00	*Price* $198.00	*Price* $210.00	*Price* $200.00
Terms 2/10/N/30 F.O.B.	*Terms* 2/10/N/30 F.O.B.	*Terms* 2/10/N/30 F.O.B.	*Terms* 2/10/N/30 F.O.B.
Delivery RR.	*Delivery* RR.	*Delivery* RR.	*Delivery* RR.

Original—to Purchasing Dept.

File Copy

Illustration 5–3

COUTRALDS, INC.	SHIP TO THIS ADDRESS UNLESS OTHERWISE INDICATED IN BODY OF PURCHASE ORDER. COUTRALDS, INC. 1300 Airport Road Harlan, Iowa 50010 Phone 515-232-3700	VENDOR NOTE: SHOW THIS P. O. NUMBER ▬▬▬ ▬▬▬ ON ALL INVOICES, PACKING SLIPS AND CERTIFICATIONS.

PURCHASE ORDER

SPECTION REQUIRED:	VENDOR SUBMIT FIRST ARTICLE FOR APPROVAL		
X VENDOR CERTIFICATION	GOVERNMENT SOURCE INSPECTION	E.C.	REQ'NR.

No. 27239

VENDOR'S NAME AND ADDRESS	REQUISITION NO.	R.R.	P.O. DATE
	ALC 4651		October 27, 19--

ALLEGHANY LUDLUM CO.
Chicago, Illinois   60607

REQUISITIONED BY	CONFIRMING WITH
JC. Kolin	

DELIVER TO	F.O.B. POINT
Harlan, Iowa	Harlan, Iowa

DELIVERY REQUIRED	SHIP VIA	CHARGE JOB/ACCT. NO.	TERMS
Nov. 15, 19--	N.Y.C. RR		3/10 eom n/60x

DELIVERY PROMISED	RESALE PERMIT	RENEGOTIABLE	BUYER	PRIORITY	GOVT. CONTRACT NO.
	YES NO	YES NO			

ITEM	QUANTITY	UNIT		UNIT PRICE	EXTENDED COST
	5	Tons	Tempered Blade Steel per Specifications attached	$200.00	$1,000.00

THIS PURCHASE ORDER IS NOT BINDING ▬▬▬ UNTIL YOUR COMPANY HAS RETURNED THE ACKNOWLEDGMENT COPY PROPERLY COMPLETED AND SIGNED.

NOTE: THE TERMS AND CONDITIONS SHOWN ON THE REVERSE SIDE HEREOF ARE APPLICABLE TO THIS ORDER AND SELLER AGREES THERETO BY ACKNOWLEDGMENT OR PERFORMANCE.

GENERAL INSTRUCTIONS TO VENDOR

1. ACKNOWLEDGMENT COPY OF THIS ORDER MUST BE SIGNED AND RETURNED, ADVISING DEFINITE SHIPPING DATE.
2. PACKING LISTS MUST ACCOMPANY EACH CASE OR PARCEL, SHOWING OUR ORDER NUMBER AND OUR COMPLETE DESCRIPTION AND PART NUMBER FOR EACH ITEM.
3. ALL ITEMS ARE SUBJECT TO INSPECTION AND ACCEPTANCE AT OUR PLANT. WHEN REQUIRED, CERTIFICATIONS MUST ACCOMPANY EACH SHIPMENT.
4. SEND INVOICES IN TRIPLICATE PROMPTLY FOR EACH SHIPMENT, SHOWING OUR ORDER NUMBER.

5. INVOICE EACH PURCHASE ORDER SEPARATELY.
6. INVOICES CANNOT BE HONORED UNLESS ACKNOWLEDGMENT COPY IS RETURNED PROPERLY COMPLETED AND SIGNED.
7. RENDER COMPLETE ITEMIZED STATEMENT MONTHLY.
8. C.O.D. SHIPMENTS WILL NOT BE ACCEPTED.
9. OVER SHIPMENTS, UNLESS SPECIFICALLY AUTHORIZED, WILL NOT BE ACCEPTED.

VENDOR'S ACKNOWLEDGMENT

THIS ORDER IS ACCEPTED SUBJECT TO ALL THE TERMS AND CONDITIONS STATED ON THE FACE AND ON THE REVERSE SIDE HEREOF.

☐ THE "DELIVERY REQUIRED" DATE SHOWN ABOVE IS THE ACKNOWLEDGED DELIVERY DATE FOR THIS ORDER.
☐ WE CANNOT MEET THE "DELIVERY REQUIRED" DATE, BUT WE DO PROMISE DELIVERY ON OR BEFORE___
☐ PRICE DATA SHOWN ABOVE IS CORRECT, EXCEPT FOR:___

BY _George Jacobson_
PURCHASING AGENT

MAIL TO:
COUTRALDS, Inc.
Harlan, Iowa 50010

FOR THE VENDOR (By)___ Date___

ACKNOWLEDGMENT—SIGN AND RETURN

90 (6-86) $

ORIGINAL -- TO VENDOR

ACKNOWLEDGMENT COPY

PURCHASING DEPT. COPY

RECEIVING DEPT. COPY

ACCOUNTING DEPT. COPY

STORES LEDGER CLERK COPY

sufficient copies are made to meet the requirements of the departments interested. Usually, one copy goes to the receiving department so that it may know what goods to expect. If the quantities are omitted from this copy and only the items are stated, the copy is called a *blind receiving report;* the receiving department must fill in the quantities received and return it to the purchasing department.

A third copy of the purchase order is sent to the department requisitioning the material, and one copy is retained by the purchasing department. However, variations from this procedure are not uncommon. For example, one large machine company finds it convenient to prepare six copies of the purchase order; three are sent to the receiving department. The receiving department uses these three extra copies in lieu of receiving reports mentioned later.

3. The *receiving report* (see Illustration 5–4) is the form prepared

Illustration 5–4. Receiving Report

QUANTITY	MATERIAL CODE	SIZE - PART NUMBER - DESCRIPTION	CARRIER WEIGHT	OUR WEIGHT GROSS	NET
40	S-4162	Tempered Blade			
		Steel — per our			
		Specification	10040	10040	10,000

ORIGINAL--PURCHASING DEPARTMENT

STORES DEPARTMENT-COPY-2

ACCOUNTING DEPARTMENT-COPY 3

RECEIVING DEPARTMENT FILE-COPY-4

to show the quantity and kind of material received on specific purchase orders. The procedure followed in preparing this report might be:

a) An examination by receiving clerk or his assistants who weigh or count material received and prepare a report indicating Date, Received from, Via, Charges, Purchase Order No., Packages, Quantity, Description, and identification by name or initial of the receiver and checker. Preparation of the report is in triplicate; the original is sent to the purchasing department so that it may be compared with the purchase order; the duplicate is sent with the material to the stores department; and the triplicate is filed by the receiving department.

Sometimes the system of control varies the number of copies of the receiving report that must be prepared, but three, as indicated above, is the *minimum.* In some firms, additional copies of the receiving report are sent to the accounting department for comparison with the invoice received and to the planning department for use in planning and scheduling production.

b) Some firms send three to five additional copies of the purchase order to the receiving department when the order is placed with the vendor. The receiving department uses these copies in place of a separate receiving report. This method saves time and expense in operating the receiving department, but it is deficient in the matter of internal control and internal check.

4. *Returned purchases report* is similar in form and content to the *receiving report.* The original goes to the purchasing department which forwards it to the accounting department for entry in the voucher register and on the voucher if it has not already been paid; one copy goes to the storeroom department for entry in the stores ledger subsidiary record; and one copy is retained by the shipping department, which has prepared the report and taken care of the shipment.

5. The *stores ledger card* (often referred to as the perpetual inventory record) is one of the basic records for material accounting in a cost system. (See Illustration 5–5.) There are several forms of this record in common use today, but basically there are three sections or divisions on this inventory card record, each with appropriate subdivisions in which to record information as to date, requisition number, purchase order number, job order number, quantity, unit price, and total cost. The three divisions are *Receipts, Issues,* and *Balance.*

When goods are received in the storeroom, entries are made in the *Receipt section.* The goods are checked against the receiving report for quantities and against a purchase order for the unit price and description before making the entries. A separate card is used, not only for each kind of material but also for each different size of the same material.

When goods are issued for use in the factory, a materials requisition form is used indicating the quantity and kind of material and the job or department in which it is to be used. This information is entered in the *Issued section* of the stores ledger card.

Illustration 5–5. Stores Ledger Card*

STORES LEDGER CARD

ARTICLE Tempered Blade Steel
AVERAGE UNIT PRICE $.10 per lb.
CLASS NO. 400
LOCATION 26 & 27

UNIT Pounds MAX. 10,000 lbs. MIN. 2,000 lbs.

On Order				On Reserve				Received					Issued					Balance			
Date	Pur. Ord. No.	Qty.		Date	Req. No.	Qty.	Date Wanted	Date	Pur. Ord. No.	Qty.	Price	Total	Date	Req. No.	Qty.	Price	Total	Date	Qty.	Price	Total
3/5	1482	10000						4/6	1482	10000	.10	1000	3/2	154	800	.12	96.00	3/1	3000	.12	360
																		3/2	2200	.12	264
																		4/6	12200 1036		1264

* Since frequently these cards are prepared on bookkeeping machines, only one date column at the extreme left may be necessary. This date column is used for all entries, no matter in which section these are made.

If goods are returned to a vendor, entries, *encircled* (contra entries), will be made in the Received section. If material is returned to the storeroom from the factory as excess, *the amount* is entered, *encircled* (contra entry), in the Issued section.

Two additional sections for *memorandum* purposes may be added— *Material on Order* and *Material Reserved.* Frequently time elapses between the placing of a replenishment order by the stores clerk and the receipt of material. To prevent the placing of duplicate orders and the accumulation of too great a supply of material on hand, large organizations have found an *On Order* section practical. In it the stores ledger clerk notes the date the order was placed, the quantity on the order, and, perhaps, the expected date of receipt. When the goods so ordered are received, a line is drawn through the memorandum item and an entry made in the *Receipts* section.

The *Reserve* section is used to indicate materials needed in the near future on a job in process. The purpose of such a column is to prevent the issuance of so much material to new jobs that a job in process, ready to use the material, must be held up in the factory until more can be ordered and received. Its purpose is to avoid delay of orders in process for want of materials. When the material reserved is issued, a line is drawn through the entry in the *Reserve* section and the appropriate entry made in the *Issued* section.

Two methods of handling the entries in the *Reserve* section are in use. Under the first method, as soon as an amount is "reserved" it is deducted from the balance at the price in effect at time of reservation, even though the goods are not issued until a later date. The balance represents not the balance on hand but the balance available for issue. When the goods are actually issued an entry is made in the *Issued* section but not in the Balance column. Furthermore, whenever a comparison of the physical inventory and the Inventory Control account is to be made with the book inventory, the latter must first be reconciled by the amount of reservations. This procedure seems unsatisfactory since the purpose of the book inventory is to provide a check against the control account and the physical inventory, and this check should be possible without further adjustment.

Under a second method the *Reserve* section is used as a memorandum in which the amount reserved is entered. Whenever a stores ledger clerk is given a requisition for material against which a reservation has been entered, he must first deduct the reservation from the balance to ascertain the amount available for issue. If the amount remaining is sufficient, the requisition is filled. If insufficient, the requisition is partially filled and the purchasing department is asked to reorder. A release of part of the reservation may be secured. *However, the reservation will in no way affect the Balance column until the materials reserved are actually issued.* The total of the Balance columns in the book inventory *at all times* is controlled without adjustment by the Stores Control account. This latter practice seems more desirable.

A variation of these methods is occasionally found. Two Balance columns are used: one a *Balance on Hand* and the other *Balance Available for Issue.* Such a form, however, makes stores accounting involved and expensive.

The form shown in Illustration 5–6 (p. 111) provides for the maximum and minimum quantities to be kept on hand. The most economical quantities to have on hand and to be purchased are determined by the purchasing department in cooperation with the production department. These limits may be changed whenever necessary. Thereafter, determination of the amount and date of an order becomes a routine matter, and the stores ledger clerk is vested with the responsibility of keeping the stock within the range of the minimum and maximum quantities.

It may not be necessary for the stores ledger clerk to wait until the minimum quantity is reached before reordering. A point may be set above the minimum at which reorders are placed. This point would take into consideration the length of time necessary to get the material from the vendor and the approximate amount to be consumed during a given period. One fundamental rule for the stores clerk is embodied in the purpose of his job: namely, to be sure production is not held up because of lack of materials and at the same time to avoid an excessive investment in inventories on the part of the firm.

Some concerns keep only a quantity book inventory. The clerical work necessary in calculating the extensions and the amount of the balances is eliminated. Requisitions of materials used are priced and extended by the cost accounting department before entries are made on the job order or departmental cost sheets.

Accounting for the Purchase and Receipt of Materials

In studying the purchase and receipt of materials, it must be remembered that there are direct, indirect, and shipping materials. Sometimes there are office supplies. These are usually kept in a storeroom and controlled through the *stores accounts.*

No accounting entries are made when a purchase requisition for materials is sent to the purchasing department. When the materials have been purchased, received, inspected, and placed in the storeroom, however, an entry is made for the purchase. After a copy of the receiv-

Illustration 5-6. Perpetual Inventory Card, Using Average Price Method

STORES LEDGER

NAME OF COMMODITY	Copper Rods	CLASS	S-W-4	CODE NO.	MAXIMUM QUANTITY	1500	MINIMUM QUANTITY	200	UNIT Pounds	SHEET NO.	48

DESCRIPTION Solid Copper Rods   SIZE 3/4"

PURCHASE ORDERS

No.	Date	Quan-tity	Purchased From
~~401~~	~~5/3~~	~~800~~	~~Brown & Co.~~
~~401~~	~~5/4~~	~~300~~	~~Brown & Co.~~
~~402~~	~~5/7~~	~~1000~~	~~Butler & Co.~~
~~403~~	~~5/15~~	~~1200~~	~~Brown & Co.~~
403	5/16	200	Brown & Co.

RECEIVED

Pur. Ord	Inv. Date	Date Rec'd	Quan-tity	Unit Del. Price	Value
401	5/3	5/4	500	$.11	$ 55 00
401	5/3	5/8	300	11.08	33 24
402	5/7	5/10	1000	.09775	97 75
403	5/15	5/16	1000	.1065	106 50

ON RESERVE

Date	Prod. Order No.	Quan-tity
5/6	6151	800
5/13	6501	200
5/14	6151	100

ISSUED

Date	Job No. or Dept.	Req. No.	Quan-tity	Unit Del. Price	Value
5/5	6150	301	600	$.105	$ 63 00
5/9	6152	302	400	.1075	43 00
5/11	6462	303	300	.10	30 00
5/12	6471	304	600	.10	60 00
5/14	6151	305	100	.10	10 00
5/17	6483	306	600	.105	63 00

BALANCE

Quan-tity	Value	Unit Cost
500	$ 50 00	$.10
1000	105 00	.105
400	42 00	.105
700	75 25	.1075
300	32 25	.1075
1300	130 00	.10
1000	100 00	.10
400	40 00	.10
300	30 00	.10
1300	136 50	.105
700	73 50	.105

ing report has been sent to the purchasing department for comparison with the purchase order and the incoming invoice, the invoice, approved as to quantities, items, and unit prices, is sent to the accounting department for record.

Purchases of materials may be entered in a multicolumn purchase journal for small business firms or in a voucher register for the larger firms. The journal entry to summarize the purchases would be:

```
Stores...............................................xxxxx
    Accounts Payable.........................................        xxxxx
    To summarize the purchases for the month.
```

Purchase returns may be entered either in red as *contra* entries in these journals or registers or in the Sundry or Miscellaneous columns of the voucher register.

Materials purchased for use on special jobs and sent directly to the factory may be charged directly to the Work-in-Process—Materials account.

Special Accounting Problems Affecting Materials Purchased

There are several problems affecting the purchase of materials to be used in manufacturing on which there is no uniform accounting practice. These include (*a*) treatment of freight-in, (*b*) accounting for material handling charges, (*c*) accounting for containers, and (*d*) treatment of purchase discounts.

Freight-In

Freight-in on materials purchased to be used in manufacturing is actually part of the cost of the materials. However, this may cause some clerical and accounting difficulties. Freight-in may be treated in one of three ways. It may be—

1. Immediately charged to the Stores Control account and also to the respective inventory cards.
2. Set up as a Freight-In account and allocated to the individual inventory cards. Subsequently the total is closed to the Stores Control account.
3. Treated as a manufacturing overhead cost; that is, it is not distributed to the Stores Control account or the inventory cards.

If freight-in is charged immediately to the Stores Control account by debiting stores in the voucher register, the total amount must be prorated and added proportionately on the perpetual inventory cards affected. This entry is made in the *Received* section of the inventory card, with a notation "Freight" if a separate column is not provided for freight in this section. The total cost of goods plus freight is extended to the Total Amount column in the *Balance* section. The addition of freight may result in the determination of unit prices of a fractional cent. This procedure involves additional clerical labor in the computation of the cost of material requisitions and may result in more clerical errors. For example, if 300 units were purchased at 12 cents each and the freight amounted to $1.75, an additional unit cost of 0.583 cents is necessary, making the unit price 12.583 cents. Many concerns find it more practical, therefore, to treat freight-in as an overhead cost item even though such treatment is not accurate.

Some concerns carry all freight-in charges to a Freight-In account. At the end of each month an entry is made closing this account into the Stores Control account and distributing the amount, on some equitable basis, to the various book inventory cards. A freight debit memorandum is sent to the stores ledger clerk informing him which accounts to charge. This method raises the same difficulties as the direct charge to the stores ledger cards at the time the goods are received.

Because of these practical difficulties, some concerns include the freight-in as one of the material handling costs. As such it may be included with other indirect costs—that is, as part of the manufacturing overhead—or treated as one of the special material handling indirect costs and charged to jobs or production on the basis of the weight or cost of the material used.

Accounting for Material Handling Charges

The term *material handling costs* refers to the expense involved in receiving, storing, issuing, and handling materials. It might be extended to include part of the cost of operating the purchasing department. Logically, such costs are part of the cost of materials to the same extent as freight-in. But the practical difficulty arises as to how to allocate this cost to the various materials. For this reason, many companies include these costs with those of manufacturing overhead and apply them to production as such. A few companies, however, have resorted to the practice of establishing *a material handling overhead rate,* similar in computation and application as the general predetermined manufacturing overhead rate, and of charging the handling cost to the material cost of production on a *weight* basis. In some firms, such as the manufacturers of rubber goods, the weight basis is used to apportion the handling charges for some of the material, and the cost basis for other materials.

Accounting for Containers

In accounting for containers two phases of the subject must be considered. First, in the purchase of material such as acids, special containers, such as carboys, are used. These are returnable. Care must be taken to segregate from the material costs the deposit required for such containers and included in the invoice. The entry in the voucher register would be:

```
Stores......................................................800.00
Deposit for Containers........................................ 40.00
    Accounts Payable..........................................          840.00
```

When the containers are returned for credit or cash, the entry would be:

```
Cash, or Accounts Payable or Accounts Receivable.....................40.00
    Deposit for Containers.......................................          40.00
```

If, however, an expensive, nonreturnable container is used for stores purchased, the cost must be merged with the cost of the material, and an average unit price ascertained for the stores thus purchased.

Second, there is the question of special containers required to market such products as perfumes or candy. Should the cost of these containers be considered as part of the cost of the article being manufactured (perfume or candy), or should these items be treated as selling and marketing costs? This raises the question of whether perfumes, on the one hand, or perfumes and containers, on the other, are being manufactured. The principle usually accepted is that when a container is necessary for the sale of the product, the container is part of the manufacturing cost. When the container is used primarily for shipment of the goods, the container is treated as a shipping and selling expense.

Purchase Discounts   Purchase discounts in this discussion refer to cash discounts allowed on the purchase of direct materials and of supplies to be used in manufacturing. There are several methods for handling purchase discounts.

1. In sound accounting theory, there is but one method: The amount of the discount should be deducted from the invoice price and the materials recorded at net cost:

```
Stores.......................................................9,900.00
    Accounts Payable..........................................          9,900.00
    Goods invoiced at $10,000 less 1 percent.
```

There cannot be any real justification for recording materials at an amount greater than their cash price. The uncertainty as to whether or not the invoice will be paid promptly and the discount taken should have no effect on the cost of the materials. When payments are not made within the discount period, the cost of deferring payment should be:

```
Purchase Discounts Lost.......................................100.00
    Accounts Payable..........................................          100.00
    To voucher additional cost.
```

2. Despite the desirability of recording invoices at net price, stores purchased are still often entered in the voucher register at invoice price ($10,000 in the above illustration), and the discount is recorded on the date of payment in the check register:

```
Accounts Payable.........................................10,000.00
    Purchase Discount.....................................           100.00
    Cash.................................................           9,900.00
    For payment.
```

In the income statement, the purchase discount may be shown as an offset to gross purchases or as financial management or other income.

Treating purchase discounts on stores as a reduction of the cost of purchases raises the same problems in maintaining the book inventories of stores as were indicated in the treatment of freight-in. Purchase discounts on stores, therefore, may be treated as a credit to the Manufacturing Overhead Control account.

At least in theory, materials purchased for manufacturing should be priced at net cost. This is an accurate figure and prevents the statement of work-in-process and finished goods inventories at a price inflated by the amount of the purchase discounts. Many governmental agencies require that the *cost of materials* on their contracts be net after deduction of benefits of any kind arising from such purchases. Such benefits are to be considered whether taken or not, as long as they are available; and they included cash discounts on purchases in excess of 1 percent.

Internal Control through Location of Storerooms

A well-recognized rule of management is that at least two persons should be involved in all transactions affecting materials—one should handle or be responsible for the handling of the materials; the other should be responsible for the records of materials. The purpose of this rule is to reduce and prevent errors, fraud, and thefts except by collusion.

The location of the book inventory records will influence the effectiveness of the division of these two activities. Where but a single storeroom is required, it is possible to have the inventory records located in the storeroom, but entries are made thereon by a stores ledger clerk as distinguished from the storekeeper. When the materials have been issued against a properly authorized requisition, a copy of this requisition is given to the stores ledger clerk for entry.

In very large plants provision is usually made for substorerooms. These are placed throughout the factory in convenient locations to permit prompt delivery of the materials needed. Although it is possible to have a separate stores ledger for each location, a single book inventory kept in the cost accounting department is usually more practical.

Copies of all receiving reports and stores requisitions are sent to this department for entry. The segregation of the handling and the record-keeping activities reduces the possibility of fraud to a minimum.

Coding Accounts for Materials Control   Every modern up-to-date accounting system uses letters, numbers, or a combination of these to characterize its accounts. Since the number of material accounts kept in the subsidiary records is very large, codes for these accounts are usually in numerical form. For example, if a firm has one hundred different material items in its storeroom, the code numbers 400 to 500 could be assigned to this group. Further subdivisions might be made as follows: 400 to 420 might refer to the lumber products used in manufacturing; 420 to 450 to the metal products; 450 to 475 to the finished parts used; and the remaining numbers to the miscellaneous items. Sometimes by use of a decimal it is possible not only to classify the material but to indicate its location. For example, 480 might be the code number for a certain type of sponge rubber used in the upholstering department of a factory. The code 480.47 could then be used to refer to this material in storeroom number 4, bin number 7.

The use of location numbers in the codes expedites the location of the material when it is to be issued and also expedites the placing of the material into the proper bins and storerooms. In one factory, for example, there are 15,000 different items in the storeroom. Without the use of a numerical code, which not only classifies the material but also indicates its location, serious delays in issuing the material would result. There is a second reason for using codes. Numerous references must be made to the various material accounts or ledger cards. By using code numbers instead of account titles, much time can be saved. For instance, less time is needed to write "Charge Account 6–3" than to write "Charge Stores Control, Lumber." Such a saving in time, repeated many times a day, becomes a worthwhile factor in reducing the cost of accounting.

The increased use of punched card accounting, punched tape transmission and recording (integrated data processing), and electronic data processing makes the use of numerical codes for material accounting and inventory control an absolute necessity.

Procedural Analysis of Material Acquisitions   The complete picture of the managerial and accounting procedure involved in material acquisitions may be illustrated by (1) a descriptive flow of work tabulation, or by (2) a diagrammatic chart (see Illustration 5–7).

FORM PROCEDURE FOR MATERIALS CONTROL—PURCHASING,
RECEIVING, AND STORING

Purchase Requisitions: Usually *two* copies are prepared in the *stores* department, and these are used as follows:

1. Copy is filed in department originating request.
2. Copy is sent to the purchasing agent for his action.

Purchase Order: *Four* copies, more or less, may be prepared in the *purchasing* department and used as follows:

1. Copy is filed in department originating request.
2. Copy is sent to the *receiving* department to enable the clerks to anticipate the arrival of the material and to make arrangements for the work in connection therewith.
3. Copy is sent to the *stores ledger clerk* so that he may know his request received favorable action.
4. Copy is filed in the *purchasing* department as its record.

Receiving Report: Usually *three* copies may be prepared by the receiving clerks, and these are used as follows:

1. Copy is sent to the *purchasing* department for comparison with purchase order and invoice.
2. Copy is sent with goods to the *stores* department as a means of internal check and as an aid in making entries on stores ledger cards.
3. Copy is kept on file in the *receiving* department.

Stores Ledger Cards: One copy of this record is maintained in the stores department. Entries for the receipts are made in the *Receipts section,* showing quantity, unit cost, total cost, and these figures are added to those in the *Balance section.*

Managerial Problems in the Material Acquisition

A review of the preceding discussion of material acquisition costs points up that to be effective management must—

a) Coordinate the sales and production through a budgetary system planning purchases, inspecting materials when received, storing materials in the most accessible and most controllable locations.

b) Maintain adequate internal control over the material acquired by means of reliable book and physical inventories.

c) Establish a clearly outlined organization chart for fixing responsibility for the acquisition of materials.

d) Establish procedures for regularly reviewing the different kinds of materials which are or may be used.

e) Regularly study and revise the most economical quantity to order— determining *when* and *how much* to acquire on any given order.

f) Simplify, combine, and eliminate the forms and paperwork used in material acquisition procedures.

g) Select well-trained, responsible personnel to supervise the material acquisitions and pay them a salary commensurate with the responsibilities involved in supervising materials, oftentimes involving millions of dollars.

Illustration 5–7. Materials Control—Purchasing, Receiving, and Storing

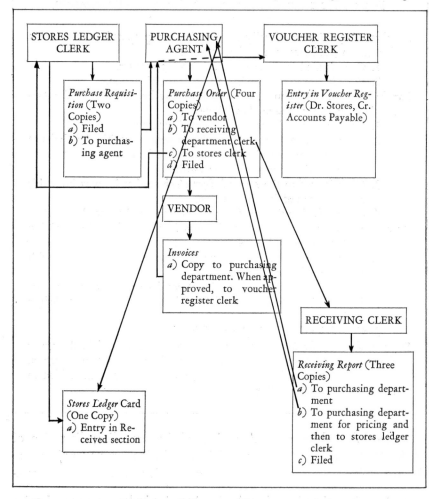

STORES LEDGER
CLERK

PURCHASING
AGENT

VOUCHER REGISTER
CLERK

Purchase Requisition (Two
Copies)
a) Filed
b) To purchasing agent

Purchase Order (Four
Copies)
a) To vendor
b) To receiving
department clerk
c) To stores clerk
d) Filed

Entry in Voucher Register (Dr. Stores, Cr.
Accounts Payable)

VENDOR

Invoices
a) Copy to purchasing
department. When approved, to voucher
register clerk

RECEIVING CLERK

Stores Ledger Card
(One Copy)
a) Entry in Received section

Receiving Report (Three
Copies)
a) To purchasing department
b) To purchasing department for pricing and
then to stores ledger
clerk
c) Filed

QUESTIONS FOR REVIEW

1. Because materials often constitute about one half of the cost to manufacture
a particular product, *material cost control* is an important managerial problem. Explain what is meant by material cost control.

2. What six requisites constitute an effective system of material cost control?

3. Why are forms an important phase of materials cost control? What forms
are a basic requirement for the proper control of the material acquisitions?

4. Outline the forms, routines, and procedures involved in the usual materials
acquisition accounting and control procedures for a firm having a good cost
accounting system.

5. Some firms use a five-section and others a three-section material inventory control card for each important item in the stores ledger. Explain the conditions which justify or warrant the use of each of these forms.

6. The location of the storeroom affects production efficiency. Discuss how this subject of location of the storeroom is important from the viewpoint of the "acquisition of materials."

7. Internal control is an important managerial responsibility in the matter of the acquisition of stores. Explain how this may be achieved at a minimum of cost.

8. Coding of accounts is more important today than ever before when the managerial responsibility for material control for a manufacturing concern is considered. Explain why this is so.

9. Investment in inventory is an important managerial problem in modern manufacturing concerns. Explain why this is so. What steps should management take to make this investment most efficient?

10. Outline the procedural analysis of material acquisitions. How may this analysis be expressed? Why is it important?

11. One phase of managerial control is the use of an engineering, planning, and routing department. Explain the function and necessity for such a department.

PROBLEMS—GROUP A

Problem 5–1. Purpose: *Transactions Affecting Materials Control*

The following transactions pertaining to materials were consummated by the Milden Corporation during the month of May:

1. Purchases of stores amounted to $140,000. All of the stores are purchased on account.

2. Requisitions processed by the storeroom showed the following:

> Direct materials issued...................$72,000
> Indirect materials issued.................. 11,000
> Shipping supplies issued...................   600

3. Defective materials in the amount of $2,300 were returned to the vendors and credit was received.

4. Invoices in the amount of $82,000 became due, and the amount less a 2 percent purchase discount was paid.

5. Paid trucking costs of $1,800. The Milden Company maintains a separate freight account.

6. Materials in the amount of $800 were issued to the maintenance department for the purpose of repairing certain machines.

7. Direct materials of $2,000 and indirect materials of $400 were returned to the storeroom.

8. The operating departments returned scrap material that had an estimated sales value of $750. Milden maintains an inventory account for scrap at sales value.

9. Material issued for parking lot repairs amounted to $1,000.

10. The scrap in the storeroom (Transaction No. 8) is sold for $720.

11. Shipping supplies in the amount of $300 were considered inferior and returned to vendor.
12. Indirect materials of $6,000 were purchased.

Record the above transactions in journal form.

Problem 5–2. Purpose: *Materials Control; Journal Entries*

The Marlin Manufacturing Company engaged in the following transactions pertaining to materials:

1. A contract ordering materials from the Carter Company was signed. Under the terms of the contract $60,000 of materials would be purchased each month for a year.
2. The current month's purchase from the Carter Company in the amount of $60,000 was received.
3. Materials amounting to $2,000 were returned to vendors.
4. The production department withdrew materials amounting to $58,000.
5. The building and administrative service section requisitioned and received $400 of materials.
6. Materials that are spoiled are returned to the storeroom and a special account "Defective Goods" is maintained for these goods. The goods are charged at estimated sales value. Spoilage that may bring $450 is brought to the storeroom during the current month. The cost of these goods was $1,800.
7. The monthly inventory account showed that actual inventory was $300 less than the perpetual inventory records.
8. A check to the Carter Company in the amount of $60,000 was issued in payment of the current month's purchases.

Prepare journal entries to record the above transactions.

Problem 5–3. Purpose: *Review of the Cost Accounting Cycle*

The Morton Machine Company produces attachments for sewing machines. On July 1 and on July 31 the following inventories appeared in the accounts:

	July 1	July 31
Stores.................................	$40,000	
Work-in-Process—Materials...........	9,000	$8,000
Work-in-Process—Labor..............	11,000	9,500
Work-in-Process—Overhead..........	11,000	9,500

The following is a summary of transactions entered into by the company during July:

1. Purchased stores in the amount of $70,000. These were purchased on account. Stores were returned to vendors in the amount of $1,500.
2. Direct materials in the amount of $50,000 were issued; $5,000 were considered excess and returned to the storeroom. Indirect materials of $10,000 were also issued.
3. The monthly payrolls were as follows:

	Gross Amount	F.I.C.A. Taxes	Federal Withholding Taxes	State Withholding Taxes
Direct labor................$130,000		$5,100	$18,000	$4,000
Indirect labor.............	14,000	550	1,600	350
Superintendence...........	3,000	–0–	420	90
Sales salaries..............	18,000	700	2,100	540
Office salaries.............	4,000	100	500	110

4. Payroll taxes in addition to the employer's share of F.I.C.A. amounted to:

> Factory share....................$5,100
> Selling share..................... 480
> Office share...................... 120

5. Actual overhead costs in addition to those already mentioned were $101,000.
6. Manufacturing overhead costs were applied to production at the rate of 100 percent direct labor costs.
7. Other expenses were as follows:

> Selling.........................$32,000
> Administrative.................. 16,000

8. Monthly sales amounted to $482,000.
9. Finished goods inventory on July 1 was $42,000 and $52,000 on July 31.

Required:

a) Prepare T-Ledgers for the following accounts:

Stores
Manufacturing Overhead Control
Finished Goods
Selling Expense

Work-in-Process (three accounts)
Manufacturing Overhead Applied
Cost of Sales
Administrative Expense

b) Enter the beginning balances in the accounts.
c) Record the transactions for the month in the accounts.
d) Prepare a statement of cost of goods sold for the month.
e) Prepare a condensed income statement for the month.

Problem 5–4. Purpose: *C.P.A. Problem on Materials Control*

You are with the controller's office of the Maine Manufacturing Company which closes its books at December 31 each year.

You are engaged in an audit of the Maine Manufacturing Company for the year ended December 31. To reduce the work load at year-end the company took its annual physical inventory under your observation on November 30, 19—. The company's inventory account, which includes raw material and work-in-process, is on a perpetual basis, and the first-in, first-out method of pricing is used. There is no finished goods inventory. The company's physical inventory revealed that the book inventory of $60,570 was understated by $3,000. To avoid distorting the interim financial statements the company decided not to adjust the book inventory until year-end except for obsolete inventory items.

Your audit revealed the following information regarding the November 30 inventory:

1. Pricing tests showed that the physical inventory was overpriced by $2,200.
2. Footing and extension errors resulted in a $150 understatement of the physical inventory.
3. Direct labor included in the physical inventory amounted to $10,000. Overhead was included at the rate of 200 percent of direct labor. You determined that the amount of direct labor was correct and the overhead rate was proper.
4. The physical inventory included obsolete materials recorded at $250. During December these obsolete materials were removed from the inventory account by a charge to Cost of Sales.

Your audit also disclosed the following information about the December 31 inventory:

1. Total debits to certain accounts during December are listed below:

	December
Purchases	$24,700
Direct labor	12,100
Manufacturing expense	25,200
Cost of sales	68,600

2. The cost of sales of $68,600 included direct labor of $13,800.
3. Normal scrap loss on established product lines is negligible. However, a special order started and completed during December had excessive scrap loss of $800 which was charged to Manufacturing Expense.

(AICPA Adapted)

PROBLEMS—GROUP B

Problem 5–5. Purpose: *Transactions Affecting Materials Control*

Transactions affecting materials for the month of January for the Wells Manufacturing Company follow:

1. Materials in the amount of $15,000 were purchased on account.
2. Direct materials in the amount of $7,500 were issued; $100 of shipping supplies and $1,000 of other indirect materials were also issued.
3. Invoices in the amount of $12,000 were paid, less the 1 percent customary purchases discount.
4. Materials in the amount of $400 were considered defective and were returned for credit to vendors.
5. Freight in the amount of $800 was paid. The freight, although on purchases, should be charged to an overhead account.
6. Indirect materials amounting to $50 and direct materials amounting to $200 were returned to the storeroom.
7. Materials issued to the repair department for sidewalk repair amounted to $100.

8. Production Department A returned scrap material that had an estimated sales value of $190. The company maintains an inventory account for scrap at sales value.
9. Materials issued for elevator repair amounted to $125.
10. Shipping supplies in the amount of $160 were returned for credit to the vendor.
11. The scrap (Transaction No. 8) was sold for $170.
12. Purchased indirect materials in the amount of $3,000.
Record the above transactions in journal form.

Problem 5–6. Purpose: *Materials Control; Journal Entries*

During the month of June, the Weston Company engaged in the following transactions:
1. A contract was signed with the Eastern Company whereby Eastern agreed to supply $125,000 of materials each month for the next six months. The price for the contract period was fixed.
2. Eastern shipped the current month's share of $125,000 of materials. These were received.
3. Inspectors found $5,000 of materials defective, and these were returned for credit to the Eastern Company.
4. Direct materials issued amounted to $98,000.
5. The maintenance department withdrew $5,000 of materials from the storeroom.
6. All spoiled materials are returned to the storeroom, and an account called "Spoilage and Scrap" is maintained for these goods. The goods are carried in the account at estimated sales value. Spoiled goods with a sales value of $2,100 are brought in during the current month. The cost of these goods was $4,000.
7. An inventory count showed actual inventory to be $1,400 below the records of the storeroom.
8. Eastern Company is paid for its current month's shipment less the 2 percent discount.
Prepare journal entries to record the above transactions.

Problem 5–7. Purpose: *Review of the Cost Accounting Cycle*

Washing machine motor subassemblies are made by the Washer Company. The following represents a summary of transactions entered into during June:
1. Material purchases amounted to $800,000. These were purchases on account.
2. Materials in the amount of $8,000 were returned to the vendor.
3. Issuance of materials was as follows:

> Direct materials................$600,000
> Indirect materials.............. 16,000

4. Direct materials in the amount of $8,000 were returned unused to the storeroom.
5. The monthly payrolls were as follows:

	Gross Amount	F.I.C.A. Taxes	Federal Withholding Taxes	State Withholding Taxes
Direct labor	$250,000	$9,200	$28,000	$7,000
Indirect labor	30,000	1,100	3,200	800
Selling salaries	35,000	1,300	4,000	900
Administrative salaries	20,000	750	2,200	600

6. The employer's share of F.I.C.A. amounted to the same amount as the employee's share. Other payroll taxes amounted to $8,500 as factory share; $1,000 as selling share; and $600 as administrative share.
7. Manufacturing overhead costs were applied to production at the rate of 90 percent of direct labor cost.
8. Overhead items in addition to indirect materials, payroll, taxes, and indirect labor amounted to $160,000.
9. Other selling expenses amounted to $50,000, and other administrative expenses were $31,000.
10. Sales amounted to $2,000,000.
11. The beginning and ending inventories were as follows:

	Beginning	Ending
Stores	$300,000	?
Work-in-process	220,000	$260,000
Finished goods	410,000	512,000

Required:

a) Prepare T-ledger accounts for Stores, Work-in-Process (one account), Factory Expense, Factory Expense Applied, Finished Goods, Cost of Goods Sold, Selling Expense, Administrative Expense.

b) Enter the beginning balances in the accounts.

c) Record the transactions for the month in the accounts.

d) Prepare a cost of goods sold statement for the month.

e) Prepare a condensed income statement for the month.

Problem 5–8. Purpose: *C.P.A. Problem on Materials Control*

Wilcox Manufacturers maintains its inventory records on a perpetual basis and uses the first-in, first-out method of inventory pricing. A physical count of the inventory showed actual inventory to be $28,785. The perpetual inventory records of stores and work-in-process showed inventory should be $30,285. There was no finished goods inventory. The above discrepancy was noted on February 28, one month before the close of the fiscal year. To avoid distorting the interim financial statements, the controller of Wilcox decided not to adjust the book inventory until year-end, except for obsolete inventory items.

Further investigation of the inventory records that yielded the above discrepancy showed that there was a footing error that resulted in a $75 understatement of the physical inventory. The physical inventory was "priced," and it was found that it was overpriced by $1,100.

Overhead was applied to the inventory at the rate of 200 percent of direct labor cost. The amount of direct labor which was included in the inventory was $5,000. This amount was found to be correct.

The physical inventory included obsolete materials recorded at $125. During March, these obsolete materials were removed from inventory and charged to "Cost of Goods Sold."

Certain amounts were charged to the following accounts during the month of March: Purchases—$12,350; Direct Labor—$6,050; Manufacturing Expense—$12,600; Cost of Goods Sold—$34,300.

The $34,300 of cost of goods sold included $6,900 of direct labor.

The manufacturing operations are such that excessive scrap loss is rare. However, on a special order completed during March, $400 of excessive scrap was charged to manufacturing expense. The amount was considered correct.

Required:

a) Determine the correct physical inventory at February 28.

b) Determine the correct physical inventory at March 31 if the February 28 inventory was $28,850. Do not let this answer prejudice your answer to (*a*) above.

c) Compute the over- or underapplied manufacturing expense, if any, at March 31.

(AICPA Adapted)

CHAPTER

6 Managerial Cost Control

of Materials Used—Issuing,

Costing, and Inventory Records

Managerial Planning, Routing, and Issuing of Materials
In the larger manufacturing organizations, production must be carefully planned, scheduled, and routed through the factory so that there will be a minimum of delay and confusion. Although the work of the planning and routing department is essentially the responsibility of the production manager, it is so closely related to the cost accounting work that the student must be familiar with its operation. The planning and routing department is frequently one of the most important departments in the factory. Its staff will have or will produce descriptions of all production or jobs to be manufactured. These descriptions are known as *production orders*—orders sent to various parts of the factory to inform the superintendent or foremen what is to be done. These production orders later become the headings or descriptions on the job order cost sheets.

The second duty of the planning and routing department is to route the work through the factory. Definite time schedules must be arranged so that the necessary materials will be delivered to the proper department just when needed—not too long beforehand, when they might interfere with other work; nor after they are required, for this would cause wasteful idle time. It is this part of the work of the planning and routing department that affects materials control. This department is also concerned with the machines required to complete the work and with the portable tools from the toolroom. Machines must be available, and tools must be delivered to expedite the work.

A careful study of the planning, routing, and scheduling of work in the factory emphasizes the necessity of this procedure. The staff of the planning and routing department plays the same important part in factory production that railroad dispatchers play in routing train services. Without the dispatchers, many collisions would result. Without the planning and routing department in the factory, some departments would be overloaded with work while others would be idle. Confusion would result. Efficient management produces the opposite state of affairs. In one large piano factory, for example, the planning and routing department is able, at any time, to tell just what orders are in the factory, in which departments they are located, and the stage of their completion. This type of *effective managerial control* plays an important part in cost accounting.

In the large assembly plants of the automobile firms, the variety of cars to be produced to meet the desires of the various customers, such as colors of body, the types of upholstery, the various electives such as power steering, automatic transmission, air conditioning, power brakes, and many other variables, makes efficient production planning a tremendous problem. Collecting orders, scheduling production, and issuing material requisitions for the large variety of parts used requires the efforts of trained personnel. The use of electronic computers has been a great help in solving these promptly and accurately. Obviously, this type of effective production control plays an important part in cost accounting.

In one large organization the production planning and engineering department performs the following functions:

1. Prepares master production orders.
2. Prepares necessary subproduction orders.
3. Prepares blueprint orders.
4. Acknowledges and checks blueprint receipts.
5. Prepares bills of material.
6. Prepares tool orders.
7. Prepares and checks laboratory records.

Cost Accounting for Materials Issued

Managerial control of the issue of materials involves the use of forms, procedural analysis, journal entries, subsidiary inventory records, and proper costing of the materials issued. Special problems arise in the taking of physical inventories, accounting for scrap, spoiled, and defective work, storing the material, and budgeting the long-term requirements. Since these problems affect the *unit costs* of production, sound and accepted accounting practices must be followed.

Forms and Reports Used in Controlling the Issuance of Materials

As in the case of the receipt and storage of materials, forms are used to fix responsibility and develop internal check and control for the issuance and costing of the materials required in the manufacturing operations. Among the forms used in the issuance and pricing of materials are the following:

1. Materials requisitions.
2. Standard bill of materials.
3. Returned materials report.
4. Scrap report.
5. Spoiled materials report.
6. Perpetual or book inventory records (stores ledger cards).

1. The *material requisition forms* are sent to the stores department whenever any materials are to be withdrawn for use in the factory. Sometimes these requisitions are prepared in a central department, that is, the planning, routing, and scheduling department. In other firms, they may be prepared by the foreman in charge of the department planning to use the material. In a few firms not having too much internal control, the form is prepared by the worker who needs the material.

This form (see Illustration 6–1) when filled out authorizes the issuance of the materials and indicates the purpose for which the materials are to be used, and it is prepared usually in duplicate or triplicate. The first two copies are sent to the stores department, and the third is kept in the department authorizing the issuance. A separate requisition may be prepared for each kind of material withdrawn, or a single requisition may be prepared to cover the issuance of a number of items. If the requisition is printed in triplicate, the stores department sends one copy to the cost accounting department so that it may be informed of the quantity and, perhaps, the cost of the materials used in production or in the maintenance of the plant and equipment. If the materials requisition slip is prepared in duplicate, the stores department must report to the cost accounting department by some other means the cost of the materials used on the various jobs. Such a report, a timesaver for the cost accounting department, may be in the form of a recapitulation of the materials requisitions by jobs, prepared by the stores clerk from his summary of materials costs to be posted to the job order cost sheets.

Some concerns make use of a requisition on which is printed each kind of material carried in stock. Whenever materials are needed in the factory, the quantity is written in the space provided. Such a form is

Illustration 6-1. Stores Requisition Slip

WALLACE MANUFACTURING CO.

DATE 3/2/--	MATERIAL REQUISITION	

WHERE USED
Stamping Department   No. B 154

ACCOUNT CHARGED
Work-in-Process Job UCS 782

QUANTITY	DESCRIPTION	PRICE	TOTAL	
800 lbs	Tempered Blade Steel			
	Spec. 482	12	96	00

RECEIVED ABOVE	APPROVED	DELIVERED BY				
P. Mascari	*J. Forbes*	*C. C. Rye*				

ENTERED COST LEDGER	ENTERED IN CAT.	PRICED	EXTENDED	CHECKED	POSTED	PUNCHED
JKC	JKC	P 7	P.7.	VC	✓	✓

Original to Stores Dept.
    Duplicate to Cost Department
        Triplicate to Planning or Originating Dept.

most advantageously used in an assembly type of manufacturing concern where most requisitions will be for finished parts.

2. In many concerns having definite standards for the quantity of material that should be used on a particular job, the planning and scheduling department will prepare a *standard bill of materials* (Illustration 6–2) which lists all the materials that will be required for the completion of a job. These materials will be sent into production either as one shipment or as scheduled. If the manufacturing operations involve merely the assembling of the parts so issued, there should be no variation from the amount issued and the amount of material used. If, however, the job has spoilage, on the one hand, or the more efficient use of material, on the other, additional requisitions may be required to make up the deficiency, or a credit memorandum will be issued for

Illustration 6–2. Standard Bill of Materials

Per 100		BILL OF MATERIALS				Stock No. *3841*	
Del. By Dept. No.	Quan.	Description	Stock No.	Del. By Dept. No.	Quan.	Description	Stock No.
12	*20*	*Sheets 18 ga. steel 36x120*					
	20	*Sheets 16 ga. steel 36x120*					
	52	*Sheets 18 ga. steel 46x 16*					
	300	*20 ga. end pieces*					
17	*100*	*Drawer fronts*	*53369*				
	100	*Drawer bodies*	*51699*				
	100	*Drawer liners*	*55572*				
18	*200*	*Case strips supports*	*59464*				
	200	*Case strips*	*13787*				
	400	*Corner sockets*	*58217*				
	200	*Braces*	*51503*				
	100	*Drawer strips*	*58216*				
	200	*Splice plates*	*57176*				
	400	*Legs*	*58218*				
	800	*Clamp plates*	*52211*				
	200	*Bronze bindings*	*4471*				
	400	*¼x¼ R. H. screws*					
	400	*⅜x16x2 Hex. head screws*					
	400	*⅜" Lock washers*					

Original—To Stores Dept.

Duplicate—To Cost Dept.

Triplicate—To Planning or Originating Dept.

excess materials returned. The use of a standard bill of materials enables the factory manager to ascertain and control the amount of waste of materials by tabulating the amounts used on the extra requisitions.

3. Because of the speed in sorting and summarizing, many firms are using punched card accounting machines in their cost accounting work. The information on the requisitions can be transmitted to a central accounting department by means of telegraphic handwriting, or common-language punched tape (teletypewriter) so that the punched card requisitions may be prepared immediately, and the work of sorting and recording the materials requisitions on job cost sheets or reports is expedited. Such punched card requisitions are shown in Illustration 6–3.

4. The *returned materials report* (see Illustration 6–4) is prepared

Illustration 6–3

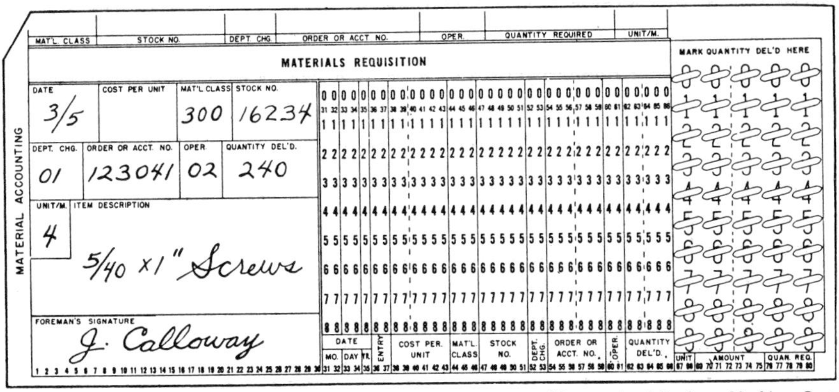

Courtesy of *International Business Machines Corp.*

Illustration 6–4. Returned Materials Report

DATE	STORES AND SUPPLIES RETURNED CREDIT MEMO.		
4/7/--			
WHERE USED		No A 4107	
Stamping Department			
ACCOUNT CHARGED			
Work-in-Process, Job #UCS782			

QUANTITY	DESCRIPTION	PRICE	TOTAL	
56 lbs.	Tempered Blade Steel			
	Spec. 482	12	6	72

RECEIVED ABOVE	APPROVED	DELIVERED BY		
C. C. Rye	J. Farber	F. Mascari		
ENTERED COST LEDGER	ENTERED IN CAT.	PRICED	EXTENDED	CHECKED	POSTED	PUNCHED
JKC	JKC	$.7.	2 7	K	✓	✓

Original--Dept. Returning material

Duplicate--Cost Dept.

Triplicate--Stores Department

in triplicate by the stores ledger clerk. It has the opposite effect of a requisition and shows the excess material returned to storeroom. One copy is sent to the department returning the materials. The second copy is sent to the cost department and acts as a credit memorandum since it reduces the charge for materials used. The third copy is kept by the stores department as a basis for an entry on the stores ledger card.

5. A *scrap report* is a form of receiving report prepared when scrap is accumulated and recorded on a perpetual inventory record. It usually contains only a quantity record which is entered in the Received section of an appropriate inventory record card. Some firms feel that since scrap has little value, no records are necessary.

6. A *spoiled material report* is similar to a scrap report, but it indicates the causes for spoilage and, if available, the costs involved in the spoilage.

7. The *book inventory cards* were discussed in detail in the previous chapter.

Entries in the Book Inventory Records   Entries in the book inventory records are made in each of five possible divisions: Receipts, Issues, Balance, Materials on Order, and Materials on Reserve.

A copy of the receiving report moves with the goods to the storeroom. Previously, a copy of the purchase order was sent to the storeroom. A comparison of these records confirms the checking already completed by the receiving department. If the stores clerk keeps a quantitative inventory, he records in the proper columns of the *Receipts* section the date, purchase order number, and quantity received. This quantity is then extended to the *Balance* section, on the same line, by adding it to the balance on the preceding line.

Should both a quantity and value inventory be kept, the stores clerk must have the unit prices and total cost of the goods received. The copy of the purchase order on hand may have had the prices inserted when the order was placed; if so, this form provides the necessary information. The usual procedure however is to send a copy of the receiving report first to the purchasing department for the insertion of the prices and then have this copy forwarded to the stores ledger clerk for posting to the inventory cards.

Unsatisfactory goods received may be returned to the vendor immediately, and the receiving report will then show the quantity actually accepted. The stores ledger will show the satisfactory goods received. But this practice is not always possible. Goods may be placed in the stock room, found unsatisfactory after some have been used in the manufacturing process, and then returned to the vendor. Since the entry for the receipt was made when the goods were placed in the storeroom, an adjustment must now be made. The returned purchase report gives the information for the entry. The usual procedure is to enter the quantity and cost of the returned purchases *in red* in the *Receipts* section and to subtract the quantity and value from the respective amounts in the *Balance* section. A few firms suggest that the entry be made in the *Issued* section; but little justification can be found for this practice since it distorts the entries on the stores ledger for the amount of material used in manufacturing.

The authorization for the issue of material by the storeskeeper is the materials requisition. A copy of this form, duly signed, is sent to the stores clerk for his record. In the *Issued* section of the stores ledger card the date, stores requisition number, production order number, quantity, unit price and total cost are entered. These figures are extended to the *Balance* section by deducting the quantity issued from the previous quantity balance, and cost of issue from the previous balance.

Upon the completion of an order, excess material may be on hand. When these are returned to the storeroom, a *returned materials* report is prepared and a copy sent to the stores clerk. On the stores ledger card the quantity and cost are entered in red in the *Issued* section and added to the units and value of the preceding balance.

Entries for freight-in and adjustments for shortages will be discussed later in this chapter.

Procedural Analysis of the Control of Materials Issued

The following flow-of-work description, together with Illustration 6–5, will facilitate the understanding of the forms procedure involved in the issuance of materials from the storeroom.

Accounting for Issuance of Materials

Costs of materials issued must be classified before they are recorded. The materials issued may be *direct materials, indirect materials,* or *packing and shipping supplies.* Furthermore, when materials are issued, there must first be a properly authorized printed form—*the stores requisition,* a copy of which is sent to the stores ledger clerk.

Accounting entries for the issuance of materials are made (1) on the stores inventory cards, (2) on the cost accounting records, and (3) on the general accounting records.

Entry on the Stores Inventory Record. The first accounting

Illustration 6-5. Materials Control—Issuance of Materials

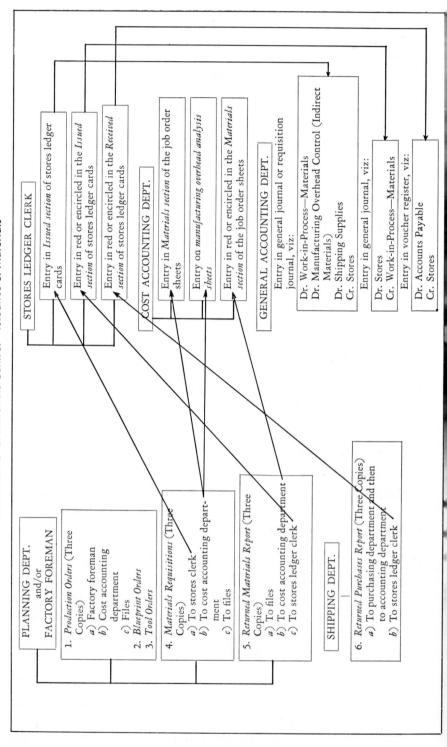

FORMS PROCEDURE FOR MATERIALS CONTROL—ISSUANCE
OF MATERIALS

Materials Requisitions: At least three copies are prepared either in the planning and routing department or in the department requiring the material. These are used as follows:

1. Copy sent to the stores department to authorize the issuance of the material.
2. Copy sent to the cost department for both direct and indirect materials.
3. Copy is retained in department requesting the material.

Returned Materials Report: At least three copies are prepared in the stores department, and these are used as follows:

1. Copy is sent to department returning the material.
2. Copy is sent to the cost accounting department for deductions in the *Material Costs* section of the job order sheets.
3. Copy is kept by the stores department for entry in red or encircled in the *Issued* section of the stores ledger cards affected, and for addition to the *Balance* section.

Returned Purchases Report: At least three copies are prepared in the shipping department, and these are used as follows:

1. Copy is sent to the purchasing department which forwards it to the accounting department for entry in the voucher register, debiting Accounts Payable and crediting Stores Control.
2. Copy is sent to the stores department for entry in red or encircled in the *Received* section of the respective stores ledger cards, and for deduction from the *Balance* section of these cards.
3. Copy is retained by the shipping department for its record.

record for any material issued from the storeroom is made in the *Issued* section of the stores inventory card and deducted from the balance in the *Balance* section. The entries are made in terms of the *quantity* as well as the *unit cost* and *total cost,* for example:

Received			Issued			Balance		
Units	Price	Total	Units	Price	Total	Units	Price	Total
						500	1.00	500.00
300	1.00	300.00				800	1.00	800.00
			250	1.00	250.00	550	1.00	550.00

Entry on Cost Accounting Records. Periodically, copies of material requisitions are sent to the cost accounting department, where they are sorted. Those for *direct materials* are sorted by job order numbers.

Those for *indirect materials* and for *shipping supplies* are sorted into separate lots. From this sorting of the requisitions, entries for the *direct materials* are made on the respective *job order sheets* in the *Materials Cost* section. The *indirect materials used* total and the cost of *shipping supplies used* are transmitted to the general accounting department for recording as *manufacturing overhead costs* and *selling expenses,* respectively.

Entries on the General Accounting Records. For the *direct materials used* and for the *indirect materials used,* a summary general journal entry is made, usually *weekly:*

> Work-in-Process—Materials............................3,690.00
> Manufacturing Overhead Control (Indirect Materials)......... 310.00
> Stores... 4,000.00

A posting to the subsidiary Manufacturing Overhead Ledger account for indirect materials is also made for the amount of $310.

For the shipping supplies, a summary general journal entry is made (with or without use of Selling Expense Control account):

> Shipping Supplies Used...................................450.00
> Stores... 450.00

It should be evident that the total in the debit to the Work-in-Process—Materials account must agree with the total of the various charges made in the *Materials Cost* sections of the different job order cost sheets.

The Requisition Journal

In some firms, use is made of a running or continuous record of the requisitions. If desirable, this may be in the form of a book of original entry. Such use is limited to firms in which the number of requisitions is small, and the amounts involved are large; otherwise it is an unnecessary duplication of clerical effort. The rulings of such a requisition journal as a book of original entry would be:

Date	Requisition Number	Job Order Number	Work-in-Process— Materials Dr.	Manufacturing Overhead Dr.	Shipping Supplies Dr.	Stores Cr.
	Totals					

This requisition journal may be primarily a memorandum record whereby the foremen or superintendent use it like a work sheet to maintain operating records and accumulate the totals. Illustration 6–6 on the following page shows not only the requisitions journal but also the accounting procedure when it is used.

Costing Materials Used in Production   The variety of materials used in different manufacturing concerns and the conditions under which these are priced when issued necessitates a constant repetition of the statement that there are many ways of doing the same thing. A cost accountant, as distinguished from a cost clerk, must be familiar with most of the methods in use and the conditions under which each may be advantageously applied.

Some of the more commonly used methods of costing or pricing requisitions in the perpetual inventory records are:

1. First-in, first-out pricing method (FIFO).
2. Last-in, first-out pricing method (LIFO).
3. Moving-average pricing method.
4. Average price at close of preceding period method.
5. Miscellaneous methods.

First-In, First-Out Method of Inventory Pricing (FIFO)   The first-in, first-out method of inventory pricing is based upon the principle that materials should be issued in the order and at the price of their original purchase. For example, if 500 pounds of copper were purchased at 40 cents a pound and, later, another lot of 750 pounds was purchased at 39 cents a pound, the first 500 pounds to be used will be charged into production at the price of 40 cents and thereafter charges will be made at 39 cents. Theoretically it is assumed that the 500 pounds will be segregated from the 750-pound lot and will be issued first. Actually, however, since the goods in both lots are identical, the goods are not separated. A careful study of this method of inventory pricing emphasizes the fact that the Balance column must be extended in such a way as to indicate clearly the quantity and price of each lot. If three or more lots are on hand at one time, the balance must be extended on three lines. This procedure is awkward if there are many such items. But, from a practical angle, few concerns will have more than two lots of materials on hand at one time unless they anticipate a rising market. The balance, therefore, normally ought not to contain more than two quantities or prices at a given date.

Illustration 6–7 (p. 139) represents the *first-in, first-out* method of costing requisitions. The same data, used in this illustration and in those

Illustration 6-6. Requisitions Journal Showing Flow of Work in Materials Control—The Issuing of Material

MATERIALS REQUISITION JOURNAL

Date	Req. No.	Description	Work-in-Process Materials Dr.	Indirect Supplies Used Dr.	Shipping Supplies Expense Dr.	Materials Cr.
Jan. 4	646	Job No. 187	$ 500.00			$ 500.00
5	647	Job No. 190	400.00			400.00
5	648	For Grinding Department		$ 50.00		50.00
7	649	Job No. 188	120.00			120.00
8	650	Shipping Supplies for week			$ 250.00	250.00
9	651	Job No. 191	60.00			60.00
		Total for week	$1,080.00	$ 50.00	$ 250.00	$1,380.00
			(45)	(50)	(55)	(46)

MATERIALS ACCOUNT

Jan. 31 Purchases V.R. $6,000.00	Jan. 9 Req. Jr. $1,380.00

WORK-IN-PROCESS MATERIALS

Jan. 31 Req. Jr. $1,080.00	

JOB ORDER COST SHEET

Job No. 187

For Stock--20 Machines Model BT2

Started 1/4

Materials	Labor	Expenses
Jan. 7 $500.00		

MATERIALS REQUISITION No. 646

for Job No. 187

Material A	$400.00
Material B	100.00
	$500.00

Date 1/4   Dept. Cutting

STORES LEDGER CARDS

Material--A   Location Bin 2

Received			Issued			Balance		
D.	O.	Price	D.	O.	Price	D.	O.	Price
			1/4		$400.00	1/1		$800.00
						1/4		400.00

Material--B   Location Bin 4

Received			Issued			Balance		
D.	O.	Price	D.	O.	Price	D.	O.	Price
			1/4		$100.00	1/1		$450.00
						1/4		350.00

Illustration 6–7. Perpetual Inventory Card—First-In, First-Out Pricing Method

RECEIPTS			ISSUES			BALANCE		
Nov. 1	600 @ 12¢	$72.00				Nov. 1	600 @ 12¢	$72.00
			Nov. 3	300 @ 12¢	$36.00	3	300 @ 12¢	36.00
			5	125 @ 12¢	15.00	5	175 @ 12¢	21.00
12	500 @ 14¢	70.00				12	175 @ 12¢	21.00
							500 @ 14¢	70.00
			14	50 @ 12¢	6.00	14	225 @ 12¢	27.00
							500 @ 14¢	70.00
			15	225 @ 12¢	27.00			
				25 @ 14¢	3.50	15	475 @ 14¢	66.50
			18	300 @ 14¢	42.00	18	175 @ 14¢	24.50
21	300 @ 13¢	39.00				21	175 @ 14¢	24.50
							300 @ 13¢	39.00

for the other inventory pricing methods which follow, cover the following transactions so that comparisons between the pricing methods can be made:

Purchases	Issues	Returns to Storeroom from Factory
Nov. 1 600 units		
	Nov. 3 300 units	
	5 125 units	
12 500 units		Nov. 14 50 units
	15 250 units	
	18 300 units	
21 300 units		

For the *first-in, first-out* method, it is claimed that since the materials are charged into production at actual cost in the order of receipt, the method is more accurate. This is one of the reasons the Internal Revenue Service favors this method. However, the Internal Revenue Service also favors this method because in a market of rising prices, income calculations include closing inventories of raw materials at more recent, higher prices and the cost of goods sold, thereby, at a lower figure. The net effect taxwise is a larger income tax to be paid currently on higher net income. (The opposite income tax effect is involved in the last-in, first-out method of costing the closing raw materials inventories.) The main disadvantage from the point of view of business is in the amount of clerical work involved in extending balances on the inventory cards if these inventory balances include materials at several different prices.

Two other problems arise in the use of this method of inventory pricing. The first is the question of returns to the vendor of merchandise found unsatisfactory some time after purchase. The vendor will always be charged with the goods *at the price at which purchased.* However, if the Balance column no longer contains goods at the price of the original purchase because all subsequent purchases were either at a higher or lower price, the entry in the stores ledger card for the return will use the price of the next available lot; the entry will be made in the *Receipts* section, circled. However, the entry in the voucher register for the return must account for the difference through an inventory adjustment entry. For example, the goods being returned are 200 units at 14 cents, but only 10-cent units are on hand according to the inventory card. The vendor must be charged with the 14-cent price, although on the inventory card, it will be at 10 cents. Therefore the adjustment entry would be:

```
Accounts Payable.................................................28.00
      Stores........................................................      20.00
      Manufacturing Overhead—Materials Adjustment...................       8.00
```

A second problem arises in the treatment of returns from the factory to the storeroom of excess materials. Assume that in the foregoing illustration all the 12-cent material and some of the 14-cent material had been issued. Thereafter, some of the material issued at 12 cents is returned to the storeroom as excess. Should it be treated as old material and placed before the remaining 14-cent material, or treated as though it were a new purchase and placed after the 14-cent material? *Theoretically,* at least, either treatment would state the previous issue of 14-cent material incorrectly, since there are still some 12-cent materials on hand which according to the first-in, first-out rule should have been allocated to this order. No fixed rule has been determined for handling such transactions because the small amounts involved in such situations do not cause much concern in business.

This rule, however, might be used: If goods are returned to the storeroom, the price used is the same as that at time of issue. If no goods have since been issued at a different price, the returned goods would be placed first in the Balance column: if goods have been issued at a different price, the returned goods are treated as though they were a new purchase and placed last.

The FIFO method of inventory pricing can be used satisfactorily where the following three conditions exist:

1. Inventories turn over rapidly.
2. Inventory is not a major factor in the profit or current asset situation.
3. The nature and type of goods used in the inventory changes frequently.

Last-In, First-Out Method (LIFO) The last-in, first-out method is predicated upon the principle that in a rising market, inventory or speculative inventory profits should not be recognized since the inventory used in production must be replaced at higher costs. Under this method the cost of current purchases of materials used in production is applied as the cost of current production. In other words, the cost of current production is charged with the cost of materials at prices which most nearly correspond in point of time with those which are being paid to replace the materials consumed.

Illustration 6–8. Perpetual Inventory Card—Last-In, First-Out Pricing Method

RECEIPTS			ISSUES			BALANCE		
Nov. 1	600 @ 12¢	$72.00				Nov. 1	600 @ 12¢	$72.00
			Nov. 3	300 @ 12¢	$36.00	3	300 @ 12¢	36.00
			5	125 @ 12¢	15.00	5	175 @ 12¢	21.00
12	500 @ 14¢	70.00				12	175 @ 12¢	21.00
							500 @ 14¢	70.00
			14	50 @ 12¢	6.00	14	225 @ 12¢	27.00
							500 @ 14¢	70.00
			15	250 @ 14¢	35.00	15	225 @ 12¢	27.00
							250 @ 14¢	35.00
			16	250 @ 14¢	35.00			
				50 @ 12¢	6.00	18	175 @ 12¢	21.00
21	300 @ 13¢	39.00				21	175 @ 12¢	21.00
							300 @ 13¢	39.00

During recent years, the last-in, first-out method of inventory pricing has come to be more widely used than ever before. This is due primarily to the steady rise in the cost of practically all materials and the rather widely held opinion that prices will probably not return to lower levels under present economic conditions and practices. To illustrate this method, the same figures used in the first-in, first-out method are used. When materials are requisitioned, the assumption is that the prices are taken from the last additions to the inventory (see Illustration 6–8).

A distinction must be made between LIFO applied as a *continuous pricing method* under a book inventory procedure (as in Illustration 6–8) and LIFO applied as a *periodic* inventory method. For example, if there had been only a *periodic* inventory of the item in the foregoing illustration, all of the 475 units in the final inventory would be priced at

12 cents under the LIFO method since the number of units in the final inventory is not greater than in the first purchase at 12 cents. The *elective* method, which may be used in computing taxable income (under certain conditions), is a periodic inventory LIFO method. Under the elective method, the units in the final inventory not in excess of those in the initial inventory are priced the same as in the initial inventory. Excess units may be priced (consistently from year to year) at earliest purchase price (or prices), at latest purchase price (or prices), or at average purchase prices.

The last-in, first-out method of inventory pricing can be used whenever it would be possible to use the first-in, first-out method or the moving-average pricing method. The practical aspects of the problem, however, suggest that some or all of the following conditions should be present:

1. That there is a continued need for substantial quantities of materials, the price of which may be subject to considerable price fluctuations.
2. That the relative value of the materials used in production is large in comparison to the total cost of the finished product.
3. That the selling prices of the finished product react rather sharply and quickly to the fluctuations in the replacement cost of the materials used.

During a period of inflation or in a rising price market, the last-in, first-out method of inventory pricing tends to reduce the amount of the stated profit and consequently decreases any taxes based on the calculation of profits. This effect is created because the so-called "inventory profits," that is, profits which have not been transformed into cash or receivables, are minimized. The costs of production and, consequently, the cost of goods sold are based upon the cost of materials most recently purchased, which is at higher prices than on the first-in, first-out basis. It results in higher cost of sales, smaller profits, and unrealistic, underpriced stores inventory on the balance sheet.

Moving-Average Method of Inventory Pricing

This method is used by firms desiring the *average cost* of units of materials rather than the actual costs. If the prices of stores fluctuate frequently, more satisfactory costs are secured by the use of the average method than by the first-in, first-out method.

The procedure for pricing on the inventory cards is as follows: Entries for the receipt and issue of materials are the same as those described for the first-in, first-out method. When materials are received, the quantity is added to the quantity in the Balance column; the cost of the material received is added to the amount of cost already shown in

Illustration 6–9. Perpetual Inventory Card
Moving-Average (after Each Purchase) Price Method

Receipts			Issues			Balance		
Nov. 1	600 @ 12¢	$72.00				Nov. 1	600 $72.00 @ 12¢	
			Nov. 3	300 @ 12¢	$36.00	3	300 36.00	
			5	125 12¢	15.00	5	175 21.00	
12	500 14¢	70.00				12	675 91.00	13.5¢
			14	(50) 12¢	(6.00)	14	725 97.00	
			15	250	13.5¢	33.75	15	475 63.25
			18	300	13.5¢	40.50	18	175 22.75
21	300 13¢	39.00				21	475 61.75	13¢

the Balance column. This total is divided by the total quantity to determine the new average price. Because the average price is determined after the total of quantity and cost are obtained, it is suggested that the unit price column in the *Balance* section be placed last. One rule to remember in using this method is *that no new average price is computed unless a new purchase is made.* For example, if the Balance column contains 1,200 units at an average price at 12 cents, and 100 units previously issued at 11½ cents are returned as excess issue, the quantity in the Balance column becomes 1,300 and the total price $155.50, but the unit price for future issues remains 12 cents until a new purchase is made. After the purchase a new average is computed—an average which will absorb the discrepancy created by the returns.

To illustrate the moving-average price method and to facilitate comparison, the same figures are used as were used for the first-in, first-out method (see Illustration 6–9).

Method of Average Price at the Close of the Preceding Month[1] Some concerns find it expedient to ascertain the average price of each kind of material on hand at the close of each month and to use this price in costing all requisitions for the following month. For such a system to function without extreme variations, the price of materials must not fluctuate too widely from month to month. Furthermore, the company must make most of its purchases on a month-to-month basis, *buying a sufficient quantity near the end of each month to carry operations for the following month.* The requisitions may be priced by the cost accounting department before they are entered on the cost sheets. This is possible because at the end of each month a list can be prepared giving the prices to be used during the following month. The stores ledger clerk records the quanti-

[1] Sometimes called "weighted average method."

ties and costs of all stores received. All requisitions are entered and computed at the determined price. It is unnecessary to extend the balance of quantity or amount after each entry. At the end of the month the total receipts are added to, and the total issues are subtracted from, the opening balance to ascertain the figures to be used in computing the unit price for the next month. The accompanying inventory card (see Illustration 6–10) shows the calculations when this method is used. The

Illustration 6–10. Perpetual Inventory Card—Average Price at Close of the Month

Receipts			Issues			Balance		
						Nov. 1	600 @ 12¢	$72.00
			Nov. 3	300 @ 12¢	$ 36.00			
			5	125 12¢	15.00			
Nov. 12	500 @ 14¢	$ 70.00	14	(50) 12¢	(6.00)			
			15	250 12¢	30.00			
			18	300 12¢	36.00			
21	300 @ 13¢	39.00						
	800	$109.00		925	$111.00	Dec. 1	475 @ 14.7¢	$70.00

figures are the same as those used in Illustration 6–9. The computations are:

Balance at beginning of November...................	600	$ 72
Purchases during month...........................	800	109
Total..	1,400	$181
Issues during month..............................	925	111
New Balance, end of November....................	475	$ 70

The price to be used during December will be 14.7 cents per unit ($70 ÷ 475 units).

If the prices of materials fluctuate widely, especially in a rising market, the resulting price figures may disrupt the accounting for the cost of materials. To illustrate an extreme case, let us assume that 1,000 pounds of materials, valued at 20 cents per pound, are on hand at the end of the month. During the following month, purchases are: 8,000 pounds at 24 cents, 7,500 pounds at 26 cents, and 10,000 pounds at 28 cents. Total requisitions for the month amount to 25,000 pounds. The resulting figures would be:

Balance on hand	at beginning..............................	1,000 lbs.	$ 200
Purchases	at 24 cents...............................	8,000	1,920
	at 26 cents...............................	7,500	1,950
	at 28 cents...............................	10,000	2,800
	Total.................................	26,500 lbs.	$6,870
Requisitions	at 20-cent average price at end of preceding month...................................	25,000	5,000
	Balance at end of month...................	1,500 lbs.	$1,870
	Average price to be used next month........		$1.246

It is evident that under such wide fluctuations it would be illogical to use $1.246 as the price for the next month. Therefore, to be practical, this method must presume that the purchasing department will buy near the end of each month sufficient material to carry on the production for the coming month.

Miscellaneous Pricing Methods   Three other methods of inventory pricing and material requisition costing used infrequently are:

1. *Market price at time of issue* regardless of purchase price. The stores clerk maintains the book inventory on a quantity basis only. Requisitions are priced in the cost accounting department either at the price of the *last purchase* or the *current market price.* The use of this method is restricted to cost accounting operated as statistical compilations since it is not generally approved by the Internal Revenue Service, nor by professional accounting societies.
2. *Standard* or *predetermined* costs for each item of material. This simplifies the accounting procedure. It is discussed in more detail in Chapter 17. Where inventories are maintained at standard costs, these must be adjusted to the actual cost basis (LIFO or FIFO) for balance sheet presentation.
3. *Base stock inventory pricing* method is similar in effect to the LIFO method. A basic quantity of material is assumed to be on hand at all times to keep production facilities operating. This basic stock is costed at the prevailing cost when the material was first acquired and is assumed it will never be used up. All purchases above this basic stock are presumed to be for current operations, not for replenishment of base stock. These purchases may be costed on any of the pricing methods previously discussed.

Obsolete Inventory Valuation   *Obsolete inventory valuation* refers to finished stock and sometimes raw materials which have become obsolete under current business operations. Changing the production models in the automotive industry obsoletes many of the finished parts or raw materials on hand; electronic improvements such as transistors have obsoleted the vacuum tubes; the lower cost of competitive production (on a cost or market basis) or newer materials might make the value of the materials in stock at less than cost; and finally the discontinuance of a product might make finished goods and even raw materials an obsolescence-valuation problem. The loss of a special customer for whom a certain product was manufactured may also result in the obsolescence-valuation of inventory. All of these situations present rare but peculiar inventory valuation problems for a manufacturing concern which must be recognized.

For management to take into consideration the obsolescent factor in inventory valuations, be it raw materials or finished parts, certain procedures may be necessary: (*a*) parts inventories should be on a comparative basis, from year to year, to ascertain the slow-moving items, and the causes therefor; (*b*) comparison should be made of items used in current production and those which cannot be used, thus indicating obsolescence; (*c*) where designs or models change regularly, parts relative to the older production should be aged on an obsolescent schedule, such as one–two years old, 80 percent; two–three years old, 60 percent of cost; three–four years old, at 40 percent of cost; and over four years, at 30 percent. This aging schedule may be determined at the time of manufacture or purchase. The adjustment in value should be taken into consideration in the period in which the obsolescence is established and recognized in the statements prepared for the Internal Revenue Service.

Comparative Results of Material Inventory Pricing Methods

A comparison of the effect of the various inventory pricing methods on business operations is a difficult matter because conditions vary so much from one manufacturing firm to another. However, it is apparent from the illustrations given of the four most common methods that inventory values at the end of the accounting period—and therefore income for the period—will vary under these methods:

```
Inventory balance—FIFO...........................................$63.50
Inventory balance—Moving average after each purchase............. 61.75
Inventory balance—Moving average at end of month................ 70.00
Inventory balance—LIFO.......................................... 60.00
```

Since this discrepancy is the result of but one item in the inventory, and since many inventories consist of thousands of different materials, it is evident that the choice of inventory pricing methods may have a significant effect on periodic profits. Even though over a period of years the differences in annual profits for a firm may tend to "average out" as the result of price fluctuations in one direction and then the other, yet the *periodic* costs of work-in-process, finished goods, and cost of sales and the *periodic* net profits are important items of information and must be computed as accurately as possible. Taxable income should be computed on the basis most favorable to the taxpayer—but within the bounds of the law. To illustrate the effect of various market conditions on the results shown by different inventory pricing methods over a period longer than one month, the table in Illustration 6–11 shows the effect

Illustration 6–11

COMPARATIVE TABLE SHOWING INVENTORY EFFECT OF VARIOUS METHODS OF
INVENTORY PRICING OVER TWO-YEAR PERIOD*

	Quantity	FIFO	Average Cost	LIFO
FIRST YEAR—PRICE TREND UPWARD				
Initial Inventory: 200 @ $1.00..........	200	$ 200.00	$ 200.00	$ 200.00
Purchases—One Contract, Installment				
Deliveries: 900 @ $1.40..............	900	1,260.00	1,260.00	1,260.00
Total Charges to Stores..........	1,100	$1,460.00	$1,460.00	$1,460.00
Issued to Production:	500			
FIFO: 200 @ $1.00..................		200.00		
300 @ 1.40..................		420.00		
Average Cost: 500 @ $1.327.........			663.50	
LIFO: 500 @ $1.40.................				700.00
Final Inventory at Cost at End of Year..	600	$ 840.00	$ 796.50	$ 760.00
SECOND YEAR—PRICE TREND DOWNWARD				
Initial Inventory:				
FIFO: 600 @ $1.40...........	600	$ 840.00		
AVERAGE: 600 @ 1.327..........			$ 796.50	
LIFO: 200 @ 1.40...........				$ 200.00
400 @ 1.00...........				560.00
Purchases: 800 @ 1.05...........	800	840.00	840.00	840.00
Total Charges to Stores..........	1,400	$1,680.00	$1,636.50	$1,600.00
Issued to Production:				
FIFO: 600 @ $1.40...........		840.00		
150 @ 1.05...........	750	157.50		
AVERAGE: 750 @ 1.169..........			876.75	
LIFO: 750 @ 1.05...........				787.50
Final Inventory at Cost at End of Second Year..............................	650	$ 682.50	$ 759.75	$ 812.50

* Adapted from J. H. March, *Cost Accounting* (New York: McGraw-Hill Book Co.)

over a period of two years, during which prices increased the first year
and decreased in the second.

If these figures were used in the final inventories of the income
statement, then the net income for the first year under the *average cost*
method would be $43.50 *less,* and under the LIFO method $80 *less,*
than under the FIFO method. However, at the end of the second year
much of this effect is offset since the net income for the second year will
be $78 *more* under the *average cost* method, and $130 *more* under the
LIFO method, than under the FIFO method. Other items in the stores
inventory would be similarly affected.

However, it should be noted that in the long-continued price increase, price declines have *not* offset price increases. As a result, the selection of one inventory pricing method as against another has had a *cumulative* effect on reported profits. Firms which chose the elective method (LIFO) early in the last two decades have consistently reported lower profits (and have paid less income tax) than similar firms using FIFO. Even now, it appears doubtful that in the foreseeable future, price declines will cancel out any important part of this tax saving. In anticipation of continued price increases (inflation, perhaps), an increasing number of firms in the manufacturing field have been changing to the LIFO method.

Factors to Be Considered in Selecting a Material Pricing Method   The factors which should be taken into consideration when choosing a materials-used costing method are as follows:

1. Methods most commonly used by the industry in which engaged; this produces a sounder competition and more comparable figures.
2. Frequency of price fluctuations and frequency of material purchases.
3. Relative value of material cost to total cost of products manufactured.
4. Frequency of raw material purchases.
5. Quantities of materials to be purchased at any one time.
6. The effect of the different pricing methods on income taxes.
7. Trend of prices and income taxes over a long period of time.
8. The possibility of using different methods for various classes of items in the inventory.

The Physical Inventory as Part of Materials Cost Control   To account properly for *materials used in manufacturing,* a perpetual or book inventory is desirable. Such an inventory enables management to prepare financial statements without the delays and expense of taking a physical inventory. Such an inventory, however, must be checked against a physical inventory to eliminate the errors that might occur where such a large amount of detailed work is involved. The physical inventory checkup may be *continuous* or *periodic.*

Under the *continuous method* (more recently called the *cycle* or *rotating method*), the counting is spread throughout the fiscal year, following a pattern used in cycle billing. Each inventory card is checked against a physical count at least once a year, sometimes three or four times. This is accomplished by counting part of the inventory each day, each week, or each month, under a systematic plan, thus avoiding the overtime and use of untrained personnel required in the annual inventory. One concern, with a book inventory of four hundred items, checks three items each day by physical count. Thus each year, every item is verified at least twice. Some firms count the *bin stock* at the time of reordering or at the time the purchase requisition is issued. Through the use of this continuous or cycle method of verifying the physical inventory, errors are quickly detected and are not carried on the books until an annual checkup is made. An early detection of errors permits a possible elimination of their cause. *The trend today is away from the annual all-at-one-time physical inventory and toward the continuous count.*

Under the *periodic* method, the entire book inventory is verified at a given date by an actual count of materials on hand. This physical inventory is usually taken near the end of the fiscal period. Some firms even suspend plant operations when this is done.

Illustration 6–12. Inventory Tag

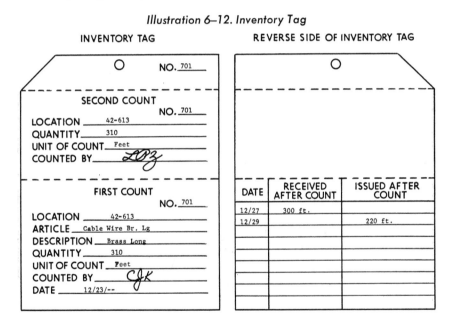

The following procedure is recommended to facilitate prompt and accurate results in taking a complete physical inventory at a given date:

1. The date of inventory should be set to conform with the date of financial records. An inventory may take several days; therefore, if the inventory is taken December 20–24 and the book inventory adjusted, the book inventory may then be accepted as correct for a balance sheet dated December 31. When the date of inventory taking has been set, every effort should be made to reduce the stocks as of that date.

A method for taking inventory in a large plant in a *single day* developed over a period of years for a number of large and small companies in the automotive, aircraft, electrical appliance, and farm equipment industries, involves a few simple steps, viz:[2]

1. Draw an easily understood diagram of each floor area in the plant to be inventoried, with sufficient copies so that each counting team will have a copy for the floor for which they are responsible.
2. Divide the manpower available for actual counting into two-man teams and prepare an assignment sheet indicating areas each team is to count. (Each area must be counted twice.)
3. List all classes of items to be counted in each area indicating whether recording is to be in pounds, barrels, dozens, etc.
4. Organize two-man teams to supervise counting in each area or group of areas, with a foreman or accountant to supervise the teams.
5. Prepare the patched (two-part) system tags for recording on a separate tag the quantity of each different class of materials found in each separate area to be inventoried. These tags must be PRENUMBERED in sequence. (See Illustration 6–12.)
6. Each supervisory team is given a sufficient quantity of tags for counting the material in its area. To control these tags, an Inventory Tag Control Schedule should be prepared, viz:

INVENTORY TAG CONTROL SCHEDULE							
Prepared By					Date:		
Building	Inventory Location Number	Assigned Foreman	Assigned Accountant	Prenumbered Inventory Tags Charged Out	Number of Tags Charged Out	Tags Ret'd Spoiled or Voided	Signature of Accountant Receiving Tags
C&C Basement	B-1	Smith	Fletcher	001–075	75		
	B-2	Black	Fletcher	076–150	75		
C&C 1st Floor	PR	Parker	Martin	151–300	150		
C&C Warehouse	W-1	Burns	Hogan	801–900	100		
No. 2 Warehouse	A-1	Mapes	Long	901–1050	150		
Yard (Skids & Drums)		White	Long	1051–1100	50		

7. Prepare and issue lists of counting instructions for the guidance of each supervisory team and counting team.
8. Have a meeting to review all typed and mimeographed instructions.
9. As early as possible on day selected, start the actual count. If tags assigned are insufficient, do not allow one team to borrow from another. Additional tags must be obtained from central control.
10. *First counting team* counts an area and attaches tags to each pile,

[2] With permission, the Tag Manufacturers Institute. System devised by G. H. Kline, General Foods Corporation.

unit, or bin counted, filling out lower section of tag, and giving it to supervisor. A *second counting team* records its figures on second section of tag, tears this off and turns it in to the supervisor, who matches these with those of the first team.

11. The accountant classifies the inventory from these tags after they have been checked—as stores, work-in-process, or finished goods.

12. The inventory sheets are prepared; the items and quantities are listed on the sheets (Illustration 6–13), priced, and extended by expert calculating machine operators. Since the possibility of mathematical error exists, a second detachable extension column is used. The first calculating machine operator places the extensions in the column at extreme right. These are totaled and detached from inventory sheets.

Illustration 6–13. Inventory Sheet

Listed By B.J.N. Extended By N.C.B. Sheet No. 14 | 14						
Priced By C.O'Brien Checked By N.B.S.						
Tag No.	Code No. of Material	Description	Quantity	Unit Price	Extended Total	Checking Total
701	a-42	Cable Wire	310 ft.	.30		93
702	C-1	Brass Caps	400	.02		8
703	c-4	Brass Studs	200	.08		16
		(other items not listed)				
750	D-3	Hand Screws	600	.01		6
				Total		543

Later, a second operator repeats the extension work and places the results in the second column from the right on the original inventory sheets. A comparison is made of the totals of each set of extension columns, and all errors are corrected.

Adjustment of Physical and Book Inventories

Certain problems of inventory valuation must be considered at the time physical inventorying is being completed.

1. If book inventory records of stores have been maintained, *quantity* differences between physical count and the clerical stock record must be reconciled. Ordinarily, these differences are shortages in stock due to such factors as breakage, spoilage, and evaporation, and to clerical errors in storeskeeping. Management must, at this point, consider the

nature of these shortages to discover weaknesses in its internal control of inventories, and even to consider theft as a possible reason for unusually large shortages.

The clerical records must be corrected to agree with the physical count, and the verified differences, usually due to normal loss in handling or to the physical nature of the stores themselves, must be recorded:

Manufacturing Overhead Control (Inventory Shortage)..................xxxx
Stores...   xxxx
To account for difference in quantity (units lost × unit price).

When shortages in stores inventories are unusually large, due to some unusual cause, then the difference may be considered a nonmanufacturing loss and charged to some special loss account and finally closed out to the Profit and Loss account.

The balance sheet valuation of *stores* inventories is usually at cost on the assumption that any differences between market price and cost price will ultimately find their way into the cost of goods completed in the normal course of manufacturing.

2. The method of accounting for losses in *finished goods* inventory values should be contrasted here with the accounting for losses in *stores* inventory. Two problems arise in handling losses in finished goods inventory values. One results, as in the case of stores inventories, from differences in quantity between physical count and book inventory records if such records have been maintained. The other arises from the balance sheet valuation of the finished goods inventory if the inventory is reported at the lower of cost or market.

The clerical records for finished goods inventories must be corrected to agree with physical count of stock, and the verified differences, usually shortages, must be recorded:

Inventory Shortages (to Profit and Loss)............................xxxx
Finished Goods...   xxxx
To record losses due to shortages in stock.

It would be a tedious and expensive task to adjust finished goods inventory records, if they exist, to the lower of cost or market, as each inventory card might possibly call for adjustment. Such a procedure is not the practical solution. To adjust to the lower of cost or market price and so reconcile the inventory ledger cards and the physical inventory at cost with the balance sheet figure, the following journal entry would be recorded:

Loss Due to Fluctuation in Inventory Value (to Profit and Loss)..........xxxx
Allowance for Decline in Inventory Values (valuation allowance).....   xxxx

The allowance would be deducted from the inventory figure at cost to report the inventory at the lower figure.

True Reserves in Relation to Inventory Valuation In an analysis of inventory values, management faces a related problem as it looks ahead to sales of finished goods. What is the prospect for future sales of the goods on hand at balance sheet date? Conservative management may take present steps to anticipate future problems.

If the business outlook for the future is good, then the inventories will be sold at prevailing or better prices in the normal course of business. If future business prospects, however, cannot be viewed with optimism, then cautious management may earmark present earnings (that is, prevent them from moving into the hands of stockholders) so as to protect the cash position of the company faced with a possible reduction of sales income derived from its finished goods stock. The journal entry to effect such a precaution is:

```
Retained Earnings...................................................xxxx
    Reserve for Possible Future Loss on Inventory Values...............   xxxx
    To earmark earnings in anticipation of a future decline.
```

This reserve is a so-called "true" reserve or an appropriation of earnings and should appear in the balance sheet as a subdivision of retained earnings.

Should the anticipated decline in market values occur, the resulting actual losses from reduced sales income would be reflected in the operational reports of that accounting period. The provision for possible loss (the reserve) would then be eliminated by a reversal entry.

Accounting for Scrap Material Scrap is salable material resulting from the primary manufacturing operations. If scrap has little value, no entry is usually made for the quantity or value until it is sold. At that time Cash or Accounts Receivable is debited and the income account, Sale of Scrap, is credited. If the value and quantity are relatively important and the scrap is to be sold, an inventory card may be set up showing the quantity and the market value. Because of the difficulty of valuation and perhaps the delay in selling the material, scrap is usually recorded as to quantity only. When the scrap material is received in the storeroom, a scrap report similar to the receiving report is made out. From this report an entry is made on the book inventory card for the scrap.

There are three possible methods of accounting for scrap sold:

1. Credit the sales prices to the material cost of the job on which scrap originated.
2. Credit the sales price to Manufacturing Overhead Control.
3. Credit the sales price as miscellaneous income.

The most accurate and ideal method is to credit the material cost of the job on which the scrap originated. But in most instances this method is not practical because the difficulty of segregating the amount of scrap occurring on the various jobs and the difficulty of valuation are too great. The cost of segregating and valuing the scrap may be greater than the amount realized from its sale.

The second most desirable method is to treat the value of the scrap as a credit to manufacturing overhead. This method reduces the cost of all the jobs passing through the department. When the scrap is placed in the storeroom, an entry is made debiting Scrap Material and crediting Manufacturing Overhead Control with the expected sales value. This procedure may raise the question of the correct price to use in recording the scrap when it is placed in the storeroom. If the market price does not fluctuate very much, the sales or market price of scrap is used when recording the scrap stored. When this scrap is sold, the journal entry would be:

```
Cash or Accounts Receivable........................................xxxx
    Scrap (or Stores Control if inventoried)............................    xxxx
    To record the sale of scrap.
```

If there is no fixed price for the scrap, some firms merely record the quantity on an inventory card, or they make no entry at all until the scrap is sold. If the practice of reducing the manufacturing overhead costs by the amount received for scrap is used, the entry made at the time of the sale would be:

```
Cash or Accounts Receivable........................................xxxx
    Manufacturing Overhead (Sale of Scrap)............................    xxxx
```

However, because the scrap may be sold in a period different from that in which it was created and because scrap has a relatively low sales value, many concerns reduce their accounting for scrap to a minimum by making only a quantity record of the scrap while it is being collected, or they make no entry at all. When the scrap is sold, the entry for the sale of scrap would be:

```
Cash or Accounts Receivable........................................xxxx
    Sale of Scrap......................................................    xxxx
```

The Sale of Scrap account is then treated as other income on the income statement.

Scrap is not always sold. For example, scrap from the manufacture of tin and zinc is sent to the storeroom to be reissued and used on other jobs. Although referred to as *scrap,* such materials actually represent a return to the storeroom of excess materials issued and should be treated as such on the inventory records. If the manufacturing processes result in genuine scrap, a new materials account can be opened for scrap and some reasonable value assigned to it; then, when it is used in manufacturing, the job may be properly charged with the cost of the scrap.

Parts scrapped while in the process of manufacture, or finished parts scrapped during assembling operations because subsequent use results in their being defective, may be included as scrap; but a more accurate cost accounting treats them as spoiled or defective material, discussed in the following section.

Nature of Spoiled and Defective Work   One problem facing many manufacturing concerns today is that of quality control. This problem involves not only manufacturing and production control through more effective supervision but also control through forms and reports on spoiled and defective work. Many manufacturers have found it to be more profitable to spend more on *Inspection Control* before the product leaves the plant than to pay for the correction of quality defects after the product has been sold.

Accounting for Spoiled and Defective Materials   A distinction is sometimes made between *spoiled* and *defective* materials. The distinction is based on the condition of the goods as it leaves the manufacturing process. *Spoiled* materials are goods which in the process of manufacture have developed some imperfection which cannot economically be corrected, and thus the goods must be sold as seconds. *Defective* materials are goods which in the process of manufacturing have developed some imperfection but which, unlike spoiled materials, can by the expenditure of additional labor, and possibly materials, be made into perfect finished articles.

The cost of spoiled goods may be handled by either of two methods: (1) the loss due to spoilage *may be charged to the production order on which the spoilage occurred,* or (2) *the spoilage loss may be charged to manufacturing overhead control and thus spread over the cost of all jobs.* If a job is produced on special order—that is, the specifications are distinct and the spoilage is clearly traceable to the work done on that order—the loss resulting from spoiled goods should be treated as a part of the cost of the job on which it occurred. If, however, the manufacturing is being done on a mass-production basis and, owing to the nature of the manufacturing processes, spoilage is the general rule though irregular in amount on the various orders, the loss arising from the spoiled goods should be treated as a *manufacturing overhead* cost and the total prorated over all the jobs by means of the manufacturing overhead rate. In either case the spoiled goods are recorded on the books at the expected sales price.

The manufacture of shirts may be used to illustrate these methods of handling the loss on spoiled goods. A job order calling for 1,200 shirts was sent through the factory. The cost elements per shirt were:

```
Materials......................................32¢
Labor.........................................80
Predetermined Manufacturing Overhead.............28
```

When the shirts were manufactured, it was found that 100 were spoiled and would have to be sold as seconds at a price of 50 cents each.

Under the first method, where the loss is charged to the specific job, the entries are as follows:

```
Work-in-Process...........................................1,680.00
    Stores...............................................          384.00
    Payroll..............................................          960.00
    Applied Manufacturing Overhead.......................          336.00
    To record cost of work put into process.

Spoiled Goods Inventory...................................   50.00
    Work-in-Process......................................           50.00
    To record the sales value of work spoiled in process.

Finished Goods............................................1,630.00
    Work-in-Process......................................        1,630.00
    To record the cost of shirts finished.
```

As a result of these entries, the total cost of manufacturing 1,100 good shirts is $1,630, at a unit price of $1.482.

When the second method is used, the entries for handling the spoilage losses are as follows:

```
Work-in-Process...........................................1,680.00
    Stores...............................................          384.00
    Payroll..............................................          960.00
    Applied Manufacturing Overhead.......................          336.00
    To record the cost of the work put into process.

Spoiled Goods Inventory...................................   50.00
Manufacturing Overhead Control (Loss on Spoiled Work).........   90.00
    Work-in-Process......................................          140.00
    To set up the inventory of spoiled goods and to charge the loss
    to the Manufacturing Overhead Control.

Finished Goods............................................1,540.00
    Work-in-Process......................................        1,540.00
    To record the cost of shirts completed.
```

As a result of these entries, the total cost of manufacturing 1,100 shirts is $1,540 at a unit cost of $1.40. A comparison of the two unit costs shows that under the first method there is a loading of $0.082 per shirt because of the loss due to the spoiled goods. It should be noted that if the spoilage on this order is representative of the average loss incurred from this cause, then the predetermined manufacturing overhead rate must be higher under the second method so that $0.082 additional will be allocated to the cost of each shirt. The *total cost* of manufacturing the shirts will not be affected by the choice of a method of allocating the indirect cost arising from the spoilage.

The rules governing the accounting for *defective work* are similar to those relating to *spoiled goods*. If the job is a special order, the additional costs caused by defective work should be charged to that job. If defective work occurs on the regular manufacturing orders, the additional costs of perfecting the goods should be set up as a part of the manufacturing overhead. It should be noted that no asset account similar to Spoiled Goods is set up. Since the defective work is subsequently perfected, the cost of making the changes is either charged to Work-in-Process or set up in an account, Loss on Defective Work, a manufacturing overhead account.

The manufacture of hand saws is given as an illustration of the entries necessary to account for defective material. One hundred dozen were put into process on a certain job order. The costs for each dozen were: materials, $12.50; labor, $26; and manufacturing overhead, $19.50. Upon the completion of the order it was found that 10 dozen were defective and had to be returned for reprocessing, which required additional labor and overhead. No additional materials were necessary. The additional labor cost was $4 and the manufacturing overhead, $3 per dozen.

Under the first method, where the additional cost *is to be charged directly to the job,* the entries are:

Work-in-Process..5,800.00		
Stores..		1,250.00
Payroll..		2,600.00
Applied Manufacturing Overhead........................		1,950.00
To charge Work-in-Process for materials, labor, and overhead used.		
Work-in-Process..	70.00	
Payroll..		40.00
Applied Manufacturing Overhead........................		30.00
To record additional labor and overhead necessary to correct defective work.		
Finished Goods..5 870.00		
Work-in-Process..		5,870.00
To record the finished goods transferred from Work-in-Process.		

The foregoing entries result in the per dozen cost of $58.70.

Under the second method *the loss due to defective work is charged to the manufacturing overhead account* and prorated over all the jobs worked on during the period. The entries for this method would be:

```
Work-in-Process.............................................5,800.00
    Stores...................................................        1,250.00
    Payroll..................................................        2,600.00
    Applied Manufacturing Overhead...........................        1,950.00
    To charge Work-in-Process for the materials, labor, and overhead
    used.

Manufacturing Overhead Control (Loss on Defective Work)........    70.00
    Payroll..................................................          40.00
    Applied Manufacturing Overhead...........................          30.00
    To charge labor and overhead due to defective work.

Finished Goods..............................................5,800.00
    Work-in-Process..........................................        5,800.00
    To record the finished goods transferred from Work-in-Process.
```

The second method results in a unit cost of $58. Again it should be noted that under the second method the predetermined manufacturing overhead rate must have included an estimated amount for expected losses due to defective work.

Controlling Scrap and Defective Work   To control scrap and defective work, many of the larger manufacturing concerns use daily or weekly defective material reports. These will show the order numbers on which the spoiled work occurred, the reason for its occurrence, why material was rejected as defective, and the cost of correcting the defects. The preparation of such reports requires time and expense, and will be justified only if over a period of time the making of these reports results in the elimination of avoidable causes and expense. Illustration 6–14 shows one type of defective work report that can be used to study and control spoilage.

Debatable Material Costs   Certain costs that may, under given circumstances, be proper additions to the cost of inventory, receive various treatments in practice as shown in the following discussion.

Packaging Costs. If the goods are packaged before being sent to the finished goods warehouse, the cost of packaging is considered part of the cost. If they are packaged just before shipment, the cost is treated as a selling and shipping expense, not part of the inventory. But the acceptance of this rule is by no means uniform. In a survey made by the Committee of Research of the N.A.A., it was found that approximately one half of the firms packaging goods at time of shipment treated this packaging cost as part of the manufacturing costs and included it in the inventories.

Storage Costs. About one half of the firms surveyed in the N.A.A. study considered the storing of goods awaiting sale *at the factory* as a

Illustration 6–14. Spoilage Report

						SALVAGE	
Machine Operator	Total Units Produced	Spoiled Work	Per Cent of Spoilage	Unit Cost of Spoilage	Total Cost of Spoilage	Labor Penalty 10%	Scrap Value 20¢ Each
401	250	13	5.2	$.36	$ 4.68	$ .46	$ 2.60
402	258	15	5.8	.36	5.40	.54	3.00
403	262	15	5.7	.36	5.40	.54	3.00
404	255	15	5.9	.36	5.40	.54	3.00
405	270	18	6.7	.36	6.48	.64	3.60
406	265	17	6.4	.36	6.12	.61	3.40
407	267	15	5.6	.36	5.40	.54	3.00
408	264	12	4.5	.36	4.32	.43	2.40
409	270	15	5.6	.36	5.40	.54	3.00
410	280	30	10.7	.36	10.80	1.08	6.00
Total	2641	165	6.2		$59.40	$5.92	$33.00

WEEKLY REPORT ON SPOILAGE

Stitching Department No. 23   Foreman C. E. Bowman

Week Ending March 30, 19—

manufacturing cost and included it in the inventory of finished goods. The other half of the firms felt that the manufacturing operations were completed when the goods were placed in the warehouse and that, therefore, warehouse or storage costs were part of the selling expenses.

Administrative Salaries. In some cases, salaries of corporate officers above the rank of factory superintendent have been included in the cost of inventories. Salaries of those officers primarily concerned with the manufacturing operations are often included as part of the manufacturing costs applicable to inventories. In a few instances, the salaries of top officials, such as president down to the controller, are prorated between the manufacturing and financial operating costs of the firm, the former thus becoming part of the inventory.

"Direct Costing." In recent years a number of companies have been experimenting with the idea of including in manufacturing cost only direct labor and direct material and those indirect manufacturing costs which fluctuate with production, excluding all fixed costs. There have been a number of instances in which firms have considered as the cost of goods manufactured, and hence the finished goods inventory, only material and labor costs. Direct costing is discussed in detail in Chapter 21.

Cost Reduction through Physical Distribution Control of Inventories[3] Inventory costs of both raw materials and finished goods are running as high as 30 cents on the dollar. This refers to the cost in capital investment to store the inventory and to protect it. Offsetting this cost is the loss due to not having enough inventory, resulting in inefficient production methods and in the case of finished goods of loss in sales and damage to the firm's competitive standing.

Inventory costs and *transportation* costs are essentially *time* costs. Both of these are closely related to each other. To reduce inventory costs, it is usually necessary to increase transportation costs. Therefore, these two costs should be correlated—time can be reduced by shortening the *transportation distance.* Inventory costs can be reduced by *location*—the costs of maintenance of goods in *procurement* and/or *distribution.* Among the location cost factors are warehousing, protective packaging, plant and warehouse locations, requirements forecasting, and order processing.

Management may be able to reduce costs by the so-called "trade-off policy"—offsetting higher costs in one area by greatly reduced costs in another area such as *production planning*—large lot buying, and low-cost transportation to prevent production downtime, yet owning and warehousing costs may be greater than the savings of large lot buying versus small lot buying more frequently delivered by airfreight. It is the *total costs* that counts.

A common and costly mistake is often made in charging the distribution costs—costs of packing, shipping room activities, and warehousing—to costs of production. Even the question of state and local personal property taxes must be considered. Closing down warehouses and resorting to direct-to-customer shipments and using higher transportation costs may result in cost reduction, provided *total costs* are studied.

The use of electronic computer techniques in modern business under

---

[3] Adapted from data from United Airlines.

a highly centralized department of purchasing and distribution might be management's answer to this cost reduction through inventory control —both of raw materials as well as finished goods, with wide-open communication among middle management personnel. An electronic computer program can be written to test all possible combinations of procurement and distribution to provide the best answer to these management problems affecting inventories.

Managerial Control of Inventories   In many large industrial concerns, the materials inventories require an investment of millions of dollars. The first requisite for effective managerial control is to have this work placed under an executive who has the authority and responsibility for the investment in inventories, the use of the materials, spoilage reports, transportation and storage costs, in addition to the usual clerical and accounting records.

The primary purpose of inventory control is to maintain a *minimum of investment in inventory, consistent with smoothly operating production schedules*. First, in managerial control, is the *materials budget* which will indicate *when* the materials should be purchased, and *how much*. The concentration of the effort in this budget should be placed on the more important materials—those purchased in quantities sufficiently large to make them account for an important part of the cost of goods manufactured. As part of this materials control, it might be wise to standardize the kinds and size of materials or parts to be purchased. A second phase of managerial control is the *systematic procedure* to be followed in purchasing, receiving, storing, issuing, and pricing the materials to be used. A by-product of this is an effective system of internal control to reduce the possibility of losses by theft. The proper coordination of the budget and the accounting procedure will result in a minimum investment in inventories, reduction in obsolete stock, and losses from fraud or theft.

One concern accomplishes part of this control by having a simple report made for each four-week period showing the balances in various inventory accounts, broken down into broad classes of products as to stores, work-in-process, processed parts, and finished goods. From this report, the upward or downward trend in inventories can be studied from period to period.

Another concern prepares annually an inventory showing in three groups the value of the material on hand: Group A, material of which there is a one-year supply on hand—this is the active material; Group B, material of which there is a two-year supply on hand—this is a slow-moving material; and Group C, material of which there is stock on

Illustration 6–15. Complete Summary and Analysis

Nature of Transaction	Forms Used	Book of Original Entry	Source of Entry	Journal Form of Entry
Ordering materials	1. Purchase requisition 2. Purchase order			
Receiving materials	1. Receiving report 2. Purchase order 3. Creditor's invoice	Voucher register	Creditor's invoice	Dr. Stores Cr. Accounts Payable
Issuing direct materials	1. Material requisition 2. Summary of stores requisitions	General journal	Summary of stores requisitions	Dr. Work-in-Process—Materials Cr. Stores
Issuing indirect materials	1. Material requisition 2. Summary of stores requisitions	General journal	Summary of stores requisitions	Dr. Manufacturing Overhead (Indirect Materials) Cr. Stores
Payment of invoice	1. Voucher check 2. Invoice	Check register	Vouchered invoice	Dr. Accounts Payable Cr. Cash
Direct materials returned to stores	1. Returned material report 2. Summary of returned materials	General journal	Summary of returned materials	Dr. Stores Cr. Work-in-Process—Materials
Indirect materials returned to stores	1. Returned material report 2. Summary of returned materials	General journal	Summary of returned materials	Dr. Stores Cr. Manufacturing Overhead (Indirect Materials)
Materials returned to vendor	1. Returned shipping report	General journal or voucher register	Returned shipping report	Dr. Accounts Payable Cr. Stores
Inventory adjustment—physical less than book	1. Stores inventory report	General journal	Stores inventory department memo	Dr. Manufacturing Overhead (Inventory Adjustment) Cr. Stores
Inventory adjustment—physical more than book	1. Stores inventory report	General journal	Stores inventory department memo	Dr. Stores Cr. Manufacturing Overhead (Inventory Adjustment)
Cost of finished parts manufactured	1. Cost memo 2. Summary of cost of finished product	General journal	Summary of cost of finished product	Dr. Finished Parts—Stores Cr. Work-in-Process—Materials Cr. Work-in-Process—Labor Cr. Work-in-Process—Manufacturing Overhead
Issuing finished parts for further use in production	1. Material requisition 2. Summary of finished parts requisitioned	General journal	Summary of material requisitions	Dr. Work-in-Process—Materials Cr. Finished Parts—Stores
Placing scrap material in storeroom	1. Scrap report 2. Summary of returned materials	None	Summary of returned materials	
Spoiled work (material cost)	1. Spoiled material report 2. Summary of spoiled work	General journal	Summary of spoiled work	Dr. Stores (scrap value) Dr. Manufacturing Overhead (Loss on Spoiled Work) Cr. Work-in-Process—Materials (original cost)

of Materials Accounting under a Cost System

Subsidiary Accounting Record (Perpetual Inventory Control)	Entry on Subsidiary Account Record	Cost Record or Summary Form Used*	Entry on Cost Record or Cost Summary†	Source of Cost Entry
Stores ledger card	Memo in ordered section			
Stores ledger card	In Received section cross out memo in Ordered section			
Stores ledger card	Issued section	Job order sheet	Material section of job sheet	Summary of stores requisitions
Stores ledger card	Issued section	Standing order or overhead work sheet	Standing order for indirect material or subsidiary overhead ledger account	Summary of stores requisitions
Stores ledger card	Received section or in RED in Issued section	Job order sheet	Entry in RED in Material section of job sheet	Summary of returned materials
Stores ledger card	Received section or in RED in Issued section	Standing order or overhead work sheet	In RED standing order for indirect material or subsidiary overhead ledger account	Summary of returned materials
Stores ledger card	Issued section or in RED in Received section			
Stores ledger card	Issued section	Standing order or overhead work sheet	Standing order for inventory adjustment or subsidiary overhead ledger account	Stores inventory dep't. memo
Stores ledger card	Received section	Standing order or overhead work sheet	In RED, standing order for inventory adjustment or subsidiary overhead ledger account	Stores inventory dep't. memo
Stores ledger card— finished parts stores	Received section	Job order sheet	Summarize finished job orders	
Finished parts stores— stores ledger card	Issued section	Job order sheet	Material section of job sheet	Summary of material requisitions
Stores ledger card	Received section quantity only	Job order sheet	In RED—Material section of job sheet	Summary of returned materials
Stores ledger card	Received section	Job order sheet, standing order or overhead work sheet	1. Standing order for loss on spoiled work or subsidiary overhead ledger account— loss on spoiled work 2. In RED, Material section	Spoiled work report

* Actual overhead work sheet.
† Subsidiary overhead ledger account.

hand for a period beyond two years—this is considered obsolete stock. Group C is written off the books completely, and for Group B an estimated loss allowance is set up. If any Group C material is later sold, it is credited directly to Miscellaneous Income. The loss for Group B is charged against current *Profit and Loss.* This policy assumes, of course, that the long-term supply indicates obsolescence and deterioration.

Many concerns use periodic spot checking on the quantities and the condition of the inventories on hand.

Tabulated Summary   Illustration 6–15 (pages 162–63) gives
of the Accounting for   a complete summary and analysis of
Materials   materials accounting under a cost system.

QUESTIONS FOR REVIEW

1. The planning, routing, scheduling, and engineering department of large manufacturing concerns is one of the basic factors in controlling the cost of materials used. Explain.

2. Distinguish between the *material requisitions* and the *standard bill of materials.* Which is preferable from the viewpoint of material control? When should the standard bill of materials be used?

3. Why is it desirable to establish maximums and minimums in the inventories of the materials used in manufacturing? What effect does this policy have on managerial control of inventories?

4. Materials issued during the week were as follows:

   Used in production.............................$12,500
   Used in factory maintenance...................... 1,500
   Used as shipping supplies........................ 3,200
   Used in building a new machine to be used in
     the factory................................... 1,600

   Indicate how each of these should be recorded in the factory journal, general journal, inventory records, job order cost sheets, and other subsidiary records.

5. A requisition journal might be effectively used in a process cost accounting system. Why? What columnar arrangements would you suggest for a four-department process plant?

6. Punched-card accounting would facilitate the clerical work attending the maintenance of a perpetual book inventory. How is this achieved? How might the maintenance of the manual inventory records be altered when the punched-card system is used?

7. The selection of a unit pricing method is a cost accounting, a sales department, and income tax problem. Under these conditions what effect does each of the following methods have on the above considerations: FIFO, LIFO, and average?

8. What are the causes of variations between the physical and the book inventories? How are adjustments for these variations recorded?

9. Why is it impractical to record freight-in and discount on materials purchased in accordance with accepted theory of accounting? Explain.

10. What are the methods of accounting for spoiled and defective work arising in the manufacturing operations? For most effective managerial control, how should accounting for these two be maintained?

PROBLEMS—GROUP A

Problem 6–1. Purpose: *Comparative Inventory Pricing Methods*

The following transactions affected material Urano in Plant No. 3 of the Nevins Manufacturing Company:

Feb. 1 Received 2,000 units at $1.10.
      2 Issued 800 units for Production Order V 890.
      3 Issued 500 units for Production Order X 352.
      6 Received 1,000 units at $1.12.
      9 Returned 100 units of the February 6 receipts; these were defective.
     11 Issued 2,000 units for Production Order V 953.
     14 Received 50 excess units from Production Order X 352.
     19 Received 1,100 units at $0.90.
     21 Issued 700 units for Production Order Y 541.
     23 Returned to vendor 100 units of the February 19 purchase.
     25 Received 400 units at $1.10.
     26 Issued 100 units for Production Order Z 101.

Required:

a) Prepare a stores ledger card with sections for Received, Issued, and Balance, using the FIFO pricing method.

b) Do the same as in (*a*) using the LIFO pricing method.

c) Do the same as in (*a*) using the moving-average pricing method.

d) Prepare general journal entries summarizing the card records. Use the LIFO card as the basis for entries.

Problem 6–2. Purpose: *Inventory Pricing Methods*

The raw material "netlon" had the following activity recorded on the bin card during October:

Oct. 1 Balance, 100 units at $1.50.
      8 Purchased 200 units at $1.60.
     11 Issued 140 units.
     12 Purchased 200 units at $1.70.
     14 Issued 190 units.
     18 Issued 100 units.
     26 Purchased 200 units at 1.40.

Required:

a) The cost of the material "netlon" that was used is determined at month-end. Compute cost of netlon used and cost of the ending inventory under the FIFO and LIFO pricing methods.

b) A new unit cost is determined after each purchase. Compute the cost of netlon used under the FIFO, LIFO, and moving-average pricing methods.

Problem 6–3. Purpose: *Defective Work Accounting*

The Narxon Company produces a copper product known as "cope." The experience of Narxon is that approximately 15 percent of copes produced are defective in some manner and are sold at greatly reduced prices.

During the month of August, the following costs were incurred by the production department manufacturing cope:

Materials...........................	$ 60,000
Labor...............................	80,000
Manufacturing overhead................	80,000
	$220,000

Two hundred twenty units of cope were manufactured, but the inspectors determined that 20 of the units were defective and that these could be sold for $500 each. The normal selling price of cope is $2,300. One hundred seventy units are sold at this price.

Prepare journal entries recording the above transactions. Assume that 15 of the 20 defective units of cope are sold at $500 each. There were no beginning inventories of finished or defective goods.

Problem 6–4.   Purpose: *Effect on Income of Inventory Pricing Methods*

The management of the National Wholesale Company is interested in the effects of various inventory valuation methods on net income. On October 1, 19—, the company had an inventory of 10,000 product units at a $10 per unit cost. Purchases and sales were made as follows:

Purchases:

October	10	10,000	@ $12	$120,000	
November	10	10,000	@ 14	140,000	
December	10	10,000	@ 16	160,000	$420,000

Sales:

October	20	5,000	@ $20	$100,000	
November	20	10,000	@ 22	220,000	
December	20	10,000	@ 24	240,000	$560,000

Selling and general expenses for the quarter ended December 31, 19—, total $150,000. Compute the net income under each assumption for the quarter ended December 31, 19—:

a) If the company employs the FIFO method.
b) If the company employs the LIFO method.
c) Discuss the pros and cons of LIFO versus FIFO from the income statement and balance sheet positions.

Problem 6–5.   Purpose: *Spoiled Goods Accounting*

The Narshall Company produces one product that sells for $15. The cost of producing the unit is:

Material......................................	$4
Labor..	2
Manufacturing overhead......................	2

During the second quarter of 19—, 300 units are spoiled and 200 are sold for $3 each.

Prepare journal entries to record the above transactions in as many ways as you think possible.

Problem 6–6. Purpose: *Journal Entries and Procedures for Spoiled Work*

The Nriad Shirt Company produces fine-quality cotton men's shirts. In the manufacturing process, there are, from time to time, a number of rejects which must be sold as seconds.

During the month of May, 19—, the firm produced, on job lot orders for stock and for special customers, 40,000 shirts. The manufacturing costs for the month were:

```
Materials, trimmings, etc........................$29,000
Direct labor costs..............................  38,000
Manufacturing overhead applied..................  19,000
```

An examination of the completed shirts indicated that 400 of them had defects and had to be sold as seconds at $2 each. The good shirts were sold at $48 a dozen. Thirty thousand of the shirts manufactured were sold.

Assuming that this firm uses a factory ledger for its costing data, record in both the general office and the factory office books in journal entry form the following:

a) Purchase of materials in the amount of $32,000.

b) Manufacturing costs, assuming that actual manufacturing overhead costs amounted to $20,160.

c) Spoiled materials costs and loss under each of the following conditions:
   (1) When the loss is not customary and is charged to all the production for the period through the manufacturing overhead account.
   (2) When loss due to spoiled work is customary and is charged to the job on which it occurred.

d) Completion and sale of good shirts under conditions in (*c*[1]) and (*c*[2]).

e) Sale of spoiled shirts for cash.

PROBLEMS—GROUP B

Problem 6–7. Purpose: *Inventory Pricing Methods*

The Xoren Manufacturing Company uses a material known as "xor" in its manufacturing process. The perpetual inventory records showed the following transactions affecting "xor" took place during June:

June 1   Balance, 2,000 @ $21

Purchases		Issues	
June 9	3,000 @ $20.50	June 12	2,500 units
13	3,000 @ 22.00	15	3,100
27	4,000 @ 23.00	19	2,000

Required:

a) Compute the cost of "xor" used and the cost of the ending inventory under the FIFO and LIFO pricing methods. Assume that the cost of the material "xor" that was used is determined at the month's end.

b) Do the same as in (*a*) above except assume that the cost of "xor" used is determined at the time the goods are used.

Problem 6–8. Purpose: *Spoiled Goods Accounting*

The Xilliam Company's product "wil" costs $10 for material, $5 for labor, and $4 in overhead. "Wil" sells for $30.

During the month of November, 1,000 units of "wil" are produced but 75 of these are spoiled and have to be sold for $5 each. Fifty of the units are actually sold in November.

Prepare journal entries to record the above transactions in as many ways as you think possible.

Problem 6–9. Purpose: *Comparative Inventory Pricing Methods*

The following affected Material X-1842 at the Xerto Company, Plant No. 2:

May 1 2,000 units at $2 was the opening balance.
     3 Issued 400 units under Requisition 453z.
     4 Purchased 1,000 units at $2.05.
     7 Issued 900 units as per Requisition 762v.
     9 Purchased 1,000 units at $2.10.
    12 Returned to vendor, 200 defective units from the May 4 purchase.
    15 Issued 1,800 units as per Requisition 871b.
    19 Purchased 500 units at $2.
    21 Received 100 excess units issued on the 15th under Requisition 871b.
    24 Issued 400 units as per Requisition 542x.
    26 Returned 50 units to vendor from the May 19 purchase.
    29 Purchased 1,000 units at $2.02.

Required:

a) Prepare a stores ledger card with sections for Received, Issued, and Balance, using the FIFO pricing method.

b) Do the same as in (*a*) using the LIFO pricing method.

c) Do the same as in (*a*) using the moving-average pricing method.

d) Prepare general journal entries summarizing the card records. Use the FIFO card as the basis for the entries.

Problem 6–10. Purpose: *Defective Work Accounting*

The Xeedone Company manufactures "wees" in a continuous process operation. Approximately 5 percent of all "wees" produced are defective and are sold for $3 each.

During a normal month when 1,000 "wees" are produced, costs are $8,000 for materials, $6,000 for labor, and $3,000 for overhead. The selling price for "wees" is $25. Fifty "wees" were defective, and 30 were sold. Nine hundred of the good "wees" were also sold.

There were no beginning inventories of finished or defective goods.

Prepare journal entries to record the above transactions.

Problem 6–11. Purpose: *Effect on Income of Inventory Pricing Methods*

The XYZ Company sells a single product. Typically, purchases are made once a month, and billings to customers are made once a month. Purchases are made on the 15th of each month and sales on the 25th. During the second quarter of 19—, the following occurred:

	Purchases	Sales
April	30,000 @ $ 7 each	20,000 @ $15 each
May	30,000 @ 10 each	30,000 @ 19 each
June	25,000 @ 13 each	30,000 @ 24 each

The inventory on hand on April 1 was 30,000 @ $6 each.

Required:

a) Compute the gross profit for the XYZ Company for the second quarter under the assumption that the FIFO pricing method is used.

b) Do the same as in (*a*) except assume that the company uses the LIFO method.

c) Which gross income is more accurate? Discuss.

Problem 6–12. Purpose: *Accounting for Defective Work*

The Factronic Instrument Company manufactures for stock a precision instrument which must meet rigid specifications for accuracy. Many units must be reworked after completion because of excess variations from the specifications.

During the month of March, 19—, 9,000 of these units were ordered and manufactured on a special job. The costs of production were:

Materials $32,000
Direct labor 45,000
Manufacturing overhead applied 18,000

Inspection disclosed 600 defective units which were returned to production. Additional costs for this work were: materials, $1,200; direct labor, $800; manufacturing overhead applied, $300.

Assuming that a factory journal is used, record in journal form the following:

a) The cost of manufacturing the original order.

b) The additional costs for correction of defects:

    (1) When it is customary to have some reworking on every large production order.

    (2) When defective work is not customary.

c) The cost of completed work.

CHAPTER

7 Accounting for Factory Payroll Costs

Nature of Payroll Accounting   The ultimate objective of all payroll accounting for a manufacturing concern is to establish (*a*) how much the worker must be paid weekly and (*b*) how this payroll cost should be allocated to the various jobs, products, or departments. Since payroll costs are second in importance to material costs, management is particularly interested in the procedures involved, the accuracy of the allocations, and the controllable and cost reduction possibilities. First, it must be understood that payroll costs are classified as *administrative* (executives and office workers), *selling* (salesmen and marketing employees), and *manufacturing* (factory workers). Generally speaking, executives and some office employees are paid by check, semimonthly or monthly, and the others are paid by check or cash on a weekly basis. While most of the factory workers are paid on an hourly basis, some firms use an incentive or efficiency basis which complicates the accounting procedures. Cost accounting for factory payrolls requires a classification of the type of work performed. There are two main groups of factory workers: *productive* or *direct labor* and *nonproductive* or *indirect labor*. *Direct labor* refers to that used in producing the article in such a manner that the cost of it can be identified *economically* with a specific job lot of goods, whereas *indirect labor costs* are those resulting from the auxiliary activities which are necessary but are not directly associated with a particular job. Among these are the payrolls for the superintendent, foremen, repairmen, factory clerical workers, and factory sweepers. However, when the cost of direct labor, even though normally it might be considered direct labor, is so small that it cannot be charged with any

170

reliable degree of accuracy to any specific job lot of goods or is so small as to involve a disproportionate amount of clerical expense in analyzing and allocating it to a specific job, the cost of such labor is merged with the indirect labor costs and treated as part of the manufacturing overhead.

Timekeeping for Payroll Purposes   Timekeeping is an important phase of industrial accounting because it is used to prove compliance with the federal and state wage and hour laws. It is also required for the computation of the payrolls and the variety of payroll tax and income tax deductions. Timekeeping is also necessary for computing the labor costs applicable to the various jobs or operations. The timekeeping records most frequently used in industry are explained below.

Time-Clock Cards. A time-clock card is an individual card for each employee on which a time clock records the "in" and "out" time each day. These cards may also contain spaces and references for computing and recording the gross earnings, deductions, and net pay. Two forms of these cards are in use: (1) the traditional form which is based upon a clock showing the hours on a normal 12-hour basis and (2) the continental clock which records the time on a 24-hour cycle. The latter is becoming increasingly important because of the ease with which the elapsed time may be computed. This form is shown in Illustration 7–1.

Job Time Tickets. In allocating the direct labor costs to specific jobs, the workman must record the time he started and the time he finished each job during the day. Two forms of the job time ticket have been used. One is an *individual job time ticket,* which is a small printed form on which is recorded the employee's name and number, department, job number on which he is working, time he started on that job, time finished, total time spent on job and rate of pay. The final computation of the cost of labor on these cards is done in the cost accounting department. In some firms, use is made of a *daily job time ticket,* on which the daily working time, at 15-minute intervals, is printed. The worker merely marks the time he starts and finishes each job and inserts the job number. This form has the advantage of showing on one form how the day's work was performed, but it has the disadvantage of requiring an analysis of the charges by jobs when they have been computed—an extra clerical task.

Several procedural improvements have been made in the use of the job time tickets. In one firm, telephones connected with a central switchboard are located throughout the plant. Whenever a worker starts a new job, he telephones the information to the clerk who records it on a

Illustration 7-1. Time-Clock Card—Continental Time

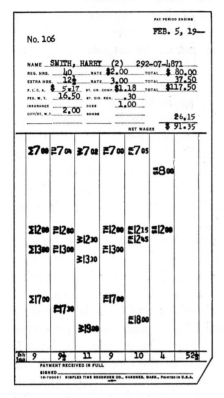

Card of Harry Smith, social security No. 292–07–4871,* with two income tax exemptions. Overtime computations are based upon regular pay for 40 hours per week and time and one half for all time over 40 hours. Mr. Smith works in a state where the employee as well as the employer contributes to the state unemployment fund (1 percent). State disability insurance deductions are at the rate of 30 cents per week. Federal and state withholding income taxes are indicated, as well as union dues of $1 per week. To compute hours worked each day on continental time, start at bottom of each column and subtract top figure. After allowing one hour for lunch, the difference represents hours worked.

punched card. When he completes the job, this information is also phoned to the operator. This saves the time of the production worker in preparing the forms and enables faster processing of the data because it is already on a punched card.

Another improvement is the use of a time clock which not only records the time the job was started and the time it was completed but also computes automatically the elapsed time. It has been estimated that use of such a clock saves the time of one cost clerk for each 200 production workers in the factory.

Payroll Taxes in Labor Accounting Procedures   Management today is concerned not only with the problems and procedures of preparing the various payrolls but also with the various deductions required by state and federal laws and union contracts. Basically, the federal and state regulations apply to two types of payroll deductions: (1) F.I.C.A. tax for social security and medicare (federal regulation); and (2) income tax deductions both federal and

---

* F.I.C.A. (social security tax) is at the revised 4.4 percent (1967–68) rate.

state, known as withholding taxes. In a few states, the state laws require an employee to pay part of the unemployment tax, in which case there must be a deduction for this employee's share. These payroll taxes are becoming increasingly important because the firm must pay these whether it sustains a profit or not. The taxes on payrolls are as follows:

1. *Federal Insurance Contributions Act Tax (F.I.C.A.)*. With few exceptions, all employees and self-employed persons are taxed on wages up to $6,600 received in any one calendar year. The *employee* and *employer* contribute equal amounts, whereas the self-employed person pays a higher amount when he files his annual federal income tax report. The following are the most recent rates which include medicare:

SOCIAL SECURITY PAYROLL TAXES INCLUDING MEDICARE

Tax Based on the First $6,600 of Yearly Earnings	*Employee and Employer (Each Must Pay)*		*Self-employed Worker*	
	Tax Rate	*Maximum Tax*	*Tax Rate*	*Maximum Tax*
1967–68	4.4 %	$290.40	6.40%	$422.40
1969–72	4.9	323.40	7.10	468.60
1973–75	5.4	356.40	7.55	498.30
1976–79	5.45	359.70	7.60	501.60
1980–86	5.55	366.30	7.70	508.20
1987 and thereafter	5.65	372.90	7.80	514.80

2. *State Unemployment Tax (S.U.T.)*.[1] This tax varies with the states. In some states the *employer* must pay the entire tax; in others, the employees are also taxed, but not necessarily at the same rate as the employer. The usual rate for many of the states is 2.7 percent of the total wages paid to any employee in any one calendar year, not exceeding a wage base of $3,000. Some states permit a merit rating which reduces this rate.

3. *Federal Unemployment Tax (F.U.T.)*. This tax is paid entirely by the employer at the rate of $8/10$ of 1 percent (0.8 percent) on all wages paid any employee in any one calendar year, not exceeding $3,000. To be subject to this tax, a firm must have four or more employees one or more days in each of 20 different weeks during the taxable year.

4. *Federal Withholding (Income) Tax (F.W.H.T.)*. This is the estimated income tax on employees which is withheld from their pay. The amount withheld depends upon the amount of the earnings and taxable status (number of exemptions) of the employee.

5. *State withholding taxes*. Increasingly the states which have income taxes are asking employers to do some of their bookkeeping work, just as the federal government does. Since the work is parallel and similar, though the rates are different, the additional computations are not too

---

[1] The Guaranteed Annual Wage (GAW) drive of labor unions will no doubt cause the state unemployment insurance rates to be revised and increased upward so that all employees will get the benefits of a GAW, under government control and supervision.

laborious. The trend in this direction is increasing; so the problem may as well be faced in present payroll accounting.

6. *City income taxes.* The collection method is not uniform but the future indicates it will follow the federal and state procedures.

It is evident that the recording and collection of these taxes involves considerable work on the part of the employer. Furthermore, the

Illustration 7-2

CALENDAR OF EMPLOYER'S DUTIES

On Hiring New Employees

For Income Tax Withholding. Ask each new employee for a withholding exemption certificate on Form W–4.

For Social Security (Federal Insurance Contributions Act) Taxes. Record the account number and name of each new employee from his social security account number card. If he has no account number, have him file application on Form SS–5.

On Each Payment of Wages to an Employee

For Income Tax Withholding. Withhold tax from each wage payment in accordance with the employee's withholding exemption certificate and the applicable withholding rate.

For Social Security Taxes. Withhold 4.4 percent from each wage payment (1967–68).

By 15th Day of Each Month

After each of the first two months of each quarter deposit both income tax withheld and employee and employer social security taxes for such month, if the total is more than $100, in a Federal Reserve bank or other authorized bank. Tax for the third month of a quarter may be either deposited or paid with the quarterly return.

On or before Each April 30, July 31, October 31, and January 31

File a quarterly return on Form 941 with the Internal Revenue Service and pay balance amount of taxes due for the previous quarter on both income tax withheld from wages and employee and employer social security taxes.

Before December 1 of Each Year

For Income Tax Withholding. Request filing of a new certificate, Form W–4, by each employee whose withholding exemptions will be different in the next year from the exemptions shown on his last certificate.

On or before Each January 31 and at End of Employment

Give each employee a withholding statement in duplicate on Form W–2, showing (1) the total wages and the amount of income tax withheld and (2) the amount of social security employee tax withheld and the amount of wages subject to this tax. If Form W–2 is not required, give statement of social security wages and employee tax deducted.

On or before January 31 of Each Year

For Income Tax Withholding. File Form W–3, Reconciliation of Income Tax Withheld from Wages, together with all District Director's copies (Copy A) of withholding statements furnished employees on Form W–2 for the preceding calendar year.

For Federal Unemployment Tax Act (F.U.T.A.) Tax. File annual return on Form 940, before January 31.

payroll taxes, the cost of which the employer must bear (not the deductions from the employee's gross pay), constitute additional labor costs, sometimes known as *fringe labor costs,* and may be an important part of the total cost of labor in manufacturing, especially when they are added to the welfare benefits paid on the workers' account as a result of union contracts. It has been estimated by some that these indirect labor costs amount to as much as 10 to 20 percent of the regular payroll.

A calendar of the duties of the present-day business firm in the matter of the federal payroll taxes is shown in Illustration 7–2.

Financial Accounting   Financial accounting for labor refers to
for Labor   the computation of the earnings of the
worker less *deductions.* Some of these deductions are authorized by law, such as the federal insurance contribution taxes, state unemployment taxes, and withholding (income) taxes. Other deductions are authorized by the worker himself or through his representatives in labor unions, such as union dues, deductions for insurance, and for the purchase of bonds. The customary forms used in the financial accounting for labor include: (1) *timecards,* previously discussed; (2) *payroll records;* (3) *voucher register;* (4) *record of individual employees' earnings;* and (5) *deductions authorization card.*

In some concerns the *payroll record* may be in the form of a bound book or loose-leaf sheets. Posting may be made directly from the payroll records, using them as books of original record, or from summary entries prepared therefrom and entered in a journal. The payroll record should contain the following information:

1. The time-clock card number assigned to the employee.
2. Name and social security number of the worker.
3. Type of work performed—sometimes necessary for compensation insurance classification and premium calculation.
4. Total hours worked.
5. Rate of pay per hour, per day, or per week.
6. Gross earnings.
7. Deductions for F.I.C.A. tax.
8. Deductions for state unemployment taxes, where such deductions are made.
9. Deductions for federal and state withholding (income) taxes.
10. Deductions for advances, insurance, and stock or bond purchases.
11. Remarks.
12. Signature of employees (usually only required in small plants). (In larger plants receipts are given out with the pay envelopes, and these must be signed and returned.)

The subject of *payroll deductions* has become increasingly important in business today, first, because of the large amount of clerical work involved in computing and recording the numerous deductions and, second, because these deductions are taking an increasingly large proportion of the workers' earnings. These deductions may be of a *fixed* nature—the same amount each payday, such as bond or insurance deductions—or may fluctuate, such as the social security and withholding tax deductions. Except for those authorized by law, the worker must authorize deductions made periodically by the employer. Such authorization is usually made on a card signed by the employee, similar to that approving the purchase of government bonds by payroll deductions.

To give effect to the payroll and to these deductions, the following entry or its equivalent will be made in the *payroll record* or a summary journal each week:

(1)

Payroll	10,500.00	
F.I.C.A. Taxes Payable (4.4%)		462.00
Employees' Insurance Premium Payable		75.00
Federal Withholding Taxes Payable		800.00
State Withholding Taxes Payable		100.00
Union Dues Payable		200.00
Employees' Bond Purchase Deposit Account		150.00
Payroll Accrued		8,713.00

Checks will be drawn to pay for the various deductions. Entries for each of these checks must first be made in the *voucher register* and then in the *check register*. For the payroll itself, the entry is given below. For the others, the same type of entry would be made.

In the *voucher register:*

(2)

Payroll Accrued	8,713.00	
Accounts Payable		8,713.00

In the *check register:*

(3)

Accounts Payable	8,713.00	
Cash		8,713.00

The voucher register has been discussed in Chapter 3. Here attention should be called to the heading of the column used to record the payroll liability. In the entry given above, the payroll record was used as a posting medium, and therefore the column in the voucher register would be headed *Payroll Accrued.* Should the payroll book be merely a memorandum record, the column heading would be *Payroll,* and the various deductions would be recorded either in special columns (credits) or in the *Sundry General Ledger, Credits* section of the voucher register.

Periodically, the payroll must be analyzed and distributed to accounts which will indicate whether it is direct labor, indirect labor (manufacturing overhead), selling expense, or administrative expense. For this the entry would be:

(4)

Work-in-Process—Labor	6,000.00	
Manufacturing Overhead Control (Indirect Labor)	1,000.00	
Selling Expenses (Sales Salaries)	1,200.00	
Administrative Expenses (Officers' Salaries)	1,000.00	
Administrative Expenses (Office Salaries)	1,300.00	
Payroll		10,500.00

To close out the Payroll account to appropriate accounts.

At least quarterly, although some firms do it monthly, it is necessary to record the employer's share of the various payroll taxes. The entry for this would be:

(5)

Payroll Taxes	829.50	
F.I.C.A. Taxes Payable (4.4%)		462.00
Federal Unemployment Taxes Payable (0.8%)		84.00
State Unemployment Taxes Payable (2.7%)		283.50

To record employer's liability for payroll taxes.

It is necessary, however, to keep a record of how much of these payroll taxes are selling expenses, how much administrative, and how much factory overhead costs. At the end of the fiscal accounting period, an entry is made to close the Payroll Tax account, viz:

(6)

Manufacturing Overhead (Payroll Taxes)	553.00	
Selling Expense (Sales Payroll Tax)	94.80	
Administrative Expense (Office Payroll Tax)	181.70	
Payroll Taxes		829.50

To close out the Payroll Tax account to appropriate expense accounts, at 7.9 percent of gross payroll.

Accruing the Payroll at the End of the Year—Split Payrolls   When the books of a firm are closed in the middle of a pay period, it may be necessary to accrue the payroll for part of the week before preparing the financial statements. Dividing the payroll in this form is known as *splitting payrolls*. Although there are two methods of handling this situation, it should be noted in each case that F.I.C.A. taxes are not accrued at the end of the period, unless the wages are actually paid in that period. If the year ends in the middle of the week and workers are not paid until the end of the week, the F.I.C.A. taxes must be computed as of the date of payment. Those who have exceeded the maximum limit in the year just ending will have to pay F.I.C.A. taxes on those earnings made in the end of the preceding year but paid for in the first week of the new year.

This problem must be considered in studying the two methods. One method is to summarize the payroll book for the part of the week ending with the closing of the fiscal year, as follows:

```
Payroll...............................................................xxxx
      Payroll Accrued...............................................         xxxx
      To record payroll accrued to date without F.I.C.A. and withholding de-
      ductions.
```

No entry is made in the voucher register, but the payroll book is ruled and closed. This entry may be made in the general journal if the payroll book is not used as a book of original entry. The payroll for the remainder of the week will then be calculated and recorded, with the F.I.C.A. deductions and the full weekly withholding tax liability. The entry is:

```
Payroll...............................................................xxxx
      F.I.C.A. Taxes Payable........................................         xxxx
      Federal Withholding Taxes Payable.............................         xxxx
      State Withholding Taxes Payable...............................         xxxx
      Payroll Accrued...............................................         xxxx
```

A single voucher is then made out for the sum of the two payroll accrued figures.

A second method is sometimes used. A voucher is prepared for the payroll up to the closing date. A second voucher is prepared for the amount of the payroll for the remainder of the week immediately following the closing date. Both voucher checks are put through the bank on the same day and thus provide the cash for the total payroll for the week.

Where the cost records are integrated with the financial accounting records, it is necessary to analyze, summarize, and record the job time tickets for the period up to the date of closing the books. The accrual for the payroll taxes to be paid by the employer must also be recorded. Since in many instances this is an impractical procedure, many firms make no attempt to reconcile the cost and the financial accounting records until the end of the fiscal accounting period.

The Use of a Payroll Clearing Account

Some accountants feel that in recording the payroll it should not be a charge to the Payroll account, since the Payroll account is a nominal account. Part of the payroll of a manufacturing concern will be transferred as direct labor to such asset accounts as work-in-process and later to finished goods. Therefore, many cost accountants in the interest of more exact terminology set up the payroll in a Payroll Clearing account—a temporary account set up until such time as the amounts which make up the payroll for the period can be distributed to the more appropriate accounts of work-in-process, manufacturing overhead, selling expense, and administrative expense.

Cost Accounting for Payrolls

The cost accounting problems involved in factory payrolls are (*a*) separating the payroll costs into those which are considered *direct labor* and those which are considered *indirect labor;* and (*b*) computing the amount of labor costs which should be charged to the specific jobs or in process costing to the various departments.

Separating the payroll costs into *direct* and *indirect* requires the use of the individual or daily job time tickets. (See Illustrations 7–3 and 7–4.) That labor which is directly applicable to the manufacturing operations

Illustration 7–3. Individual Job Time Ticket

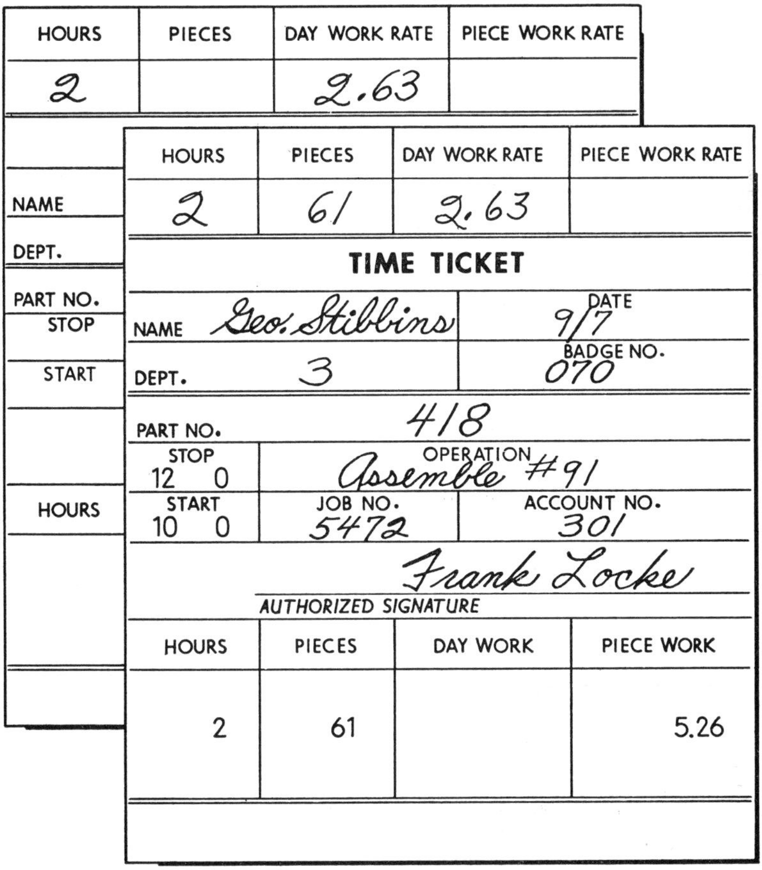
HOURS | PIECES | DAY WORK RATE | PIECE WORK RATE
2 | | 2.63 |
NAME
DEPT.
PART NO.
STOP
START
HOURS

HOURS	PIECES	DAY WORK RATE	PIECE WORK RATE
2	61	2.63	

TIME TICKET

NAME Geo. Stibbins — DATE 9/7
DEPT. 3 — BADGE NO. 070
PART NO. 418
STOP 12 0 — OPERATION Assemble #91
START 10 0 — JOB NO. 5472 — ACCOUNT NO. 301
Frank Locke
AUTHORIZED SIGNATURE

HOURS	PIECES	DAY WORK	PIECE WORK
2	61		5.26

of a specific product is known as direct labor. Generally speaking all other factory labor costs are *indirect,* but for managerial control, these should be classified under the headings of supervision, inspection, maintenance, idle time, and others.

Illustration 7–4. Payroll Calculations Derived from Daily Job Time Tickets

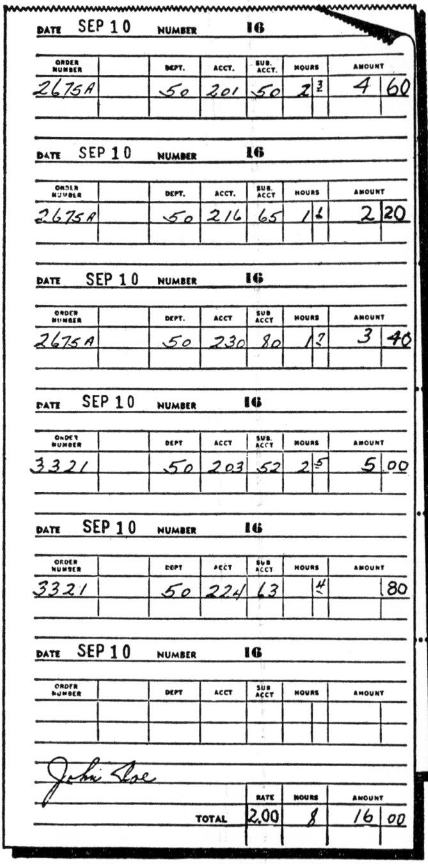

When daily job time tickets are used, an analysis of these tickets must be made in the cost accounting department to compute the amount applicable to the various jobs. (See Illustration 7–5.)

When individual job time tickets are used, these can be sorted by job numbers, totaled on the adding machine and then posted to the respective cost accounting sheets.

When costs are kept on a departmental or process basis instead of by jobs, no distinction is made between the direct and indirect labor. The total departmental payroll, both direct and indirect, is charged to the departmental work-in-process cost.

Since both the materials requisitions and the labor time tickets require a great amount of sorting and tabulating and posting to the cost sheets, many of the larger firms have recorded these requisitions and time tickets on punched cards, thus facilitating and expediting the clerical work involved.

Diagrammatically, labor cost accounting can be summarized as shown in Illustration 7–6.

Procedural Analysis of Payroll Accounting

A complete picture of the procedural sequence of payroll accounting is shown in Illustration 7–7 which gives the tabulation of transactions, forms, books of original entry, cost record entries and their sources.

Illustration 7–5. Daily Job Time Recapitulation Sheet

								DATE MARCH 5, 19--
	DAILY JOB TIME REPORT RECAPITULATION SHEET							
	JOB NUMBERS							
EMPLOYEE NO.	760	763	768	770	774	IDLE TIME	REPAIRS	TOTAL
J. JONES 201	14 00		3 60		2 00	2 00		21 60
A. SMITH 202		15 00		7 00				22 00
C. BROWN 203	8 00		4 00	4 00	4 00			20 00
C. BUTLER 204		10 00	11 00		60	3 60	1 80	27 00
TOTALS	182 00	216 00	140 00	72 00	90 00	18 00	27 00	740 00

Illustration 7–6

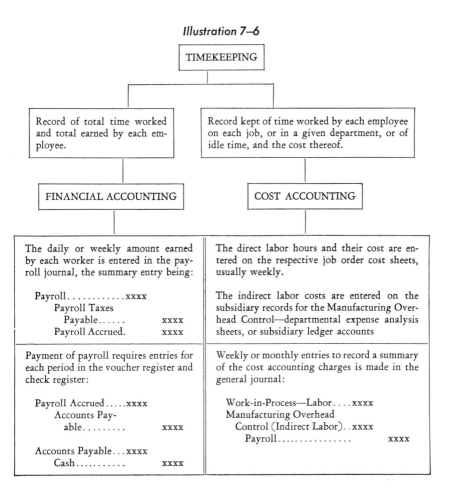

TIMEKEEPING

Record of total time worked and total earned by each employee.

Record kept of time worked by each employee on each job, or in a given department, or of idle time, and the cost thereof.

FINANCIAL ACCOUNTING

COST ACCOUNTING

The daily or weekly amount earned by each worker is entered in the payroll journal, the summary entry being:

```
Payroll...........xxxx
    Payroll Taxes
      Payable......        xxxx
    Payroll Accrued.       xxxx
```

Payment of payroll requires entries for each period in the voucher register and check register:

```
Payroll Accrued.....xxxx
    Accounts Pay-
      able........        xxxx
Accounts Payable...xxxx
    Cash..........        xxxx
```

The direct labor hours and their cost are entered on the respective job order cost sheets, usually weekly.

The indirect labor costs are entered on the subsidiary records for the Manufacturing Overhead Control—departmental expense analysis sheets, or subsidiary ledger accounts

Weekly or monthly entries to record a summary of the cost accounting charges is made in the general journal:

```
Work-in-Process—Labor....xxxx
Manufacturing Overhead
    Control (Indirect Labor)..xxxx
      Payroll...............        xxxx
```

Illustration 7–7. Summary of Labor Accounting and Procedure

Transaction	Forms Used	Book of Original Entry	Source of Entry	Entry in Journal Form	Entry on Cost Record or Summary	Source of Cost Record Entry
1. To record the payroll at end of each week	a) Time-clock cards b) Payroll record	a) Payroll book	a) Time-clock cards b) Payroll summary	(1) Dr. Payroll Cr. F.I.C.A. Taxes Payable Cr. Federal W.H. Taxes Payable Cr. State W.H. Taxes Payable Cr. Payroll Accrued		
2. To voucher and pay wages	a) Payroll sheet b) Employees' individual ledger cards	a) Voucher register b) Check register	a) Payroll sheet	(2) Dr. Payroll Accrued Cr. Accounts Payable (3) Dr. Accounts Payable Cr. Cash		
3. To record distribution of payroll	a) Job time tickets b) Payroll recapitulation sheet of job time tickets	a) General journal	a) Recapitulation of job time tickets	(4) Dr. Work-in-Process Labor Dr. Mfg. Overhead—Indirect Labor Cr. Payroll	a) Direct Labor section of job order cost sheets b) Standing order sheet for indirect labor costs.	a) Recapitulation sheet of job time ticket
4. To record employer's payroll taxes	a) Payroll sheet	a) General journal	a) Payroll sheet	(5) Dr. Mfg. Overhead (Payroll Taxes) Cr. F.I.C.A. Taxes Payable Cr. Federal U.T. Payable Cr. State U.T. Payable	a) Standing order sheet	

Special Payroll Cost Accounting Problems Five special problems affecting payroll costs should receive attention by management. These are (1) treatment of overtime bonus or shift bonus; (2) costs of pensions for factory workers; (3) the guaranteed annual wage; (4) vacation, holiday, and bonus pay; and (5) setup costs.

Overtime bonus payments are treated in various ways. Some firms treat the overtime bonus as an element of cost (manufacturing overhead), and it is therefore reflected in the inventory values of the work-in-process and finished goods. Other firms exclude all overtime premium payments from the cost of manufacturing. The obvious reason for this latter practice is that if there is overtime in one period and not in another, the costs are not comparable when used as a measure of production efficiency.

Where the overtime bonus is *included in the inventory costs,* the procedures followed vary. Two methods of accomplishing this have been used. Some firms treat the overtime bonus as part of the *direct labor costs* and thereby add it directly to the job order or department for which the work is done. This method undoubtedly distorts the direct labor costs when similar jobs are compared, especially if some incur overtime and others do not. Therefore, a more acceptable procedure is to include all overtime bonus payments for factory labor as an element of *manufacturing overhead,* prorating it equitably over all work done during a given period. Firms which exclude overtime bonus as a part of the cost of manufacturing usually record the bonus in a separate account which is closed directly into the Profit and Loss account.

Similar treatment is accorded the premium paid workers employed on the late afternoon or night shifts.

Whatever the disposition of these excess labor costs, it must be remembered that the type of product manufactured frequently determines the treatment of this cost. In a shipyard, it is a simple matter to allocate overtime costs directly to the job. On the other hand, if a variety of products are being manufactured, it is not so simple. The particular job being worked on in overtime may just be a matter of chance, and therefore distorted costs result if this job is penalized. There seems to be a growing tendency, however, to include all overtime premiums in manufacturing overhead or to spread them by including them in standard costs rather than penalizing the job "caught" in the overtime. Care should be taken in the treatment of overtime if manufacturing overhead is applied to production on the basis of a percentage of labor costs, for in such cases the bonus payment arising from overtime must not be included in the direct labor costs. Similarly, if manufacturing overhead is applied to production on a labor hour basis, care should be taken that only the regular hours are used (not the time-and-one-half hours) in applying the manufacturing overhead.

Pension costs for factory workers vary widely with the different firms because of the fact that some are funded and others are not; some are contributory and some are retroactive in their coverage. Basically the total estimated cost of providing employee's pensions should be accrued *ratably* over the period of active service from the date the pension plan is installed until the worker retires. The cost of the pension plan is an *element of labor cost.* However contributions for pensions or the accrual of costs for the *current service* may be (1) charged entirely to *general and administrative expenses* on the theory that it is a cost which cannot be reasonably allocated and it is to the benefit of the entire company; (2) allocated to the *cost of the department* in which the employee works (this penalizes the department having the oldest employees); or (3) allocated to cost *departmentally as a percentage of the total payrolls.* This third method is in the form of applied overhead for the factory workers and does not penalize the department having the largest proportion of old employees. It is also comparable to the treatment of other employee welfare benefits, such as lunchroom, hospital service, etc. There is, however, the additional question of treatment of the payments or *accruals for pensions for past service.* These may be treated as follows:

1. Treat the charge as a *nonrecurring* or *other expense,* since it will not recur.
2. Charge *general or administrative expense;* even though it is an extraordinary charge, it is nevertheless a cost of administering the business.
3. Allocate *either directly or proportionally to the various departments* as an element of *indirect cost,* in the same fashion as the current charges. This may destroy the comparability of costs from period to period and weaken the managerial control resulting from such a comparison.

In substance, then, it seems that *current* pension costs for factory workers should be treated similarly to other *manufacturing overhead costs* and applied to production on a labor cost basis. Charges for *past service* might well be placed on the books as a *nonrecurring expense.*

The Guaranteed Annual Wage (GAW) is a recent innovation in manufacturing plants where the unions have attempted, and succeeded in part, in obtaining unemployment benefits beyond those granted by the state unemployment laws. The plans vary. Some firms have had guaranteed employment for years. Most of these are process manufacturing plants, not job order plants. For a job order plant to have a guaranteed annual wage whereby the worker is paid for any unemployment during a given year is almost a managerial impossibility. An analysis of the economic implications of such a plan will readily reveal its managerial difficulties.

Some of the recent acceptances of the GAW principle have provided that the employer pay into a fund a certain amount for each hour that an employee works in his firm, with a top limit to the size of the fund. In some instances, the firm has paid in or will pay in a lump sum at a given date. After a waiting period of one or two weeks, the employee will receive from this fund up to 60 or 65 percent of his weekly wage for a period not exceeding 26 weeks. The 60 or 65 percent of his weekly wage will be decreased by any amount that the employee will receive from any state unemployment fund.

Thus the GAW becomes a supplement to the state unemployment insurance tax laws. The legal or restrictive clauses are not important here. Until a wider adoption of the GAW plans and more uniformity is developed, the best that can be hoped for is that the cost will be limited to a fixed amount per hour, no matter how the fund is to be administered or distributed. Ultimately, the GAW will probably result in a higher state unemployment tax, so that all firms will come under the benefits presently available only to the employees of the larger firms which have signed union agreements covering the GAW. In other words, as the state unemployment insurance plans raise their taxes and benefits to the worker, there will be less need for GAW; the state will assume that responsibility to the worker.

Where a corporation must pay into the fund for the GAW benefits, the problem of accounting for these payments arises. One large corporation has merely added the hourly payment (5 cents) to the regular earnings rate for the employee, increasing the direct labor or indirect labor costs accordingly; the journal entry therefor being as follows:

```
Payroll...............................................100,000.00
   F.I.C.A. Taxes Payable (4.4%)............................     4,400.00
   Federal Withholding Taxes Payable.......................    18,000.00
   State Withholding Taxes Payable.........................     1,250.00
   GAW Fund Payable.......................................     2,500.00
   Accounts Payable.......................................    73,850.00
   To record the payroll for the period.
```

This probably is the most accurate method, since the 5 cents per hour contribution to the fund is merely an increase in the labor costs. The Internal Revenue Service has thus far allowed the firm to deduct as a manufacturing cost the 5 cents per hour thus contributed, and the employee is not required to include in his income for income tax purposes, the 5 cents per hour paid into the fund on his account. The employee however is taxed on the supplemental payment when he receives the money.

In some firms, the agreement with the union has established a GAW fund, independent of the union and the employer, in which an amount is deposited to the credit of each individual employee in much the same fashion as a savings account. If the employee leaves the firm, he is entitled to his "deposit." If he is unemployed, the fund is used to pay unemployment wages. This arrangement is somewhat different from a fund which is trusteed and from which the employee gets nothing if he leaves his present employment or if he dies. Under the "savings" type of unemployment insurance, the amount thus contributed is, no doubt, not only a deduction for the employer but also taxable income for the employee in the year of contribution to the fund.

If the GAW goes far enough in industry, each firm will know exactly what its total labor cost for the year will be whether or not there is any production. Thus direct labor tends to become a *fixed cost* rather than a variable cost.

Vacation, Holiday, and Bonus Payments   Although there are several methods of treating these payments in a cost accounting system, probably the most satisfactory is as an element of the indirect labor costs, and thus as a charge to the manufacturing overhead costs. Along with this treatment, some firms accrue these labor costs on the basis of the labor budget estimates. An entry to illustrate this procedure would be:

```
Work-in-Process—Labor..........................................600.00
Manufacturing Overhead (Indirect Labor)........................... 40.00
Manufacturing Overhead (Bonus).................................... 30.00
Manufacturing Overhead (Holiday and Vacation Pay)................. 80.00
    Payroll......................................................            670.00
    Liability for Vacation and Holiday Pay.......................             80.00
```

Setup Time Costs   Oftentimes, considerable time and labor costs may be required to set up the machines, conveyor systems, and other facilities before production on a particular job can be started. The costs thus incurred are known as *setup costs*. There are several methods of treating these costs in the accounting records: (1) treat the costs as part of the *direct labor costs* on the job, since it is a direct cost but not direct labor; (2) treat it as a *direct cost of the job* but under a separate heading—*setup costs*—thus showing the cost of manufacturing under four divisions—direct material, direct labor, setup costs, and manufacturing overhead; and (3) treat the costs as part of the manufacturing overhead. This method would not be very accurate if some jobs had more and others less, proportionately, of such costs.

Managerial Aspects of Labor Cost Accounting

A manufacturer is engaged primarily in converting raw materials into a finished salable product. One major factor in this conversion process is labor cost. Management's main problem is to control and reduce the labor costs so that the business operations will be more successful in terms of greater profits. This managerial control of labor costs can be most effective through:

1. Production planning.
2. Use of labor standards.
3. Use of labor budget.
4. Use of labor performance reports.
5. Study of the probable effectiveness of wage incentive systems.
6. Reduction in cost of labor cost accounting.

Production planning and cost accounting are closely related. Without production planning, cost accounting becomes merely a clerical compilation of useless figures. Without a sound cost accounting system, production planning loses most of its managerial control effectiveness.

There are three phases of production planning—*product engineering; process engineering;* and *planning, scheduling, and routing.*

Product engineering has as its function the creation of new products or the improvement in the design or construction of current products. The purpose of product engineering is to increase the sales potential of the products either by a more attractive design, a more substantial product at the same price, or the same product at a lower price. This increase in sales may be achieved by reducing the cost of an article by using cheaper material, or less material, or redesigning the product so that less labor will be required in its production. Product engineering for many concerns is a continuous business function. However, it may precede, parallel, or follow the work of the cost accounting department. While it is essentially an engineering function, product engineering measures the effectiveness of its work through the figures compiled by the cost accounting department.

Process engineering is closely associated with product engineering and cost accounting in aiding management to create a finished product at the lowest possible cost. Process engineering refers to the setting up of the proper machines, dies, and flow of work so that the minimum of labor will be required in the manufacture of a high-quality product. In most instances, it results in simplifying the manufacturing operations through the use of more automatic machinery and tools. Naturally, the processes of manufacturing cannot be organized until the product has been properly designed or engineered. Then the cost accounting department measures the effectiveness of the work through the presentation of the unit costs. There are many illustrations of how product engineering and process engineering have worked together to reduce the cost of labor required. For example, designing all-steel automobile bodies eliminated the labor operations of sewing or attaching waterproof tops to cars; designing cars so that the fenders and the body of the car are one continuous piece of steel eliminated the labor operations previously required in bolting the fenders to the body; and casting the entire motor block as one piece instead of two, eliminated the labor operation of bolting the two pieces together. Every industry has numerous illustrations of how product and process engineering have worked together to reduce not only the cost of materials but the labor costs as well. *But it is the task of the cost accounting department to measure the effectiveness of this work.*

Product engineering and process engineering are not always sufficient to manufacture an article at the lowest possible cost. Much confusion, idle time, and other inefficiencies may occur in the factory operations unless all work is carefully *planned, routed,* and *scheduled,* so that the work will flow uninterruptedly from one department to another. This phase of production control is usually directed by a group of engineers who are responsible for having the machines, tools, and manpower available for the work to be done. The machines must be properly set up in time so that the men will not be idle waiting for the work or the machines. Materials must be available when needed to avoid the delays and inefficiencies resulting from bottlenecks in the flow of work. Definite time schedules must be adhered to so that any interruptions or breakdowns in the schedule will be quickly located and eliminated.

Both the process engineering and the planning, scheduling, and routing of work in the factory must make use of *labor standards.* By means of time-and-motion studies for each operation, a firm is able to compute how much, under normal operating conditions, a worker should be able to produce; and on the basis of this computation, it should know how many workmen should be hired to do a certain volume of work. Without such standards management is at a loss to know whether in spite of all appearances to the contrary the workmen are actually turning out the work in the volume that is expected of them. These standards will not be set until as a result of time-and-motion studies the most efficient machines and operations have been installed and developed. Labor standards are primarily time standards. When the planning, scheduling, and routing department knows how long it will take to complete certain operations, it will be able to schedule and route the work through the factory with the minimum of delay or confusion. A simple standard time sheet for the manufacture of a guard is shown in Illustration 7–8.

Illustration 7-8. Process Sheet—Specifications and Routing

PROCESS SHEET - SPECIFICATIONS & ROUTING

SHEET 1 of 1

PART NO. 33018	PART NAME GUARD	
WRITTEN BY NAVARRD	CHECKED BY E.J.MILLER	APPROVED H.I.D.

MATERIAL DESCRIPTION .032 X 2 3/8 X 3 3/8 -52-S AL.ALLOY (PINK-BLUE)

SUB.ASSMB.USED ON 33000 RELEASE APPROVAL A.E.N. ENG.RELEASE

DATE 5-31- DATE RELEASED TO PROD.CONTROL 5-26-

MAT.SPEC.NO. 1103 MAT.CODE NO. 26233 ENG.CHANGE ORDER NO. ENG.CHANGE DATE

OPER. NO.	OPERATION DESCRIPTION	DEPT.	GROUP	MACH.	EQUIPMENT DESCRIPTION — TOOL, JIG, GAGE OR FIXTURE NUMBER & DESCRIPTION	PIECES PER HR.	STD. HRS. PER 100 PIECES	CLASS	STD. SET-UP TIME	NORMAL MCH. HRS. PER 100 PCS.	NORMAL MAN HRS. PER 100 PCS.
1	PIERCE AND BLANK	414	6	517	#3½ TOLEDO PUNCH PRESS PIERCING AND BLANKING P & D / T.41624 BOLSTER 1003	600	.166	T	.5	.166	.166
2	FORM	414	6	1181	#3½ TOLEDO PUNCH PRESS FORMING P & D 41625 / BOLSTER 1001 CHECKING GAUGE 48695	333	.300	T	.5	.300	.300
3	BURR AND WASH	440			POLISHING JACK TANK	200	.500	T	-	-	.500
4	INSPECT	475			BENCH CHECKING GAUGE 48695	200	.500	T	-	-	.500
5	ANODIZE AS PER SPEC. #26 (SEND OUTSIDE)										

TIME & LABOR STANDARDS

DATE OF LAST PREVIOUS CHANGE

Closely related to the time standards and the production schedules is the *labor budget*. Production schedules must be made several weeks to a month in advance, and when the standards of producing each unit are used, it is possible to prepare and use a labor budget in controlling costs. Such a labor budget is given in Illustration 7–9.

Illustration 7–9

MOTOR ASSEMBLY DEPARTMENT
LABOR BUDGET
For the Month of December, 19—
Issued November 24, 19—

Production Order Nos.	Units Scheduled	Direct Labor Hours per Unit	Total Direct Labor Hours for Month
D-481	2,000	2	4,000
D-482	2,100	2	4,200
D-483	2,100	2	4,200
D-484	1,800	2	3,600
			16,000

LABOR BUDGET		
Fixed:		
Supervision.....................................$ 1,800.00		640
Clerical...................................... 1,250.00		400
Total Fixed Labor Budget...............$ 3,050.00		1,040
Variable:		
Direct Labor, 16,000 Hours @ $2.50..........$40,000.00		16,000
Other Indirect Labor, 800 Hours @ $1.50...... 1,200.00		800
Total Variable Labor Budget............$41,200.00		16,800
Total Labor Budget, Based on 40-Hour Week, plus 5% for Absence:		
Fixed Labor..............................$ 3,050.00		1,040
Variable Labor............................ 41,200.00		16,800
5% for Absence...........................		892
Total.....................................$44,250.00		18,732
Number of Workers, 40 Hours per Week..................		469

Performance reports are a necessary part of a managerial control and cost control. To be most effective, these reports should be given to the departmental foremen for their attention and action. A good foreman will make careful use of these reports in improving the work in his department. Two illustrations are given of production reports: (1) a weekly or daily departmental *efficiency* report (Illustration 7–10), which shows the efficiency of each worker; it requires a great deal of clerical work and is therefore expensive but, if properly used, should pay big dividends in increased production; and (2) departmental labor *cost* (Illustration 7–11), showing the weekly actual and standard labor costs, with variations from standard together with the causes therefor.

Illustration 7–10. Departmental Efficiency Report

DEPARTMENTAL EFFICIENCY REPORT

Department No. 78   Week Ending April 12, 19—

Ford A. Waters, Foreman

No.	Name	This Week	Last Week	Previous Month	Remarks
401	J. Columbus	96%	98%	95%	O.K.
402	R. Donlon	99%	100%	100%	O.K.
403	C. Cohen	90%	92%	95%	O.K.
404	R. Burton	100%	100%	102%	Exceptional Worker
405	F. George	100%	96%	98%	O.K.
406	A. Flint	70%	76%	80%	New Worker Not Familiar with Machine
407	M. Barb	80%	85%	90%	Machine Repairs
408	S. Chensi	80%	82%	80%	Delayed Waiting For Work
	Average	89.3%	91%	92.5%	

90% to 100% operating efficiency considered good. Above or below this figure some comment should be made in "remarks" column.

Illustration 7–11. Labor Cost Report

DEPARTMENTAL LABOR COST REPORT

Department No. 16   Foreman L. E. Falconer

Production 200—Model 4-F   Week Ending March 8, 19—

Operations	Actual Labor Cost	Standard Labor Cost	Variation from Standard	Remarks
Planing	$1,210.00	$1,190.00	+$20.00	Waiting for Material
Drilling	1,300.00	1,250.00	+ 50.00	Machine Repairs
Cutting	1,120.00	1,120.00	—	O.K.
Bolting	1,150.00	1,175.00	− 25.00	Use of Special Tools —Revise Standards
Spraying	150.00	150.00	—	O.K.
Total	$4,930.00	$4,885.00	+$45.00	

Other labor reports of production may be prepared, but it is important that a checkup be made of what use the foremen make of these reports.

Incentive Wage Systems as a Phase of Managerial Control of Labor Costs

Management can reduce the per unit cost for the *fixed overhead* charges if it can increase the number of units produced in a given period of time. To offer the workers some inducement to increase production, a variety of incentive wage systems have been introduced—from the simple straight piece rate to the more complicated graduated bonus system. All incentive systems are a variation of the straight piece-rate system—payment of wages for *output* rather than for time alone. Because of the minimum wage and hour laws, and also to offer encouragement to the use of an incentive system, most incentive plans guarantee the worker a minimum hourly wage even if his production does not justify it. A good incentive system, in times of high production, will help create wholesome labor relations through increased earnings. However, in many industries, unions oppose the use of these systems. In others, such as the garment and shoe industries, the unions work out the piece rates in cooperation with the manufacturer. One large shoe manufacturing corporation has had as many as 250,000 different piece rates in its agreement with the union.

An incentive system to be successful must have these characteristics:

1. It must be easy for the workman to understand.
2. Rates must be set fairly so that the exceptional worker can increase his earnings accordingly.
3. The standards of production must be guaranteed.
4. There must be enough work to keep the workers busy.
5. There must be a guaranteed minimum and payment for holidays.

The basic principle underlying incentive wage systems is the *reduction of the fixed overhead cost per unit* by increasing the quantity of production in a given period of time. Some incentive wage systems also attempt to reduce the unit cost of labor by using a graduated incentive rate.

Four types of incentive wages systems are generally used: (*a*) straight piecework, (*b*) efficiency systems, (*c*) point systems, and (*d*) group bonus system. Illustration 7–12 on the following pages uses a simple example in computing the earnings under the more commonly known incentive wage systems, viz:

Standard production per hour.....................................60 pieces
Hourly rate of pay... $1.80
Minimum hourly wage except for the Taylor System ($1.40)........ 1.80

Illustration 7–12. Comparative Table of Five Common Incentive Wage Systems

TAYLOR DIFFERENTIAL PIECE-RATE

TAYLOR DIFFERENTIAL PIECE-RATE system uses two piece rates—a low rate for the poorer worker, and a higher rate for better production. Although no minimum is guaranteed, the wage and hour laws require a $1.40 minimum payment per hour.

System / Production per Hour	Rate per Piece	Total Pay per Hour	Pay per Piece	Overhead per Hour	Overhead per Piece	Total Overhead and Labor per Piece
30 pcs.	$0.015	$1.40*	$0.0466	$1.50	$0.03	$0.0956
50	0.015	1.40	0.028	1.50	0.03	0.058
59	0.015	1.40	0.0237	1.50	0.0254	0.0491
60	0.03	1.80	0.03	1.50	0.025	0.055
80	0.03	2.40	0.03	1.50	0.01875	0.04875
100	0.03	3.00	0.03	1.50	0.015	0.045

*Minimum per hour when illustration was prepared.

HALSEY PREMIUM WAGE

HALSEY PREMIUM WAGE system guarantees a minimum wage per hour. The worker is paid for a percentage of time saved in producing more than the standard quantity. In this illustration, the payment is for 50% of time saved.

System / Production per Hour	Hourly Wage	Total Pay	Pay per Piece	Overhead per Hour	Overhead per Piece	Total Overhead and Labor per Piece
30 pcs.	$1.80	$1.80	$0.06	$1.50	$0.03	$0.11
50	1.80	1.80	0.036	1.50	0.03	0.066
59	1.80	1.80	0.0305	1.50	0.0254	0.0559
60	1.80	1.80	0.03	1.50	0.025	0.055
80	1.80	2.10	0.02625	1.50	0.01875	0.045
100	1.80	2.40	0.024	1.50	0.015	0.039

POINT SYSTEMS

POINT SYSTEMS of wage payment such as Bedaux, Mannit, Kim, etc. Production is converted in "B's," Mannits, etc., which represent amount of work that should be done in one minute. Worker should earn 60 B's an hour. Excess production is paid for at ¾ usual piece rate, the other ¼ going to supervisor or foreman. Minimum guaranteed is $1.80.

Production per Hour	No. of B's Credit	Pay per B Unit	Total Pay	Pay per Piece	Overhead per Hour	Overhead per Piece	Total Overhead and Labor per Piece
30 pcs.	30	$0.03	$1.80	$0.06	$1.50	$0.05	$0.11
50	50	0.03	1.80	0.036	1.50	0.03	0.066
59	59	0.03	1.80	0.0305	1.50	0.0254	0.0559
60	60	0.03	1.80	0.030	1.50	0.025	0.055
80	80	60 X $0.03 / 20 X $0.02¼*	2.25	{0.028125 / 0.001875*}	1.50	0.01875	0.04875
		20 X $0.00¾*	0.15				
100	100	60 X $0.03 / 40 X $0.02¼*	2.70	{0.027 / 0.003*}	1.50	0.015	0.045
		40 X $0.00¾*	0.30				

* Bonus shared by indirect workers.

Illustration 7–12. Comparative Table of Five Common Incentive Wage Systems (Continued)

	Production per Hour	Hourly Wage	Total Pay per Hour	Pay per Piece	Bonus Rate	Overhead per Hour	Overhead per Piece	Total Overhead & Labor per Piece
STANDARD TIME SYSTEM—Gantt task and Bonus. There is a set time for each task or job and a fairly high standard. When worker achieves this standard he gets a bonus which is a percentage of his earnings. Minimum hourly pay is guaranteed.	30 pcs.	$1.80	$1.80	$0.06		$1.50	$0.05	$0.11
	50	1.80	1.80	0.036		1.50	0.03	0.066
	59	1.80	1.80	0.0305		1.50	0.0254	0.0559
	60	1.80	2.16	0.036	20%	1.50	0.025	0.061
	80	1.80	2.88	0.036	60%	1.50	0.01875	0.05475
	100	1.80	3.60	0.036	100%	1.50	0.015	0.051

	Efficiency Percentage	Bonus of Base Pay	Hourly Rate if Base Pay Is $1.80 per Hour	Overhead per Hour	Total Cost	Units Produced	Total Unit Cost
GRADUATED BONUS SYSTEM—Emerson, Wennerlund, etc. Increasing bonus rate based upon pay, as production per hour increases. Minimum hourly rate is guaranteed.	66⅔%	5%	$1.89	$1.50	$3.39	40	$0.08475
	80	10%	1.98	1.50	3.48	48	0.0725
	100	20%	2.16	1.50	3.66	60	0.061
	125	50%	2.70 (75 minutes + 20%)	1.50	4.20	75	0.056
	166⅔%	100%	3.60 (100 minutes + 20%)	1.50	5.10	100	0.051

In a study in 1963, it was reported that only about 26 percent of the industrial firms were using incentive systems. This number will probably decrease in the future due to (*a*) union opposition, (*b*) the effect of the wage and hour laws, and (*c*) increased automation whereby the volume of production is controlled by the machine or conveyor systems.

Group Bonus Pay System   Some firms use an incentive system under which several employees are paid a bonus collectively, and this bonus is distributed on some equitable basis. The reasons for a group bonus are: (1) it develops cooperation among the group of workers, particularly where the work of one may delay the work in some subsequent operation; (2) it reduces the amount of clerical work involved in computing bonuses—that is, a bonus is figured for group production, not for each individual's production; and (3) it reduces the amount of supervision necessary. The group bonus system has found definite application in the large automobile factories where the conveyorized organization is used,

Illustration 7–13. Group Bonus Pay Sheet

GROUP PAY SHEET						
DEPARTMENT Assembling				WEEK ENDING SEPTEMBER 30		
Name	Clock No.	Total Hours	Hourly Base Rate	Total Base Earnings (Hrs. × Rate)	Bonus	Total Pay
Paul Brown	203	50	$1.84	$ 92.00	$11.79	$103.79
Walter Kahn	204	49	1.60	78.40	10.05	88.45
Frank Smith	205	50	1.50	75.00	9.62	84.62
John Norman	206	45	1.50	67.50	8.65	76.15
Edward Hastie	207	46	1.00	46.00	5.90	51.90
		Total		$358.90	$46.01	$404.91

PRODUCTION ORDER NO.   525   ACCOUNT NO.   62
DESCRIPTION   Assembly of C. S. PRESS   QUANTITY   10
GROUP ALLOWANCE (For completed job)....................................$404.91
GROUP BASE EARNINGS..$358.90
GROUP BONUS (To be distributed)...$ 46.01
PERCENT OF BONUS TO BASE EARNINGS............................ 12.82%

and in other assembly types of business, such as washing machine, radio, and refrigerator manufacturing.

The Wennerlund, the Bedaux, and the Halsey systems have been applied to the group plan. Bonuses are generally computed on the weekly or monthly production to avoid periods of speedup and periods of slow production. If all the workers in a group are doing the same kind of work and receiving the same basic pay, the bonus can be figured on the output and distributed equally. If the workers do not perform the same kind of work and do not receive the same rate of pay, the bonus will be distributed in proportion to the time earnings for each task, as shown in Illustration 7–13.

Payroll and Labor Cost Accounting Illustrated
To illustrate the sequence, as well as the entries, affecting both the financial and the cost accounting for payroll, the following transactions will be recorded in general journal form, with indications of the books of original entry used and the subsidiary records affected. *Since the more common practice is to treat payroll taxes, overtime, and other fringe benefits as manufacturing overhead,* not as part of the direct labor costs, this procedure is followed in the illustration.

a) The payroll period is for the month of January, 19—

JANUARY, 19—						
SUN.	MON.	TUE.	WED.	THURS.	FRI.	SAT.
1	2	3	4	5	6	7
8	9	10	11	12	13	14
15	16	17	18	19	20	21
22	23	24	25	26	27	28
29	30	31				

b) The workers are paid on Wednesday of each week for wages earned through the preceding Saturday.

The December 31 (past) payroll amounted to $20,000 and was journalized on that date as: Dr. Payroll, $20,000; Cr. Payroll Accrued, $20,000. The workers were paid on January 4 when the other payroll liabilities (federal withholding tax, $4,000; state withholding tax, $1,000; and F.I.C.A. tax $1,760) were recorded as deductions and accruals.

c) Payroll figures for salaries and labor costs for the month of January, 19—, were:

For Week Ended				
	Jan. 7	Jan. 14	Jan. 21	Jan. 28
Direct labor costs....................	$12,000.00	$11,000.00	$10,500.00	$13,000.00
Indirect labor costs..................	6,200.00	6,300.00	5,800.00	5,900.00
Sales salaries.......................	8,000.00	8,000.00	8,000.00	8,000.00
Office and administrative salaries........	3,000.00	3,000.00	3,000.00	3,000.00
Total.........................	$29,200.00	$28,300.00	$27,300.00	$29,900.00
Federal withholding taxes payable.......	6,200.00	5,800.00	5,700.00	6,400.00
State withholding taxes payable.........	1,420.00	1,360.00	1,350.00	1,480.00
F.I.C.A. taxes payable (4.4%)	1,284.80	1,245.20	1,201.20	1,315.60

d) Payroll accrued for the period January 30 and 31 inclusive, amounted to $13,000, of which amount, direct labor costs were $6,600; indirect labor, $2,400; sales salaries, $2,600; and office salaries, $1,400.

e) The employer's payroll taxes recorded monthly at the following rates: *F.I.C.A.,* 4.4 percent; *state unemployment,* 2.7 percent; *federal unemployment tax,* 0.8 percent. The employees are subject to the F.I.C.A. tax deduction at the rate of 4.4 percent, recorded in the payroll journal. However, this deduction is made at the time of *payment,* that is, *only for wages actually paid.* Therefore, for accrued payroll at the end of the fiscal period, no payroll deductions are recorded for the accrual. The F.I.C.A. tax is deducted on the pay received during the first week of the new year, even though some of that pay was earned in the preceding year, and exceeded the maximum limit, which presently is $6,600. It is the time of payment, not the time of earning, that fixes the tax deduction date for F.I.C.A. tax.

The entries on pages 198–200 illustrate the payroll and tax accounting for the first month of the year. (At this time, no employee has yet earned the maximum amount taxable under the various payroll tax laws.)

Reducing the Clerical Cost of Labor Cost Accounting

Calculating the elapsed time on jobs, sorting the tickets by jobs, and preparing the cost sheets with a minimum of delay involves a great amount of clerical time and expense. Machines have been used to reduce the costs. The Calculagraph is a time recorder which computes automatically the elapsed time on any job time ticket, in hours and fractions of an hour. (See Illustration 7–14 on p. 201.) When used in conjunction with *time and payroll tables,* the computation of the dollars and cents cost of the time used on a job is expedited. Further, if the job time ticket is in the form of an IBM prepunched job time ticket, the sorting by jobs and subsequent tabula-

Date	Entry	Book of Original Entry

19—
Jan. 4
	Payroll Accrued.........................14,275.00
	    Accounts Payable*.................. 14,275.00
	    To voucher payroll of December 31.
		Voucher register

4	Accounts Payable.......................14,275.00
	    Cash............................. 14,275.00
	    Payment of December 31 payroll.
		Check register

4	Payroll Accrued......................... 5,880.00
	    Federal Withholding Taxes Payable.... 4,000.00
	    State Withholding Taxes Payable...... 1,000.00
	    F.I.C.A. Taxes Payable.............. 880.00
	    To record payroll deductions on December 31 payroll in year of payment.
	    (Employer's payroll taxes on above payroll may be assumed to have been accrued at year-end.)
		Payroll journal

7	Payroll...............................29,200.00
	    Federal Withholding Taxes Payable.... 6,200.00
	    State Withholding Taxes Payable...... 1,420.00
	    F.I.C.A. Taxes Payable (4.4%)....... 1,284.80
	    Payroll Accrued.................... 20,295.20
	    Payroll liabilities, week ended 1/7.
		Payroll journal

7	Work-in-Process—Labor.................12,000.00
	    Manufacturing Overhead (Indirect Labor).. 6,200.00
	    Selling Expense (Sales Salaries)........... 8,000.00
	    Administrative Expense (Office Salaries).... 3,000.00
	    Payroll.......................... 29,200.00
	    Distribution of weekly payroll.†
		General journal

11	Payroll Accrued.......................20,295.20
	    Accounts Payable.................. 20,295.20
	    To voucher payroll of January 7.
		Voucher register

11	Accounts Payable......................20,295.20
	    Cash............................. 20,295.20
	    Payment of January 7 payroll.
		Check register

14	Payroll...............................28,300.00
	    Federal Withholding Taxes Payable... 5,800.00
	    State Withholding Taxes Payable..... 1,360.00
	    F.I.C.A. Taxes Payable (4.4%)....... 1,245.20
	    Payroll Accrued.................... 19,894.80
	    Payroll liabilities.
		Payroll journal

	Work-in-Process—Labor.................11,000.00
	    Manufacturing Overhead (Indirect Labor).. 6,300.00
	    Selling Expenses (Sales Salaries)........... 8,000.00
	    Administrative Expense (Office Salaries)... 3,000.00
	    Payroll.......................... 28,300.00
	    Distribution of payroll.
		General journal

* The vouchering for payment of the tax liabilities of the previous year have not been included in this illustrative problem.

† Some firms reduce the clerical work by distributing the labor costs monthly instead of weekly.

Date	Entry		Book of Original Entry
19—			
Jan. 18	Payroll Accrued........................19,894.80 Accounts Payable...................	19,894.80	
	To voucher payroll of January 14.		Voucher register
	Accounts Payable......................19,894.80 Cash............................	19,894.80	
	Payment of January 14 payroll.		Check register
21	Payroll.............................27,300.00 Federal Withholding Taxes Payable... State Withholding Taxes Payable...... F.I.C.A. Taxes Payable (4.4%)....... Payroll Accrued...................	5,700.00 1,350.00 1,201.20 19,048.80	
	Payroll liabilities, week ended 1/21.		Payroll journal
21	Work-in-Process—Labor.................10,500.00 Manufacturing Overhead (Indirect Labor).. 5,800.00 Selling Expense (Sales Salaries)........... 8,000.00 Administrative Expense (Office Salaries)... 3,000.00 Payroll...........................	27,300.00	
	Distribution of payroll.		General journal
25	Payroll Accrued........................19,048.80 Accounts Payable...................	19,048.80	
	To voucher payroll of January 21.		Voucher register
25	Accounts Payable......................19,048.80 Cash............................	19,048.80	
	Payment of January 21 payroll.		Check register
28	Payroll.............................29,900.00 Federal Withholding Taxes Payable... State Withholding Taxes Payable...... F.I.C.A. Taxes Payable (4.4%)....... Payroll Accrued...................	6,400.00 1,480.00 1,315.60 20,704.40	
	Payroll liabilities, week ended 1/28.		Payroll journal
28	Work-in-Process—Labor.................13,000.00 Manufacturing Overhead (Indirect Labor).. 5,900.00 Sales Expense (Sales Salaries)............ 8,000.00 Administrative Expense (Office Salaries).... 3,000.00 Payroll...........................	29,900.00	
	Distribution of payroll.		General journal
31	Payroll.............................13,000.00 Payroll Accrued...................	13,000.00	
	Accrual for January 30 and 31.		Payroll journal
31	Work-in-Process—Labor................. 6,600.00 Manufacturing Overhead (Indirect Labor).. 2,400.00 Selling Expense (Sales Salaries)........... 2,600.00 Administrative Expense (Office Salaries)... 1,400.00 Payroll...........................	13,000.00	
	Distribution of payroll accrued, two days.		General journal

Date	Entry	Book of Original Entry
19—		

Jan. 31	Manufacturing Overhead (Payroll Taxes)... 5,585.30
	Selling Expense (Payroll Taxes)........... 2,528.00
	Administrative Expense (Payroll Taxes).... 948.00
	    F.I.C.A. Taxes Payable (4.4%)........ 5,046.80
	    State Unemployment Taxes Payable.... 3,096.90
	    Federal Unemployment Taxes Payable.. 917.60
	Payroll taxes for payrolls of January 7,
	14, 21, and 28:
		General Journal

	Factory	Selling	Office	Total
F.I.C.A.	$3,110.80	$1,408.00	$528.00	$5,046.80
S.U.T.	1,908.90	864.00	324.00	3,096.90
F.U.T.	565.60	256.00	96.00	917.60
	$5,585.30	$2,528.00	$948.00	$9,061.30

Date	Entry	Book of Original Entry

31	Manufacturing Overhead (Payroll Taxes)... 711.00
	Selling Expense (Payroll Taxes)........... 205.40
	Administrative Expense (Payroll Taxes).... 110.60
	    F.I.C.A. Taxes Payable (4.4%)........ 572.00
	    State Unemployment Taxes Payable
	    (2.7%)............................. 351.00
	    Federal Unemployment Taxes Payable
	    (0.8%)............................. 104.00
	Accruals for January 30 and 31.
		General journal

Feb. 1	(Month-end entries for two-day payroll may be reversed, and then included in the next weekly payroll.)	General journal
15	F.I.C.A. Taxes Payable...................11,853.60 Federal Withholding Taxes Payable.......28,100.00 Accounts Payable*.................. 39,953.60 To voucher social security and withhold- ing tax liabilities on payrolls paid in Jan- uary.	Voucher register
15	Accounts Payable.......................39,953.60 Cash.............................. 39,953.60 Payment to federal depositary.	Check register

* The total includes liabilities for the last December payroll paid on January 4, but not the payroll tax liabilities on payroll for the January 30 and 31 payroll accrual.

tion of results become even more efficient and less costly. A second method of reducing the cost of job labor costing is to combine the daily "in" and "out" time-clock card with the *individual* daily job time tickets (Illustration 7–15). The top portion of this card shows the daily "in" and "out" time record for payroll purposes. The remainder of the card shows the perforated sections to be used when time stamped for the daily job time cost computations. In this illustration, Henry Jones worked on the third shift, starting at 6:00 A.M. and ending at 2:12

Illustration 7–14. Job Time Ticket Prepared on Calculagraph

ELAPSED TIME			**COMMENCED**		Workman No 38

					Time Allowed
Boring	Drilling	Grinding	Planing	Tapping	
Chipping	Facing	Milling ✓	Roughing	Threading	Premium Credit
Cutting Off	Filing	Mounting	Shaping	Turning	Foreman

Quantity_____ Total Time_____ Rate_____ Cost_____

This Calculagraph record shows that workman No. 38 commenced work at 8:24 A.M., that he was performing a milling operation on Job No. 530, and that he was employed 5.3 hours.

P.M. The first job on which he worked was 201. He is being paid $2 per hour. On this job he worked 1.3 hours, earning $2.60.

A third method of reducing the clerical work of cost accounting requires the use of the Tel-Autograph sending and receiving machines. Each worker writes on the shop machine information regarding job work, and this information is shown on a machine in the cost accounting office, from which items are posted to individual payroll and job order cost records.

A fourth method, which is surprisingly prevalent, is the use of payroll tables which show the earnings for any number of hours or fractional hours, at almost any hourly rate. These tables range in cost from $5 to as much as $600, but they seem to justify their cost in the amount of clerical labor saved.

A fifth method has been discussed in the use of telephones in reporting the time a job was started and again when it was completed.

Punched-card accounting has long been useful in computing, sorting, and summarizing labor costs by jobs for prompt analysis. More recently, dictating machines, tape recorders, and intercom systems for central time recording have expedited the cost accounting for labor on various jobs.

By using a computer it is possible to reduce payroll accounting

Illustration 7–15. Combination Daily Time-Clock and Individual Job Time Ticket

```
51171
50-759
HENRY JONES
N° 3    SHIFT GROUP EXTRA CARD NOS.    2.2  1.2  0.0
                                        2.2  1.0  0.0
SIGN HERE
        Henry Jones
TOTAL HOURS  7 3|    TOTAL AMOUNT  14.40
CHARGE  201   OPER. NO.  50   N° 51171
QUANTITY  120   RATE
HOURS  13   RATE   2.60
CHARGE  216   OPLN. NO.  65   N° 51171
QUANTITY  60   RATE
HOURS  7   RATE   1.40
CHARGE  230   OPER. NO.  80   N° 51171
QUANTITY  140   RATE
HOURS  9   RATE   1.80
CHARGE  203   OPLN. NO.  52   N° 51171
QUANTITY  80   RATE
HOURS  15   RATE   3.00
CHARGE  224   OPER. NO.  63   N° 51171
QUANTITY  177   RATE
HOURS  16   RATE   3.20
CHARGE  218   OPER. NO.  71   N° 51171
QUANTITY      RATE
HOURS  12   RATE   2.40
```

and job cost accounting for labor to one simple operation—turning a key in a slot. This of course is applicable only for firms large enough to be customers of a *data processing center*—about 250 workers is the break-even point for operating this system. It is a substitute for the slow manual time clocks and manual payroll accounting.

The system consists of a recording console and pairs of key transmitting stations, any number of which can be placed throughout the factory. One transmitting station of each pair is an "IN" station and the other an "OUT" station. Every worker has his own key made of plastic harder than steel. When he comes to work he inserts the key in the hole in the nearest "IN" station to his work and turns it. At the end of the day or at noon if he goes out of the building for lunch, the worker turns his key in the "OUT" station. The time signals transmitted to the console are punched on a tape along with the worker's code number. The punched tape is forwarded to the data processing center where it goes through a computer. The computer has been programmed (instructed via magnetic tape) to match the code number with the worker's name, his hourly rate, and hours worked during the week, to calculate his pay. It is programmed to figure regular time as well as overtime with proper pay rates separately for each type of time. Thus this arrangement supersedes the use of time clocks for payroll accounting.

For job order costs, this same arrangement has application. The time in which a job is started is similarly recorded with a code for the job number. When the work has been completed by the employee on the job, the "OUT" key is inserted. The analysis of this tape with its costs and hours by the programmed tape will serve as a basis for reporting the actual labor costs and the estimated labor costs. If standards have been set for the normal amount of hours that a job should require, the difference between the actual and standard hours can be computed and used for managerial control.

QUESTIONS FOR REVIEW

1. What are the three phases of accounting for labor for a manufacturing company? How may each of these be mechanized?

2. Indirect labor costs are responsible for an increasing proportion of the labor cost of manufacturing. List the various indirect labor costs and indicate what management can do to control these.

3. What is meant by the fixed costs of labor? Since these are increasing, what effect should this have on the cost accounting for labor?

4. Managerial control of labor costs involves consideration of six factors. What are these?

5. What effect will automation have on the cost accounting for labor costs in manufacturing plants?

6. Management needs labor cost reports to measure the efficiency of its factory operations. What are some of these reports and how can management use them?

7. The payroll of the Northland Company for the month of April totaled $25,000. This amount included $1,200 for superintendence, $3,500 for indirect labor, $1,250 for overtime bonuses, $300 for idle time, $950 for office salaries, and $2,160 for sales salaries. The federal withholding taxes were $5,400; state withholding taxes, $900. F.I.C.A. taxes are at the rate of 4.4 percent. Prepare all the entries in journal form affecting the financial and cost accounting for this payroll.

8. What is the Guaranteed Annual Wage (GAW)? If this plan should receive increased use in business, what effect will its use have on labor cost accounting?

9. Pension costs for factory workers are becoming increasingly common in modern business. Explain the cost and financial accounting problems and treatment of these costs.

10. Indicate the various methods by which the cost of the clerical work in labor cost accounting may be reduced.

PROBLEMS—GROUP A

Problem 7-1. Purpose: *Computation of Payroll Costs and Deductions*

The payroll data of the assembly department of the Optimum Company for the week ended May 29 follows:

	Exemptions per W-4	Hours Worked	Wage Rate
J. Johnson	2	40	$3.00
K. Lewis	3	41	2.50
V. Lawrence	4	40	3.25
G. Giles	0	42	2.00
Y. Lamm	3	44	2.40
A. Regent	1	42	3.00
P. Lattimore	5	45	2.80
T. Holland	2	39	2.00
P. Jones	1	41	3.40

The federal withholding system used at Optimum is to allow $13 times the number of exemptions to be subtracted from gross wages. The difference is subject to withholding at the rate of 14 percent.

The F.I.C.A. rate is 4.4 percent. State unemployment tax is 2.7 percent. Federal unemployment tax is 0.4 percent.

Overtime at 1½ times the regular rate is paid on all hours worked over 40. Union dues of $2 per week are deducted from all employees.

Required:

a) Prepare a payroll record for the above department. Use the following columns:

Name of Employee	Overtime Bonus
Exemptions	Federal Withholding Tax
Hours Worked	F.I.C.A.
Rate of Pay	Union Dues
Gross Earnings	Net Wages
Regular Earnings	

b) Total the payroll sheet and prepare the necessary journal entries.

c) Prepare a journal entry recording payment of the wages on June 2.

Problem 7–2. Purpose: *Overtime Bonus Computations*

The Oldham Company operates a machine shop where tools are produced on a job order basis. During the month of October, it is necessary to incur overtime labor costs in manufacturing an order for the Kent Company. The amount of the overtime is $3,400. The other manufacturing costs of the job to Kent amounted to $16,000 of which $5,000 was direct labor. The total direct labor for the month was $50,000. Overhead is applied to production on the basis of direct labor dollars.

Required:

a) What is the cost of the order made for the Kent Company?

b) Is there an alternate to the cost you determined in (*a*)?

c) Under what conditions would you use each of the alternates you developed in (*a*) or (*b*)?

Problem 7–3. Purpose: *Estimating Labor Costs*

The Olsom Manufacturing Company is contemplating building a new plant in Stinesville. Before a decision can be made as to whether or not to build, management is interested in determining the labor costs and the related costs covering payroll taxes and fringe benefits.

Two products will be produced at the new plant if it is built. Product A will take 10 labor hours to complete a unit, and product B, 20 hours. These times are for the first six months, after which it is estimated that the time may be reduced by 6 percent. It is estimated that employee turnover will be such that a reduction in work force by 6 percent after six months will create no burden or hardship.

The normal work period in Stinesville will be eight hours per day, five days per week, 50 weeks per year.

Tentative plans call for the production at Stinesville of 50,000 units of A during the first six months and 40,000 units of B. The same production is also budgeted for the second six months of the year.

The wage rate can be expected to be $3 per hour.

The payroll taxes are estimated to be 4.4 percent F.I.C.A. on $6,600 wages; unemployment insurance taxes, 3.1 percent of $3,000 wages.

Each employee will receive two weeks of paid vacation pay and eight paid holidays during the year.

Contributions by the employer for pension plans, etc., are expected to total $20 per month, per employee.

Required:

a) How many employees should Olsom hire for the first six months? For the second six months?

b) Compute the direct labor cost for the year.

c) Compute all of the other related labor costs for the year.

Problem 7–4. **Purpose:** *Summarizing Payroll Transactions*

The following accounts appeared in the Oliphant Corporation's ledger on June 15, 19—:

Federal Withholding Taxes Payable (June 1–June 15 accumulation)....................$4,000
F.I.C.A. Taxes Payable (June 1–June 15 accumulation representing employees' and employer's share)... 1,500
State Unemployment Insurance Taxes Payable (2.7% all paid by employer) (April 1–June 15 accumulation)... 6,500
Federal Unemployment Insurance Taxes Payable (0.4% all paid by employer) (April 1–June 15 accumulation)... 1,310

The payroll records for June 15–29 payroll period show factory employees earned $36,000 with $3,900 withheld as federal withholding tax. Sales and office personnel earned $7,500 with $820 withheld.

The F.I.C.A. rate is 4.4 percent.

As of June 30, no employee earned over $3,000 since the plant was closed for a strike during the early part of the year.

Required:

a) Journalize the June 29 payroll and record payment of the wages on July 3.

b) Journalize the employer's payroll tax liability at June 29.

c) Journalize the entry recording payment of the amount due for F.I.C.A. and federal withholding taxes. Payment was made on July 12.

d) Journalize the entry recording payment of the quarterly amount due on the state unemployment tax.

Problem 7–5. **Purpose:** *Summary and Distribution of Payroll*

The Orange Manufacturing Company produces items on a job order basis in four producing departments and three service departments. Payroll is computed weekly, and the factory payroll for the week ended January 8 showed the following:

Department	No. of Employees	Total Hours	Total Payroll	Overtime Premium	Federal Withholding Tax
Department A.........5		250	$980	$40	$130
Department B.........5		210	750	35	108
Department C.........3		100	360	40	55
Department D.........2		85	300	62	52
Toolroom.............2		84	126	3	18
Storeroom............2		80	120		16
Shipping.............3		120	188		22

The payroll of the sales and administrative offices amounted to $1,400 with federal withholding tax of $305.

Payroll deductions are made for withholding and F.I.C.A. taxes and union dues of $1.50 per week. The latter is applicable to factory employees only.

The employer also contributes 3 percent of payroll to a pension plan. The accrual is made monthly at the same time that the payroll taxes are accrued. The F.I.C.A. rate is 4.4 percent, and other payroll taxes amount to 3.1 percent.

A recapitulation of the job time tickets for the week of January 8 indicated:

Job Order No.	Dept. A	Dept. B	Dept. C	Dept. D
2 F 42...............$150		$120	$ 60	$ 45
3 F 56............... 120		105	50	35
3 G 48............... 160		130	65	55
4 M 64............... 135		105	45	40
3 G 72............... 100		80	30	25
5 L 10............... 145		90	40	30
6 K 12............... 110		70	20	..
Total............$920		$700	$310	$230

From the above information, prepare journal entries in logical sequence on both the factory office and the general office books to record (a) summary of the payroll journals, (b) payment of workers, (c) distribution of the payrolls, and (d) the employer's liability for payroll taxes and other fringe benefits.

PROBLEMS—GROUP B

Problem 7–6. Purpose: *Summary of Payroll; Distribution of Payroll Costs; No Separate Factory Books*

The Yorkshire Company operates a small factory in which the cost accounting is integrated with the financial records. No separate factory ledger is used.

The factory workers are unionized, but the office and sales personnel do not belong to the union. Shipping department and finished goods stock room employees are classified as sales department employees but are members of the union.

The payroll book is a book of original entry. Payroll deductions include union dues of $2.10. The employer's liability for payroll includes a fringe benefit for disability insurance of 30 cents per week for every union member, and life insurance $1.00 per week.

The accrued liabilities on payroll as at March 24, are: federal unemployment taxes, $150; F.I.C.A. tax, $750; state unemployment tax, $1,320; and accumulated withholding taxes, $2,600.

The payroll for the week ended March 31, 19—, has been summarized as follows:

Department	No. of Workers	Total Labor Hours	Total Payroll	Overtime Bonus	Federal Withholding Taxes
Department No. 1	12	510	$1,000.00	$ 55.00	$195.00
Department No. 2	9	400	800.00	40.00	150.00
Department No. 3	6	240	500.00	....	105.00
Department No. 4	5	200	480.00	20.00	70.00
Toolroom	2	84	129.00	13.00	25.00
Storeroom	2	80	120.00	....	23.60
Finished stock room	1	40	60.00	....	12.40
Shipping department	2	80	136.00	....	28.00
Sales office	3	...	450.00	....	78.00
General office	8	...	600.00	....	100.00
Total	50	1,634	$4,275.00	$128.00	$787.00

A recapitulation of the job time tickets for the week of March 31, indicated:

Job Order No.	Dept. No. 1	Dept. No. 2	Dept. No. 3	Dept. No. 4
M 4-1	$150	$120	$ 83	$160
M 4-2	130	110	70	50
M 4-3	148	115	78	58
M 4-4	122	95	62	40
M 4-5	180	130	87	62
M 4-6	120	80	60	50
M 4-7	80	50	25	..
Total	$930	$700	$465	$420

Payroll tax rates are as follows:

F.I.C.A. 4.4%
State unemployment tax 2.7
Federal unemployment tax 0.4

Journalize the following transactions:
a) The recording of the payroll.
b) Payment of amount due employees.
c) Payment of union dues withheld by union.
d) The recording of the employer's payroll taxes and fringe benefits.
e) The distribution of the payroll.

Problem 7-7. Purpose: *Estimating Labor Costs*

The Yantic Company is considering the possibility of adding a new wing to its present factory building to manufacture a new product known as "yan." Management is obviously interested in the production cost of "yan," and you have been delegated with the task of computing the labor cost of producing a unit of "yan." Labor cost in this case includes not only the direct labor cost but also includes payroll taxes and costs of fringe benefits. You determine the following:

> 10 units per hour may be manufactured in the proposed plant during the first one-half year of the plant's operation; after that, employees will be more efficient and will be able to produce 12 per hour.
> The proposal calls for hiring 300 persons at a rate of $2.80 per hour.
> Management feels that the output from the 300 persons can be sold.
> Payroll taxes are expected to average at about 7 percent of total wages. The Yantic Company also expects to contribute 5 percent of wages into a pension plan.
> The average workweek is 40 hours, and the company plans to operate for 50 weeks less the normal seven holidays which will be paid days. Each employee will also receive two weeks' vacation pay.

Required:

   a) Compute the direct labor cost for the year in total.
   b) Compute the total cost of payroll taxes and fringe benefits.
   c) Compute the direct labor cost per unit of "yan."
   d) Compute the cost of payroll taxes and fringe benefits per unit of "yan."
   e) Compute the unit cost of labor and the related cost per unit of "yan."

Problem 7-8. Purpose: *Overtime Premium Computations*

The Young Furniture Company manufactured 200 desks on special order for the State University. The following costs were incurred on the order:

$$
\begin{aligned}
&\text{Materials}\dots\dots\dots\dots\dots\dots\$8,000\\
&\text{Direct labor}\dots\dots\dots\dots\dots\ 5,000\\
&\text{Overhead}\dots\dots\dots\dots\dots\dots\ 3,000
\end{aligned}
$$

In addition, the Young Furniture Company incurred $800 of overtime premium costs on manufacturing the desks, as it was essential that they be delivered in time for September school opening.

The cost accounting system at Young's is such that overhead is applied to jobs on the basis of direct labor dollars. The job of making desks for the University took 1,000 of the 9,000 hours worked during the period.

Required:

   a) Determine the unit cost of manufacturing a desk.
   b) Is there an alternate to the unit cost determined in (*a*)?
   c) When would you use the cost developed in (*a*)? In (*b*)?

Problem 7-9. Purpose: *Computation of Payroll Costs and Deductions*

The finishing department's payroll of the Yarman Machine Company for the week ended January 14 follows:

	Exemp- tion Class	Hours Worked	Wage Rate
B. Vincent..................... 3	3	42	$2.00
Z. Davis....................... 1	1	38	2.50
A. Lomar...................... 5	5	44	3.00
E. Murphy..................... 2	2	43	3.50
C. Weeks...................... 0	0	41	2.80
Q. Hornblower................. 4	4	40	3.40
V. Blarney.................... 1	1	42	3.60
D. Finnegan................... 2	2	40	3.20

Other data:

Compute withholding by multiplying $13 times the number of exemptions and subtracting this number from the wages. Take 14 percent as withholding from the balance.

An overtime premium is paid on all hours worked over 40. Life insurance premiums of $3 per week are deducted from each employee. The payroll tax rates are:

$$\text{F.I.C.A.} \dots\dots\dots\dots\dots\dots\dots\dots\dots 4.4\%$$
$$\text{State unemployment tax} \dots\dots\dots\dots 2.7$$
$$\text{Federal unemployment tax} \dots\dots\dots 0.4$$

Required:

a) Prepare a payroll record for the finishing department. Head columns in the following manner:

Name of Employee	Overtime Premium
Exemptions	Federal Withholding Tax
Hours Worked	F.I.C.A.
Rate	Life Insurance
Gross Earnings	Net Wages
Regular Earnings	

b) Prepare the journal entries recording the payroll, payment of wages, and the recording of the employer's share of the payroll taxes.

Problem 7–10. Purpose: *Summarizing Payroll Transactions*

The general ledger of the Yarborough Corporation contained the following accounts on September 15, 19—:

Federal Withholding Taxes Payable	F.I.C.A. Taxes Payable
8,200	3,100 (includes employee and employer share)

State Unemployment Taxes Payable	Federal Unemployment Taxes Payable
12,500	2,500

Factory employees earned $70,000 from September 16–September 30, and $7,800 was withheld as federal withholding tax. Sales and administrative wages for the same period amounted to $10,000 with $1,000 withheld.

The F.I.C.A. rate is 4.4 percent. The state unemployment tax rate is 2.7 percent and the federal unemployment tax rate is 0.4 percent.

Required:

a) Prepare journal entries recording the payroll, the employer's payroll tax liability, and payment of the wages.

b) Prepare journal entries recording the payment of the amount due for F.I.C.A. and withholding taxes.

c) Prepare a journal entry recording the quarterly payment of the amount due on the state unemployment tax.

CHAPTER

8 | Manufacturing Overhead

Applied to Production

Nature of Indirect Manufacturing Costs   In the conversion of direct material into a finished product, direct labor and a large number of indirect costs are incurred. These indirect costs are summarized in the *manufacturing overhead control account,* supported by a subsidiary ledger for the detailed indirect cost accounts. Manufacturing overhead is sometimes termed *factory expense, factory burden,* or *factory on-cost.* Since many of the indirect manufacturing costs will not be known and recorded until the end of the *fiscal accounting period,* it has become necessary to charge most jobs or the departmental work-in-process accounts with an *estimated* amount for the manufacturing overhead. Furthermore, the *actual* overhead fluctuates so much *from month to month* that the results from using the actual overhead rate for each month would be misleading from the standpoint of valuing inventories and measuring operating efficiency.

Therefore, a predetermined rate is computed at the beginning of the year based upon the budgeted manufacturing overhead and the budgeted production for the year. This rate is used in computing the amount of overhead to be charged to the jobs or departmental work-in-process accounts during the year. Periodically, entries are made charging the work-in-process accounts and crediting a temporary account known as the *applied manufacturing overhead.*

Classification of the Various Indirect Manufacturing Costs   Manufacturing overhead may be classified, according to the nature of the item, as fixed, variable, and semivariable, or as general overhead and departmental overhead. In addition, there is an underlying classification of these indirect costs under three primary headings: *indirect materials and supplies, indirect labor payroll costs,* and *other indirect costs.* The heading *other indirect costs* is too broad to be handled effectively for managerial control. It is therefore subdivided further into the following groups: (1) maintenance; (2) fixed charges; (3) power, heat, and light; (4) special service department costs; and (5) sundry indirect costs. To illustrate more specifically the various items which may appear in each group, the following lists are given:

INDIRECT MATERIALS

Shop supplies
Factory office supplies
Fuel
Nondurable tools
Lubricants
Unabsorbed freight and cartage

INDIRECT LABOR

Superintendence
Foremen
Inspectors
Factory clerical workers, timekeepers, etc.
Helpers and laborers
Storekeepers and assistants
Chauffeurs and drivers
Overtime payments of bonuses
Elevator operators
Idle time
Athletics
Sickness pay

OTHER INDIRECT COSTS

Maintenance

Building maintenance
Machinery and tool maintenance
Furniture and fixture maintenance
Transportation system maintenance
Patterns
Auto and delivery equipment
   maintenance

Fixed Charges

Depreciation
Taxes
Insurance
Shop vacations
Group insurance
Taking inventory
Pensions
Rentals

Power, Heat, and Light

Operating employees
Operating supplies
Maintenance of equipment
Fixed charges

Special Service Department Costs

Purchasing department
Receiving department
Storekeeping department
Cost accounting department
Medical department
Cafeteria department
Police and protection

Sundry Overhead Costs

Royalties	Interest on investment (when used)
Apportioned administrative expenses	Defective material losses
Special taxes, such as payroll, process-	Spoiled goods
ing, and even income taxes	Direct material inventory losses

Manufacturing overhead costs have also been classified as *fixed, vari-ble, semivariable,* and *semifixed.* Total fixed manufacturing costs remain more or less constant in amount, regardless of the volume of production. Total variable costs fluctuate with, and in the same manner as, the volume of production, whereas semivariable costs fluctuate with the volume of production but not in the same manner—rather, by periodic steps. *The per unit cost of fixed overhead decreases in a given period as the number of units produced increases.* Few indirect costs are exactly fixed or 100 percent variable. Many of them are somewhere in between.

The following indirect costs may generally be classified as below:

Fixed Costs	*Variable Costs*
Rent	Compensation insurance
Taxes	Heat, light, and power
Fire insurance	Supplies
Depreciation	Repairs
Superintendence	Spoilage
	Freight-in
Semivariable Costs	Taxes on payroll
Inspection	
Indirect labor	*Semifixed Costs*
Factory clerical help	Rent
Supervision	Taxes
	Insurance

Calculating the Predetermined Manufacturing Overhead Rate   To calculate a predetermined overhead rate, the accountant must first of all determine whether there should be a single rate covering all the departments of a factory or whether there should be separate rates for each department. In a small plant with only a few departments similar in organization, all departments using either machine or hand labor exclusively, and each product moving through all departments, a single rate might be practical. However, if some departments use machine work and others handwork, and if all the products do not go through all the departments, then in the interest of more accurate costs, it is advisable to have a predetermined overhead rate for each productive department in the factory. The procedure followed when manufacturing overhead is applied on a departmental basis is similar to that when but a single rate is used for the entire factory.

When the detailed budget of indirect factory costs is prepared for the coming year, this estimate assumes that there must also be an estimate of the *volume of production.* This volume may be expressed in terms of (1) units produced, (2) direct labor hours, (3) direct labor costs, (4) machine-hours, or (5) material costs.

If only a single product is being manufactured, it is possible to use the *units-produced* method. If a number of different products are manufactured, however, this method becomes impractical, and some common base must be used to measure the volume of production such as labor hours, labor costs, or machine-hours.

Dividing the volume of production into the budgeted or estimated manufacturing overhead will produce the *predetermined overhead rate, expressed either as dollars* per unit, per direct labor hour, or per machine-hour, or as a *percent* of the direct labor costs, or material costs.

Although the method may seem simple, the effectiveness of the cost system depends upon the reliability of *two estimates*—the indirect costs and the volume of production—both of which may be grossly miscalculated. As a result of long years of experience and through the use of carefully prepared budgets of sales and indirect costs, cost accountants have been able to calculate predetermined overhead rates with a surprising degree of accuracy.

Normal Operating Conditions and the Manufacturing Overhead Rates

When the manufacturer estimates his volume of production, he must do so in terms of *normal operating conditions,* since these affect the method of calculating a predetermined rate for manufacturing overhead. Accountants, engineers, and top management are not always in agreement as to the exact meaning of this term.

There are three concepts of normal operating conditions: (1) *total or ideal plant capacity,* (2) *practical plant capacity,* and (3) *expected actual volume.* When all is said and done, management must decide how it will measure the efficiency of its production.

Some accountants feel that in calculating the predetermined overhead rate the estimated volume of production should be the *maximum* or *total plant capacity.* In other words, if the plant has a full operating capacity at maximum efficiency (no idle time or machine breakdown) of 10,000 units even though business and factory conditions indicate that only 6,000 units will be produced, the former figure should be used in computing the predetermined factory overhead rate. It is obvious that the use of the 10,000 figure will result in applied manufacturing over-head very much less than the actual overhead, but these accountants maintain that the *underapplied* manufacturing overhead is due to *idle plant capacity* and is a proper charge to the Profit and Loss account. They consider it a management loss or expense chargeable either to the *sales* department because of its inability to sell the maximum amount of goods which would have kept the plant busy at capacity or to the *production* department for having too great an investment in plant and equipment or for not properly supervising the workmen or equipment to prevent machine breakdown and idle time. This basis is usually a *long-term*—five- or ten-year—measure of efficiency.

Other accountants maintain that few plants operate continuously at the maximum plant capacity. Therefore, they compute the predeter-mined overhead rates on the basis of *practical plant capacity.* This volume is based on the production estimated when the employees work on a regular shift, the usual number of hours per week, with due allowance for human inability to achieve maximum, 60-minutes-per-hour production, for machine breakdown, idle time, and other delays and interruptions which prevent maximum production. Some account-ants estimate this volume at about 80 percent of the ideal or maximum volume. This procedure is also a long-term measure of efficiency.

A more reasonable interpretation of *normal operating conditions,* the one used in computing the predetermined rates in this text, assumes production at the *expected actual volume* for a period of a year or less. This volume may be based upon past performance, adjusted to the present business and economic outlook. The sales budget is usually the determining factor. This method results in an accurate measurement of managerial efficiency over a short period of time.

Top management must decide what basis should be used in measur-ing the effectiveness of production. So long as top management realizes that there are several bases on which to compute the predetermined overhead rate and then uses this information in analyzing the results as indicated by the over- or underapplied overhead, an intelligent interpre-tation of managerial efficiency will be possible.

For example:

1. If the estimate of maximum plant capacity for the next five years is 200,000 hours, 240,000 hours, 300,000 hours, 320,000 hours, and 400,000 hours, then the *ideal normal* plant capacity will average 292,000 hours. Over the period of the next five years, management must strive to equal this figure during the first two years and should attempt to exceed it during the last three years. The production results will be interpreted in the light of the five-year period.

2. If the plant has 100 machines and there is a 15 percent allowance for delays, machine breakdowns, etc., the *practical plant capacity* would be computed as follows:

100 machines × 40 hours per week × 50 weeks per year . . . . 200,000 hours
Less: 15% for idle machines, etc. 30,000
Practical Plant Capacity for Computing the Predetermined Overhead Rate . . . 170,000 hours

This practical plant capacity is based on the *ability to produce,* not necessarily the ability to sell.

3. It is assumed that the sales prospects indicate that during the coming year 5,000 units will be sold, that no attempt will be made to build up the finished goods inventory, and that 30 machine-hours will be required to produce each unit. The estimated capacity based upon *expected actual volume* (which in turn is based upon *estimated sales*) is 150,000 machine-hours.

In a year in which there is low production, the use of expected actual capacity will result in a high rate which is meaningless from the standpoint of measuring production efficiency and misleading in helping to set sales prices. When production is low, a higher rate would give the impression that a higher selling price is necessary; this would cause production to drop even lower. The effect of the capacity level on the manufacturing overhead rates may be illustrated as follows:

	Ideal	Practical	Expected Actual
Operating capacity	100%	85%	70%
Direct labor hours	1,000	850	700
Budgeted manufacturing overhead costs:			
Fixed	$2,000	$2,000	$2,000
Variable	2,000	1,700	1,400
Total	$4,000	$3,700	$3,400
Predetermined overhead rate	$4.00	$4.35	$4.85

Characteristics of a Good Base for Computing Predetermined Overhead Rates

The characteristics of a good base on which to compute the predetermined overhead rates are:

1. It should be computed easily.
2. It should be inexpensive to use in applying it to the cost of production.

3. It should have some relation to the time factor involved in many indirect costs (*period costs*).
4. It should be computed on a departmental basis, if possible, so that the causes of variations may be localized.
5. It should be reasonably accurate, that is, representative of the estimated overhead costs applicable to each unit.

In a survey conducted by the National Association of Accountants in one important industrial area, it was discovered that the methods of applying manufacturing overhead most commonly used were: *percentage of direct labor costs,* 41 percent of the firms surveyed; *per direct labor hour,* 11 percent; *per machine-hour,* 4 percent; *per unit rate,* 9 percent; and all other methods, 35 percent.

Bases for Application of Manufacturing Overhead to Production

Allocation of manufacturing overhead with reasonable accuracy over production for a month or a year is one of the major problems confronting a cost accountant and involves much study of cost data.

In ascertaining such a rate, manufacturing overhead is estimated for a given period and divided by the estimated base. In the following illustrations, a single-unit factory is assumed, undivided into production centers or departments. The methods used for a single-department factory, however, are also applicable to the individual departments or the operating units of production centers of a factory.

The bases used in determining the manufacturing overhead rate applicable to the cost of manufacturing are:

1. Unit.
2. Material costs.
3. Labor costs.
4. Prime costs.
5. Labor hours.
6. Machine-hours.
7. Machine-hours plus a supplementary rate.
8. Moving average.

Since production conditions and management control in business firms vary, each of the foregoing methods of applying manufacturing overhead will find application in some instances. To illustrate how each of these rates is computed, the following facts are assumed:

The *budgeted manufacturing overhead* for the year is:

Fixed	$ 96,000	
Variable	360,000	$456,000
The estimated *number of units* to be produced in this period		120,000 units
The estimated *direct material costs* are		$240,000
The estimated *direct labor costs* are		$360,000
The estimated *prime cost* is		$600,000
The estimated *direct labor hours* are		180,000 man-hours
The estimated *machine-hours* are		84,000 machine-hours

The computation of the manufacturing overhead rates on the various bases is illustrated with only a blanket figure rather than a separate one for fixed and for variable manufacturing overhead.

Unit Basis   One of the simplest methods of distributing manufacturing overhead is on the per unit basis. The unit might be a pound, a foot, a machine, a hundred pieces, or, under the Bedaux incentive pay system, a "B." The formula for the determination of the rate is:

$$\frac{\text{Estimated manufacturing overhead}}{\text{Estimated number of units}} = \text{Overhead rate per unit. } (R)$$

Using the figures given above, the unit burden rate is:

$$R = \frac{\$456,000}{120,000 \text{ units}} = \$3.80 \text{ per unit.}$$

The unit method of applying overhead is used most satisfactorily in small manufacturing concerns having relatively simple manufacturing processes or in large concerns manufacturing few articles in large quantities.

In foundry cost accounting, some firms use a predetermined rate based on the units of production (pounds of castings). Where a variety of castings are produced, the various products are grouped into classes, depending upon the size, and a predetermined rate per pound of casting is computed for each class.

Material Cost Basis   Some concerns find that a percentage of the cost of material used in production is a satisfactory method of determining the amount to add to the cost of direct materials and direct labor in computing the cost of manufacturing. The formula for determining the rate is:

$$R = \frac{\text{Estimated manufacturing overhead, \$456,000}}{\text{Estimated cost of material to be used, \$240,000}} = 190\% \text{ of material cost.}$$

This method is found in concerns *using materials of approximately the same value in each article being manufactured and also in concerns where the amount of material used per hour is uniform in value,* as in a firm whose output is controlled by automatic machines.

This method has limitations, however. First, since most of the factory overhead, such as superintendence, heat, light, power, insurance, rent, taxes, depreciation, and indirect labor, is consumed on a *time basis,* the value of the materials used must bear some direct relation to the amount of time used in manufacturing. This relationship is possible where the output is controlled by machines and where the cost of materials involved is more or less the same for each unit produced.

To illustrate the inaccuracies which may occur in the use of the material cost method when the cost of the materials consumed per hour or per day is not approximately the same, consider the jewelry manufacturer who uses, in the manufacture of rings of similar design, silver costing 40 cents per ounce, gold at $35 per ounce, and platinum at $65 an ounce. Rings to be manufactured from these three metals will require approximately the same amount of time and the same quantity of metal. Labor costs should be the same for each ring, since the designs are similar. If manufacturing overhead were charged to production on the basis of time, the applied overhead *should be essentially the same for each ring.* But the absence of any relationship between the time consumed in making the ring and the cost of materials used is shown by the following figures:

	Silver	Gold	Platinum
100 rings, materials............................	$20	$300	$520
100 rings, labor.................................	25	30	30
100 rings, overhead (10% of material costs).......	2	30	52
	$47	$360	$602

Although the amount of time used on each of these jobs was approximately the same and therefore the amount of the indirect overhead consumed on a time basis should also be the same, the resulting overhead applied on a materials cost basis varies widely.

From a theoretical viewpoint this method of computing the manufacturing overhead applicable to a given job is quite incorrect, but firms using this method argue that since the cost of the articles varies, the selling prices will vary accordingly and on the higher priced articles the amount of profit should be greater. Therefore, the amount of overhead to be borne by these higher priced articles should be greater. This is a practical answer, but it is not correct from an accounting viewpoint.

Labor Cost Basis The labor cost basis follows closely the materials cost method. Concerns having the same hourly pay rate for all direct laborers can best use this method. The formula is:

$$R = \frac{\text{Estimated manufacturing overhead, } \$456,000}{\text{Estimated labor costs, } \$360,000} = 126\tfrac{2}{3}\% \text{ of labor costs.}$$

The weakness of this method is apparent. If one skilled worker is paid $2.20 per hour and another worker who is more skilled but not necessarily performing the same kind of work is paid $3.30 per hour, the amount of overhead charged for the second worker per hour would be 1½ times as much as the first. Yet when both have worked one hour they have used about the same amount of manufacturing overhead on a time basis. Simplicity of operation seems to be the main argument for such a method, and it finds very wide application. Since most workers in the same department will probably receive the same rate of pay, this method will be most practical when a separate rate is calculated for each department.

Prime Cost Basis   The prime cost method is rather arbitrary and has the same weaknesses as the materials and the labor cost methods. Theoretically, it could be used where the increased cost of direct materials is offset by a proportionate decrease in the direct labor cost per article due to a proportionate decrease in the amount of time used by such workers. Such conditions, however, do not exist in business. The most that can be said for such a method is that it is simple and arbitrary—not sound.

The formula used in determining the rate is:

$$R = \frac{\text{Estimated manufacturing overhead, \$456,000}}{\text{Estimated prime cost of production, \$600,000}} = 76\% \text{ of prime cost.}$$

Labor Hour Basis   To overcome the theoretical objections of the first three methods, some firms have resorted to the use of labor hours as a base for ascertaining the overhead rate. The labor hour method considers the time factor in applying overhead but involves additional clerical expense in computing the labor hours used on each job. It is sometimes known as the *man-hour* rate and can be effectively used where the work is of a manual and skilled nature, such as carpentering, painting, grinding, riveting, drilling, polishing, and assembling.

The formula used in determining the rate is:

$$R = \frac{\text{Estimated manufacturing overhead, \$456,000}}{\text{Estimated number of man-hours, 180,000}} = \$2.53\frac{1}{3} \text{ per man-hour.}$$

Machine-Hour Basis   The machine-hour basis is similar to the labor hour method and is used where the work is performed primarily on machines. In many concerns a large proportion of the manufacturing overhead is made up of depreciation on machines, power, and repairs to machines; overhead can therefore be charged more accurately to production on a machine-hour basis. The method does require additional clerical expense in computing the machine-hours on each job.

The formula used in computing the rate is:

$$R = \frac{\text{Estimated manufacturing overhead, \$456,000}}{\text{Estimated machine-hours, 84,000}} = \$5.42\frac{6}{7} \text{ per machine-hour.}$$

As in the case of the labor-cost-basis method, this machine-hour method can be used to advantage when a concern wishes to compute and apply manufacturing overhead to production on a departmental basis and where in some departments it might be desirable to use the percentage of labor cost method and in others the machine-hour method. It should be emphasized that both the labor hour and the machine-hour methods are desirable because they consider the time factor which influences the amounts of many overhead cost items.

Machine-Hour Plus a Supplementary Rate   The use of the machine-hour rate for applying manufacturing overhead is sometimes modified by a second, or "supplementary," rate. Under this method, there is a machine-hour rate for applying the overhead to production, and at the end of each month or year, the overapplied or underapplied manufacturing overhead is distributed by the use of a supplementary rate. This supplementary rate serves to correct the error in the predetermined rate; and when it has been used to take care of this adjustment, there no longer is any overapplied or underapplied overhead.

The objections to the use of this procedure are apparent. First, it is costly to readjust the job sheets for a given period, particularly when there are a great number of them. Second, the final costs on each job must be held up until the end of the month or the end of the year, when the adjustments by the supplementary rate are made. Finally, the particular value of this method is somewhat doubtful. If the overhead rates are carefully computed at the beginning of each period, the amount of the overapplied or underapplied manufacturing overhead should not be very large and this can be conveniently closed into the Cost of Goods Sold account.

There is a second interpretation of the *machine-hour rate plus a supplementary rate*. Where the factory has been departmentalized, it is possible to have a machine-hour rate for the various departments. In calculating this rate, only those indirect costs which originate in or are chargeable directly to the respective departments are used. In other words, the machine-hour rate is a direct departmental overhead rate. For all other manufacturing overhead, that is, general factory overhead, a second or supplementary rate can be used. This rate will be the same for the entire factory. Therefore, on each job sheet, in addition to the overhead applied on the basis of machine-hours, there will appear a second charge at the supplementary rate.

Moving-Average Method

This method uses actual figures for the past 12 months in ascertaining overhead rates. No estimated or predetermined overhead figures are necessary. Actual manufacturing overhead for the past 12 months is totaled and averaged (by dividing by 12). The resulting average represents the amount of manufacturing overhead applicable to production for the following month. The overhead rate may be based upon the material cost, labor cost, labor hour, machine-hour, or production unit. However, this method has very little application in business today.

Using More Than One Manufacturing Overhead Rate in Costing Production

In the interest of more accurate costing, some firms compute and use more than one manufacturing overhead rate in place of a single rate. This multirate procedure may involve several approaches:

1. *Departmental versus a single predetermined rate.* Instead of using a single plantwide rate, many firms analyze the manufacturing overhead costs by departments and then compute a separate rate for the work done in each department. These departmental rates usually apply only to the producing departments. The detailed procedure is discussed in more detail later in this chapter.
2. *Special rates for material handling costs.* In firms where materials are used only in some of the departments, it is felt that the material handling costs—freight-in, storage, inventory recordings, delivery to factory costs, etc.—are really part of the costs of the materials used, and as such should be charged to the departments using the material on some predetermined rate basis such as a percent of the cost of materials used.
3. *General administrative expense costs* of a multiplant organization often requires the allocation of some of these costs to the various manufacturing plants. These must then be absorbed by the cost of manufacturing in these plants. This can best be done by a separate rate, unless the amount is included with the general factory overhead costs.
4. *Separate fixed and variable overhead cost rates.* In order to create the maximum control over the manufacturing costs, many firms analyze their overhead costs into the fixed and variable elements, using separate rates for each group.

Departmentalization of the Manufacturing Overhead

Computing overhead rates on a departmental basis results in better cost control by localizing the variations from the budgeted and the actual costs. A *department or a production center* of a factory for cost accounting purposes has been defined as a group of machines or workers performing similar operations. For example, a group of employees working at benches assembling vacuum cleaners would be considered the *assembly department;* a group of men operating a large stamping machine would be considered the *stamping department;* and a group of employees painting the final product might be described as the *painting* or *finishing* department. Departments must be further classified as *producing* or *service* departments. A producing department is one in which the actual manufacturing operations are performed such as cutting, assembling, drilling, and painting. Service departments are those whose activities are necessary to facilitate the manufacturing operations, but in which no manufacturing work is actually performed, such as the materials handling department, the powerhouse activities, maintenance and repair of plant and equipment department, factory toolroom, factory hospital, and factory lunchroom. Since the service departments do not involve *directly* the manufacturing operations, it will be necessary to apply the overhead of the service departments on some rational basis. It may be done under three possible arrangements:

1. *Reciprocal basis* under which the service department expenses are distributed to the various other departments so that when it is completed, the entire manufacturing overhead costs are distributed to the *producing* departments.
2. *Direct basis* under which the manufacturing overhead costs are allocated only to the producing departments, with none to the service departments—thus making it unnecessary to redistribute the service department overhead costs to the producing departments.
3. *Nonreciprocal basis* under which there is an accumulation of the service departments overhead costs and under which a separate rate is computed for each service department as well as for each producing department.

However, although there are three basic methods for use in allocating the manufacturing overhead, the only practical method is the reciprocal method under which all the service department overhead costs are redistributed to the producing departments, and thus when completed, there are predetermined rates only for the producing departments.

Procedure Used in Departmentalizing Indirect Factory Costs

The procedure to be followed in departmentalizing manufacturing overhead may be outlined as follows:

A. SETTING DEPARTMENTAL RATES

1. Prepare a list of the estimated or budgeted overhead costs for the entire plant.
2. Decide what bases are to be used in allocating the various costs to the departments, service as well as production (such as floor space, production hours, etc.).
3. Prepare a factory survey (statistical summary) of these bases and use this information to distribute the budgeted overhead costs to the various departments.
4. Transfer the service department costs to the producing department so that all the budgeted costs will be assigned to producing departments only.
5. Estimate the number of labor hours, machine-hours, etc., to be used as the denominator in calculating departmental rates.
6. Compute the predetermined rates by dividing the estimated departmental overhead by the estimated base.

B. APPLYING OVERHEAD RATES

1. Apply the predetermined overhead rates to the finished jobs and the work-in-process on a departmental basis.

C. RECORDING ACTUAL OVERHEAD COSTS

1. Record overhead actually incurred in the Manufacturing Overhead Control account, posting details to the subsidiary ledger.
2. Prepare a work sheet analysis similar to the one used in distributing estimated costs by departments.
3. Calculate the over- or underapplied manufacturing overhead by department and dispose of this difference at the close of the fiscal year.

To amplify the procedures listed above, the following discussion should be carefully examined.

A–1 and A–2. Bases for Allocating and Prorating Manufacturing Overhead Departmentally. The first step in prorating the manufacturing overhead departmentally is the preparation of a list of the estimated or budgeted overhead costs for the entire plant, as shown in Illustration 8–1. After this has been done, the cost accountant is faced with the problem of allocating these costs departmentally. Some of these overhead costs may be allocated *directly* to the various departments, both producing and service, since they may arise solely within the department affected or may be measured as a departmental direct charge. Others are plantwide charges which must be *prorated* to the various departments on some equitable basis.

Those *indirect costs* which can be charged directly to the departments affected may be items such as indirect materials and indirect labor; electricity where each department has a meter measuring arrangement; payroll taxes and compensation insurance costs based upon departmental payrolls; and depreciation charges based upon departmental equipment investment. The procedure of departmentalization of indirect costs directly to the departments affected is known as *allocation.*

Some indirect costs, however, do not lend themselves to accurate allocation. These must be prorated, and the results must be approximately correct. For example, in prorating the building maintenance costs, such as rent, taxes, insurance, and repairs, it is assumed that each location in the building is of equal value and that by using the square footage as a basis, a reasonable distribution of these costs to the various departments can be computed. There are many other charges which must be similarly treated.

Except for those indirect costs whose allocation is obtained by direct measurement, the basic procedure for allocating or prorating factory

Illustration 8–1. Budgeted Overhead Costs and Bases for Allocation

Cost Item	Amount	Basis of Distribution to Departments
Indirect materials	$11,000	Estimated departmental use
Indirect labor	5,600	Estimated departmental use
Superintendence	5,000	Number of workers
Fire insurance on machinery	1,200	Value of equipment in department
Compensation insurance	1,600	Estimated department payroll
Light	800	Kilowatt-hours
Power	2,400	Horsepower-hours
Fuel	1,000	Heat Service Department in total
Repairs to machinery	4,000	To Maintenance Department in total
Depreciation of machinery	4,200	Value of equipment in each department
Rent	2,400	Square footage
Total Estimated Overhead Costs	$39,200	

overhead requires the preparation of a *factory survey* which will give the information about the number of square feet, the number of employees, the investment, and other facts necessary for indirect cost distribution. Illustration 8–2 presents some suggested bases for overhead cost distribution.

A–3. Factory Survey for the Distribution of Indirect Costs to the Departments. After the bases for distribution have been agreed upon for a plant, a survey of the factory and adjoining facilities is made to ascertain how each of these bases affects each of the departments. The facts presented in the survey are first used in allocating the estimated indirect costs to the departments so that the predetermined departmental overhead rates may be computed. *The same survey is used as a basis for allocating or prorating the actual indirect costs to the departmental overhead accounts,* through a departmental analysis sheet or a work sheet.

This survey may be used year after year with slight adjustments for such items as investments, payroll, or electricity used. In using this

*Illustration 8–2. Bases of Departmentalization
of Factory Overhead Costs*

Basis of Distribution	Indirect Costs Distributed on this Basis
Square footage	Rent of factory Taxes on factory Depreciation of factory buildings Repairs to factory buildings Fire insurance on buildings Heat expense, where separately charged
Number of employees	Superintendence Factory lunchroom costs Factory hospital costs Cost accounting costs Toolroom costs
Pay of employees	Compensation insurance Payroll taxes
Rated capacity	Light (when not metered for each department)
Horsepower-hours	Power (when not metered for each department)
Investment in equipment	Fire insurance on machinery Depreciation on machinery Machinery repairs (if not charged directly) Personal property taxes
Direct departmental charges	Indirect labor Machinery repairs
Number of electric light bulbs	Light charges are distributed on this basis if all bulbs are of a uniform wattage

survey it is necessary to estimate the total indirect manufacturing costs for a given period. A large number of these estimated costs, such as rent, insurance, superintendence, depreciation, etc., may be determined exactly.

A hypothetical factory situation is set up to illustrate the nature of a survey (see Illustration 8–3). There are four departments actually engaged in the manufacturing processes and three service departments: the maintenance and repair department, air-conditioning service, and heating service. It is assumed that the power is purchased rather than manufactured. The bases for prorating the estimated manufacturing overhead for the year are as given in Illustration 8–3.

The item of rent is used to illustrate how these estimated indirect costs are prorated to the departments in conjunction with a survey.

Department A occupies 400 square feet out of a total of 3,000. This department, therefore, would be charged with 400/3,000 of $2,400, or $320; Department B, with an area of 500 square feet, would be charged with 500/3,000 of $2,400, or $400; etc.

A similar prorating method is used for each of the other indirect costs.

A–4. Transfer the Service Department Overhead Costs to the Producing Departments. Although a few firms use a separate predetermined rate for each of the service departments, this procedure is not practical because it becomes too complicated. Therefore, in most factories the budgeted manufacturing overhead costs for the service

Illustration 8–3. Factory Survey for Year 19—

Department	Basis					
	Square Feet	No. of Employees	Total Pay to Employees	KW Hours	H.P. Hours	Investment
Producing Department A	400	10	$12,000	800	3,200	$10,000
Producing Department B	500	10	10,000	800	800	5,000
Producing Department C	600	15	20,000	1,200		1,000
Producing Department D	800	20	30,000	2,000	1,600	7,500
Maintenance service	300	5	4,000	100	200	2,500
Air-conditioning service	200	3	2,000	50	100	1,000
Heating service	200	2	2,000	50	100	1,000
Total	3,000	65	$80,000	5,000	6,000	$28,000

departments are prorated to the producing departments on the basis rendered to the respective departments. When the producing departments have been charged with all the prorated indirect costs as well as the *service* department's costs, a predetermined manufacturing overhead rate is calculated for each producing department, for use in determining the overhead charges to be entered on the job order cost sheets.

The apportionment of the service department overhead costs to the other departments may sometimes cause difficulty because some of the service departments may render service to other service departments. To avoid too many complications, the *sequence* in which the service department manufacturing overhead is to be distributed to the producing departments must be established. For example, the maintenance of equipment department serves not only the producing departments but also the other service departments; the air-conditioning and heating departments do likewise. A safe rule to follow in apportioning service department costs is to *first* close out the amount for that service department which affects the *greatest number of other service departments*. If such a distinction is not possible, as in the case above, close first the amount for the service department which involves *the largest amount of costs*. Once a service department overhead has been closed, no further items are distributed to it.

A list of estimated indirect costs shown in Illustration 8–1, together with the proration to the service and producing departments, is shown in the tabulation of Illustration 8–4. The proration is based upon the factory survey shown in Illustration 8–3.

In the table of distribution given in Illustration 8–4, the amount of maintenance department costs was distributed first because it involved the largest amount. The basis of distribution to the other departments was the *equipment investment* in each department. After the amount for the maintenance department costs was closed, the air-conditioning department costs were distributed. It should be noted that the amount distributed to the other departments included not only the original amount of $2,171.60 but the additional amount of $300 charged from the distribution of the maintenance department overhead. Air-conditioning costs were distributed to the other departments on the basis of *square footage*. Although the usual basis for distributing air-conditioning and heat costs is the cubic footage, square footage is equally satisfactory if the ceilings are of a uniform height. Heating department costs were distributed to the producing departments, but the amount so distributed included the costs added from the maintenance and air-conditioning departments.

A–5 and A–6. Computing the Departmental Predetermined Overhead Rate. When the budgeted overhead costs have been properly allocated to the producing departments (including the distribution of the service departments overhead costs), then a predetermined overhead rate must be computed for each producing department. To do this, management must decide what base is to be used in the various departments for this overhead application. It might be: *a percent of labor costs; a dollar and cents rate per direct labor hour; or a dollar and cents rates per machine-hour.* This then necessitates the *estimate* of the labor costs, the labor hours, or the machine-hours for the period covered by the budgeted overhead costs. In Illustration 8–5, the manufacturing overhead rates are computed departmentally. In this illustration, it was estimated that in Department A there would be 11,500 direct labor hours; in Department B, $30,464 direct labor costs; in Department C, $41,598 direct labor costs; and in Department D, 47,400 machine hours. Using this information together with the allocation of the budgeted

Illustration 8–4. The Departmentalization of the Estimated Indirect Manufacturing Costs for the Year 19—

Cost Item	Service Departments			Producing Departments				Total
	Maintenance	Air Con.	Heating	A	B	C	D	
Indirect material	$1,000.00	$ 700.00	$ 300.00	$ 2,000.00	$1,200.00	$3,000.00	$ 2,800.00	$11,000.00
Indirect labor	1,200.00	800.00	1,100.00	700.00	800.00	1,000.00	1,000.00	5,600.00
Superintendence*	384.60	230.75	153.85	769.25	769.25	1,153.80	1,538.80	5,000.00
Fire insurance on machinery*	107.15	42.85	42.85	428.55	214.30	42.85	321.45	1,200.00
Compensation insurance	80.00	40.00	40.00	240.00	200.00	400.00	600.00	1,600.00
Light	16.00	8.00	8.00	128.00	128.00	192.00	320.00	800.00
Power	80.00	40.00	40.00	1,280.00	320.00		640.00	2,400.00
Fuel			1,000.00					1,000.00
Repairs to machinery	4,000.00							4,000.00
Depreciation of machinery	375.00	150.00	150.00	1,500.00	750.00	150.00	1,125.00	4,200.00
Rent	240.00	160.00	160.00	320.00	400.00	480.00	640.00	2,400.00
Total	$7,482.75	$2,171.60	$2,994.70					$39,200.00
Maintenance*		300.00	300.00	2,982.75	1,500.00	300.00	2,100.00	$ 7,482.75
Total		$2,471.60						
Air conditioning*			200.00	400.00	500.00	600.00	771.60	$ 2,471.60
Total			$3,494.70					
Heating*				665.00	835.00	1,000.00	994.70	$ 3,494.70
Total				$11,413.55	$7,616.55	$8,318.65	$11,851.25	$39,200.00
Basis of predetermining rate				11,500 direct labor hours	$30,464.00 direct labor costs	$41,598.00 direct labor costs	47,400 machine-hours	
Predetermined departmental overhead rates				$1.00 per labor hour	25% of direct labor costs	20% of direct labor costs*	25¢ per machine-hour	

* Approximated calculations of the distributions

Illustration 8–5. Computation of Predetermined Overhead Rates

Department	Predetermined Overhead	Basis of Predetermining Rate	Predetermined Overhead Rate on Departmental Basis*
Producing Department A	$11,413.55	11,500 direct labor hours	$1 per labor-hour*
Producing Department B	7,616.55	$30,464 direct labor costs	25% of direct labor costs*
Producing Department C	8,318.65	$41,598 direct labor costs	20% of direct labor costs
Producing Department D	11,851.25	47,400 machine-hours	25¢ per machine-hour

* Approximate calculation.

overhead costs as shown in Illustration 8–4, it is possible to compute the departmental overhead rates as shown in Illustration 8–5 as follows:

Producing Department A.........$1 per man-hour
Producing Department B......... 25% of direct labor costs
Producing Department C......... 20% of direct labor costs
Producing Department D......... 25¢ per machine-hour

B–1. Applying Manufacturing Overhead Costs Departmentally. When departmental overhead rates are used, the design of the job order sheets must be changed so that the overhead may be recorded in separate columns representing the different departments (Illustration 8–6). In this illustration, manufacturing overhead is applied departmentally:

Machine Department No. 1 on the basis of machine-hours.
Machine Department No. 2 on the basis of machine-hours.
Assembling department on the basis of labor hours.
Finishing department as a percent of labor costs.

Since in Machine Departments No. 1 and No. 2 it is necessary to record the machine-hours and in Assembling the labor hours, space must be provided for recording this data in the Payroll section of the job order cost sheet. Parallel columns are then provided for recording the manufacturing overhead.

Paralleling this procedure, applied manufacturing overhead accounts must be maintained for each producing department. The entry, made weekly or monthly, to record the applied manufacturing overhead would be:

Work-in-Process—Manufacturing Overhead......................6,000.00
    Applied Manufacturing Overhead—Department No. 1.........   600.00
    Applied Manufacturing Overhead—Department No. 2.........   100.00
    Applied Manufacturing Overhead—Assembling...............   1,500.00
    Applied Manufacturing Overhead—Finishing................   3,800.00
    To record overhead applied to production.

Illustration 8–6. Cost of Production Report Showing Manufacturing Overhead and Labor Costs Departmentalized

PRODUCTION ORDER & JOB ORDER COST SHEET

FOR Browning Mfg Co JOB NUMBER 10-142

ADDRESS Houston, Texas DATE Oct 20, 19--

DESCRIPTION 5 Special Machines CUSTOMER'S NUMBER OM-7-487

DATE COMPLETED Nov. 11. 19- SELLING PRICE $6500.00 TOTAL COST $3172.00 UNIT COST $634.40

DATE	DIRECT LABOR COSTS — MACH. DEPT. #1 Mach. Hrs.	Amount	MACH. DEPT. #2 Mach. Hrs.	Amount	ASSEMBLING Labor Hrs.	Amount	FINISHING Amount	MATERIAL COSTS Date	Req. No.	Amount
Oct 28	30	90.00	10	33.00				Oct 20	651	160.00
Nov 4	25	80.00	10	33.00	32	100.00		30	658	200.00
Nov 11					60	200.00	600.00	Nov 7	690	400.00
Totals		170.00		66.00		300.00	600.00			760.00

DATE	APPLIED MANUFACTURING OVERHEAD COSTS — MACH. DEPT. #1 Hrs.	R.	Amt.	MACH. DEPT. #2 Hrs.	R.	Amount	ASSEMBLING Hrs.	R.	Amount	FINISHING Cost	%	Amt.	SUMMARY Cost Element	Amount
Oct 28	30	2.00	60.00	10	1.80	18.00							MATERIAL	760.00
Nov 4	25	2.00	50.00	10	1.80	18.00	32	2.50	80.00				LABOR #1	170.00
Nov 11							60	2.50	150.00	600.00	150%	900.00	LABOR #2	66.00
													LABOR #3	300.00
													LABOR #4	600.00
													O.H. #1	110.00
													O.H. #2	36.00
													O.H. #3	230.00
													O.H. #4	900.00
Total			110.00			36.00			230.00			900.00	TOTAL COST	3172.00

The above entry is a summary of the applied overhead costs recorded on the job order cost sheets for the period.

C–1, C–2, and C–3. Recording the Actual Manufacturing Overhead Costs. The procedures, problems, and methods of recording the actual overhead costs will be discussed in Chapter 9 which follows.

Analyzing Overhead Costs into Their Fixed and Variable Elements

As previously indicated, *fixed overhead* costs do not fluctuate in response to fluctuations in volume. They may fluctuate from period to period. In fact, fixed overhead costs may exist when there is no production at all. *Variable* overhead costs fluctuate in the same direction and usually proportionately with the volume of production. *Semivariable* overhead costs while fluctuating in the same direction as volume, do so in less than the proportional changes in volume of production, and frequently in "steps" rather than in a continuous manner. It might be assumed that since a *basic* figure for semivariable overhead will exist with a minimum volume of production, this cost could be considered fixed.

On the theory that factory management and supervision has little or no control over the fixed or period overhead costs but has considerable control over the variable overhead costs, it becomes necessary to separate manufacturing overhead costs into their fixed and variable elements. This separation and the subsequent comparison of these costs from period to period, or from job to job, will provide a more reliable measurement of the managerial achievements in cost reduction through the variable overhead. By examining the flucatation in costs and production of the semivariable overhead item of *inspection costs*—Illustration 8–7, showing figures arranged in order of the volume of production, not chronologically—it is possible to compute the increase in costs due to increase in volume of production—the *variable* element of the cost. To illustrate, the following data are used:

Month	Volume of Production	Inspection Costs
January	120,000 units	$ 8,000
February	120,000	8,000
March	145,000	9,500
April	142,000	9,300
May	150,000	9,800
June	130,000	8,300
July	135,000	8,750
August	157,000	10,392
September	155,000	10,200
October	100,000	7,000
November	140,000	9,200
December	140,000	9,200

The increase in the volume of production of 57,000 units over the base or minimum figure of the October production of 100,000 resulted in an increase in the inspection costs of $3,392, or the equivalent of 5.95 cents per unit ($3,392 ÷ 57,000 units). This 5.95 cents is assumed to be the *average* variable cost since it fluctuated with the

Illustration 8–7. Analysis of the Inspection Costs for the Previous Year

Month	Volume of Production (Units)	Cost of Inspection	Increase in Volume of Production (Units)	Increase in Cost of Production Due to Inspection Costs
October	100,000	$ 7,000	...	...
January	120,000	8,000	20,000	$1,000
February	120,000	8,000	...	...
June	130,000	8,300	10,000	300
July	135,000	8,750	5,000	450
November	140,000	9,200	5,000	450
December	140,000	9,200	...	...
April	142,000	9,300	2,000	100
March	145,000	9,500	3,000	200
May	150,000	9,800	5,000	300
September	155,000	10,200	5,000	400
August	157,000	10,392	2,000	192
Total			57,000	$3,392

volume of production. In prorating the inspection costs for each month between the fixed and variable amounts the actual production is multiplied by this variable cost per unit, and the balance is considered the *fixed* inspection cost. It should be noted that this is merely a mathematical procedure for dividing the costs into the controllable and noncontrollable factors. To illustrate this proration:

```
Production for October, 100,000 units, variable cost @ 5.95¢......$5,950
Balance is fixed cost.........................................  1,050
    Total Inspection Cost......................................$7,000
```

On the basis of these computations, it will be assumed that for each month the *fixed* portion of the inspection costs will be $1,050, and the balance variable. Following this procedure, it is possible to prepare a budget of the estimated manufacturing overhead costs, showing the fixed and variable parts of each item, and thereafter to compute a separate rate for the fixed and variable items, or a combined rate. Since management is interested in the *controllability* of the variable portion of the various manufacturing overhead costs, separation into two parts is desirable. The analysis of manufacturing overhead shown in Illustration 8–8 has been prepared in a manner similar to that just described, showing what part of each cost is considered fixed and what part is considered variable.

Illustration 8–8. Analysis of Manufacturing Overhead Estimated for Year Ending December 31, 19—

Overhead Cost Item	Fixed	Variable	Total
Indirect materials..............................		$12,000	$ 12,000
Fuel..$ 6,000		2,000	8,000
Superintendence............................... 12,000			12,000
Inspection................................... 12,600		2,500	15,100
Material handling............................. 6,000		4,000	10,000
Indirect labor................................		14,000	14,000
Payroll taxes................................. 1,300		900	2,200
Maintenance of buildings........................ 3,000			3,000
Repairs and maintenance of equipment............		7,000	7,000
Telephone and telegraph....................... 500		2,500	3,000
Depreciation—machinery and equipment........... 10,000			10,000
Workmen's compensation insurance............... 200		800	1,000
Light.. 500		3,500	4,000
Power.......................................		12,000	12,000
Rent.. 10,800			10,800
Small tools..................................		5,200	5,200
Total................................$62,900		$66,400	$129,300

In addition to the previous method of separating the semivariable and semifixed overhead into the fixed and variable portions (known as the high-low method), two other methods are used: (1) the scattergraph method and (2) the method of least squares.

Illustration 8–9. Scattergraph of Fixed and Variable Overhead Costs

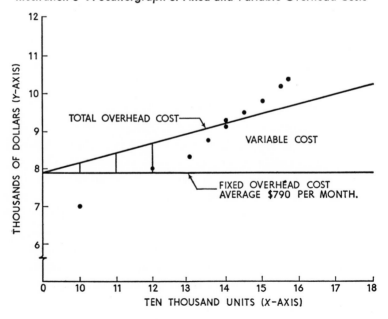

The *scattergraph method* involves the plotting of the cost and volume data on a sheet of graph paper and fitting a line by sight to these data (see Illustration 8–9). The fixed element can be read from the graph at the point where the overhead cost line crosses the Y-axis. Examining this graph, the following situations exist:

	Fixed Overhead	Variable	Total
January	$790	$7,200	$7,990
February	790	7,200	7,990
March	790	8,700	9,490

As is evident, these figures are approximate but would come out exactly were precise mathematical calculations involved. Here, the application and theory are important. Calculating the variable overhead cost on a unit basis results in a figure of approximately 60 cents per unit.

The least squares method of separating overhead costs into their fixed and variable elements is an application of statistics to accounting. This mathematical method eliminates the guesswork used in the scattergraph method, since it is unlikely that the 12 points in a scattergraph will result in a straight line. In this method, the line is determined by means of the statistical technique of least squares. The line represents a situation in which the sum of the squared deviations is a minimum. Two simultaneous linear equations are necessary to determine the fixed cost element and the variable cost per unit of activity. For any given month, the mathematical implication of these formulae is:

Fixed overhead cost + (Unit variable overhead allowance × Production)
= Total overhead.

The linear equations are:

(1) $$\Sigma XY = a\Sigma X + b\Sigma X^2$$
(2) $$\Sigma Y = na + b\Sigma X$$

in which

X = number of units of production.
Y = total overhead cost at a given level of production.
n = number of observations (months).
a = fixed cost amount.
b = variable cost per unit of production.

To illustrate this method of least squares, the data given for the scattergraph are used and will be tabulated in accordance with the formulae requirements (see Illustration 8–10).

Illustration 8–10

Month	X Units of Production (Thousands)	Y Inspection Costs	XY	X²
January..........................	120	$ 8,000	$ 960,000	$ 14,400
February.........................	120	8,000	960,000	14,400
March............................	145	9,500	1,377,500	21,025
April............................	140	9,300	1,302,000	19,600
May..............................	150	9,800	1,470,000	22,500
June.............................	130	8,300	1,079,000	16,900
July.............................	135	8,750	1,181,250	18,225
August...........................	157	10,390	1,631,230	24,649
September........................	155	10,200	1,581,000	24,025
October..........................	100	7,000	700,000	10,000
November.........................	140	9,200	1,288,000	19,600
December.........................	140	9,200	1,288,000	19,600
	1,632	$107,640	$14,817,980	$224,924

Using this data in the formula, the equations would be:

(1)
$$\Sigma XY = a(\Sigma X) + b(\Sigma X^2)$$
$$\$14,817,980 = a(1,632) + b(224,924)$$

(2)
$$\Sigma Y = na + b(\Sigma X)$$
$$\$107,640 = 12a + 1,632b$$

Solving these two simultaneous equations, a will be the fixed inspection costs for the month, or $810[1] and b will be the variable cost per thousand units of production or $60.[1]

A shortcut procedure for the least squares method would be as shown in Illustration 8–11.

The variable rate per thousand units of production is as follows:

$$\frac{178,940}{2,972} = 60.$$

The fixed element per month is computed as follows: Average total cost per month minus average total variable cost per month equals the total fixed cost per month.

$$8,970 - (60 \times 136) = \$810 \text{ approximate.}$$

---

[1] Approximate figures.

Illustration 8–11

Month	(1) Difference from Average of Units of Production 1,632 ÷ 12 = 136	(2) Column (1) Squared	(3) Difference from Average of Inspection Costs $107,640 ÷ 12 = $8,970	(4) Column 1 × Column 3
January	−16	256	$ −970	15,520
February	−16	256	−970	15,520
March	+9	81	530	4,770
April	+4	16	330	1,320
May	+14	196	830	11,620
June	−6	36	−670	4,020
July	−1	1	−220	220
August	+21	441	1,420	29,820
September	+19	361	1,230	23,370
October	−36	1,296	−1,970	70,920
November	+4	16	230	920
December	+4	16	230	920
Total	0	2,972	0	178,940

It should be noted that the high-low, statistical scattergraph, and least squares methods of separating fixed and variable costs are all based on an analysis of past performance. From a control standpoint, this may perpetuate waste and inefficiency. We should encourage a fresh, engineering point of view which looks at what costs should be rather than what they were.

Controlling Costs through the Use of a Flexible Manufacturing Overhead Budget

Introductory budgetary procedure was discussed in Chapter 4. A budget is a plan of action. It is used to measure actual results. Material and labor costs are variable costs and therefore subject to control. Manufacturing overhead may be fixed with a limited amount of cost control or it may be flexible, in which case it is the area in which major cost control can be exercised. Therefore the manufacturing overhead budget is made up of two parts—the fixed and flexible costs. The fixed part is comparable to the static budget; the flexible part is the one which varies with production and is therefore subject to a certain amount of supervisory control.

Overhead rates are usually determined and used for a definite period of time—usually on an annual basis, subject to correction if they are extremely out of line with actual conditions.

By preparing and using a flexible manufacturing overhead budget as shown in Illustration 8–12, it is possible to compare the actual operating results with those that should have occurred because of fluctuating volume of production. From this comparison, it is possible to determine whether the variations in overhead costs are due to volume of production or to the cost of the overhead—thus serving as a tool of managerial control of costs.

In Illustration 8–12, if it is assumed that at the start of the

Illustration 8–12

FLEXIBLE MANUFACTURING OVERHEAD COST BUDGET

FOR THE CUTTING DEPARTMENT*

For Year Ending December 31, 19—

Element of Overhead	Operating Capacity				
	40%	60%	80%	100%	110%
Variable overhead costs:					
Indirect materials........	$ 4,800	$ 7,200	$ 9,600	$ 12,000	$ 13,200
Fuel.................	800†	1,000†	1,500†	2,000†	2,200†
Inspection.............	0	200†	300†	500†	600†
Materials handling.......	1,500†	2,600†	3,000†	4,000†	4,500†
Indirect labor...........	5,000	8,000	11,200	14,000	15,500
Payroll taxes...........	360†	540†	720†	900†	1,000†
Equipment repairs and maintenance..........	2,640	4,260	5,580	7,000	7,500
Telephone and telegraph	1,000†	1,500†	2,000†	2,500†	2,800†
Compensation insurance..	300†	500†	650†	800†	900†
Light..................	1,400†	2,100†	2,800†	3,500†	3,800†
Power.................	4,800	7,200	9,600	12,000	13,200
Small tools.............	2,000	3,000	4,000	5,200	5,800
Total Variable Costs	$ 24,600	$ 38,100	$ 50,950	$ 64,400	$ 71,000
Fixed overhead costs:					
Fuel.................				$ 6,000‡	
Superintendence.........				12,000	
Inspection.............				8,000‡	
Materials handling.......				6,000‡	
Payroll taxes...........				1,300‡	
Building maintenance....				3,000	
Telephone and telegraph				500‡	
Depreciation—equipment				10,000	
Compensation insurance..				200‡	
Light..................				500‡	
Rent..................				10,800	
Total Fixed Overhead........	$ 58,300	$ 58,300	$ 58,300	$ 58,300	$ 58,300
Estimated direct labor costs.................	$140,000	$190,000	$250,000	$300,000	$340,000
Predetermined rate—variable	1.76%	2.00%	2.04%	2.15%	2.09%
Predetermined rate—fixed	4.16%	3.07%	2.33%	1.94%	1.71%

* Similar schedules must be prepared for each producing department.
† Variable portion of semivariable overhead costs.
‡ Fixed portion of semivariable overhead costs.

accounting period the plant would be operating at 80 percent capacity during the coming year, then the predetermined rates for overhead would be 2.04 percent for the variable overhead and 2.33 percent of labor costs for the fixed overhead. These would be used during the coming year. Any over- or underapplied manufacturing overhead would then be reconciled to the overhead costs and the predetermined rates, to ascertain how much of the variation was due to costs and how much to the volume of production. The foremen would have some definite plan for measuring their operating efficiency.

QUESTIONS FOR REVIEW

1. Why is it necessary to classify manufacturing overhead as fixed, variable, semifixed, and semivariable? How can this distinction be recognized in the accounting records?

2. What is meant by normal *operating conditions?* Why is this information important in manufacturing overhead accounting?

3. Predetermined overhead rates are rarely accurate. Why are they used? When are they determined?

4. In calculating the predetermined rate for manufacturing overhead, the estimated overhead is divided by the estimated volume. How is *volume* indicated in manufacturing operations?

5. *Volume* of production is considered the *base* upon which manufacturing overhead is calculated and applied to production. In considering the *volume,* indicate:
   a) The two major groups into which volume may be classified.
   b) Which of these two groups seems more accurate?
   c) Which volumes are used by the majority of business firms today? Why?

6. Are predetermined rates required in process cost accounting? Explain.

7. *Supplementary rate* has been variously described in cost accounting. What are the various meanings of supplementary rate of manufacturing overhead?

8. Under what conditions do you feel that a separate manufacturing overhead rate should be used for the *material handling costs?* When do you feel that a separate rate should not be used?

9. Some firms use more than one manufacturing overhead rate in costing production. Under what conditions would it seem desirable to use more than one rate? Illustrate your answers.

10. The Progressive Machine Company has been subletting some of its manufacturing operations. By installing a single filling and sealing machine at a cost of $30,000, automatically controlled, all the work can be performed which was previously sublet at a savings of $3,000 in cost for the volume previously produced. However, this machine is used only four hours a day throughout the week because of its automatic and high-speed capacity.

All other machine centers compute their manufacturing overhead on an eight-hour day, 40 hours per week. How do you feel that the manufacturing overhead rate for this department should be determined so that no inequities will result?

PROBLEMS—GROUP A

Problem 8–1.   Purpose: *Various Methods of Applying Manufacturing Overhead*

The Peterson Manufacturing Company opened a new plant in Elletsville where tools and dies will be manufactured on a job order basis. Management is currently making a study of the various possibilities of applying the manufacturing overhead to production.

The planning budget for the year contained the following:

Direct materials	$144,000
Direct labor	218,000
Direct labor hours	60,000
Machine hours	50,000
Manufacturing overhead	218,000

There was no work-in-process at the beginning of the period. Actual data for the first month of operations follow:

Job	Material	Labor Dollars	Labor Hours	Machine-Hours	Status at End of Month
456x	$ 1,800	$ 1,200	350	220	Completed
457x	1,200	850	200	220	Completed
458x	850	600	170	300	Completed
459x	1,000	700	180	120	Completed
460x	16,000	10,700	1,500	1,100	In process
416x	1,500	950	240	460	Completed
417x	2,200	1,500	360	310	In process

Required:

a) Calculate predetermined overhead rates based upon each of the following:

   (1) Direct labor hours.
   (2) Direct labor dollars.
   (3) Machine-hours.
   (4) Prime cost.

b) Compute the cost of completing Jobs 457x and 459x using each of the four rates computed in (*a*).

c) Compute the over- or underapplied overhead for each of the four methods under the assumption that the actual overhead for the month was $16,000.

Problem 8–2.   Purpose: *Determination of Predetermined Overhead Rate*

The Parker Chemical Corporation produces a chemical known as "par" at its Plant No. 10. The plant has three producing departments and a general factory service department.

A flexible overhead budget for the coming month has been set as follows for each of the departments:

> Department A............$1.00 per labor hour plus $15,000
> Department B........... 0.50 per labor dollar plus $6,000
> Department C............ 1.50 per labor hour plus $8,000
> General factory........... 0.20 per labor hour plus $7,000

The general factory overhead is allocated to the producing departments on the basis of labor hours.

The budgeted production to be used in establishment of rates is as follows:

	Labor Hours	Labor Dollars
Department A............	16,000	$50,000
Department B............	9,000	26,000
Department C............	5,000	12,000

The actual experience for the month of April resulted in the following:

	Labor Hours	Labor Dollars	Direct Overhead
Department A...............	14,000	$46,000	$21,000
Department B...............	10,000	27,000	13,100
Department C...............	4,000	11,000	13,900
General factory..............			16,000

Required:

a) Compute the predetermined overhead rates for each of the departments.

b) Compute the over- or underapplied overhead for each of the departments.

c) Prepare journal entries recording overhead transactions for the month.

Problem 8–3.   Purpose: *Determining Overhead Rates Using Flexible Budget*

The Powell Furniture Company manufactures chairs on a continuous process operation in three producing departments: cutting, assembling, and painting. The overhead costs for the period have been budgeted as follows:

	Variable Costs	Fixed Costs
Cutting.................	$12,000	$20,000
Assembling.............	24,000	14,000
Painting................	8,000	9,000

The normal production for the period is 8,000 chairs.

Required:

a) Compute the predetermined rate for overhead for each of the departments based upon normal production.

b) Compute the predetermined rate for overhead for each of the departments based upon the assumption that the plant will operate at 70 percent of capacity during the coming period.

c) Explain the difference in rates computed in (*a*) and (*b*).

Problem 8–4. Purpose: *Computing Manufacturing Overhead Rates*

The budget committee of the Pelham Corporation is in the process of preparing the annual budget for the next fiscal year. You have been called in to aid in the development of predetermined overhead rates for the producing departments as the direct overhead charges for each of the departments has already been determined.

The planing and machine departments will use labor dollars for applying manufacturing overhead to the department, while the assembling and finishing departments will use a labor hour basis.

Service department costs will be allocated with the following basic considerations in mind: material handling costs will be prorated upon the estimated cost of materials used; the toolroom costs on the number of employees in the producing departments; and the factory office costs equally to all other departments. These departmental costs will be distributed in the reverse order of their listing in the plant survey.

PLANT SURVEY

Department	Area in Square Feet	Value of Machinery and Equipment	Estimated Materials to Be Used	Horse-power Rate	Direct Labor Hours	Direct Labor Costs	Number Em-ployees
Planing............	6,000	$36,000	$ 4,000	300	50,000	$ 30,000	24
Machining..........	8,000	40,000	12,000	240	50,000	75,000	30
Assembling........	12,000	12,000	2,000	100	30,000	35,000	18
Finishing..........	4,000	6,000	6,000	160	20,000	40,000	12
Material handling...	3,000	2,000	.....	...	......	......	6
Toolroom..........	2,000	.....	.....	...	......	......	2
Factory office.......	1,000	.....	.....	...	......	......	4
	36,000	$96,000	$24,000	800	150,000	$180,000	96

Budgeted manufacturing overhead costs for the year 19—:

```
Salary of superintendent..................................$14,000
Real estate taxes on factory..............................  6,000
Depreciation of machinery and equipment...................  30,000
Factory building insurance................................    600
Repairs to machinery and equipment........................  4,500
Repairs to factory building...............................    720
Fire insurance on machinery and equipment.................    600
Depreciation of factory building..........................  8,000
Compensation insurance ($2 per $100)......................  3,600
Power.....................................................  3,600
Fuel, heat, and light.....................................  2,400
Factory office salaries, including payroll tax............  10,500
Factory office expenses...................................  2,000
Indirect materials used:
  Planing.................................................    500
  Machining...............................................    400
  Assembling..............................................    600
  Finishing...............................................    800
Indirect labor costs, overtime bonus, and payroll taxes:
  Planing.................................................  1,800
  Machining...............................................  2,000
  Assembling..............................................  3,600
  Finishing...............................................  2,400
  Material handling.......................................  10,000
  Toolroom................................................  4,800
```

Required:

a) Prepare a work sheet to distribute budgeted manufacturing overhead to the producing and service departments.

b) Compute the predetermined manufacturing overhead rates for each of the producing departments on both the labor hour and the labor cost bases.

Problem 8–5. Purpose: *Cost Accounting Procedure for Distributing Manufacturing Overhead*

The Air Products Company operates two producing units, an electrolytic unit and a liquefaction unit, each of which when operating produces at capacity.

1. *Electrolytic Unit.* This unit produces one volume of oxygen and two volumes of hydrogen simultaneously, and this production ratio is maintained throughout whenever the unit operates. The unit consists of a number of metal tanks, or "cells," containing electrodes carrying low-voltage, high-amperage electrical currents.

Water is a compound of oxygen and hydrogen. The positive electrical terminal in each cell attracts oxygen; the negative terminal attracts hydrogen. They bubble off as gases and are collected commercially pure at the rate of 800 cubic feet of oxygen and 1,600 cubic feet of hydrogen per hour. Distilled water is continuously added to the cells.

The operating record of the unit for the year was:

```
7,100 hours producing both gases
  500 hours producing hydrogen only, all oxygen escaping because empty cylinders
      were not available
  400 hours producing oxygen only, all hydrogen escaping for the same reason
  760 hours idle, repair, etc.
8,760 hours, being 365 days of 24 hours
```

The entire cost of operating the electrolytic unit during the year was $48,000, which includes depreciation. Since the above production ratio of 1 to 2 is constant, this cost is to be apportioned between the two gases on the basis of volume actually produced by the unit. The production cost value of the gases lost is to be treated as a deduction from the gross profit on sales.

2. *Liquefaction Unit.* The liquefaction unit separates atmospheric air (containing 20 percent oxygen and 80 percent nitrogen) by mechanical means. Air is compressed and expanded, and the temperature lowered to about 300° Fahrenheit below zero, which liquefies the air. The unit produces liquid air at a uniform rate.

Oxygen and nitrogen boil (leave the liquid air as gases) at different temperatures, and one or the other (but not both together) is collected commercially pure. The operating record of the unit during the year was:

Oxygen—7,200 hours at the rate of 1,000 cubic feet per hour.
Nitrogen—1,200 hours at the rate of 1,333⅓ cubic feet per hour.

The operating cost of the liquefaction unit, including depreciation, aggregated $30,240 for the year. Because of the uniform rate of production, this cost is to be apportioned between the two gases on the basis of the number of hours operating.

3. *Compressing and Filling.* The gases are filled into steel cylinders, each of which is always used for the same gas. They are all of the same capacity (except the oxygen 110's), and they are filled at a uniform pressure by three very similar compressors, each compressing only one gas. However, the gases differ in compressibility, and the cylinder contents are as shown below.

The cost of compression was $13,480 for the year, including depreciation of the compressors; and the cost is to be allocated to the gases produced on the basis of cubic feet compressed.

The cost of filling, that is, connecting and disconnecting cylinders at the charging line, amounted to $5,643 and is the same for each cylinder, large or small. During the year, 6,000 small oxygen cylinders were filled.

4. *Cylinders.* Each cylinder is always refilled with the same gas. They are always returned when empty, and no charge is made for their use. The following data are given concerning the number of cylinders owned (all in service) and their depreciation:

	Contents Cu. Ft.	Number Owned	Depreciation	
			Rate	Amount
Hydrogen............190	190	5,120	$2.09	$10,700.80
Oxygen............220	220	10,260	2.09	21,443.40
Oxygen............110	110	1,508	1.32	1,990.56
Nitrogen............200	200	1,662	2.09	3,473.58

5. *Other Data.* At the beginning of the year there were on hand 310 full nitrogen cylinders, of which the contents of 62,000 cubic feet were carried forward at the previous year's cost of $0.424 per 100 cubic feet, or $262.88. All other cylinders were on hand empty.

At the end of the year, 200 full small oxygen cylinders were on hand; their contents, 22,000 cubic feet, are carried forward at the average year's cost. All other cylinders were on hand empty.

All gases are valued for inventory purposes at average cost before charging depreciation of cylinders.

The average sales prices of the gases were as follows:

> Hydrogen (in large cylinders): $0.80 per 100 cubic feet.
> Oxygen (in large cylinders): $1.00 per 100 cubic feet.
> Oxygen (in small cylinders): $1.20 per 100 cubic feet.
> Nitrogen (in large cylinders): $1.20 per 100 cubic feet.

The total of all selling, general, and executive expenses and of interest and taxes was $76,375.

From the foregoing information prepare the following statements:

a) Cost of production and sales.

b) Net income.

Also show the calculations of operating data and the apportionment of costs.

(Adapted from AICPA Uniform Examination)

PROBLEMS—GROUP B

Problem 8–6. Purpose: *Determination of Predetermined Overhead Rates*

The Zeron Corporation manufactures a product called "zeron" in a continuous process, in mixing, cooking, and cooling departments. A general plant service department serves all of the three producing departments.

A flexible overhead budget for the coming month has been determined for each of the departments as follows:

> Mixing......................$0.50 per labor dollar plus $5,500
> Cooking..................... 0.90 per labor hour plus $7,000
> Cooling..................... 1.05 per labor hour plus $3,200
> General plant service......... 0.30 per direct labor hour of each of the
> producing departments plus $8,000

The general plant service department is allocated to the producing departments on the basis of labor dollars.

Twelve thousand labor hours are budgeted for mixing, 8,000 for cooking, and 4,000 for cooling. Estimated labor costs for the month are:

> Mixing............$30,000
> Cooking........... 21,000
> Cooling............ 15,000

Actual data for the month showed:

	Mixing	Cooking	Cooling	General Plant
Labor hours...........	13,000	8,500	4,200	
Labor dollars..........$33,000		$23,000	$15,200	
Direct overhead........$20,000		$15,100	$12,900	$15,300

Required:

  a) Compute the predetermined overhead rates for each of the departments.
  b) Prepare journal entries recording overhead transactions for the month.
  c) Compute the over- or underapplied overhead for each of the departments.

Problem 8–7.   Purpose: *Various Methods of Applying Manufacturing Overhead*

The Ziles Company operates a printing plant where trade publications are printed to order. Management is not satisfied with the manner in which the manufacturing overhead has been applied to jobs and is currently studying the subject. Management is interested in examining overhead rates determined in various manners.

Actual data for the past month follows:

Job No.	Materials	Labor Dollars	Labor Hours	Machine-Hours	Status at End of Month
3091.....................	$17,000	$11,000	2,400	1,220	Completed
3092.....................	11,000	7,500	3,000	1,250	Completed
3093.....................	7,500	5,000	1,900	900	Completed
3094.....................	9,000	6,000	2,200	1,120	Completed
3095.....................	98,000	97,000	29,000	9,600	In process
3096.....................	15,000	9,500	3,100	1,400	Completed

The operating budget for the current year included:

Direct materials......................	$1,542,000
Direct labor.........................	$2,042,000
Direct labor hours....................	720,000
Machine-hours........................	125,000
Manufacturing overhead..............	$2,042,000

There was no work-in-process inventory at the beginning of the month.

Required:

  a) Calculate the predetermined manufacturing overhead rates based upon each of the following: direct labor hours, direct labor dollars, machine-hours, prime cost.
  b) Compute the cost of completing jobs 3091 and 3093 using each of the four rates computed in (*a*).
  c) Actual overhead for the month was $156,000. Compute the over- or underapplied overhead for each of the four methods.

Problem 8–8.   Purpose: *Determining Overhead Rates Using Flexible Budget*

Plant No. 2 of the Zyphon Company manufactures, in three departments, a chemical solution known as "zyp." Overhead costs have been analyzed and categorized as fixed and variable. As a result the flexible budget for the period is as follows:

	Fixed Costs	Variable Costs
Department A...................	$16,000	$ 6,000
Department B...................	21,000	21,000
Department C...................	23,000	33,000

Production at normal capacity is estimated to be 60,000 gallons of "zyp."

Required:

a) Compute the predetermined overhead rate for each of the departments at normal capacity.

b) Compute the predetermined overhead rate for each of the departments at 85 percent of capacity—the expected level of operations during the coming period.

c) Why is there a difference between the rates computed in (*a*) and (*b*) above? Explain.

Problem 8–9.   Purpose: *Computing Manufacturing Overhead Rates*

The budget committee of the Zonson Company has recently made a survey of the factory as part of its assignment to prepare an operating budget for the coming calendar year, 19—. In order to compute predetermined overhead rates for the producing departments of the factory, the data herein presented has been assembled:

Department	Area in Square Feet	Value of Machinery and Equipment	Estimated Materials to Be Used	Horse-power Rate	Direct Labor Hours	Direct Labor Costs	Number of Em-ployees
Department I......... 9,000		$40,000	$80,000	600	36,000	$70,000	18
Department II.........12,000		60,000	6,000	300	30,000	50,000	12
Assembling.......... 9,000		10,000	4,000	500	24,000	40,000	8
Finishing............ 6,000		8,000	10,000	100	10,000	20,000	8
Material handling..... 6,000		3,000	...				3
Toolroom........... 4,000		26,000	...				2
Factory office........ 2,000		3,000	...				3

Material handling costs are prorated on the basis of the cost of materials used, the toolroom on the basis of the number of employees in the producing departments, and the factory office equally to all the departments. Allocate factory office cost first, toolroom second, material handling last.

BUDGETED MANUFACTURING OVERHEAD

Rent of factory.................	$12,000	Factory office salaries, including	
Superintendent's salary..........	12,000	taxes........................	$12,000
Depreciation of equipment......	19,200	Factory office expenses...........	2,000
Repairs to machinery...........	3,500	Indirect materials used:	
Fire insurance on machinery and		Dept. I......................	500
equipment..................	800	Dept. II.....................	600
Compensation insurance ($2 per		Assembling..................	400
$100 of direct labor)..........	3,600	Finishing....................	300
Power.......................	4,500		
Fuel (light and heat)..........	4,800		

Indirect labor, overtime bonus, and factory payroll taxes: Dept. I, $2,000; Dept. II, $3,000; assembling, $2,500; finishing, $1,500; material handling, $8,200; toolroom, $5,800.

Prepare:

a) Work sheet to distribute budgeted manufacturing overhead to the producing and service departments.

b) Computation of predetermined overhead rates for the producing departments. Overhead is applied on labor hours basis.

Problem 8–10.   Purpose: *C.P.A. Problem: Revision of Departmental Overhead Rates*

The Zellan Manufacturing Company has decided to change its method of distributing factory burden to its products, all of which are manufactured on special order.

Required:

a) Develop appropriate departmental overhead rates based on the operations of the company for the first half of 1968.

b) Illustrate their use by determining the cost of Job Order No. 685 by using these new rates.

The trial balance of the factory ledger of the company for the six months ended June 30, 1968, is as follows:

	Debit	*Credit*
Materials and manufacturing supplies.........................	$ 85,321	
Work-in-process—material.................................	86,105	
Work-in-process—labor...................................	82,872	
Work-in-process—manufacturing overhead.....................	161,480	
Indirect labor...	41,740	
Factory rent...	2,400	
Insurance—machinery and equipment.........................	4,216	
Compensation insurance...................................	2,486	
Superintendence..	6,000	
Factory clerical salaries...................................	4,950	
Machinery maintenance and repairs..........................	31,010	
Depreciation of machinery and equipment....................	42,800	
Fuel..	3,172	
Electricity...	2,178	
Manufacturing supplies used................................	3,617	
Social security taxes......................................	9,210	
Factory office supplies.....................................	879	
Miscellaneous factory expense..............................	1,212	
Manufacturing overhead applied.............................		$158,200
General ledger control.....................................		413,448
	$571,648	$571,648

Additional data:

The manufacturing operations are carried on in three producing departments, A, B, and C, with the aid of two service departments, numbered 1 and 2, respectively. Other data are as follows:

	Total	A	B	C	1	2
				Departments		
Plant floor space, square feet....	30,000	10,000	5,000	2,000	7,500	5,500
Number of employees..........	109	50	20	4	25	10
Number of labor hours.........	113,360	52,000	20,800	4,160	26,000	10,400
Number of machine-hours.......	47,952	31,912	9,640	560	5,840	....
Salaries and wages............$	161,317	$ 76,180	$ 28,472	$ 9,975	$ 37,230	$ 9,460
Cost of machinery and equipment.................$	1,019,047	$623,225	$250,960	$20,210	$112,862	$11,790
Annual depreciation rates.......		8%	8%	10%	10%	20%

In developing overhead rates, expenses not distributed in the above table shall be distributed to departments as follows:

On the basis of floor space: factory rent, fuel, one fourth of electricity.

On the basis of salaries and wages: compensation insurance, superintendence, manufacturing supplies used, social security taxes, factory office supplies, miscellaneous factory expense.

On the basis of investment in machinery and equipment: insurance—machinery and equipment, machinery maintenance and repairs, three fourths of electricity.

Factory clerical salaries and $4,500 of indirect labor are charged to Department No. 2. The balance of indirect labor is charged to Department No. 1.

Expenses of Department No. 1 are to be distributed one tenth to Department No. 2 and the balance to all other departments on the basis of machine-hours.

Expenses of Department No. 2 are to be distributed to Departments A, B, and C, on the basis of labor hours.

The departmental burden rates are to be based on machine-hours for Departments A and B, and on labor hours for Department C.

Data applicable to Job Order No. 685: material, $487.92; direct labor, $465; machine-hours—50 hours from Department A and 12 hours from Department B; labor hours—20 hours from Department C.

(AICPA)

Problem 8–11 . Purpose: *Separating Overhead Costs into Their Fixed and Variable Elements*

The following data represents the direct labor hours and inspection costs for the year for the Maxilion Manufacturing Company. This firm is interested in managerial control in allocating the inspection costs to the departments after separating them into their fixed and variable elements. From this data you are asked to compute the fixed overhead rate and the variable overhead rates using (*a*) the high-low method and (*b*) the shortcut least squares method:

Month	Direct Labor Hours	Inspection Costs
January	1,800	$ 6,000
February	2,000	6,400
March	3,200	8,400
April	4,000	10,000
May	2,800	7,800
June	4,800	12,000
July	5,000	13,000
August	3,800	9,600
September	4,500	11,000
October	5,300	13,800
November	4,200	10,400
December	3,000	8,000
Total	44,400	$116,400

CHAPTER

9 | Accounting for the Actual

Manufacturing Overhead Costs

Accumulating Actual Manufacturing Overhead Costs In the previous chapter, discussion was centered upon estimating the manufacturing overhead costs on a departmental basis and applying them to production by means of a predetermined rate. Departmentalizing these indirect costs, as well as separating them into their fixed and variable amounts, results in better managerial control through more accurate costs on a job or production in a process type of manufacturing operations. Additional predetermined rates are sometimes used for materials handling charges and for central administration costs, thus providing even more accurate costs.

Predetermined overhead costs were considered first in the preceding chapter because they are used before the actual manufacturing overhead are or could be accumulated. The actual manufacturing overhead costs are accumulated during the fiscal period, and some are not recorded until the end of the fiscal period. In most instances, a *manufacturing overhead control account* is used, supported by a subsidiary ledger of the individual overhead costs. How these costs are recorded in the various books of original entry will be discussed later in this chapter. A careful analysis of the various manufacturing overhead costs will indicate that these may be grouped under five headings: (1) indirect labor, (2) indirect materials, (3) valuation charges, (4) items for which cash must be expended, and (5) accruals and deferrals. Entries in journal form to illustrate the recording of these charges (these entries assume that no separate factory journal is used) are as follows:

251

Nature of Overhead Cost	Book in Which Recorded	Journal Entry to Record Overhead Cost Item		
1. Indirect labor	General journal	Mfg. Overhead Control (Indirect Labor)............	200.00	
		Work-in-Process—Direct Labor.................	8,000.00	
		Payroll...............		8,200.00
2. Indirect materials used	General journal	Mfg. Overhead Control (Indirect Materials)........	500.00	
		Work-in-Process—Materials..11,000.00		
		Stores...............		11,500.00
3. Depreciation or valuation charges	General journal	Mfg. Overhead Control (Depreciation).............	800.00	
		Allowance for Depreciation...........		800.00
4. Indirect costs involving payment of cash	Voucher register	Mfg. Overhead Control (Power Costs)...........	900.00	
		Accounts Payable......		900.00
5. Expiration of prepaid expense	General journal	Mfg. Overhead Control (Insurance Costs)...........	520.00	
		Prepaid Insurance.......		520.00
6. Accrued charges	General journal	Mfg. Overhead Control (Taxes).................	560.00	
		Accrued Taxes Payable..		560.00

Recording and Posting the Manufacturing Overhead Costs

When a control account is used, postings must also be made to the subsidiary ledger for the detailed amounts. This will be accomplished by using special columns in the books of original entry and in exceptional cases by means of split postings. An analysis of the five types of manufacturing overhead cost entries just listed indicates that entries for these are made in the voucher register and in the general journal. Special columns for the manufacturing overhead are provided in each of these journals. This is illustrated in the paragraphs that follow.

Voucher Register

A debit column is provided for the manufacturing overhead (see Illustration 9–1). The total of this column is posted to the manufacturing overhead control account. The individual items are posted to the respective subsidiary ledger account. Since there are many different individual overhead costs, the nature of the expense is indicated by a code number. Assume that the code number of the Manufacturing Overhead Control account is 900 and the subsidiary ledger accounts are:

Illustration 9–1. Voucher Register Illustrating Entries Made for the Manufacturing Overhead Costs When No Factory Journal Is Used

Date	Explanation	Voucher No.	Paid Date	Paid Check No.	Accounts Payable, Cr.	Stores, Dr. Code	Stores, Dr. Amount	Payroll, Dr.	F.I.C.A. Taxes Payable, Cr.	Federal Withholding Taxes Payable, Cr.	State Withholding Taxes Payable, Cr.	Factory Overhead, Dr. Code	Factory Overhead, Dr. Amount	Selling Expense, Dr.	Administrative Expense, Dr.	Miscellaneous Accounts Dr.	Miscellaneous Accounts Cr.	L.F.	Explanation
Apr. 4	Aetna Realty Co.	100	4/4	210	800 00							903	800 00						
5		101																	
6		102																	
8	Morton Repairs Co.	103			260 00							906	260 00						
9		104																	
11		105																	
11		106																	
12	General Power Co.	107	4/15	270	480 00							907	480 00						
12		108																	
12		109																	
13		110																	
14		111																	
												√	4,840 00						
													(42)						

901 Indirect Materials
902 Indirect Labor
903 Rent of Factory
904 Depreciation of Equipment
905 Factory Insurance
906 Machine Repairs
907 Heat, Light, and Power

Examining the partial illustration of the voucher register, it will be noted that on April 4, the factory rent was paid. Entry is made in the Voucher Payable column, Cr., and a debit to the Manufacturing Overhead. Since the rent code number is 903, this is indicated in the proper column. This figure will be posted to the subsidiary ledger account for Factory Rent. Similarly entries are made for Machine Repairs, Code 906, and Heat, Light, and Power, Code 907. At the end of the month, the total in this column is posted to the Manufacturing Overhead Control account, thus agreeing with the total of the postings to the subsidiary ledger accounts.

Factory Journal Entries and Postings   In this illustration of the procedure, it is assumed that a separate factory journal is used. Entries are made in this journal for the manufacturing overhead costs, with a separate amount and code column for these charges to permit the dual postings (see Illustration 9–2). Sample entries are made for the indirect labor, indirect materials, depreciation transferred from the general office records, and the expired insurance also transferred from the general office.

The individual figures for indirect materials ($300), indirect labor ($800), depreciation ($480), and insurance ($160) are posted to the respective subsidiary ledger accounts, and the total of $4,600 is posted to the manufacturing overhead control account.

Posting to the Subsidiary Manufacturing Overhead Accounts   As has been indicated previously, the summary figures for the manufacturing overhead are maintained in the *Manufacturing Overhead Control account*. Since a subsidiary ledger is maintained, posting arrangements must be made for posting to these subsidiary ledger accounts. The following arrangements indicate the various methods of postings to the subsidiary ledger for manufacturing overhead:

1. Entries in sufficient detail in the *general journal* and the *voucher register* so that dual postings can be made—special columnar totals to the Manufacturing Overhead Control account and the subsidiary ledger postings by means of code numbers in the special columns.

2. Prepare *factory journal or transfer vouchers* in sufficient detail so that the entries may be made therefrom in the subsidiary ledgers.

3. Send the *original invoice* for the manufacturing overhead charge to the subsidiary ledger clerk so that he may make the entry therefrom. It would be better, however, to use the method of (2) whereby all charges to the subsidiary ledger are vouchered in a uniform manner.

4. Place the subsidiary ledger charge on a punched card and have these accumulated from time to time for entry on the subsidiary ledgers.

Illustration 9–2. Factory Journal Illustrating Entries Made for the Manufacturing Overhead Costs

General Ledger, Dr.	Manufacturing Overhead Control, Dr.		Factory Ledger, Dr.	L.F.	Account and Explanation	L.F.	Factory Ledger, Cr.	General Ledger, Cr.
	Code	Amount						
			4,000 00		Jan. 6 Work-in-Process— Materials			
	901	300 00			Indirect Materials Stores Used during week.		4,300 00	
			5,000 00		6 Work-in-Process— Labor			
	902	800 00			Indirect Labor Payroll For week.		5,800 00	
	904	480 00			31 Depreciation General Ledger For period.	√		480 00
	905	160 00			31 Insurance—Factory General Ledger Expired for month.	√		160 00
10,000 00		4,600 00	30,000 00				38,000 00	6,600 00
(21)		(10)	(√)				(√)	(21)

When these procedures have been followed and completed, the Manufacturing Overhead Control account will show in total the details shown in the subsidiary ledger accounts. The columnar postings to the Manufacturing Overhead Control account will be as follows:

Manufacturing Overhead Control Account

Dec. 31	G J.	4,500.00	Dec. 31	Applied mfg. overhead	10,000.00
31	V R.	8,000.00			

Applied Manufacturing Overhead Account

Dec. 31	Closed to Mfg. Overhead Control account	10,000.00	Dec. 31	Applied to production	10,000.00

Departmentalization of the Actual Manufacturing Overhead. It has been emphasized in the previous discussion that the predetermined rates for manufacturing overhead and the applied manufacturing overhead should, in the interest of more accurate costing and better managerial control of the manufacturing operations, be departmentalized. Therefore, for comparative purposes, the *actual* manufacturing overhead must also be recorded on a departmental basis. The most practical method of doing this is by means of the *work sheet method,* paralleling the procedure used in departmentalizing the estimated manufacturing overhead.

Under this method, a controlling account is set up for the total of the actual manufacturing overhead costs, with a subsidiary ledger for the individual expense accounts. At the end of the fiscal accounting period, a list of the individual manufacturing overhead accounts is entered on a work sheet on which there is a distribution column for each of the producing and service departments of the plant. *Using the same survey of plant facilities as was necessary in departmentalizing the estimated manufacturing overhead costs,* these overhead costs are then prorated or allocated to the various departments, the amounts being entered in the appropriate departmental columns.

Since the service departments do not involve any manufacturing operations, it is necessary to redistribute their overhead costs to the various departments to the extent to which these service departments render service to the other departments.

When this work sheet has been completed, *all* of the manufacturing overhead costs will have been allocated to the producing departments. In the following illustration, the total amount of the manufacturing overhead at the end of the accounting period was $108,902. The various overhead cost items are listed, and these have been allocated to the producing and service departments on the bases indicated in the plant survey. However, the amounts allocated to the *service departments* must then be redistributed to the other departments as shown, resulting in a *final* total, departmentally, of the actual manufacturing overhead as illustrated (see Illustration 9–3).

```
Cutting department........................................$ 47,821.24
Planing department........................................  28,457.03
Assembling department.....................................  17,923.57
Finishing department......................................  14,700.16
     Total Actual Manufacturing Overhead...................$108,902.00
```

When these actual departmental overhead cost figures are compared with the applied departmental manufacturing overhead costs, the over- or underapplied departmental manufacturing overhead is computed. This *applied* and the *over- or underapplied* departmentally may also be shown on this work sheet, as illustrated.

The journal entry to close the Manufacturing Overhead Control account into the various departmental manufacturing overhead accounts as shown on the work sheet would be:

```
Manufacturing Overhead—Cutting Department................47,821.24
Manufacturing Overhead—Planing Department................28,457.03
Manufacturing Overhead—Assembling.......................17,923.57
Manufacturing Overhead—Finishing........................14,700.16
     Manufacturing Overhead Control.......................        108,902.00
     To close the manufacturing overhead control account per work
     sheet.
```

To visualize the sequence of the entries made to record and departmentalize the *actual* manufacturing overhead, Illustration 9–4 is given. A study of this illustration reveals the following procedures:

1. Manufacturing overhead is recorded in a subsidiary ledger.
2. The Manufacturing Overhead Control account is a controlling account for the subsidiary ledger.
3. The Manufacturing Overhead Control account is closed into the departmental overhead accounts, both service and producing departments, by a journal entry. The figures used in this entry are obtained from a work sheet showing distribution of the actual manufacturing overhead.
4. The service department overhead accounts are closed into the producing department overhead accounts by a journal entry.

Illustration 9-3.

JOHANNSON MANUFACTURING COMPANY

Work Sheet for the Proration of the Actual Manufacturing Overhead Costs
For the Year Ended December 31, 19—

Basis for Apportioning Various Overhead Costs		Total Amount	Cutting Dept.	Planing Dept.	Assembling Dept.	Finishing Dept.	Material Handling Dept.	Toolroom	Factory Office
No. of employees	Superintendent's salary	12,000.00	3,600.00	3,000.00	2,000.00	1,400.00	800.00	400.00	800.00
Area	Taxes on building	6,000.00	1,500.00	1,250.00	1,000.00	750.00	750.00	500.00	250.00
Investment	Depreciation of equipment	30,600.00	12,000.00	8,000.00	2,000.00	1,600.00	400.00	6,000.00	600.00
Area	Insurance of plant	600.00	150.00	125.00	100.00	75.00	75.00	50.00	25.00
Investment	Repairs to machinery	4,590.00	1,800.00	1,200.00	300.00	240.00	60.00	900.00	90.00
Area	Repairs to plant	400.00	100.00	83.33	66.67	50.00	50.00	33.33	16.67
Investment	Fire ins., machinery and equip.	612.00	240.00	160.00	40.00	32.00	8.00	120.00	12.00
Area	Depreciation of plant	5,000.00	1,250.00	1,041.67	833.33	625.00	625.00	416.67	208.33
Payroll	Compensation insurance	3,600.00	1,360.00	1,000.00	840.00	400.00			
Horsepower	Power costs	4,800.00	1,920.00	1,280.00	960.00	640.00			
Direct	Factory office salaries	10,500.00							10,500.00
Area	Fuel, heat, and light	2,400.00	600.00	500.00	400.00	300.00	300.00	200.00	100.00
Direct	Factory office expenses	2,000.00							2,000.00
Direct	Indirect materials used	2,000.00	500.00	300.00	600.00	600.00			
Direct	Indirect labor costs	23,800.00	1,800.00	2,000.00	2,400.00	2,800.00	10,000.00	4,800.00	
	Total	108,902.00	26,820.00	19,940.00	11,540.00	9,512.00	13,068.00	13,420.00	14,602.00
No. of employees	Factory office costs	14,602.00	4,693.50	3,911.25	2,607.50	1,825.25	1,043.00	521.50	
							14,111.00		
Cost of materials used	Material handling costs	14,111.00	11,288.80	423.33	987.77	1,411.10			
No. of employees	Toolroom costs	13,941.50	5,018.94	4,182.45	2,788.30	1,951.81		13,941.50	
	Total	108,902.00	47,821.24	28,457.03	17,923.57	14,700.16			
	Applied manufacturing overhead	112,902.00	45,821.24	31,457.03	18,923.57	16,700.16			
	Over- ( ) or underapplied mfg. overhead	(4,000.00)	2,000.00	(3,000.00)	(1,000.00)	(2,000.00)			

Subsidiary Ledger, and Work Sheet Are Used

DEPARTMENTAL OVERHEAD ACCOUNTS

Manufacturing Overhead--Dept. A

Manufacturing Overhead--Dept. B

Manufacturing Overhead--Dept. C

Manufacturing Overhead--Dept. D

Manufacturing Overhead--Dept. X

Manufacturing Overhead--Dept. Y

Manufacturing Overhead--Dept. Z

WORK SHEET DISTRIBUTION OF THE ACTUAL MANUFACTURING OVERHEAD (AS RECORDED IN SUBSIDIARY LEDGER ACCOUNTS).

Overhead Cost	Total Amount	Departments						
		A	B	C	D	X	Y	Z
I. M.								
I. L.								
Supt.								
F. I.								
L. H., & P.								
Fuel								
Deprec.								
Rent								
X								
Y								
Z								

Manufacturing Overhead Control Account

Indirect Materials
Indirect Labor
Superintendence
Fire Insurance
Light, Heat & Power
Fuel
Depreciation
Rent

Subsidiary Ledger Accounts

Indirect Materials Account

Superintendence

Light, Heat & Power

Depreciation

Indirect Labor

Fire Insurance

Fuel

Rent

A specific illustration of the journal entry made to close the controlling account into the departmental accounts is given below:

```
Manufacturing Overhead—Department A.........................7,000.00
Manufacturing Overhead—Department B.........................4,550.00
Manufacturing Overhead—Department C.........................6,400.00
Manufacturing Overhead—Department D.........................8,000.00
Manufacturing Overhead—Department X.........................7,000.00
Manufacturing Overhead—Department Y.........................2,600.00
Manufacturing Overhead—Department Z.........................  880.00
    Manufacturing Overhead Control.........................          36,430.00
    To close Manufacturing Overhead account as per standing order
    sheets.
```

Following the procedure used with the estimated manufacturing overhead, the distributions to Departments X, Y, and Z Manufacturing Overhead accounts must be closed into the accounts of the producing departments, either singly or jointly. A summary of departmental distributions from work sheet is presented in Illustration 9–5 with the subsequent distribution of service department overhead so that the journal entries to close the service department overhead accounts may be understood more readily.

On the basis of this summary the individual entries necessary to close overhead accounts of Departments X, Y, and Z are:

(1)
```
Manufacturing Overhead—Department A.........................2,800.00
Manufacturing Overhead—Department B.........................1,500.00
Manufacturing Overhead—Department C.........................  300.00
Manufacturing Overhead—Department D.........................2,200.00
Manufacturing Overhead—Department Y.........................  100.00
Manufacturing Overhead—Department Z.........................  100.00
    Manufacturing Overhead—Department X.....................          7,000.00
    To close the overhead costs of Department X into the other depart-
    ments.
```

(2)
```
Manufacturing Overhead—Department A.........................  450.00
Manufacturing Overhead—Department B.........................  600.00
Manufacturing Overhead—Department C.........................  650.00
Manufacturing Overhead—Department D.........................  800.00
Manufacturing Overhead—Department Z.........................  200.00
    Manufacturing Overhead—Department Y.....................          2,700.00
    To close the overhead costs of Department Y into the other depart-
    ments.
```

(3)
```
Manufacturing Overhead—Department A.........................  280.00
Manufacturing Overhead—Department B.........................  340.00
Manufacturing Overhead—Department C.........................  390.00
Manufacturing Overhead—Department D.........................  170.00
    Manufacturing Overhead—Department Z.....................          1,180.00
    To close the overhead costs of Department Z into the producing de-
    partments.
```

Illustration 9–5. Showing the Method of Transferring the Service Department Overhead into the Producing Department Overhead

	Department							Total
	X	Y	Z	A	B	C	D	
Total....................	$7,000.00	$2,600.00	$ 880.00	$ 7,000.00	$4,550.00	$6,400.00	$ 8,000.00	$36,430.00
Service Department X, overhead costs........		100.00	100.00	2,800.00	1,500.00	300.00	2,200.00	7,000.00
Total....................		$2,700.00						
Service Department Y, overhead costs........			200.00	450.00	600.00	650.00	800.00	$ 2,700.00
Total..................			$1,180.00					
Service Department Z, overhead costs........				280.00	340.00	390.00	170.00	$ 1,180.00
				$10,530.00	$6,990.00	$7,740.00	$11,170.00	$36,430.00

However since these data appear on the work sheet, the foregoing entries are usually combined into a single entry, that is, the three service department overhead accounts are closed simultaneously as follows:

```
Manufacturing Overhead—Department A..........................3,530.00
Manufacturing Overhead—Department B..........................2,440.00
Manufacturing Overhead—Department C..........................1,340.00
Manufacturing Overhead—Department D..........................3,170.00
Manufacturing Overhead—Department Y..........................  100.00
Manufacturing Overhead—Department Z..........................  300.00
    Manufacturing Overhead—Department X....................          7,000.00
    Manufacturing Overhead—Department Y....................          2,700.00
    Manufacturing Overhead—Department Z....................          1,180.00
    To close the service department overhead cost accounts into the pro-
    ducing departments.
```

In fact, some accountants avoid entirely the use of manufacturing overhead *accounts* for the service departments. The work sheet is completed showing the allocation of the actual manufacturing overhead to both producing and service departments, and then the redistribution of the service department overhead costs to the other departments. Then when the journal entry is made to close out the manufacturing overhead control, the charges are made directly and only to the producing departments, viz:

```
Manufacturing Overhead—Department A......................10,530.00
Manufacturing Overhead—Department B...................... 6,990.00
Manufacturing Overhead—Department C...................... 7,740.00
Manufacturing Overhead—Department D......................11,170.00
    Manufacturing Overhead Control.........................       36,430.00
    To close out the manufacturing control as per work sheet.
```

Alternative Method of Treating Service Department Overhead

Sometimes some of the service department overhead is analyzed into its fixed and variable portions, such as heat, light, and power costs (powerhouse). The fixed portion is distributed to the other departments on the basis of area, number of lights, or horsepower. The variable portion is distributed to the other departments on the basis of services rendered or actual consumption. This method has certain advantages because of its greater accuracy, especially in those instances where the production and usage is not uniform throughout the plant. In some firms, some service department overhead costs are not redistributed to the other departments but instead a separate or supplementary rate is calculated for the service department involved. This rate is used as an additional overhead costing on the job sheets. Using this method will result in an over- or underapplied manufacturing overhead for the service department involved. This method has found limited application, since it is difficult to determine how much of the service department costs should be charged to a specific job without incurring a large amount of additional clerical work.

Over- and Underapplied Departmental Manufacturing Overhead

The departmental manufacturing overhead discussed thus far covers three phases of the subject: (1) *estimated manufacturing overhead,* from which the predetermined departmental rates are computed; (2) *applied manufacturing overhead,* which represents the departmental amounts charged to the work-in-process on the job order cost sheets by means of rate computed in (1), and (3) *actual departmental manufacturing overhead,* which is ascertained from the work sheet analysis. The difference between the actual manufacturing overhead and the applied manufacturing overhead accounts for each *producing* (and sometimes *service*) department represents the over- or underapplied manufacturing overhead. The localization of errors in the estimate permits better managerial control of the overhead cost element. At the end of the accounting period, the applied departmental overhead accounts are closed into the actual departmental overhead accounts. Periodically a statement may be prepared, as shown in Illustration 9–6, showing the actual and the applied manufacturing overhead and the resulting variance for each producing department.

The over- or underapplied manufacturing overhead on a departmental basis is disposed of in the same manner as previously discussed for indirect costs not departmentalized. In this illustration, to close out the

Illustration 9–6

		MARTIN MANUFACTURING CO. Summary of the Actual and Applied Manufacturing Overhead January 1, 19— to December 31, 19—			
		Actual Manufacturing Overhead Charges			
	Dept. A	Dept. B	Dept. C	Dept. D	Total
Indirect material................	$ 1,989.00	$1,256.00	$2,800.00	$ 3,110.00	$ 9,155.00
Indirect labor..................	700.00	800.00	1,000.00	....	2,500.00
Superintendence................	769.25	769.25	1,153.80	1,538.50	4,230.80
Fire insurance..................	428.55	214.30	42.85	321.45	1,007.15
Compensation insurance..........	250.00	200.00	450.00	700.00	1,600.00
Light.........................	128.00	128.00	192.00	320.00	768.00
Power........................	1,280.00	320.00	....	640.00	2,240.00
Depreciation on machinery........	1,500.00	750.00	150.00	1,125.00	3,525.00
Rent.........................	320.00	400.00	480.00	640.00	1,840.00
Apportioned charges (service depts.).....................	3,050.00	2,800.00	1,000.00	3,865.00	10,715.00
Total actual overhead......	$10,414.80	$7,637.55	$7,268.65	$12,259.95	$37,580.95
Less: Applied mfg. overhead.........	10,366.08	7,740.15	7,378.85	12,331.60	37,816.68
Balance underapplied............	$ 48.72	....	....	....	....
Balance overapplied.............	....	$ 102.60	$ 110.20	$ 71.65	$ 235.73

variation to the Cost of Goods Sold account, the following entry is necessary:

```
Manufacturing Overhead—Department B...........................102.60
Manufacturing Overhead—Department C...........................110.20
Manufacturing Overhead—Department D........................... 71.65
    Manufacturing Overhead—Department A......................        48.72
    Cost of Goods Sold......................................        235.73
    To close the balances in the departmental overhead accounts into the
    Cost of Goods Sold account.
```

A similar procedure may be followed if it is desired at the end of the fiscal accounting period to close the over- or underapplied manufacturing overhead on a departmental basis to the Work-in-Process, Finished Goods, and Cost of Goods Sold accounts.

Closing out the over- or underapplied manufacturing overhead either into the Cost of Goods Sold account, or prorated to the Work-in-Process, Finished Goods, and Cost of Sales account is usually not done until the end of the fiscal accounting period. This is true, since the over- or underapplied manufacturing overhead of one month may be offset by the reverse over- or underapplied manufacturing overhead of the following month. It is the over- or underapplied manufacturing overhead at the end of the fiscal accounting period that must be considered, not the monthly fluctuations, which may be only temporary.

Analyzing the Over- and Underapplied Manufacturing Overhead

Management wants to know why there was an over- or underapplied manufacturing overhead. This analysis becomes more effective if the overhead is first separated into its *fixed* and *variable* elements. In either instance, the causes for the over- or underapplied overhead may be traced to incorrect estimates of the *volume* of production expressed in terms of labor hours or labor costs, or incorrect estimates of the *cost* of the overhead items, or a combination of both of these factors (see Illustration 9–7).

To illustrate this analysis, the following facts are assumed:

	Fixed Overhead	Variable Overhead
Estimated (budget) overhead............	$24,000	$14,400
Budgeted plant capacity................	24,000 labor hours	24,000 labor hours
Predetermined rate....................	$1	$0.60
Actual overhead.......................	$25,440	$12,000
Actual labor hours (volume)............	25,000 labor hours	25,000 labor hours
Applied overhead:		
25,000 hrs. × $1.00..................	$25,000	
25,000 hrs. × $0.60..................		15,000
Underapplied overhead (Dr.)...........	$440	
Overapplied overhead (Cr.).............		$3,000

Illustration 9–7. Analysis of the Over- and Underapplied Manufacturing Overhead

VARIATIONS DUE TO COST FACTORS

	Fixed Overhead	Variable Overhead	Total
Budgeted overhead................	$24,000	$14,400	
Actual overhead..................	25,440	12,000	
Difference due to costs:			
Favorable (Cr.)................		$ 2,400 (Cr.)	
Unfavorable (Dr.)..............	$ 1,440 (Dr.)		$ 960 (Cr.)

VARIATIONS DUE TO VOLUME OF PRODUCTION

	Fixed Overhead	Variable Overhead	Total
Budgeted labor hours.............	24,000 hrs.	24,000 hrs.	
Actual production hours...........	25,000	25,000	
Excess productions (favorable)......	1,000 hrs.	1,000 hrs.	
Variation due to volume:			
1,000 hrs. × $1.00 (Cr.)........	$ 1,000 (Cr.)		
1,000 hrs. × $0.60 (Cr.)........		$ 600 (Cr.)	$1,600 (Cr.)
Net underapplied (unfavorable).....	$ 440 (Dr.)		
Net overapplied (favorable)........		$ 3,000 (Cr.)	$2,560 (Cr.)

Special Manufacturing Overhead Problems Special attention must be given to the allocation of some of the manufacturing overhead costs to the various departments. Among these items are:

Factory rent costs are a fixed manufacturing overhead cost, usually distributed departmentally on a square footage basis. When the building is owned, a charge equivalent to rent is sometimes built up out of the following: property taxes, insurance, depreciation, and maintenance and repair charges.

Light, heat, and power costs may be incurred by a direct charge from the utility company. In that event, the allocation is simple: *light* on the basis of kilowatt-hours and/or the number of bulbs in each department; *heat* on the basis of square or cubic feet in each department, or the number of radiators; *power* on the basis of the number of machines in each department, or the machine-hours of production, or the horse-power hours used.

If however, the firm has its own powerhouse, then more accurate cost accounting would divide the powerhouse house costs into its *fixed* elements (taxes, insurance, depreciation, and maintenance) and the *variable* costs (cost of actual power production) and prorate these to the various departments.

Taxes as manufacturing overhead creates no particular problem as far as taxes on plant and payroll taxes are concerned. But in recent years, a lively discussion has arisen as to the advisability of including state and federal income taxes in the cost of production. Some writers in the Bulletins of the National Association of Accountants and in a study made by the National Industrial Conference Board have recommended the inclusion of these taxes in manufacturing costs. This recommendation has not as yet had very wide acceptance.

Indirect materials consist of materials not directly identifiable with the product—materials such as repair and replacement parts, packing materials, and cleaning and polishing supplies. Where large supplies of these materials are kept on hand, control through the use of inventory cards and requisition forms is desirable, the charges for indirect materials used being made direct to the departmental overhead accounts.

Tools and *tool expense* require special consideration. If a large quantity of tools is consumed in production, inventories may be taken monthly to determine the charge to manufacturing overhead. Some firms carry the tool inventory at a fixed basic figure, and all replacements of tools are treated as an overhead cost at the time of purchase.

Indirect labor is work which is not applied directly to the product and which cannot be charged to specific jobs or lots, such as work done by shop foremen, repairmen, sweepers, clerks, janitors, and timekeepers. Indirect labor may include labor costs for idle time due to lack of materials, nonfunctioning machinery, or any other cause which prevents men ordinarily engaged in direct labor from working on the product if such costs are not recorded in a separate Idle or Delay Time account.

In the case of *insurance,* a diversity of opinion exists as to whether or not the various insurance costs should be included in the computation of manufacturing costs. Some insurance, such as against forgery, holdup, and robbery, is treated as administrative expense. These do not affect the factory operations directly. Insurance costs paid on automobiles may be variously treated. Insurance on trucks used for outgoing shipments is selling expense; insurance on trucks used to carry materials to the factory is factory overhead or part of the freight and cartage-in. If the trucks are used for both in and out shipments, it will become necessary to prorate on some equitable basis all the delivery expenses (including the insurance) between manufacturing overhead and selling expenses. Premiums for group life insurance and compensation insurance are treated as factory overhead costs if they are calculated on the wages paid employees in the factory, as selling expenses if on wages paid sales employees, and as administrative expenses if paid on wages of office force. The insurance costs applying to the factory payroll should be apportioned departmentally on the basis of departmental payrolls. The costs of fire and sprinkler insurance covering the factory equipment and materials used in manufacturing are treated as manufacturing overhead. If such insurance covers the finished stock, its cost is part of the selling expenses. The cost of fire insurance on the materials used in manufacturing is merged with the other storeroom costs and becomes part of the prorated charges of the service department. The cost of fire insurance and sprinkler leakage insurance on the buildings will be prorated over the departmental overhead accounts, usually on the basis of area occupied by each department. Some of these costs may be allocated to a sales department or an administrative department if such departments are located in the same building as the factory operations.

Conversion or *reconversion* costs raise a serious problem for many manufacturers. The cost of rearranging the plant and reinstalling machinery and lines of production may either be capitalized and written off over a long period of time or treated as a charge to be written off over the current year's production. The attitude of the Internal Revenue Service has not been definite in this matter. Until the time when a definite legal ruling is obtained, it would seem reasonable and conservative to write off the conversion or reconversion cost over the shortest possible period. It would therefore be an element of manufacturing cost and part of the manufacturing overhead for the current period. It would destroy the comparability of costs for that year with the subsequent years when no such charge will occur.

Normal *inventory shrinkages* in stores, resulting from evaporation, breakage, obsolescence, etc., are legitimate charges to production costs as manufacturing overhead. They are often discovered when inventory count is reconciled with perpetual inventory cards. Extraordinarily large losses, however, resulting from unforeseen, unusual circumstances would be charged to a special loss account with an appropriate title and then closed out to the Profit and Loss account. Raw materials market price changes call for no special consideration as price changes will be reflected in the costs of the period of use rather than the period of purchase.

The allocation of the indirect costs of a number of *special services* sometimes raises a problem. The costs of the *medical department, the cafeteria department* (loss due to costs being greater than income), *welfare department, general supervision, cost department, timekeeping and payroll, and the employment department* may well be distributed on the basis of either the number of employees or man-hours. *Purchasing department* costs and *storeroom* costs may well be allocated to the departments on the basis of tonnage or value of materials used in the various departments. Some accountants recommend the allocation on the basis of man-hours, but there seems little justification for this practice except perhaps its simplicity and the small amount involved. *General engineering costs,* unless identified with special jobs or currently manufactured products, may be capitalized and charged to some capital asset or deferred charge. *Building elevator* and *building operation costs* should be collected into one summary account and allocated on the basis of square footage. *Police, fire, and watchman service costs* should no doubt be prorated on the basis of the value of the property in each department—that is, investment. *Interest on investment,* a problem of much debatable importance, is discussed on pages 273–74.

Depreciation as Manufacturing Overhead Cost

Depreciation is not a method of evaluation of property but rather a method of allocating the cost of property to operating periods.

The Internal Revenue Code recognizes this allocation in the calculation of taxable income, and several methods of calculating the depreciation charge are permissible. The Internal Revenue Code of 1954 has focused attention on the so-called *accelerated* methods of depreciation with their income tax advantages to the manufacturer.

Formerly the *straight-line* method (cost less scrap value divided by the estimated life of the asset) was considered the most satisfactory method; now because of income tax and cash savings effected by the *sum-of-years' digits* and the *fixed-percentage-of-diminishing-value* meth-

Illustration 9–8

COMPARATIVE METHODS OF DEPRECIATION

As Authorized in Sec. 167 of Internal Revenue Code of 1954
(Illustrative Case. Item Cost of $100,000 with Ten-Year Estimated Useful Life.
Salvage Not Considered.)

Ten-Year Life	Straight Line		Maximum Permissible Declining Balance*		Sum of the Digits		
	Annual Charge	Cumulative Allowance	Annual Charge	Cumulative Allowance	Sum Digits	Annual Charge	Cumulative Allowance
1............	$10,000	$ 10,000	$20,000	$20,000	10	$18,182	$ 18,182
2............	10,000	20,000	16,000	36,000	9	16,364	34,546
3............	10,000	30,000	12,800	48,800	8	14,545	49,091
4............	10,000	40,000	10,240	59,040	7	12,727	61,818
5............	10,000	50,000	8,192	67,232	6	10,909	72,727
6............	10,000	60,000	6,554	73,786	5	9,091	81,818
7............	10,000	70,000	5,243	79,029	4	7,273	89,091
8............	10,000	80,000	4,194	83,223	3	5,455	94,546
9............	10,000	90,000	3,355	86,578	2	3,636	98,182
10............	10,000	100,000	2,684	89,262	1	1,818	100,000
					55		

* Maximum rate cannot exceed twice the straight-line rate.

Prepared by American Appraisal Company

ods, their use has increased. These two methods, forms of accelerated depreciation, permit a larger write-off in the earlier years of life of the asset than would be permissible under the straight-line method. Illustrations 9–8 and 9–9 present the comparative depreciation costs for the three methods most frequently used under the new income tax regulations.

A change to one of the newer permissible methods will also raise some interesting and important questions: Do the higher depreciation charges in the earlier years, as part of manufacturing overhead, increase the cost of manufacturing to the extent that a selling price higher than that of competitors will become necessary? Are the current costs unduly burdened by the higher depreciation charges, and will some future periods benefit from the resulting lower manufacturing overhead charges?

Illustration 9–9

COMPARATIVE METHODS OF DEPRECIATION

As Authorized in Sec. 167 of Internal Revenue Code of 1954

(Salvage Cost Not Considered. Item Cost, $100,000. Ten-Year Basis.)

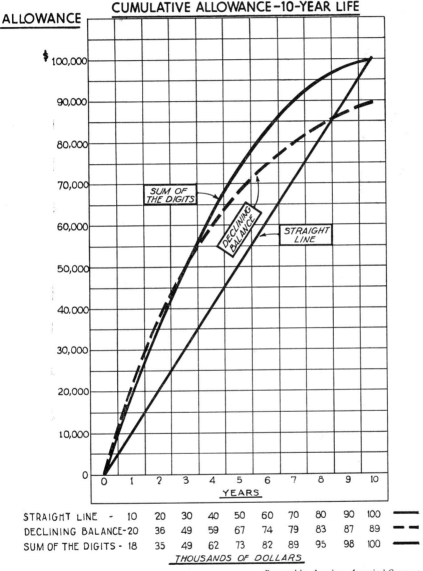

STRAIGHT LINE -	10	20	30	40	50	60	70	80	90	100	▬▬
DECLINING BALANCE-	20	36	49	59	67	74	79	83	87	89	▬ ▬
SUM OF THE DIGITS -	18	35	49	62	73	82	89	95	98	100	▬▬

THOUSANDS OF DOLLARS

Prepared by American Appraisal Company

Furthermore, the law permits the manufacturer using the declining-balance method to change to the straight-line method at any time, but this is not possible with the sum-of-years'-digits method. It becomes, therefore, a serious problem of management to select the method of depreciation which will most effectively reflect comparable costs, so that management may measure the effectiveness of production by plants, divisions, and products. These are some of the situations which may arise:

1. A product with a level sales trend will have few major capital requirements, whereas one with a rapid growth or with many style changes will have frequent major additions to capital requirements.
2. A narrow profit product produced on a highly mechanized line could well be changed into a losing product if a major addition in or replacement of equipment is to be made and a higher rate of depreciation used.
3. If replacements and additions occur at different times in various units of a company, then it will be a long time before all the fixed assets in all the plants of a company are on the same basis of depreciation.
4. Increased mechanization through greater application of automation in manufacturing will greatly increase the amount of depreciation application to cost of manufacturing, since a greater investment in machines and other equipment will be required. The importance of automation in planning for the future cannot be overemphasized.

Accuracy of Declining Balance versus Straight-Line Depreciation Method

It must be restated here that depreciation is not a method of evaluating property but rather a method of allocating the cost of property to operating periods and finally to the product. The most logical and reasonable basis for allocating this cost would seem to be in relation to the net value of the service rendered in the various operating periods. *This assumption leads to the conclusion that depreciation should be on some declining-amount basis for several reasons:*

1. When property is purchased, it is with the expectation that the volume of production and the earnings for the reasonably immediate future will justify the purchase. It is not ordinarily expected that the property will be uniformly useful over its entire estimated life.
2. The physical efficiency of property ordinarily declines over its useful life, reducing gradually the quantity and/or the quality of its service. This may involve the loss of precision, more time out for repairs, and other factors. There are, however, some situations where this is not true. For example in the paper-making industry, the paper machines increase their efficiency for many years after their installation, producing more paper of a better quality.
3. There is the gradual encroachment of obsolescence, which reduces the value of even the same quantity and quality of service rendered in the successive periods.
4. Repairs and maintenance tend to increase each year, and reduce the net value of the service rendered in successive periods.

Which declining-balance method should be used is still a difficult problem. In addition to the two methods—fixed-percentage-of-diminishing-value and sum-of-years'-digits method—there is the multiple-straight-line-principle under which 150 percent of the straight-line method can be used during the first half of the useful life and only 50 percent of the straight-line rate for the last half; or 150 percent of straight-line during first third of useful life, 100 percent during second third, and 50 percent during the last third. The ultimate in the application of the multiple-straight-line method is a constantly declining rate with a uniform change each year—such as 145 percent of the straight-line rate or 14½ percent the first year, 135 percent or 13½ percent the second year, and 125 percent or 12½ percent the third year, etc., until in the last year of a 10-year asset it would be 5½ percent of the cost. The sum-of-years'-digits method is a very specific, inflexible application of this method.

In any given situation the method selected should be one which achieves best the following objectives: it should reflect best the periodic decline in the net value of the service rendered; it should produce the best cost figures for managerial purposes, including replacement policies; and, other things being equal, it should involve the least administrative and accounting costs. But the selection of a declining-amount method in a given situation and its application present extremely more difficult problems than those involved in the straight-line method.

A continuation of the straight-line method results in substantial errors in cost allocation greater than any that are likely to result from selection and application of any declining-amount method that seems reasonably appropriate to the given situation. For cost accounting to have any managerial significance, it is necessary to use the declining-amount method not only for post-1953 assets but for those acquired earlier. But because of the conflict of tax accounting, straight-line book accounting, and more accurate cost accounting through a declining-amount method (other than fixed-percentage-of-diminishing-value, or of sum-of-years'-digits method), most firms will probably continue to use the straight-line method for cost accounting.

Guideline Lives for Depreciation
Not only is the selection of the method of depreciation important to the manufacturer but the determination of the *useful life* is also relevant.

In 1962, the Treasury Department issued Revenue Procedure 62–21 (later amended) which introduced the concept of *Guideline Life*. A taxpayer could adopt Guideline Lives for depreciating his assets without having to substantiate these lives as long as his replacement policy was consistent with the Guidelines. Generally, the useful lives in the 75 categories permitted under the Guidelines were liberal.

The fact that a Guideline Life has been adopted for tax purposes does not necessarily mean that the same useful life should be used in computing depreciation on the accounting records of the company. The useful life used by the company in its record keeping should be that which clearly approaches reality, and guidelines are supposed to be realistic.

Investment Credit and Depreciation Costs   Fixed asset accounting was complicated even further by the Revenue Act of 1962 and amended by the Revenue Act of 1964 when an *investment credit* was introduced. The credit which is a subtraction from the income tax payable in a given year amounts to 7 percent of the cost of qualified depreciable fixed assets. The credit does not have to be subtracted from the asset in computing depreciation for tax purposes.

The treatment of the investment credit on the records of a company has split the ranks of the American Institute of Certified Public Accountants. The dispute hinges on whether the credit should be subtracted from the *tax expense per books* all in *one year* or should be spread *over the* life of the asset. Both methods are currently acceptable.

If the investment credit is prorated over the life of the asset, the effect is that of reducing overhead costs. For example, an asset with a 10-year life is purchased for $1,000 and a $70 credit is taken in the year of purchase (this is mandatory under the law). If $7 of the credit is amortized each year, the effect is to reduce depreciation by $7.

If the investment credit is not amortized but considered as a benefit in the year of the asset's purchase, the entire $70 increases the net income in the year of purchase and overhead is not affected.

Reconciling Cost, Book, and Tax Accounting Depreciation Methods   The retention of the straight-line depreciation for book accounting, with the adoption of a declining-amount method for income tax purposes, ordinarily demands the use of an account, *Deferred Income Taxes Payable.* In years when the depreciation deduction for tax purposes exceeds book depreciation, there should be added to this estimated liability an amount equal to this difference times the effective tax rate, with an offsetting charge to an expense account in lieu of taxes. In years when the book depreciation exceeds the depreciation deduction for tax purposes, there should be deducted from this estimate an amount equal to this difference times the effective tax rate, with an offsetting credit to an account which is contra to tax expense. This procedure is consistent with that recommended by the Committee on Accounting Procedure of the American Institute of Certified Public Accountants.

Interest on Investment as a Cost Element One of the controversial subjects in cost accounting is the treatment of *interest on investment.* Although some cost accountants are quite emphatic in stating that interest should or should not be included as an element in cost accounting, it must be pointed out here that interest on investment is one of those doubtful items which must be omitted from cost for some purposes and must be included in cost for other purposes. The items to be included in or excluded from cost depend entirely upon the purpose for which the cost figure is to be used. There is no such thing as *a* correct cost figure for *all* purposes.

Interest on investment as an element of cost refers to the amount to be included in the manufacturing overhead as a charge for the capital used in production. It assumes that if this capital had not been used in the business it would have been invested and would have earned a return called "interest on investment." The rate or amount of the return is an economic concept defined as the income derived from capital with a minimum of risk involved in the investment. This *economic* concept of interest, when applied to accounting, raises several difficulties.

The first difficulty lies in the definition of *investment.* Investment is not used with the same meaning by all concerns. For some, investment has been defined as the value of inventories plus the value of fixed assets less allowance for depreciation; for others, investment has been defined as the sum of all the assets except intangibles and investments in securities; for others it may be any variation of these values. A second difficulty is created by the question: *What rate of interest represents the economic concept of a return on investment with a minimum of risk?* There is a tendency to use 6 percent, although the rate is unreasonably high in the light of the foregoing definition and limitation.

Many cost accountants have raised arguments favoring or opposing the inclusion of interest as an element of cost, assuming that a uniform procedure should be followed by all. This is not true. There are conditions under which interest on investment as an element of cost might be used; there are others in which it should not be used. Where interest on investment is to be included as part of the manufacturing overhead, it is probably better to treat costs as *statistical data.* The books will then not have to be adjusted when the cost statements, in which interest on investment is not permitted to appear, are to be prepared.

If costs are treated as statistical data and are not controlled by entries on the general accounting books, the interest item is recorded on the cost sheets as part of the manufacturing overhead, but no journal entries are made. If, however, the costs are controlled by the general accounting records, journal entries to record the interest on investment are:

(1)

Manufacturing Overhead Control (Interest Cost)........................xxxx
    Interest on Investment...xxxx
        To record the interest on investment charge as an element of cost.

(2)

Interest on Investment..xxxx
    Retained Earnings..xxxx
        To record the amount of interest applicable to the cost of goods sold.

The effect of these two entries is to divide the usual net profit of a business into two parts: (1) interest on investment, which through the Manufacturing Overhead account increases the cost of goods manufactured and through the Retained Earnings account increases the net income; and (2) the *remaining* net income arising from the difference between the increased cost of goods manufactured and sold (increase due to the addition of interest on investment as an element of cost) and the selling price. If interest on investment were not used, the net income would equal the sum of the two parts thus mentioned.

Trade associations favor the inclusion of interest on investment because it provides a more uniform and accurate comparison of manufacturing efficiency of the various members. The interest charge acts as a measure of the effect of capital in large- and small-scale business operations.

In most accounting work there is no need for inclusion of interest on investment. The Internal Revenue Service does not permit the inclusion of interest on investment as an element of cost. For them the inclusion of interest on investment inflates costs and because of the larger inventories, it understates the profits.

For managerial use, interest may or may not be included as an element of cost, but the treatment of interest must be consistent from year to year. If the firm owns and operates several plants with varying investments in plants and machinery, the inclusion of interest as an element of cost would allow a more reliable comparison of the relative efficiency of each than would its exclusion and a better comparison of the relative costs of manufacturing the different products. Very few concerns are organized in this manner. A survey of the members of the National Association of Accountants indicated that for this reason about four out of every five oppose the inclusion of interest on investment as a manufacturing cost.

Diagrammatic Summary of Manufacturing Overhead Accounting
In order to visualize the complete sequence of the application of manufacturing overhead to production from the time the costs are incurred until they have been charged to a job order, Illustration 9–10 is presented on the following page.

A Recapitulation of What Management Must Do Relative to Manufacturing Overhead
From the discussion in this and the preceding chapter, it becomes apparent that management, through its cost accounting division, must make certain decisions relative to the calculation and application of manufacturing overhead to production. Among these, but not necessarily in the order given, are the following:

1. Analysis of indirect costs into fixed (period) and variable, and the subsequent preparation of a flexible overhead budget.
2. Determination of whether the overhead costs are to be applied to the cost of production on an overall-plant, departmental, or work-center basis.
3. Determination of whether the costs of service departments are to be (*a*) collected by service departments or allocated directly to the producing departments or (*b*) distributed to production by means of a supplementary overhead rate.
4. The determination of the effect of calendar variations on the predetermined overhead rate.
5. Determination of the basis on which to apply overhead cost to production.
6. Determination of the accounting disposition of the over- or underapplied overhead costs whether on a factorywide or departmental basis.
7. Analysis of the causes of the manufacturing overhead variations into *cost* and *volume* factors.
8. Determination of method of correcting grossly inaccurate predetermined overhead rates.

Managerial Control of Manufacturing Overhead Costs
Compilation of manufacturing overhead data, with its many ramifications, is but one important phase of the work of the cost accountant. Another, and probably more important phase, is the prodding of management to use these data to create a more efficient plant.

Illustration 9-10. Diagrammatic Summary of Manufacturing Overhead Accounting

Transaction	Forms Used	Book of Original Entry	Source of Entry	Journal Form of Entry	Cost Record or Summary Form Used	Entry on Cost Record or Summary Form
Recording indirect labor costs	Time tickets and recapitulation sheet	General journal	Recapitulation sheet	Dr. Mfg. Overhead Control (Indirect Labor) Cr. Payroll	Standing order sheet or subsidiary ledger	
Recording indirect materials used costs	Material requisitions	Requisition journal or general journal	Requisition journal or requisitions	Dr. Mfg. Overhead Control (Indirect Material Used) Cr. Stores	Standing order sheet or subsidiary ledger	
Incurring factory overhead through (1) Payment of cash	Voucher check	Voucher register	Invoice	Dr. Manufacturing Overhead Control (Heat, Light, and Power, Etc.) Cr. Accounts Payable; Dr. Accounts Payable Cr. Cash	Standing order sheet or subsidiary ledger	
(2) Decreasing prepaid charges		General journal	Memorandum	Dr. Manufacturing Overhead Control (Insurance, Etc.) Cr. Prepaid Expense	Standing order sheet or subsidiary ledger	
(3) Depreciation valuation charges		General journal	Memorandum	Dr. Manufacturing Overhead Control (Depreciation) Cr. Allowance for Depreciation	Standing order sheet or subsidiary ledger	
Distribution of manufacturing overhead to service and producing depts.	Summary of standing orders or work sheet analysis	General journal	Summary of standing orders or work sheet	Dr. Producing Dept. Overhead Accounts Service Dept. Overhead Accounts Cr. Manufacturing Overhead Control		
Distribution of service dept. overhead	Summary of standing orders or work sheet analysis	General journal	Summary of standing orders or work sheet	Dr. Producing Dept. Overhead Accounts Cr. Service Dept. Overhead Accounts		
Manufacturing overhead applied to production	Summary of applied manufacturing overhead	General journal	Summary of applied manufacturing overhead	Dr. Work-in-Process—Mfg. Overhead Cr. Applied Mfg. Overhead—Producing Depts.	Job order sheet	Entry in the Applied Mfg. Overhead section of job order sheets

Illustration 9–11. Controllable Overhead Report

CONTROLLABLE OVERHEAD REPORT
80% Operating Capacity

Department No. 62—Drill Press   For Month Ending April 30, 19—

F. A. Butler, Foreman   80% Capacity O.R.

Expense	Actual This Month	Budget This Month	Difference for Month Between Actual and Budget	Actual Year to Date	Budget Year to Date
Power & Light	$ 50.00	$ 52.00	$ 2.00*		
Inspection	60.00	60.00	—		
Indirect Labor	245.00	250.00	5.00*		
Supplies	110.00	108.00	2.00†		
Repairs	65.00	60.00	5.00†		
Spoilage	40.00	47.00	7.00*		
Tool Expense	50.00	54.00	4.00*		
Total Variable	$ 620.00	$ 631.00	$11.00*		
Fixed Charges	870.00	870.00	—		
Total	$1,490.00	$1,501.00	$11.00*		
Direct Labor Hours	4,800	4,810	10*		

* Decrease.
† Increase.

Illustration 9–12. Idle Machine Report

IDLE MACHINE REPORT   For month ending July 31, 19——

DEPARTMENT #106   CUTTING   Foreman: A. B. Howard

Machine Number	Standard Hours	Actual Hours			Idle Hours							% of Standard	Burden Rate for Idle Time	Cost of Idle Time	Remarks
		Regular	Over Time	Total	No Operator	No Materials	Repairs	Awaiting Set up	Awaiting Tools	Awaiting Instructions	Total				
C-102	160	160		160											O K.
C-103	160	150		150	10						10	6.25	$3.10	$31.00	Material held up in drilling dep't.
C-104	160	160		160											
F-110	160	140		140		20					20	12.5	1.80	36.00	Improper Scheduling
F-111	130	160	15	175									1.80	27.00*	To make up loss of Mach. #110.
F-112	130	125		130			3	2			5	3.85	1.80	9.00	Job instructions not on hand.
Total	900	895	15	915	10	20	3	2		35		2.77		31.00	

. * Credit for overtime.

Effective reports form the link between the factory and top management, and the preparation of many of these reports is often in the hands of the cost accountant. Among these reports, those on manufacturing overhead rank high as aids in possible effective control of some of the factory costs.

Effective manufacturing overhead reports must be in the hands of management promptly if the information is to be meaningful and usable. These reports must pinpoint to management the expected and actual costs with a study of possible reasons for differences. These differences between actual and applied overhead must be departmentalized wherever feasible to further localize performance.

Departmental foremen, too, are an important part of the management team in the collection of information in their respective departments. Two reports from the factory in Illustrations 9–11 and 9–12 emphasize the position of the factory foreman in managerial control. Foremen are also important in the later analysis and study of the cost data for their departments. Failure to reach expected goals must be sought in large measure at the operational level in the factory, in factors such as careless operation, inexperience, wasted time, idle men, idle machines, poor machines, poor lighting, poor tools, poor materials, spoilage and waste of materials, and even in poor supervision.

As manufacturing plants grow in size, and the relationship of top management and factory personnel becomes more impersonal, these various reports, including those on manufacturing overhead, take on added significance in the line of communication between the factory and the executive offices.

QUESTIONS FOR REVIEW

1. Departmentalization of overhead costs is necessary because it produces more accurate costs and better managerial control. On the basis of this statement—

    a) What is a department?

    b) Why should the term "production center" be used in place of "department"?

    c) How may departments be classified? Why is this necessary?

2. What five steps are necessary in departmentalization of the manufacturing overhead costs?

3. A factory or plant survey of plant facilities is basic in departmentalizing manufacturing overhead. When is it made; when changed; and with what manufacturing overhead is it used?

4. What two methods might be used in allocating manufacturing overhead which belongs to the service departments? Which is preferable? Why?

5. Over- or underapplied manufacturing overhead may be analyzed into two possible causes. What are they? How are they computed?

6. The budgeted manufacturing overhead of the Calcutta Manufacturing Company is $50,000. The predetermined rate is $2 per direct labor hour. The actual manufacturing overhead for the period is $56,350. The applied manufacturing overhead is $54,000. Compute the over- or underapplied manufacturing overhead and indicate the causes therefor.

7. The Superior Manufacturing Company's production fluctuates seasonally during the different months of the year. This results in large amount of underapplied manufacturing overhead during the slack periods. How should the underapplied manufacturing overhead be shown on the *monthly* financial statements? Explain.

8. What factors should be considered in selecting an effective predetermined manufacturing overhead rate?

9. What method of computing depreciation of plant and equipment seems most desirable from a cost accounting viewpoint? What is the most satisfactory method of solving the cost accounting problem raised by the unequal depreciation amounts resulting when the sum-of-years' digits and the fixed-percentage-of-diminishing-value methods are used?

10. Manufacturing overhead is usually recorded in a control account. Explain how the subsidiary records for departmentalizing the overhead may be maintained. What effect does such a control account have on the books of original entry?

PROBLEMS—GROUP A

Problem 9–1. Purpose: *Determination of Over- and Underapplied Manufacturing Overhead*

The Quickmike Company purchases parts and assembles typewriters. The planning budget for the month of January calls for the following:

```
Estimated production...........3,000 typewriters
Material cost.................. $120,000
Labor cost.....................  240,000
Indirect materials.............   21,000
Indirect labor.................   32,000
Superintendence................    6,000
Heat, light, power.............    4,000
Depreciation...................    6,000
Insurance and taxes............    8,000
Sundry overhead costs..........    7,000
```

Manufacturing overhead is applied to production on the basis of the number of units manufactured.

During the month of January, 2,800 typewriters were produced and 2,000 were sold at a price of $300 each.

Unit costs for materials and labor were the same as budgeted. Actual manufacturing overhead costs incurred were $82,000.

There were no work-in-process inventories at the beginning or end of the period.

Required:

a) Prepare journal entries to record the above information.

b) Determine the over- or underapplied manufacturing overhead. Charge the over- or underapplied overhead to cost of goods sold.

Problem 9–2. Purpose: *Summary Journal Entries to Departmentalize Manufacturing Overhead*

The Quensen Woodworks Company operates its factory with three producing and three service departments. The departmental overhead costs have been recorded for the month of August, 19—, as shown below:

Costs	Cutting	Assembling	Finishing	Store-room	Mainte-nance	Tool-room	Total
Indirect material..........$	400	$ 500	$ 500	$ 200	$1,000	$ 100	$ 2,700
Indirect labor..............	800	400	600	300	1,000	200	3,300
Taxes, plant...............	200	200	300	200	250	150	1,300
Insurance..................	100	200	200	250	250	150	1,150
Depreciation, plant........	300	200	100	100	150	200	1,050
Depreciation, equipment....	400	180	120	500	200	300	1,700
Heat and light.............	100	200	140	60	100	100	700
Power.....................	250	150	200	...	100	...	700
Superintendence............	150	100	100	50	180	120	700
Plant repairs..............	50	40	30	60	120	...	300
Miscellaneous..............	150	130	110	80	150	80	700
Total................$	2,900	$2,300	$2,400	$1,800	$3,500	$1,400	$14,300
Maintenance department....	1,000	700	900	500		400	
Toolroom.................	750	550	350	150	$1,800		
Storeroom................	1,700	500	250	$2,450			
Total................$	6,350	$4,050	$3,900				$14,300
Applied overhead.........	6,000	4,000	4,150				14,150
Differences...........$	350	$ 50	$ 250*				$ 150

* Overapplied.

Journalize (*a*) to close the Manufacturing Overhead Control account, (*b*) to distribute service department costs, (*c*) to apply manufacturing overhead to production, and (*d*) to close over- and underapplied manufacturing overhead. (Reminder: Journal entry (*d*) is usually a year-end entry only.)

Problem 9–3. Purpose: *Manufacturing Overhead Variance Analysis*

The manufacturing overhead of the Queens Company is applied on the basis of direct labor hours. Eight thousand direct labor hours is considered as normal capacity of the Queens Company which manufactures a line of candy dishes.

Budgeted manufacturing overhead at normal capacity is as follows:

	Variable Cost	Fixed Cost
Indirect labor..............................	$1,000	$2,000
Superintendence............................		3,000
Heat, light, and power......................	1,000	1,500
Supplies....................................	900	
Depreciation of building and equipment........		2,000
Taxes on building and equipment..............		500
Maintenance................................		400
Repairs....................................	1,000	500
Insurance..................................		600

The actual number of hours worked in May was 9,000, and the following overhead costs were incurred:

Indirect labor	$2,800
Superintendence	3,000
Heat, light, and power	2,900
Supplies	1,100
Depreciation on building and equipment	2,000
Taxes on building and equipment	500
Maintenance	600
Repairs	1,600
Insurance	700

Required:

a) Compute the predetermined manufacturing overhead rate for the month.

b) Compute the manufacturing overhead applied during the month.

c) Compute the over- or underapplied manufacturing overhead.

d) Prepare a schedule showing the manufacturing overhead variations and the causes of the over- or underapplied overhead.

Problem 9–4. Purpose: *Correction of the Predetermined Manufacturing Overhead Rate*

The Quixote Manufacturing Company uses a predetermined rate for applying manufacturing overhead to production. The nature of the business is such that direct labor hours is used as the basis. The predetermined rate was set last December by the use of the following data:

Budgeted manufacturing overhead	$140,000
Estimated direct labor hours	70,000

A flood during January hindered production for the first quarter. Only 8,000 direct labor hours were worked during the first three months. Estimates are that 40,000 labor hours will be the total worked hours during the last nine months of the year. The estimated manufacturing overhead for the entire year has been revised to $120,000. Management is anxious to know if some corrective action may be taken.

Required:

a) Journalize the manufacturing overhead applied under the original rate during the first quarter. Correct retroactively, the rate for these three months.

b) Compute a new rate for manufacturing overhead if no retroactive action is taken.

c) Comment on the methods used in (a) and (b).

Problem 9–5. Purpose: *Analysis of Causes of Over- or Underapplied Overhead*

The following items are determinable from the records of the Qwowen Company for the year 19—.

Budgeted manufacturing overhead for the year	$186,000
Predetermined manufacturing overhead rate	$2.50 per machine-hour
Actual manufacturing overhead	$202,000
Actual machine-hours	82,100 hours

Required:

a) Compute the over- or underapplied manufacturing overhead for the year.

b) Isolate as many variances as you can in attempting to explain the over- or underapplied manufacturing overhead.

PROBLEMS—GROUP B

Problem 9–6. Purpose: *Analysis of Causes of Over- or Underapplied Manufacturing Overhead*

The Abernathy Corporation's cost records contained the following items which pertained to manufacturing overhead for the year 19—:

Predetermined manufacturing overhead rate..................$2 per direct labor hour
Budgeted manufacturing overhead for the year............... $3,650,000
Actual manufacturing overhead............................ $3,640,000
Actual direct labor hours worked.........................   1,840,000 hours

Required:

a) Determine the amount of over- or underapplied manufacturing overhead, if any.

b) Explain in as much detail as possible, the causes of the over- or underapplied overhead determined in (*a*).

Problem 9–7. Purpose: *Determination of Over- and Underapplied Overhead*

The Alpine Company assembles floor polishers from the parts that it purchases. During the month of October, 4,000 polishers were produced and 3,000 of these were sold at a price of $99.50. There were no inventories at the beginning or end of the period.

The planning budget for October had called for the production of 4,500 polishers at the following costs:

Materials...............................$90,000
Labor................................... 45,000
Superintendence.........................   5,000
Supplies................................   8,000
Indirect labor.......................... 12,000
Depreciation............................   4,000
Heat, light, and power..................   3,000
Other overhead costs.................... 16,000

A predetermined rate is used for manufacturing overhead, and the rate is determined on the basis of the number of units manufactured.

The actual manufacturing overhead costs for October were $43,000. There was no change in unit costs of material and labor from the budget.

Required:

a) Record the above information in general journal form.

b) Determine the over- or underapplied manufacturing overhead. Charge the over- or underapplied manufacturing overhead to cost of goods sold.

Problem 9–8. Purpose: *Overhead Variance Analysis*

The Appleton Company manufactures a line of radios and TV sets. In its cost accounting operation, it was decided to apply manufacturing overhead on the basis of direct labor dollars.

During June, when actual direct labor was $925,000, the following manufacturing overhead costs were incurred:

Superintendence	$250,000
Indirect labor	290,000
Supplies	120,000
Heat, light, and power	280,000
Depreciation	200,000
Taxes	150,000
Maintenance and repairs	130,000
Insurance	50,000

A predetermined manufacturing overhead rate had been established at a normal capacity of $1,200,000 of direct labor dollars. The budgeted manufacturing overhead at normal capacity had been budgeted as follows:

	Variable Cost	*Fixed Cost*
Superintendence		$250,000
Indirect labor	$240,000	40,000
Supplies	120,000	
Heat, light, and power	140,000	200,000
Depreciation		200,000
Taxes		150,000
Maintenance and repairs	60,000	100,000
Insurance		40,000

Required:

a) Calculate the predetermined manufacturing overhead rate and compute the applied manufacturing overhead for the month.

b) Compute the over- or underapplied manufacturing overhead.

c) Prepare a schedule showing the manufacturing overhead variations and the causes therefor.

Problem 9–9. Purpose: *Correction of the Predetermined Manufacturing Overhead Rate*

Some years ago, the management of the Ames Manufacturing Company adopted machine-hours as the basis for allocating manufacturing overhead to production with the use of a predetermined rate. A new rate is set each year just before the start of the company's fiscal year. The predetermined rate for the current year was set by using the following:

Estimated machine-hours	120,000
Budgeted overhead costs	$360,000

A strike at one of the major suppliers of materials forced a cutback during the first three months of operations. Seven thousand machine-hours were worked during the entire first quarter. Management expects to operate for 70,000 machine-hours for the rest of the year. A survey was conducted, and it is now expected that total overhead for the year will amount to $290,000.

Management personnel ask you whether or not a new rate for overhead should be computed.

Required:

a) Prepare a journal entry applying overhead during the first three months at the original rate.

b) Correct retroactively, the rate for these three months.

c) Compute a new rate for manufacturing overhead if no retroactive action is taken.

d) Comment on the methods used in (*b*) and (*c*).

Problem 9–10.   Purpose: *Journal Entries to Departmentalize Manufacturing Overhead*

Qeweller, Inc., maintains a factory which has three producing departments and two service departments. The cost accounts are maintained at the factory. Departmental overhead cost (standing order) sheets are used to accumulate the manufacturing overhead charges for all the departments. The data for the month of July, 19—, have now been assembled and summarized as follows:

QEWELLER, INC.

SUMMARY OF STANDING ORDERS AND APPLIED MANUFACTURING OVERHEAD

Month of July, 19—

Overhead Cost	Grinding Dept.	Machining Dept.	Finishing Dept.	Power-house	Toolroom	Total
Indirect material......$	2,000	$1,000	$1,200	$4,000	$ 800	$ 9,000
Indirect labor.........	3,000	2,500	1,750	2,000	600	9,850
Superintendence......	200	400	100	200	100	1,000
Rent................	200	120	180	200	100	800
Insurance...........	80	50	70	100	50	350
Depreciation........	150	200	150	150	100	750
Repairs.............	60	70	20	150	20	320
Miscellaneous.......	200	150	100	200	150	800
Total..........$	5,890	$4,490	$3,570	$7,000	$1,920	$22,870
Powerhouse.........	3,500	2,000	1,000		500	
Toolroom...........	1,000	1,200	220		$2,420	
Total..........$	10,390	$7,690	$4,790			$22,870
Overhead applied.....	12,000	7,000	5,000			24,000
Difference........$	1,610*	$ 690	$ 210*			$ 1,130*

* Overapplied.

Journalize (*a*) to close the Manufacturing Overhead Control account, (*b*) to distribute service department costs, (*c*) to apply manufacturing overhead to production, and (*d*) to close over- and underapplied manufacturing overhead. (Reminder: Journal entry (*d*) is usually a year-end entry only.)

Problem 9–11. Purpose: *C.P.A. Problem: Revision of Departmental Overhead Rates*

The Quaverly Manufacturing Company has decided to change its method of distributing factory burden to its products, all of which are manufactured on special order.

Required:

a) Develop appropriate departmental rates based on the operations of the company for the first half of 1968.

b) Illustrate their use by determining the cost of Job Order No. 685 by using these new rates.

The trial balance of the factory ledger of the company for the six months ended June 30, 1968, is as follows:

	Debit	*Credit*
Materials and manufacturing supplies	$ 85,321	
Work-in-process—material	86,105	
Work-in-process—labor	82,872	
Work-in-process—manufacturing overhead	161,480	
Indirect labor	41,740	
Factory rent	2,400	
Insurance—machinery and equipment	4,216	
Compensation insurance	2,486	
Superintendence	6,000	
Factory clerical salaries	4,950	
Machinery maintenance and repairs	31,010	
Depreciation of machinery and equipment	42,800	
Fuel	3,172	
Electricity	2,178	
Manufacturing supplies used	3,617	
Social security taxes	9,210	
Factory office supplies	879	
Miscellaneous factory expense	1,212	
Manufacturing overhead applied		$158,200
General ledger control		413,448
	$571,648	$571,648

Additional data:

The manufacturing operations are carried on in three producing departments, A, B, and C, with the aid of two service departments, numbered 1 and 2, respectively. Other data are as follows:

	Total	*A*	*B*	*C*	*1*	*2*
Plant floor space, square feet	30,000	10,000	5,000	2,000	7,500	5,500
Number of employees	109	50	20	4	25	10
Number of labor hours	113,360	52,000	20,800	4,160	26,000	10,400
Number of machine-hours	47,952	31,912	9,640	560	5,840	....
Salaries and wages	$ 161,317	$ 76,180	$ 28,472	$ 9,975	$ 37,230	$ 9,460
Cost of machinery and equipment	$1,019,047	$623,225	$250,960	$20,210	$112,862	$11,790
Annual depreciation rates		8%	8%	10%	10%	20%

In developing burden rates, expenses not distributed in the above table shall be distributed to departments as follows:

On the basis of floor space: factory rent, fuel, one fourth of electricity.

On the basis of salaries and wages: compensation insurance, superintendence, manufacturing supplies used, social security taxes, factory office supplies, miscellaneous factory expense.

On the basis of investment in machinery and equipment: insurance—machinery and equipment, machinery maintenance and repairs, three fourths of electricity.

Factory clerical salaries and $4,500 of indirect labor are charged to Department No. 2. The balance of indirect labor is charged to Department No. 1.

Expenses of Department No. 1 are to be distributed one tenth to Department No. 2 and the balance to all other departments on the basis of machine-hours.

Expenses of Department No. 2 are to be distributed to Departments A, B, and C, on the basis of labor hours.

The departmental burden rates are to be based on machine-hours for Departments A and B, and on labor hours for Department C.

Data applicable to Job Order No. 685: material, $487.92; direct labor, $465; machine-hours—50 hours for Department A and 12 hours for Department B; labor hours—20 hours for Department C.

(AICPA)

SECTION III

Principles and Practices of Process Cost Accounting

The large number of firms engaged in manufacturing operations in which costs are computed on a departmental or process basis necessitates a separate treatment of the cost accounting procedures for this group.

The subject has been carefully divided into chapters and topics to make this comprehensive in coverage yet simplified for easy understanding and learning.

Six chapters are devoted to this coverage: (1) Basic Process Cost Accounting Principles and Practices; (2) Special Problems of Process Cost Accounting Including the Average Method of Treating the Initial Work-in-Process Inventory; (3) The FIFO Method of Costing the Initial Work-in-Process Inventory; (4) Simplified Process Cost Procedures; (5) Coproduct, Joint Product, and By-product Cost Accounting Procedures; and (6) Simplifying Cost Accounting through Estimated Costs.

CHAPTER

10 | Process Cost Accounting

Procedures—Part I

Basic Principles and Practices

Definition and Nature Process costs are best understood when
of Process Costs they are compared with specific job order
costs. Under a system of specific job order
costs, the materials, labor, and manufacturing overhead are accumulated
by jobs or lots. Unit costs are not available until the job or lot is
completed. When the job is completed, unit costs are calculated by
dividing the total cost of work done on the job by the number of
completed units produced. Each job is usually independent of every
other job; and costs may vary considerably from job to job, even when
the same product is being manufactured.

On the other hand, process cost accounting is used by a firm manufacturing products in a more or less continuous flow, without reference to
specific orders or lots. Emphasis is placed on *production for a given
period*—a day, a week, or a month—and this period of time may be
comparable to the job or lot in specific order cost accounting. Furthermore, the continuous nature of the production usually implies that in
many concerns there will be work-in-process inventories at the beginning and at the end of the given period. This gives rise to the problem
of how to treat the work-in-process in computing unit costs. Emphasis in
process cost accounting is therefore placed on the *period of time* and on
the *number of units* (or quantity) completed and in process. The
continuous nature of the production also means that unit costs are in
reality daily, weekly, or monthly *average* costs.

Furthermore, since the products are manufactured on a continuous
basis, the factory production is generally for warehouse stocks, not for

specific customers. The quantities to be produced will be governed to a large extent by the estimated sales or demand for the products.

Industries to which the process cost accounting system may be applied vary widely in such matters as (1) the number of products; (2) the length of the production cycle; (3) the number of operations or departments involved; (4) the number of departments in which materials must be added, and whether these materials increase the number of units being produced or merely alter the units already in production; (5) the amount of shrinkage or waste; and, finally (6), whether or not at the end of the month there is any work-in-process. These factors determine whether the continuous process cost accounting system will be a simple or a complicated procedure.

To indicate the diversity of operations to which process cost accounting procedure is applicable, the following list of types of firms which use a continuous process cost accounting system is given:

Manufacturing	*Mining*	*Public Utilities*
Textiles	Coal mining	Gas manufacturing
Sugar refineries	Copper mining	Electricity producers
Bakeries	Salt production	
Petroleum products		
All other types of chemical manufacturers		
Rubber goods producers		
Plastics		

Classification of Process Cost Manufacturers By attempting to visualize the manufacturing conditions under which process operations may be conducted, the understanding of process cost accounting is simplified. First of all, process manufacturers may produce but a single product on a continuous basis, or they may produce a variety of products. These may be further subdivided, as outlined below for cost accounting purposes, into:

1. Firms manufacturing a *single product* continuously. This single product may be produced in one department or in several consecutive departments. Single-product continuous process costs may be further classified into those in which:

    a) *Materials to be processed are placed into production only in the initial department.* All subsequent departments merely add labor and manufacturing overhead to the cost of manufacturing.

    b) Materials to be processed are placed into production, not only in the initial department but *also* in some of the subsequent departments. This additional material may either *increase the number of units being manufactured* or merely increase the unit costs but not the number of units being produced.

    c) *There is no work-in-process inventory in any of the departments* at the end of the cost accounting period. The simpler the manufacturing processes and the more perishable the product, the less likely it is that there will be any work-in-process inventory at the end of the period. And if there is no work-in-process inventory at the end, the simpler becomes the computation of unit process costs.

d) *There is a work-in-process inventory in at least some of the departments* at the end of the cost accounting period. The longer the manufacturing production cycle and the more involved the manufacturing operations, the more likely it is that there will be some unfinished work in some of the departments at the end of the cost accounting period. For example, bread bakeries, ice-cream manufacturers, and food canners usually complete all work placed in process before computing unit costs. There are no work-in-process inventories for these firms. But in oil refineries, gas and electric utility firms, steel mills, and textile manufacturers, the operations invariably involve some unfinished work-in-process no matter when the costs are summarized. These work-in-process inventories complicate the computation in the cost accounting work.

2. Firms manufacturing *more than one product* on a continuous basis. There are several possible conditions which may exist here:

a) *Separate products are produced in different departments which have no relation to each other.* This is the same as a number of single-product firms. Cost accounting procedure would be the same as though each product were produced in a separate factory.

b) *Separate products are produced, but the second product uses some of the first product in its manufacturing operations.* In a fertilizer plant, acid phosphate is produced in one department. Some of this is sold, and the rest is used in manufacturing fertilizer. This does not raise very serious cost problems since the effect is the same as though each product were made in separate departments. However, it becomes necessary to determine the costs of the acid phosphate before any cost can be computed for the fertilizer.

c) *A number of products are produced.* In the course of manufacturing operations the work done in one department is transferred to several departments, after which further production results in several products. This type of continuous process manufacture is used by rubber manufacturers, oil refineries, and industrial chemical producers and involves essentially the problem of prorating costs to several coproducts.

The cost accounting problems raised by these variations in manufacturing processes and the methods of handling them will be discussed in this and the following chapters. This chapter and part of the next will be concerned primarily with a single-product factory. In the following chapter, costing of multiple products will be discussed.

Process Cost Accounting Procedures   Process costs are in reality daily, weekly, or monthly *average* costs. In order to emphasize this *average* characteristic, there are certain procedures which must be stressed at this time. These are as follows:

1. Material, labor, and manufacturing overhead costs are accumulated and re-corded by *departments* or *processes*. However, the cost accounting pro-cedure differs slightly from that of specific job order cost accounting, viz:

   a) *Material Costs.* Stores ledger cards may be kept for each kind of ma-terial. Material requisitions may be used but are not necessary. In place of them, so-called *consumption reports* are kept by either the stores or the manufacturing departments. Since the same materials are used in the same departments time after time, the use of consumption reports simplifies the accounting; in effect, they take the place of recapitulation sheets in job order costs. Furthermore, in process cost accounting, no distinction is ordinarily made between direct and indirect materials. In some concerns the materials are actually stored in or near the depart-ments in which they are to be used, thus simplifying the handling and issuing of the material and the recording of the material consumed. Since in many concerns all materials used in manufacturing are to be placed in manufacturing in the initial department, the procedure for handling material costs will be controlled by this department.

   The accounting entries to record the use of materials in production are a charge to the work-in-process account for the department in which used. Entries are made periodically, usually weekly or monthly, viz:

Work-in-Process—Dept. A...............................	3,200.00	
Work-in-Process—Dept. B...............................	1,800.00	
Work-in-Process—Dept. C...............................	2,000.00	
Stores Control.......................................		7,000.00

   To summarize the materials used in production as indicated by the departmental (or factory) consumption reports for month.

   b) *Labor Costs.* No distinction is usually made between direct and in-direct labor. Job time tickets are not necessary. Payrolls are prepared by departments or production centers and provide the labor cost for manu-facturing during a certain period. Although most labor is on an hourly basis, piece-rate work may also be involved.

   The accounting entry for both direct and indirect labor costs will be a charge to the departmental work-in-process accounts, viz:

Work-in-Process—Dept. A...............................	4,000.00	
Work-in-Process—Dept. B...............................	3,000.00	
Work-in-Process—Dept. C...............................	2,000.00	
Payroll or Payroll Clearing Account......................		9,000.00

   To allocate the payroll of the factory to the departments for the month.

   Although not a necessary record, but for purposes of control, the simple form of labor distribution shown in Illustration 10–1 might be set up on a pegboard so that the departmental sheets may be over-lapped. For control purposes, direct and indirect labor costs are herein separated.

   c) *Manufacturing Overhead.* In process cost accounting, manufacturing overhead may be charged to the various departments on a predeter-

Illustration 10–1. Labor Distribution Sheets

LABOR DISTRIBUTION

FOR MONTH ENDING _March_

CLASSIFICATION	DEPARTMENT A HOURS	DEPARTMENT A AMOUNT	DEPARTMENT B HOURS	DEPARTMENT B AMOUNT	DEPARTMENT C HOURS	DEPARTMENT C AMOUNT
DEPARTMENTAL PAYROLL						
HOURS WORKED	2,800	4,000 00	2,200	3,000 00	1,700	2,000 00
REGULAR EARNINGS		2,800 00		2,750 00		1,700 00
OVERTIME BONUS PAY		900 00		150 00		100 00
VACATION PAY		300 00		100 00		200 00
TOTAL WAGES		4,000 00		3,000 00		2,000 00
PAYROLL DISTRIBUTION						
DIRECT LABOR HOURS	2,600		1,950		1,600	
DIRECT LABOR REGULAR EARNINGS		2,600 00		2,500 00		1,600 00
INDIRECT LABOR HOURS	200		250		100	
INDIRECT LABOR COSTS: REGULAR		200 00		250 00		100 00
OVERTIME BONUS		900 00		150 00		100 00
VACATION PAY		300 00		100 00		200 00
TOTALS–HOURS	2,800		2,200		1,700	
TOTALS–PAY		4,000 00		3,000 00		2,000 00

mined basis, the same as in job order costing. However, it is not customary to do so in those process industries where the very evenness and regularity of the continuous flow of production automatically "normalizes" the amount of the *actual* manufacturing overhead. Under these circumstances, the use of a predetermined normal rate of applied manufacturing overhead is unnecessary. However, if the process work is not produced uniformly throughout an accounting period, costs may fluctuate considerably from period to period unless a predetermined overhead rate is used. This is also true if the work is on a seasonal plan. Therefore, when production varies from period to period or from season to season, such as in a canning plant or in a coal mine or meatpacking plant, the use of a predetermined rate is desirable in the interest of more "normal" costs. Another problem arises in the concurrent manufacture of several products (or various sizes, shapes, or weights of the same product) in the same departments or cost centers. Here the application of manufacturing overhead to the various products on a predetermined basis cannot be on the basis of the number of units but must be on some suitably weighted method.

It should be further noted that some process manufacturing concerns keep separate accounts for *fixed manufacturing overhead* and for *variable manufacturing overhead*. The variable overhead may then be charged *directly* into the departmental work-in-process accounts, and the fixed overhead may be prorated on a *predetermined rate* to the production for the period. Such proration would assume, as in standard costs, that idle capacity should be considered in measuring efficiency and that part of the underapplied manufacturing overhead should be charged against management as their responsibility. Proration would therefore be based upon normal production capacity.

It should be noted, however, that there is an increasing trend toward the use of a predetermined overhead rate in process cost accounting because it permits more satisfactory comparisons of unit costs from period to period.

The entry for the manufacturing overhead charged to production would be:

```
Work-in-Process—Dept. A...................................3,150.00
Work-in-Process—Dept. B...................................2,000.00
Work-in-Process—Dept. C...................................1,800.00
    Manufacturing Overhead Control........................    6,950.00
    To record the distribution of the manufacturing overhead to the
    departmental accounts and production.
```

If a predetermined overhead rate is used, the entry would be:

```
Work-in-Process—Dept. A...................................3,150.00
Work-in-Process—Dept. B...................................2,000.00
Work-in-Process—Dept. C...................................1,800.00
    Applied Manufacturing Overhead........................    6,950.00
    To record the application of overhead to work-in-process on pre-
    determined departmental rates.
```

2. The second characteristic of process cost accounting has already been indicated. Costs are kept on a *time basis,* not on a job basis. That is, material, labor, and manufacturing overhead costs are summarized daily, weekly, or monthly, as required by the individual needs of any particular firm.

3. A third characteristic of process cost accounting relates to the summary report of costs made weekly, daily, or monthly. It is known as a *cost of production report* and covers the cost of materials, labor, and manufacturing overhead for a *definite period* of time on a *departmental* basis.

4. A fourth characteristic of process cost accounting is that the cost of production must always contain a *quantity of production report,* either as an integral part or a supplementary report. This will show the number of units started or received into production, the number completed, in process, lost, and transferred out of the department, viz:

QUANTITY OF PRODUCTION REPORT DEPARTMENT I For Month of January, 19—		
Put into Process—to Be Accounted For...................		60,000 lbs.
Accounted for as Follows:		
Completed and Transferred to Dept. II..................	45,000 lbs.	
Work-in-Process (1/31/—).............................	15,000 lbs.	
Lost in Production...................................	0	
Total Accounted For................................		60,000 lbs.

There is usually some provision for the recording of the *unit cost* for each department. This may be recorded by the departments only or by each element within each department followed by the total for that department.

The Summary Cost of Production Report
The form of the summary cost of production reports for process costs is not standardized. The form depends upon the type and number of products being manufactured and the number of departments through which the material must pass in the course of production. Any logical presentation of data which will cover the characteristics just given is acceptable. The type of cost of production report illustrated in this chapter is readily adaptable to most process cost accounting situations.

To illustrate the cost of production report, the following departmental data of the Alton Manufacturing Company for the month of January are given:

In Department I:
Sixty thousand pounds of material costing $18,000 were put into process.
Payroll cost for the month was $7,500.
Overhead costs for month were $2,500.
Forty-five thousand pounds were completed and transferred to Department II. Fifteen thousand pounds are still in process. On this work-in-process, all necessary material for the finished product has been used, but it was considered one-third complete as to labor and manufacturing overhead costs.

In Department II:
Payroll costs were $10,500.
Overhead costs were $5,600.
Of the 45,000 pounds received in the department from Department I, 25,000 pounds were completed and transferred to Department III; 5,000 pounds were completed and still in Department II; 15,000 pounds are still in process, being considered one-third complete as to labor and manufacturing overhead costs in Department II.

In Department III:
Payroll costs were $4,400.
Overhead costs were $3,080.
Of the 25,000 pounds received in this department from Department II, 20,000 pounds were completed and sent to the stock room and 5,000 pounds are still in process and are estimated to be 40 percent complete as to labor and manufacturing overhead costs.

In Illustration 10–2 these data are shown on the summary cost of production report. The form of this illustration is flexible enough to be

Illustration 10-2

ALTON MANUFACTURING COMPANY
SUMMARY COST OF PRODUCTION REPORT
For Month of January, 19—

	Department I		Department II		Department III		Totals	
	Cost	Per Unit	Cost	Per Unit	Cost	Per Unit	Cost	Per Unit
COST IN PRECEDING DEPARTMENT:								
Transferred in during Month			$22,500.00	$0.50	$24,000.00	$0.96	xxx	xxx
Additional Cost for Lost Units				xx		xx	xx	xx
COST IN CURRENT DEPARTMENT:								
Material Costs	$18,000.00	$0.30	$10,500.00	$0.30	$ 4,400.00	$0.20	$18,000.00	$0.30
Labor Costs	7,500.00	0.15	5,600.00	0.16	3,080.00	0.14	22,400.00	0.65
Manufacturing Overhead Costs*	2,500.00	0.05					11,180.00	0.35
Total Departmental Costs	$28,000.00	$0.50	$16,100.00	$0.46	$ 7,480.00	$0.34	$51,580.00	$1.30
CUMULATIVE COST TOTAL	$28,000.00	$0.50	$38,600.00	$0.96	$31,480.00	$1.30	$51,580.00	$1.30
Transferred to Next Department	$22,500.00	$0.50	$24,000.00	$0.96	$26,000.00	$1.30		
Work-in-Process:								
Completed and on Hand, 1/31/—	0		4,800.00	0.96	0			
Work-in-Process, 1/31/—	5,500.00		9,800.00		5,480.00			
CUMULATIVE COST DISTRIBUTION	$28,000.00		$38,600.00		$31,480.00			

QUANTITY OF PRODUCTION REPORT (In Pounds)

	Department I	Department II	Department III
QUANTITY TO BE ACCOUNTED FOR:			
Completed and on Hand, 1/1/—			
Work-in-Process, 1/1/—			
Put into Process or Received from Preceding Departments	60,000	45,000	25,000
To Be Accounted For	60,000	45,000	25,000
QUANTITY ACCOUNTED FOR AS FOLLOWS:			
Transferred to Next Department	45,000	25,000	20,000
Work-in-Process:			
Completed and on Hand, 1/31/—	0	5,000	0
Work-in-Process, 1/31/—	15,000	15,000	5,000
(Stage of Completion			
Material Costs	(100%)	0	0
Labor Costs	(33⅓%)	(33⅓%)	(40%)
Mfg. Overhead Costs)	(33⅓%)	(33⅓%)	(40%)
Lost or Spoiled Production	0	0	0
Total Accounted For	60,000	45,000	25,000

readily adaptable to most process industries. The characteristics of this summary cost of production report which should be noted are these:

1. For each department the costs are shown separately for each element, namely, material, labor, and manufacturing overhead. These costs are shown in total and on a *per unit* basis.
2. An analysis is made of the total costs of production in each department. This analysis shows: the cost of production transferred to the next department; the cost of work completed and not transferred; and the unfinished work, or work-in-process, in the department. In later reports, the problem of units lost in production will be introduced.
3. A *quantity of production report* is necessary for the computation of unit costs. This report will show for each department the quantity received and to be accounted for and the disposition of the quantity thus received.

In the preparation of this summary cost of production report, the following three factors must be considered:

1. The nature of the *units of production.*
2. The computation of *unit costs* through the medium of *equivalent production.*
3. The treatment of interdepartmental transfers.

These factors will be discussed in connection with Illustration 10–2.

Nature of Units of Production in Process Cost Procedures

In a process type of industry, the costs of production are reduced not only to the unit basis but in most instances to *units by elements of cost,* that is, the cost for materials, labor, and manufacturing overhead in each department. The units of manufacture are variously expressed, e.g.:

In the production of ice cream, *gallons* of milk and cream, *pounds* of sugar and gelatin, and *ounces* of flavoring are mixed to produce *gallons, quarts,* and *pints* of the finished product. It is evident that the *units of the materials* used in manufacturing are not the deciding factors used in computing the *unit costs* of production. It is rather the *units of the completed production in each department*—in this instance, gallons of ice cream.

In the production of paint products, *pounds* of lead, zinc, and titanium are mixed with *gallons* of linseed oil, dryers, and solvents to produce *gallons* of paint. The units of production must be that of the completed units—gallons of paint.

In the manufacture of cement, *tons* of rock and shale are combined with other materials to produce *bags* or *barrels* of cement. The *bags* or *barrels* are units of production used in computing unit costs, not the tons of rock and shale.

So, whenever and wherever in this discussion the quantity report is used, the figures given refer to the *units* being produced—the units of the finished production in each department. These may change from department to department. Therefore, in most process manufacturing firms, little attention is given to the number of units put into process unless these are expressed in the same terms as the completed units. Production for each department is usually analyzed into:

1. Units completed and transferred to a subsequent department.
2. Units completed but remaining in the department (not yet transferred).
3. Units still in process, for which an estimate must be made of the stage of completion.

From this quantitative analysis of departmental production, unit costs can be computed. In the illustration given, all production, including the materials put into process, is expressed in terms of pounds. This simplifies the computation of unit costs.

Computation of Unit Costs through Equivalent Production   Because in process cost accounting many firms will have some unfinished work at the end of the accounting period, it is necessary to convert this work-in-process to *equivalent* finished units. The problem of *equivalent production* arises *only* in those plants in which there is some unfinished work (work-in-process) at the end of the period for which the cost of production report is being prepared. It is necessary to compute the equivalent production so that unit costs may be calculated. To indicate how the equivalent production is computed and used in determining the units costs by elements, reference is made to the summary cost of production report (Illustration 10–2, p. 296).

In Department I, 60,000 pounds of material were put into production. Since both the completed and work-in-process *units of production* already are complete as far as the material costs are concerned, and since no units of production were lost or spoiled in the manufacturing, the equivalent production for the *material costs* is 60,000 units, as follows:

```
Completed and transferred to the next department.............45,000 lbs. (units)
In process but complete as far as materials costs are concerned. .15,000
    Equivalent Production...................................60,000 lbs. (units)
```

Dividing these 60,000 units into the $18,000 material cost results in a *unit* cost for materials in Department I of 30 cents.

The computation of unit costs for the elements of labor and manufacturing overhead is different, viz:

Forty-five thousand units were completed and transferred to Department II. As far as labor and manufacturing overhead costs are concerned, these units are equivalent to 45,000 finished units.

Fifteen thousand units are still in the process in Department I and are *estimated* to be one-third complete in the matter of labor and manufacturing overhead costs. These 15,000 are therefore *equivalent to* 5,000 finished units for these two elements of cost.

The total equivalent production in Department I for these two cost elements is therefore 50,000 units (45,000 + 5,000). Dividing the labor costs ($7,500) and the manufacturing overhead costs ($2,500) by this equivalent production (50,000) results in unit costs of 15 cents and 5 cents for labor and manufacturing overhead, respectively.

It is obvious that without the computation of an *equivalent production* it would not be possible to calculate the unit costs for labor and manufacturing overhead.

Determining the Stage of Completion of Work-in-Process The methods of determining or estimating the stage of completion of the work-in-process differs with industries. For some firms, it is possible to compute quite accurately the time it would take in a given department to complete the manufacture of a product. This may be done by determining *the* number of machine operations required, the length of time for each operation, or the number of man-hours required for the complete manufacturing cycle in a given department, and by computing the number which have already been used on the work-in-process. In other firms this is not so exact, and therefore an estimate or average must be used. For example, in the textile industry, where many departments are involved, instead of computing a separate "stage of completion" for each department, it is assumed that all work-in-process at the end of any given period is either one-half or one-third complete. In the manufacture of some products which require a carefully controlled period of aging, curing, or chemical action, it is possible to have separate batches or quantities started from day to day. The progress of these quantities, separately recorded, can furnish a fairly reliable figure of the stage of completion. For example, assume that one product requires three days for completion in a given department and that each day a new lot is started. At the end of the accounting period, some of the material will be one-third complete, some will be two-thirds complete, and the remainder will be completed. The determination of a reliable "stage of completion" is an important factor in the calculation of dependable unit cost figures in process industries. However, since in many cases the applied manufacturing overhead is based upon labor hours or labor costs, the same ratio or stage of completion is used for manufacturing overhead costs as is used for labor costs.

Applying these principles to the labor and overhead costs in the second and third departments, the computation of unit costs is as follows:

Department II

25,000 units completed and transferred, equivalent to	. . . .	25,000 units
5,000 units completed and on hand, equivalent to	. . . .	5,000
15,000 units ⅓ complete, equivalent to	. . . .	5,000
Equivalent Production for Labor and Overhead	. . . .	35,000 units

Dividing 35,000 units into $10,500 (labor costs) and $5,600 (overhead costs) results in unit costs as follows:

$0.30 per unit for labor costs in Department II, and $0.16 per unit for overhead costs in Department II.

Department III

20,000 units completed and transferred, equivalent to	. . . .	20,000 units
5,000 units in process, 40% complete, equivalent to	. . . .	2,000
Total Equivalent Production for Labor and Overhead	. . . .	22,000 units

Dividing 22,000 units into $4,400 (labor costs) and $3,080 (overhead costs) results in unit costs as follows:

$0.20 per unit for labor costs and $0.14 per unit for overhead costs in Department III.

Treatment of Interdepartmental Transfers

Some concerns have a separate cost of production report for each department on which are recorded the costs for the material, labor, and overhead for that particular department, together with the quantity of production statistics—quantity of units received into the department, quantity completed and transferred out, quantity in process at end of period, units lost or spoiled. Periodically, the cost accounting department prepares a composite summary report of the costs and quantity of production for the entire plant. This summary report will show the interdepartmental transfers.

The simplest treatment is shown in Illustration 10–2, in which the cost data is shown in *sequential flow* from one department to another, as well as the analysis in each department of work completed and transferred out; work completed and on hand; work-in-process at end of the period; together with the quantity statement for each of these costs plus the quantity lost or spoiled. Since this method is simple and logical, the entries for it will be illustrated in the subsequent discussion. The flow chart for this procedure is illustrated on page 301.

Accounting Entries Involved in Departmental Transfers

By this time, the reader must realize that most of the departmental or process cost accounting consists of mathematical computations. The few accounting entries required refer to the departmental transfers. To illustrate these entries as

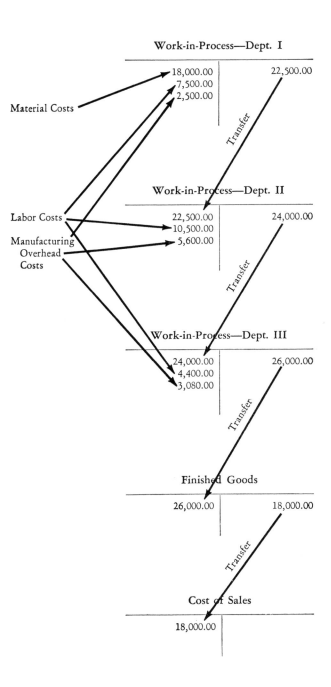

Work-in-Process—Dept. I

18,000.00	22,500.00
7,500.00	
2,500.00	

Material Costs

Transfer

Work-in-Process—Dept. II

22,500.00	24,000.00
10,500.00	
5,600.00	

Labor Costs

Manufacturing
Overhead
Costs

Transfer

Work-in-Process—Dept. III

24,000.00	26,000.00
4,400.00	
3,080.00	

Transfer

Finished Goods

26,000.00	18,000.00

Transfer

Cost of Sales

18,000.00

taken from the summary cost of production report (Illustration 10–2), the following are given. It should be noted, however, that the amounts of *the departmental transfers are calculated by using the unit costs which have been computed and accumulated and the quantities which have been transferred.*

(1)

Work-in-Process—Dept. I	28,000.00	
Stores Control		18,000.00
Payroll		7,500.00
Manufacturing Overhead Control		2,500.00

To record cost of materials, labor, and overhead used in Dept. I during January.

(2)[1]

Work-in-Process—Dept. II	22,500.00	
Work-in-Process—Dept. I		22,500.00

To record cost of work transferred to Dept. II from Dept. I (45,000 pounds X $0.50).

(3)

Work-in-Process—Dept. II	16,100.00	
Payroll		10,500.00
Manufacturing Overhead Control		5,600.00

To record costs incurred in Dept. II during January.

(4)[2]

Work-in-Process—Dept. III	31,480.00	
Work-in-Process—Dept. II		24,000.00
Payroll		4,400.00
Manufacturing Overhead Control		3,080.00

To record the transfer and the departmental costs for Dept. III during the month of January (25,000 pounds X $0.96).

(5)

Finished Goods	26,000.00	
Work-in-Process—Dept. III		26,000.00

To record cost of work completed and sent to finished goods stock room (20,000 pounds X $1.30).

If these entries are posted to the various accounts, the balances in departmental work-in-process accounts represent the work-in-process inventories in each department. *It should be noted that work completed but not transferred out of a department is part of the work-in-process inventory of that department,* viz:

Work-in-Process—Dept. I

(1)		28,000.00	(2)		22,500.00

---

[1] Two separate entries are made to record costs in Department II—one for departmental transfer and one for additional costs in department during month. These two entries may be combined as illustrated in next footnote.

[2] Both the departmental transfer and the departmental costs are combined into a single entry.

Work-in-Process—Dept. II

| (2) | 22,500.00 | (4) | 24,000.00 |
| (3) | 16,100.00 | | |

Work-in-Process—Dept. III

| (4) | 31,480.00 | (5) | 26,000.00 |

Finished Goods

| (5) | 26,000.00 | | |

It is possible to verify the accuracy of the work-in-process inventories in each department by mathematical computations, viz:

Department I

Material costs of work-in-process:
15,000 units 100% complete, at $0.30......................$4,500
Labor and overhead costs in process:
15,000 units ⅓ complete, at $0.15.......................... 750
15,000 units ⅓ complete, at $0.05.......................... 250
Total... $ 5,500

Department II

15,000 units in process:
Cost in preceding department (Dept. I):
15,000 units 100% complete, at $0.50.....................$7,500
Cost in Dept. II (labor and overhead ⅓ complete):
15,000 units ⅓ complete, at $0.30........................ 1,500
15,000 units ⅓ complete, at $0.16........................ 800
Total cost of unfinished units........................ $ 9,800
5,000 units completed but not transferred out:
Cost in preceding department (Dept. I):
5,000 units 100% complete, at $0.50.....................$2,500
Cost in Dept. II (labor and overhead 100% complete):
5,000 units 100% complete, at $0.30...................... 1,500
5,000 units 100% complete, at $0.16...................... 800   4,800
Total Cost of Inventory............................. $14,600

Department III

5,000 units in process:
Cost in preceding departments (Depts. I and II):
5,000 units 100% complete, at $0.96.....................$4,800
Cost in Dept. III (labor and overhead 40% complete):
5,000 units 40% complete, at $0.20........................ 400
5,000 units 40% complete, at $0.14........................ 280
Total... $ 5,480

An alternative method of recording the information shown on the summary cost of production report makes use of but a single factory-wide Work-in-Process account, leaving the departmental details on the departmental cost reports. The figures would be taken from the Total column shown on the summary cost of production report. Referring to the same illustration used previously, the journal entries under this method would be:

(1)

Work-in-Process..51,580.00		
Stores...	18,000.00	
Payroll..	22,400.00	
Manufacturing Overhead Control............................	11,180.00	

To summarize cost of production for month per cost of production report.

(2)

Finished Goods..26,000.00	
Work-in-Process..	26,000.00

To record cost of work completed and placed in stock room during January.

This alternative method may be too condensed for most cost accountants. However, if the supporting cost reports are sufficiently detailed, this method can probably be used satisfactorily.

Special Accounting Problems Arising in Process Cost Accounting

In view of the wide variety of conditions under which process cost accounting might operate, a number of special problems will arise. These will be discussed in detail in this and in subsequent chapters. Among these problems are:

1. The *effect of lost units* (whether due to spoilage or shrinkage), on process cost accounting. These units may be lost at the beginning, during, or at the end of the departmental manufacturing operations. This problem of lost units must be further analyzed to determine:

   a) The *effect on the unit costs* in the department in which the loss occurs, and

   b) The *effect on the cumulative unit costs.*

2. The *meaning of* and the *methods of computing the final work-in-process* inventories. Two methods can be used, and these check each other:

   a) The *account-balance* method, and

   b) The *analyzed-by-elements* method.

3. The accounting treatment of *materials added to production in any department after the first.* These materials may:

   a) *Increase* the number of the units in production, or

   b) *Not* affect the number of the units in production.

4. The treatment of the *work-in-process inventory* at the beginning of the period when computing unit costs. Two methods are used:

   a) The *average method;* and

   b) The *first-in, first-out method* (FIFO).

5. *Simplified process* cost accounting for the *average method* eliminating lost unit costing, adjustment for work-in-process inventory at beginning, and for added materials increasing volume of production.
6. The proration of costs when *multiple products* are manufactured simultaneously in a given department and complete segregation of operations and costs is not possible. Sometimes this problem is referred to *as joint-product* or *coproduct* accounting.
7. The effect of *by-products* on process cost accounting.

Effect of Lost Units on Process Cost Accounting   Lost or spoiled units occur in some industries due to shrinkage, evaporation, or defective work. Lost or spoiled units do not affect the *total* costs of manufacturing during a given period but do increase the *unit* costs. This increase in unit costs is due to the fact that the cost of the work done on the lost units must be absorbed by the remaining good units, thus increasing the unit costs of these good units.

The problem of lost unit cost accounting involves two phases: (*a*) the cost of the work done on the lost units in the *department in which the loss or spoilage occurs,* and (*b*) the cost of the work done on the lost units in the *preceding departments.*

The cost of work done on the lost units in the department in which the loss occurs is handled quite simply. By omitting the lost unit quantity from the production in that department, a smaller equivalent production results. Dividing a smaller quantity into the material, labor, and overhead costs yields a *higher per unit cost* for each element.

The unit cost of the work done on the lost units in preceding departments is computed as follows:

a) Determine the *cost* of the work transferred into the department, including those subsequently lost or spoiled.
b) Divide this cost by the remaining good units (after deducting those spoiled or lost). This gives the corrected *cost per unit* for preceding departments.
c) Subtracting from this *corrected unit cost,* the unit cost of the units when transferred in gives the lost unit cost.

Another method, which is perhaps easier to compute, is as follows:

a) Multiply the *lost units* by the *unit cost* for the preceding departments.
b) Divide this result by the remaining good units (those received from preceding department less spoiled units) to obtain the lost unit cost.

Illustration of the Computation of Lost Unit Costs   The *lost unit cost* may be recorded as a separate element of cost on the cost of production report. To illustrate the computation of the lost unit costs and the effect of these lost unit costs on the cost of production report and the work-in-process inventory, the summary cost of production report of the Alton Manufacturing Company, previously given for the month of January, is again used; but the quantity of production figures has been changed to provide for the lost units. The material costs have been changed to simplify the computations.

Illustration 10–3

ANALYSIS OF COST OF PRODUCTION DATA

For Month of January, 19—

QUANTITY OF PRODUCTION DATA (In Pounds)

	Department I	Department II	Department III
QUANTITY TO BE ACCOUNTED FOR:			
Put into Process....................	60,000		
Received in Department.............		45,000	25,000
To Be Accounted For............	60,000	45,000	25,000
QUANTITY ACCOUNTED FOR AS FOLLOWS:			
Completed and Transferred to Next Department.......................	45,000	25,000	20,000
Completed and on Hand in Department..	.....	5,000	.....
Work-in-Process:			
Material, 100% Complete, Labor and Overhead, 50% Complete........	10,000		
Labor and Overhead, 33⅓% Complete		15,000	
Labor and Overhead, 50% Complete.			4,000
Lost or Spoiled Production...........	5,000	0	1,000
Total Accounted For............	60,000	45,000	25,000

DEPARTMENTAL COST OF PRODUCTION DATA

	Department I	Department II	Department III
Material Costs........................	$16,500.00	....	....
Labor Costs..........................	7,500.00	$10,500.00	$4,400.00
Manufacturing Overhead (Direct and Apportioned)........................	2,500.00	5,600.00	3,080.00
Total Departmental Costs........	$26,500.00	$16,100.00	$7,480.00

The data relating to the summary cost of production report are shown in Illustration 10–3. The summary cost of production report for January for these data is given in Illustration 10–4. The computations for the departments are as shown on page 308.

Illustration 10-4

ALTON MANUFACTURING COMPANY
SUMMARY COST OF PRODUCTION REPORT
For Month of January, 19—

	Department I		Department II		Department III		Totals	
	Cost	Per Unit	Cost	Per Unit	Cost	Per Unit	Cost	Per Unit
COST IN PRECEDING DEPARTMENT:								
Transferred in during Month			$22,500.00	$0.50	$24,000.00	$0.96	xxx	xxx
Additional Cost for Lost Units					xx	0.04		$0.04
Adjusted Unit Cost Total			$22,500.00	$0.50	$24,000.00	$1.00		$0.04
COST IN CURRENT DEPARTMENT:								
Material Costs	$16,500.00	$0.30	$10,500.00	$0.30	$ 4,400.00	$0.20	$16,500.00	$0.30
Labor Costs	7,500.00	0.15	5,600.00	0.16	3,080.00	0.14	22,400.00	0.65
Manufacturing Overhead Costs	2,500.00	0.05					11,180.00	0.35
Total Departmental Costs	$26,500.00	$0.50	$16,100.00	$0.46	$ 7,480.00	$0.34	$50,080.00	$1.30
CUMULATIVE COST TOTAL	$26,500.00	xx	$38,600.00	xx	$31,480.00	xx	$50,080.00	xx
Transferred to Next Department	$22,500.00	$0.50	$24,000.00	$0.96	$26,800.00	$1.34	$26,800.00	$1.34
Work-in-Process:								
Completed and on Hand, 1/31/—			4,800.00				4,800.00	
Work-in-Process, 1/31/—	4,000.00		9,800.00	0.96	4,680.00		18,480.00	xx
CUMULATIVE COST DISTRIBUTION	$26,500.00		$38,600.00		$31,480.00		$50,080.00	

QUANTITY OF PRODUCTION REPORT (In Pounds)

	Department I	Department II	Department III
QUANTITY TO BE ACCOUNTED FOR:			
Completed and on Hand, 1/1/—			
Work-in-Process, 1/1/—			
Put into Process or Received from Preceding Departments	60,000	45,000	25,000
To Be Accounted For	60,000	45,000	25,000
QUANTITY ACCOUNTED FOR AS FOLLOWS:			
Transferred to Next Department	45,000	25,000	20,000
Work-in-Process:			
Completed and on Hand, 1/31/—*	0	5,000	0
Work-in-Process, 1/31/—*	10,000(½)	15,000(⅓)	4,000(½)
Lost or Spoiled Production	5,000	0	1,000
Total Accounted For	60,000	45,000	25,000

* Figures in parentheses indicate stage of completion of work-in-process for labor and overhead.

Department I

Equivalent production for material costs is:

Completed and transferred to next department............45,000 units
In process but complete as to material costs...............10,000
    Equivalent Production for Material Costs............55,000 units

$$\frac{\$16,500}{55,000 \text{ units}} = \$0.30 \text{ unit cost for material.}$$

Equivalent production for labor and overhead costs is:

Completed and transferred...............................45,000 lbs.
In process, ½ complete, 10,000 pounds, equal to.............. 5,000
    Equivalent Production............................50,000 lbs.

$$\frac{\$7,500}{50,000 \text{ lbs.}} = \$0.15 \text{ unit cost for labor.}$$

$$\frac{\$2,500}{50,000 \text{ lbs.}} = \$0.05 \text{ unit cost for overhead.}$$

By omitting the 5,000 pounds lost in production, the equivalent production is a smaller quantity. Dividing by a smaller quantity results in a larger unit cost. Computation of work-in-process inventory, January 31, in Department I:

10,000 lbs. × 100% × $0.30 (material cost).................$3,000
10,000 lbs. × 50% × $0.15 (labor cost)..................... 750
10,000 lbs. × 50% × $0.05 (overhead cost)................. 250
    Work-in-Process Inventory, Dept. I.....................$4,000

Department II

Equivalent production for labor and overhead costs is:

Completed and transferred...............................25,000 lbs.
Completed and on hand................................... 5,000
In process, ⅓ complete (15,000 × ⅓).................... 5,000
    Equivalent Production............................35,000 lbs.

$$\frac{\$10,500}{35,000 \text{ lbs.}} = \$0.30 \text{ unit cost for labor.}$$

$$\frac{\$5,600}{35,000 \text{ lbs.}} = \$0.16 \text{ unit cost for overhead.}$$

Computation of work-in-process inventory, January 31, Department II:

5,000 lbs., complete as to Depts. I and II @ $0.96............$ 4,800
15,000 lbs., cost in Dept. I..............@ 0.50.............. 7,500
15,000 lbs. × ⅓ × $0.30, Dept. II (labor cost)............... 1,500
15,000 lbs. × ⅓ × $0.16, Dept. II (overhead cost)............ 800
    Work-in-Process Inventory, Dept. II.....................$14,600

Department III

Equivalent production for labor and overhead, omitting the 1,000 pounds lost in production, is 20,000 pounds plus one half of 4,000 pounds, or 22,000 pounds. The cost of the work done on the 1,000 pounds in Department III *only* is automatically absorbed by dividing by a smaller quantity with the following resulting unit costs in Department III:

$$\frac{\$4,400}{22,000 \text{ lbs.}} = \$0.20 \text{ unit cost for labor.}$$

$$\frac{\$3,080}{22,000 \text{ lbs.}} = \$0.14 \text{ unit cost for overhead.}$$

Computation of the additional *unit cost* for work done in Departments I and II on the lost units is as follows:

1,000 pounds × the cumulative cost for Departments I and II ($0.50 plus $0.46) or $0.96 equals $960.
Dividing this figure ($960) by the remaining good units that came into Department III (25,000 pounds less 1,000), 24,000 pounds, results in an additional unit cost of $0.04 for the lost units.

Computation of the work-in-process inventory, January 31, Department III:

```
4,000 lbs. × $0.96 (cost in Depts. I and II).....................$3,840
4,000 lbs. × $0.04—in additional cost for first two departments for
   lost units.....................................................  160
      Total costs for Depts. I and II............................$4,000
4,000 lbs. × ½ × $0.20 (for labor cost in Dept. III)............  400
4,000 lbs. × ½ × $0.14 (for overhead cost in Dept. III).........  280
      Work-in-Process Inventory, Dept. III.......................$4,680
```

Illustration of Accounting Entries Covering Process Cost Accounting Cycle

The accounting entries in journal form to record the production costs and the interdepartmental transfers for the month of January would be as follows:

(1)
```
Work-in-Process—Dept. I.................................26,500.00
   Stores...................................................        16,500.00
   Payroll..................................................         7,500.00
   Manufacturing Overhead Control..........................         2,500.00
   To record the cost of work put into process in Dept. I in January.
```

(2)
```
Work-in-Process—Dept. II................................38,600.00
   Work-in-Process—Dept. I.................................        22,500.00
   Payroll..................................................        10,500.00
   Manufacturing Overhead Control..........................         5,600.00
   To record the transfer from Dept. I of 45,000 units at 50 cents and
   the charges for payroll and manufacturing overhead during Janu-
   ary in Dept. II.
```

(3)

```
Work-in-Process—Dept. III...................................31,480.00
    Work-in-Process—Dept. II.............................          24,000.00
    Payroll..............................................           4,400.00
    Manufacturing Overhead Control.......................           3,080.00
    To record the transfer from Dept. II of 25,000 units at 96 cents, and
    the charges for payroll and manufacturing overhead during Janu-
    ary in Dept. III.
```

(4)

```
Finished Goods............................................26,800.00
    Work-in-Process—Dept. III............................          26,800.00
    To record the transfer to finished stock room 20,000 units at $1.34.
```

If a summary entry is to be made for the entire month's operation with but a single Work-in-Process account, not on a departmental basis, the following journal entries might be used:

(1)

```
Work-in-Process..........................................50,080.00
    Stores...............................................          16,500.00
    Payroll..............................................          22,400.00
    Manufacturing Overhead Control.......................          11,180.00
    To record operating costs for the month.
```

(2)

```
Finished Goods...........................................26,800.00
    Work-in-Process......................................          26,800.00
    To record cost of the finished work—20,000 units at $1.34.
```

An Alternative Method of Recording Finished Goods for a Process Cost Accounting Firm

An alternative method of recording the finished goods for a firm using a process cost accounting system eliminates the departmental transfers. This is accomplished by computing the *final work-in-process inventory in each department* from the individual or summary cost of production reports and transferring the balance in the work-in-process accounts to the Finished Goods account. The accounting effect is the same as when there are departmental transfers. The departmental transfer method is more desirable because it is more logical and follows the data shown on the cost of production report. It also is probably less prone to mistakes, since there must be detailed verification on the cost of production reports as indicated by the details which make up the "CUMULATIVE COST TOTAL ACCOUNTED FOR" in each departmental column. To illustrate the entry to be made when there are no departmental transfer entries, the illustration of cost of production report (Illustration 10–4) for the month of January is used. Exclusive of the departmental transfers, the charges to the three departmental work-in-process accounts and the amount of the final work-in-process inventories are given so that the amount of the charge to the Finished Goods account may be computed, viz:

Department	Charges to Work-in-Process Account	Final Work-in-Process Inventory	Difference as Charge to Finished Goods Account
Work-in-Process—Dept. I......	$26,500	$ 4,000	$22,500
Work-in-Process—Dept. II.....	16,100	14,600	1,500
Work-in-Process—Dept. III....	7,480	4,680	2,800

The journal entry to record this without departmental transfers would then be:

```
Finished Goods.........................................26,800.00
    Work-in-Process—Dept. I..............................        22,500.00
    Work-in-Process—Dept. II.............................         1,500.00
    Work-in-Process—Dept. III............................         2,800.00
    To record cost of finished goods for the month.
```

An Alternative Treatment of Lost Unit Costs

There is an alternative method of treating lost unit costs which can be adapted to some manufacturing concerns. This method attempts to treat as an *additional manufacturing overhead cost,* listed separately in the department in which the lost units occur, the *lost unit cost* resulting from the work done on the lost units in the preceding departments. As such, it would have to be apportioned on the basis of *equivalent production for the department in which the loss occurs.* In other words, both the final work-in-process inventory and the units completed, whether transferred or not, would have as elements of costs (unit figures assumed):

```
Materials.................................................$0.40
Labor costs............................................... 0.30
Manufacturing overhead.................................... 0.20
Lost unit cost............................................ 0.04
    Total Unit Cost.......................................$0.94
```

The uncompleted units in this department will be charged only for the pro rata share of the lost unit cost. This seems more accurate than some of the other methods discussed, since should there be any additional lost units in the subsequent period in which the work-in-process units are to be completed, these work-in-process units will have to be charged with an additional pro rata share of such lost unit cost.

To illustrate this method, reference is made to the preceding cost of production report, Department III, for the month of January (see page 307).

Costs would be computed in the same manner as before for Department III, namely, 20 cents and 14 cents for labor and manufacturing overhead, respectively. However, the lost unit cost for work done in the preceding departments, namely, 1,000 units at 96 cents, or $960, would be apportioned as manufacturing overhead over the equivalent production of:

```
Units completed and transferred............................20,000
In process, ½ complete as to manufacturing overhead (4,000 × ½)..  2,000
    Equivalent Production....................................22,000
```

The lost unit costs, which would now appear as a second manufacturing overhead unit cost arising from the loss of units, would then be $960 ÷ 22,000 units, or $0.043636, and would be recorded on the cost of production report. This method commends itself by the fact that it can be used for lost units under any conditions in any department, and, furthermore, it is consistent with the theory that the lost unit cost resulting from accumulated costs in preceding departments is actually an additional manufacturing overhead cost for the department in which the loss occurs.

Unit Costs When Units Are Lost at Beginning or End of Departmental Operations For the most part, when units are lost at the beginning or at the end of operations, it implies an inspection of finished production and a rejection of spoiled work. This inspection and rejection may be made before or after unit costs have been computed for departmental operations.

To illustrate the effect on unit costs of these two procedures, the following data are assumed for Department II, for the month of May:

```
Units received from Dept. I, 12,000 with a cost of.............$18,000  ($1.50 each)
Costs in Dept. II for month of May:
    Labor...............................................  2,700
    Overhead............................................  4,500
                                                        $25,200
```

```
Production figures:
    Units transferred to Dept. III...................... 7,000 units
    Units completed and on hand......................... 1,000
    Work-in-process, ⅓ complete as to labor and overhead.. 3,000
    Units lost in production............................ 1,000
                                                        12,000 units
```

If the lost units were discarded before computing the unit costs, the quantity to be accounted for would be based on a total of 11,000 and unit costs would be:

Adjusted unit costs for Dept. I ($18,000.00 ÷ 11,000)......$1.6363 (l.u. cost $0.1363)
Labor costs in Dept. II, equivalent production of 9,000
  ($2,700.00 ÷ 9,000).................................... 0.30
Manufacturing overhead costs in Dept. II ($4,500.00 ÷ 9,000) 0.50
    Total Unit Cost of Goods Transferred.................$2.4363

This figure would be the same as that computed when the units are lost *during* the operations.

If, however, the units are not rejected until *after* the unit costs have been computed (impractical as this may seem), then the adjustment will affect only the finished units, viz:

Unit cost in Dept. I ($18,000.00 ÷ 12,000)................................$1.50
Labor costs in Dept. II (the lost units are considered as finished units)
  ($2,700.00 ÷ 10,000)... 0.27
Manufacturing overhead cost in Dept. II ($4,500.00 ÷ 10,000)................ 0.45
                   $2.22

There were 7,000 finished units *transferred.* Of the 9,000 units finished, 1,000 were rejected as spoiled. Therefore, their cost must be absorbed by the remaining good units (8,000), since some of the present work-in-process in Department II may turn out to be spoiled at the end of June. The resulting unit cost is $2.4975 (9,000 × $2.22 ÷ 8,000), as compared with the figure of $2.4363 previously computed.

Should the lost units not be discovered until the *beginning of operations* in Department III, the same effect would be created in the unit costs as when they were discovered after the cost of production for Department II for May was completed, making the unit cost for work in the preceding departments (that is, I and II), $2.4975.

Normal and Abnormal Spoilage in Production   In Chapter 6 reference was made to loss on spoiled work and shrinkage with particular reference to job order costs. In a continuous process plant the problem of controlling lost or spoiled work becomes even more important. *Normal* loss from evaporation, shrinkage, or spoilage is absorbed in the cost of the remaining good production during the current period. Although for control purposes, it is possible to compute a separate *lost unit cost* for each department including the first, usually, as illustrated in this chapter, the unit cost is shown on the production reports only for all the departments except the first. The purpose of this separate computation of lost or spoiled unit costs is for managerial control. This *lost unit cost* is added to the regular unit costs in each department, as previously illustrated on the production reports in this chapter. From time to time, however, some unforeseen factors may cause an abnormal quantity of spoilage in production. Because of the unforeseen and unexpected nature of this loss, it should not be included in the normal manufacturing cost computations but should be charged directly to the Profit and Loss account. This will exclude the amount from the Finished Goods account. The amount so charged should be at a *unit cost* based on an equivalent production which would include these abnormal lost units. The credit for this loss would be to the work-in-process account involved.

The Methods of Computing the Work-in-Process Inventory in Process Costing

If separate work-in-process accounts are kept for each department, the work-in-process inventories are likewise calculated on a departmental basis. The work-in-process inventory in any department, except the final manufacturing operation, will include not only the unfinished work but also the *work completed but not yet transferred* out of the department. This becomes apparent when one realizes that one method of determining the work-in-process inventory is merely to use the balances in the respective departmental or the factorywide work-in-process accounts. A second method, and one which should be used to verify the balances in the work-in-process accounts, requires detailed computations using the unit costs shown on the cost of production report for each of the elements as shown on page 303.

Two or More Products from the Same Material Prepared in First Department

One type of problem arises in process cost accounting where certain material is processed in the initial department and is then used in the second and third departments to prepare *simultaneously two different products*. It is sometimes termed a "tree problem" because from one trunk, two branches or products are developed. The simplest method of solving a problem of this type is to treat the cost of production of the basic material in Department I as a separate one-department problem. Then separate cost of production reports are prepared for each of the two different products. The cost of the materials received from Department I is treated in Department II for either product as though it were purchased from an outsider. Thus it will be merged with whatever other materials are used in Department II. Hence no separate computation or unit cost figures will appear in Department II for lost units. The effect of this procedure is to make three separate problems summarized on one or two cost of production reports: one problem for costing the production in Department I; and one problem each, for Product A, covering the costing in Departments II and III; and one for Product B, covering the costing in Departments II and III. To illustrate this procedure diagrammatically, the following illustration should be studied.

To illustrate the solution of such a problem and the resulting cost of production reports (Illustration 10–5A), the data of production shown in Illustration 10–5 must be considered.

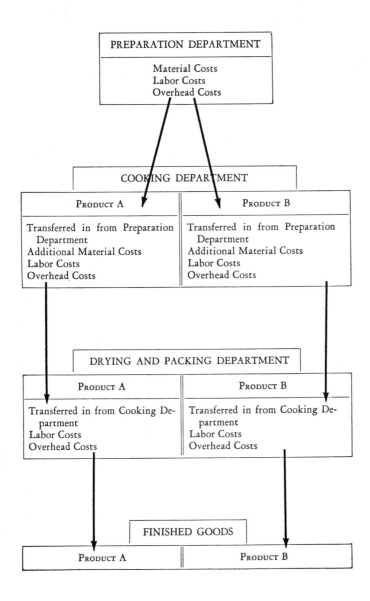

Illustration 10–5

ANALYSIS OF COST OF PRODUCTION DATA

For Month of March, 19—

QUANTITY OF PRODUCTION DATA (In Pounds)

	Preparation Department, Dept. I	Cooking Department, Dept. II		Drying and Packing, Dept. III	
		Product A	Product B	Product A	Product B
QUANTITY TO BE ACCOUNTED FOR:					
Put into Production	100,000	22,000	18,000	0	0
Received in dept., from preceding dept.	0	38,000	32,000	45,000	30,000
To Be Accounted For	100,000	60,000	50,000	45,000	30,000
QUANTITY ACCOUNTED FOR AS FOLLOWS:					
Finished and Transferred:					
Product A	38,000				
Product B	32,000				
Total	70,000	45,000	30,000	35,000	20,000
Work-in-Process, 3/31/—:					
All Materials, $3/5$ Labor and Overhead	25,000				
All Materials, $1/2$ Labor and Overhead		10,000	16,000		
All Materials, $3/4$ Labor and Overhead					
$5/7$ Labor and Overhead				7,000	8,000
$1/2$ Labor and Overhead				3,000	2,000
Lost or Spoiled Production	5,000	5,000	4,000		
Total Accounted For	100,000	60,000	50,000	45,000	30,000

Illustration 10-5—(Continued)

COSTS OF PRODUCTION
For Month of March, 19—

	Preparation Department, Dept. I	Cooking Department, Dept. II		Drying and Packing, Dept. III	
		Product A	Product B	Product A	Product B
Material Costs................	$19,000.00	$26,500.00	$12,800.00	0	0
Labor Costs..................	34,000.00	24,000.00	25,200.00	$18,000.00	$ 7,680.00
Manufacturing Overhead Costs....	12,750.00	10,000.00	4,200.00	4,800.00	2,400.00
Total Departmental Costs....	$65,750.00	$60,500.00	$42,200.00	$22,800.00	$10,080.00

Illustration 10–5A

SUMMARY COST OF PRODUCTION REPORT—PREPARATION DEPARTMENT
For Month of March, 19—

	Total	Per Unit
COSTS IN DEPARTMENT DURING WEEK:		
Material Costs*	$19,000.00	$0.20
Labor Costs†	34,000.00	0.40
Manufacturing Overhead Costs‡	12,750.00	0.15
Total Departmental Costs	$65,750.00	$0.75
CUMULATIVE COST TOTAL ANALYSIS:		
Finished and Transferred:		
Product A	$28,500.00	
Product B	24,000.00	
Work-in-Process, 3/31—:		
Materials (25,000 × $0.20)	5,000.00	
Labor (25,000 × ⅗ × $0.40)	6,000.00	
Manufacturing Overhead (25,000 × ⅗ × $0.15)	2,250.00	
Cumulative Cost Accounted For	$65,750.00	

* $19,000.00 ÷ (70,000 units + 25,000 units) = $0.20
† $34,000.00 ÷ [70,000 units + ⅗ (25,000)] = $0.40
‡ $12,750.00 ÷ [70,000 units + ⅗ (25,000)] = $0.15

SUMMARY COST OF PRODUCTION REPORT
For Month of March, 19—

	COOKING DEPARTMENT				DRYING AND PACKING DEPARTMENT			
	Product A		Product B		Product A		Product B	
	Total Cost	Unit Cost	Total Cost	Unit Cost	Total Cost	Unit	Total	Unit
COST IN PRECEDING DEPARTMENT:								
Transferred into Department during Month					$75,600.00	$1.68	$45,000.00	$1.50
Additional Costs for Lost Units					xx	0.12	xx	0.1071
Adjusted Unit Cost Total					$75,600.00	$1.80	$45,000.00	$1.6071
COST IN CURRENT DEPARTMENT:								
Material from Preparation Department	$28,500.00		$24,000.00					
Additional Materials Added in This Department	26,500.00		12,800.00					
Total Material Costs	$55,000.00	$1.00	$36,800.00	$0.80	xxx		xxx	
Labor Costs	24,000.00	0.48	25,200.00	0.60	$18,000.00	$0.45	$ 7,680.00	$0.32
Manufacturing Overhead Costs	10,000.00	0.20	4,200.00	0.10	4,800.00	0.12	2,400.00	0.10
Total Departmental Costs	$89,000.00	$1.68	$66,200.00	$1.50	$22,800.00	$0.57	$10,080.00	$0.42
CUMULATIVE COST TOTAL	$89,000.00	$1.68	$66,200.00	$1.50	$98,400.00	$2.37	$55,080.00	$2.0271
Finished and Transferred	$75,600.00		$45,000.00		$82,950.00		$40,542.00	
Finished and on Hand	0		0		0		0	
Work-in-Process, 3/31/—:								
Preceding Department Cost					11,760.00		12,000.00	
Lost Unit Cost					840.00		856.80	
Material Costs	10,000.00		12,800.00		0		0	
Labor Costs	2,400.00		7,200.00		2,250.00		1,280.00	
Manufacturing Overhead Costs	1,000.00		1,200.00		600.00		400.00	
CUMULATIVE COST TOTAL ANALYSIS	$89,000.00		$66,200.00		$98,400.00		$55,078.80*	

* Error of $1.20 due to rounding.

Alternative Cost of Production Report for Two Products from Same Material in Department I

Instead of using a cost of production report showing the costs of the two products on a *departmental* basis as given in this chapter previously, it is possible to prepare such a report on a *product* rather than on a *departmental* basis. In that event, the rearrangement of the columns would be as follows:

COST DESCRIPTION	PRODUCT A				PRODUCT B			
	Cooking Dept.		Drying and Packing		Cooking Dept.		Drying and Packing	
	Total	Unit	Total	Unit	Total	Unit	Total	Unit

The ultimate figures would be the same as previously given, but the emphasis in the cost of production report is on the products not on the departments.

QUESTIONS FOR REVIEW

1. What characteristics distinguish process costs from job order costs?
2. In some process plants, the units put into production are often different from those transferred out of a given department. How must the term "units of production" be interpreted in process cost accounting? Why?
3. In a multiproduct firm, what is the basic cost accounting problem?
4. What is the simplest method of determining the work-in-process in any given department? What alternative method may be used in checking this work-in-process inventory?
5. What is the meaning and purpose of "equivalent production"? Under what conditions would it be unnecessary to compute the equivalent production?
6. In Department I, the output for the week was as follows:

```
Completed and transferred out..........................30,000 units
Completed and not transferred.........................10,000
Work-in-process on which all the materials and one fourth of
    the labor and overhead had been applied................20,000
Units lost in production............................ 5,000
```

Compute the equivalent production for materials, labor, and manufacturing overhead. How many units were started into production?

7. The cost of the work done on the lost units in the department in which

these units are lost is not considered separately in process cost accounting. Explain this statement.

8. When units are lost in a department after the first in a process cost accounting plant, the *unit* cost of the work received from the preceding department must be adjusted. Explain two methods of computing this adjustment.

9. Department II received 15,000 units from Department I at a unit cost of $2.80. In Department II, 12,000 of these units were completed and transferred to Department III, 2,000 were in process, one-fourth complete as to labor and overhead, and 1,000 units were lost. Compute the corrected unit cost for Department I. What is the lost unit cost in Department II for work done in Department I?

10. The unit costs in Department II are as follows:

Corrected unit costs for Dept. I	$2.50	$25,000
Labor costs	2.00	16,000
Manufacturing overhead costs	1.00	8,000

Total number of units received from Department I, 12,000, of which 2,000 were lost. Work-in-process at the end of the period was 3,000 units, one-third complete as to labor and overhead. All completed work was transferred to Department III. Prepare the journal entries to record the transactions affecting Department II.

PROBLEMS—GROUP A

Problem 10–1. Purpose: *Cost of Production Report and Journal Entries for a Three-Department Factory; Lost Units in Department I Only*

The Raymond Manufacturing Company produces a single product which goes through three departments successively, with materials used only in the first department.

The production statistics for the week ending June 5, 19—, were as follows:

	Dept. I	Dept. II	Dept. III
Completed and transferred out	50,000 units	30,000 units	21,000 units
Completed and not transferred out	10,000	5,000	0
Work-in-process, all materials, one-third labor and overhead	30,000	15,000	9,000
Lost in production	10,000	0	0

During the week, the first of its operations, materials used, cost $36,000. The labor and overhead costs incurred in the three departments were as follows:

	Dept. I	Dept. II	Dept. III
Labor costs	$56,000	$28,000	$60,000
Manufacturing overhead costs	35,000	40,000	45,000

On the basis of these data, prepare a cost of production report for the week, showing the unit costs by elements in each department, the cumulative unit costs, and the work-in-process inventory in each department in analyzed form.

Prepare journal entries to cover the entire manufacturing cycle for this week.

Problem 10–2. Purpose: *Cost of Production Report; Journal Entries; Lost Units in All Departments*

The Relland Manufacturing Company operates a plant on the continuous process manufacturing basis, with a single product going through three producing departments. Materials are used in the initial department only. There is no work-in-process inventory at the beginning of the month.

In Department I, 80,000 units were started into production, of which 60,000 were completed and transferred to the second department; 15,000 units were in process at the end of the month on which all the materials have been applied and two thirds of the labor and overhead. The remaining units were spoiled or lost in the manufacturing operations.

In Department II, 50,000 units were completed and transferred to Department III, 5,000 were completed but not transferred, 3,000 were still in process estimated to be one-third complete as to labor and overhead. The remaining units were lost in production.

In Department III, 35,000 units were completed and sent to the finished stock room, 10,000 were still in process, 40 percent complete as to labor and manufacturing overhead, and 5,000 units were lost or spoiled in production.

The operating costs departmentally were as follows:

	Dept. I	Dept. II	Dept. III
Material costs	$ 97,500	0	0
Labor costs	56,000	$61,600	$39,000
Manufacturing overhead	14,000	30,800	7,800
	$167,500	$92,400	$46,800

From this information, you are asked to prepare:

a) Cost of production report showing unit costs by elements; cumulative costs both on a unit cost and total basis.

b) Journal entries to cover the cost accounting cycle.

Problem 10–3. Purpose: *Process Costing When Two Products Are Manufactured Simultaneously from Material Received from the Initial Department*

The Rilson Manufacturing Company has three producing departments. In Department I, the material being manufactured is sent to Department II where Products A and B are manufactured simultaneously. This segregation of costs and products is continued in the third department.

The quantity statements and costs for the production for the month of May were as follows:

	Department I	Department II Product A	Department II Product B	Department III Product A	Department III Product B
Started into production or received from preceding dept..............	150,000 units	70,000	44,000	50,000	30,000
In process, 100% complete for materials, 40% complete for labor and overhead........................	30,000	15,000	10,000	15,000	7,000
Transferred out:					
Product A.......................	70,000	50,000		33,000	
Product B.......................	44,000		30,000		20,000
Lost or Spoiled..................	6,000	5,000	4,000	2,000	3,000
Total.......................	150,000	70,000	44,000	50,000	30,000

Costs for this period:

	Department I	Department II Product A	Department II Product B	Department III Product A	Department III Product B
Materials......................	$ 72,000	0	0	0	0
Labor.........................	75,600	$39,200	$20,400	$31,200	$20,520
Mfg. overhead................	50,400	16,800	13,600	15,600	13,680
Total.....................	$198,000	$56,000	$34,000	$46,800	$34,200

From this information, you are asked to prepare a composite cost of production report similar to the following form:

	Department I	Product A Dept. II	Product A Dept. III	Product B Dept. II	Product B Dept. III
Materials...............					
Labor.................					
Mfg. overhead.........					

Using one work-in-process account for each department, prepare journal entries to cover the manufacturing cycle for this report.

Problem 10–4. Purpose: *C.P.A. Problem Involving a Simple Process Cost Accounting Situation; Cost of Production Report; Added Materials in a Department after the First Does Not Increase Volume*

The Resistor Tool Company manufactures on a continuous basis a single electrical product which goes through two manufacturing departments: *machining* and *assembling*. Although materials are added in each department, no increase in the number of units being manufactured results therefrom.

During the month of May, production records showed for the machining department:

Units put into production..200,000
Units completed and transferred to assembling department....................160,000
Units in process, 100% complete as to material, but 25% complete as to
  labor and overhead... 40,000

The costs of manufacturing for May in the machining department were:

Material costs.......................................$240,000
Labor costs.. 136,000
Manufacturing overhead costs........................ 114,750

In the assembling department, 120,000 units were completed and transferred to finished stock room, 30,000 units were in process, 100 percent complete as to material but two-thirds complete as to labor and manufacturing overhead. Five thousand units were discarded as defective and will be sold as scrap material sometime in the future, at a nominal value. Of the 10,000 units lost in production, one half of the prescribed labor had been applied, but all of the material. *No overhead was charged to the spoiled work.*

The cost of the lost units should be treated as additional overhead cost in the assembling department. Cost of spoilage *all charged to Finished Units.*

Costs of manufacturing for May in the assembling department were:

Material costs.......................................$153,600
Labor costs.. 163,125
Manufacturing overhead costs........................ 49,795*

* Does not include any charges for work done on the spoiled units.

There was no work-in-process inventory in either department at the beginning of the month of May.

From these data you are asked to prepare:

a) Statement showing unit costs in each department and cumulatively for the production for the month of May.

b) A schedule showing the details of the work-in-process inventory in each department.

(Adapted from an AICPA Uniform Examination)

Problem 10–5. Purpose: *Journal Entries Covering the Cost Accounting Cycle for a Three-Department Process Plant*

The following cost of production report has been submitted to you for your consideration and analysis. On the basis of this report, you are asked to prepare and explain the journal entries which will record the accounting information covering the cycle from the use of materials until the completed product has been recorded.

RANICE MANUFACTURING COMPANY

SUMMARY COST OF PRODUCTION REPORT

For Week Ending July 17, 19—

	Department I		Department II		Department III	
	Total Cost	Unit Cost	Total Cost	Unit Cost	Total Cost	Unit Cost
Cost in Preceding Department:						
Transferred into Department during Week..........................			4,500	0.45	5,200.00	0.80
Additional Cost for Lost Units......				0.05		0.06⅔
Adjusted and Corrected Unit Cost Total.........................			4,500	0.50	5,200.00	0.86⅔
Cost in Current Department:						
Cost in Department during Week:						
Material Costs..................	2,520	0.18	900	0.10	1,500.00	0.25
Labor Costs....................	1,440	0.12	1,200	0.15	780.00	0.15
Mfg. Overhead Costs............	1,800	0.15	400	0.05	520.00	0.10
Total Cost in Current Dept.......	5,760	0.45	2,500	0.30	2,800.00	0.50
CUMULATIVE COST TOTAL.......	5,760	0.45	7,000	0.80	8,000.00	1.36⅔
Work Completed and Transferred Out	4,500		5,200	0.80	6,833.33	
Work-in-Process, July 17, 19—:						
Completed but Not Transferred Out	0		400		0	
Work-in-Process, Cost in Preceding Department......................			1,000		866.67	
Work-in-Process, Materials........	720		200		250.00	
Work-in-Process, Labor............	240		150		30.00	
Work-in-Process, Mfg. Overhead....	300		50		20.00	
CUMULATIVE COST TOTAL ACCOUNTED FOR...............	5,760		7,000		8,000.00	

PROBLEMS—GROUP B

Problem 10–6. Purpose: *Cost of Production Report; Lost Units in First Department Only; Work-in-Process in Analyzed Form; Journal Entries*

The Barton Manufacturing Company operates a continuous process plant with three producing departments in which a single product is manufactured. Materials are used only in the first department, in which department there is usually a loss in volume due to spillage and evaporation.

Production reports are prepared weekly. For the first week's operations, the following represent the accounting data:

Department	Materials	Labor	Manufacturing Overhead
I	$142,500	$34,000	$17,000
II	0	28,000	14,000
III	0	30,000	10,000
	$142,500	$92,000	$41,000

The quantities of production statistics were as follows:

	Dept. I	Dept. II	Dept. III
Units completed and transferred	75,000 units	60,000 units	45,000 units
Units completed, not transferred	5,000	5,000	0
Work-in-process, June 12, 19—:			
100% material, ⅓ labor and overhead	15,000		
½ labor and overhead		10,000	
⅓ labor and overhead			15,000
Units lost in production	5,000	0	0

From these data, you are asked to prepare:

a) Cost of production report.

b) Statement of work-in-process inventory in each department in analyzed form.

c) Journal entries to record the manufacturing cycle.

Problem 10–7. Purpose: *Cost of Production Report; Journal Entries; Lost Units in All Departments*

The Brenner Manufacturing Company produces a single product on a continuous basis. For the first week of its operations, ending August 7, materials were used in Department I, costing $60,000. The labor and overhead costs in this initial department for this period were $46,800 and $13,000, respectively.

Of the 80,000 units started into production August 2 in Department I, 60,000 units were completed and transferred to Department II, 15,000 were in process, 100 percent complete as to material costs and one-third complete as to labor and overhead. The remaining units were lost in production.

The labor and overhead costs for Departments II and III for this period were:

Department	Labor Costs	Overhead Costs
II	$16,000	$12,000
III	28,500	24,700
Total	$44,500	$36,700

The production statistics for this period were as follows:

	Dept. II	Dept. III
Units completed and transferred to next department................................	45,000 units	30,000 units
Units completed, not transferred................	3,000	0
Work-in-process, August 7, 19—:		
25% complete as to labor and overhead costs....................................	8,000	
66⅔% complete as to labor and overhead costs....................................		12,000
Units lost in production........................	4,000	3,000
Total................................	60,000 units	45,000 units

You are asked to prepare in good form a cost of production report for the week ending August 7, showing the unit costs by elements, by departments, and cumulatively, as well as the total costs. Supplement this report with a schedule of the work-in-process inventories in analyzed form for each department and the journal entries to record the accounting cycle.

Problem 10–8. **Purpose:** *Process Costing Two Products Manufactured Simultaneously from Material Received from Department I*

The Brockway Food Processing Company is engaged in the canning and freeze-packing of fresh fruits and vegetables throughout the year. Sometimes the materials to be processed has to be shipped long distances, although the tendency is to have processing plants located near the source of materials. Some of the plants have to be closed down during the slack season. In each plant, the organization and procedures are similar.

Materials are handled in the incoming or preparation department and then shipped either to the canning kitchens or to the freezing department. Cost of production schedules are simply prepared on a weekly basis.

During one of the weekly periods, the following was the data supplied by the preparation department:

Quantity of material received for processing................	150,000 lbs.
Shipped to the canning department........................	80,000
Shipped to the freezing department........................	60,000
In process, all material, but ¼ labor and overhead..........	8,000
Waste, spoilage, and rejected............................	2,000

The costs in this department were as follows:

Materials..	$6,660
Labor costs..	3,195
Manufacturing overhead costs......................	1,775

The production statistics for the canning and freezing departments were as follows:

	Canning	Freezing
Quantity completed and packed....................	65,000 lbs.	50,000 lbs.
Quantity in process, all material:		
⅓ labor and overhead...........................	12,000	
¼ labor and overhead...........................		8,000
Spoilage, waste, and loss........................	3,000	2,000

The cost statistics for the canning and freezing departments were as follows:

	Canning	Freezing
Materials (does not increase volume of production—units).....$3,350		$4,060
Payroll costs... 2,760		1,820
Manufacturing overhead costs............................. 966		624

On the basis of this information, you are asked to prepare a cost of production report using the following form:

	Preparation Dept.	Canning Dept.	Freezing Dept.
Material Costs or Received from Previous Dept. Additional Material Costs Labor Costs Mfg. Overhead Costs			

Problem 10–9. Purpose: *Cost of Production for a Single-Department, Single-Product Firm, So That Inventory Values May Be Verified on the Basis of Cost or Market, Whichever Is Lower*

The Bavlon Manufacturing Company produces a single product in its one-department factory. It values its inventories at cost or market, whichever is lower, both for the finished goods, work-in-process, and defective work. At December 31, 19—, the market price of the finished goods and work-in-process was considerably above the cost. However, the market price of the defective work (sold as seconds) was $1 per unit.

Manufacturing operations require that materials are added to the production line *at the start* of the process, and manufacturing overhead is applied at the rate of 80 *percent of the direct labor costs.*

From the company's accounting and other records, the following information is obtained:

Description	Units	Costs Materials	Direct Labor
Beginning inventory, January 1, 19—............100,000		$100,000	$160,000
Additional units started during year.............500,000		550,000	997,500
Units completed during year:			
Good units..............................500,000			
Defective units.......................... 10,000			
Finished goods inventory, December 31, includes the 10,000 defective units..................			

Defective units occur at the end of the process, that is, at the point of final inspection of finished units.

The company's records further show the following inventories as of December 31, 19—:

Finished goods inventory, 110,000 units, valued at.............$504,900
Work-in-process inventory, 90,000 units, 50% completed........ 330,480

From this information, you are asked to prepare schedules showing:
a) Effective or equivalent production.

b) Unit costs of production of materials, labor, and manufacturing overhead.

c) Pricing of inventories of finished goods, defective units, and work-in-process.

Also prepare such journal entries, if any, to correctly state the inventory valuation of *finished goods* and *work-in-process,* ignoring income tax considerations.

(Adapted from an AICPA Examination)

Problem 10–10. Purpose: *Journal Entries Covering the Cost Accounting Cycle for a Three-Department Process Plant*

The following cost of production report of the Bruner Manufacturing Company has been submitted to you for the week ending July 31, 19—. You are asked to prepare the journal entries to record the manufacturing cycle of this report.

BRUNER MANUFACTURING CO.
SUMMARY COST OF PRODUCTION REPORT
For Week Ending July 31, 19—

	Department I		Department II		Department III	
	Total Cost	Unit Cost	Total Cost	Unit Cost	Total Cost	Unit Cost
Cost in Preceding Department:						
Transferred into Department during Week..............			14,520	0.66	19,890.00	1.326
Additional Cost for Lost Units....			0	0.066	0	0.094714
Corrected Unit Cost Total....			14,520	0.726	19,890.00	1.420714
Cost in Current Department:						
Cost in Department during Week:						
Material Costs................	6,720	0.24	7,000	0.35	2,800.00	0.20
Labor Costs..................	7,800	0.30	1,700	0.10	3,600.00	0.30
Mfg. Overhead Costs..........	3,120	0.12	2,550	0.15	1,440.00	0.12
Total Cost in Current Dept....	17,640	0.66	11,250	0.60	7,840.00	0.62
CUMULATIVE COST TOTAL.....	17,640	0.66	25,770	1.326	27,730.00	2.040714
Work Completed and Transferred Out.......................	14,520	0.66	19,890	1.326	20,407.14	2.040714
Work-in-Process, July 31, 19—:						
Completed but Not Transferred Out.......................	1,980					
Cost in Preceding Departments....	0		3,630		5,682.86	
Work-in-Process, Materials.......	720		1,750		800.00	
Work-in-Process, Labor..........	300		200		600.00	
Work-in-Process, Mfg. Overhead..	120		300		240.00	
Total Work-in-Process..........	3,120		5,880		7,322.86	
CUMULATIVE COST TOTAL ACCOUNTED FOR..........	17,640		25,770		27,730.00	

CHAPTER

Process Cost Accounting Pro-cedures—Part II

II Special Problems Including the Average Method of Treating the Initial Work-in-Process Inventory

Introductory Review   In the preceding chapter the problems of process cost accounting were presented with emphasis upon the fact that these costs are characteristically distinguished *by a departmental cost statement, for a definite period of time,* supplemented by *a quantity of production report.* Furthermore, the problems of computing unit costs by using *equivalent production* were emphasized, together with the effect of *lost units* on process cost accounting. The methods of computing the *work-in-process* inventories were discussed.

In this chapter, the discussion will be limited to a *single product firm* and will consider the problems of:

1. Accounting treatment and the computation of unit costs when *materials are added* to production in a department after the first, and when these—
    a) Do not increase the number of units in production, and
    b) Do increase the number of units in production.
2. Computation of *lost unit costs* when materials are added in a department after the first and increase the volume of production.
3. The *average cost method* of treating the *work-in-process inventory* at the beginning of the accounting period.
4. Computation of *lost unit costs* when there is an *initial work-in-process inventory.*

These topics are most important because they cover comprehensively the subject of average process costs. Most process cost accounting is average costing, not FIFO.

Process Cost Accounting Procedures When Materials Are Added to Production in a Department after the First

In many process type plants all the necessary materials are placed into production in the initial manufacturing department, and thereafter it is merely a matter of addition of factory labor and overhead in the other departments to complete the work. In other plants, additional materials may be required in departments after the first. When additional materials are added, two possible situations may result:

1. The additional materials may merely change the nature or character of the product being manufactured but *will not add to the number of units being produced*. This would be the case in the manufacture of toys by the continuous process method, whereby, in departments after the first, materials are added to color the toys or ornaments are added to embellish them but neither of these materials—paint and ornaments—increases the number of toys being produced.
2. The additional materials may add to the quantity being produced, thus increasing the number of units. In the manufacture of paints, the addition of oils, dryers, pigments, etc., in a department after the first will increase the number of gallons being produced.

The procedure to be followed when the additional material *does not increase* the number of units being produced is similar to that previously described, except that in the departments after the first there will be an additional element of cost (materials) for which a unit cost must be computed. If, however, the addition of materials increases the *number of units being produced,* the unit costs for the preceding departments must be adjusted when cumulative unit costs are being computed. For example, 25,000 gallons were received from Department I, at a unit cost of 30 cents, total cost $7,500. In Department II, 5,000 additional gallons of material were added, making the production in Department II on the basis of 30,000 gallons. In determining the *cumulative* unit cost, the total cost for Department I ($7,500) must be spread over 30,000 units now in production, making the adjusted unit cost for Department I, 25 cents ($7,500 ÷ 30,000 gallons). In the second department, the unit costs will be computed on the basis of the actual production of 30,000 gallons. However, in computing *cumulative unit costs* for the first and second departments, the *adjusted* unit cost for the first department must be used. This same adjusted unit cost for the first department must be used in computing the *work-in-process inventory in the second department.*

Illustration of Cost of Production Report When Added Materials Do Not Increase Number of Units in Production

For the sake of illustration and comparison, as well as a proper understanding of the effect that additional material has upon the number of units of production, the cost of production statement in Illustration 11–2 is for a situation in which the materials *do not increase* the number of units in production. In Illustration 11–3 essentially the same data will be used to indicate the effect on the cost accounting when the additional materials do *increase* the number of units being produced.

The data used in Illustration 11–2 are:

	Dept. I	Dept. II
Costs of production:		
Material costs	$48,000	$ 5,400
Labor costs	25,000	8,000
Manufacturing overhead costs	10,000	3,000
Total	$83,000	$16,400
Quantity production figures:		
Started in production	15,000 units	6,000 units
Added materials—no increase in units	0	0
To Be Accounted For	15,000 units	6,000 units
Transferred to next department	6,000 units	4,000 units
Completed and on hand	2,000	0
Work-in-process: complete as to material, ½ complete as to labor and overhead	4,000	2,000
Lost in production	3,000	0
Total Accounted For	15,000 units	6,000 units

The cost of production report for this information is shown in Illustration 11–2. It should be noted that the added material in Department II does not require the adjustment of the unit cost for work done in Department I, since the added material *did not increase* the number of units in production. The computation of the equivalent production and the unit costs for this method is shown in Illustration 11–1.

Illustration of Cost of Production When Added Materials Increase the Number of Units in Production

Using essentially the same data as in Illustration 11–2 except that in Department II the additional material used increases the number of units in production by 3,000, the following cost of production report and supporting tabulation of computations are given. Because the added materials in Department II do increase the number of units in production, there is required an adjustment of the *unit cost* for Department I; the *detailed computations of the*

Illustration 11–1

COMPUTATION OF EQUIVALENT PRODUCTION AND UNIT COSTS, WHEN ADDED
MATERIALS DO NOT INCREASE NUMBER OF UNITS ÍN PRODUCTION

	Computation of Equivalent Production	Computation of Unit Costs
Department I:		
Material..............................	12,000 units	$48,000 ÷ 12,000 units $4.00
Labor and overhead:		
Completed and transferred..............	6,000 units	
Completed and on hand................	2,000	
In process, ½ complete (4,000 × ½).....	2,000	
	10,000 units	
Labor costs............................		25,000 ÷ 10,000 units 2.50
Overhead costs.........................		10,000 ÷ 10,000 units 1.00
Total Unit Costs.....................		$7.50
Department II:		
Material..............................	6,000 units	$5,400 ÷ 6,000 units $0.90
Labor and overhead:		
Completed and transferred..............	4,000 units	
In process, ½ complete (2,000 × ½).....	1,000	
	5,000 units	
Labor costs............................		8,000 ÷ 5,000 units 1.60
Overhead costs........................		3,000 ÷ 5,000 units 0.60
Total Unit Costs.....................		$3.10

work-in-process inventory in Department II are shown, as well as the *journal entries covering* the cycle of production. See Illustrations 11–2 and 11–4. Because of the increase in number of units in Department II due to added materials, the total costs of units transferred to Department II must be spread over a larger number of units, thus adjusting the unit cost for Department I to a lower figure in the cumulation, e.g.:

Transferred to Dept. II.............................$45,000.00 ÷ 6,000 units $7.50
Increase in units due to added materials.............   3,000
Adjusted unit cost for Dept. I, for work in Dept. II...$45,000.00 ÷ 9,000 units $5.00

When this figure of $5 is added to the unit costs of $1.975 for Department II, the cumulative unit cost for the finished production is $6.975. This figure must be used when computing the work-in-process inventory in Department II at the end of January, as is illustrated in the following:

Work-in-process inventory, Dept. II, Company B:

2,000 units (adjusted unit cost for Dept. I)	@ $5.00..............	$10,000
2,000 units, material costs, Dept. II	@ 0.60..............	1,200
2,000 units, labor costs, Dept. II (½ × $1.00)	@ 0.50..............	1,000
2,000 units, overhead costs, Dept. II (½ × $0.375) @ 0.1875............		375
Total Work-in-Process Inventory, Dept. II.......................		$12,575

Illustration 11–2

COMPANY A MANUFACTURING COMPANY
SUMMARY COST OF PRODUCTION REPORT
For the Month of January, 19—
(Additional Material in Department II Does Not Increase Quantity of Production)

	Department I		Department II	
	Cost	Per Unit	Cost	Per Unit
COSTS FOR THE MONTH OF JANUARY:				
Material Costs........................	$48,000.00	$4.00	$ 5,400.00	$ 0.90
Labor Costs..........................	25,000.00	2.50	8,000.00	1.60
Manufacturing Overhead Costs...........	10,000.00	1.00	3,000.00	0.60
Total Costs in January..............	$83,000.00	$7.50	$16,400.00	$ 3.10
Completed and on Hand, 1/1/—.........				
Work-in-Process, 1/1/—................				
Transferred into Department in January....			45,000.00	7.50
CUMULATIVE TOTAL COST............	$83,000.00	$7.50	$61,400.00	$10.60
Transferred to Next Department.............	$45,000.00	$7.50	$42,400.00	$10.60
Completed and on Hand, 1/31/—...........	15,000.00	7.50		
Work-in-Process, 1/31/—.................	23,000.00	5.75	19,000.00	9.50
CUMULATIVE COST DISTRIBUTION....	$83,000.00	xxx	$61,400.00	xxx

QUANTITY PRODUCTION REPORT (In Pounds)

QUANTITY TO BE ACCOUNTED FOR:		
Completed and on Hand, 1/1/—...............................		
Work-in-Process, 1/1/—......................................		
Put into Production in January....................................	15,000	
Received from Preceding Departments...........................		6,000
To Be Accounted For...	15,000	6,000
QUANTITY ACCOUNTED FOR AS FOLLOWS:		
Transferred to Next Department...............................	6,000	4,000
Completed and on Hand, 1/31/—...............................	2,000	
Work-in-Process, 1/31/—...................................	4,000	2,000
Material Costs..	(100%)*	(100%)
Labor Costs...	(50%)	(50%)
Overhead Costs..	(50%)	(50%)
Lost or Spoiled in Production..................................	3,000	
Total Accounted For.......................................	15,000	6,000

* Indicates degree of completion of work-in-process.

Journal entries to summarize the data presented on the cost of production report for Company B (Illustration 11–4) where added materials increase the number of units being manufactured would be:

(1)

Work-in-Process—Dept. I............................83,000.00		
Stores..	48,000.00	
Payroll...	25,000.00	
Manufacturing Overhead...............................	10,000.00	
To record costs for January in Dept. I.		

(2)

Work-in-Process—Dept. II...........................61,400.00		
Work-in-Process—Dept. I...............................	45,000.00	
Stores..	5,400.00	
Payroll...	8,000.00	
Manufacturing Overhead...............................	3,000.00	
To record costs for January in Dept. II including transfer from Dept. I.		

(3)

Finished Goods.......................................48,825.00		
Work-in-Process—Dept. II.............................	48,825.00	
To record the cost of work completed and placed in stock room.		

Illustration 11–3

COMPUTATION OF EQUIVALENT PRODUCTION AND UNIT COSTS WHEN ADDED MATERIALS INCREASE THE NUMBER OF UNITS IN PRODUCTION

	Computation of Equivalent Production	Computation of Unit Costs	
Department I:			
Material............................	12,000 units	$48,000 ÷ 12,000 units	$4.00
Labor and overhead:			
Completed and transferred.............	6,000 units		
Completed and on hand...............	2,000		
In process, ½ complete (4,000 × ½)....	2,000		
	10,000 units		
Labor costs........................		25,000 ÷ 10,000 units	2.50
Overhead costs......................		10,000 ÷ 10,000 units	1.00
Total Unit Costs..................			$7.50
Department II:			
Material............................	9,000 units	$5,400 ÷ 9,000 units	$0.60
Labor and overhead:			
Completed and transferred.............	7,000 units		
In process, ½ complete (2,000 × ½)....	1,000		
	8,000 units		
Labor costs........................		8,000 ÷ 8,000 units	1.00
Overhead costs......................		3,000 ÷ 8,000 units	0.375
Total Unit Costs..................			$1.975

Illustration 11–4

COMPANY B MANUFACTURING COMPANY

SUMMARY COST OF PRODUCTION REPORT

For the Month of January, 19—

(Material Added in Department II Increases the Number of Units Being Produced)

	Department I		Department II	
	Cost	Per Unit	Cost	Per Unit
COSTS FOR THE MONTH OF JANUARY:				
Material Costs.........................	$48,000.00	$4.00	$ 5,400.00	$0.60
Labor Costs............................	25,000.00	2.50	8,000.00	1.00
Manufacturing Overhead Costs............	10,000.00	1.00	3,000.00	0.375
Total Costs in January................	$83,000.00	$7.50	$16,400.00	$1.975
Completed and on Hand, 1/1/—..........				
Work-in-Process, 1/1/—.................				
Transferred into Department in January......			45,000.00	5.00*
CUMULATIVE TOTAL COST..............	$83,000.00	$7.50	$61,400.00	$6.975
Transferred to Next Department..............	$45,000.00	$7.50	$48,825.00	$6.9750
Completed and on Hand, 1/31/—.............	15,000.00	7.50		
Work-in-Process, 1/31/—.................	23,000.00	5.75	12,575.00	6.2875
CUMULATIVE COST DISTRIBUTION......	$83,000.00	xxx	$61,400.00	xxx

* Adjusted for added material.

QUANTITY PRODUCTION REPORT (In Pounds)

QUANTITY TO BE ACCOUNTED FOR:		
Completed and on Hand, 1/1/—...............................		
Work-in-Process. 1/1/—..................................		
Put into Production in January.............................	15,000	3,000
Received from Preceding Departments........................		6,000
To Be Accounted For......................................	15,000	9,000
QUANTITY ACCOUNTED FOR AS FOLLOWS:		
Transferred to Next Department.............................	6,000	7,000
Completed and on Hand, 1/31/—..............................	2,000	
Work-in-Process, 1/31/—.....................................	4,000	2,000
Material Costs.......................................	(100%)*	(100%)
Labor Costs...	(50%)	(50%)
Overhead Costs......................................	(50%)	(50%)
Lost or Spoiled in Production................................	3,000	
Total Accounted For.................................	15,000	9,000

* Indicates degree of completion of work-in-process.

Effect of Lost Units on Added Materials Costs

In any department after the first, lost units require an adjustment of the unit costs for the preceding departments before calculating the cumulative unit cost. This adjustment is affected by the addition of materials which increase the number of units in production. The basic rule to remember when computing lost unit costs in a department after the first when materials are added which increase the number of units in production is:

> *If the number of units are increased in a department after the first because of added materials, the unit cost for the preceding departments must FIRST be adjusted for the added materials before computing the lost unit cost.*

The computation of lost unit costs in the department when materials are added and the increased number of units being manufactured necessitates *first* computing the *adjusted unit cost for the preceding departments,* and then using this adjusted unit cost in computing the lost unit cost, is as follows:

In Department III the cost and production figures for the month of March were:

15,000 units	Cost in preceding departments: total	$30,000	unit cost	$2

Costs in Department III, added material increasing number of units in production:

10,000 units	Material costs (100% complete) total	$11,500	unit cost	$0.50
	Labor costs (⅓ complete) total	2,100	unit cost	0.10
	Overhead costs (⅓ complete) total	6,300	unit cost	0.30
25,000 units	Total to Be Accounted For	$49,900		$2.90

Of the 25,000 units to be accounted for in Department III, the results showed:

Completed and transferred.................................20,000 units
In process, all material, one-third labor and overhead........... 3,000
Lost in production... 2,000
Total Accounted For.....................................25,000 units

The *adjusted unit cost* for the first two departments after giving effect to the added materials would be:

15,000 units + 10,000 units = 25,000 units, divided into $30,000 = $1.20.

The *lost unit cost* can now be computed using the $1.20 figure, e.g.:

(2,000 units × $1.20) ÷ 23,000 units = $0.1043 as the lost unit cost.

Thus the *total adjusted and corrected unit* cost for the two preceding departments, taking into consideration both the added materials and the lost units, is $1.3043 ($1.20 + $0.1043). Again, it should be emphasized that it is FIRST necessary to adjust the previous department's unit cost for added material before computing the lost unit cost.

Treatment of the Work-in-Process Inventory at the Beginning of the Process Accounting Period

The treatment of the initial work-in-process inventory is important because it affects the computation of the unit costs in a department. Two characteristics of the initial work-in-process inventory must be recognized:

1. Because of the different stage of completion of the initial work-in-process inventory as far as material, labor, and manufacturing overhead costs are concerned, this initial work-in-process inventory will be shown on the cost of production report in *analyzed form,* that is, separate figures will be shown for the work-in-process—material, work-in-process—labor, and work-in-process—manufacturing overhead.
2. In the work-in-process inventory in the first manufacturing department, these figures represent the total cost of this inventory. In the subsequent departments, the work-in-process inventory must also include a cost figure for the work done on this inventory in the *preceding departments.*

An examination of the detailed computation of the work-in-process inventories as shown in Chapter 10, page 303, illustrates the figures here referred to.

There are two accounting treatments of this beginning work-in-process inventory when computing unit costs. The first, and probably more popular because it is characteristic of the nature of the process costs (average costs), is known as the *average cost method.* This method involves the merging of the departmental costs, *by elements,* of the initial work-in-process inventory with the costs incurred in the department during the month and dividing the total cost by elements thus computed by an equivalent production based upon the sum of units in process at the beginning of the period and the units put into production during this period. *A second method,* known as *first-in, first-out* (FIFO), is predicated on the assumption that the costs for the current period will be used first to complete the initial work-in-process and then will be applied against the new production. This method will be treated separately in the following chapter.

The Average Cost Method of Treating the Initial Work-in-Process Inventory— Department I

To illustrate the *average cost method,* the cost of production report for Department I of the Alton Manufacturing Company is prepared for the month of February. It is assumed that there were in process, February 1, 10,000 pounds (units) on which *all the material* and *one half of the labor and manufacturing overhead* had already been applied in January. The costs of this work-in-process inventory as taken from the January Department I cost of production report were:

Material costs...$3,000	
Labor costs.. 750	
Manufacturing overhead costs.................................... 250	

During February, 76,000 pounds (units) were started. The costs of material were $22,600; labor costs were $9,000; and manufacturing overhead amounted to $3,650. The quantity statement showed these results for the month's operation (these include the 10,000 units in process at the beginning):

Finished and transferred to Dept. II.............................60,000 lbs. (units)	
In process, February 28 (all the material complete, but only ¼ complete as to labor and overhead)...............................20,000	
Lost in the process of manufacturing during February............. 6,000	
Total to Be Accounted For...............................86,000 lbs. (units)	

The departmental cost statement prepared on February 28 from this information for Department I is shown in Illustration 11–5. In studying this production report the work-in-process on February 1 requires our attention first. The amount, $4,000, is in analyzed form; *that is, the cost for each element is given.* In computing the unit costs for the month of February it is, therefore, a simple matter to add the cost of materials used in production for the month to the cost of material in the in-process inventory February 1 to get the *total material cost* and then to divide this figure by the *equivalent material production* to get the unit cost for material. For example, the computations would be:

	Quantity	Cost Value
In process, February 1......................10,000 lbs.		$ 3,000
Put into process during February...............76,000		22,600
Total...................................86,000 lbs.		$25,600
Units lost................................. 6,000		
Equivalent Production....................80,000 lbs.		$25,600

Dividing the equivalent production for material in Department I for February (80,000 units) into the total cost ($3,000 + $22,600) of $25,600 results in an average unit cost for materials in Department I for the month of February of $0.32.

Illustration 11–5

DEPARTMENT I

COST PRODUCTION REPORT

For Month of February, 19—

	Total Cost	Unit Cost
COST IN PRECEDING DEPARTMENT:		
Work-in-Process, 2/1/—..........................	0	
Transferred into Department during Month..........	0	
Total.......................................	0	
Additional Cost for Lost Units....................	xx	0
Adjusted and Corrected Unit Cost Total..........	0	0
COST IN CURRENT DEPARTMENT:		
Work-in-Process, 2/1/—:		
Material Costs..............................	$ 3,000.00	
Labor Costs.................................	750.00	
Manufacturing Overhead Costs....................	250.00	
Cost in Department during Month:		
Material Costs..............................	22,600.00	$0.32
Labor Costs.................................	9,000.00	0.15
Manufacturing Overhead Costs..................	3,650.00	0.06
Total Cost in Current Department...............	$39,250.00	$0.53
CUMULATIVE COST TOTAL.....................	$39,250.00	$0.53
Work Completed and Transferred Out:..................	$31,800.00	
Work-in-Process, 2/28/—:		
Completed but Not Transferred Out.................	0	
Work-in-Process—Materials.......................	$ 6,400.00	
Work-in-Process—Labor..........................	750.00	
Work-in-Process—Manufacturing Overhead..........	300.00	
Total Work-in-Process.......................	$ 7,450.00	
CUMULATIVE COST TOTAL ACCOUNTED FOR....	$39,250.00	

QUANTITY PRODUCTION REPORT (In Pounds)*

QUANTITY TO BE ACCOUNTED FOR:	
Pounds-in-Process, 2/1/—..	10,000
Put into Process during February................................	76,000
To Be Accounted For..	86,000
QUANTITY ACCOUNTED FOR AS FOLLOWS:	
Completed and Transferred to Dept. II............................	60,000
Completed and on Hand..	0
Work-in-Process (All Material, ¼ Labor, ¼ Manufacturing Overhead)	20,000
Lost or Spoiled in Production....................................	6,000
Total Accounted For..	86,000

* For the computation of the equivalent production see page 339.

A similar procedure is followed in computing the unit costs in Department I for labor and overhead for the month of February, viz:

	Actual Production (Including W-I-P at the Beginning of Month)	Equivalent Production	Total Cost, Including W-I-P at Beginning of Month	Unit Cost
Completed............................	60,000 units	60,000		
In process, Feb. 28, ¼ complete...........	20,000	5,000		
Lost in production.....................	6,000	0		
Total...........................	86,000 units	65,000		
Labor costs ($750 + $9,000).............			$9,750	
Labor unit cost ($9,750 ÷ 65,000).........				$0.15
Overhead costs ($250 + $3,650)...........			$3,900	
Overhead unit cost ($3,900 ÷ 65,000).....				$0.06

Summary of Procedure in Department I Using Average Cost Method for Initial Work-in-Process

To summarize the procedure based upon the above, when there is a work-in-process inventory at the beginning of the accounting period, the following is given:

1. The inventory of the initial work-in-process must be stated in analyzed form—that is, separate figures for materials cost, labor cost, and manufacturing overhead cost.
2. The number of units in the initial inventory are added to the units received into the department during the period, giving the total units to be considered.
3. The cost in the initial inventory of the work-in-process for each element of cost is added to the corresponding cost for the same element for work performed during the period, thus obtaining the total cost for each element.
4. Dividing the total costs obtained in 3 by the corresponding equivalent production for each element gives the *average unit departmental cost* for that element.

The Average Method of Treating the Initial Work-in-Process Inventory— Department II

Continuing the previous illustration, the data summarizing the cost of production for February in Department II are tabulated and the cost of production report for Department II is presented. See Illustrations 11–6 and 11–7.

Illustration 11–6

DEPARTMENT II

	Quantity	Cost Value
February 1, 19—		
Completed and on hand (not transferred in January) (to be issued on first-in, first-out basis).................	5,000 lbs.	@ $0.96 $ 4,800
In process..	15,000	
Cost in Dept. I in January........................		7,500
Cost in Dept. II in January:		
Labor...		1,500
Overhead......................................		800
Costs during February:		
Received in dept. during February, costs for Dept. I.....	60,000	@ 0.53 31,800
Costs for labor in Dept. II.........................		18,100
Costs for overhead in Dept. II......................		11,100
To Be Accounted For............................	80,000 lbs.	$75,600
Accounted for as follows:		
Transferred to Dept. III:		
Completed and on hand at beginning (2/1/—)........	5,000 lbs.	
Completed during month..........................	65,000	
Work-in-process, 2/28/—(½ complete)...............	10,000	
Accounted for during February...................	80,000 lbs.	

The following explanations are necessary to understand the figures and computations relating to Illustration 11–7:

1. The 5,000 pounds on hand and complete in Dept. II, February 1, are not used in computing any unit costs. They represent merely the first 5,000 units to be transferred to Dept. III during February.
2. There were 15,000 pounds in process February 1. The cost of these in Dept. I for work done on them in January was............................... $ 7,500
3. Received from Dept. I during February were 60,000 pounds which cost in Dept. I.. 31,800
4. The total cost for work done in Dept. I for those units worked on in Dept. II during February was $39,300 for 75,000 pounds (60,000 + 15,000). This resulted in an *average unit cost* of production for Dept. I of............. 0.524
5. To compute the unit costs for labor and overhead in Dept. II the *equivalent production* must be computed for the sum of the units in process at beginning of period and the units received into the department during February 15,000 + 60,000. This equivalent production is 65,000 units + ½ (10,000).. 70,000 lbs.
6. To compute the *unit cost* for labor and for overhead, the equivalent production (70,000) must be divided respectively into the total labor cost and total overhead cost used on this production, e.g.:
   - Labor: $1,500 + $18,100 = $19,600 ÷ 70,000 units................. $0.28
   - Overhead: $ 800 + $11,100 = $11,900 ÷ 70,000 units................. 0.17
7. The *work-in-process inventory, February 28,* in Dept. II is 10,000 pounds, complete as far as Dept. I is concerned but ½ complete as far as labor and overhead costs in Dept. II are involved. This is computed:
   - For Dept. I Cost: 10,000 pounds × $0.524..........................$5,240
   - For Dept. II Cost:
     - Labor....................10,000 × ½ × $0.28................. 1,400
     - Overhead................10,000 × ½ × $0.17................ 850 $7,490

Illustration 11–7
DEPARTMENT II
COST PRODUCTION REPORT
For Month of February, 19—

	Total Cost	Unit Cost
COST IN PRECEDING DEPARTMENT:		
Work-in-Process, 2/1/—....................................	$ 7,500.00	$0.50
Transferred into Department during Month.....................	31,800.00	0.53
Total...	$39,300.00	$0.524*
Additional Cost for Lost Units..............................	xx	0
Adjusted and Corrected Unit Cost Total....................	$39,300.00	$0.524
COST IN CURRENT DEPARTMENT:		
Work-in-Process, 2/1/—:		
Material Costs..	0	
Labor Costs...	$ 1,500.00	
Manufacturing Overhead Costs............................	800.00	
Cost in Department during Month:†		
Material Costs..	0	
Labor Costs...	18,100.00	$0.28
Manufacturing Overhead Costs............................	11,100.00	0.17
Total Cost in Current Department.......	$31,500.00	$0.45
Cost of Goods Completed in January but Not Transferred (5,000 at $0.96)...	$ 4,800.00	
CUMULATIVE COST TOTAL...............................	{$70,800.00} {4,800.00}	$0.974 0.96
Work Completed and Transferred Out:		
5,000 @ $0.96...	$ 4,800.00	
65,000 @ $0.974..	63,310.00	
Work-in-Process, 2/28/—:		
Completed but Not Transferred Out..........................	0	
Cost in Dept. I..	$ 5,240.00	
Work-in-Process—Materials................................	0	
Work-in-Process—Labor...................................	1,400.00	
Work-in-Process—Manufacturing Overhead..................	850.00	
Total Work-in-Process................................	$ 7,490.00	
CUMULATIVE COST TOTAL ACCOUNTED FOR.............	$75,600.00	

* Average unit price ($39,300.00 ÷ 75,000 pounds).
† Equivalent production of 70,000 pounds (see page 342).

Illustration 11–7—(Continued)

QUANTITY PRODUCTION REPORT (In Pounds)

QUANTITY TO BE ACCOUNTED FOR:	
Pounds-in-Process, 2/1/—...	15,000
Pounds Completed but Not Transferred, 2/1/—......................	5,000
Put into Process during February (from Dept. I)....................	60,000
To Be Accounted For......................................	80,000
QUANTITY ACCOUNTED FOR AS FOLLOWS:	
Pounds Completed and Transferred to Dept. III......................	70,000
Completed and on Hand...	0
Work-in-Process (½ Labor, ½ Manufacturing Overhead).............	10,000
Lost or Spoiled in Production......................................	0
Total Accounted For...	80,000

The Average Method of Treating the Initial Work-in-Process Inventory in Department III

Continuing the previous illustration, the data summarizing the cost of production for February in Department III are tabulated and the cost of production report for Department III is presented. See Illustrations 11–8 and 11–9.

Illustration 11–8

DEPARTMENT III

	Quantity	Cost Value	
February 1, 19—			
In process: Cost in Depts. I and II in January.........	4,000 lbs.	@ $1.00	$ 4,000
Cost in Dept. III in January:			
Labor..............................			400
Overhead...........................			280
Costs during February:			
Received in Dept. III during February, costs for			
Depts. I and II..............................	{ 5,000	@ 0.96	4,800
	{ 65,000	@ 0.974	63,310
Costs for labor in Dept. III......................			14,300
Costs for overhead in Dept. III..................			10,220
To Be Accounted For......................	74,000 lbs.		$97,310
Accounted for as follows:			
Transferred to finished goods stock room...........	69,000 lbs.		
Work-in-process, ¼ complete as to labor and overhead	4,000		
Lost in production.............................	1,000		
Accounted for during February................	74,000 lbs.		

Illustration 11–9

DEPARTMENT III

COST PRODUCTION REPORT

For Month of February, 19—

	Total Cost	Unit Cost
COST IN PRECEDING DEPARTMENT:		
Work-in-Process, 2/1/—(4,000 @ $1.00)..................	$ 4,000.00	
Transferred into Department during Month................	68,110.00	
Total...	$72,110.00	$0.97446
Additional Cost for Lost Units (1,000 × $0.97446 ÷ 73,000 lbs.)	xx	0.013349
Adjusted and Corrected Unit Cost Total...............	$72,110.00	$0.987809
COST IN CURRENT DEPARTMENT:		
Work-in-Process, 2/1/—:		
Material Costs......................................	0	
Labor Costs..	$ 400.00	
Manufacturing Overhead Costs.......................	280.00	
Cost in Department during February:*		
Material Costs......................................	0	
Labor Costs..	14,300.00	$0.21
Manufacturing Overhead Costs.......................	10,220.00	0.15
Total Cost in Current Department...................	$25,200.00	$0.36
CUMULATIVE COST TOTAL...........................	$97,310.00	$1.347809
Work Completed and Transferred Out (69,000 @ $1.347809)....	$92,998.82	
Work-in-Process, 2/28/—:		
Completed but Not Transferred Out......................	0	
Cost in Depts. I and II (4,000 @ $0.97446)................	$ 3,897.84	
Lost Unit Cost (4,000 @ $0.013349)......................	53.40	
Work-in-Process—Material, Dept. III.....................	0	
Work-in-Process—Labor, Dept. III.......................	210.00	
Work-in-Process—Mfg. Overhead, Dept. III...............	150.00	
Total Work-in-Process.............................	$ 4,311.24	
CUMULATIVE COST TOTAL ACCOUNTED FOR.........	$97,310.06	

* Equivalent production, 70,000 pounds.
† Discrepancy of $0.06 due to decimals in unit costs.

Illustration 11–9—(Continued)
QUANTITY PRODUCTION REPORT (In Pounds)

QUANTITY TO BE ACCOUNTED FOR:	
In Process, 2/1/—	4,000
Put into Process (from Dept. II) during February	70,000
To Be Accounted For	74,000
QUANTITY ACCOUNTED FOR AS FOLLOWS:	
Completed and Transferred to Finished Goods Stock Room	69,000
In Process (¼ Labor, ¼ Manufacturing Overhead)	4,000
Lost in Process of Manufacturing	1,000
Total Accounted For	74,000

The following explanations are necessary to understand the figures and computations shown on Illustration 11–9:

1. The 4,000 pounds in process *February 1*, cost per unit in the two preceding departments $0.96 plus $0.04 for lost units, total $1. (See Dept. III report for January, Chapter 10, page 307.
   4,000 pounds @ $1 .... $ 4,000
2. The cost of the *labor* and *overhead* applied in *January* to the 4,000 units in process February 1 amounted to:
   Labor cost 400
   Manufacturing overhead lost 280
3. Received into Dept. III from Dept. II during February:
   5,000 lbs. at $0.96 .... $ 4,800
   65,000 lbs. at $0.974 63,310
   70,000 lbs. $68,110
4. The equivalent production for labor and overhead for work done in Dept. III during February was [69,000 + ¼(4,000)] .... 70,000 lbs.
5. The unit costs for labor and overhead in Dept. III for work done in February was as follows:
   Labor: $14,300 + $400 = $14,700 ÷ 70,000 lbs. $0.21
   Overhead: $10,220 + $280 = $10,500 ÷ 70,000 lbs. 0.15
6. The lost unit cost is computed by multiplying 1,000 units lost by the average cost of $0.97446 for Depts. I and II, and dividing the product by the remaining good units:
   (1,000 × $0.97446) ÷ (74,000 lbs. − 1,000 lbs.) .... $ 0.013349

A Complete Cost of Production Report Illustrating the Average Method of Costing Initial Work-in-Process Inventory

A cost of production report for the entire factory for the month of February is shown in Illustration 11–10. This represents the composite report of the three individual departmental reports just discussed, and it is the result of the cost accounting department's work in consolidating the various reports submitted by each department.

Illustration 11–10

ALTON MANUFACTURING COMPANY
SUMMARY COST OF PRODUCTION STATEMENT
For Month of February, 19—

	Department I		Department II		Department III	
	Cost	Per Unit	Cost	Per Unit	Cost	Per Unit
COST TRANSFERRED FROM PRECEDING DEPARTMENTS:						
Work-in-Process, 2/1/—........	0		$ 7,500.00	$0.50	$ 4,000.00	$1.00
Transferred into Department during February................	0		31,800.00	0.53	4,800.00	0.96
Transferred into Department during February................	0		0	0	63,310.00	0.974
Total Cost of Work Done in Preceding Departments....	0		$39,300.00	$0.524*	$72,110.00	$0.97446
Additional Costs for Lost Units.....		0		0		$0.013349
						0.987809
COSTS IN DEPARTMENT:						
Work-in-Process, 2/1/—:						
Material Cost...............	$ 3,000.00		0		0	
Labor Cost.................	750.00		$ 1,500.00		$ 400.00	
Manufacturing Overhead Cost.	250.00		800.00		280.00	
Costs for the Month of February:						
Material Costs..............	22,600.00	$0.32	0		0	
Labor Costs................	9,000.00	0.15	18,100.00	$0.28	14,300.00	$0.21
Manufacturing Overhead Costs.	3,650.00	0.06	11,100.00	0.17	10,220.00	0.15
Total Departmental Costs....	$39,250.00	$0.53	$31,500.00	$0.45	$25,200.00	$0.36
Cost of Goods Completed in January but Not Transferred......			$ 4,800.00	$0.96		
CUMULATIVE COST TOTAL....	$39,250.00	$0.53	{$70,800.00 4,800.00	$0.974 0.96}	$97,310.00	$1.347809
Transferred to Next Department....	$31,800.00		$68,110.00		0	
Work-in-Process, 2/28/—:						
Cost in Preceding Departments...	0		$ 5,240.00		$ 3,897.84	
Lost Unit Costs................	0		0		53.40	
Material Cost.................	$ 6,400.00		0		0	
Labor Cost...................	750.00		1,400.00		210.00	
Manufacturing Overhead Cost....	300.00		850.00		150.00	
Total Work-in-Process......	$ 7,450.00		$ 7,490.00		$ 4,311.24	
Transferred to Finished Goods Stock Room.................	0		0		$92,998.82	
CUMULATIVE COST TOTAL....	$39,250.00		$75,600.00		$97,310.06†	

* Average unit price ($39,300.00 + 75,000 pounds).   † Discrepancy of $0.06 due to decimals in unit costs.

Illustration 11–10—(Continued)

QUANTITY PRODUCTION REPORT (In Pounds)

QUANTITY TO BE ACCOUNTED FOR:			
Pounds-in-Process, 2/1/—......................	10,000	20,000	4,000
Put into Process during February...............	76,000	60,000	70,000
To Be Accounted For......................	86,000	80,000	74,000
QUANTITY ACCOUNTED FOR AS FOLLOWS:			
Completed and Transferred to Next Department...	60,000	70,000	0
Completed and on Hand, 2/1/—................	0	0	0
Work-in-Process, 2/1/—......................	20,000‡	10,000§	4,000**
Lost or Spoiled in Production..................	6,000	0	1,000
Completed and Transferred to Finished Goods Stock Room..	0	0	69,000
Total Accounted For......................	86,000	80,000	74,000

‡ All material, ¼ labor, ¼ manufacturing overhead. ** One-fourth labor, ¼ manufacturing overhead.
§ One-half labor, ½ manufacturing overhead.

Accounting Entries Covering Cycle of Costing for Month of February
To record the information shown on Illustration 11–10—that is, the cycle of production for the month of February where there is an *initial work-in-process inventory* treated on the *average cost method*—the following entries in journal form are given, supplemented by the three departmental work-in-process ledger accounts and the Finished Goods account:

Balances in the work-in-process accounts, February 1, 19—:
Work-in-Process—Dept. I.................................$4,000
Work-in-Process—Dept. II:
Completed but not transferred out........................ 4,800⎫
Partially completed work............................... 9,800⎭
Work-in-Process—Dept. III............................. 4,680

(1)
Work-in-Process—Dept. I.....................................35,250.00
Stores.. 22,600.00
Payroll... 9,000.00
Manufacturing Overhead............................... 3,650.00
To record costs in department for February.

(2)
Work-in-Process—Dept. II.....................................61,000.00
Work-in-Process—Dept. I............................... 31,800.00
Payroll... 18,100.00
Manufacturing Overhead............................... 11,100.00
To record costs in Dept. II during February.

(3)

Work-in-Process—Dept. III.....................................92,630.00
    Work-in-Process—Dept. II...............................   68,110.00
    Payroll...   14,300.00
    Manufacturing Overhead.................................   10,220.00
    To record costs in Dept. III for February.

(4)

Finished Goods..92,998.82
    Work-in-Process—Dept. III.............................   92,998.82
    To record cost of work completed during February.

Work-in-Process—Dept. I			
2/1 Balance 4,000.00	2/28 (2)	31,800.00	
2/28 (1) 35,250.00			

Work-in-Process—Dept. II		
2/1 Balance:	2/28 (3)	68,110.00
Com-pleted 4,800.00		
2/1 Uncom-pleted 9,800.00		
2/28 (2) 61,000.00		

Work-in-Process—Dept. III		
2/1 Balance 4,680.00	(4)	92,998.82
2/28 (3) 92,630.00		

Finished Goods	
2/28 (4) 92,998.82	

Computation of Lost Unit Costs When There Is an Initial Work-in-Process Inventory

In any department after the first, lost unit cost computations are affected not only by the addition of materials which increase the volume of production but also by work-in-process inventory at the beginning of the period. The basic rule to follow when computing lost unit costs in a department after the first when there is an initial work-in-process inventory is:

When there is a work-in-process inventory at the beginning of the period, it is not possible to determine whether the lost units came from this inventory or from the units received into the department during the period. Therefore, all the units must be considered when calculating the *lost unit cost*. This means *computing an average unit cost* for the work done in the preceding departments, BEFORE computing the lost unit cost.

If there is a work-in-process inventory at the beginning of the period in any department after the first, an *average unit cost* must be computed for that portion of this inventory which represents the cost in the preceding departments, plus the cost of the units received into the department during the period, before computing the *lost unit cost addition*. For example:

In Department II, the work-in-process inventory at the beginning of the month was as follows:

10,000 units	Cost in Dept. I..	$15,000
	Labor cost in Dept. II...................................	4,000
	Overhead cost in Dept. II...............................	3,000
15,000 units	Received into Dept. II during the month. Cost for work done in	
	Dept. I..	24,000

Of the 25,000 units worked on in Department II, during the current month the production statistics were:

Completed and transferred............	20,000 units
In process.........................	3,000
Lost in production..................	2,000
Total........................	25,000 units

Since it is not known whether the 2,000 units lost were part of the 10,000 or part of the 15,000 lot, it is necessary to compute an *average unit cost* for Department I *before* calculating the lost unit cost, e.g.:

10,000 units...	Work-in-process..	$15,000
15,000 units...	Received from Dept. I during month......................	24,000
25,000 units...	Total Cost for Dept. I................................	$39,000

Average unit cost of manufacture for Department I is

$39,000 ÷ 25,000 units = $1.56.
Lost unit cost (2,000 units × $1.56) ÷ 23,000 units = $0.136.

Thus the unit cost for Department I, corrected for units lost in Department II, would be $1.696 ($1.56 + $0.136).

QUESTIONS FOR REVIEW

1. What is meant by the statement that the initial work-in-process inventory must be stated in analyzed form? Why is this necessary?

2. In what respect does the initial work-in-process inventory in the second department differ from that in the first department?

3. There are two methods of treating the initial work-in-process inventory in a continuous process plant. Distinguish between these two methods. Which is the more accurate? Explain. Which is used more by business firms?

4. The initial work-in-process in Department I of a firm consists of 10,000 units on which 80 percent of the required material has been applied. During the current period, 90,000 additional units were started into production. At

the end of the period, there were in process 15,000 units on which 60 percent of the required material had been applied. The remaining units were transferred to the next department, there being no lost units in this department. Compute the equivalent production for materials in this department for this period when the average method is used.

5. When materials are added to production in a department after the first in a manufacturing plant, two possible situations may arise affecting the volume of production. What are these? What effect does each method have on the unit costs for the preceding departments?

6. Compare the effect on the unit costs for the preceding department when (*a*) materials are added in a department after the first that does *not* increase the volume of production; (*b*) when the added material increases the volume of production; and (*c*) when there are lost units in the department after the first.

7. When material is added in a department after the first and this increases the volume of production, and there are also lost units in this department, which should be computed first—the adjustment for added material or the correction for lost units?

8. In Department II, 40,000 units were received from Department I at a unit cost of $1.60. Materials creating an additional 25,000 units were added in this department. As a result of the manufacturing operations in this second department, 13,000 units were lost or spoiled. Compute, in a single calculation, the adjusted and corrected unit costs for Department I.

9. What journal entry is made for the adjustment of the unit cost for the preceding departments when materials are added which increase the volume of production? Explain.

10. In Department II, 20,000 units were received from Department I at a total cost of $40,000. In Department II, the volume of production increased to 25,000 units due to added materials at an additional unit cost of $3. As a result of the manufacturing operations in Department II, 1,250 units were spoiled. What is the adjusted unit cost for Department I for the added materials; the corrected unit cost for the lost units; and the corrected and adjusted unit costs for both added materials and lost units?

PROBLEMS—GROUP A

Problem 11–1. Purpose: *Cost of Production Report When Materials Are Added in All Departments Without Increasing Volume of Production; Lost Units in All Departments*

For the week ending June 11, 19—, the production statistics for the Sampson Manufacturing Company were as follows:

	Dept. I	Dept. II	Dept. III
Material costs........................	$40,000	$9,120	$4,600
Labor costs.........................	28,500	8,592	5,300
Manufacturing overhead..............	9,500	2,864	2,120

Quantity of production results were:

	Dept. I	Dept. II	Dept. III
Completed and transferred out..........	16,000 units	12,000 units	10,000 units
Completed and on hand................	2,000	1,000	0
Work-in-process:			
100% complete as to materials, 50% labor and overhead................	2,000		
100% materials, 60% labor and overhead............................		2,200	
100% materials, 40% labor and overhead............................			1,500
Lost or spoiled in production...........	2,000	800	500

From this information, you are asked to prepare:

a) Cost of production report for the week.

b) Journal entries to record the manufacturing cycle.

c) Statement of work-in-process inventories in each department in analyzed form.

Problem 11-2. Purpose: *Cost of Production When Materials Added in All Departments, Increasing Volume of Production; Lost Units in All Departments*

The Signal Supply Company operates a process plant producing a single product in three manufacturing departments. The operating data for the first week of its operations were as follows:

Department I: Material costs, $180,000; labor costs, $147,200; and manufacturing overhead costs, $36,800. Units completed and transferred out, 80,000; work-in-process, 100 percent complete as to materials, 60 percent complete as to labor and overhead, 20,000 units; and lost in production, 2,000 units.

Department II: Material costs, $138,000; labor costs, $88,000; and manufacturing overhead costs, $33,000. The added materials increased the volume of production by 40,000 units. In this department, 100,000 units were completed and transferred out; 15,000 units were in process, 100 percent complete as to materials but two-thirds complete as to labor and overhead; and 5,000 units were lost.

Department III: Material costs, $110,000; labor costs, $90,000; and manufacturing overhead costs, $50,000. Added materials increased the volume of production by 20,000 units. Work completed and transferred to the finished goods stock room amounted to 80,000 units; in process 100 percent complete as to materials and one-third complete as to labor and overhead amounted to 30,000 units. Lost units were 10,000.

On the basis of this information, you are asked to prepare:

a) Cost of production report.

b) Journal entries to cover the manufacturing cycle.

c) Detailed statement of the work-in-process inventory at the end of the week.

Problem 11-3. Purpose: *Cost of Production Report for Firm Using Average Method of Treating Initial Work-in-Process Inventories; No Added Materials; Lost Units in All Departments*

The Schuyler Manufacturing Company has three producing departments and completes on a process cost accounting system a single product. It uses the average method in treating its initial work-in-process inventories.
On May 4 the work-in-process inventories were as follows:

	Dept. I	Dept. II	Dept. III
Units in process.....................	30,000 units	35,000 units	40,000 units
Costs of these units:			
Preceding departments.............	0	$42,000	$88,000
Material costs....................$15,000		0	0
Labor costs......................	8,680	4,200	6,000
Overhead costs...................	3,550	2,020	3,200

For the week ending May 11, the production statistics were:

	Dept. I	Dept. II	Dept. III
Units put into production............100,000 units			
Completed and transferred out........105,000		110,000 units	120,000 units
Units in process, 5/11................	20,000	27,000	25,000
Stage of completion of work-in-process, 5/11:			
Materials.........................	100%	0	0
Labor and overhead...............	40%	33⅓%	80%
Units lost in production.............	5,000 units	3,000 units	5,000 units
Costs during the week:			
Materials........................$75,000		0	0
Labor costs......................	32,000	$91,000	$92,000
Overhead costs...................	13,400	17,020	22,000

From this information you are asked to prepare:
a) Cost of production report.
b) Journal entries to record the manufacturing operations.
c) Work-in-process inventories, May 11, in analyzed form by departments.

Problem 11–4. Purpose: *Cost Production for Firm Using Average Method of Treating Initial Work-in-Process Inventories for a Firm Using Process Costing; Added Materials Increasing Volume of Production; Lost Units in First Department Only*

The Sampson Manufacturing Company uses a process cost accounting system, reporting weekly. Work-in-process inventories are averaged with the current production.

The operating results for the three departments for the week ending August 8 were as follows:

Department I: In process, August 1, there were 12,000 units. Materials used during week ending August 8, provided 60,000 additional units. Of this quantity, 61,000 units were completed and transferred to Department II. On August 8, there were in process, 9,000 units on which all the material and one third of the labor and overhead had been applied. The remaining units were spoiled and had to be rejected.

The costs were: Work-in-process, 8/1/—: materials, $6,500; labor, $2,400; and overhead, $900. During the week the costs incurred were: materials, $74,000; labor, $39,200; and overhead, $11,900.

Department II: In process, August 1, 8,000 units. Materials added to increase volume of production amounted to 23,000 units. The material was accounted for as follows: finished and transferred to Department III, 80,000 units. In process, complete as to material, and 50 percent as to labor and overhead, 12,000 units.

Operating costs for the week of August 8 were as follows: Work-in-process, 8/1/—: cost in preceding department, $14,400; materials used, $34,000; labor costs, $7,200; and overhead costs, $6,200. Additional costs incurred during week were: materials, $150,000; labor, $44,400; and overhead, $28,200.

Department III: In process, August 1, 5,000 units. Added materials, 21,250 units. Of this quantity, 96,250 units were completed and sent to the finished stock room; 10,000 units were still in process, on which all the material and 40 percent of the labor and overhead had been applied.

Costs for this week's production were: Work-in-process, 8/1/—: cost in the preceding departments, $24,000; materials, $15,000; labor, $12,100; and overhead, $2,025. Additional costs for the week were: materials, $70,000; labor, $48,050; and overhead, $8,000.

From this information, you are asked to prepare:

a) Cost of production report for the week ending August 8, 19—.

b) Journal entries to record the manufacturing operations.

c) Statement of the work-in-process inventories, 8/8/—, in analyzed form by departments.

Problem 11–5. Purpose: *Cost of Production Report Using Average Method of Treating Initial Work-in-Process Inventories; Added Materials Increasing Volume of Production; Lost Units in All Departments*

The Simpson Supply Company uses the average method of costing its initial work-in-process inventory in its process manufacturing cost system. It produces a single product which goes through two departments.

For the week April 5 to April 12, the production statistics were as follows:

MANUFACTURING COSTS

	Dept. I	Dept. II
Work-in-process, 4/5/—:		
Costs in preceding department..............	0	$ 35,000
Material costs............................$	30,000	12,000
Labor costs................................	11,200	5,000
Manufacturing overhead....................	5,025	3,600
Costs for week of 4/12:		
Material costs............................	157,500	150,000
Labor costs................................	30,200	55,000
Manufacturing overhead costs................	19,125	44,400

The units produced during the week of April 12 were as follows:

	Dept. I	Dept. II
Work-in-process, 4/5/—..................15,000 units		10,000 units
Increase in volume due to added materials.........65,000		26,000
Work completed and transferred out during week of		
4/12/—.......................................55,000		70,000
Work completed and not transferred out.............. 5,000		0
Work-in-process, 4/12/—:		
All material, 60% of labor and overhead applied.....15,000		
All material, 50% of labor and overhead applied.....		20,000
Units lost in production........................... 5,000		1,000

On the basis of these statistics, you are asked to prepare:
a) Cost of production report for week of April 12, 19—.
b) Journal entries covering the manufacturing cycle.
c) Work-in-process inventories by departments in analyzed form.

Problem 11–6. **Purpose:** *Computation of Unit Process Costs; Comparative Statements; Final Inventories*

The Security Manufacturing Company has been in operation for one year. It manufactures asbestos cement pipe in lengths of four feet. It has the necessary equipment to also produce the following sizes: 18-inch, 24-inch, 30-inch, and 36-inch.

The company has one basic machine to produce pipe. Only one size is made during each working day of eight hours, the last hour of which is used by the crew for cleanup and, as necessary, to change the machine so that a different size can be made the following day. Production during the first year was limited to sizes from 18-inch to 30-inch inclusive.

You are informed that there is a ready outlet for 36-inch pipe if it were to be produced. The company has prepared a net income schedule for the year just ended, as follows:

NET INCOME SCHEDULE

Sales...		$58,000
Raw material purchases.............................$17,657		
Direct labor....................................... 13,255		
Freight-in... 2,447		
Delivery expense................................... 3,582		
Depreciation:		
Factory building................................. 600		
Office building.................................. 280		
Factory machinery............................... 3,000		
Office furniture and fixtures..................... 200		
Electric power purchased for factory............... 1,519		
Shop supplies...................................... 2,550		
Office supplies and expenses....................... 1,000		
Office salaries.................................... 5,200		
Telephone and telegraph........................... 375		
Factory repairs and maintenance.................... 2,175		
Commissions on sales............................... 2,700		
Other factory expenses............................. 760		
Miscellaneous general expense...................... 200		
Raw materials inventory—year-end..................		1,630
Finished goods inventory, year-end at estimated cost of $10 per ton..		5,990
Profit for the year................................ 8,120		
	$65,620	$65,620

Your review of the records discloses the following data as to production and sales:

PRODUCTION AND SALES DATA

INVENTORY, 12/31

Pipe Diameter	Produced (Feet)	Sold (Feet)	Inventory Feet	Pounds per Foot	Total Weight	Average Production per Day (Feet)	Selling Price per Foot
18″	7,200	6,200	1,000	150	150,000	120	$2.20
24″	10,200	8,120	2,080	250	520,000	100	3.00
30″	6,320	5,000	1,320	400	528,000	80	4.00
					1,198,000		

Material cost in finished pipe is found to be the same per ton throughout the year regardless of size. Labor and overhead were incurred uniformly throughout the year. The plant foreman tells you that test runs have indicated that 36-inch pipe would weigh 500 pounds per foot and that production should average 64 feet per day. The 36-inch pipe will sell for $5 per foot.

From this information, you are asked to:

a) (1) Compute the cost of each size of pipe produced during the year on a per foot basis including material, labor, and manufacturing overhead.

(2) Prepare a schedule showing which size pipe would be most profitable to produce.

(3) Compute the value of the closing inventory of pipe for each size.

b) Prepare an estimate of the cost of production of 36-inch pipe and compare the gross profit from producing it with that from producing other sizes. (Carry computations to three decimal places.)

(Adapted from an AICPA Uniform Examination)

PROBLEMS—GROUP B

Problem 11-7. Purpose: *Cost of Production Report for Firm in Which Materials Are Added in a Department after the First but No Increase in Volume of Production; Lost Units in All Departments*

The Creston Manufacturing Company operates a process cost type of plant with three producing departments. For the first week of its operations, ending June 26, the following data are presented to you. From this you are asked to prepare in good form: (a) cost of production report; (b) journal entries to cover the manufacturing cycle; and (c) detailed schedule of the work-in-process inventory at the end of the week.

	Dept. I	Dept. II	Dept. III
Material costs	$46,400	$18,000	$14,000
Labor costs	18,900	8,500	5,850
Manufacturing overhead	8,100	3,400	2,600

Production statistics obtained from the departmental reports were:

	Dept. I	Dept. II	Dept. III
Completed and transferred out	22,000 units	15,000 units	12,000 units
Completed and not transferred out	3,000	0	0
Work-in-process, 6/26/—:			
100% complete as to materials, 50% complete as to labor and overhead	4,000		
100% complete as to materials, 40% complete as to labor and overhead		5,000	
100% complete as to materials, 50% complete as to labor and overhead			2,000
Units lost in production	1,000	2,000	1,000

Problem 11–8.   Purpose: *Cost of Production Report When Materials Are Added in All Departments, Increasing the Volume of Production; Lost Units in All Departments*

J. Cramer & Company, manufacturers of a single product in its three departments, submits the following quantity of production results for the first week of its operations, ending July 24, 19—:

	Dept. I	Dept. II	Dept. III
Started into production	150,000 units		
Quantity of materials added increasing the volume		50,000 units	40,000 units
Completed and transferred	100,000	120,000	130,000
Completed and not transferred out	10,000	0	0
Work-in-process, 7/24/—:			
Materials 100% complete, labor and overhead 33⅓%	30,000		
Materials 100% complete, labor and overhead 50%		24,000	
Materials 100% complete, labor and overhead 40%			25,000
Lost in production	10,000	6,000	5,000

The operating costs for this week were as follows:

	Dept. I	Dept. II	Dept. III
Material costs	$175,000	$288,000	$263,500
Labor costs	96,000	79,200	119,000
Overhead costs	36,000	26,400	21,000

On the basis of this information, you are asked to prepare:

a) Cost of production report.

b) Journal entries to cover the manufacturing cycle.

c) Work-in-process inventories in analyzed form for each department.

Problem 11–9. Purpose: *Cost of Production Report Using Average Method of Treating Initial Work-in-Process Inventories; Lost Units in All Departments; Added Materials No Increase*

The Curtis Plastics Products Company uses the average method of treating its work-in-process inventory in its process manufacturing plant cost system.

Under date of June 20, 19—, the work-in-process inventories were as follows:

	Dept. I	Dept. II	Dept. III
Units in process............	6,000 units	12,000 units	9,000 units
Stage of completion........	100% material	100% material	100% material
	20% labor and	25% labor and	33⅓% labor and
	overhead	overhead	overhead
Costs of this inventory:			
Preceding department......	0	$30,000	$36,000
Material costs...........$8,000		4,000	3,000
Labor costs..............	3,000	2,200	1,800
Overhead costs...........	800	825	1,160

The operating data for the week ending June 27 were as follows:

	Dept. I	Dept. II	Dept. III
Completed and transferred out........	50,000 units	54,000 units	52,000 units
Work-in-process, 6/27/—............	15,000 units	6,000 units	8,000 units
Stage of completion:			
Materials........................	100%	100%	100%
Labor and manufacturing overhead..	33⅓%	25%	50%
Lost units........................	1,000 units	2,000 units	3,000 units
Material costs.....................$89,500		$50,000	$45,000
Labor costs.......................	41,000	20,000	29,000
Overhead costs....................	15,700	7,500	19,000

On the basis of this information, you are asked to prepare:

a) Cost of production report.

b) Journal entries to cover the manufacturing cycle.

c) Work-in-process inventory in analyzed form for each department.

Problem 11–10. Purpose: *Cost Computations for Firm Using the Average Method of Treating the Initial Work-in-Process Inventories; Added Materials Increasing Volume of Production; Lost Units in First Department Only*

The Central Manufacturing Company operates a plant on a continuous process basis, costing its initial work-in-process inventory on the average basis. The following data represents the operating results for the week ending July 15, 19—. You are asked to prepare (*a*) cost of production report for week ending July 15; (*b*) journal entries to record the operating results; and (*c*) a work-in-process inventory statement, July 15, in analyzed form by departments.

The volume of production for the week of July 15 was as follows:

	Dept. I	Dept. II	Dept. III
Work-in-process, 7/8/—.............	10,000 units	20,000 units	30,000 units
Put into production during week.....100,000			
Added materials increasing volume of			
production.......................		25,000	40,000
Completed and transferred...........	80,000	90,000	140,000
Completed, not transferred..........	5,000	10,000	0
Work-in-process, 7/15/—:			
Materials, 100%; labor and over-			
head, 40%.....................	20,000		
Materials, 100%; labor and over-			
head, 60%.....................		25,000	
Materials, 100%; labor and over-			
head, 80%.....................			20,000
Lost in production.................	5,000	0	0

The costs of production incurred during the week of July 15 were:

	Dept. I	Dept. II	Dept. III
Work-in-process, 7/8/—:			
Cost in preceding depts...................	0	$40,000	$120,000
Material costs.........................$	6,000	4,000	14,000
Labor costs...........................	4,750	3,000	5,600
Overhead costs........................	1,600	1,500	1,200
Current costs:			
Materials costs........................	125,250	96,000	146,000
Labor costs...........................	65,000	89,000	56,800
Manufacturing overhead.................	17,000	44,500	14,400

Problem 11–11. Purpose: *Cost of Production for Process Manufacturing Firm Using Average Method of Treating Work-in-Process Inventories; Added Materials Increasing Volume of Production; Lost Units in All Departments*

The cost accounting data for the Charleton Supply Company for the week ending March 8 was as follows:

Department I: In process, March 1, 20,000 units which had cost for materials, $16,000; labor, $8,400; and overhead, $2,200. During the week ending March 8, additional materials for producing 75,000 units were issued. As a result of the manufacturing operations, 80,000 units were completed and transferred to Department II, 12,000 units were still in process March 8 with all materials and two-thirds labor and overhead applied, and 3,000 units were spoiled and rejected during the week.

The costs during the week were: materials, $85,200; labor, $64,848; and overhead, $11,752.

Department II: In process, March 1, 10,000 units which had cost for preceding department, $20,000; materials, $16,400; labor, $7,420; and overhead, $1,730. During week additional materials were used increasing the volume by 22,500 units. Units completed and transferred to finished stock room were 94,000 units. In process, March 8, were 15,000 units on which all the materials and one third of the labor and overhead had been applied. The remaining units were lost. Costs during this week were: materials, $114,400; labor, $67,820; and overhead, $22,030.

From these data, you are asked to prepare:

a) Cost of production report.

b) Journal entries to record the manufacturing operations.

c) Work-in-process inventory, August 8, 19—, in analyzed form by departments.

Problem 11–12. Purpose: *Partial Cost of Production for Firm Using Average Method of Treating Initial Work-in-Process Inventory When Materials Are Added in All Departments Increasing Volume of Production; Lost Units in All Departments*

The Carter Supply Company produces a single product in a process type of manufacturing operations. Three departments constitute the plant operations. Materials are added in each department increasing the volume of production. There is usually some work-in-process at the end of each week's operations. Spoilage which is discarded occurs in each department.

The following statistics represent the results for the second and third departments. You are asked to prepare a partial cost of production report for these two departments for the week ending June 12; journal entries for these operations; and a work-in-process inventory statement in analyzed form for each department.

The volume of production for the week of June 12 was as follows:

	Dept. II	Dept. III
Work-in-process, 6/5	12,000 units	10,000 units
Received from preceding department	40,000	70,000
Added materials increasing volume of production	26,000	20,000
Completed and transferred out	70,000	80,000
Work-in-process, 6/12/—:		
All materials, 50% of labor and overhead applied	6,000	
All materials, 25% labor and overhead applied		16,000
Units lost or spoiled	2,000	4,000

The costs of the operations for the week of June 12 were:

	Dept. II	Dept. III
Work-in-process, 6/5/—:		
Cost in preceding depts	$ 24,000	$ 52,000
Material costs	16,000	12,800
Labor costs	9,000	4,000
Manufacturing overhead	4,200	2,100
Received from preceding depts	84,000	(?)
Costs during week of 6/12/—:		
Material costs	136,000	160,000
Labor costs	64,000	50,600
Manufacturing overhead	32,300	27,300

Problem 11-13.   Purpose: *C.P.A. Problem Requiring Cost of Production Calculations and Reports*

The Calleck Company manufactures a single product on a continuous basis. This product is sold under the patented trade name of MELBO.

The manufacturing operation is as follows:

Material K, a metal, is stamped to form a part which is assembled with one of the purchased parts "X." The unit is then machined and cleaned, after which it is assembled with two units of part "Y" to form the finished device known as a "MELBO." Spray priming and enameling is the final operation.

Time and motion studies indicate that of the total time required for the manufacture of a unit, the first operation required 25 percent of the labor cost; the first assembly an additional 25 percent; machining and cleaning, 12.5 percent; the second assembly, 25 percent; and painting, 12.5 percent. Manufacturing expense is considered to follow the same pattern by operations as does labor.

The following data are presented to you as of October 31, ——, the end of the first month of operation:

```
Material K purchased—100,000 lbs.............................$25,000
Part X purchased—80,000 units................................ 16,000
Part Y purchased—150,000 units............................... 15,000
Primer and enamel used.......................................  1,072
Direct labor—cost............................................ 45,415
Manufacturing expenses....................................... 24,905
```

Unit Quantity

```
Units finished and sent to finished goods warehouse...........67,000
Units assembled but not painted.............................. 5,000
Units ready for the second assembly.......................... 3,000
Inventories at the end of the month:
  Finished units............................................. 7,500
  Material K (lbs.).......................................... 5,800
  Part X (units of part X)................................... 5,000
  Part Y (units of part Y)................................... 6,000
  MELBOS in process (units).................................. 8,000
```

Required:

a) A schedule of equivalent labor production.

b) A schedule of total and unit costs incurred in production for:

   (1) Each kind of material.

   (2) Labor cost.

   (3) Manufacturing overhead.

   (4) Total cost of production.

c) A schedule of detailed material, labor, and manufacturing costs assigned to the units left in process.

(Adapted from an AICPA Uniform Examination)

CHAPTER

12 Process Cost Accounting Procedures—Part III FIFO Method of Costing the Initial Work-in-Process Inventory

Nature of FIFO Method of Costing the Initial Work-in-Process Inventory

As a substitute for the average method of treating the initial work-in-process inventory in process cost accounting as discussed in the preceding chapter, some accountants feel that the FIFO (first-in, first-out) method of cost accounting is more accurate. The underlying principle of the FIFO method of treating the initial work-in-process inventory is that the costs expended in any department for materials, labor, and manufacturing overhead must *first* be applied to the completion of the work-in-process inventory at the beginning of the accounting period, and then to the new production. *If this principle is followed, then it must be assumed that the FINAL work-in-process inventory in any department will be costed at the unit costs of the latest or new production,* not at an average cost figure as in the previous chapter. This procedure also implies that the first transfer out of any department will reflect the costs of the *initial* work-in-process inventory.

The conditions under which it is possible to use the FIFO method of costing the initial work-in-process inventory vary from firm to firm. Three types of situations are considered as possibly practical for the use of this method, viz:

1. The lot of production represented by the initial work-in-process is kept separately throughout the manufacturing operations, not only in the costing in the department in which presently located but in the transfer from department to department. It is almost like job-lot costing applied to a process industry. Some pharmaceutical product manufacturers are known to use this method. It becomes increasingly complicated if there are many producing departments, each one having some work-

in-process at the beginning. It is probably the most accurate method, but also the most expensive to operate. For example if there were three operating departments in a firm, the *finished goods produced* would show separate costs for the following, in the final department:

> Work-in-Process, Dept. I, at beginning of period
> *New* Production, Dept. I, carried through Depts. II and III
> Work-in-Process, Dept. II, at beginning of period
> Work-in-Process, Dept. III, at beginning of period

This method is practical only if there are no added materials in any departments after the first which would increase the number of units in production, and if there are no lost units in any department after the first. This method might be termed "pure FIFO" since it keeps separately the costs of production for each initial work-in-process inventory.

2. When there are *lost units* in any department after the first, it is not possible to identify these lost units either with the initial work-in-process inventory or the new production received into the department. Therefore, where there are *lost units* in any department after the first, a *modified FIFO* procedure must be followed—that is, the costs of the preceding department, though separately stated for the initial work-in-process inventory and the new production received into the department, *must now be averaged* before *computing the lost unit cost adjustment*. Thereafter, in computing the total cost of goods transferred out of a department, the final work-in-process inventory in that department must be computed at the latest unit costs for that department, and the balance of the total costs for the department is considered the total cost of the goods transferred out. Dividing this total cost by the number of units transferred results in the unit cost of the transfer—actually it is an average cost figure.

3. When there are *added materials* in a department after the first, which added material increases the number of units in production, it is desirable to follow a procedure similar to that used when there are lost units—using the average costs of the transfer into a department before computing the *adjusted unit cost* resulting from the added materials.

Each of these methods will be discussed and illustrated in more detail.

Method No. 1: Using the FIFO method in costing the initial work-in-process inventory when there are no lost units except in first department and no added materials in a department after the first increasing the volume of production.

This method might be termed "pure FIFO" since the work-in-process inventories at the beginning of the period and the new production are separately costed on the first-in, first-out basis, that is, the work-in-process must first be completed before considering the cost of the new production.

To explain and illustrate this method, the quantity and cost of production statistics are shown separately for Departments I and II, before consolidating them into a single summary cost of production report for the month of March.

Department I

In Department I, on March 1, there were in process, 5,000 units, 100 percent complete as to materials, 60 percent complete as to labor and overhead costs. The material, labor, and overhead costs were $10,000, $3,000, and $1,800, respectively.

During March, 45,000 additional units were started into production.

Additional costs of production during March were: materials, $107,500; payroll, $4,100; and manufacturing overhead, $8,200.

During March, 40,000 units were transferred out of the department—5,000 of the units in process at the beginning of the month and 35,000 new production. In process, March 31, 100 percent complete as to materials and 50 percent complete as to labor and overhead costs, were 8,000 units. Lost in production during March, 2,000 units.

From the preceding information, it is necessary to compute the equivalent production for material, labor, and overhead costs. On the FIFO basis, this equivalent production is made up of *three items:*

1. Equivalent units to complete *initial* work-in-process.
2. Equivalent units of other work completed during period.
3. Equivalent units of *final* work-in-process inventory.

For Department I *the equivalent production for the costs incurred and the unit costs* would be:

	Equivalent Production	
	Materials	Labor and Overhead
1. To complete work-in-process, March 1..............	0	2,000 units
2. Units completed during March in addition to work-in-process, March 1.........................	35,000 units	35,000
3 Work-in-process, March 31:		
Materials, 8,000 × 100%......................	8,000	
Labor and Manufacturing Overhead, 8,000 × ½....		4,000
Total Equivalent Production...................	43,000 units	41,000 units
4. Costs incurred:		
Materials.....................................$107,500		
Labor..		$4,100
Manufacturing Overhead......................		8,200
5. Dividing by equivalent production, the unit costs would be:		
Materials.....................................	$2.50	
Labor..		$0.10
Manufacturing Overhead......................		0.20

The units transferred out of Department I totaled 40,000, of which 5,000 were in process at beginning of month and 35,000 were new production. To compute the cost of *units transferred out of Department I* during March, using the FIFO method, the following calculations are required:

Units		Costs
5,000	Costs on March 1	$ 14,800
	Labor costs during March, 5,000 × 40% × $0.10	200
	Manufacturing overhead costs during March, 5,000 × 40% × $0.20...	400
	Total cost to complete 5,000 units	$ 15,400
35,000	Costs during March, all new production, 35,000 × 100% × $2.80.....	98,000
40,000	Total Transferred Out of Department I during March	$113,400

To compute the work-in-process inventory on March 31, the following calculations are used:

Material-in-process: 8,000 units × 100% × $2.50	$20,000
Labor-in-process: 8,000 units × 50% × $0.10	400
Overhead-in-process: 8,000 units × 50% × $0.20	800
Total Work-in-Process, Dept. I, March 31	$21,200

The cost of production report for Department I for the month of March, using the FIFO method of accounting for the initial work-in-process inventory, is as shown in Illustration 12–1.

Continuing the illustration given previously for Department I, the production statistics for *Department II* for the month of March were:

In process on March 1, 6,000 units, 30 percent complete as to labor and manufacturing overhead costs in Department II. The costs for this in-process inventory, March 1, were: costs in Department I, $17,100; labor costs in Department II, $5,400; and overhead costs in Department II, $3,000.

During March, there were received into Department II:

5,000 units	Costs per production report for Dept. I	$ 15,400	$3.08
35,000	Costs per production report for Dept. I	98,000	2.80
40,000 units	Total	$113,400	

Additional costs of production in Department II during March were:

Payroll costs	$115,020
Manufacturing overhead costs	38,340

During March, 42,000 units were transferred out of Department II. This total was made up of:

6,000 units in process in Dept. II on March 1
5,000 units representing first lot from Dept. I during March
31,000 units second lot received from Dept. I during March
42,000 units—total completed
4,000 units—in process in Dept. II, March 31, 60% complete as to labor and manufacturing overhead.
46,000 units—Total quantity to be accounted for in Dept. II during March

Illustration 12–1

DEPARTMENT I

COST OF PRODUCTION REPORT

For Month of March, 19—

	Total Cost	Unit Cost
COST IN CURRENT DEPARTMENT:.....................		
Work-in-Process, 3/1/—:		
Material Costs..	$ 10,000.00	$2.00
Labor Costs..	3,000.00	0.60
Manufacturing Overhead Costs........................	1,800.00	0.36
Cost in Department during Month:		
Material Costs..	107,500.00	2.50
Labor Costs..	4,100.00	0.10
Manufacturing Overhead Costs........................	8,200.00	0.20
Total Cost in Current Department.....................	$134,600.00	$2.80
CUMULATIVE COST TOTAL.............................	$134,600.00	
Work Completed and Transferred Out: 5,000 @............... {	$ 15,400.00	$3.08
35,000 @............... {	98,000.00	2.80
Work-in-Process, 3/31/—:		
Completed but Not Transferred Out.....................	0	
Work-in-Process—Materials (8,000 × 100% × $2.50)...........	$ 20,000.00	
Work-in-Process—Labor (8,000 × ½ × $0.10)...............	400.00	
Work-in-Process—Manufacturing Overhead: (8,000 × ½ × $0.20).	800.00	
Total Work-in-Process................................	$ 21,200.00	
CUMULATIVE COST TOTAL ACCOUNTED FOR..............	$134,600.00	

QUANTITY OF PRODUCTION REPORT (In Pounds)

QUANTITY TO BE ACCOUNTED FOR:	
Work-in-Process, 3/1/—..	5,000
Put into Production or Received from Preceding Departments...............	45,000
To Be Accounted For..	50,000
QUANTITY ACCOUNTED FOR AS FOLLOWS:	
Transferred to Next Department..................................... {	5,000
	35,000
Completed but Not Transferred Out..................................	0
Uncompleted Work-in-Process.......................................	8,000
Units Lost in Production...	2,000
Total Accounted For..	50,000
Equivalent Production:	
Material...	43,000
Labor and Manufacturing Overhead...................................	41,000

On the basis of the foregoing information, it is necessary to compute the equivalent production for labor and overhead costs in the same manner as for Department I, when the FIFO procedure was to be followed, namely:

1. Equivalent units to complete *initial* work-in-process in Dept. II.
2. Equivalent units of other work completed in Dept. II during March.
3. Equivalent units of *final* work-in-process inventory in Dept. II, March 31.

See Illustration 12–2.

Illustration 12–2

DEPARTMENT II

COST OF PRODUCTION REPORT

For Month of March, 19—

	Total Cost	Unit Cost
COST IN PRECEDING DEPARTMENT:		
Work-in-Process, 3/1/—, (6,000 units @ $2.85)...............	$ 17,100.00	$2.85
Transferred into Department during Month: { 5,000..........	15,400.00	3.08
{ 35,000..........	98,000.00	2.80
Total Cost in Preceding Department................	$130,500.00	
COST IN CURRENT DEPARTMENT:		
Work-in-Process, 3/1/—:		
Material Costs..	0	
Labor Costs..	$ 5,400.00	
Manufacturing Overhead Costs..........................	3,000.00	
Cost in Department during Month:		
Material Costs..	0	
Labor Costs..	115,020.00	$2.70
Manufacturing Overhead Costs..........................	38,340.00	0.90
Total Cost in Current Department......................	$161,760.00	
CUMULATIVE COST TOTAL............................	$292,260.00	
Work Completed and Transferred Out: 6,000.................	$ 40,620.00	$6.77 ⎫
5,000.................	33,400.00	6.68 ⎬
31,000.................	198,400.00	6.40 ⎭
Work-in-Process, 3/31/—:		
Completed but Not Transferred Out......................	0	
Cost in Preceding Department...........................	$ 11,200.00	$2.80
Work-in-Process—Materials..............................	0	
Work-in-Process—Labor (4,000 × 60% × $2.70).............	6,480.00	1.62
Work-in-Process—Manufacturing Overhead (4,000 × 60% × $0.90)..	2,160.00	0.54
Total Work-in-Process..............................	$ 19,840.00	
CUMULATIVE COST TOTAL ACCOUNTED FOR...........	$292,260.00	

QUANTITY PRODUCTION REPORT (In Pounds)

QUANTITY TO BE ACCOUNTED FOR:	
Work-in-Process, 3/1/—..	6,000 units
Put into Production or Received from Preceding Departments............	40,000
To Be Accounted For..	46,000
QUANTITY ACCOUNTED FOR AS FOLLOWS:	
Transferred to Next Department................................. {	6,000
	5,000
	31,000
Completed but Not Transferred Out..............................	0
Uncompleted Work-in-Process...................................	4,000
Units Lost in Production.......................................	0
Total Accounted For......................................	46,000
Equivalent Production:	
Material..	0
Labor and Manufacturing Overhead..............................	42,600

For Department II the equivalent production and unit costs for the total costs
incurred during March are as follows:

Labor and
Manufacturing
Overhead: To complete *initial* work-in-process, March 1, 6,000 units × 70%.... 4,200 units
Units completed in addition to initial work-in-process inventory
(42,000 units − 6,000 units)................................36,000
Equivalent production of *final* work-in-process inventory, March 31,
4,000 units × 60%... 2,400
Equivalent Production for Labor and Manufacturing Overhead
in Dept. II during March..............................42,600 units

The unit costs for labor and manufacturing overhead in Department
II for the month of March can now be computed as follows:

Labor: $115,020 ÷ 42,600 = $2.70
Manufacturing Overhead: $38,340 ÷ 42,600 = $0.90

To compute the cost of units transferred out of Department II on the
pure FIFO basis, each separate lot of production must be considered on
the basis of the appropriate costs. In this instance, three separate batches
or quantities must be considered in the following order, viz:

Quantity in Process in Department II, March 1

6,000 units	Costs in Dept. I during February @ $2.85....................$ 17,100	
	Costs in Dept. II during February:	
	Work-in-Process—Labor.................................	5,400
	Work-in-Process—Manufacturing Overhead................	3,000
	Costs to complete in Dept. II during March:	
	Labor costs: 6,000 × 70% × $2.70........................	11,340
	Mfg. overhead costs: 6,000 × 70% × $0.90................	3,780
		$ 40,620

Transferred into Department II during March

5,000	Costs in Dept. I during February and March @ $3.08.........$ 15,400	
	Costs in Dept. II during March:	
	Labor costs: 5,000 × $2.70.............................	13,500
	Mfg. overhead costs: 5,000 × $0.90......................	4,500
		$ 33,400
31,000	Costs in Dept. I during March @ $2.80......................$ 86,800	
	Costs in Dept. II during March:	
	Labor costs: 31,000 × $2.70.............................	83,700
	Mfg. overhead costs: 31,000 × $0.90......................	27,900
		$198,400
42,000 units	Total Transferred Out of Department II during March......$272,420	

The computation of the final (March 31) work-in-process inventory in Department II is as follows:

4,000 units	Cost in Dept. I in March, 4,000 units × $2.80..........$11,200	
	Costs in Dept. II during March:	
	Labor costs: 4,000 × 60% × $2.70..................	6,480
	Mfg. overhead costs: 4,000 × 60% × $0.90..........	2,160
4,000 units	Total Work-in-Process, Dept. II, March 31.........$19,840	

Illustration 12–3 shows the summary results of cost and production for the two departments for March. It must be evident that where the "pure FIFO" method is used, keeping track of the various lots of production becomes more complicated as the number of manufacturing departments increase. For example, the material transferred out of Department II is made up of three different lots; those that will be transferred out of Department III will be four different lots; and so on. This makes for cumbersome cost accounting. Therefore, the modified FIFO method, as described in the following pages, is used more frequently by those firms planning to use the FIFO method of costing the initial work-in-process inventories.

Method No. 2: Handling initial work-in-process inventory on a FIFO basis when there are lost units in a department after the first.

When there are lost units in a department after the first, it is not always possible in a process plant to ascertain definitely whether these lost units came from the initial work-in-process inventory or from the units transferred into the department during the current period. Furthermore, as indicated previously, using the pure FIFO method becomes increasingly complicated as the number of producing departments becomes larger. Therefore, a modified FIFO procedure is devised, as follows:

1. The *final* work-in-process inventory in any department will be valued at this month's or the current manufacturing costs.
2. The amount transferred from any department is determined by subtracting from the *total* costs of manufacturing, the *final* work-

Illustration 12–3

SUMMARY COST OF PRODUCTION REPORT

For Month of March, 19—

	Department I Total Cost	Department I Unit Cost	Department II Total Cost	Department II Unit Cost
COST IN PRECEDING DEPARTMENT:				
Work-in-Process, 3/1/—, 6,000 @ $2.85...			$ 17,100.00	$2.85
Transferred into Department during				
Month 5,000.....................			$ 15,400.00	$3.08
35,000.....................			98,000.00	2.80
COST IN CURRENT DEPARTMENT:				
Work-in-Process, 3/1/—:				
Material Costs......................	$ 10,000.00	$2.00	0	
Labor Costs......................	3,000.00	0.60	$ 5,400.00	
Manufacturing Overhead Costs........	1,800.00	0.36	3,000.00	
Cost in Department during Month:				
Material Costs......................	107,500.00	2.50	0	
Labor Costs......................	4,100.00	0.10	115,020.00	$2.70
Manufacturing Overhead Costs........	8,200.00	0.20	38,340.00	0.90
Total Cost in Current Department....	$134,600.00	$2.80	$161,760.00	$3.60
CUMULATIVE COST TOTAL..........	$134,600.00		$292,260.00	
Work Completed and Transferred Out:......	$ 15,400.00	$3.08	$ 40,620.00	$6.77
	98,000.00	2.80	33,400.00	6.68
			198,400.00	6.40
Work-in-Process, 3/31/—:				
Completed but Not Transferred Out......	0		0	
Cost in Preceding Department...........	0		$ 11,200.00	$2.80
Work-in-Process—Materials.............	$ 20,000.00		0	
Work-in-Process—Labor...............	400.00		6,480.00	1.62
Work-in-Process—Manufacturing Overhead...........................	800.00		2,160.00	0.54
Total Work-in-Process...............	$ 21,200.00		$ 19,840.00	
CUMULATIVE COST TOTAL ACCOUNTED FOR.....................	$134,600.00		$292,260.00	

QUANTITY OF PRODUCTION REPORT (In Pounds)

	Department I	Department II
QUANTITY TO BE ACCOUNTED FOR:		
Work-in-Process, 3/1/—.............................	5,000 units	6,000 units
Put into Production or Received from Preceding Departments...	45,000	40,000
To Be Accounted For...............................	50,000 units	46,000 units
QUANTITY ACCOUNTED FOR AS FOLLOWS:		
Transferred to Next Department.....................	5,000	6,000
	35,000	5,000
		31,000
Completed but Not Transferred Out...................	0	0
Uncompleted Work-in-Process......................	8,000	4,000
Units Lost in Production............................	2,000	0
Total Accounted For............................	50,000	46,000

in-process inventory. Without separating this figure into separate lots, the transfer becomes a composite figure of the initial work-in-process inventory and the new production.

3. To obtain the *unit cost* of the transfer, the quantity transferred is divided into the total cost of the transfer. This actually is an *average unit cost* of the transfer.

If there are lost units in the second or a subsequent department, *the costs for the preceding departments* of the initial work-in-process inventory and the units transferred into the department during the period must be averaged before *computing the lost unit cost adjustment.*

To illustrate the procedure involved in this method of costing the *initial work-in-process inventory* and the computation of the *lost unit cost adjustment,* the following cost data for the month of February will be considered:

QUANTITY OF PRODUCTION DATA FOR MONTH OF FEBRUARY

	Department I	Department II	Department III
In Process, Feb. 1, All Materials, ½ Labor and Overhead Costs.	10,000 units		
In Process, Feb. 1, ⅛ Labor and Overhead Costs.		15,000 units	
In Process, Feb. 1, ½ Labor and Overhead Costs.			4,000 units
Put into Production during February.	76,000		
QUANTITY ACCOUNTED FOR AS FOLLOWS:			
Transferred to Next Department.	60,000 units	65,000 units	64,000 units
In Process, Feb. 28, All Materials, ¼ Labor and Overhead Costs.	20,000		
In Process, Feb. 28, ½ Labor and Overhead Costs.		8,000	
In Process, Feb. 28, ¼ Labor and Overhead Costs.			4,000
Lost in Production.	6,000	2,000	1,000
Total Accounted For.	86,000 units	75,000 units	69,000 units

The cost of production statistics for the three producing departments for the month of February were:

	Dept. I	Dept. II	Dept. III
Work-in-process, 2/1/—:			
Cost in preceding departments.	0	$ 7,400	$ 4,000
Material costs in department.	$ 3,000	0	0
Labor costs in department.	750	1,500	400
Mfg. overhead costs in department.	250	800	280
Costs during month of February:			
Material costs.	23,100	0	0
Labor costs.	9,000	17,920	13,860
Mfg. overhead costs.	3,600	11,520	9,450

Illustration 12–4

SUMMARY COST OF PRODUCTION REPORT
For Month of February, 19—

FIFO METHOD WITH LOST UNITS IN ALL DEPARTMENTS

	Department I		Department II		Department III	
	Total Cost	Unit Cost	Total Cost	Unit Cost	Total Cost	Unit Cost
COST IN PRECEDING DEPARTMENT:						
Work-in-Process, 2/1/—.............	0		$ 7,400.00		$ 4,000.00	$1.00
Transferred into Department during Month.........................	0		32,050.00		65,026.71	1.00041
Total.......................	0		$39,450.00	$0.5260	$69,026.71	$1.000371
Adjusted Unit Cost for Added Materials	0		0	0	xx	0
Additional Cost for Lost Units........	0		x	0.014411	xx	$0.0147115
Adjusted and Corrected Unit Cost Total......................	0		$39,450.00	$0.540411	$69,026.71	$1.0150987
COST IN CURRENT DEPARTMENT:						
Work-in-Process, 2/1/—:						
Material Costs...................	$ 3,000.00	$0.30	0		$ 400.00	$0.10
Labor Costs....................	750.00	0.075	$ 1,500.00	$0.030		
Manufacturing Overhead Costs......	250.00	0.025	800.00	0.016	280.00	0.07
Cost in Department during Month:						
Material Costs...................	23,100.00	0.33	0	0	0	0
Labor Costs....................	9,000.00	0.15	17,920.00	0.28	13,860.00	0.22
Manufacturing Overhead Costs......	3,600.00	0.06	11,520.00	0.18	9,450.00	0.15
Total Cost in Current Department.	$39,700.00	$0.54	$31,740.00	$0.46	$23,990.00	$0.37
CUMULATIVE COST TOTAL......	$39,700.00		$71,190.00		$93,016.71	
Work Completed and Transferred Out....	$32,050.00	$0.53416	$65,026.71	$1.00041	$88,586.32	$1.3850987*
Work-in-Process, 2/28/—:						
Completed but Not Transferred Out....	0		0		0	
Cost in Preceding Department.......			$ 4,323.29	$0.540411	$ 4,060.39	$1.0150987
Work-in-Process—Materials..........	$6,600.00		0		0	
Work-in-Process—Labor.............	750.00		1,120.00		220.00	
Work-in-Process—Manufacturing Overhead.......................	300.00		720.00		150.00	
Total Work in Process...........	$ 7,650.00		$ 6,163.29		$ 4,430.39	
CUMULATIVE COST TOTAL ACCOUNTED FOR.................	$39,700.00		$71,190.00		$93,016.71	

QUANTITY OF PRODUCTION (In Pounds)

	Department I	Department II	Department III
QUANTITY TO BE ACCOUNTED FOR:			
Completed and on Hand, 2/1/—...... Work-in-Process, 2/1/—.............	0 10,000(½)	0 15,000(⅓)	0 4,000(½)
Put into Production or Received from Preceding Departments...........	76,000	60,000	65,000
To Be Accounted For...........	86,000	75,000	69,000
QUANTITY ACCOUNTED FOR AS FOLLOWS:			
Transferred to Next Department......	{10,000 {50,000	{15,000 {50,000	{ 4,000 {60,000
Completed but Not Transferred Out....			
Uncompleted Work-in-Process.......	20,000(¼)	8,000(½)	4,000(¼)
Units Lost in Production............	6,000	2,000	1,000
Total Accounted For...........	86,000	75,000	69,000
Equivalent Production:			
Material..........................	70,000	0	0
Labor and Manufacturing Overhead....	60,000	64,000	63,000

* Figures may not be exact due to rounding.

On the basis of this data, Illustration 12–4, showing the summary cost of production for the month of February is prepared. In this it must be emphasized that the FIFO principle requires *that the costs of production for the current period must first be used to complete the initial work-in-process inventory, and then be applied to the new production.*

Equivalent Production and Unit Cost Computations for Department I:

Materials: To complete initial work-in-process inventory   0
New production for month . . . . 50,000 units
Work-in-process inventory, Feb. 28, 100% complete as to materials 20,000

      Equivalent Production for Materials for Dept. I . . . . 70,000 units

      Dividing 70,000 into $23,100 results in a unit cost for materials in Dept.
      I for February production of $0.33

Labor and
Overhead: To complete initial work-in-process inventory, already ½ complete,
      10,000 × ½ . . . . 5,000 units
New completed production for the month 50,000
In process, Feb. 28, ¼ completed: 20,000 × ¼ 5,000

      Equivalent Production for Labor and Overhead for Dept. I . . . . 60,000 units

      Dividing 60,000 into $9,000 results in unit cost for labor in Dept. I for
      February production of $0.15
      Dividing 60,000 into $3,600 results in unit cost for overhead in Dept. I
      for February production of 0.06

Equivalent Production and Unit Cost Computations for Department II:

Labor and
Overhead: To complete initial work-in-process inventory, already ⅓ complete,
      15,000 × ⅔ . . . . 10,000 units
New completed production for month 50,000
In process, Feb. 28, ½ completed: 8,000 × ½ 4,000

      Equivalent Production for Labor and Overhead for Dept. II . . . . 64,000 units

      Dividing 64,000 into $17,920 results in a unit cost for labor in Dept. II
      for February production of $0.28
      Dividing 64,000 into $11,520 results in a unit cost for overhead in Dept.
      II for February production of 0.18

Equivalent Production and Unit Cost Computations for Department III:

Labor and
Overhead: To complete initial work-in-process inventory, already ½ complete,
      4,000 × ½ . . . . 2,000 units
New production for the month, completed 60,000
Equivalent production for work-in-process, Feb. 28, 4,000 × ¼ 1,000

      Equivalent Production for Labor and Overhead for Dept. III . . . . . . 63,000 units

      Dividing 63,000 into $13,860 results in a unit cost for labor in Dept. III
      for February production of $0.22
      Dividing 63,000 into $9,450 results in a unit cost for overhead in Dept.
      III for February production of 0.15

Thus the unit costs within each department are computed by using the equivalent production resulting from first completing the initial work-in-process and then considering the new production. Now with further reference to the figures on Illustration 12–4, it is necessary to compute the transfers out of the department and the unit costs for lost units in departments after the first.

When the FIFO method of treating the initial work-in-process inventory is in use and there are lost units in any department after the first, the following rules or principles should govern the procedure after computing the unit costs for each element of cost in each department:

1. Compute the final work-in-process inventory, *not* including "units completed but not transferred out," in any department. Subtract this amount from the total *cumulative* costs of manufacturing. The difference represents the total costs of the *units completed.* Computing a unit cost for the completed units and multiplying by the number of units transferred out of the department will result in the cost of work transferred out of the department.

2. If there are lost units in any department after the first, it is necessary to compute the average *unit cost for the preceding departments* before attempting to compute the lost unit cost. This average is made up of the costs of the preceding department for the work-in-process at the beginning, plus the new production received into the department during the month, divided by the total units of the initial work-in-process inventory and units received into the department. When this corrected unit cost (which includes the lost unit cost) has been computed for the preceding departments, and the unit costs in the department have been calculated, it is then possible to compute the work-in-process inventory at the end of the month in any department. Deducting this amount from the total cumulative costs results in the total cost of completed units. From this it is a simple matter to compute the unit cost of the work transferred to the next department.

These two principles will now be applied specifically to Illustration 12–4.

Dept. I: Total cumulative cost of manufacturing amounted to.... $39,700.00
            Final work-in-process inventory, 2/28/—:
            Material costs: 20,000 × 100% × $0.33............$ 6,600.00
            Labor costs: 20,000 × ¼ × $0.15.................   750.00
            Mfg. overhead costs: 20,000 × ¼ × $0.06..........   300.00   7,650.00
            Completed and Transferred to Dept. II........... $32,050.00

Dept. II: *Average cost for Dept. I:*
            Work-in-process inventory, 2/1/—, 15,000 units......$ 7,400.00
            Received in dept. during February, 60,000 units....... 32,050.00
                Total, 75,000 units.........................$39,450.00 $ 0.5260
            Lost unit cost adjustment, 2,000 × $0.5260 ÷ 73,000
                units...   0.014411
                Corrected unit cost for Dept. I................. $ 0.540411
                Total cumulative cost of manufacturing, Depts. I
                    and II.................................... $71,190.00
            Final work-in-process inventory, 2/28/—, Dept. II:
            Cost in Dept. I, adjusted: 8,000 × 100% × $0.540411 ..$ 4,323.29
            Labor cost, Dept. II: 8,000 × ½ × $0.28............ 1,120.00
            Mfg. overhead cost, Dept. II: 8,000 × ½ × $0.18....   720.00   6,163.29
            Completed and Transferred to Dept. III......... $65,026.71

Dept. III: Average cost for Depts. I and II:

Work-in-process inventory, 2/1/— 4,000 units	$ 4,000.00		
Received in dept. during Feb......65,000	65,026.71		
Total.....................69,000 units	$69,026.71	$	1.000386
Lost unit cost adjustment: 1,000 × $1.000386 ÷ 68,000			
units...			0.0147115
Corrected unit cost for Depts. I and II.............		$	1.0150975
Total cumulative cost of manufacturing, Depts. I,			
II, and III................................		$93,016.71	

Final work-in-process inventory, 2/28/—, Dept. III:

Cost in Depts. I and II adjusted: 4,000 × 100% ×			
$1.0150975...................................$ 4,060.39			
Labor cost, Dept. III: 4,000 × ¼ × $0.22..........	220.00		
Mfg. overhead cost, Dept. III: 4,000 × ¼ × $0.15...	150.00	4,430.39	
Completed and Transferred as Finished Goods....		$88,586.32	

Method No. 3: Handling initial work-in-process inventory on FIFO basis when there are added materials in departments after the first increasing the volume of production. Also lost units in departments after the first.

The procedure followed under such circumstances is similar to that described in Method No. 2 when there are lost units in each department. The unit cost for the work done in the preceding departments must be adjusted *after* obtaining an *average* unit cost for the preceding department for the initial work-in-process inventory and the goods transferred into the department during the current period. If there are also lost units in such a situation, the adjustment for the lost units is made *after the adjustment for the added materials.* Thus here again, when materials are added in a department after the first, increasing the volume of production, the *computation of unit costs adjusted and corrected for added materials and lost units if any, for the preceding departments is on the average basis, not FIFO.*

The methods and procedures involved can best be explained by using an illustration similar to that used for Method No. 2. Illustration 12–6 presents the data and unit costs discussed in these paragraphs for the month of March. Note the data in Illustration 12–5.

The cost of production statistics for the three producing departments for month of March were:

	Dept. I	Dept. II	Dept. III
Work-in-process, 3/1/—:			
Cost in preceding departments..........	0	$ 9,400	$ 33,000
Material costs in department...........	$ 5,700	10,500	17,800
Labor costs in department.............	1,700	540	660
Mfg. overhead costs in department......	740	1,020	1,480
Costs during month of March:			
Material costs......................	56,000	111,600	153,000
Labor costs........................	31,920	14,500	16,800
Mfg. overhead costs.................	13,300	30,450	42,000

Illustration 12–5

QUANTITY OF PRODUCTION DATA FOR MONTH OF MARCH

Initial Work-in-Process Inventory on FIFO Plan

Added Materials in All Departments Increasing Volume of Production

Lost Units in All Departments

	Depart-ment I	Depart-ment II	Depart-ment III
In Process, March 1, All Materials, $\frac{2}{3}$ Labor and Overhead Costs...............	3,000 units		
In Process, March 1, All Materials, $\frac{1}{3}$ Labor and Overhead Costs..............		3,000 units	
In Process, March 1, All Materials, $\frac{1}{2}$ Labor and Overhead Costs..............			4,000 units
Put into Production during March........	30,000		
Added Materials Increasing Volume of Production............................		6,000	8,000
QUANTITY ACCOUNTED FOR AS FOLLOWS:			
Transferred to Next Department.........	27,000	28,000	28,000
In Process, March 31, All Materials, $\frac{2}{5}$ Labor and Overhead Costs...........	4,000		
In Process, March 31, All Materials, $\frac{1}{3}$ Labor and Overhead Costs...........		6,000	
In Process, March 31, All Materials, $\frac{1}{5}$ Labor and Overhead Costs...........			10,000
Lost in Production...................	2,000	2,000	2,000
Total Accounted For..............	33,000 units	36,000 units	40,000 units

On the basis of this data, Illustration 12–6, summary cost of production for the month of March has been prepared. It must be repeated again that in this illustration, the FIFO principle requires that the costs of production for the current period must first be used to complete the initial work-in-process inventory and then be applied toward the new production. It must also be emphasized that to obtain the cost of the production completed in any department, the final work-in-process inventory must be computed at the latest unit costs. This work-in-process inventory is then deducted from the total cumulative manufacturing costs to obtain the cost of the completed production. From this cost of completed production it is now possible to compute the unit cost of the completed production transferred to the next department. This procedure will now be illustrated.

Equivalent Production and Unit Cost Computations for Department I:

Materials: To complete initial work-in-process inventory....................... 0
New production for month......................................24,000 units
Work-in-process, March 31, 4,000 units × 100%..................... 4,000

Equivalent Production for Materials, Dept. I....................28,000 units

Dividing $56,000 by the equivalent production of 28,000 units, results in
a unit cost for materials of..$2.00

Labor and
Overhead: To complete initial work-in-process inventory, already ⅔ complete,
3,000 × ⅓... 1,000 units
New production for period...24,000
Work-in-process inventory, March 31, 4,000 × ⅖.................. 1,600
    Equivalent Production for Labor and Overhead for Dept. I........26,600 units

Dividing 26,600 units into $31,920 results in a unit cost for labor in Dept.
I for March production of.......................................$1.20
Dividing 26,600 units into $13,300 results in a unit cost for overhead in
Dept. I for March of... 0.50

Equivalent Production and Unit Cost Computations for Department II:

Materials: To complete initial work-in-process inventory........................ 0
New production for month...25,000 units
Work-in-process inventory, March 31, 6,000 × 100%................. 6,000
    Equivalent Production for Materials, Dept. II...................31,000 units

Dividing $111,600 by equivalent production of 31,000 units results in a unit
cost for materials of...$3.60

Labor and
Overhead: To complete initial work-in-process inventory, already ⅓ complete,
3,000 × ⅔... 2,000 units
New production for period...25,000
Work-in-process inventory, March 31, 6,000 × ⅓.................. 2,000
    Equivalent Production for Labor and Overhead for Dept. II.......29,000 units

Dividing $14,500 by the equivalent production of 29,000 units results in a
unit cost for labor in Dept. II for March production of.............$0.50
Dividing $30,450 by the equivalent production of 29,000 units results in a
unit cost for overhead in Dept. II for March production of.......... 1.05

Equivalent Production and Unit Cost Computations for Department III:

Materials: To complete initial work-in-process inventory........................ 0
New production for month of March...............................24,000 units
Work-in-process, March 31, 10,000 × 100%.......................10,000
    Equivalent Production for Materials, Dept. III..................34,000 units

Dividing 34,000 units into $153,000 results in a unit cost for materials in
Dept. III for March...$4.50

Labor and
Overhead: To complete initial work-in-process inventory, already ½ complete,
4,000 × ½... 2,000 units
New production for month of March...............................24,000
Work-in-process inventory, March 31, 10,000 × ⅕.................. 2,000
    Equivalent Production for Labor and Overhead for Dept. III.......28,000 units

Dividing $16,800 by 28,000 units results in a unit cost for labor in Dept. III
for March production of.......................................$0.60
Dividing $42,000 by 28,000 units results in a unit cost for overhead in Dept.
III for March production of.................................... 1.50

As in the previous illustration, the unit costs thus computed are based upon the equivalent production resulting from first completing the initial work-in-process, and then considering the new production. With reference to Illustration 12–5, it is necessary to compute the transfers out of the departments by using the latest costs for the final work-in-process inventories and deducting this figure from the total cumulative costs, as follows:

Illustration 12–6

SUMMARY COST OF PRODUCTION REPORT
For Month of March, 19—

FIFO METHOD WITH ADDED MATERIALS AND LOST UNITS IN ALL DEPARTMENTS

	Department I		Department II		Department III	
	Total Cost	Unit Cost	Total Cost	Unit Cost	Total Cost	Unit Cost
COST IN PRECEDING DEPARTMENT:						
Work-in-Process, 3/1/—.............	0		$ 9,400.00		$ 33,000.00	$8.25
Transferred into Department during Month.........................	0		98,640.00		232,884.13	8.31729
Total........................	0		$108,040.00	$3.60133	$265,884.13	$8.30888
Adjusted Unit Cost for Added Materials.	0		xx	3.00111	xx	$6.647103
Additional Cost for Lost Units........	0		xx	0.176535	xx	0.3498475
Adjusted and Corrected Unit Cost Total......................	0		$108,040.00	$3.177645	$265,884.13	$6.9969505
COST IN CURRENT DEPARTMENT:						
Work-in-Process, 3/1/—:						
Material Costs.................	$ 5,700.00	$1.90	$ 10,500.00	$3.50	$ 17,800.00	$4.45
Labor Costs...................	1,700.00	0.85	540.00	0.54	660.00	0.33
Manufacturing Overhead Costs.....	740.00	0.37	1,020.00	1.02	1,480.00	0.74
Cost in Department during Month:						
Material Costs....................	56,000.00	2.00	111,600.00	3.60	153,000.00	4.50
Labor Costs.....................	31,920.00	1.20	14,500.00	0.50	16,800.00	0.60
Manufacturing Overhead Costs.....	13,300.00	0.50	30,450.00	1.05	42,000.00	1.50
Total Cost in Current Department..	$109,360.00	$3.70	$168,610.00	$5.15	$231,740.00	$6.60
CUMULATIVE COST TOTAL.......	$109,360.00		$276,650.00		$497,624.13	
Work Completed and Transferred Out:....	$ 98,640.00	$3.6533	$232,884.13	$8.31729	$378,454.62	
Work-in-Process, 3/1/—:						
Completed but Not Transferred Out....	0		0		0	
Cost in Preceding Department........	0		$ 19,065.87		$ 69,969.51	
Work-in-Process—Materials..........	$ 8,000.00		21,600.00		45,000.00	
Work-in-Process—Labor.............	1,920.00		1,000.00		1,200.00	
Work-in-Process—Manufacturing Overhead.........................	800.00		2,100.00		3,000.00	
Total Work-in-Process...........	$ 10,720.00		$ 43,765.87		$119,169.51	
CUMULATIVE COST TOTAL ACCOUNTED FOR..................	$109,360.00		$276,650.00		$497,624.13	

QUANTITY OF PRODUCTION REPORT (In Pounds)

	Department I	Department II	Department III
QUANTITY TO BE ACCOUNTED FOR:			
Completed and on Hand, 3/1/—.......	0	0	0
Work-in-Process, 3/1/—.............	3,000(⅔)	3,000(⅓)	4,000(½)
Put into Product on or Received from Preceding Departments............	30,000	27,000	28,000
Increase in Production Due to Added Materials.......................	0	6,000	8,000
To Be Accounted For.............	33,000	36,000	40,000
QUANTITY ACCOUNTED FOR AS FOLLOWS:			
Transferred to Next Department.......	{ 3,000 { 24,000	{ 3,000 { 25,000	{ 4,000 { 24,000
Completed but Not Transferred Out....	0	0	0
Uncompleted Work-in-Process.........	4,000(⅖)	6,000(⅓)	10,000(⅕)
Units Lost in Production.............	2,000	2,000	2,000
Total Accounted For.............	33,000	36,000	40,000
Equivalent Production:			
Material........................	28,000	31,000	34,000
Labor and Manufacturing Overhead....	26,600	29,000	28,000

Note: Figures may not be exact due to rounding.

Dept. I: Total cumulative cost of manufacturing for March..... $109,360.00
Final work-in-process inventory, 3/31/—:
 Material costs: 4,000 × 100% × $2................$ 8,000.00
 Labor costs: 4,000 × ⅖ × $1.20.................. 1,920.00
 Mfg. overhead costs: 4,000 × ⅖ × $0.50..........   800.00   10,720.00
  Completed and Transferred to Dept. II.......... $ 98,640.00

Dept. II: *Average, adjusted, and corrected cost for Dept. I:*
 Work-in-process inventory, 3/1/—, 3,000 units $ 9,400.00
 Received in Dept. II during March ..27,000   98,640.00
  Total......................30,000 units $108,040.00
 Average unit cost before adjustment for added materials.. $ 3.60133
 Adjustment for added materials: 30,000 + 6,000 divided into $108,040, adjusted unit cost of........ $ 3.00111
 Lost unit cost adjustment: 2,000 × $3.00111 divided by 34,000 units (36,000 − 2,000)..............   0.176535
 Adjusted and corrected unit costs for Dept. I........ $ 3.177645
 Total cumulative cost for March for Depts. I and II.... $276,650.00
Final work-in-process inventory, 3/31/—, Dept. II:
 Cost in Dept. I, adjusted and corrected: 6,000 × 100% × $3.177645................................$ 19,065.87
 Material costs in Dept. II: 6,000 × 100% × $3.60.... 21,600.00
 Labor costs: 6,000 × ⅓ × $0.50.................. 1,000.00
 Mfg. overhead costs: 6,000 × ⅓ × $1.05.......... 2,100.00   43,765.87
  Completed and Transferred to Dept. III........ $232,884.13

Dept. III: *Average, adjusted, and corrected cost for Depts. II and III:*
 Work-in-process inventory, 3/1/—, 4,000 units $ 33,000.00
 Received in Dept. III during March 28,000   232,884.13
 Increase in units by added materials   8,000
  Total units worked on........40,000 units
 Less: Lost units................. 2,000
  Total goods production.......38,000 units $265,884.13
 Dividing $265,884.13 by 38,000 units results in an adjusted and corrected unit cost for Depts. I and II of...$6.9969505
 Total cumulative cost of manufacturing, Depts. I, II and III... $497,624.13
Final work-in-process inventory, March 31, Dept. III:
 Cost in Depts. I and II, adjusted and corrected:
 10,000 × 100% × $6.9969505..................$ 69,969.51
 Material costs in Dept. III: 10,000 × 100% × $4.50.. 45,000.00
 Labor costs in Dept. III: 10,000 × ⅕ × $0.60....... 1,200.00
 Mfg. overhead costs, Dept. III: 10,000 × ⅕ × $1.50   3,000.00
  Total final work-in-process inventory, Dept. III, March 31..............................   119,169.51
 Cost of Finished Goods Transferred Out of Dept. III... $378,454.62

QUESTIONS FOR REVIEW

1. FIFO method of treating the initial work-in-process inventories becomes impractical as the number of departments increases. Explain this statement.

2. Distinguish between "pure" and "modified" FIFO.

3. Why does the "pure" FIFO method of treating the initial work-in-process inventory have such limited application?

4. What problems arise in the FIFO method of treating the initial work-in-process inventory when there are lost units in a department after the first?

5. When there are both added materials increasing the volume of production and lost units in a department after the first, what is the sequence of the unit cost adjustments? Why?

6. The initial work-in-process in Department II was composed of 20,000 units, 80 percent complete as to materials, 60 percent complete as to labor and overhead. During the week, 70,000 units were completed, 30,000 were still in process, 75 percent complete as to materials and 50 percent complete as to labor and overhead. When the FIFO method of treating the initial work-in-process inventory is used, what are the equivalent productions for materials and labor and overhead for this week's production?

7. As of April 12, the total cumulative costs for Departments I and II were $78,000. In Department II, the corrected unit costs for work done in Department I were $1.30. The unit costs in Department II were materials, $0.48; labor, $0.14; and overhead $0.13. There were 5,000 units in process in Department II, 60 percent complete as to materials, 40 percent complete as to labor and overhead. What was the cost of the work transferred out of Department II if the FIFO method of treating the initial work-in-process inventory is used?

8. What is the simplest formula to use to obtain the *adjusted and corrected* unit cost in Department III when there are added materials increasing the volume of production and lost units in this department?

9. In Department I the work in process at the beginning of the week amounted to 30,000 units, 80 percent complete as to materials, 60 percent complete as to labor and overhead costing. Costs incurred in the previous week for this work-in-process were $14,400 for materials, $9,000 for labor, and $3,600 for overhead. Unit costs computed for this and additional production were materials, $0.65; labor, $0.48; and overhead, $0.24. What was the cost of these 30,000 units when transferred to Department II?

10. A firm has some work-in-process in each department, uses pure FIFO method of treating the initial work-in-process inventories. How many separate computations must be made for the material transferred out of the third department?

PROBLEMS—GROUP A

Problem 12–1. Purpose: *Cost of Production Statement When Pure FIFO Method of Costing Initial Work-in-Process Inventories Is Used*

The Tranball Manufacturing Company prepares weekly cost of production reports for its two-department process type of plant. It uses the FIFO method of costing its initial work-in-process inventories. From the following cost and production data, you are asked to prepare (*a*) statement of the equivalent production for each department for the various elements of cost; (*b*) cost of production report for the week ending June 14, 19—; (*c*) schedule of work-in-process in analyzed form for each department, June 14, 19—; and (*d*) journal entries to record the manufacturing operations.

	Dept. I	Dept. II
Work-in-process, June 7, 19—:		
Units in process, 70% as to material, and 25% complete as to labor and overhead...16,000 units		
Units in process, one-third complete as to labor and overhead....................		24,000 units
Units put into production during week.....50,000		
Transferred out of the department during the week..............................60,000		74,000
Work-in-process, June 14, 19—:		
Materials, 80%; labor and overhead, 40% complete........................... 6,000		
Labor and overhead 30% complete........		10,000

Costs of the manufacturing:

	Dept. I	Dept. II
Work-in-process, June 7, 19—:		
Cost in preceding department.........		$62,400
Material costs in department........	$17,920	0
Labor costs in department...........	3,120	9,600
Overhead costs in department........	1,400	2,800
Costs for week of June 14, 19—:		
Material costs......................	96,480	0
Labor costs........................	48,300	89,700
Overhead costs.....................	22,540	20,700

Problem 12–2. Purpose: *Cost of Production Report, Using Modified FIFO Method of Treating Initial Work-in-Process Inventories When Materials Are Added Increasing Volume of Production; No Lost Units*

The Thurmond Supply Company operates a two-department process type of plant. It uses a modified FIFO method in costing its initial work-in-process inventories. Materials are added in the second department increasing the volume of production.

The production statistics for the week ending May 24, 19—, were as follows:

	Dept. I	Dept. II
Work-in-process, May 17, 19—:		
Units in process, 90% material, 40% labor and overhead....................20,000 units		
Units in process, 80% material, 80% labor and overhead..................		15,000 units
Increase in volume of production due to added material.....................60,000		25,000
Transferred out of department...........65,000		85,000
Work-in-process, May 24, 19—:		
Units on which 80% of materials and 60% of labor and overhead had been applied...........................15,000		
Units on which all the material and 40% of the labor and overhead had been applied.............................		20,000

The costs of production for the week of May 24, 19—, were:

	Dept. I	Dept. II
Work-in-process, May 17, 19—:		
Cost in preceding department.........		$30,000
Material costs......................$18,000		13,500
Labor costs........................ 3,000		5,000
Overhead costs...................... 1,000		3,600
Costs during week of May 24, 19—:		
Material costs...................... 64,900		86,400
Labor costs........................ 52,800		46,170
Overhead costs..................... 19,800		25,650

From this information you are asked to prepare:

a) Statement of the equivalent production for each element of cost in each department.

b) Cost of production report for the week.

c) Work-in-process inventories, May 24, for each department in analyzed form;

d) Journal entries to record the manufacturing operations.

Problem 12–3. Purpose: *Using Modified FIFO Method of Costing the Initial Work-in-Process Inventories When There Are Lost Units in All Departments; Cost of Production Report*

The Tremont Manufacturing Company operates a two-department plant, manufacturing a single product on a continuous basis. Units are lost in each department during the manufacturing operations. The work-in-process at the beginning of each week is costed on the FIFO basis. Cost of production reports are prepared weekly.

For the week of September 6–13, the following operating data have been obtained from the departmental reports:

Department I: On September 6, there were in process 10,000 units on which 75 percent of the necessary material and one fourth of the labor and overhead had been applied. The costs of this inventory of September 6 were: materials, $12,500; labor, $3,000; and manufacturing overhead, $1,000.

During the week additional materials costing $84,150 representing 60,000 units were added in this department. The labor and overhead costs for the week of September 13 were $61,930 and $25,898 respectively.

During the week 4,000 units were lost in production. In process were 12,000 units on which 80 percent of the material and 40 percent of the labor and overhead had been applied.

Department II: On September 6, there were in process 7,000 units on which 30 percent of the labor and manufacturing overhead had been applied. As of this date, the costs of these units for the preceding department were $21,000; labor and overhead costs were $1,640 and $1,134 respectively.

The labor and manufacturing overhead costs for the week of September 13 in this department were $48,510 and $29,106 respectively.

Fifty thousand units were completed and sent to the finished stock room; 10,000 were in process on which 60 percent of the labor and overhead had been applied; the remaining units, 1,000, were spoiled and rejected in the operations.

From this information, you are asked to prepare:

a) Cost of production report for the week of September 13.

b) Journal entries to record the manufacturing operations.

c) Work-in-process inventory, September 13, in analyzed form by departments.

d) Statement of the equivalent production for the elements in each department.

Problem 12–4. Purpose: *Comparative Cost of Production Reports Showing Operating Results When the FIFO Method and the AVERAGE Method Are Used in Costing the Initial Work-in-Process Inventories; Added Materials Increasing the Volume of Production; Lost Units in Second Department*

The Traslow Manufacturing Company operates a two-department, single-product plant in which materials are added in the second department, increasing the volume of production. Cost of production reports are prepared weekly. There is work-in-process in each department at the end of each week.

In order to ascertain the differences in unit costs and work-in-process inventories, you are asked to prepare (*a*) cost of production reports for both the FIFO and the AVERAGE methods of treating initial work-in-process inventories; and (*b*) statement of the work-in-process inventories in each department in analyzed form under each method.

	Dept. I	Dept. II
Work-in-process, April 10, 19—:		
80% materials, 50% labor and overhead applied......	6,000 units	
60% materials, 40% labor and overhead applied......		18,000 units
Additional units put into process.....................30,000		
Increase in volume due to added materials............		12,000
Completed and transferred out......................28,000		45,000
Work-in-process, April 17, 19—:		
All materials, 60% labor and overhead..............	7,000	
All materials, 30% labor and overhead..............		10,000
Lost in production................................	1,000	3,000

Costs of production were:

	Dept. I	Dept. II
Work-in-process, April 10, 19—:		
Costs in preceding departments............................		$39,600
Costs in current department:		
Material...$ 6,200		11,040
Labor...	1,500	5,560
Manufacturing overhead...............................	500	2,000
Costs during week of April 17, 19—:		
Material...	39,260	50,000
Labor..	17,520	37,440
Manufacturing overhead...............................	4,380	14,040

Problem 12–5. Purpose: *Cost of Production Report for Process Industry Firm Using FIFO Method of Costing Initial Work-in-Process Inventories*

The B. C. Tresh Company is engaged in the manufacture of a single product in a continuous process plant. From the information given, you are asked to prepare a summary of costs and production for October, 19—. In costing units out of each department, the *first-in, first-out method* is used.

The two producing departments are numbered I and II. Overhead is allocated to Department I in total and is applied on a labor dollar basis to production in the department; the cost of direct labor is accumulated for each of two separate processes performed within the department, which processes are identified as A and B. Material is used at various stages of production as follows: Material L is placed in process at the beginning of work in Department I (i.e., at the beginning of Process A); Material T is put into process at the beginning of the second process (Process B) in Department I.

No materials are added in Department II. When the production of Process A reaches Process B, it is mixed with Material T.

Costing of production is on a pound basis in Department I but on a unit basis in Department II. A unit has a weight of 80 pounds at the start of processing in Department II. There is a weight loss in Department I, all of which takes place in the second (B) process. There is a normal loss of units in Department II due to units being found to be defective upon final inspection in the department. These defective units have no salvage value.

The following data cover the operations for the month of October, 19—:

DEPARTMENT I

	Work-in-Process 10/1/— (Pounds)	Work-in-Process 10/31/— (Pounds)	Transferred to Department II (Pounds)
Process A	2,000	3,000	...
Process B	4,000	2,000	36,000

During October, 25,000 pounds of Material L, costing $4,250, were issued to Process A, and 12,000 pounds of Material T, costing $2,720, were issued to Process B.

Labor cost during October for Process A was $13,832 and for Process B was $14,878. Overhead is 100 percent of labor cost. Work on the inventory in Process A as of October 1, 19—, had been 40 percent completed. The cost of material, labor, and overhead had amounted to $1,284. The inventory in Process B had been 60 percent completed in that process and had an accumulated total cost of $5,384. The inventories on October 31, 19—, were 50 percent complete in both processes.

DEPARTMENT II

In Department II there were 250 units in process on October 1, 19—, which were estimated to be 50 percent completed. Their accumulated cost was $70,001.20. During the month the cost of labor was $53,560 and overhead was applied at 150 percent of labor cost. During October, 500 units were completed, of which 400 were transferred to finished goods stores. There are 160 unfinished units in the department on October 31, 19—, which are five-eighths complete as to this department.

(Adapted from an AICPA Uniform Examination)

Problem 12–6. Purpose: *Computation of FIFO and AVERAGE Costing Methods of Work-in-Process Inventories*

The Triplett Process Company manufactures one product, processing it through two processes—No. 1 and No. 2.

For each unit of Process No. 1 output, two units of raw material X are put in *at the start* of processing. For each unit of Process No. 2 output, three cans of raw material Y are put in *at the end* of processing. Two pounds of Process No. 1 output are placed in at the start of Process No. 2 for each unit of finished goods started.

Spoilage generally occurs in Process No. 2 when processing is approximately 50 percent complete.

In-process accounts are maintained for raw material, conversion costs, and prior department costs.

The company uses FIFO basis for inventory valuation for Process No. 1 and finished goods, and AVERAGE cost for inventory valuation for Process No. 2.

Data for March:

1. Units transferred:

From Process No. 1 to Process No. 2......................2,200 lbs.
From Process No. 2 to finished goods...................... 900 gals.
From finished goods to cost of goods sold................... 600 gals.

2. Units spoiled in Process No. 2—100 gallons.
3. Raw material unit costs: X—$1.51 per unit; Y—$2 per can.
4. Conversion costs: Process No. 1—$3,344; Process No. 2—$4,010.
5. Spoilage recovery: $100 (treated as cost reduction).
6. Inventory data:

	Process No. 1		Process No. 2		Finished Goods	
	Initial	Final	Initial	Final	Initial	Final
Units........................	200	300	200	300	700	1,000
Fraction complete conversion costs......	½	⅓	½	⅔		
Valuation:........................					$13,300	
Materials........................	$560		0			
Conversion costs....................	$108		$ 390			
Prior department costs...............			$2,200			

Required:

Journalize March entries to record the transfer of costs from Process No. 1 to Process No. 2, from Process No. 2 to finished goods, and from finished goods to cost of goods sold. Prepare schedules of computations to support entries.

(Adapted from an AICPA Uniform Examination)

PROBLEMS—GROUP B

Problem 12–7. Purpose: *Cost of Production Report Using Pure FIFO Method of Costing Initial Work-in-Process Inventory*

The Duncan Manufacturing Company uses a process cost accounting system in its two-department, single-product plant. Initial work-in-process inventories are costed on the FIFO basis on the weekly cost of production reports.

On the basis of the costs and production statistics given, you are asked to prepare (*a*) a statement of the equivalent production by elements for each department; (*b*) a cost of production report for the week ending March 10, 19—; (*c*) a schedule of the work-in-process inventories, March 10, 19—, in analyzed form for each department; and (*d*) journal entries to record the manufacturing operations for the week.

	Dept. I	Dept. II
Work-in-process inventory, 3/3/—:	20,000 units	30,000 units
Stage of completion:		
Materials	80%	0
Labor and overhead	60%	50%
Units put into production or received from the preceding		
department	60,000 units	64,000 units
Work-in-process inventory, 3/10/—:	16,000 units	20,000 units
Stage of completion:		
Materials	75%	0
Labor and overhead	50%	70%
Transferred out of department	64,000 units	74,000 units
Cost of work-in-process, 3/3/—:		
Cost in preceding department	0	$60,000
Material costs	$ 32,000	0
Labor costs	7,000	18,000
Manufacturing overhead costs	5,000	7,500
Costs for the week of 3/10/—:		
Material costs	110,250	0
Labor costs	33,000	94,900
Manufacturing overhead costs	24,750	40,150

Problem 12–8. Purpose: *Cost of Production Report for Firm Using Modified FIFO Method of Costing Initial Work-in-Process Inventory; Added Materials Increasing Volume of Production*

The Drawson Manufacturing Company operates a two-department process plant producing a single product. This firm uses a modified type of costing the initial work-in-process inventory on a FIFO basis, preparing cost of production reports weekly. On the basis of the information given, you are asked to prepare (*a*) schedule of the equivalent productions in each department; (*b*) cost of production report; (*c*) journal entries to summarize the week's manufacturing operations; and (*d*) schedule of the work-in-process in analyzed form in each department, January 13, 19—.

Department I: On January 6, 19—, there were in process 12,000 units on which 90 percent of the material and 60 percent of the labor and overhead had been applied. The costs of this inventory were: material, $21,600; labor, $10,800; and overhead, $2,880. During the week of January 13, 60,000 units were put into production. The operating costs for the week were: materials, $125,840; labor, $101,660; overhead, $17,940.

During the week ending January 13, 60,000 units were completed and transferred to Department II; 10,000 were still in process, 80 percent complete as to material and 70 percent complete as to labor and overhead. *Department II:* On January 6, 19—, there were in process, 15,000 units on which 50 percent of the material and 40 percent of the labor and overhead had been applied. The costs of this inventory as of 1/6/— were: costs in Department I, $61,400; material costs, $7,200; labor costs, $9,800; and overhead costs, $1,520. Materials added in this department increased the volume by 25,000 units. Of the total production, 82,000 units were completed and sent to the stock room; 18,000 were in process on which 70 percent of the material and 50 percent of the labor and overhead had been applied.

The operating costs in Department II during the week of January 13 were: materials, $95,810; labor, $137,700; and manufacturing overhead, $23,800.

Problem 12–9. Purpose: *Completion of a Partial Cost of Production Report for Firm Having an Initial Work-in-Process Inventory Costed on the FIFO Basis; Added Materials and Lost Units in All Departments*

The Driscoll Plastic Products Company manufactures a single product in its three operating departments. The following represents the costs and production statistics for the month of September of Departments II and III. This firm uses a modified FIFO method in costing its initial work-in-process inventories.

From this you are asked to prepare a partial cost of production report for Departments II and III, supplementing it with a statement of the equivalent production in each department and journal entries to record the operating data.

Production Costs	Dept. II	Dept. III
Costs of units received from Department I during September............$91,600		
Work-in-process, 9/1/—:		
Costs in preceding departments......................................	27,200	$18,900
Material costs...	0	4,800
Labor costs...	4,800	1,400
Manufacturing overhead costs.....................................	1,400	280
Costs during September:		
Material costs...	0	32,430
Labor costs...	31,640	21,300
Manufacturing overhead costs.....................................	8,588	4,260

The quantities produced, transferred, and in process during the month were:

Volume of Production Statistics	Department II	Department III
Units in process, September 1, 60% complete as to labor and overhead...10,000 units		
Units in process, September 1, 80% complete as to materials, 40% complete as to labor and overhead.....................		5,000 units
Received from preceding department during September..........24,000		25,000
Increase in production due to added materials..................		6,000
Units completed and transferred out during September..........25,000		28,000
Units in process, 9/30, 45% complete as to labor and overhead... 8,000		
Units in process, 9/30, 70% complete as to materials, 40% complete as to labor and overhead.....................		6,000
Units lost or spoiled in production........................... 1,000		2,000

Problem 12–10. Purpose: *Comparative Cost of Production Reports for Modified FIFO and AVERAGE Method of Treating the Initial Work-in-Process Inventories; Added Materials Do Not Increase Volume of Production; Lost Units*

The Dunbar Manufacturing Company operates a three-department, single-product plant on a continuous basis, preparing monthly statements of the cost of production. Since the manufacturing cycle results in some uncompleted work-in-process at the end of each month, the firm is anxious to learn what difference in the unit costs would result if the FIFO method versus the AVERAGE method were used in costing the initial inventories of the work-in-process.

To answer the questions thus raised, you are asked to prepare two cost of production reports for the month of October—one using the FIFO method and the other the AVERAGE method of costing the initial work-in-process inventories. The costs of production for the month of October were as follows:

	Mixing Dept.	Refining Dept.	Finishing and Packing Dept.
Work-in-process, October 1, 19—:			
Cost in preceding department..............	0	$ 9,070	$ 8,260
Material costs...........................$	3,000	3,000	3,000
Labor costs..............................	1,200	1,500	1,800
Manufacturing overhead costs..............	1,000	1,200	1,500
Costs during month of October:			
Material costs...........................	57,760	45,500	81,250
Labor costs.............................	48,100	37,400	54,900
Manufacturing overhead costs..............	39,960	28,560	57,340

The production statistics for the month of October were as follows:

	Mixing Dept.	Refining Dept.	Finishing and Packing Dept.
Work-in-process, October 1, 19—:			
All materials, 50% labor and manufacturing overhead................................	4,000 units		
All materials, 60% labor and manufacturing overhead................................		5,000 units	
All materials, 40% labor and manufacturing overhead................................			2,500 units
Put into production increasing number of units..80,000		0	0
Completed and transferred out of department....72,000		65,000	60,000
Work-in-process, October 31, 19—:			
All materials, 50% labor and overhead....... 8,000			
All materials, 60% labor and overhead.......		10,000	
All materials, 40% labor and overhead.......			5,000
Lost in production......................... 4,000		2,000	2,500

Problem 12–11.   Purpose: *C.P.A. Problem on Process Cost Accounting Using FIFO Method of Costing Initial Work-in-Process Inventory*

The Dwine Extract Company produces flavoring extracts and spices for food products. The company has been successfully operated for many years and carries an extensive line, but vanilla extract is its major product.

Vanilla extract is produced in two processes of percolating and mixing. In the percolating process, chopping of vanilla beans, percolating, and drying operations are carried out, while the mixing process has only the mixing operation. Inventories are carried in percolating tanks and in storage tanks both before and after mixing process.

In the chopping operations, a sufficient number of beans are chopped for one batch of extract and placed in the percolator. Ten percolators are used, so that the production of the extract is continuous. The extract is piped from the percolator to storage tanks, while the residue is carried to a dryer. The alcohol in the residue is recovered in the drying process and returned to storage. The dried residue is then discarded as waste.

Eleven hundred pounds of beans are chopped and sent to the percolator, where 405 gallons of alcohol and sufficient water to make the mixture total 1,000 gallons are added to make one batch of extract. Eight hundred gallons of extract, 45 percent alcohol, is produced in each batch, the remainder going to the dryer, or is lost in the percolating process. Thirty-five gallons of alcohol are ordinarily recovered from the dryer for each batch.

The 45 percent strength vanilla extract is then placed in storage tanks to await further processing. From these storage tanks, 400 gallons are drawn at a time and piped into a mixing tank where it is mixed with a sugar and water solution. When completely mixed, the alcohol content has been reduced to 36 percent.

The sugar and water solution is prepared by mixing 10 pounds of sugar with each gallon of water in the mixing tank. The contents of the mixing tank are then piped into storage tanks and, from there, piped to another location for packaging. For the purpose of this problem, the storage tanks containing the 36 percent strength extract are to be considered the finished goods stage.

Since labor is not a material item in the production of vanilla extract, wages are charged to burden. Manufacturing expenses are accumulated in two burden accounts, one for the percolating process, and one for the mixing process. Storage and chopping costs are treated as a part of the burden costs of their respective processes. These costs are then allocated to production in each process. Burden incurred for the period was as follows:

Percolating process..$32,832
Mixing process.. 12,800

Alcohol costs 50 cents a gallon from the supplier, but a federal tax of $20.50 is levied on each gallon purchased. A rebate of $19 a gallon of alcohol is allowed for all alcohol used in the production of extract. Usage is determined by applying the percentage strength of the quantity of extract piped to the packaging operations. Amounts of recoverable tax are excluded from these inventories and from manufacturing cost but are recorded in a separate account.

The first-in, first-out method is followed for inventories in the percolating process, but the weighted average method is used for all other inventories, including those in storage tanks.

Periodic inventories have been taken, the results of which are as follows:

December 31, 1967

In process, percolators, ½ finished	4 batches	$6,370
Storage tanks, 45% strength	3,200 gallons	6,268
Mixing process	None	
Storage tanks, 36% strength	2,000 gallons	3,544

December 31, 1968

In process, percolators, ½ finished	8 batches
Storage tanks, 45% strength	4,000 gallons
Mixing process	None
Storage tanks, 36% strength	2,500 gallons

During the year's operations, 130 batches were started in the percolators; 100,000 gallons of 45 percent strength extract was piped into the mixing process and 250,000 pounds of sugar were added to the solution. Average cost of vanilla beans was 50 cents a pound, while sugar cost 5 cents a pound.

You are to prepare:

a) Manufacturing statement showing costs, units, and prices by processes.

b) Computations showing the rebate to be claimed from the federal government for the period and the amount of deferrable tax applicable to the inventories which have not gone to the packaging department.

(Adapted from an AICPA Uniform Examination)

CHAPTER

13   Process Cost Accounting—Part IV

Simplified Procedures

Introduction   This chapter has been prepared for those students and instructors who because of the limit of time wish to make a practical but more limited study of the process cost accounting. The procedure described is not as exact as that in the preceding chapters but can be used for small process plants. This method is not, however, adaptable to the solution of some of the more complicated problems appearing on the C.P.A. examinations. It ignores the FIFO principles and stresses primarily averaging costs, but it can be used in all instances, even where there are lost units, initial work-in-process inventories, or added materials increasing the volume of production.

Basic Principles   Using this simplified process cost accounting assumes that each department is treated as a separate plant. Whatever materials are received from a preceding department are considered as though they were purchased at cost from an outsider. Work received from a preceding department becomes part of the *material costs* in the receiving department. No separate lost unit costs are computed, since each department is treated as though it were the initial and only manufacturing department.

Illustrative Work Sheets and Accounting Entries   To properly understand this simplified method of process costing, it is necessary to use two months' operations, the first being the initial operations, and the second being the continuation of the first. For this reason the illustrations show

391

first the cost of production report and computations for the month of January, and second the continuation for February.

Operating data for the month of January were:

	Dept. I	Dept. II	Dept. III
Costs, not including transfers:			
Material costs..........................	$16,500		$10,000*
Labor costs.............................	7,500	$10,500	6,400
Manufacturing overhead.................	2,500	5,600	4,480
Production quantity statistics (pounds):			
Material put into production............60,000 lbs.			10,000 lbs.*
			(Increase in volume)
Completed and transferred out............45,000		25,000 lbs.	30,000
Completed and not transferred out........ 0		5,000	0
Work-in-process........................10,000		15,000	4,000
Stage of completion of work-in-process:			
Materials...............................	100%	100%	100%
Labor..................................	50	33⅓	50
Overhead...............................	50	33⅓	50
Lost in production.......................	5,000 lbs.	0	1,000 lbs.

* Increase in volume.

The cost of production report prepared from these data under the simplified method is shown in Illustration 13–1. It should be noted that the transfers from one department to another become part of the material costs of the department in which they are received.

Computations for this work sheet:

Department I, Unit Costs

Equivalent production for materials: 45,000 completed
                                         10,000 in process 100% complete
                                         55,000 units

Cost of materials, $16,500, resulting in a unit cost of $0.30 ($16,500/55,000).
Equivalent production for labor and overhead: 45,000 completed
    10,000 units × 50%.......................... 5,000 in process
                                                 50,000 units

Cost of labor, $7,500, resulting in labor unit cost of $0.15 ($7,500/50,000).
Cost of overhead, $2,500, resulting in overhead unit cost of $0.05 ($2,500/50,000).
Transferred to Department II, 45,000 units × $0.50, or $22,500.
In process, January 31:
    Materials: 10,000 × 100% × $0.30 = $3,000
    Labor: 10,000 × 50% × 0.15 =   750
    Overhead: 10,000 × 50% × 0.05 =   250
                                         $4,000

Department II, Unit Costs

Equivalent production for materials: 25,000 completed and transferred
                                             5,000 completed and on hand
                                            15,000 in process, 100% complete
                                            ‾‾‾‾‾‾
                                            45,000 units

Material costs, $22,500, resulting in unit cost of $0.50 ($22,500/45,000).
Equivalent production for labor and overhead: 25,000 completed, transferred
                                             5,000 completed, on hand
15,000 units × 33⅓% .... 5,000 in process
                                            ‾‾‾‾‾‾
                                            35,000 units

Labor costs, $10,500, resulting in labor unit cost of $0.30 ($10,500/35,000).
Overhead costs, $5,600, resulting in overhead unit cost of $0.16 ($5,600/35,000).
Transferred to Department III, 25,000 units × $0.96, or $24,000.
In process, Department II, January 31:
   Materials: 15,000 × 100% × $0.50   = $7,500
   Labor: 15,000 × 33⅓% × $0.30 = 1,500
   Overhead: 15,000 × 33⅓% × $0.16 =   800
                                        ‾‾‾‾‾‾
                                         $9,800

Department III, Unit Costs

Equivalent production for materials: 30,000 completed, transferred
                                             4,000 in process, 100% complete
                                            ‾‾‾‾‾‾
                                            34,000 units

Material costs, $10,000 plus $24,000, resulting in a unit cost of $1 ($34,000/
34,000 units).
Equivalent production for labor and overhead: 30,000 completed, transferred
4,000 units × 50% .... 2,000 in process
                                            ‾‾‾‾‾‾
                                            32,000 units

Labor costs, $6,400, resulting in unit cost of $0.20 ($6,400/32,000).
Overhead costs, $4,480, resulting in unit cost of $0.14 ($4,480/32,000).

Accounting entries for month of January:

(1)

Work-in-Process—Dept. I 26,500.00		
Stores		16,500.00
Payroll		7,500.00
Manufacturing Overhead		2,500.00

To summarize cost of production in Dept. I for the month of
January.

(2)

Work-in-Process—Dept. II 38,600.00		
Work-in-Process—Dept. I		22,500.00
Payroll		10,500.00
Manufacturing Overhead		5,600.00

To summarize the cost of production in Dept. II during January.

(3)

Work-in-Process—Dept. III 44,880.00		
Work-in-Process—Dept. II		24,000.00
Stores		10,000.00
Payroll		6,400.00
Manufacturing Overhead		4,480.00

To summarize cost of production in Dept. III, including added
materials increasing volume of production, for month of
January.

Illustration 13–1
COST OF PRODUCTION REPORT
For Month of January
(First Month of Operations)

	Department I		Department II		Department III	
	Total	Unit Cost	Total	Unit Cost	Total	Unit Cost
WORK-IN-PROCESS AT BEGINNING OF MONTH, JANUARY 2, 19—:						
Material Costs.........................	0		0		0	
Labor Costs..........................	0		0		0	
Manufacturing Overhead Costs........	0		0		0	
COSTS DURING THE MONTH:						
Material Costs.........................	$16,500.00	$0.30	$22,500.00	$0.50	($10,000.00*) 24,000.00	$1.00
Labor Costs..........................	7,500.00	0.15	10,500.00	0.30	6,400.00	0.20
Manufacturing Overhead Costs........	2,500.00	0.05	5,600.00	0.16	4,480.00	0.14
TOTAL COSTS TO BE ACCOUNTED FOR.....	$26,500.00	$0.50	$38,600.00	$0.96	$44,880.00	$1.34
Completed and Transferred Out........	$22,500.00	$0.50	$24,000.00	$0.96	$40,200.00	$1.34
Completed and on Hand...............	0		4,800.00	0.96	0	
Work-in-Process at End of Month, January 31, 19—:						
Material...........................	3,000.00		7,500.00		4,000.00	
Labor.............................	750.00		1,500.00		400.00	
Manufacturing Overhead.............	250.00		800.00		280.00	
CUMULATIVE TOTAL COST ACCOUNTED FOR......	$26,500.00		$38,600.00		$44,880.00	

* Added material increases volume of production.

QUANTITY OF PRODUCTION REPORT (In Pounds)

Work-in-Process at Beginning of Month, January 1, 19—	0		0	0
Put into or Received in Production during Month	60,000		45,000	{10,000* {25,000
To Be Accounted For	60,000		45,000	35,000
Completed and Transferred Out during Month	45,000		25,000	30,000
Completed and on Hand at End of Month	0		5,000	0
Work-in-Process at End of Month	10,000		15,000	4,000
Materials	100%		100%	100%
Labor	50%		33⅓%	50%
Manufacturing Overhead	50%		33⅓%	50%
Lost or Spoiled in Production	5,000		0	1,000
Total Accounted For	60,000		45,000	35,000

* Added material increasing volume of production.

(4)

```
Finished Goods.........................................40,200.00
    Work-in-Process—Dept. III.............................        40,200.00
    To record the cost of work completed and sent to finished goods
    stock room.
```

In continuing this illustration for the second month of operations (February), the final work-in-process inventories in the respective departments, January 31, become the initial inventories for the work during the month of February. During the month of February, the same elimination of the separate statement of the departmental transfers, and separate lost unit costs computation is followed. All transfers become part of the material costs in the department in which received.

The operating data for the month of February are as follows (*costs not including transfers*):

	Dept. I	Dept. II	Dept. III
Work-in-process, 2/1/19—:			
Completed and on hand	0	$ 4,800	0
Material costs	$ 3,000	7,500	$ 4,000
Labor costs	750	1,500	400
Manufacturing overhead	250	800	280
Additional manufacturing costs:			
Material costs	21,320	0	0
Labor costs	11,202	19,620	14,720
Manufacturing overhead	5,726	9,760	8,540
Production statistics for February:			
Units in process, 2/1/19—	10,000 units	5,000 ⎱ units 15,000 ⎰	4,000 units
New production started	70,000		
Completed and transferred out	60,000	5,000 ⎱ 60,000 ⎰	58,000
Work-in-process, 2/28/19—	16,000	10,000	10,000

	Dept. I	Dept. II	Dept. III
Stage of completion, work-in-process:			
Materials	100%	100%	100%
Labor	40%	60%	50%
Manufacturing overhead	40%	60%	50%
Lost in production	4,000 units	5,000 units	1,000 units

The cost of production report from these data under the simplified costing method is shown in Illustration 13–2.

Accounting entries for February: Following the entries made at the end of January, the following entries summarize the cost accounting work for February:

(1*a*)

Work-in-Process—Dept. I..................................38,248.00		
Stores...		21,320.00
Payroll..		11,202.00
Manufacturing Overhead..............................		5,726.00

To summarize the cost of production in Dept. I during the month of February.

(2*a*)

Work-in-Process—Dept. II.................................64,780.00		
Work-in-Process—Dept. I.............................		35,400.00
Payroll..		19,620.00
Manufacturing Overhead..............................		9,760.00

To summarize the manufacturing costs in Dept. II during February.

(3*a*)

Work-in-Process—Dept. III...............................93,630.00		
Work-in-Process—Dept. II............................		70,370.00
Payroll..		14,720.00
Manufacturing Overhead..............................		8,540.00

To summarize the manufacturing costs in Dept. III for the month of February.

(4*a*)

Finished Goods...85,473.23		
Work-in-Process—Dept. III...........................		85,473.23

To record the cost of goods completed and transferred to finished goods stock room during February.

LEDGER ACCOUNTS

Work-in-Process—Dept. I

Jan. 31 (1) 26,500.00	Jan. 31 (2) 22,500.00
Feb. 28 (1*a*) 38,248.00	Feb. 28 (2*a*) 35,400.00

Balance, $6,848.00*

*W-I-P—
Mat.	$5,120.00
Labor	1,152.00
O.H.	576.00
	$6,848.00

Work-in-Process—Dept. II

Jan. 31 (2) 38,600.00	Jan. 31 (3) 24,000.00
Feb. 28 (2*a*) 64,780.00	Feb. 28 (3*a*) 70,370.00

Balance, $9,010.00†

†W-I-P—
Mat.	$6,130.00
Labor	1,920.00
O.H.	960.00
	$9,010.00

Work-in-Process—Dept. III

Jan. 31 (3) 44,880.00	Jan. 31 (4) 40,200.00
Feb. 28 (3*a*) 93,630.00	Feb. 28 (4*a*) 85,473.23

Balance, $12,836.77‡

‡W-I-P—
Mat.	$10,936.77
Labor	1,200.00
O.H.	700.00
	$12,836.77

Finished Goods

Jan. 31 (4) 40,200.00	
Feb. 28 (4*a*) 85,473.23	

Illustration 13–2

COST OF PRODUCTION REPORT

For Month of February (Second Month)

	Department I		Department II		Department III	
	Total	Unit Cost	Total	Unit Cost	Total	Unit Cost
WORK-IN-PROCESS AT BEGINNING OF MONTH, FEBRUARY 1, 19—:						
Material Costs	$ 3,000.00		$ 7,500.00		$ 4,000.00	
Labor Costs	750.00		1,500.00		400.00	
Manufacturing Overhead Costs	250.00		800.00		280.00	
Completed and on Hand			4,800.00			
COSTS DURING THE MONTH:						
Material Costs	21,320.00	$0.32	35,400.00	$0.61286	{ 4,800.00 / 65,571.60	$1.0937
Labor Costs	11,202.00	0.18	19,620.00	0.32	14,720.00	0.24
Manufacturing Overhead Costs	5,726.00	0.09	9,760.00	0.16	8,540.00	0.14
TOTAL COSTS TO BE ACCOUNTED FOR	$42,248.00	$0.59	$79,380.00	$1.09286	$98,311.60	$1.4737
Completed and Transferred Out	$35,400.00	$0.59	{ $ 4,800.00 / 65,571.60	$0.96 / 1.09284	$85,474.60	$1.4737
Completed and on Hand	0					
Work-in-Process at End of Month, February 28, 19—:						
Material	5,120.00		6,128.60		10,937.00	
Labor	1,152.00		1,920.00		1,200.00	
Manufacturing Overhead	576.00		960.00		700.00	
CUMULATIVE TOTAL COST ACCOUNTED FOR	$42,248.00		$79,380.20*		$98,311.60	

* Error of $0.20 due to rounding.

QUANTITY OF PRODUCTION REPORT (In Pounds)

Work-in-Process at Beginning of Month, February 1, 19— ..	10,000	{ 5,000	{ 4,000
Put into or Received in Production during Month..........	70,000	{ 15,000	{ 5,000
		{ 60,000	{ 60,000
To Be Accounted For.................	80,000	80,000	69,000
Completed and Transferred Out during Month..........	60,000	{ 5,000	58,000
Completed and on Hand at End of Month............	0	{ 60,000	
Work-in-Process at End of Month, February 28, 19—:			
Materials......................	16,000	10,000	10,000
Labor.........................	100%	100%	100%
Manufacturing Overhead.........	40%	60%	50%
	40%	60%	50%
Lost or Spoiled in Production.........	4,000	5,000	1,000
Total Accounted For...........	80,000	80,000	69,000

An Evaluation of This Simplified Process Costing

This procedure has certain phases which might recommend its use. It is simple to understand and operate. It is particularly adaptable to a single-product cumulative type of manufacturing such as the production of cement or bricks. If there were a prompt and reliable method of recording the cost of the departmental transfers, this method would enable the individual departmental cost reports to be prepared under each foreman's supervision. Otherwise, a composite cost of production report could only be prepared in the central cost accounting department.

Lacking the individual figures (unit costs) for lost units eliminates a certain amount of information for managerial control and necessitates an analysis of the comparative figures.

The cost of operating this type of cost accounting system is less than the more involved procedures previously dismissed. Offsetting this advantage, the lack of detailed unit cost figures makes the final unit cost figures less exact. However, since process costs are at best average costs, and since even using the FIFO method as contrasted with the AVERAGE method results in such small unit costs differences, it is doubtful that the accuracy question has much validity.

This simplified method *cannot* be used in some of the more complicated and involved problems which have appeared on professional examinations in which the theory of cost accounting was often more important than the practical applications to business situations.

QUESTIONS FOR REVIEW

1. What basic principle underlies all simplified process cost accounting?
2. In any department after the first, *lost units* are disregarded in the cost computations. Explain why this is so.
3. Under the simplified process accounting procedure, in any department after the first, there is no separate unit cost for the work done in the preceding departments. Explain.
4. How are materials added in a department after the first increasing the volume of production treated under the simplified process procedure?
5. When the simplified cost procedures are used, it is not possible to use the FIFO method of handling the initial work-in-process inventory. Explain why this is so.
6. Simplified process cost accounting has been described as the *maximum* average method. What does this mean? What effect does this have on the accuracy of the unit costs of production?
7. Is it desirable in process cost accounting to have a separate unit cost for the work done in the preceding departments? Explain. Under what circumstances would your answer be different?

8. Under what conditions do you think simplified cost accounting procedures should be used for a process type of industry?

9. What effect do the simplified process cost accounting procedures have on the initial and final work-in-process inventories?

10. What effect on managerial control does the use of simplified process cost accounting procedures have?

PROBLEMS—GROUP A

Problem 13–1. Purpose: *Simplified Process Cost Accounting in Three-Department Factory; Adding Materials Increasing Volume of Production; No Lost Units*

The Union Manufacturing Company operates a three-department plant on a continuous process cycle. Materials are added in each department increasing the volume of production.

The costs of production for the month of July were:

	Dept. I	Dept. II	Dept. III
Material costs	$72,000	$52,000	$127,500
Labor costs	38,500	58,800	84,800
Manufacturing overhead	16,500	24,500	26,500

The volume-of-production statistics were:

Department I:
Finished and transferred out .... 40,000 units
In process, 80% complete as to materials, 60% complete as to
  labor and overhead 25,000
Department II:
Increase in volume due to added materials 10,000
Finished and transferred out 45,000
In process, 100% of materials, 80% labor and overhead 5,000
Department III:
Increase in volume due to added materials 15,000
Finished and transferred out 50,000
In process, 50% material, 30% labor and overhead 10,000

On the basis of this information, you are asked to prepare:

a) Cost of production report using the simplified process cost accounting procedure.

b) Journal entries to record the manufacturing operations.

Problem 13–2. Purpose: *Cost of Production Report; Simplified Cost Accounting Procedures; Lost Units in All Departments; Materials Added Only in First Department*

The Utopia Manufacturing Company operates a three-department factory in which a single product is completed. Materials are used only in the first department, and there is some loss or spoilage in each department. A simplified cost accounting procedure is used.

The following represent the production and costs for the month of October, there being no work-in-process inventory at the beginning of the month:

Department I:
Units completed and transferred.....60,000	Material costs.....................$160,000
Units in process, 100% material, 40%	Labor costs....................... 81,600
labor and overhead..............20,000	Overhead costs.................... 23,800
Units lost in production...........10,000	

Department II:
Units completed and transferred.....45,000	Material costs.................... 0
Units in process, 60% complete as to	Labor costs....................... 68,850
labor and overhead..............10,000	Overhead costs.................... 30,600
Units lost in production........... 5,000	

Department III:
Units completed and transferred.....40,000	Material costs.................... 0
Units in process, 25% complete as to	Labor costs....................... 38,540
labor and overhead.............. 4,000	Overhead costs.................... 10,660
Units lost in production........... 1,000	

On the basis of this information you are asked to prepare:

a) Cost of production using the simplified process cost accounting method.

b) Journal entries to record the accounting transactions.

Problem 13-3. Purpose: *Simplified Process Cost Accounting for a Three-Department Factory; Added Materials Increasing Volume and Lost Units in All Departments*

The Uhrless Supply Company operates a three-department process type of plant. Materials are added in each department to increase the volume of production of its single product. Some units are lost or spoiled in each department.

From the data given, you are asked to prepare (*a*) cost of production report using the simplified process cost accounting procedures, and (*b*) journal entries to record the operations.

Department I:
Finished and transferred out....75,000 units	Material costs.....................$195,650
Work-in-process, 80% complete	Labor costs....................... 47,850
as to materials, 60% for labor	Overhead costs.................... 26,100
and overhead................20,000	
Units lost in production........ 5,000	

Department II:
Completed and transferred out..80,000 units	Material costs.....................$101,800
In process, 60% of materials,	Labor costs....................... 102,000
50% labor and overhead......10,000	Overhead costs.................... 38,250
Units lost in production........ 4,000	

Department III:
Finished and transferred out....92,000 units	Materials costs....................$164,000
Work-in-process, 100% complete	Labor costs....................... 69,696
as to materials, 60% complete	Overhead costs.................... 27,104
as to labor and overhead..... 8,000	
Units lost or spoiled........... 6,000	

Problem 13-4. Purpose: *Simplified Process Cost Accounting in a Two-Department Factory; Added Materials Increasing Volume Compared with the Average Method of Costing*

The Unified Manufacturing Company has a two-department process plant in which its single product is manufactured.

For the month of April, the following data represent the manufacturing operations:

No work-in-process inventory on April 1, 19—.

Department I:
Work completed and transferred out..................... 10,000 units
In process, April 30, 100% of materials, and 40% labor and overhead.. 3,000 units
Costs in Department I:
Materials......................................$10,920
Labor... 3,024
Manufacturing overhead............................ 1,456
Department II:
Work completed and transferred out................... 19,000 units
In process, 80% complete as to materials, 60% complete as to labor and overhead............................ 3,500 units
Costs in Department II:
Materials......................................$26,840
Labor... 13,082
Manufacturing overhead............................ 5,908

On the basis of this information, you are asked to prepare:

a) Cost of production report using the simplified method of process cost accounting.

b) Cost of production report using the average method of process cost accounting.

Problem 13–5. Purpose: *Simplified Process Cost Accounting in Two-Department Factory; Added Materials Increasing Volume of Production and Lost Units in All Departments; Compared with Average Method of Costing*

The Uppan Company operates a two-department factory on a process basis in which materials are used in each department increasing the volume of production and in which units are lost or spoiled in both departments.

There was no work-in-process at the beginning of the month of November.

The operating costs for these two operating departments for November were:

	Dept. I	Dept. II
Material costs................................	$16,614	$6,150
Labor costs......................................	7,344	4,750
Manufacturing overhead costs....................	1,620	1,425

The units produced during this month were:

Department I:
Started into production..............................14,000 units
Completed and transferred out........................ 9,000
Work-in-process, November 30, 19—, 90% materials, and 60% labor and overhead applied..................... 3,000
Lost in production................................... 2,000
Department II:
Added materials increasing volume of production.......... 3,000
Completed and transferred out......................... 8,000
Work-in-process, November 30, 19—, on which 100% of the materials and 50% of the labor and overhead had been applied.. 3,000
Units lost or spoiled in production..................... 1,000

On the basis of this information you are asked to prepare:

a) Cost of production using the simplified method of process costing.

b) Cost of production using the average method of process costing.

PROBLEMS—GROUP B

Problem 13–6. Purpose: *Simplified Process Cost Accounting in Three-Department Factory; Added Materials Increasing Volume of Production; No Lost Units*

The Elson Chemical Company operates a three-department continuous process plant in which materials are added in the third department increasing the volume of production. No lost units in any department. No work-in-process at the beginning of the month of March for which these figures were compiled.

The volume of production for the month of March was:

Department I:
Completed and transferred out..........................50,000 units
In process, 60% complete as to materials and 40% complete
   as to labor and overhead.............................10,000
Department II:
Completed and transferred out..........................45,000
In process, 80% complete as to labor and overhead........ 5,000
Department III:
Completed and transferred out..........................50,000
In process, 80% complete as to materials and 60% complete
   as to labor and overhead.............................10,000
The additional materials used in this department increased
   the volume of production by..........................15,000

The operating costs for the month of March were:

	Dept. I	Dept. II	Dept. III
Material costs......................	$56,000	0	$68,950
Labor costs........................	43,200	$33,600	61,600
Manufacturing overhead..............	13,500	11,200	22,400

On the basis of this information, you are asked to prepare:

a) Cost of production report using the simplified process cost accounting procedure.

b) Journal entries to record the manufacturing operations.

Problem 13–7. Purpose: *Simplified Process Cost Accounting in a Three-Department Factory; Lost Units in All Departments; Materials Added in the Initial Department*

The Elliott Manufacturing Company operates a three-department continuous process plant, manufacturing a single product. Materials are used only in the first department. In all departments some units must be rejected as spoiled and discarded.

The operating data for the month of May were as follows:

There was no work-in-process on May 1.

Department I:

Units completed and transferred out...............80,000	Material costs........$200,000
Work-in-process, May 31, on which all materials and	Labor costs.......... 73,600
60% of the labor and overhead had been applied. .20,000	Overhead costs....... 13,800
Units rejected as spoiled........................ 5,000	

Department II:

Units completed and transferred out...............62,000	Material costs........ 0
Work-in-process, 50% complete as to labor and over-	Labor costs.......... 33,600
head....................................15,000	Overhead costs....... 11,815
Units rejected as defective...................... 3,000	

Department III:

Units completed and transferred out...............50,000	Material costs........ 0
Work-in-process, May 31, 60% complete as to labor	Labor costs.......... 14,000
and overhead...............................10,000	Overhead costs....... 8,400
Units lost through spoilage..................... 2,000	

On the basis of this information, you are asked to prepare:

a) Cost of production report using the simplified process cost accounting procedure.

b) Journal entries to record the manufacturing operations.

Problem 13–8.   Purpose: *Simplified Process Cost Accounting for Firm Having Three Departments; Materials Used in All Departments, Increasing Volume of Production; Lost Units in All Departments*

The E-Z-O Manufacturing Company operates a three-department process plant in which materials are used in each department, increasing the number of units being produced. In each department some units are lost through spoilage and evaporation.

For the month of November, the following are the operating statistics (no work-in-process, November 1, 19—) :

Department I:

The costs in Department I were materials, $53,600; labor, $9,600; and manufacturing overhead, $3,200.

In this department, 40,000 units were completed and transferred to Department II, 30,000 were in process on which 90 percent of the material and 80 percent of the labor and overhead had been applied. Units lost totaled 2,000.

Department II:

The costs in this department amounted to $51,800 for materials, $27,450 for labor, and $12,200 for manufacturing overhead. Making allowance for the increase in the volume of production due to added materials, there were finished and transferred to Department III, 48,000 units; in process November 30, on which all of the materials and 65 percent of the labor and overhead had been applied, 20,000 units. Lost in production in this department were 7,000 units.

Department III:

The costs in this department were materials, $34,500; labor, $22,240; and manufacturing overhead, $8,340. Making allowance for the increase in the volume of production due to added materials, 50,000 units were completed and transferred to the finished stock room; 8,000 were in process, 100 percent complete as to materials and 70 percent complete as to labor and overhead. Units lost totaled 4,000.

On the basis of this information, you are asked to prepare:

a) Cost of production report for the month of November, using the simplified process accounting procedure.

b) Journal entries to record the manufacturing operations.

Problem 13-9. Purpose: *Simplified Process Cost Accounting in Two-Department Factory; Added Materials Increasing the Volume of Production; Comparison with Average Cost Procedure*

The J. B. Ellis Company operates a two-department plant on a continuous process plan. It produces a single article. For the month of October, the operating data were (no work-in-process, October 1, 19—):

Department I:

Units completed and transferred to Department II totaled, 15,000. On October 31, 19—, there were 5,000 units in process, 80 percent complete as to materials and 50 percent complete as to labor and overhead. Units lost or spoiled totaled 2,000.

Operating costs for the month of October in Department I were: materials, $14,250; labor, $6,125; and manufacturing overhead, $1,750.

Department II:

Materials were added in this department to increase the volume of production by 5,000 units. During the month of October, 18,000 units were completed; there were in process, October 31, 19—, 2,000 units on which all of the necessary materials and 60 percent of the labor and overhead had been applied. There were no lost units in this department during the month.

Operating costs for the month of October in Department II were: materials, $4,200; labor, $9,600; and manufacturing overhead, $3,456.

On the basis of this information, you are asked to prepare:

a) Cost of production report using the simplified process cost procedure.

b) Cost of production report using the average cost accounting procedure.

Problem 13-10. Purpose: *Simplified Process Accounting in Two-Department Factory; Added Materials Increasing the Volume of Production; Lost Units in Each Department; Comparison with Averge Process Cost Accounting*

The ERICO Manufacturing Company in its two-department factory creates a single product for which it has a special patent. Materials are used in each department, increasing the volume of production.

There was no work-in-process at the beginning of the month of May.

Other operating data obtained from the books and records showed:

Department I:

Units completed and transferred out...	8,000
Units in process May 31 on which 80% of the materials and 60% of the labor and overhead had been applied...	6,000
Units lost or spoiled in production..	1,000
Operating costs were:	
Materials..	$16,896
Labor...	9,048
Manufacturing overhead..	4,060

Department II:

Units completed and transferred out.. 9,000
Units in process, 100% complete as to materials and 70% complete as to labor and overhead... 1,600
Units lost in production... 200
Operating costs were:
Materials...$16,970
Labor... 4,554
Manufacturing overhead... 1,012

On the basis of this information, you are asked to prepare:

a) Cost of production report using the simplified process cost accounting procedures.

b) Cost of production report using the average process cost accounting procedures.

CHAPTER

14 : Process Cost Accounting—Part V

Cost Accounting for Coproducts,

Joint Products, and By-products

Nature of Joint Products, Coproducts, and By-products Joint costs may be interpreted in two distinct ways: (1) *joint overhead costs* which must be apportioned to various departments, whether these apply to a job order or a continuous process manufacturing plant; and (2) *joint product costs* under which the processing of one or more raw materials may result in a variety of products. This variety may result in coproducts, joint products, or by-products, depending upon the importance of the sales value of each, the manufacturing operations involved, or the attitude of management in attempting to control costs as these relate to the sales income. It is therefore apparent that distinctions be made between these three terms: *joint products, coproducts,* and *by-products.* In the previous discussion and descriptions of cost accounting methods and procedures, ample attention has been given to the allocation and proration of joint overhead costs. In this chapter attention will be focused on the accounting principles and procedures relating to costing these three products.

Definitions of Terms To clarify the discussion which follows, it is necessary to define and distinguish between the various multiple products. These products may be grouped under two headings: (1) *joint* and/or *coproducts,* and (2) *by-products.* The accounting principles and procedures will be developed under these two headings.

Joint products are two or more products manufactured simultaneously by a common or series of processing operations. The quantity and sales value of each product are such that none of them may be properly designated as the main product. Illustrations of joint products are found in the meat-packing industry in which hams, ribs, etc., are obtained in the slaughter of pigs; and when linseed oil and cake are obtained from linseed oil processing. In each of these illustrations, the joint products are obtained from the *same source* or the *same raw material. Coproducts,* if and when a distinction must be made, refer to the production of two or more products at the same time, but not necessarily from the same processing operations or the same raw material. For example, in lumbering operations, it is possible to obtain oak, pine, and walnut boards *at the same time,* but from different trees (raw material).

By-products are produced under conditions similar to those of joint or coproducts—that is, from common processing operations. However, where there are *by-products,* the distinction between the various types of products is made on the basis of the relative importance of the *quantity and value of each.* A *by-product* is essentially the *secondary* result of manufacturing operations. A rather arbitrary rule has been suggested in interpreting the meaning of "secondary"—if the value of a product is less than 10 percent of the total value of all products, it could be considered a *by-product,* not a *coproduct* or *joint product.* What may be considered as a by-product for one firm may be the main product of another, and vice versa. For example, in large cities where the demand for manufactured gas for cooking and heating is important, the main product is gas and the by-products, coke, tar, etc.; whereas in Connelsville, Pennsylvania, where the demand in the steel mills for coke is large, coke is the main product and gas becomes one of the by-products. *Time* as well as *location* frequently alters the by-product picture. Many years ago, gasoline was the by-product of the oil industry, when kerosene was the main product; later the reverse was true; and finally after 1928, gasoline and heating oils were both important enough relatively to be considered as joint products.

Characteristics of Joint or Coproducts   Sometimes in manufacturing operations multiple products result because of different sizes of the same product, or various grades, or various styles. *Joint* and *coproducts* are to be distinguished from these multiple products in several respects:

1. The joint or coproduct must be the *primary* objective of the manufacturing operations.
2. The sales value of the joint or coproduct must be *relatively high* if it is to be compared with a by-product resulting at the same time.

3. In the case of certain joint products, the manufacturer must produce *all* of the products of a certain process, if he produces any of them. For example, in meat-packing there will always be hams, sausage, and bacon every time a pig is slaughtered.
4. In certain joint products, the manufacturer has no control over the *relative* quantities of the various products that will result. From each pig that is slaughtered, there will be two hams, two shoulders, etc., no more and no less.

In spite of these definitions and limitations, expediency rather than accurate accounting often determines whether a multiple product is to be treated as a joint product or a by-product.

Problems in Costing Joint and By-products There are a number of problems which arise in the accounting for joint and by-products, the solution of which creates a variety of different costs even for the same products. Among these problems are:

1. Some firms, either because of clerical costs or lack of sufficient volume of production, find it impractical to develop systems and accounting for apportioning the costs between the several products except on some approximate or arbitrary basis. This results in costs which vary widely for the same products with different firms.
2. The volume and selling price of the by-product do not justify spending the money to determine its cost. Therefore many by-products are treated and sold as scrap.
3. Sometimes the manufacturing operations are such that it is difficult to measure with any degree of accuracy the amount of labor and overhead applicable to the various products.
4. Management does not understand why reasonably accurate costs should be determined for the joint products and the by-products. Not only is this necessary to help fix selling prices but also to determine the advisability of extending the manufacturing operations to develop new joint products.

Classification of Joint or Multiple Product Cost Procedures There are a variety of conditions under which process manufacturing firms operate when several products are being manufactured. Among these are:

a) Several different products are manufactured, each in a different department having no relation to the others.

The accounting procedures under these conditions are similar to those existing where each product is manufactured in a separate factory. The problems would be the same, therefore, as those in a firm manufacturing a single product. These have been discussed previously.

b) Several products are manufactured, each in a different depart-ment, but part of at least one of the products is used in the manufacture of one or more of the other products.

In this situation part of, say, the first product is completed and sent to the finished stock room while the remainder is forwarded to one or more of the departments making the other products. Although the accounting procedures are similar to those for a single-product firm, the analysis of the disposition of the costs of production of each product will show on the cost of production report the quantity and cost figures for part or all of the following:

1. Work completed and transferred to the finished goods stock room.
2. Work completed and transferred to other manufacturing departments.
3. Work completed but still in the department.
4. Work-in-process.
5. Lost in production.

Work completed in one department and received in subsequent depart-ments for use in other products will be treated as though purchased from an outside firm. The costs for the second and third departments or for other products will be computed in a manner similar to the single-product firm except that the costs for these products cannot be computed until the costs for preceding departments have been determined.

c) A number of products are being manufactured either simulta-neously in the same department or in different departments from the same materials purchased from the outside or prepared in another department.

These are sometimes known as *coproducts* or *joint products*. It is with this last phase of process cost accounting that this chapter is primarily concerned. The major problem in this type of work is the method of prorating or allocating the costs between the various products with some degree of accuracy.

Prorating Costs When Several Products Are Being Manufactured   This is one of the major problems of mul-tiple product process costing. Different methods of proration will produce differ-ent costs. The important principle to keep in mind is that the method be reasonable and reliable and result in fairly accurate costs for each product. Otherwise the manufacturer is not in a position to measure accurately the profitableness of the various products being made and sold.

Since the *materials* used in manufacturing usually have a direct relationship to the volume of production of the various products, materials are therefore a basic influence on the method of prorating costs equitably among the various products. Firms using *multiple product cost procedures* may be grouped accordingly, viz:

1. Firms in which the use of a *single raw material* may result in several finished products, such as the chemical industries, lumber producers, and meat-packing plants.
2. Firms in which *several raw materials* are used in the production of *two or more products.*

One Raw Material Is Used to Produce Several Products

There are three methods of prorating the costs for multiple products: (1) on a quantity basis, (2) on a weighted average or market value basis, and (3) by formula. If the *units of production* (such as gallons, pounds, tons, etc.) are the same for all products, it is possible to prorate the material costs and labor costs, and also the overhead costs of their *joint production,* on a *unit or quantity* basis.

In the production of several products from a single source, such as crude oil in the refining business, the quantity of each product extracted can be used as the basis of cost proration of the material costs, or labor costs, or both. To illustrate this proration, it is assumed that 10,000 barrels of crude oil were run through the refinery, from which the quantity of each product resulting from the refining after deducting the loss of 200 barrels from the manufacturing operations was:

Product	Quantity	Percent
Gasoline	2,600 bbls.	26.52%
Benzine	200	2.04
Kerosene	1,000	10.21
Lubricating oil	300	3.06
Fuel oil	5,000	51.03
Gas oil	300	3.06
Miscellaneous	400	4.08
Total	9,800 bbls.	100.00%
Loss	200	
	10,000 bbls.	

If these percentages are fairly uniform, they may be used regularly in apportioning the cost of materials used. Labor may be apportioned similarly, unless a more specific and accurate method can be developed.

A schedule of the cost allocation for this particular run for materials is illustrated, assuming the total cost of $26,000 ($2.60 per barrel):

Product	Quantity after Loss	Percent of Total	Cost of Material Allocated
Gasoline...................	2,600 bbls.	26.52%	$ 6,895.20
Benzine...................	200	2.04	530.40
Kerosene...................	1,000	10.21	2,654.60
Lubricating oil.............	300	3.06	795.60
Fuel oil...................	5,000	51.03	13,267.80
Gas oil....................	300	3.06	795.60
Miscellaneous..............	400	4.08	1,060.80
Total................	9,800 bbls.	100.00%	$26,000.00

But since this method of proration is not always useful, that is, since some products may be more valuable than others, and also because in some concerns the *units* of the manufacturing products are not always the same, some firms use the *weighted average* (sometimes known as the *market value*) method. The quantity of production is weighted (multiplied) by the *average sales price* or assumed market price before computing the proportion of the total cost for material and/or labor applicable to each product.

For example, in extensive copper mining, it may be assumed that the gold, silver, and other valuable metals being produced are coproducts (as contrasted with the term "by-product") of the mining operations. Copper production is expressed in pounds or tons, whereas the silver and gold are in ounces. Furthermore, the great disparity in the sales prices of the products would indicate that some method which gave some consideration to the sales prices as well as the quantities would be more equitable. Copper sells for 33 cents per pound; gold, $40 an ounce; and silver, 85 cents an ounce.

To illustrate this method, it is assumed that the costs of mining for the period amounted to $4,445,000, for which 18,000,000 pounds of copper, 3,000,000 ounces of silver, and 10,000 ounces of gold were produced. Taking into consideration the market prices of each of these products, the apportionment of costs on the basis of a weighted average would be as follows:

```
Copper.........18,000,000 lbs. at $ 0.33...........$5,940,000
Silver.......... 3,000,000 oz. at   0.85........... 2,550,000
Gold........... 	 10,000 oz. at 40.00...........   400,000
                                                   $8,890,000
```

It will be noted that the cost of production, $4,445,000, is 50 percent of the weighted average or hypothetical sales price allocation of the finished products ($8,890,000). Therefore in allocating the costs of production of the various coproducts, 50 percent of the sales value of the respective products provides the cost figures, e.g.:

50% of $5,940,000 is	$2,970,000	Cost of copper produced
50% of 2,550,000 is	1,275,000	Cost of silver produced
50% of 400,000 is	200,000	Cost of gold produced
Total Cost of Production	$4,445,000	

In other words, when this method is used, the first step is to compute the total costs of production of all the products. Then compute the estimated sales income to be derived from the total sales of this production. Determine the ratio of the total *cost of production to the total sales income.* This ratio multiplied by the sales income for the various products gives the cost allocation for the respective products. The cost allocation for the respective products divided by the volume of production for the respective products results in the *unit cost* of production for each product: e.g., 18,000,000 pounds of copper produced at an allocated *cost* of $2,970,000 results in a unit cost of 16½ cents per pound.

It should be noted that no matter what cost allocation is made, the total income for the firm when the entire output has been sold will be the same. In other words, only the unit profit is affected, not the total profit. If all the production is not sold, it will have an interim effect on the valuing of the work-in-process or finished goods inventories.

A third method is to prorate the costs in any department on a theoretical or formula basis. For example, it is agreed that during a given period, for every 5,000 pounds of production of certain material there will be 3,000 pounds of Product A and 1,800 pounds of Product B, with 200 pounds lost. This would establish a ratio of 18/48 for Product B and 30/48 for Product A, to be used in prorating the material costs and, if necessary, the labor and overhead costs of all joint production of Products A and B.

Several Raw Materials Are Used to Produce Several Products   Where several raw materials are used to produce several products, the situation may be one in which (1) all the materials are used in one department, with the production of the several products in that department being sent to the finished stock room or to other departments for additional processing; or (2) some of the material is used in one department to manufacture several products, and then in the next department additional material is used to continue the production of one or more of the products of the first department. In either case, it is a problem of adapting the methods previously discussed to the multiproduction. This may be accomplished by using an *average quantity basis* in each department if the relative value of each product does not differ too greatly and the unit of production is the same for each product. Otherwise, a *weighted average* or *formula basis* might be used. Most of these calculations and apportionments will be shown on the cost of production reports. Only the totals will appear in the ledger accounts for work-in-process and finished goods. Wherever possible, the costs should be allocated directly to the products. The chemical industries, in particular, are subject to a great deal of criticism for the methods used in the allocation of costs to several products. Because of the complexity of the operations, it is frequently difficult to obtain reasonably accurate costs. The best that can be hoped for is an honest statement or interpretation of the relation existing between the various products being manufactured. For example, one of the large manufacturers of photographic film devoted part of its activities to the manufacture of educational films. Because of an incorrect allocation of costs to the educational film division, this firm could not meet competitive prices, with the result that it had on several occasions planned to discontinue a necessary phase of its industrial work. Any good cost accountant could have discovered this situation in a few hours of work and perhaps expanded a profitable activity so that the firm's total profit would have been increased.

**By-products
Cost Accounting**

By-products present an accounting problem in many continuous process manufacturing plants. The main feature distinguishing a by-product from the main product and from scrap is one of relative value, the by-product being a secondary result of operations. Usually, if the value of the product is less than 10 percent of the total value of all products, it may be considered a by-product. By-products in some industries become the main products of others.

Illustrations of by-products are:

Industry	*Main Product*	*By-products*
1. Gas...................	Gas....................	Coke, tar, and ammonia
2. Coke..................	Coke....................	Gas, tar, and ammonia
3. Copper mining, smelting..	Copper...................	Silver and gold
4. Meat-packing...........	Dressed meats............	Hides and trimmings
5. Milling................	Flour....................	Feed, bran, and cereals
6. Soap..................	Soap....................	Glycerine
7. Leather tanning.........	Tanned leather...........	Split leather

By-products are sometimes classified as (1) those requiring no further processing after separation from the main product, and (2) those requiring additional processing after separation from the main product.

By-products vary greatly in importance in the various industries. In some concerns the sales value of the by-product is so small relatively that the by-product becomes practically synonymous with scrap. In others, the sales value becomes so important that it may be questionable whether the product is a by-product or a joint product. Such wide variations in the nature of by-products result in equally divergent accounting treatments.

There are five methods of by-product accounting:

a) Treat sales of by-product as other income.
b) Treat sales of by-product as reduction in cost of main product.
c) Treat by-product as having no cost at time of separation but charge by-product with all costs after separation.
d) Record cost of by-product before and after separation from main product.
e) Reversal cost method (sales price method).

a) *Treat Sales of By-product as Other Income.* If the value of the by-product is comparatively small, many manufacturers treat the by-product as though it were scrap material, and a *quantity* inventory may be set up as the by-products are recovered. When the by-product is sold, an entry is made, which in journalized form is:

```
Accounts Receivable..................................................xxxx
    By-product Sales.................................................          xxxx
    To record sale of by-products.
```

On the income statement, by-product sales are treated as an item in the *Other Income* section. Although this method is not very accurate, it is inexpensive and simple and is used in instances where the market value of the by-product is *small* and does not, therefore, warrant setting up inventory and sales accounts for by-products.

b) *Treat Sales of By-product as a Reduction of the Cost of the Main Product.* There are a variety of conditions under which this procedure may be followed, viz:

1. Reduce the cost of the main product by the total estimated income from by-product.
2. Reduce the cost of the main product by the total estimated income from by-product less the selling expenses to be incurred therefrom.
3. Reduce the cost of the main product by the total estimated income from by-product less the selling expenses and an estimated amount for profit.

In each of these situations, it is assumed that the by-product has a small but readily ascertainable sales value. In the first of these situations, the by-product recoveries are set up in the Stores account at the estimated sales value, with a credit to the work-in-process account of the department in which the by-product was created, e.g.:

```
By-product Stores.............................................1,200.00
    Work-in-Process, Dept. B...................................        1,200.00
    To record the by-product at the estimated sales value.
```

This situation develops a complication if the subsequent sales price of the by-product is different from the inventory value. A simple treatment under such conditions is to credit or charge the difference to *Profit and Loss on Sale of By-product.* This method is not usable when the by-product requires further processing after separation. In the second situation, where allowance is to be made for selling expenses incurred with the disposition of the by-product, the credit to the work-in-process account will be reduced accordingly, e.g.:

```
Sales value of the by-product recoveries.............$1,200
Less: Selling expenses to be incurred................   120

Amount to be credited to the work-in-process of the
    main product....................................$1,080
```

In the third situation, where an allowance will also be made for an estimated profit on the sale of by-product, the credit will be further reduced before making the entry, e.g.:

```
Sales price of by-product..................................    $1,200
Selling expenses...................................$120
Estimated profit...................................  60      180

Amount to be credited to the cost of main product...........    $1,020
```

c) ***Treat By-product as Having No Cost at Time of Separation but Charge By-product with All Costs after Separation.*** This method should be used when the by-product requires further processing after separation and when the by-product has no salable value at time of separation. This method overstates the cost of the main product and understates the cost of the by-product, but it is used for practical reasons rather than for theoretical accuracy.

The journal entry to record this is:

```
By-product Costs.............................................xxxx
    Direct Labor.............................................        xxxx
    Materials...............................................        xxxx
    Overhead................................................        xxxx
    To charge by-products with cost for processing after separation.
```

Sales of by-products may be recorded as:

(1)
```
Accounts Receivable.........................................xxxx
    Sale of By-product......................................        xxxx
```

or

(2)
```
Accounts Receivable.........................................xxxx
    By-product Costs........................................        xxxx
    Profit and Loss on Sale of By-products..................        xxxx
```

d) Recording Cost of By-product or Joint Product before and after Separation from Main Product. This method is used when the by-product has a relatively high value—equivalent to a coproduct or joint product—and requires additional processing after separation from the main product. By some this method is called *joint* product cost accounting.

It is the most accurate method but also more costly. Therefore, the value of the by-product must warrant the expenditure incurred. It is considered as a method of by-product accounting only when the nature of product or its value *obviously* makes the product a by-product. Otherwise, it is a method of the previously discussed joint product accounting.

Apportioning the costs before separation between the main product and the by-product is one problem of this method. The bases of this apportionment are similar to those of joint products, namely:

1. The value of the by-product and main product.
2. A standard of quantity—such as gallons, bushels, or pounds—common to both.
3. A weighted average of the quantity weighted by the sales price. This is necessary when the sales values vary widely or when the main product and by-product do not have a common unit of measurement.
4. Approximation.

Journal entries at time of separation are:

```
By-product Costs.................................................xxxx
Main Product Costs..............................................xxxx
     Work-in-Process—Dept. B.......................................     xxxx
     To record costs at time of separation.
```

Thereafter, individual cost reports are used for each product containing charges for the materials, labor, and overhead necessary for their completion.

e) Reversal Cost Method (Sales Price Method). The purpose of this method is *to compute the amount of the costs before separation* that should be charged to a by-product or a coproduct. The procedure is to work back from the selling price, making allowance for a fixed percentage for profit, selling, and administrative expenses, and then to deduct the costs applicable to the by-product or coproduct after separation from the main product. The resulting balance is the amount of the costs before separation which should be applied to the by-product or coproduct.

To illustrate more specifically, it is assumed that the costs of manufacturing before the separation of the products were $25,600. The main product is known as Alpha. Two by-products are manufactured, known as Creatna and Pyrota. The sales prices of the by-products per ton are $50 and $80, respectively; selling and administrative expenses are estimated at 25 percent of the selling price; net profit, 10 percent of selling price. After separation from the main product the costs of manufacturing each ton are $9.50 and $14, respectively. You are asked to compute the amount of the cost per ton before separation that should be allocated to each by-product and thus credited to the main product.

The following illustrations indicate the method of computing this amount:

	By-product Creatna	By-product Pyrota
Sales price per ton...................................	$50.00	$80.00
Net profit, 10%; selling and administrative expenses, 25%...	17.50	28.00
Cost to manufacture................................	$32.50	$52.00
Costs after separation.............................	9.50	14.00
Amount of costs before separation for which main product should be credited, per ton basis.....................	$23.00	$38.00

The final per ton costs can be multiplied by the production for the given period to determine the total credit to the main product for costs before separation which should be applicable to the by-products.

This reversal cost method can be used not only in by-product cost accounting but also with coproducts.

Federal Income Tax Regulations Affecting Joint and By-product Costs

Federal income tax laws affecting joint products are quite broad and general. The tax laws affect multiple product cost accounting because the unsold product becomes part of the final inventory. Therefore it is necessary to compute its value in determining the net profit for the period. The following is a statement of accepted practice in inventorying joint or by-product costs:

A taxpayer engaged in mining or manufacturing who by a single process or uniform series of processes derives a product of two or more kinds, sizes, or grades, the unit cost of which is substantially alike, and who in conformity to a recognized trade practice allocates an amount of cost to each kind, size or grade of product, which in the aggregate will absorb the total cost of production, may use such allocated cost as a basis for pricing inventories, provided such allocation bears a reasonable relation to the respective selling values of the different kinds of product.

This seems to indicate that the government will accept any of the methods discussed in this chapter if they represent accepted trade practices, and if the manufacturer and his accountant can justify his method as being reasonably accurate.

Summary of Coproduct and By-product Accounting

Except for costs after separation, it cannot be said that in the case of coproducts there is profit on one product and a loss on the other. Tracing costs before separation does not seem to accomplish very much because it cannot be said that one product is made independently of the other. Both from the viewpoint of cost and inventory valuation, costs are apportioned on the basis of their market value. The theory back of this is that neither product could be made without the other, and it is assumed that, except for special competitive conditions, the same rate of profit should be maintained on each product.

By-products, on the other hand, arise under such a variety of conditions that no one method will fit all situations. The importance, dollar-wise, of the by-products will determine the treatment as separate source of income, or a reduction in the cost of the main product.

Managerial Decision Aspects of Joint and By-product Costing

The preceding discussion has covered the accounting aspects of joint and by-product costing. The decision of which method to use in allocating the costs before separation of one product from the other is somewhat varied and even arbitrary. Management is faced with two main problems in joint and by-product costing—namely, the cost basis to use in pricing the salable product and the extent to which the firm should expand its manufacturing operations after separation to make a better or a new salable product.

How much costs before separation should be allocated to each product will no doubt involve (1) the volume of each product; (2) the competitive price situation for each product; and (3) price differential if one or both of the products were to be processed further. Since each of these factors differs with each type of business activity, no fixed rules can be promulgated. However, in Chapter 22, a study of the *cost-volume-price* relationship of various manufactured products is given. These same principles will apply not only to joint products but also to by-products. Management may however take into consideration the income tax impact of the various methods of cost allocation. If one of the products is not readily marketable and has a high profit rate but a long storage life before being sold, it might be wise to allocate a greater proportion of the cost before separation to the other product which is more readily salable, assuming of course that the allocation method is reasonable. Sometimes the decision to process a product further after separation from a common source may be determined by (1) plant facilities available for further processing; (2) additional investment if any in equipment or factory space, to process further; and (3) whether the additional profit from further processing warrants the above investment. If not, then the product can be sold at the time of separation either as a joint product or as a by-product. The determining factor is the *profit impact*.

QUESTIONS FOR REVIEW

1. Distinguish between coproducts and joint products. How important is this distinction in cost accounting? What are some of the objections or difficulties which make some manufacturers avoid joint or by-product cost accounting?

2. A manufacturer produces several products, one of which is of small volume but has a relatively high sales value. The manufacturer feels that it is not important enough to spend money to compute the cost of making this product. He therefore treats the sales income of this product as other income when sold. Explain the fallacy of this procedure.

3. What are the three classifications of multiple product cost procedures? Which is the more important and why? What is the major accounting problem in this important classification?

4. What three methods of cost proration among multiple products can be used?

5. How does the use of several raw materials in multiple product manufacture complicate the cost accounting work?

6. Three joint products are manufactured by the Suffern Chemical Company, a manufacturer of powdered chemical cleaners. There were no inventories at the beginning of the period. For the month of September the production and sales statistics were:

Product	Production Units	Sales Units	Dollar Sales
Floorenzo.............	12,000	10,000	$380,000
Linolenzo.............	20,000	15,000	150,000
Tilenzo...............	18,000	16,000	320,000

The selling prices at the end of the month have had to be adjusted because of competitive conditions and are now F, $40; L, $12.50; and T, $25.

The cost of manufacturing for the month of September was $306, 800.

On the basis of these figures, prepare a schedule showing the cost of sales and the final inventories of finished goods, if it is assumed that the sales prices as operating at the end of month will be continued for the remainder of the year.

7. The Insect Destruction Company produces two chemicals jointly. For the month of October, the production data were:

Joint manufacturing costs......................................$50,000
Beetle DM Powder, 15,000 lbs., sales price..................... 37,500
Antkill FM Powder 20,000 lbs., sales price.................... 22,000

The company can process Antkill FM Powder and produce a multikill product for an additional cost of $11,000 to obtain 25,000 pounds of product MULTI X which can be sold for $35,000. Should the company change its manufacturing and marketing policy to produce the new product C?

8. What rather arbitrary rule can be used to identify a product as a by-product when no other information is available? What two major classifications are used to describe by-products?

9. By-products may be described as those which do not require further processing after separation and those which do. What methods of accounting are used in each of these instances?

10. What complication arises in accounting for a by-product that requires additional processing after separation?

11. What is the purpose of the "reversal sales" method of accounting for by-products or coproducts?

12. What is the attitude of the federal income tax authorities toward multiple product cost accounting procedures?

PROBLEMS—GROUP A

Problem 14–1. Purpose: *Statements of Cost of Goods Manufactured; Cost of Sales and Final Inventories by Products*

The Vernam Chemical Company processed 2,200 tons of raw materials for which it paid $170 a ton. For every 110 tons of material, 99 tons of output were obtained. From the materials thus used, the following three products were obtained, all of the same consistency but slightly different thickness and width, in the following proportions:

```
Product A...................... 50%, salable at $380 per ton
Product B...................... 30%, salable at  280 per ton
Product C...................... 20%, salable at  230 per ton
```

The labor and overhead costs were $59,400.

During this period, the sales were 900 tons of Product A, 400 tons of Product B, and 300 tons of Product C.

From these data you are asked to compute the cost of goods manufactured, the cost of goods sold, and the amount of the final inventories. There were no work-in-process inventories either at the beginning or end of the accounting period, and no finished goods inventory at the beginning of the period. Use the weighted average method of apportioning costs.

Problem 14–2. Purpose: *Cost of Production Report for Coproducts; Statement of Operations for the Coproducts*

A chemical company manufactures two products from the same ingredients, viz: Every 2,000 pounds of raw material produces 1,000 pounds of Product A and 800 pounds of Product B; of the latter product, however, 50 percent is waste and unsalable. The plant is divided into the following three departments:

Raw material department,
    Grinding and mixing.
Conversion Department A,
    Converting Product A into salable form.
Conversion Department B,
    Converting Product B into salable form.

The raw materials consumed in the raw material department amounted to 2,000,000 pounds and cost $0.08 per pound. The departmental expenses are as follows:

Expenses	Dept. Raw Material	Conversion Dept. A	Conversion Dept. B
Labor..	$ 70,000	$ 75,000	$25,000
Heat, light, and power..........................	15,000	18,000	9,000
Depreciation...................................	2,500	15,000	17,000
Machinery maintenance.........................	3,500	12,000	12,000
Rent..	16,000	20,000	9,000
Insurance......................................	3,000	5,000	8,000
Departmental expense..........................	10,000	15,000	12,000
	$120,000	$160,000	$92,000

The selling and administrative expenses applicable to both products amount to 20 percent of their cost. Product A sells for $0.60 per pound less discounts of 25 percent and 10 percent. Product B sells for $0.70 per pound less a 10 percent discount.

From this information you are asked to—

a) Prepare a production report showing unit costs for each product.

b) Prepare a statement indicating for management the profitableness of each product.

(Adapted New York C.P.A. Examination)

Problem 14–3. Purpose: *Cost of Production Report for Two Products Being Manufactured Simultaneously from the Same Materials Previously Prepared in Initial Department; Journal Entries*

The Vickers Manufacturing Company produces two products simultaneously from the same material previously manufactured in the initial department. The three departments are: *preparation, aging,* and *purifying and packing.* The two products being manufactured are termed, *Product A* and *Product B.* The additional costs for materials in the second and third manufacturing departments do not result in any increase in the volume of production.

The quantity of production statistics for the month of October were as follows:

	Preparation Dept.	Aging Dept.	Purifying and Packing Dept.
Started into production........................200,000		0	0
Completed and transferred out:			
For Product A............................. 90,000		60,000	35,000
For Product B............................. 60,000		45,000	35,000
In process, 100% materials, 40% labor and overhead...................................... 40,000			
In process, 100% materials, 60% labor and overhead, Product A......................		25,000	20,000
In process, 100% materials, 70% labor and overhead, Product B......................		10,000	8,000
Balance lost in production..................... 10,000		?	?

The cost of production statistics were as follows:

Department	Materials		Labor		Overhead	
	Product A	Product B	Product A	Product B	Product A	Product B
Preparation...........	$285,000		$249,000		$124,500	
Aging................	$11,000	$ 6,000	$7,500	$7,800	$15,000	$26,000
Purifying and packing...	27,500	43,000	7,050	6,090	9,400	8,120

From this information you are asked to prepare:

a) A cost of production report for each product emphasizing the departmental costs.

b) Journal entries to record the costs of production and completion, assuming one work-in-process account for each department.

Problem 14–4. Purpose: *Computation of Unit Costs for Main Product When By-product Results; Proration of Costs by Products and by Departments*

In the production of a main product and its one by-product a manufacturer utilizes six production departments. Raw material when placed in process passes first through the reduction department in which it is fused to a clinker mass. Then it passes to the grinding department and next to the mixing department. From the mixing department it passes to the extraction department at which point the by-product emerges. Both products next pass to the finishing department and to the packing department.

Raw material when placed in process is composed of two items as follows:

    X 45% costing..$110 per ton
    Y 55% costing..   70 per ton

Material storage and handling cost is computed at 8 percent of material cost.

In the mixing department one ton of additional materials (chemicals) is added for each ton transferred from the grinding department. This additional ton is composed of the following quantities and costs:

    (1) 25% costing...$ 40 per ton
    (2) 60% costing...   80 per ton
    (3) 15% costing... 160 per ton

Direct labor cost is computed on tonnage handled in each department.

Direct department expense and indirect department expense are computed as a percentage of direct labor cost.

The following are the direct labor costs and expense percentages:

Department	Direct Labor per Ton	Direct Dept. Expense	Indirect Dept. Expense
Reducing.....................................	$20	40%	30%
Grinding.....................................	22	150	30
Mixing.......................................	30	250	30
Extraction...................................	24	200	30
Finishing....................................	50	60	30
Packing......................................	36	40	30

In the extraction process 80 percent of material placed in process becomes the main product. Of the remaining portion sent to the finishing department along with the main product, two thirds comes out as completed by-product. There is no loss in finishing the main product.

Since it takes approximately twice as long to finish the by-product as it does the main product, finishing costs will be twice as much also. Therefore the quantity of by-product is doubled to get a basis for apportioning the finishing costs between the main product and the by-product. The *cost of the main product is credited* with the "profit" on the by-product in the ratio of one ton of by-product for six tons of main product.

By-product is sold at a net profit of $96 a ton, after giving consideration to its share of factory costs. No commercial expenses are assigned to the by-product.

Main product is sold for $900 per ton. Main product is charged with commercial expenses at the rate of 15 percent of sales price.

Determine the profit per ton of main product sales.

From this information you are asked to prepare:

a) Cost statement showing per unit computations (per ton) by departments.

b) Statement showing credit for by-product per ton of main product.

c) The profit per ton of main product sales.

Problem 14–5. Purpose: *By-product Costs with Treatment as Reduction of Cost of Main Product; and Also By-product Costs Both before and after Separation from Main Product*

The Vellman Corporation produces a special metal product known as Rareboloy which sells for $1,400 per ton. The manufacturing operations are on a continuous process and cover four successive departments: *reducing and grinding, mixing, extracting,* and *finishing.* Materials are used in the reducing and grinding department and in the mixing department. In the latter department, the additional materials increase the number of units being produced.

Production data for the month of January were as follows:

Department	Material Costs	Labor Costs	Overhead Costs
Reducing and grinding department:			
600,000 lbs. of material A @ 8¢........	$48,000	$ 40 per ton	$50 per ton
1,800,000 lbs. of material B @ 5¢.......	90,000		
Mixing department:			
500,000 lbs. of material C @ 4¢........	20,000		
750,000 lbs. of material D @ 6¢.........	45,000	$ 36 per ton	200% of labor costs
250,000 lbs. of material E @ 12¢........	30,000		
Extracting department.....................	0	$ 30 per ton	$65 per ton
Finishing department.....................	0	$100 per ton for main product	$85 per ton of finished product

The production in the extracting department is as follows: 60 percent *Rareboloy,* and the balance, a by-product, known as *Sensimetal.* Both of these semifinished metals are sent to the finishing department.

In the finishing department, 45 percent of the material used in making Sensimetal is lost, the balance becoming the by-product. In the finishing department, four times as much labor is used in completing a ton of Rareboloy as in *making the ton of Sensimetal.*

Selling and administrative expenses are estimated at 15 percent of the selling price of the main product. No charge for selling and administrative expenses is made for the by-product.

The Rareboloy sells for $1,400 per ton; the by-product, Sensimetal, for $150 per ton.

From this information you are asked to prepare a statement of the cost of production and an income statement for the month of January: (*a*) when the by-product income is treated as a reduction in the cost of the Rareboloy; and (*b*) when costs before and after separation are computed for each product.

Problem 14–6. Purpose: *Coproduct Cost Accounting with By-product; Cost of Production Report on the FIFO Basis*

The Vardon Company is a manufacturer, producing two principal products known as XO and MO. Incidental to the production of these products, it produces a by-product known as Bypo. The company has three producing departments which it identifies as Departments 101, 201, and 301. Raw materials A and B are started in process in Department 101. Upon completion of processing in that department, one fifth of the material is by-product and is transferred directly to stock. One third of the remaining output of Department 101 goes to Department 201 where it is made into XO, and the other two thirds goes to Department 301 where it becomes MO. The processing of XO in Department 201 results in a gain in weight of material transferred into the department of 50 percent due to the addition of water at the start of the processing. There is no gain or loss of weight in the other processes.

The company considers the income from Bypo, after allowing 5 cents per pound for estimated selling and delivery costs, to be a reduction of the cost of the two principal products. The company assigns Department 101 costs to the two principal products in proportion to their net sales value at point of separation, computed by deducting costs to be incurred in subsequent processes from the sales value of the products.

The following information concerns the operations during April, 19—:

INVENTORIES

	March 31 Quantity (*Pounds*)	March 31 Value	April 30 Quantity (*Pounds*)
Department 101...........................	None	......	None
Department 201...........................	800	$17,160	1,000
Department 301...........................	200	2,340	360
Finished stock—XO........................	300	7,260	800
Finished stock—MO........................	1,200	18,550	700
Finished stock—Bypo......................	None	......	None

Inventories in process are estimated to be one-half complete in Departments 201 and 301, both at the first and last of the month.

COSTS

	Material Used	Labor and Burden
Department 101	$134,090	$87,442
Department 201	....	31,950
Department 301	....	61,880

The material used in Department 101 weighed 18,000 pounds.

SALES PRICES

XO	$29.50 per lb.
MO	17.50 per lb.
Bypo	0.50 per lb.

Prices as of April 30 are unchanged from those in effect during the month.

You are to prepare the following statements covering the operations of the Vardon Company. Present all supporting computations in good form.

a) Statement showing costs and production by departments for the month of April. The company uses first-in, first-out to cost out production.

b) A schedule of inventory values for work-in-process and finished goods as of April 30.

(American Institute of Accountants Examination)

Problem 14–7. Purpose: *Reversal Sales Method of Prorating Costs before Separation to Main and By-products*

In the manufacturing operations of the Volmer Manufacturing Company, three products result through additional work after separation. Two of these are main or important products and are known as Products A and B, and one of these known as Product X is a by-product.

Heretofore, the by-product and Product B were charged only with costs after separation from Product A, because of the difficulties of prorating the costs before separation. This resulted in a high rate of profit for Products B and X and a low return for Product A.

The production manager feels that more reliable figures would be obtained if the costs before separation from Product A were prorated to all products on some equitable basis.

The total costs before separation are $159,000. The costs after separation were as follows:

Product A	$350,000
Product B	200,000
By-product X	5,600

Production for the period with sales prices are as follows:

200,000 pounds of Product A, salable at $4.00
200,000 pounds of Product B, salable at $2.20
30,000 pounds of By-product X salable at $1.20

Estimated and expected *net* profit for Product A is 15 percent of selling price; for Product B, 12½ percent of selling price; and for By-product X, 10 percent.

Selling and administrative expenses for all products are estimated at 30 percent of the selling price.

From this information you are asked to prepare:

a) A schedule of production costs showing proration before separation by using the reversal sales method.

b) A comparative income statement for all three products.

PROBLEMS—GROUP B

Problem 14–8. Purpose: *Journal Entries and Statements for Coproduct and By-product Accounting—Sales Value Method of Cost Apportionment*

The Fosterale Manufacturing Company produces three products: Alpha, Gamma, and By-product Reta.

The production outline is as follows:

Department I—Materials, labor, and overhead are used to prepare the basic materials from which all products emerge.

Department II—Product Alpha is completed using some of the material from Department I.

Department III—Product Gamma is completed by using some of the material from Department I.

The By-product Reta comes out of Department I and requires no further processing.

Cost and operating data were:

1. Materials put into production in Department I, cost $24,000
2. Conversion costs:
   Department I..............................$16,000
   Department II............................. 7,140
   Department III............................   450
3. Production and sales statistics:

Product	Quantity Produced	Quantity Sold	Selling and Administrative Costs per Unit	Average Selling Price per Unit
Alpha....................	10,000	8,000	$0.60	$6.00
Gamma..................	4,500	3,000	0.40	3.00
Reta....................	1,000	900	0.05	0.50

4. Costs are assigned to Products Alpha and Gamma on the basis of the sales value and the By-product Reta on the basis of reduction of main product.
5. In assigning costs to the by-product, the company makes an allowance of 10 percent profit in addition to selling and administrative expenses.

From this you are asked to prepare:

a) Journal entries to record the manufacturing operations.

b) Statement showing the cost allocation for each product, the cost of sales, and the finished goods inventories at the end of the period.

Problem 14-9.   Purpose: *Joint Product Costs; Allocation of Costs to Different Products; Statement of Profit and Loss by Products and in Total*

The Fortran Lumber Company purchases hardwood logs and manufactures certain kinds of lumber from them. It divides its production into three general classes: Grades A, B, and C, in addition to the scrap products which include slabs, sawdust, etc.

Raw material is purchased at flat prices for large lots, and in some cases one lot includes logs from which two or more grades of lumber are produced.

Inventories of each grade of finished lumber are carried at cost. Cost of sales for each grade are based on opening inventories and monthly production costs. Production costs are apportioned so that the unit costs of the three grades of lumber for each month are proportionate to sales prices at the end of the month. No net profit is allocated to scrap sales, but it is estimated that the ratios of selling and general expenses to production costs in connection with scrap are the same as those that would be applicable with respect to A, B, and C grades of lumber before credit to production costs for scrap produced.

Inventories at January 1, 19—, were:

```
Raw materials—logs......................................$9,000
Supplies................................................. 1,000
Grade A—220,000 feet..................................... 4,840
Grade B—300,000 feet..................................... 5,400
Grade C—400,000 feet..................................... 6,000
Scrap (at sales prices less percentage for selling and administrative
    expenses)............................................   420
```

Sales, costs, and expenses for the month of January, 19—, were as follows:

```
Sales—Grade A, 120,000 feet.............................$ 3,600
Sales—Grade B, 240,000 feet............................. 6,000
Sales—Grade C, 200,000 feet............................. 4,200
Sales—scrap.............................................   100
Logs purchased.......................................... 10,000
Supplies purchased......................................   600
Mill salaries and wages................................. 1,950
Other mill expenses.....................................   700
Sales department salaries and expenses.................. 1,000
General and administrative expenses.....................   400
```

The inventories at January 31, 19—, were as follows:

```
Raw materials—logs......................................$16,400
Supplies................................................ 1,250
Grade A.................................................160,000 feet
Grade B.................................................180,000 feet
Grade C.................................................290,000 feet
Scrap (at sales price less % for selling and administrative expenses).$   650
```

There was no material in process, either at the beginning or end of the month.

The sales prices at January 31, 19—, were as follows:

```
Grade A.................................................$30 per 1,000 feet
Grade B................................................. 25 per 1,000 feet
Grade C................................................. 21 per 1,000 feet
```

Selling and administrative expenses ($1,400) are allocated in part to the scrap on the basis of production cost. This means that $20 of the sales of scrap is included in the cost of scrap. The costs of the shipments of all lumber are on the basis of the average cost of the initial inventory and the costs of production for the period even though cost of sales actually are all from the initial inventory.

From this information you are asked to prepare

a) Statement of production costs.

b) Statement of scrap produced.

c) Statement of allocation of production costs to various grades of lumber.

d) Statement of profit and loss by products (grades of lumber).

Problem 14–10.   Purpose: *Coproduct Cost Accounting after Split-Off in First Department*

From the information below, prepare the following statements, supported by whatever explanatory schedules you consider necessary:

a) Statement to show at what list price and at what net price per pound YIP should be sold.

b) Statement to show at what list price and at what net price per gallon ZIP should be sold.

c) Condensed income statement to show, separately and combined, the results of operations in YIP and ZIP, on the assumption that the entire quantity of each product manufactured will be sold at the respective prices indicated in the statements prepared in (*a*) and (*b*), above, and that selling, administrative, and general expenses are to be included at the same estimate as is allowed in setting such prices.

Fremco, Inc., has perfected a process for producing from the three raw materials, A, B, and C, two chemical compounds, YIP and ZIP.

The raw materials are required in the following proportions by weight:

```
A.............................................. 3 parts
B.............................................. 5
C.............................................. 2
                                              _____
                                              10 parts
                                              ==========
```

The following diagram illustrates the manufacturing process:

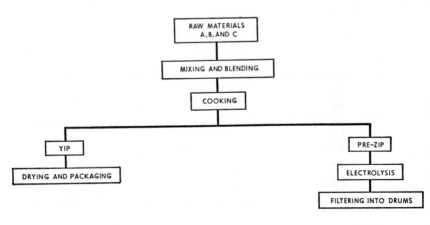

One hundred thousand (100,000) pounds of raw material will be processed. The unit costs of the three raw materials are as follows:

A.....................................$ 2 per pound
B..................................... 50 per ton
C..................................... 4 per gallon

Other costs of production are estimated to be:

Mixing, blending, and cooking...................................$16,090
Additional costs applicable to YIP (drying and packaging).......... 4,660
Additional costs applicable to ZIP (electrolysis and filtering into drums) 6,920

The cooking process reduces the weight of the combined raw materials by 40 percent. Out of 100,000 pounds of original raw materials, 20,000 pounds of pre-ZIP are obtained. Of the pre-ZIP electrolyzed, 25 percent becomes a non-marketable precipitate, the remainder as a liquid, being filtered into 50-gallon drums without further attention.

The cost of drums, which are returnable and for which customers are to be charged specifically, is not to be included in either the cost or price of ZIP.

Each product is to be sold on the basis of a list price, less 35 percent and 10 percent. Of the net selling price of each product, 25 percent is to be allowed for selling, administrative, and general expenses, including provision for income tax, and 20 percent for net profit after provision for all costs and expenses.

The company has never marketed either of the products but has demonstrated the existence of markets for both if they can be manufactured to sell at suitable prices. Its experience in producing both these and other chemicals leads it to believe that the above estimates of cost relative to the processing of 100,000 pounds of the three raw materials combined are reliable as a basis for setting a price for each of the products to be manufactured therefrom.

Note: One gallon of ZIP weighs 7.5 pounds. One gallon of raw material C weighs 8 pounds.

(American Institute of Accountants)

Problem 14–11.   Purpose: *By-product Accounting Whereby the By-product Recoveries Reduce the Cost of the Main Product*

The Frumelt-Conda Mining Company operates a copper mining property in which the operations are (1) *mining,* (2) *milling* and *ore reduction,* and (3) *smelting* and *refining.* In the mining, there are always some by-products. The firm is not sure whether it should treat the by-product recoveries as a reduction of the cost of main product or as other income.

From the information given, you are asked to prepare:

a) A profit and loss statement when the *estimated income* from the by-products of gold and silver is treated *as a reduction in the cost of the main product.*

b) A profit and loss statement when the income from gold and silver is treated as *Other Income.*

The departmental costs for the six months ended June 30, 19—, are as follows:

Elements of Costs	Mining Dept.	Milling Dept.	Smelting Dept.	Total
Supplies and materials............$	150,000	$200,000	$100,000	$ 450,000
Labor costs.....................	500,000	350,000	180,000	1,030,000
Coal...........................	50,000	40,000	30,000	120,000
Power..........................	100,000	20,000	40,000	160,000
Depletion of mine...............	1,000,000	....	....	1,000,000
Other expenses..................	190,000	100,000	60,000	350,000
	$1,990,000	$710,000	$410,000	$3,110.000

The production for the six months' period showed:

```
Copper produced...........................................20,000 tons
Silver....................................................12,500 lbs.
Gold...................................................... 1,000 oz.
```

The cost of the work still in the smelters was estimated at $50,000.

Sales for the period: 17,000 tons at 40 cents a pound for copper
11,250 pounds of silver at 92 cents an ounce
1,000 ounces of gold at $40 an ounce

Selling expenses for the period were $450,000, and administrative expenses were $75,000.

Problem 14–12. Purpose: *By-product Cost Accounting with Costs Both before and after Separation*

The Farvin Chemical Company's main product is known as Protextin. In its manufacture a by-product results which can be sold to farmers and nurserymen after slight additional processing.

On the basis of the information given, you are asked to prepare pro forma profit and loss statements (assuming all the production is sold) under the following conditions:

a) When the by-product is charged only with the costs after separation.

b) When the costs before separation are allocated to the main product and the by-product on a quantity basis.

c) When the costs before separation are allocated to the main product and the by-product on a weighted average basis.

The costs of production for the six months' period ending October 31 were:

	Before Separation	After Separation Main Product	After Separation By-product
Material costs........................	$380,000	$ 84,000	$12,000
Labor costs..........................	209,000	806,400	36,000
Manufacturing overhead costs..........	111,000	192,000	6,000
Total........................	$700,000	$1,082,400	$54,000

The quantity of production indicated the following statistics:

	Before Separation	After Separation Main Product	After Separation By-product
Started into production	300,000 lbs.		
Transferred to main product	220,000		
Transferred for by-product	60,000		
Lost in production	20,000		
Finished and transferred to stock room		180,000 lbs.	50,000 lbs.
In Process, all materials, ⅔ labor and overhead applied		30,000	
Lost in production		10,000	10,000

The selling price of the main product is $25 per pound, and of the by-product, $3 per pound. The selling and administrative expenses applicable to the two products, assuming the sale of the entire production for the period, would be:

Main product	$150,000
By-product	12,000

Problem 14–13.   Purpose: *Cost Statements for Metal Smelting Company; Joint Product Costing*

From the following data prepare a statement of operating results of the Farmer Mining and Milling Company in October that will show the operations on the company's own account and its activities in furnishing milling services to others, both for zinc and for lead concentrates. Present all supporting schedules. Carry computations to the third decimal.

The Farmer Mining and Milling Company operates several mines and a mill for concentrating ore. The ore as it comes from the mines must be concentrated in the mill before being shipped to the smelters. The resulting zinc and lead concentrates amount to about 5 percent to 7 percent of the original weight. Both kinds of concentrates go through substantially the same milling processes. Zinc concentrates contain about 60 percent zinc, while lead concentrates contain about 80 percent lead.

The company, in addition to milling the rock produced in its own mines, does commercial milling for other mines in the neighborhood, accepting as compensation 20 percent of the concentrates produced. The amount of concentrates produced from the ores thus brought in is determined by assaying each carload of rock as it is received. This is necessary because (*a*) the ores from different mines differ in richness and (*b*) it is not practicable to mill different batches of ore separately.

The mining land and ore deposits are not owned by the company. A royalty of 12 percent of the selling price of concentrates produced from company ores must be paid to the owners. This royalty accrues as the concentrates are sold. royalty expense being charged and accounts payable credited at the end of the month in which sales are made.

The company develops its own power, which is used 40 percent for mining operations and 60 percent in the mill.

Inventories of partially mined rock and of rock in process in the mill are constant and may be ignored for the purposes of this problem.

The following operating data are presented:

Cost of mining....................................$31,356
Cost of milling.................................. 11,326
Cost of power................................... 6,292
General management........................... 5,586
                                                $54,560

(The above costs include all labor, supplies, expenses, and depreciation.)

It is understood that the mining and milling expenses will be apportioned to the cost of zinc and lead concentrates on the basis of their sales value (known as the "joint product method") and that the general management expenses will not be absorbed in the production costs.

Cost and production data showed:

	Tons	Valued at—
Mined rock on hand October 1............................	500	$ 615
Rock mined and brought to the surface in October..........	27,600	
Mined rock on hand October 31..........................	1,500	
Rock owned by others milled in October.................	4,600	
Concentrates on hand October 1:		
Zinc—own product only.............................	150	3,900
Lead—own product only.............................	50	1,800
Concentrates produced in October, both own and for others:		
Zinc...	1,810	
Lead...	187	
Concentrates delivered to others after retaining company's share:		
Zinc...	216	
Lead...	24	
Concentrates on hand October 31:		
Zinc—own product only.............................	125	
Lead—own product only.............................	20	
Sales of concentrates in October:		
Zinc...		66,379
Lead...		11,001
Market price per ton of concentrates October 31:		
Zinc...		42
Lead...		58

(American Institute of Accountants Uniform Examination)

Problem 14–14. Purpose: *Computation of By-product Costs*

The Falstaff Laboratories, Inc., manufactures the chemical product *Zoom* sold to the automobile industry at $4.25 a pound. The manufacturing process is departmentalized as follows:

Department 1—mixing
Department 2—cooking
Department 3—cooling
Department 4—packing

Materials X, Y, and Z are issued from stores twice daily for production runs, which are controlled by number and date.

In Department 1, materials X, Y, and Z are weighed and mixed in accordance with a secret formula. In Department 2 the mixture is cooked and 10 percent of the mixture is lost in evaporation at the end of the departmental process. The cooking process requires several hours, and immediately upon completion the vats containing the remaining 90 percent of the mixture are conveyed on belts through several rooms of different temperatures comprising the cooling department. In the final stages of this department, the top 80 percent of the mixture is poured out and transferred to Department 4 where it is poured into barrels for shipment. The 20 percent of the mixture that represents impurities and sediments resulting from the cooling process is sold in bulk as a by-product called W for a nominal selling price of $1 a pound.

Variation in the length of time in the cooling process or in the temperatures can result in increasing the percentage of by-product to as high as 30 percent of the Department 3 mixture, but the minimum by-product always will be 20 percent.

The research division of the company has discovered a prospective use for the by-product in another field, but it would require the setting up of an additional department and an investment of additional capital to handle a further manufacturing process. This new by-product (Clora-W) would sell for $5 a pound. To produce this product one-half pound of new material is added to each pound of the sediment obtained from Department 3. However, processing causes a 40 percent shrinkage of the resulting mixture. Processing Clora-W will add the following additional costs:

Material to be added.........................$	0.50 per pound
Variable processing costs.....................	1.10 per pound of input
Fixed processing costs.......................	3,092.00 per month

Material issued to Department No. 1:

> X 8,000 lbs. at $1.00
> Y 3,000 lbs. at 1.10
> Z 1,000 lbs. at 0.70

Processing costs:

Department 1..............................	$0.37 per pound of departmental input
Department 2..............................	0.38 per pound of departmental input
Department 3..............................	0.45 per pound of departmental input
Department 4..............................	0.45 per pound of departmental input

All processing costs in Department 4 may be considered as variable.

Required:

Based on the following cost data and production figures for a one-month period, the management requests you to prepare statements showing total manufacturing cost and gross profit for each of the following situations, assuming that all production is sold:

a) By-product W produced at a rate of 20 percent of Department 3 mixture.

b) By-product Clora-W produced at each of the following percentages of Department 3 mixture: (1) 20 percent, and (2) 30 percent.

(Uniform C.P.A. Examination of A.I.A.)

Problem 14–15. Purpose: *C.P.A. Problem of Accounting for Coproducts and By-products Requiring Processing after Separation*

The Filips Manufacturing Company produces one principal product designated MILINE. Incidental to its manufacture, two additional products result: COPINE and BOLINE. Material is started in Process No. 1, and three products come out of this process. MILINE is processed further through Department II; COPINE is processed further through Department III; while BOLINE is sold without further processing.

There were no work-in-process inventories either at the beginning or the end of the period. Operating costs were materials put into process in Department I, $12,000. Conversion costs (labor and overhead) were: Department I, $8,000; Department II, $4,000; and Department III, $300. These costs were for the month of February.

Production and sales data for the month of February were:

Product	Quantity Produced	Quantity Sold	February Average Sales Price	Market Price February 28
MILINE	5,000	4,000	$6.00	$6.00
COPINE	3,000	2,000	1.00	0.90
BOLINE	1,000	900	0.50	0.55

Selling and administrative expenses are related to the quantity sold. It is estimated that next period selling and administrative costs will be the same as February actual:

MILINE	$2,000
COPINE	800
BOLINE	36

Standard net profit on COPINE is 10 percent of sales, whereas no profit or loss is realized on BOLINE sales.

Required:

a) Compute value of the BOLINE inventory and the costs transferred from Department I to the BOLINE units during February.

b) Compute the value of the COPINE inventory and the costs transferred from Department I to COPINE units during February.

c) Copy and complete the following entries:

Work-in-Process—Dept. I.....................................
Work-in-Process—Dept. II....................................
Work-in-Process—Dept. III...................................
    Stores and Conversion Costs................................

Work-in-Process—Dept. II....................................
Work-in-Process—Dept. III...................................
BOLINE Inventory Account....................................
    Work-in-Process—Dept. I...................................

Finished Goods—MILINE..

Work-in-Process—Dept. II..

Finished Goods—COPINE...

Work-in-Process—Dept. III.......................................

Cash..

Sales—MILINE...

Cost of Goods Sold—MILINE...

Finished Goods—MILINE..

Cash..

Sales—COPINE...

Cost of Goods Sold—COPINE...

Finished Goods—COPINE..

Cash..

BOLINE Inventory...

Selling and Administrative Expenses............................

d) Copy and complete the following income statement:

	MILINE	COPINE	BOLINE	Total
Sales............................				
Less: Cost of goods sold..............				
Gross profit on sales.................				
Less: Selling and administrative expenses.......................				
Net Income for Month of February.....				

(Adapted from an AICPA Uniform Examination)

CHAPTER

15 | Simplifying Cost Accounting

| Through Estimated Costs

Nature of Cost Estimates

Some firms have simplified their cost work and records through the use of an *estimated cost system.* It is a form of *predetermined costs* used by firms who must calculate their costs in estimated form in advance of the actual manufacture of the goods, or the completion of a special construction contract, for the purpose of subsequent comparison with actual costs. The estimated cost figures actually appear in the Work-in-Process, Finished Goods, and Cost of Goods Sold accounts, though they must later be adjusted to the actual cost figures. Manufacturers of clothing, shoes, and furniture, among others, may use estimated costs. Contractors engaged in construction and engineering work also use a modified form of estimated costs.

Cost estimates are sometimes known as *formula costs,* especially in firms engaged in the manufacture of chemicals, patent medicines, or candy.

Cost estimates are also known as *predetermined costs,* since the cost of each element of cost—materials, labor, and manufacturing overhead—is estimated and computed before the manufacturing operations are started. Such an interpretation has led many cost accountants to believe that estimated costs are merely a type of standard costs. However, the difference between standard and estimated costs will be indicated later in the chapter.

There are two basic reasons for having estimated costs:

1. The nature of the manufacturing and selling operations requires the determination of selling prices sometime in advance of the actual manufacturing. Orders for men's suits and for shoes, for example, are

taken months in advance of actual production and shipment. To fix the selling prices, estimates of cost must be prepared.

2. The use of an estimated cost accounting system reduces the expense of the clerical work of cost keeping because most requisitions and job time tickets are eliminated. It is true that the cost figures obtained under an estimated cost system are not so accurate nor so reliable as those obtained under the historical job order cost method. Estimated costs represent a practical method adapted to peculiar business conditions, i.e., advance sale of goods not yet manufactured.

The disadvantage of a slight inaccuracy in costs may be greatly outweighed by the advantage of a much smaller clerical expense in cost keeping.

Managerial Implications of Estimated Costs

Two managerial aspects of estimated costs should be discussed before proceeding with the accounting treatment of estimated costs. These are (1) budgetary aspects of estimated costs, including PERT; and (2) engineering aspects of estimated costs.

Cost estimating especially in the large manufacturing plants must be performed by carefully trained personnel. They must be familiar with the product engineering and design, manufacturing operations, and possess a knowledge of methods of cost allocations especially of the *fixed and variable* manufacturing overhead. Cost estimating is a form of forecasting under certain given conditions, and as such is closely akin to budgeting. Cost estimating procedures require a comparison of the estimates with the actual costs and a study of the differences. In this respect, it parallels budgeting when budgeted figures are compared with the actual figures. In recent years, a newer production and cost accounting procedure known as PERT (program evaluation and review technique) for planning, scheduling, and controlling complex manufacturing or construction projects has been developed. This also is an important phase of estimating costs and is closely related to budgeting.

The factors involved in cost estimates emphasize the engineering background that an estimator should possess. For example, for reliable estimates to be developed, he should have complete drawings and specifications of the product to be manufactured, the approximate volume of production, and a budget of the material, labor, and overhead costs. These must be supplemented by a knowledge of the manufacturing operations. Use will be made of previous estimates and previous actual cost records. When these characteristics have been accepted, a definite organization for estimating should be set up. Usually a centralized department organized under the supervision of the general manager has proven most effective.

Determination of Cost Estimates

Cost estimates are usually broken down into estimates of the elements of cost, viz: materials, labor, fixed charges, and apportioned charges. These estimates may be secured from records of past experience, from computations, from mathematical or chemical formulas, or simply from approximations. They must be computed for each different product. If there are many different products, the use of an estimating cost procedure becomes as expensive as a more complete system, with results that may be less accurate.

Estimates are prepared at the beginning of the manufacturing season; at the beginning of a fiscal period; or in the case of construction work, such as shipbuilding and tunnels, bridge, or building construction, when the contract is accepted.

The most common method of preparing estimates is by the *elements of cost,* viz:

ESTIMATED COST PER UNIT OF MANUFACTURING

Men's Fine Suits—Style J-47

```
Materials used................................................$13.25
Supplies (linings, buttons, etc.)...................................  3.75
Labor.......................................................  10.00
Factory overhead (50% of labor cost)............................   5.00
    Total...................................................$32.00
```

Whether or not this detail is necessary will depend upon the method or possibility of verifying *actual* figures with the *estimates.* In the case above, it is presumed that verification by the elements of cost will be possible and desirable.

Sometimes verification of actual with estimated costs will be on the basis of *elements of cost* figured departmentally and sometimes by *total costs.*

The figures given above are again presented to illustrate the estimates based upon the elements of costs, but this time they are analyzed on a departmental basis:

ESTIMATED COST PER UNIT OF MANUFACTURING

Men's Fine Suits—Style J-47

	Cutting Department	Tailoring Department	Total
Materials used........................	$13.25	....	$13.25
Supplies (linings, buttons, etc.).............	....	$ 3.75	3.75
Labor................................	3.00	7.00	10.00
Factory overhead (50% of labor)...........	1.50	3.50	5.00
Total............................	$17.75	$14.25	$32.00

If the verification of estimates is by total costs, the figure $32 is used without reference to the figures for material cost, labor cost, or overhead cost. Emphasis should again be laid on the fact that the nature of the estimates is governed by the method to be used in verifying actual costs with the estimates.

Many concerns have specially prepared forms on which the estimated figures are inserted. These forms are adapted to the products and processes of the particular business and thus simplify the estimating work. These estimated cost sheets may be used for computing the selling prices or for the purpose of recording the costs on an estimated basis. However, it is possible to have an estimated cost sheet and still use job order costs or process costs as a matter of record.

Illustration 15–1 shows a sample of an estimated cost sheet used in a plastics concern and is given as an illustration because of its completeness.

Responsibility for Setting Estimated Costs

Setting estimated costs is primarily an engineering job, supplemented by aid from the purchasing, budget, and accounting departments. Product design or improvements will be made by the engineering department aided by the sales or marketing divisions. Effective production procedures and flow of work will be estimated or established by the engineers and the factory supervisory force. Occasionally test runs may be used in the factory in which a large volume of production is anticipated. Through these test runs, the speed of production and the estimated labor costs can be established, and if necessary revisions in the flow of work through the factory can be made. Time and motion studies may be necessary also to determine estimated labor costs. By means of sales and production budgets and manufacturing overhead budgets, careful estimates can be made of the per unit overhead costs. These budgets require the cooperation of the engineering, factory supervisory, and the accounting and budget personnel. How expensive this procedure for setting the standards is will be determined by the scope of the manufacturing operations, the volume and variety of products, and thoroughness with which it is done. This cost of determining estimates must be weighed against the savings resulting from the use of an estimated cost accounting system as compared with a traditional, integrated cost accounting system.

Learning or Improvement Curve in Cost Estimating

With the event of automating machinery and the progressive assembly line, *direct labor costs* tend to decrease as the employees become more experienced. In a competitive price situation, the manufacturer must be able to estimate

Illustration 15–1

DETROIT MACOID CORPORATION
COST ESTIMATE SHEET FOR PLASTICS

Acme Motor Car Co.

Address: *Detroit*   Date: *April 30,*

Name of Part: *Knob*   Part No. *S-4930*

Description	Quantity	Unit Cost	Total Cost	Cost per C Pcs.
Material Cost				
Material Delivered	79.00	70	55.30	
Credits: Sprue 15.5%	12.25	45	5.51	
Scrap 0.3%	0.25	45	0.11	
Burn 11.4%	9.00	0	0	
Total Credits	21.5	26	5.62	
Net Material Cost	57.5	.864	49.68	.998
Production				
Gross 100.0%	5,006			
Scrap 0.5%	27			
Burn %	0			
Total Scrap 0.5%	27			
Net Prod. Pieces 99.5%	4,979			

	Hours	Rate	Total Cost	Cost Per C Pcs.
Labor and Burden Cost				
Molding Labor	17	4.00	68.00	1.366
Finishing Labor			70.00	1.406
Finishing Burdens 75%			52.50	1.054
Total Operating Cost			190.50	3.826

Summary:				
Statistics:	‖ Material Cost		49.68	0.998
Number in Mold 2	‖ Operation Cost		190.50	3.826
Mach. Prod. per Hr. 290	‖ Cost of Inserts		10.01	0.20
Wgt. of 1 Piece 5 Grams	‖			
Wgt. of C Pieces 500 Grams	‖Total Cost Without Molds		250.19	5.025
Material No. AW1702 M.S.	‖Sales & Adm. @ 30%		72.05	1.447
Estimator	‖ Mold Cost @ 10,000 Pcs.			5.000
Est. Mold Cost $500.00	‖ Mold Cost @ 50,000 Pcs.			1.000
	‖ Mold Cost @ 100,000 Pcs.			0.500

Prices Quoted	Cost	Profit	Price	‖Total Cost @ 10,000 Pcs.			11.472
Without Dies	$ 6.472	0.647	7.12	‖Total Cost @ 50,000 Pcs.			7.472
With Dies @ 10 M.	11.472	1.294	12.766	‖Total Cost @ 100,000 Pcs.			6.972
With Dies @ 50 M.	7.472	0.970	8.442	‖Remarks: *Prices and costs are in terms of C pieces*			
With Dies @ 100 M.	6.972	0.647	7.619	‖			

*Taken, with permission, from "Cost Accounting in the Plastic Molding Industry," by Robert W. Peden, N.A.(C.)A. Bulletin, Vol. XX, No. 9.

this change in direct labor costs. Several studies have been made of the influence of *learning with practice* on direct labor costs. In the large-scale manufacturing of television sets, it was found that

a) The larger the group size, that is, the length of the assembly line, the more complex the learning curve, since the line cannot progress faster than the slowest worker.

b) The more complex the operations, the longer it takes to improve the volume of production.

c) The extent of change in work procedures or flow of work from previous operations will influence the relearning.

d) Wage incentives influence the speed in which to achieve maximum production.

e) Supervisory pressure and union restrictions affect the speed of the learning process and the improved production.

f) Labor turnover rate and level of operators' skill influence the learning curve. If there is a constant labor turnover, the slowdown of the newer, inexperienced workers affects the volume of production.

In an estimating cost system, the work measurement engineers set the standard production at 100 percent efficiency as the ultimate objective of the production line, as well as the initial production of the inexperienced workers. As the employees become more experienced in their tasks, the ultimate objective may be approached. However, this is restricted if there is a large labor turnover resulting in a constant retraining of new employees.

Studies seem to indicate that as the employee on an assembly line or at a production area becomes more experienced, the time required for a task may be reduced 15 percent to 40 percent with the most common reduction about 20 percent. The learning curve is based on the principle that as the cumulative quantities double, the average time per unit should decrease 20 percent as illustrated:

		Time in Minutes		
Production in Units	*Cumulative Production*	*Cumulative*	*% Improvement of Previous Production*	*Time per Unit (Minutes)*
10	10	600	0	60
20	30	1,440	80%*	48
40	70	2,688	80	38.4
80	150	4,608	80	30.72
160	310	7,619	80	24.58
320	630	12,512	80	19.86

* Twenty percent improvement in production time.

The graph in Illustration 15–2 shows the effect of these changes in production and time.

It should be noted that the relationship between the assembly labor hours and the machine-hours generally determines the percentage decline in unit costs—the higher the ratio of assembly labor to total cost, the greater the decline in unit costs.

The learning curves are used as the basis for setting prices in such large-scale industries as the automobile, television industries, and in subcontracting at fair prices in the aerospace industries. It also is an important consideration in budgeting labor costs for the factory.

Illustration 15–2. Learning Curve Showing 20 Percent Time Reduction

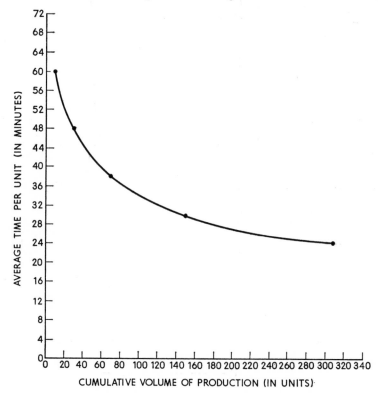

CUMULATIVE VOLUME OF PRODUCTION (IN UNITS)

Accounting Procedures for Estimated Costs   The estimated cost procedures discussed here are those which are used as the basis of the journal entries with a minimum of clerical expense. They may be summarized briefly as—

1. Charge the *work-in-process* for the *actual* costs of materials, labor, and manufacturing overhead incurred.
2. Charge the *finished goods* and cost of *sales accounts* for the *estimated* cost of the goods completed or sold, crediting either the *work-in-process* or *finished goods* accounts accordingly.
3. Take a physical inventory of the work-in-process at *estimated costs.* Find the difference between this figure and the amounts in the work-in-process accounts and transfer the differences to the *Adjustment account.* (These differences represent the errors due to incorrect estimates.)
4. Prorate the amount of the adjustments to the work-in-process, finished goods, and cost of goods sold, usually on the basis of units.

Applying these four rules of procedure to the specific elements of costs, the following discussion is given:

1. Materials Accounting. Purchases of materials are recorded in the voucher register by debiting the Stores account and crediting Accounts Payable. Where practical, a perpetual or book inventory of stores should be maintained. When the foregoing debit to Stores is posted at the end of the fiscal period—whether it be a month, six months, or a year—the Stores account will contain on the debit side the *inventory of materials at the beginning of the period and the purchases for the period.*

Thereafter, materials will be issued to the factory upon properly authorized requisitions specifying the quantities only, not the prices. These requisitions are not recorded unless a perpetual inventory is kept. At the end of a month, six months, or a yearly period, a physical inventory is taken of the direct materials on hand. The difference between the inventory of materials at the beginning of the period plus the purchases during the period and the inventory of the materials at the end of the period represents the cost of the materials used. This figure is used for the following entry:

```
Work-in-Process—Materials.........................................xxxx
    Stores......................................................      xxxx
```

The value stated in this entry is presumed to be *actual cost of the materials used.*

2. Labor Accounting. The *actual cost* of the factory labor, both direct and indirect, is transferred to the Work-in-Process—Labor account at the end of the fiscal accounting period.

3. Manufacturing Overhead Cost Accounting. This follows the same procedure as that for the labor accounting, namely, the transfer of the *actual overhead costs* to the work-in-process account at the end of the period.

4. Finished Goods Accounting. This is recorded at the end of the fiscal period by debiting the Finished Goods account and crediting the Work-in-Process account for the *estimated cost* of the goods completed. viz:

```
Finished Goods.......................................................xxxx
    Work-in-Process—Materials....................................   xxxx
    Work-in-Process—Labor........................................    xxxx
    Work-in-Process—Mfg. Overhead..............................     xxxx
```

When this entry is posted, the Finished Goods account will represent the *estimated cost value* of the finished work, but the work-in-process accounts will have debit figures on an *actual* cost basis and credit figures on an *estimated* cost basis.

5. Cost of Sales Accounting. Since the Finished Goods account has debit figures at the estimated costs, the transfers to the Cost of Sales account must of necessity be at the estimated costs, the entry being:

```
Cost of Sales (estimated cost)..........................................xxxx
    Finished Goods (estimated cost)................................    xxxx
```

At this stage of the accounting work, the estimated and actual costs of the accounting entries would be as follows:

Work-in-Process

Materials used *at actual*	xxxx	Finished goods *at estimated*	xxxx
Payroll costs *at actual*	xxxx		
Overhead costs *at actual*	xxxx		

Finished Goods

From work-in-process *at estimated*	xxxx	Cost of sales *at estimated*	xxxx

Cost of Sales

From finished goods *at estimated*	xxxx

Since the Work-in-Process account is the only account of the three above in which the debit (at actual) and the credit (at estimated costs) are not on the same cost basis, some adjustment of this conflict is necessary so that the Work-in-Process account will be on a comparable basis with the Finished Goods and Cost of Sales accounts in which both the debit and credit are at estimated costs.

6. Determining the Variation from Estimates. To adjust the conflict of bases indicated in the work-in-process accounts, a physical inventory is taken of the work-in-process priced at the *estimated cost value* for the *proportion of work done.* This physical inventory uses the *equivalent production* method described in chapters on process costs. For example, if the estimated cost of manufacturing a suit of clothes is:

```
Materials and supplies............................................$17
Labor...........................................................  10
Factory overhead (50% of labor)...................................   5
                                                                  ---
                                                                  $32
```

and the physical inventory of work-in-process showed 200 suits on which all the necessary material but only one fourth of the labor and overhead had been added, then the value of the inventory at estimated costs for the proportion of work done is calculated thus:

200 suits at $17 (material)..	$3,400
200 suits at ¼ of $10 (labor)..	500
200 suits at ¼ of $5 (for overhead).................................	250
Inventory of Work-in-Process for Proportion of Work Done.......	$4,150

The difference between this physical inventory of work-in-process priced at *estimated costs* and the inventory of work-in-process as recorded in the work-in-process accounts represents the *variation due to incorrect estimate.* This error may be adjusted in several ways:

a) The error may be spread over the *cost* of the effective production for the period, i.e., over the work-in-process, finished goods, and cost of sales priced at *estimated cost value.* This method has the effect of correcting the estimates and adjusting the inventories which will appear on the balance sheet and are used in determining the cost of goods sold on the income statement. When this adjustment has been made, the work-in-process inventory, the finished goods inventory, and the cost of sales will then be stated at the amounts that would have been secured if the original estimates had been correct and therefore had coincided with the actual costs.

b) The error may be spread over the cost of the work-in-process, finished goods, and cost of goods sold on the basis of the *number* of completed units or equivalent units. This method has the same effect as the first, but the error is corrected on the basis of *quantities* rather than *costs.*

To summarize the accounting procedure of an estimated cost system: (1) charge the Work-in-Process account with the *actual* cost of materials, labor, and overhead used in production; (2) charge the Finished Goods account, crediting the Work-in-Process account, for the *estimated* cost of work completed; (3) take a physical inventory of work-in-process at *estimated cost;* and (4) find the difference between the book and physical inventory of work-in-process and prorate the error over work-in-process, finished goods, and cost of goods sold on the basis of estimated cost or on the basis of equivalent production quantity of each.

Illustrations of Estimated Cost Accounting   Since the accounting for estimated costs revolves around the method of handling the work-in-process, illustrations of estimated cost procedures must be classified on the basis of the work-in-process accounts. Accounting procedures have therefore been classified according to the following work-in-process conditions: (1) the use of a single Work-in-Process account; (2) the use of a Work-in-Process account for each element of cost—

material, labor, and manufacturing overhead; (3) the use of a single
Work-in-Process account for each producing department; and (4) the
use of a Work-in-Process account for each element of cost in each
producing department.

To a certain extent, these methods overlap. Furthermore, the accounting work is considerably simplified if at the end of the cost accounting
period no unfinished work remains in process; under such conditions,
the variations from estimates can be closed out to the finished goods
inventory and the cost of goods sold on the basis of the number of units
manufactured and sold during the period if a single product is being
manufactured. Illustrations of the accounting procedure will be given
for (2) since that overlaps and practically includes (1), and for (4)
which overlaps and includes (3).

The Use of a Work-in-Process Account for Each Element of Cost

The estimated cost sheet for producing article B is:

ESTIMATED COSTS—ARTICLE B

Materials and supplies	$ 4
Labor	5
Manufacturing overhead	3
Total Estimated Cost	$12

From the books and records the following information was secured:

Inventory of materials and supplies, September 1	$ 1,200
Purchases of materials and supplies during September	15,800
A physical inventory of materials and supplies on September 30	600
Sales for the month	60,000
Payroll for month	16,310
Manufacturing overhead, including indirect labor	11,900

The production records for the month of September showed that
4,000 units were started into production. Of these, 3,000 were
completed and 1,000 were still in process. But of the unfinished work,
all the required material had been applied but only one half of the
required labor and overhead. Of the units completed, 2,500 were sold at
$24 each.

Entries in journal form to record the transactions for the month and
the ledger accounts prepared therefrom would be as follows:

(1)

Materials and Supplies	15,800.00	
Accounts Payable		15,800.00
To record purchases for the month.		

(2)

Work-in-Process—Materials...............................	16,400.00	
Materials and Supplies................................		16,400.00

To record the actual cost of materials and supplies used. Computed as follows: inventory at beginning plus purchases, minus inventory at end, or $1,200 + $15,800 − $600 = $16,400.

(3)

Work-in-Process—Labor.................................	16,310.00	
Payroll...		16,310.00

To close out the payroll into the work-in-process.

(4)

Work-in-Process—Manufacturing Overhead..................	11,900.00	
Manufacturing Overhead.............................		11,900.00

To close out the manufacturing overhead to the work-in-process.

(5)

Finished Goods...	36,000.00	
Work-in-Process—Materials...........................		12,000.00
Work-in-Process—Payroll.............................		15,000.00
Work-in-Process—Manufacturing Overhead..............		9,000.00

To record the value of the finished goods computed on the basis of estimated costs, 3,000 units at a total cost of $12 each.

(6)

Cost of Sales..	30,000.00	
Finished Goods......................................		30,000.00

Twenty-five hundred units sold at an estimated cost of $12 each, or a total value of $30,000.

(7)

Accounts Receivable....................................	60,000.00	
Sales..		60,000.00

Twenty-five hundred units sold at a selling price of $24 each, or $60,000.

It is now necessary to adjust the Work-in-Process, Finished Goods, and Cost of Goods Sold accounts for any variations between actual costs and estimated costs. Before doing so, it is advisable to post the foregoing transactions to determine the status of each of the ledger accounts. To the ledger accounts on the following pages there have been posted not only the foregoing transactions but also certain adjusting entries not yet discussed. By ignoring these adjustment entries for the moment, it is possible for the student to determine the status of each ledger account at this point in the procedure.

Materials and Supplies

Sept.	1	Inventory	1,200.00	Sept. 30	Used (2)	16,400.00
	30	Purchases (1)	15,800.00	30	Balance	600.00
			17,000.00			17,000.00
Sept.	30	Inventory	600.00			

Accounts Payable

	Sept. 30	Purchases (1)	15,800.00
	30	Payroll direct labor	16,310.00

Work-in-Process—Materials

Sept. 30	Materials (2)	16,400.00	Sept. 30	Finished goods (5)	12,000.00
30	Adjust (9a)	100.00	30	Adjust (8a)	400.00
			30	Balance	4,100.00
		16,500.00			16,500.00
Sept. 30	Inventory	4,100.00			

Work-in-Process—Labor

Sept. 30	Payroll direct labor (3)	16,310.00	Sept. 30	Finished goods (5)	15,000.00
30	Adjust (8b)	1,190.00	30	Adjust (9b)	170.00
			30	Balance	2,330.00
		17,500.00			17,500.00
Sept. 30	Inventory	2,330.00			

Payroll

Sept. 30	Accounts payable	16,310.00	Sept. 30	To close (3)	16,310.00

Work-in-Process—Manufacturing Overhead

Sept. 30	Applied (4)	11,900.00	Sept. 30	Finished goods (5)	9,000.00
30	Adjust (9c)	200.00	30	Adjust (8c)	1,400.00
			30	Balance	1,700.00
		12,100.00			12,100.00
Sept. 30	Inventory	1,700.00			

Finished Goods

Sept. 30	Completed (5)	36,000.00	Sept. 30	Sold (6)	30,000.00
30	Adjust (9a)	50.00	30	Adjust (9b)	170.00
30	Adjust (9c)	200.00	30	Balance	6,080.00
		36,250.00			36,250.00
Sept. 30	Inventory	6,080.00			

Cost of Sales

Sept. 30	Finished goods (6)	30,000.00	Sept. 30 Adjust (9b) 850.00
30	Adjust (9a)	250.00	
30	Adjust (9c)	1,000.00	

Accounts Receivable

Sept. 30 Sales (7)	60,000.00

Sales

	Sept. 30 Accts. rec. (7) 60,000.00

The *book* inventory of work-in-process as of September 30 (before adjustment for errors in estimates) and the physical inventory priced at estimated cost are presented in Illustration 15–3.

Illustration 15–3

	Present Book Inventory as Shown in the Accounts	Computed Inventory on Estimated Cost Basis	Variation
Work-in-process—materials..........................$4,400	....	....
Work-in-process—materials (1,000 equivalent production at $4 each unit).............................	$4,000	$ 400*
Work-in-process—labor............................. 1,310	....	....
Work-in-process—labor (1,000 units ½ completed at $5)	2,500	1,190†
Work-in-process—manufacturing overhead............ 2,900	....	....
Work-in-process—manufacturing overhead (1,000 units ½ completed at $3).............................	1,500	1,400*

* Indicates estimated costs too low.
† Indicates estimated costs too high.

In order to adjust the balances in the work-in-process accounts to an estimated cost basis, the variations shown above are transferred to an Adjustment account. The necessary entries are:

(8a)

Adjustment Account...	400.00	
Work-in-Process—Materials...............................		400.00

(8b)

Work-in-Process—Labor......................................1,190.00		
Adjustment Account......................................		1,190.00

(8c)

Adjustment Account...	1,400.00	
Work-in-Process—Manufacturing Overhead.................		1,400.00

To adjust the work-in-process accounts to the estimated cost figures. Separate entries were made for each, since each figure will have to be prorated separately later.

When these entries have been posted, the work-in-process accounts will be costed on the same basis as the Finished Goods and the Cost of Sales accounts—*the estimated cost basis.* Therefore, the Adjustment account must be prorated over all of these accounts in order to bring them to the amounts that would be there if the estimated costs had been absolutely correct. Entries are made for each adjustment separately, and proration may be on the basis of equivalent units or cost values; in this case, the results on either basis are the same. The entries are:

(9a)

Work-in-Process—Materials....................................	100.00	
Finished Goods...	50.00	
Cost of Sales..	250.00	
Adjustment Account......................................		400.00

To prorate the material cost variation arising from estimates that were too low. The ratio used was work-in-process, 1,000; finished goods, 500; cost of sales, 2,500; these figures represent the number of units or equivalent production for the material cost.

(9b)

Adjustment Account...	1,190.00	
Work-in-Process—Labor....................................		170.00
Finished Goods...		170.00
Cost of Sales...		850.00

To prorate the labor cost variation arising from estimates which were too high. The ratio used was work-in-process, 500 (1,000 × ½ complete); finished goods, 500; and cost of sales, 2,500; these figures represent the number of units or the equivalent production for the labor cost.

(9c)

Work-in-Process—Manufacturing Overhead.....................	200.00	
Finished Goods...	200.00	
Cost of Sales..	1,000.00	
Adjustment Account......................................		1,400.00

To prorate the manufacturing overhead cost variation arising from estimates which were too low. The ratio used was the same as that for labor.

The Adjustment account is not always used; instead, the net amount taken from or added to the Work-in-Process account is prorated directly to the Finished Goods and Cost of Sales accounts.

The statements suggested for use with estimated costs are of a managerial type; that is, they are used by management to evaluate the results of their estimates. The statements sent to stockholders or used for financial purposes show only the actual costs, that is, the costs after adjustment. The managerial statements prepared when estimated costs are used are shown in Illustrations 15–4 and 15–5; these are based on the amounts in the foregoing entries.

Illustration 15–4. One Form of Cost of Goods Manufactured Statement When Estimated Costs Are Used

Schedule B-1

ALTON MANUFACTURING COMPANY
SCHEDULE OF COST OF GOODS MANUFACTURED
For Month of September, 19—

Material Cost, at Estimate			$16,000.00
Labor Cost, at Estimate			17,500.00
Manufacturing Overhead Cost, at Estimate			10,500.00
Total Estimated Cost			$44,000.00
Adjustments:			
Material Cost, at Actual	$16,400.00		
Material Cost, at Estimate	16,000.00		
Underestimate		$ 400.00	
Manufacturing Overhead, at Actual	$11,900.00		
Manufacturing Overhead, at Estimate	10,500.00		
Underestimate		1,400.00	
Total Underestimate		$1,800.00	
Labor, at Actual	$16,310.00		
Labor, at Estimate	17,500.00		
Total Overestimate		1,190.00	
Net Underestimate			610.00
Actual Manufacturing Cost Put into Production			$44,610.00
Less: Inventory, Work-in-Process:			
Material Cost, at Estimate	$ 4,000.00		
Labor Cost, at Estimate	2,500.00		
Manufacturing Overhead, at Estimate	1,500.00		
Total at Estimate	$ 8,000.00		
Add: Adjustment for Underestimate:			
Material	$100.00		
Labor	170.00*		
Manufacturing Overhead	200.00	130.00	
Adjusted Work-in-Process Inventory			8,130.00
Actual Cost of Goods Manufactured to Exhibit B, Income Statement			$36,480.00

* Overestimated figures.

Illustration 15–5.   A Second Form of Cost of Goods Manufactured Statement When Estimated Costs Are Used

Schedule B-1

ALTON MANUFACTURING COMPANY

SCHEDULE OF COST OF GOODS MANUFACTURED
For Month of September, 19—

	Estimated Cost	Adjustment Cost	Actual Cost
Material Costs.........................	$16,000.00	$ 400.00	$16,400.00
Labor Costs............................	17,500.00	1,190.00*	16,310.00
Manufacturing Overhead Costs............	10,500.00	1,400.00	11,900.00
Total..............................	$44,000.00	$ 610.00	
Total Actual Manufacturing Cost......................................			$44,610.00
Less: Inventory of Work-in-Process:			
Material Costs.........................	$ 4,000.00	$ 100.00	
Labor Costs...........................	2,500.00	170.00*	
Manufacturing Overhead Costs..........	1,500.00	200.00	
Total..............................	$ 8,000.00	$ 130.00	8,130.00
Actual Cost of Goods Manufactured.....................................			$36,480.00

* Overestimated figures.

Exhibit B

ALTON MANUFACTURING COMPANY

INCOME STATEMENT
For Month of September, 19—

Sales..			$60,000.00
Cost of Sales:			
Cost of Goods Manufactured per Schedule B-1...............		$36,480.00	
Less: Inventory of Finished Goods:			
At estimate...............................	$6,000.00		
Add: Adjustments:			
Material...........................$ 50.00			
Labor............................ 170.00*			
Manufacturing Overhead............ 200.00			
Net Underestimate.................·———	80.00		
		6,080.00	
Cost of Sales, at actual (adjusted).....................................			30,400.00
Gross Profit on Sales...			$29,600.00†

* Overestimate.
† From this figure must be subtracted the selling and administrative expenses.

Estimated Costs Where the Work-in-Process Is Kept by Elements of Costs and by Departments A more complicated cost accounting situation arises where the manufacturing operations go through several departments and where the work-in-process accounts are maintained by elements of cost for each department. To illustrate the procedure, the following information, entries, and ledger accounts are used.

The estimated cost card for manufacturing a certain article is represented in Illustration 15–6.

Illustration 15–6

Estimated Cost Card No. 8			Date of Estimate
Product X-Y Style: Large			9/1/—
	Dept. A	Dept. B	Total by Elements
Materials and Supplies:			
5 yds. of material @ $0.60	$ 3.00		
Supplies	0.60		$ 3.60
Labor:			
2 hours @ $1.50	3.00		
1½ hours @ $1.20	1.80		
3 hours @ $1.60		$4.80	9.60
Manufacturing Overhead:			
3½ hours @ $0.80	2.80		
50% of $4.80		2.40	5.20
Total Estimated Cost	$11.20	$7.20	$18.40

From the books of record the following data have been ascertained:

Inventory of materials and supplies at beginning of month	$ 1,300
Purchases of materials and supplies during month	13,260
Materials and supplies on hand at the end of the month (determined by physical inventory)	2,500
Sales for the month	50,000

Departmental Charges for the Month	Dept. A	Dept. B	Total
Direct labor payroll*	$13,300	$13,500	$26,800
Indirect labor payroll*	210	230	440
Fixed charges	4,026	3,000	7,026
Apportioned manufacturing overhead costs	4,820	3,200	8,020

* In this illustration, factory payroll is separated into direct and indirect labor, the latter being part of overhead.

Illustration 15–7 shows the production record for the month.

Illustration 15–7

	Dept. A	Dept. B	Total
Number of units in process at the beginning of the month—all materials and supplies have been issued against them, but labor and overhead averaged 60% completion...............	100	200	
Number of units completed during month including those in process at the beginning.......3,000		3,100	
Units in process at the end of month on which all the material had been issued, but labor and overhead averaged 40% completion........	200	100	
Number of units sold..........................			2,500

Solution

The value of the initial inventory of the work-in-process is analyzed and computed as shown in Illustration 15–8:

Illustration 15–8

	Dept. A	Dept. B Transfer Account	Dept. B
Materials and supplies:			
100 units at $3.60..............................$360			
200 units at 3.60..............................		$ 720	
Labor:			
100 units × 60% × $4.80......................... 288			
200 units × 100% × 4.80.........................		960	
200 units × 60% × 4.80.........................			$576
Factory overhead:			
100 units × 60% × $2.80......................... 168			
200 units × 100% × 2.80.........................		560	
200 units × 60% × 2.40.........................			288
Total Initial Work-in-Process Inventories.........$816		$2,240	$864

The journal entries necessary to record some of the transactions for the month to illustrate the procedures of estimated cost are:

(1)

Purchases—Materials and Supplies.............................13,260.00
    Accounts Payable..   13,260.00
    To record the purchases of materials and supplies for the month.

(2)

Work-in-Process—Materials, Dept. A	12,060.00	
Materials and Supplies		12,060.00

To record the actual cost of the materials and supplies used, computed as follows: inventory at beginning plus purchases, minus inventory at end, or $1,300 + $13,260 − $2,500 = $12,060.

(3)

Work-in-Process—Labor, Dept. A	13,300.00	
Work-in-Process—Manufacturing Overhead, Dept. A	210.00	
Payroll Accrued		13,510.00

To record actual amounts expended for payroll in Dept. A, for both direct and indirect labor.

(4)

Work-in-Process—Manufacturing Overhead, Dept. A	8,846.00	
Manufacturing Overhead		8,846.00

To record the actual fixed and apportioned manufacturing overhead incurred during the month.

(5)

Work-in-Process—Transfer Account, Dept. B[1]	33,600.00	
Work-in-Process—Materials, Dept. A		10,800.00
Work-in-Process—Labor, Dept. A		14,400.00
Work-in-Process—Manufacturing Overhead, Dept. A		8,400.00

By the use of the Work-in-Process—Transfer account, to record the cost of the goods transferred to Dept. B, computed on the basis of 3,000 units which were transferred to Dept. B from Dept. A:

Materials................3,000 @ $3.60 = $10,800
Labor...................3,000 @ 4.80 = 14,400
Manufacturing overhead.....3,000 @ 2.80 =   8,400

(6)

Work-in-Process—Labor, Dept. B	13,500.00	
Work-in-Process—Manufacturing Overhead, Dept. B	230.00	
Payroll Accrued		13,730.00

To record actual amounts expended for payroll during month in Dept. B, both direct and indirect labor.

(7)

Work-in-Process—Manufacturing Overhead, Dept. B	6,200.00	
Manufacturing Overhead		6,200.00

To record the actual fixed and apportioned manufacturing overhead incurred during the month in Dept. B.

(8)

Finished Goods	57,040.00	
Work-in-Process—Transfer Account, Dept. B		34,720.00
Work-in-Process—Labor, Dept. B		14,880.00
Work-in-Process—Manufacturing Overhead, Dept. B		7,440.00

To record the value of the finished goods transferred from Dept. B. 3,100 units at a cost as follows: Dept. A at $11.20; labor, Dept. B, $4.80; and manufacturing overhead, Dept. B, $2.40.

(9)

Costs of Sales	46,000.00	
Finished Goods		46,000.00

To record the sale of 2,500 units at an estimated cost of $18.40 each, or total, $46,000.

---

[1] When a *Work-in-Process—Transfer account* is used, this account is considered as the Finished Goods account when related to the work done in Department A, and as the Work-in-Process—Materials account when related to the work done in Department B.

(10)

```
Accounts Receivable..............................................50,000.00
    Sales..................................................              50,000.00
    To record the selling price of the goods sold during the month.
```

The final inventory of work-in-process in analyzed form, priced at *estimated cost* per unit, is calculated as shown in Illustration 15–9.

Illustration 15–9

	Dept. A	*Dept. B Transfer Account	Dept. B
Materials and supplies:			
200 units @ $3.60............................	$ 720		
100 units @ 3.60............................		$ 360	
Labor:			
200 units 40% × $3.00........................	240		
200 units 40% × 1.80........................	144		
100 units 100% × $3.00........................		300	
100 units 100% × 1.80........................		180	
100 units × 40% × $4.80.....................			$192
Factory overhead:			
200 units × 40% × $2.80.......................	224		
100 units 100% × $2.80........................		280	
100 units × 40% × $2.40.....................			96
Total Closing Work-in-Process Inventories, at estimated cost.........................	$1,328	$1,120	$288

* This Transfer account is similar in theory to the Finished Goods account of Department A. Adjustments must first be made for Department A before considering adjustments for Department B accounts.

In order to ascertain the variation between the work-in-process inventory accounts at estimated cost, as shown above, and the *book* inventory of the work-in-process accounts, it is necessary to reconstruct the accounts from the entries made during and at the end of the period:

Work-in-Process—Materials, Dept. A

Inventory at beginning	360.00	(5)	10,800.00
(2)	12,060.00	Balance	1,620.00
	12,420.00		12,420.00
Balance before adjustment	1,620.00		

Work-in-Process—Labor, Dept. A

Inventory at beginning	288.00	(5)	14,400.00
(3)	13,300.00		
Balance	812.00		
	14,400.00		14,400.00
		Balance before adjustment	812.00

Work-in-Process—Manufacturing Overhead, Dept. A

Inventory at beginning	168.00	(5)	8,400.00
(3)	210.00	Balance	824.00
(4)	8,846.00		
	9,224.00		9,224.00
Balance before adjustment	824.00		

Work-in-Process—Transfer Account, Dept. B

Inventory at the beginning	2,240.00	(8)	34,720.00
(5)	33,600.00	Balance	1,120.00
	35,840.00		35,840.00
Balance before adjustment	1,120.00		

Work-in-Process—Labor, Dept. B

Inventory at beginning	576.00	(8)	14,880.00
(6)	13,500.00		
Balance	804.00		
	14,880.00		14,880.00
		Balance before adjustment	804.00

Work-in-Process—Manufacturing Overhead, Dept. B

Inventory at beginning	288.00	(8)	7,440.00
(6)	230.00		
(7)	6,200.00		
Balance	722.00		
	7,440.00		7,440.00
		Balance before adjustment	722.00

Finished Goods

(8)	57,040.00	(9)	46,000.00

Cost of Sales

(9)	46,000.00		

A comparative summary of the book inventory of the work-in-process taken from the foregoing accounts and the work-in-process computed on the basis of *estimated costs* (see schedule, page 458) presents the figures shown in Illustration 15–10, but attention is directed to the fact

Illustration 15–10

Account	Book Inventory Taken from the Accounts	Computed Inventory on Estimated Cost Basis per Schedule, p. 458	Variation
Work-in-Process—Materials Department A	$1,620	$ 720	$ 900†
Work-in-Process—Labor Department A	812 Cr.	384	1,196‡
Work-in-Process—Mfg. Overhead Department A	824	224	600†
Work-in-Process—Transfer Account Department B	1,120	1,120	0*
Work-in-Process—Labor Department B	804 Cr.	192	996‡
Work-in-Process—Mfg. Overhead Department B	722 Cr.	96	818‡

* Before adjustment for Department A variations.
† Indicates estimates too low.
‡ Indicates estimates too high.

that the Work-in-Process—Transfer Account, Department B, shows no variation and will not until adjustments have been made in Department A.

As previously stated, the variations from estimates may be closed out by apportioning the amounts to the Work-in-Process, Finished Goods, and Cost of Sales accounts or by transferring the entire amount to the Cost of Sales account. The former seems more desirable for estimated costs; the latter more practical for standard costs. The use of an Adjustment or Estimated Cost Variation account simplifies the accounting work. The entry to transfer the variations to the Adjustment account is:

(11)

Work-in-Process—Labor, Dept. A................................1,196.00		
Work-in-Process—Labor, Dept. B.............................. 996.00		
Work-in-Process—Manufacturing Overhead, Dept. B.............. 818.00		
Work-in-Process—Materials, Dept. A........................	900.00	
Work-in-Process—Manufacturing Overhead, Dept. A...........	600.00	
Adjustment Account..	1,510.00	

To transfer the estimated cost variations to the Adjustment account, thus leaving the balances in all work-in-process accounts at estimated cost.

Although the Adjustment account may be closed by apportioning the amount to the Work-in-Process, Finished Goods, and Cost of Sales accounts on the basis of the equivalent number of units produced in each, it is usually easier, where the accounting for estimated costs is quite involved, as in this instance, to make the corrections of the estimated costs on the basis of the estimated cost values in each account.

In order to do this, the amount of each variation must be apportioned between the Work-in-Process accounts, the Finished Goods account, and the Cost of Goods Sold account. The simplest way to do this is to set up a detailed tabulation showing the estimated cost figures in each account, and then to compute the proration. In this tabulation, for example, the variation in the Work-in-Process—Materials, Department A, is $900 (see Illustration 15–11). The balances at estimated material cost in the respective accounts are:

Work-in-Process—Materials, Dept. A (see p. 458)......................$ 720	
Work-in-Process—Transfer account, Dept. B (see p. 458)................ 360	
Finished Goods, 600 units at $3.60 (see estimated cost sheet, p. 455)...... 2,160	
Cost of Goods Sold, 2,500 units at $3.60 (see cost sheet, p. 455).......... 9,000	
Total Basis of Proration for Material Cost Variation................$12,240	

The same procedure is followed for labor costs in Department A, labor costs in Department B, manufacturing overhead in Department A, and manufacturing overhead in Department B. Illustration 15–12 (p. 463) shows the estimated cost figures now in the accounts, the amount of the adjustments, and the verification.

Below is the summary adjustment entry which should be made to close out the variations of the estimated costs from the actual costs (in other words, to adjust the estimated figures to the actual):

Work-in-Process—Materials, Dept. A 52.94	
Work-in-Process—Manufacturing Overhead, Dept. A.............. 14.63	
Work-in-Process—Transfer Account, Dept. B..................... 8.29	
Adjustment Account..1,510.06	
Work-in-Process—Labor, Dept. A..........................	29.18
Work-in-Process—Labor, Dept. B...........................	12.69
Work-in-Process—Manufacturing Overhead, Dept. B..........	10.42
Finished Goods...	296.81
Cost of Sales...	1,236.82

Illustration 15–11

TABULATION SHOWING THE ESTIMATED COST FIGURES IN THE VARIOUS ACCOUNTS, THE AMOUNT OF THE ADJUSTMENTS AND THE ADJUSTED TOTAL (ACTUAL) FOR EACH ACCOUNT

	MATERIAL PUT INTO PROCESS IN DEPARTMENT A			LABOR COSTS IN DEPARTMENT A			LABOR COSTS IN DEPARTMENT B			MANUFACTURING OVERHEAD, DEPARTMENT A			MANUFACTURING OVERHEAD, DEPARTMENT B		
	Balance at Estimated	Adjustment*	Adjusted to Actual	Balance at Estimated	Adjustment	Adjusted to Actual	Balance at Estimated	Adjustment	Adjusted to Actual	Balance at Estimated	Adjustment	Adjusted to Actual	Balance at Estimated	Adjustment	Adjusted to Actual
Department A...........	$ 720.00	$ 52.94	$ 772.94	$ 384.00	$ 29.18*	$ 354.82				$ 224.00	$ 14.63	$ 238.63			
Department B—Transfer...........	360.00	26.47	386.47	480.00	36.47*	443.53				280.00	18.29	298.29			
Department B...........							$ 192.00	$ 12.69*	$ 179.31				$ 96.00	$ 10.42*	$ 85.58
Finished Goods: 600 @ $3.60 600 @ 4.80 600 @ 4.80 600 @ 2.80 600 @ 2.40	2,160.00	158.83	2,318.83	2,880.00	218.79*	2,661.21	2,880.00	190.30*	2,689.70	1,680.00	109.76	1,789.76	1,440.00	156.31*	1,283.69
Cost of Goods Sold: 2,500 @ $3.60 2,500 @ 4.80 2,500 @ 4.80 2,500 @ 2.80 2,500 @ 2.40	9,000.00	661.77	9,661.77	12,000.00	911.64*	11,088.36	12,000.00	792.96*	11,207.04	7,000.00	457.31	7,457.31	6,000.00	651.30*	5,348.70
TOTAL...........	$12,240.00	$900.01	$13,140.01	$15,744.00	$1,196.08*	$14,547.92	$15,072.00	$995.95*	$14,076.05	$9,184.00	$599.99	$9,783.99	$7,536.00	$818.03*	$6,717.97

* Credit.

COMPUTATIONS

$ 900.00 / 12,240.00 = .07353	$ 1,196.00 / 15,744.00 = .07597	$ 996.00 / 15,072.00 = .06608	$ 600.00 / 9,184.00 = .06533	$ 818.00 / 7,536.00 = .10855

$ 720.00 X .07353 = $ 52.94
360.00 X .07353 = 26.47
2,160.00 X .07353 = 158.83
9,000.00 X .07353 = 661.77
$900.01

$ 384.00 X .07597 = $ 29.18
480.00 X .07597 = 36.47
2,880.00 X .07597 = 218.79
12,000.00 X .07597 = 911.64
$1,196.08

$ 192.00 X .06608 = $ 12.69
2,880.00 X .06608 = 190.30
12,000.00 X .06608 = 792.96
$995.95

$ 224.00 X .06533 = $ 14.63
280.00 X .06533 = 18.29
1,680.00 X .06533 = 109.76
7,000.00 X .06533 = 457.31
$599.99

$ 96.00 X .10855 = $ 10.42
1,440.00 X .10855 = 156.31
6,000.00 X .10855 = 651.30
$818.03

Illustration 15–12

TABLE SHOWING THE SUMMARY OF ADJUSTMENTS OF ESTIMATED COSTS TO ACTUAL
(Prepared from tabulation on page 462)

Account	Amount of Adjustment	Work-in-Process Accounts						Finished Goods	Cost of Goods Sold
		Materials, Dept A	Labor, Dept. A	Overhead, Dept. A	Transfer Account, Dept. B	Labor, Dept. B	Overhead, Dept. B		
Materials Used in Department A...	$ 900.01 Dr.	$52.94			$26.47			$158.83	$ 661.77
Labor Used in Department A......	1,196.08 Cr.		$29.18*		36.47*			218.79*	911.64*
Manufacturing Overhead, Department A........	599.99 Dr.			$14.63	18.29			109.76	457.31
Labor Used in Department B......	995.95 Cr.					$12.69*		190.30*	792.96*
Manufacturing Overhead, Department B........	818.03 Cr.						$10.42*	156.31*	651.30*
	$1,510.06 Cr.	$52.94	$29.18*	$14.63	$ 8.29	$12.69*	$10.42*	$296.81*	$1,236.82*

* Credit.

When this entry is posted, the inventory accounts will all have been adjusted to correct the error caused by inaccurate estimates. The same procedure will be followed at the close of each succeeding accounting period. However, the Transfer account may cause some difficulty if after adjustment for this period the estimated costs for the next period are revised. In that event the adjustment must be made on the basis of the revised estimates and the actual costs as adjusted for the previous period.

Estimated Costs When Two or More Products Are Manufactured When two or more products are manufactured at the same time, a similar procedure as discussed above is followed. A separate Work-in-Process account for each product is necessary however.

Since the total cost of the materials used is determined by computation, i.e., inventory at beginning plus purchases minus inventory at the end, some method must be used whereby the material costs are allocated to the several work-in-process accounts. If the same quantity of each product is produced, a ratio of the estimated material cost of each may be used. For example:

Estimated Costs	Product A	Product B
Material....................	$ 7	$ 3
Labor......................	6	5
Overhead..................	4	4
	$17	$12

Materials used for the period cost $8,500. The *same number of units* of Product A and Product B were started into process. Material costs are charged to the Work-in-Process—Product A and Product B accounts on a 70 percent and 30 percent basis, i.e., on the basis of unit cost of material for each. If the volume started into process for each product is not the same, the estimated value of the material to be used in each product must be weighted by the quantity started into process and be used in calculating the percentages for apportioning the actual material costs for a given period.

A similar procedure is followed in apportioning the actual labor and manufacturing overhead costs to Work-in-Process—Product A and Product B accounts. *Physical* inventories of the Work-in-Process—Product A and Product B, taken at estimated costs and compared with the book inventories, indicate the amount of the material, labor, and overhead adjustment. The adjustment is made to the

Work-in-Process and Finished Goods accounts in the manner previously discussed for each product on the basis of the percentages previously used. For example, the materials adjustment for the work-in-process is $1,200. Of this amount, 70 percent is applicable to Product A and 30 percent to Product B.

This procedure becomes quite complicated, especially when many different products are produced at the same time. A more complete historical or standard cost system would not be much more expensive to operate than such a complicated estimated cost system, and the results would certainly be more satisfactory.

If a number of similar products of varying *sizes* or *styles* are manufactured, apportioning the amount of the adjustments to the various styles or sizes is impractical. The adjustments are then made through the accounts representing the work-in-process, finished goods, and cost of sales for the *total* production of a given period.

PERT-Time and PERT-Cost as a Phase of Estimating Costs

PERT began as a technique to help solve the problems of developing the Polaris Missile by setting out in logical fashion the sequence and time of the steps necessary for the completion of the project. PERT is a recent tool of management associated with cost control. PERT, defined as Program Evaluation and Review Technique, is a development of the governmental agencies for cost control of defensive purchases and contracts. In 1961 PERT was used for only 19 percent of private commercial work. By 1963, PERT users showed over 50 percent in private commercial work, and in a study of 44 companies, it was found that time savings for more than 75 percent of the firms ranged from 10 percent to more than 31 percent. PERT has been used in designing, developing, and using new machines; streamlining paperwork systems; and scheduling commercial aircraft transport production.

PERT must be separated into its two elements—PERT-Time and PERT-Cost. PERT may also be described as a phase of systems management aiming at greater efficiency through lower costs. It is therefore an important element of cost accounting especially in the area of estimated costs and budgeting.

PERT-Time is the basic analysis by management of the problem of producing a maximum volume with a minimum delay of time. PERT-Time is based on the principle that there may be a number of operations which can be completed simultaneously rather than sequentially, thus reducing the time of the finished product manufacture when the simultaneous operations are merged. The planning of the sequence and merging of the various operations is known as the Critical Path Method (CPM). The integration of the sequence and merging is shown in the PERT-Network.

PERT-Time Operations   The culmination of PERT-Time is a diagram known as the network, which represents the beginning and ending of activities representing a finished product or finished project. The activities represent the various tasks to complete the job and are timed. The sequence and flow of these tasks follows the critical path outlined by management and engineering. The network is a well-thought-out plan upon which is superimposed the activities time and the flow of work. The most satisfactory achievement indicates the maximum time required to complete the job along the critical path.

The network (see Illustration 15–13) pictures all the activities which must be performed before the final product is completed. It also pictures the times required for each so that the date of completion can be set. Thus a budget is projected, and the probable costs are estimated. PERT-Cost is part of this budget program, but it is based upon activity time, not on the fiscal accounting period. Emphasis is placed on the

Illustration 15–13. Critical Path Network—The Plan

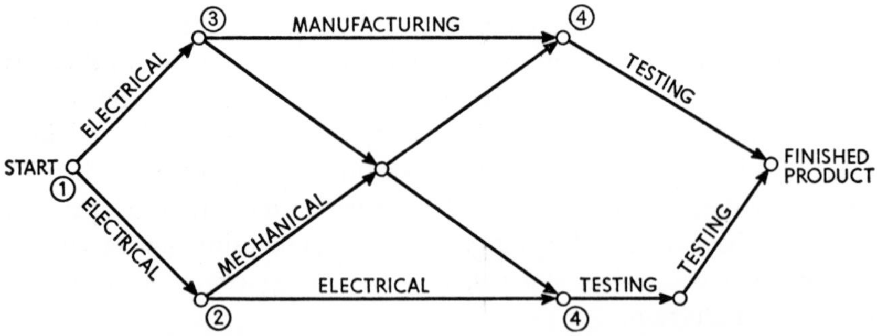

projected work packages, not the annual budget. It is predicated on *activity time*—the time to complete a project or some phase of the project. This network diagram is the cornerstone of PERT-Time. It is a logical plan incorporating the events and activities. In this illustration, the work packages might be:

1. Electrical work.
2. Mechanical work.
3. Assembling (Manufacturing).
4. Testing.

The costs can be estimated once the network has been established. These costs can be estimated in various ways: (1) a single expected actual cost estimate; (2) a triple cost estimate as the *best estimate,* the *most likely estimate,* and the most *pessimistic* costs; or (3) the *optimum* time for completing the project with the resulting effect on costs.

The Critical Path Network indicates the plan or flow of work of operations, indicating those that can be completed simultaneously. A second network should be prepared indicating the time requirements for each activity and the optimum time for completing the project. (See Illustration 15–14.)

Two of the electrical activities can be completed simultaneously, thus saving 100 hours. Some of the mechanical, manufacturing, assembling, and electrical work can be completed simultaneously, as can some of the testing. The maximum time should be electrical, 120 hours; manufacturing, 210 hours; testing, 60 hours—total 390 hours when allowance is made for simultaneous manufacturing activities.

Illustration 15–14. The Network—Time Estimate

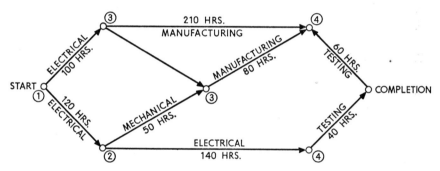

Once this time estimate has been computed, it is possible to prepare a manufacturing schedule indicating the operations, the time when the various activities are to be started and completed, and the date of completion. All of these seem to be estimated costs and budgeted operations.

PERT-Costs

As may have been noted, PERT-Cost is the managerial tool which must be coordinated with PERT-Time in estimating costs in project planning and control. PERT-Cost results not only in financial reporting both on the cost accounting and individual manager's level but it is basic in decision making in the planning and managerial control phases of the project. Some of the problems of PERT-Cost which have not yet been resolved are:

1. A lack of sophisticated analysis of costs for decision making in many firms.
2. Lack of historical cost data for many of the projects involved in the network because the products have not been manufactured previously.

3. Since PERT-Time often overlaps the fiscal accounting period, there may be a conflict in reconciling PERT-Costs with those of the fiscal accounting period.

QUESTIONS FOR REVIEW

1. Explain the advisability of using estimated costs by the following business firms: (*a*) manufacturer of specially designed drilling and stamping machines; (*b*) manufacturer of washing machines; (*c*) manufacturer of missile projectors for the government on a cost plus a fixed fee basis; (*d*) a commercial building contractor erecting a 20-story office building requiring a year and one half for completion.

2. What conditions and advantages warrant the use of an estimated costing procedure?

3. How are cost estimates usually determined?

4. Outline the steps to be followed in the accounting procedure for estimated costs when a single product is being manufactured. What changes will be made in this procedure if there is no work-in-process inventory at the end of the accounting period?

5. What is the purpose of the adjustment account? The transfer account?

6. What procedure will be followed if no adjustment account is to be used? What procedure will be followed if no transfer account is to be used?

7. Are material requisitions necessary if an estimated cost system is used? Explain. Does this provide adequate internal control of inventories?

8. The Reliable Machine Company uses an estimated cost accounting system in the manufacture of its single product. At the end of each accounting period, the firm uses its estimated cost of manufacturing corrected for the current operations for the next manufacturing period. During the current period, 12,000 units were started, 9,000 completed, 8,000 sold. In process at the end of the period, 90 percent complete as to materials, 40 percent complete as to labor and overhead costs, 3,000 units.

   Material costs were $765,000; labor costs, $463,300; and overhead costs, $182,280.

   The estimated costs per machine were: materials, $65; labor, $45; and overhead costs, $20.

   Compute the amount of the adjustment (total) for materials, labor, and overhead.

9. Why does the estimated cost procedure seem impractical when a large number of different products are being manufactured?

10. How will the cost of materials be determined when an estimated cost accounting system is used when there is no perpetual (book) inventory, no requisitions, and two different products are being manufactured at the same time?

PROBLEMS—GROUP A

Problem 15–1. Purpose: *Estimated Costs for Single Product; Journal Entries; T-Ledger Accounts; Cost of Goods Sold Statement*

The Waltron Machine Company uses an estimated cost system in manufacturing its single product. The estimated cost per unit during the first year of its operations were:

Material costs......................	$40
Labor costs........................	15
Manufacturing overhead..............	3
	$58

The seasonal nature of the sales of this product requires that production be concentrated in the period through August and November of each year. Other products are manufactured during the off season.

During the first season, 1,500 machines were started into production, of which 1,200 were completed and 1,000 were sold. The unfinished production had 80 percent of the materials and 50 percent of the labor and overhead applied.

From the books of the firm, the following additional information has been obtained:

Materials inventory, August 1, carried over from previous business operations amounted to...	$41,620
Materials on hand, November 30, the date of this problem.................	30,000
Materials purchased during the period, 8/1–11/30.........................	50,300
Factory payroll...	22,950
Manufacturing overhead costs...	3,105

From this information, you are asked to prepare:

a) Entries in journal form to record the manufacturing operations, using three work-in-process accounts, one each for materials, labor, and manufacturing overhead, and adjustment account, a finished goods account, and a cost of sales account.

b) Post to the T-ledger accounts.

c) Prepare a statement of the cost of goods sold.

d) Calculate the estimated costs for the next year assuming that the operating conditions will be the same as for this season.

Problem 15–2. Purpose: *Estimated Cost Accounting for Two Products Manufactured in a Single Department; Journal Entries and T-Ledger Accounts*

The Worth Manufacturing Company produces ladies' and children's coats using essentially the same materials and labor operations in each. This firm has two lines of merchandise: one for the spring and summer line, being manufactured in the fall of each year, and the fall and winter lines being produced during the spring of each year.

Estimated costs are kept separately for each season's production since the materials, styles, and labor operations vary from season to season. For the spring and summer line being produced from July 1 through December 1, 19—, the estimated cost sheets indicated the following costs and estimates:

Element of Costs	Ladies' Coats	Children's Coats
Material costs..........................	$30	$15
Labor costs.............................	40	10
Manufacturing overhead costs.............	10	5
Total................................	$80	$30

The costs incurred during this season's production were as follows:

Materials on hand, July 1......................................$12,600
Materials on hand, December 1............................ 8,003
Materials purchased during this period..................... 46,580
Payroll costs for the period.............................. 50,912
Manufacturing overhead costs incurred.................... 15,170

All costs are to be prorated to the two products on the basis of the weighted average of the estimated costs and the units of production.
The volume of production for the season was:

	Ladies' Coats	Children's Coats
Number of coats started.............................1,000		1,500
Number of coats completed......................... 800		1,200
In process, December 1, 100% complete as to materials,		
60% complete as to labor and overhead............. 200		
In process December 1, 100% complete as to materials,		
80% complete as to labor and overhead.............		300
Number of units sold............................. 800		1,000

From this information, you are asked to prepare:

a) Journal entries to record the manufacturing operations, maintaining separate work-in-process accounts for each product.

b) Post to T-ledger accounts.

c) Journal entries to close out the Adjustment account into the Work-in-Process, Finished Goods, and Cost of Sales accounts.

Problem 15–3.   Purpose: *Estimated Cost Accounting Procedures When Three Products Are Being Manufactured Simultaneously; Journal Entries and T-Ledger Accounts*

The Willians Products Company manufactures three different products simultaneously. The factory is not departmentalized, so costs are computed on an estimated basis as though the plant were a single operating unit.

For the coming year, the estimated costs for each of the three products are as follows:

Element of Cost	Product 1	Product 2	Product 3
Material costs..........................$ 50		$ 80	$ 75
Labor costs........................... 30		50	60
Manufacturing overhead costs............ 20		30	25
Total...............................$100		$160	$160

Three work-in-process accounts are kept—one for each element of cost: Work-in-Process—Materials; Work-in-Process—Labor; and Work-in-Process—Manufacturing Overhead.

Inventories on hand at the beginning of the year were:

Materials..$6,500
Finished goods (adjusted to actual for the preceding period):
    Product 1................................20 @ $ 95
    Product 2................................10 @ 170
    Product 3................................15 @ 150

During the year, the production statistics were as follows:

	Product 1	Product 2	Product 3
Started into production.....................200	160	300
Completed..............................160	130	260
In process at end of period................ 40	30	40
Stage of completion of work-in-process:		
Materials............................100%	100%	100%
Labor................................ 50%	33⅓%	25%
Manufacturing overhead................ 50%	33⅓%	25%
Sales, on FIFO basis....................160	125	260

Transactions for the period were as follows:

Materials purchased......................$65,000
Labor costs............................. 27,000
Manufacturing overhead costs............ 12,000
Materials inventory at end of period.......   8,000

All costs for materials, labor, and manufacturing overhead are prorated to the various products on the basis of the weighted average of the EQUIVALENT production and the estimated costs.

You are asked on the basis of this information to prepare:

a) Journal entries to record costs of production and to close out the Adjustment account into the Work-in-Process, Finished Goods, and Cost of Sales accounts.

b) T-ledger accounts showing the results of manufacturing.

Problem 15–4. Purpose: *Estimated Cost Accounting Problem Involving a Single Product but TWO Manufacturing Departments; Use of a Transfer Account; Journal Entries and T-Ledger Accounts.*

The Wuros Manufacturing Company produces a single product which goes through two manufacturing departments. Costs are on an estimated basis, but they are kept separate by departments. Work-in-process accounts are kept by elements of costs for each department. Materials are used only in the initial department.

The estimated costs for each unit for the coming period are as follows:

Cost Element	Dept. A	Dept. B
Material costs.................................$ 70	0
Labor costs.................................... 50	$40
Manufacturing overhead costs.................... 20	20
Total.....................................$140	$60

The quantity of production statistics for the period were as follows:

No work-in-process at the beginning of the period
Started into production in Department A......................1,500 units
Completed in Department A and transferred to Department B......1,000
Completed in Department B and transferred to finished goods store-
    room... 900
Work-in-process:
    Department A, all material, 60% labor and overhead........... 500
    Department B, 50% labor and overhead...................... 100

Operating costs and supplementary data obtained from the records of the company indicated the following:

Materials inventory at beginning of period..................$ 14,000
Materials purchased during period.......................... 120,000
Payroll costs, Department A............................... 63,180
Payroll costs, Department B............................... 39,995
Manufacturing overhead costs, Department A................ 24,180
Manufacturing overhead costs, Department B................ 17,480
Materials inventory at end of accounting period.............. 26,000
Units sold during period..................................   720 units

From this data you are asked to prepare:

a) Journal entries to record the manufacturing operations, prorating the adjustments to the Work-in-Process, Finished Goods, and Cost of Sales.

b) T-ledger accounts from the journal entries.

Problem 15–5.   Purpose: *C.P.A. Problem Involving Statements of Estimated Costs for a Process Industry*

From the following information concerning the Walton Company, prepare a statement showing the estimated cost of producing 13,500 tons of X product for the purposes of bidding on a government contract.

The Walton Company manufactures X, a main product, and YAPPO, a by-product. Product X is produced and sold by the ton (2,000 pounds). The raw materials used in production consists of three ingredients: "H," "I," and "J," contained in both the finished main product and in the finished by-product in proportion and at estimated cost per ton set forth as follows:

"H," 40% at $8 per ton;	"I," 36% at $5 per ton;	"J," 24% at $7 per ton.

The contract for 13,500 tons of Product X represents 60 percent of the budgeted 1968 production of X by the Walton Company.

The main Product X is manufactured through four operating departments, viz:

Department I. Materials "H" and "I" are put into production at the beginning of operations. Completed work is transferred to Department II.

Department II. Material "H" suffers a 5 percent loss in weight due to evaporation, at the end of the processing in this department, and 10 percent of the remaining work-in-process is sold as waste at a nominal amount of $6 per ton. Completed work is transferred to Department III.

Department III. Material "J" is mixed with the material received from Department II at the beginning of operations in this department. Material "J" loses 4 percent of its original weight due to evaporation at the end of operations in Department III.

Department IV. In this final department, the material is separated into the main Product X and the By-product YAPPO in the proportion of 80 percent and 20 percent, respectively, and such products are placed in salable form.

Estimated direct labor costs per ton on a departmental basis, and the manufacturing overhead costs at normal capacity (i.e., 75 percent of total plant capacity of 25,000 tons annually of X) is as follows:

Department	Direct Labor per Ton	Variable Overhead	Fixed Overhead
I.	$5.00	$ 60,000	$30,000
II.	2.50	62,000	18,000
III.	3.00	50,000	20,000
IV.	4.00	40,000	16,000
Total		$212,000	$84,000

At normal capacity level, general manufacturing overhead costs applicable to the factory as a whole amounts to $60,000, of which 40 percent is fixed. It is expected that the units called for by the government contract, coupled with the company's curtailed production during 1968, will reach 90 percent of total plant capacity measured in finished units of Product X.

By-product YAPPO is expected to sell for an estimated $20 per ton before deductions for handling, selling, and administrative expenses of $2.50 per ton. (Carry all computations correct to two decimal places.)

(Adapted from an AICPA Uniform Examination)

Problem 15–6.   Purpose: *C.P.A. Problem Using Estimated Cost Statement in Cost Analysis*

The Worthington Manufacturing Company is engaged in the production of piece goods and has no cost system. Its sales were made on the basis of estimated costs, adding 15 percent to estimated direct cost to cover overhead, then adding to the total so estimated a profit equal to 12 percent of the selling price. At the end of the year 19—, the trial balance was as follows:

Buildings	$ 276,000	
Machinery	310,000	
Spools and other similar items	33,000	
Accounts receivable	110,000	
Accounts payable		$ 27,000
Allowances for depreciation to January 1, 19—:		
Buildings		36,000
Machinery		71,000
Sales		2,013,000
Inventory—January 1, 19—	157,000	
Purchases—raw material	1,200,000	
Labor—direct	480,000	
Labor—foremen, etc.	213,000	
Office payroll	76,000	
Factory overhead	280,000	
Office and administration expenses	113,000	
Capital stock		1,000,000
Cash in bank	18,000	
Retained earnings—January 1, 19—		119,000
	$3,266,000	$3,266,000

An estimated cost, which may be taken as representative of all the estimated costs, was as follows:

Cost per yard:
Raw material..................................$0.89
Weaving—piecework............................ 0.38
Winding, warping, etc......................... 0.03
Foremen and supervision....................... 0.10
                                             $1.40
Factory and office overhead—15% of $1.40.......... 0.21
                                             $1.61
Profit—12% of $1.83............................. 0.22
    Selling Price per Yard........................$1.83

Inventories were principally of raw material, and for the present purpose may be considered as consisting entirely of raw material at cost. The inventory at December 31, 19—, was valued at $376,000.

The annual rate of depreciation on buildings was 2 percent, and on machinery, 7½ percent; spools, etc., were not depreciated; replacements were charged to operations (factory overhead).

Before the books were closed, it was realized that a heavy loss had been sustained. Suggestions were made—a defalcation, material stolen, etc.

What was the amount of the loss and to what do you ascribe it? Indicate briefly what is needed to prevent a repetition of such conditions.

(Adapted from AICPA Uniform Examination)

PROBLEMS—GROUP B

Problem 15–7. Purpose: *Estimated Costs for a Single-Product, One-Department Factory; Journal Entries; T-Ledger Accounts; and Cost of Goods Sold Statement*

The Frothburg Manufacturing Company maintains an estimated cost accounting system for the manufacture of its single product in a nondepartmentalized plant. The estimated costs for this product is adjusted from year to year on the basis of the previous year's cost experience. For the ensuing year, this cost card shows for each unit of production the following:

Material costs.......................$25
Labor costs.......................... 15
Manufacturing overhead costs.......... 10 $50

The cost and production statistics for the year which ended June 30, 19—, were as follows:

Work-in-process at the beginning of the year: 100 units in process on which 70 percent of the materials and 50 percent of the labor and manufacturing overhead had been applied. This inventory had been adjusted to the actual costs of the preceding period with the resulting figures:

Work-in-process—materials...........................$1,750
Work-in-process—labor.............................. 750
Work-in-process—manufacturing overhead............. 500 $3,000

During the year, the production statistics indicated the following:

Additional units started into production....................7,400 units
In process at end of year (June 30, 19—) 100% complete as to ma-
terials and 60% complete as to labor and manufacturing over-
head..1,000
Finished machines on hand at end of year.................. 300
Units sold during the year...............................   ?
(There were no finished units on hand at the beginning of the
year.)

During the year the following transactions were recorded:

Materials purchased...............................$260,000
Payroll costs in factory........................... 84,450
Manufacturing overhead costs incurred.............. 68,660
Materials inventory at beginning of year........... 18,000
Materials inventory at end of year................. 77,250

In this firm, the initial work-in-process inventory is averaged in with the costs for the current period.

From this information, you are asked to:

a) Prepare entries in journal form to record the manufacturing operations for the year.

b) Set up T-ledger accounts for stores, payroll, manufacturing overhead, finished goods, cost of sales, and the three work-in-process accounts and an adjustment account.

c) Prepare a cost of goods sold statement.

d) Prepare an adjusted estimated cost per unit statement for the next year.

Problem 15–8. Purpose: *Estimated Costs, Journal Entries, and T-Ledger Accounts When Two Products Are Manufactured Simultaneously*

In the plant of the Grander Manufacturing Company, two products are manufactured simultaneously, more or less continuously throughout the year. The estimated costs for these two products for the coming year are:

Element of Cost	Product A	Product B
Material costs..........................	$ 6	$ 5
Labor costs.............................	4	5
Manufacturing overhead costs..............	2	3
Total..............................	$12	$13

The production statistics for the year were as follows:

	Product A	Product B
Units in process at beginning of year.........	0	0
Started into production during year..........8,000 units		6,000 units
Completed during the year.................6,500		5,000
Sold during the year.....................5,500		4,800
In process at end of year:		
80% complete as to materials, 50% complete as to labor and overhead..........1,200		
70% complete as to materials, 60% complete as to labor and overhead.........		1,000
Lost or spoiled in production.............. 300		

The production costs for the year to be allocated to the two products on the basis of the weighted average of the equivalent production of the good units and the estimated cost of each were as follows:

Materials purchased during the year..................$96,480
Payroll in factory during the year..................... 47,940
Manufacturing overhead incurred during year.......... 24,800
Materials on hand at end of year..................... 15,894
No materials inventory at beginning of year.

From this information, you are asked to prepare:

a) Journal entries to record the manufacturing operations, closing out the Adjustment account into the Work-in-Process, Finished Goods, and Cost of Sales for each product.

b) T-ledger accounts for these journal entries.

Problem 15–9. Purpose: *Estimated Costs for Single Product Manufactured in Two Successive Departments; Journal Entries; T-Ledger Accounts; Transfer Account; Initial Work-in-Process Inventory*

The Gem Company manufactures a single product which goes through two manufacturing operations. Estimated costs are used with separate work-in-process accounts for each department. Materials used in the initial department only. The estimated costs for each unit on a departmental basis are as follows for the coming year:

Cost Element	Dept. A	Dept. B
Cost from Department A..................... 0		$170
Material costs............................$100		0
Labor costs.............................. 50		40
Manufacturing overhead costs.............. 20		15
Total.................................$170		$225

At the beginning of the year, there were in process 150 units in Department A, on which 80 percent of the material and 50 percent of the labor and overhead had been applied. The costs incurred on this work-in-process inventory were: materials, $12,000; labor, $3,750; and overhead, $1,500. There was no work-in-process inventory at the beginning in Department B. The work-in-process inventory is treated on the average cost basis with the new production.

The quantity production statistics for the year were as follows:

	Dept. A	Dept. B
Units in process at the beginning of the period..............................	150 units	
New production started during period........	2,350	
Completed and transferred to Dept. B........	2,200	
Units in process at end of year:		
90% materials used, 40% of labor and overhead applied.........................	300	
80% labor and overhead applied...........		500 units
Completed and transferred to finished goods...		1,700
Units sold during the year.................		1,500

Manufacturing costs incurred during the year were:

Materials inventory at beginning of year.....................	$ 30,000
Materials purchased during the year........................	210,000
Materials inventory at end of year.........................	42,050
Payroll costs in Department A.............................	117,850
Payroll costs in Department B.............................	87,150
Manufacturing overhead costs in Department A...............	35,540
Manufacturing overhead costs in Department B...............	30,450

From these data you are asked to prepare:

a) Journal entries to record the manufacturing operations, prorating the adjustment amounts. Use a transfer account.

b) Post to T-ledger accounts.

Problem 15–10. Purpose: *C.P.A. Problem Using Estimated Cost Procedures*

On the basis of the following data, prepare a statement of factory accounts, showing costs, variances, and inventory balances.

The Groten Manufacturing Company has a contract to manufacture 10,000 units of Product COPON, a regular-line product, for a lump-sum price. This price was determined on the basis of estimates of manufacturing cost, selling, administrative, and general expenses, and provision for net profit.

The management desires to check manufacturing cost estimates against corresponding actual costs through the factory accounting records and decides to make use of procedures followed under estimated cost systems in which estimated and actual costs are reflected in opposition in cost accounts and variations are developed thereby. These comparisons are to be made monthly so that differences between estimated and actual costs can be detected and controlled currently.

Product COPON has been manufactured by two major processes developed in the fabricating and finishing departments. Estimated costs per unit of product for each of these departments follow:

PRODUCT COPON

Estimated Cost per Unit

	Fabricating Department			Finishing Department		
	Quantity or Time	Estimated Value	Total	Quantity or Time	Estimated Value	Total
Direct materials............3 units		$1.20	$3.60	....	.....	.....
Direct labor...............2 hours		0.90	1.80	1.5 hours	$1.00	$1.50
Manufacturing overhead....2 hours		0.60	1.20	1.5 hours	0.50	0.75
Total................			$6.60			$2.25

Product and cost data for operations during the first month under the contract are as follows:

	⟶Fabricating Department⟶	⟶Finishing Department⟶
Beginning inventory:		
Quantity.............................	200 units	80 units
Average state of completion.............	35%	55%
Costs:		
Direct materials......................$720		
Transfer materials from fabricating department.........................		$528
Direct labor......................... 126		66
Manufacturing overhead.............. 84	$ 930	33 $ 627
Materials purchased and issued............	9,100	
Direct labor incurred.....................	3,810	3,860
Manufacturing overhead incurred..........	3,180	2,105
Ending inventory:		
Quantity.............................	300 units	240 units
Average state of completion.............	60%	70%

Note. The amounts in the above tabulation are at actual cost, with the exception of the beginning inventories which are stated at estimated cost.

During the month, 2,000 units were completed of which 1,800 were shipped to the purchaser under contract. Goods are assumed to be produced and sold on a first-in, first-out basis.

(Adapted from an AICPA Uniform Examination)

Problem 15–11.   Purpose: *C.P.A. Problem Involving Journal Entries, Ledger Accounts, and Adjustments for Estimated Costs*

The Gilcrest Manufacturing Company estimates its cost for a unit of its product DABON to consist of the following:

Material—5 pounds @ $1.22 per pound
Labor—7 hours @ $1.30 per hour

Overhead is applied on a direct labor cost basis and need not be considered in this problem.

The company takes the raw materials purchased into inventory of raw materials at $1.22 per pound, recording any difference between that price and actual purchase cost in a Price Variation—Materials account. The actual raw material used is issued to production at $1.22 per pound. The material cost and the actual direct labor cost for the month are recorded in separate work-in-process accounts. Finished Goods Inventory is debited, and these process accounts are credited with the estimated cost of completed units. At the end of the month the Finished Goods account and the work-in-process accounts are adjusted to actual cost by spreading the differences between actual costs and estimated costs over the accounts in proportion to the amounts of estimated costs applicable to each of the accounts. Material price variation is spread over inventory of raw materials, work-in-process, and finished goods in the same manner as other variations, but the amount applicable to inventory of raw materials is left in the variation account.

Account balances after adjustment for March 31, but before adjustment to actual costs for April 30, were as follows:

Account	Debit Balances 3/31/— after Adjustment	Debit Balances 4/30/— before Adjustment
Inventory of Raw Materials	$10,485.90	$10,673.78
Price Variation—Materials	723.55	973.28
Work-in-Process—Materials	770.80	1,091.90
Work-in-Process—Labor	731.15	758.94

The 3/31/— balance of Work-in-Process—Materials includes $49.78 of price variation. Status of the work-in-process was as follows:

	March 31, 19—		April 30, 19—	
	Units	% Completed	Units	% Completed
Materials	60	50	50	30
Materials	80	90	100	75
Labor	60	25	50	10
Labor	80	80	100	60

During the month of April, 19—, 510 units of product DABON were completed and transferred to Finished Goods.

You are to set up skeleton ledger accounts for all of the accounts affected by these transactions and prepare and post the adjustment necessary for the company at the end of April, 19—.

(Adapted from an AICPA Uniform Examination)

SECTION IV

Managerial Control through the Use of Cost Accounting Data and Procedures

In the preceding chapters, the principles and practices of job order and process cost accounting were discussed. These two subjects are basic in the study of cost accounting. However a knowledge of them is merely a prerequisite for the practical use of cost accounting, namely, managerial control and analysis.

In this section, emphasis is on management's use of cost information for control purposes—that is, to increase the firm's profit. To develop this material within the limits of classroom procedure and the experience of the students, the following topics are discussed:

> *The Comprehensive Budget*
> *Standard Costs*
> *Managerial Reports and Graphs*
> *Profit Planning through Direct Costing*
> *Profit Planning through Break-Even Charts and Profit/Volume Relationships*
> *Profit Planning through Differential and Comparative Cost Analysis*
> *Distribution Cost Analysis*
> *Nonmanufacturing Cost Analyses*

CHAPTER

16 : The Comprehensive Budget

Introduction   In this chapter, the discussion of Chapter 4 pertaining to the comprehensive budget is continued. Chapter 4 concerned itself with the basics of planning for operations. This discussion is continued with the use of a detailed illustration of the operating budget. The steps involved in building the budget were pointed out.

The comprehensive budget includes not only an operating budget but also the cash budget and the capital expenditures budget. Both of these are covered in detail in this chapter.

The Operating Budget Illustrated   To help the understanding of the complete budget plan, an illustration is used to show the interrelation of the various budgets thus prepared.

The Jordan Manufacturing Company produces three products, A, B, and C, similar in size and weight. These products are sold to dealers. Six salesmen operate in territory 1 and four salesmen in territory 2, under the direction of the sales manager, who supervises the sales function from the home office. Some sales are also made direct from the warehouse, adjacent to the home office.

The sales budget in summary form is presented in Illustration 16–1.

This budget was prepared from a compilation of the monthly sales estimates, supported by detailed estimates of the *quantities* to be sold.

From the sales figure of $800,000 the budget director is able to compute the desired net income in order to place a limit on the total amount of costs and expenses. If it is assumed that the net income on these sales should be $56,000, or 7 percent, then the balance of $744,000 represents the limit on cost of production plus operating expenses.

The cost of production budget corresponding to the above sales would appear in summary form as shown in Illustration 16–2.

Illustration 16–1

SALES INCOME BUDGET FOR YEAR ENDED DECEMBER 31, 19—

Territory	Net Sales	Product A	Product B	Product C
1..................	$300,000.00	$150,000.00	$100,000.00	$ 50,000.00
2..................	400,000.00	120,000.00	200,000.00	80,000.00
Warehouse.........	100,000.00	60,000.00	30,000.00	10,000.00
Total..........	$800,000.00	$330,000.00	$330,000.00	$140,000.00

Illustration 16–2

ESTIMATED COST OF PRODUCTION FOR YEAR ENDED DECEMBER 31, 19—

Cost Element	Total	Product A	Product B	Product C
Materials.........................	$194,000	$ 80,000	$ 90,000	$24,000
Labor.............................	296,000	120,000	120,000	56,000
Manufacturing overhead..............	74,000	30,000	30,000	14,000
Total........................	$564,000	$230,000	$240,000	$94,000

Illustration 16–3

ANALYSIS OF ESTIMATED UNIT PRODUCTION COSTS BY DEPARTMENTS
For the Year 19—

	Total	Cutting Department	Stamping Department	Finishing Department
Product A:				
Material.....................	$3.20	$3.00	....	$0.20
Labor.......................	4.80	2.00	$1.00	1.80
Manufacturing Overhead.......	1.20	0.50	0.25	0.45
Total....................	$9.20	$5.50	$1.25	$2.45
Product B:				
Material.....................	$3.60	$3.00	....	$0.60
Labor.......................	4.80	2.00	$1.00	1.80
Manufacturing Overhead.......	1.20	0.50	0.25	0.45
Total....................	$9.60	$5.50	$1.25	$2.85
Product C:				
Material.....................	$1.20	$0.90	....	$0.30
Labor.......................	2.80	1.60	$0.40	0.80
Manufacturing Overhead.......	0.70	0.40	0.10	0.20
Total....................	$4.70	$2.90	$0.50	$1.30

However, this is merely a condensed summary of the detailed reports, which would include: (1) a schedule of estimated production costs by elements per unit in each *department,* i.e., the material and labor and overhead costs; and (2) a detailed manufacturing overhead budget, broken down into variable, fixed, and semivariable overhead costs. These two important schedules are shown in Illustrations 16–3 and 16–4.

Illustration 16–4

BUDGET ESTIMATE OF MANUFACTURING OVERHEAD COSTS

For the Year Ended December 31, 19—

	Total	Producing Departments			Service Departments	
		Cutting	Stamping	Finishing	X	Y
Variable Overhead Costs:						
Indirect Materials.......	$ 2,000.00	$ 300.00	$ 200.00	$ 1,000.00	$ 350.00	$ 150.00
Indirect Labor..........	10,000.00	1,000.00	500.00	1,000.00	3,750.00	3,750.00
Fuel..................	2,500.00	500.00	400.00	300.00	650.00	650.00
Light and Power........	3,000.00	1,300.00	900.00	200.00	300.00	300.00
Compensation Insurance..	7,000.00	3,000.00	1,500.00	1,000.00	750.00	750.00
Telephone and Telegraph.	500.00	100.00	....	....	200.00	200.00
Fixed and Semivariable:						
Rent of Factory.........	5,000.00	1,400.00	900.00	900.00	900.00	900.00
Fire Insurance..........	4,000.00	1,000.00	800.00	900.00	600.00	700.00
Superintendence........	20,000.00	7,000.00	2,000.00	7,000.00	2,000.00	2,000.00
Depreciation...........	10,000.00	3,500.00	1,000.00	2,300.00	1,500.00	1,700.00
General Administrative Expenses............	5,000.00	1,100.00	800.00	700.00	1,400.00	1,000.00
Amortization of Patents..	5,000.00	3,000.00	....	2,000.00	....	....
Total..............						
	$74,000.00				$12,400.00	$12,100.00
Apportioned Charges, Department X........	$12,400.00	5,000.00	3,000.00	4,400.00		
Apportioned Charges, Department Y........	12,100.00	4,800.00	2,500.00	4,800.00		
	$74,000.00	$33,000.00	$14,500.00	$26,500.00		

The analysis of estimated unit costs (see Illustration 16–4), coupled with the number of units to be produced, as indicated by estimated sales, should give the total estimated cost of production for the year, reanalyzed by months.

A *manufacturing overhead cost budget* may be used so that effective budgetary control is realized. As indicated in the first half of this text, it is practically necessary for a manufacturer to estimate his manufacturing overhead costs and his production for the year in order to calculate a predetermined rate for applying manufacturing overhead to production costs. *This implies a budgetary process.* By use of special forms, the actual and budgeted figures should be compared frequently and cumulatively to note variations and the reasons therefor. Similar procedures can be followed for selling and administrative expenses or for distribution costs. To make the illustration complete, both the manufacturing overhead and the selling and administrative expense budgets are shown; see Illustrations 16–4 and 16–5. To be most effective, these budgets must first be prepared on a *monthly basis, by departments.*

Illustration 16–5

BUDGET ESTIMATES OF SELLING AND ADMINISTRATIVE EXPENSES
For the Year Ended December 31, 19—

	Total	Selling Expenses	Administrative Expenses
Variable Expenses:			
Traveling Expenses...............	$ 5,000.00	$ 4,000.00	$ 1,000.00
Office Expenses..................	14,000.00	6,000.00	8,000.00
Warehouse Expenses.............	16,000.00	16,000.00	....
Delivery Costs...................	15,000.00	15,000.00	....
Postage........................	4,000.00	2,250.00	1,750.00
Telephone & Telegraph...........	8,000.00	5,000.00	3,000.00
Office Supplies.................	3,000.00	750.00	2,250.00
Miscellaneous...................	2,000.00	1,000.00	1,000.00
Total Variable Expenses.......	$ 67,000.00	$ 50,000.00	$ 17,000.00
Fixed and Semi-Variable:			
Salaries........................	$ 60,000.00	$ 30,000.00	$ 30,000.00
Rent...........................	25,000.00	15,000.00	10,000.00
Administration..................	10,000.00	4,000.00	6,000.00
Insurance......................	8,000.00	6,000.00	2,000.00
Depreciation...................	10,000.00	7,500.00	2,500.00
Total Fixed Expenses.........	$113,000.00	$ 62,500.00	$ 50,500.00
Total Expenses	$180,000.00	$112,500.00	$ 67,500.00

Once the budget has been completed to this point, it is possible to project the income statement for the period and break it down into monthly statements for comparisons with the actual operating results. When the budget is prepared, only the first columns can be completed. As the actual figures are received, they may be inserted and the variations computed and analyzed. Illustration 16–6 shows how the budgeted and actual figures of the income statement may be compared and analyzed.

The analysis of the departmental manufacturing overhead requires a study of the variations, in addition to facts indicated in the Remarks column. Manufacturing overhead variations are caused, in part, by

Illustration 16–6

ESTIMATED INCOME STATEMENT

For the Year Ended December 31, 19—

	Budget		Actual		Difference†		Remarks
	Amount	%	Amount	%	Amount	%	
Net Sales............	$800,000.00	100.0	$900,000.00	100.0	$100,000.00	12.5	
Cost of Sales.........	560,000.00*	70.0	650,000.00	72.2	90,000.00	16.0	
Gross Profit on Sales..	$240,000.00	30.0	$250,000.00	27.8	$ 10,000.00	4.16	
Selling Expenses......	$112,500.00	14.06	$135,000.00	15.0	$ 22,500.00	20.0	
Administrative Expenses..........	67,500.00	8.44	63,000.00	7.0	4,500.00†	6.6†	
Total Expenses.......	$180,000.00	22.50	$198,000.00	22.0	$ 18,000.00	10.0	
Operating Income....	$ 60,000.00	7.5	$ 52,000.00	5.8	$ 8,000.00†	13.3†	
Financial Expenses...	4,000.00	.5	4,500.00	.5	500.00	12.5	
Estimated Net Income (7% of Sales)......	$ 56,000.00	7.0	$ 47,500.00	5.27	$ 8,500.00†	15.1†	

* Inventory of Finished Goods, $4,000.00.
† Indicates decrease.

inefficiency of production; that is, more hours may have been required to complete a job than were provided for. In addition, there may be further variations because the overhead incurred might cost more than was anticipated and is known as a *budget overhead variation*. If the plant as a unit operates at a greater capacity than was anticipated in the production budget, there will be a favorable variation because of greater plant activity. This is known as a *capacity variation*. The sum of the budget variation and the capacity variation, whether positive or negative, will equal the over- or underapplied manufacturing overhead for the period. Controlling overhead costs by such an analysis is a fundamental purpose of a budget. It enables management to understand why there are variations, and then to act in correcting unfavorable procedures. Illustrations 16–7 and 16–8 are examples of reports pointing out variations. In the chapter on standard costs, methods of how to compute them will be illustrated and methods showing how to place responsibility for their existence so that corrective action may be taken will be discussed.

To illustrate the flexible budgets, sets of facts paralleling those given for the static budget are used but changed where necessary. Reduced to a

Illustration 16–7

BUDGETARY REPORT ON MANUFACTURING OVERHEAD COSTS

For Month Ending March 31, 19—

Department: Cutting   Foreman: Allen K. Marmon

Costs	Budget This Month	Actual This Month	Variation This Month	Budget Year to Date	Actual Year to Date	Variation Year to Date	Remarks
Variable Overhead Costs:							
Indirect Materials	$ 25.00	$ 30.00	+$ 5.00	$ 75.00	$ 90.00	+$ 15.00	
Indirect Labor	83.33	83.33		250.00	240.00	− 10.00	
Fuel	46.67	50.00	+ 3.33	140.00	160.00	+ 20.00	Weather conditions
Light and Power	108.33	120.00	+ 11.67	325.00	450.00	+ 125.00	Special orders
Compensation Insurance	250.00	270.00	+ 20.00	750.00	800.00	+ 50.00	Higher wages
Telephone and Telegraph	8.33	7.00	− 1.33	25.00	20.00	− 5.00	
Fixed and Semivariable:							
Rent of Factory	116.67	116.67		350.00	350.00		
Fire Insurance	83.33	83.33		250.00	250.00		
Superintendence	583.33	583.33		1,750.00	1,750.00		
Depreciation	291.60	291.60		875.00	875.00		
General Administration	91.67	85.00	− 6.67	275.00	210.00	− 65.00	Salary cuts
Amortization—Patents	250.00	250.00		750.00	750.00		
Apportioned Charges, Department X	416.67	380.00	− 36.67	1,250.00	1,300.00	+ 50.00	See schedule
Apportioned Charges, Department Y	400.00	450.00	+ 50.00	1,200.00	1,220.00	+ 20.00	See schedule
Total	$2,754.93	$2,800.26	+$45.33	$8,265.00	$8,465.00	+$200.00	

Illustration 16–8

BUDGETARY REPORT ON PRODUCTION COSTS
BY PRODUCTS AND BY ELEMENTS OF COSTS*
For Month Ending March 31, 19—

Cost Elements	Budget for Month	Actual Cost for Month	Variation	Remarks
Material Cost:				
Product A..........	$ 6,666.67	$ 7,000.00	+$ 333.33	
Product B..........	7,500.00	7,600.00	+ 100.00	
Product C..........	2,000.00	2,000.00	....	
Labor Cost:				
Product A..........	10,000.00	11,000.00	+ 1,000.00	
Product B..........	10,000.00	12,000.00	+ 2,000.00	Strike
Product C..........	4,666.67	5,000.00	+ 333.33	
Manufacturing Over-head Cost:				
Product A..........	2,500.00	2,750.00	+ 250.00	
Product B..........	2,500.00	3,000.00	+ 500.00	
Product C..........	1,166.66	1,250.00	+ 83.34	
Total..........	$47,000.00	$51,600.00	+$4,600.00	

* These may be further analyzed by departments. The extent to which analyses and comparisons will be made will depend upon the size of the organization and the amount the company is willing to spend for budgetary control.

monthly basis, the flexible sales budget for the Jordan Manufacturing Company would appear as shown in Illustration 16–9.

The flexible cost of production budgets involve a great amount of detailed budgeting. A standard direct material cost budget is prepared.

Illustration 16–9

MONTHLY FLEXIBLE SALES BUDGET*
FOR THE JORDAN MANUFACTURING COMPANY
For Year 19—
(Approximate Figures)

Product	Operating Capacity					
	40%	60%	80%	100%†	120%	140%
Product A..........	$ 11,000.00	$ 16,500.00	$ 22,000.00	$ 27,500.00	$ 33,000.00	$ 38,500.00
Product B..........	11,000.00	16,500.00	22,000.00	27,500.00	33,000.00	38,500.00
Product C..........	4,666.67	7,000.00	9,333.33	11,666.67	14,000.00	16,333.33
Monthly Total.......	$ 26,666.67	$ 40,000.00	$ 53,333.33	$ 66,666.67	$ 80,000.00	$ 93,333.33
Annual Total*......	$320,000.00	$480,000.00	$640,000.00	$800,000.00	$960,000.00	$1,120,000.00

* These figures arrived at by considering the budget of standard quantities for each month and the standard selling prices (standard price × standard quantities = foregoing figures).
† Compare this annual figure with the static budget figure given on page 484. The 100% operating capacity figure is the same as the static budget figure.

The material cost per unit will usually be the same no matter what the operating capacity. The same is true of the per unit direct labor costs. These figures will be comparable to those appearing on the standard cost sheets for the various products. The per unit manufacturing overhead, particularly the fixed and semivariable overhead costs, will tend to be affected by different operating capacities. Therefore, for the computation of unit manufacturing overhead costs, the flexible or sliding budget

Illustration 16–10

STANDARD DIRECT MATERIAL COST BUDGET

For Year Ending December 31, 19—

Standard Quantity	Description of Material	Standard Price	Department in Which Used	Product A	Product B	Product C
3...............	Sheet Steel	$1.00	Cutting	$3.00	$3.00	....
1...............	Sheet Steel	.90	Cutting	....	....	$ .90
12...............	Rivets	.10	Finishing	.10	.10	.10
4 oz.............	Enamel	.10	Finishing	.10	.10	....
1 set............	Fittings	.40	Finishing	....	.40	....
8 oz.............	Wax	.20	Finishing	....	....	.20
Standard Unit Cost....	....	....	....	$3.20	$3.60	$1.20

Illustration 16–11

STANDARD DIRECT LABOR COST BUDGET

For Year Ending December 31, 19—

Standard Quantity	Description of Labor Operation	Standard Rate	Department in Which Used	Product A	Product B	Product C
4 hours...........	Cutting Machine	$2.50	Cutting	$ 5.00	$ 5.00	....
4 hours...........	Cutting Machine	2.40	Cutting	....	....	$ 9.60
2 hours...........	Stamping Machine	2.50	Stamping	2.50	2.50	....
1 hour............	Stamping Machine	2.40	Stamping	....	....	2.40
4 hours...........	Finishing Work	2.45	Finishing	4.90	4.90	....
2 hours...........	Finishing Work	2.40	Finishing	....	....	4.80
Standard Unit Labor Cost......	....	....	....	$12.40	$12.40	$16.80

is of paramount importance. To illustrate the standard material and labor budgets, as taken from the table on page 484, Illustrations 16–10 and 16–11 are presented. Illustration 16–12 presents the flexible manufacturing overhead budget.

It should be pointed out that the flexible overhead budget found in Illustration 16–12 is but one way of showing a flexible budget. Illustration 16–12 presents the elements of overhead at certain selected levels of operating capacity, i.e., at 40, 60, 80, 100, 120, and 140 percent of capacity. Another way of stating the flexible budget is in fixed and

Illustration 16–12

FLEXIBLE MONTHLY MANUFACTURING OVERHEAD COST BUDGET
FOR CUTTING DEPARTMENT*
For Year Ending December 31, 19—

Element of Overhead	Operating Capacity					
	40%	60%	80%	100% (Std)	120%	140%
Variable Overhead Costs:						
Indirect Materials.....	$ 100.00	$ 150.00	$ 200.00	$ 250.00	$ 300.00	$ 350.00
Indirect Labor.........	333.30	518.00	666.70	833.30	1,036.00	1,166.70
Fuel...................				466.70		
Light and Power.......	450.00	600.00	860.00	1,083.30	1,180.00	1,500.00
Compensation Insurance	1,000.00	1,400.00	1,900.00	2,500.00	3,000.00	3,200.00
Telegraph and Telephone..............	30.00	49.00	70.00	83.30	96.70	112.00
Apportioned Overhead Costs:						
Department X.......	4,100.00	4,100.00	4,166.70	4,166.70	4,166.70	4,220.00
Department Y.......	3,900.00	3,900.00	4,000.00	4,000.00	4,000.00	4,100.00
Variable Overhead Total.	$ 9,913.30	$10,717.00	$ 11,863.40	$ 13,383.30	$ 13,779.40	$ 14,648.70
Fixed and Semivariable:						
Rent of Factory.......	$ 1,166.70	$ 1,166.70	$ 1,166.70	$ 1,166.70	$ 1,166.70	$ 1,166.70
Fire Insurance........	833.30	833.30	833.30	833.30	900.00	900.00
Superintendence......	583.33	583.33	583.33	583.33	583.33	583.33
Depreciation of Equipment..............	2,916.70	2,916.70	2,916.70	2,916.70	3,000.00	3,000.00
Administrative Expenses..............	850.00	850.00	916.70	916.70	916.70	1,000.00
Amortization of Patents	250.00	250.00	250.00	250.00	250.00	250.00
Semivariable and Fixed Overhead Total.......	$ 6,600.03	$ 6,600.03	$ 6,666.73	$ 6,666.73	$ 6,816.73	$ 6,900.03
Estimated Direct Labor Costs................	$50,000.00	$60,000.00	$110,000.00	$120,000.00	$140,000.00	$150,000.00
Standard Rate—Variable Overhead............	19.83%	17.86%	10.78%	11.15%	9.84%	9.76%
Standard Rate—Semivariable and Fixed Overhead............	13.20%	11.00%	6.06%	5.55%	4.87%	4.6%

* Similar schedules must be prepared for each producing department.

variable components. Each cost is analyzed and its fixed and variable
components isolated. For example, fuel expense in the assembly department may be $350 at the 5,000 direct labor hour level and $440 at the
8,000 direct labor hour level. Analysis of the cost by the use of the
high-low point method of separating fixed and variable components
discloses variable costs of $0.30 per direct labor hour and fixed costs of
$200. Budgeting for fuel cost is then possible for any level between
5,000 and 8,000 direct labor hours. Illustration 16–13 presents a

Illustration 16–13

FLEXIBLE MONTHLY MANUFACTURING OVERHEAD COST
BUDGET FOR ASSEMBLY DEPARTMENT
For Year Ending December 31, 19—

	Variable per Labor Hour	Fixed
Indirect material............................	$0.50	
Indirect labor..............................	1.50	$4,000
Fuel......................................	0.30	200
Light and power............................	0.20	300
Rent.....................................		800
Fire insurance.............................		600
Depreciation..............................		700
Other expenses............................	0.10	600
	$2.60	$7,200

flexible budget for a department where each of the costs has been analyzed in a manner similar to fuel cost:

The flexible budget thus becomes $7,200 plus $2.60 per labor hour.

Once these standards and budgets have been prepared by determining the anticipated operating capacity for any month at the beginning of the month, it is possible to prepare a standard cost of production budget. To illustrate, assume that the firm will operate at 60 percent capacity during March. Compiling figures at the 60 percent capacity rate, the standard cost of production per unit for this month should be as shown in Illustration 16–14.

Illustration 16–14

STANDARD COST OF PRODUCTION BUDGET
Reduced to Unit Cost Basis

Month: March, 19—   Operating Capacity: 60%

Cost Element and Department	Product A	Product B	Product C
Material—Cutting Department...................	$ 3.00	$ 3.00	$ 0.90
Material—Finishing Department..................	0.20	0.60	0.30
Labor—Cutting Department.....................	5.00	5.00	9.60
Labor—Stamping Department...................	2.50	2.50	2.40
Labor—Finishing Department...................	4.90	4.90	4.80
Manufacturing Overhead—Cutting Department (28.86% × $5.00 or $9.60)...................	1.44	1.44	2.77
Manufacturing Overhead—Stamping Department (36% × $2.50 or $2.40).....................	0.90	0.90	0.86
Manufacturing Overhead—Finishing Department (35% × $4.90 or $4.80).....................	1.72	1.72	1.68
Total Standard Unit Costs......................	$19.66	$20.06	$23.31
Standard Quantity of Production................	100	150	200

Flexible distribution cost budgets can be prepared in a manner similar to that followed in preparing the flexible manufacturing overhead budgets. Ideally, the distribution costs budget is broken down into the groups of expenses, as indicated in Chapter 24 on distribution cost analysis and accounting.

Capacity to Produce Defined   Production engineers, managers, and cost accountants have different concepts of "capacity" and the measurement of effective manufacturing operations. *Theoretical capacity,* used at times by the engineers, indicates the maximum production possible if a plant or department is operating at full speed with few or no interruptions, delays, or breakdowns—that is, at 100 percent efficiency. Since this concept is Utopian in nature, with little chance for realization, most firms use a more *practical capacity* of perhaps 75 percent to 85 percent of the theoretical capacity. But to many even this seems unrealistic for short-term measurement of manufacturing efficiency. The expected sales volume plus the inventory requirements are factors used to determine the budgeted capacity to produce. This capacity to produce is usually referred to as *normal capacity.* In estimating both the practical capacity and the expected sales volume, management must take into consideration the effect of *idle capacity* (usable but not operative because of depressed sales conditions) and *excess capacity* (for which no present or immediate future use is available). Excess capacity can usually be eliminated by selling or leasing part of the plant or equipment, or by developing new products. Both idle capacity and excess capacity affect manufacturing overhead costs and must be properly interpreted to measure managerial effectiveness. Theoretical capacity includes idle and excess capacity in measuring plant efficiency.

Normal Capacity as a Budget Factor   It has been noted that the *normal* capacity used determines the budgeted costs, the standard unit cost of production, and the projected profit goal. This normal capacity must take into consideration both the long-term business plans and budget, and the more immediate short-term sales and production results. The latter must be considered in measuring the achievement possibilities of the long-term budgets.

Normal capacity must first be budgeted on a plantwide basis and then, for effective operation control, broken down by plants and departments so that no departments will be overloaded, or vice versa. This may require overtime, additional shifts, subcontracting, or purchase of additional equipment in some departments to provide a smooth production schedule. The basic purpose of establishing normal capacity is to permit the preparation of a reliable, effective plantwide budget. The by-products of this objective are a flexible departmental overhead budget and rates, the standard cost of production, the scheduling of production, the establishing of sales prices, etc. For proper control, management must know which costs and expenses are variable and which are fixed; and it must receive adequate cost reports and analyses to aid in reducing costs and increasing net income.

Problem of Separating Costs into Fixed and Variable   The flexible budget presents the estimated indirect costs, both manufacturing and selling and administrative, at varying levels of production. For those costs which are fixed, management can only plan to increase the volume of production so that the per unit cost will be reduced. But many costs

Illustration 16–15

Month	Volume of Production (D. L. Hrs.)	Inspection Costs	Increase in Volume (D. L. Hrs.)	Increase in Costs
January	5,000	$ 6,000	0	0
June	5,300	6,000	300	0
March	5,800	6,400	500	$ 400
April	6,400	6,700	600	300
July	7,000	7,000	600	300
August	7,500	7,600	500	600
February	7,800	7,600	300	0
May	8,000	8,200	200	600
October	8,500	8,800	500	600
November	9,000	9,500	500	700
September	9,500	10,000	500	500
December	10,000	10,600	500	600
Total	89,800	$94,400	5,000	$4,600

which are semivariable in nature contain some elements of fixed and variable costs. For example, even with a minimum of production, some *inspection* costs must be incurred. As production increases, it may become necessary to increase this cost, but not immediately or consistently with each increase in volume. *The relation of the increase in inspection costs to the increase in the volume of production must be established by management so that the variable part of the cost may be separated from the basic or fixed amount.* In the chapter on applied manufacturing overhead, a method of allocation was discussed and illustrated. In substance, it indicated that the *increase of any indirect cost* divided by the corresponding *increase in the volume of production* would result in the *average variable unit cost increase.*

Illustration 16–15 represents the inspection costs for the past year, arranged in the order of volume of production. The total increases on a month-to-month basis were 5,000 direct labor hours (representing the volume) and $4,600 for inspection costs. Interpreting this for budget preparation, it can be assumed that 92 cents per direct labor hour represents the variable portion of inspection costs, and when used with the *greatest volume* of production, it is possible to calculate the *fixed* amount of inspection costs. To illustrate, the inspection costs for December, the month having the greatest volume, are $10,600. The volume of production is 10,000 hours. Since the variable cost per hour

Illustration 16–16

RECAPITULATION OF INSPECTION COSTS

Month	Volume (D. L. Hrs.)	Total Costs	Fixed	Variable*
January	5,000	$ 6,000	$ 1,400	$ 4,600
February	7,800	7,600	1,400	6,200
March	5,800	6,400	1,400	5,000
April	6,400	6,700	1,400	5,300
May	8,000	8,200	1,400	6,800
June	5,300	6,000	1,400	4,600
July	7,000	7,000	1,400	5,600
August	7,500	7,600	1,400	6,200
September	9,500	10,000	1,400	8,600
October	8,500	8,800	1,400	7,400
November	9,000	9,500	1,400	8,100
December	10,000	10,600	1,400	9,200
Total	89,800	$94,400	$16,800	$77,600

*Note: From a practical viewpoint, such wide fluctuations would not occur in business. Such fluctuations are used here for illustrative purposes only.

is 92 cents for 10,000 hours, this would be $9,200, leaving a fixed cost of $1,400 ($10,600 — $9,200). The same result can be achieved by using the lowest volume of production, 5,000 hours. Five thousand hours at 92 cents for the variable cost would produce a total variable cost of $4,600, which if subtracted from the $6,000 would result in a fixed cost of $1,400. (See Illustration 16–16.)

A much quicker way of obtaining the same result would be to consider the *high-low* production figures and costs and use the difference to compute the variable portion of the costs. Using the same data, the figures would be:

Highest production for period	10,000 D. L. Hrs.	Costs	$10,600
Lowest production for period	5,000 D. L. Hrs.	Costs	6,000
Difference	5,000 D. L. Hrs.		$ 4,600

Variable rate for inspections equals $4,600/5,000 hours, or 92 cents per direct labor hour.

Statistical or Scatter-graph Method of Computing Variable Overhead Costs

Although the high-low average method of allocating the variable portion of semi-variable costs of overhead is one of the simplest methods, some prefer the use of the statistical scattergraph technique for accomplishing the same results. The statistical scattergraph technique determines the trend line for the two sets of data being compared. The method results in the determination of the regression line and is in fact a visual presentation of the correlation between two sets of data.

The steps involved in this method to separate the controllable and variable amount from that which is considered fixed would be as follows, using the same illustrative figures for inspection costs as previously given (see Illustration 16–17):

Illustration 16–17

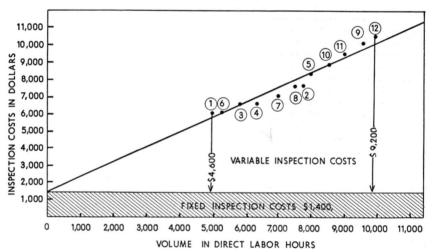

Numbers indicate the month for which figures were plotted.

1. The vertical scale (*y*-axis) is used for plotting the total inspection costs, and the horizontal scale (*x*-axis) is used for the volume of production—direct labor hours.
2. A trend line is drawn through the plotted positions so that roughly there are as many plotted points above as below the line. This represents the variable portion of the overhead costs for inspection.
3. The fixed overhead cost can now be indicated by drawing a horizontal line from point A, the intersection of the variable overhead line and the zero point of the volume of production (direct labor hours). This intersection represents the fixed inspection costs for any volume of production.

4. The variable inspection cost for any volume of production can now be determined by finding the difference between the fixed cost, $1,400, and the plotted inspection cost for that volume. For example, March would be $6,400 − $1,400, or $5,000. $5,000/5,800 direct labor hours = 86 cents per direct labor hour.

Managerial Significance of Separating the Semivariable Overhead Costs into Its Two Components   Some, but not necessarily all, of the variable elements of manufacturing overhead, selling, and administrative expenses may be controllable—that is, subject to reduction. To properly evaluate managerial effectiveness in cost reduction, it is first necessary to separate the *semivariable* overhead costs into that which is relatively fixed and beyond the control of the *supervisory* staff, and that which is variable and may be subject to reduction.

Therefore, in most effective cost accounting systems some form of budgetary procedure must be used in which projected costs and realized costs will be compared. Since in many concerns production fluctuates from month to month, or from season to season, a *flexible budget* not only for the manufacturing overhead but also for selling and administrative expenses is desirable. This will permit better managerial control through comparisons of the budgeted and actual costs and expenses at various volumes of production and sales.

The principles of flexible manufacturing overhead budgets are continued in the use of *standard or predetermined costs.* As will be discussed in the following chapters, standard costs are detailed figures of what the material, labor, and manufacturing overhead costs should be under normal operating conditions. This *estimated cost* presumes forecasting or budgeting material and labor costs in addition to manufacturing overhead. For a proper *control of costs,* there should be standard costs—*estimated costs under normal operating conditions*—which can be compared with the *actual costs* in order to control manufacturing operations.

The same principles apply to a study of the *distribution* and *administration cost analyses.* It is, therefore, fundamental that the reader understand the need for a budgetary system and the method of preparing and using it as a management tool in reducing the cost of production and distribution in order to increase income.

The specific relationships of the budget department and the cost accounting department may therefore be listed as follows:

1. The establishment of *predetermined manufacturing overhead cost rates.*
2. The preparation and use of *standard costs* (predetermined costs) for materials, labor, and also manufacturing overhead.

3. The preparation and control of predetermined distribution and administration costs.
4. The preparation of reports showing the comparison of budgeted cost figures with actual costs.
5. The use of forecasting charts—the break-even graph—showing the point at which a certain sales volume and its profit will break even with the expenses and costs.

Cash Budget

An important aspect of the budgeting process is the preparation of a cash budget. A cash budget is a schedule showing where cash will be expected to come from and where cash may be expected to go, i.e., it is a statement of expected cash receipts and disbursements.

Many companies have avoided the preparation of cash budgets or have prepared these but once a year. This may result in the company's inability to carry on certain activities with the further result that the potential profit of the company may be reduced. For example, a company may be delayed in expanding a product line because necessary funds may not be available at the desired time. Arrangements to obtain funds often have to be made well in advance. Similarly, a company may find itself with large sums of cash for relatively short periods of time. These funds could be invested. A properly prepared cash budget will point out shortages and excesses so that management can do something about them.

The length of time for which cash budgets should be prepared will vary from company to company. Generally, cash budgets should be prepared a year in advance on monthly or perhaps even weekly bases.

Importance of the Cash Budget

The preparation and then the possible revisions of the cash budget are important steps in the budgeting process. All activities that the business firm undertakes are based upon the premise that adequate cash will be available at the proper time to meet payrolls, invoice due dates, etc. The cash budget will provide the information on cash availability. The operating budget will become "operational" and can be implemented only after the cash budget has been prepared and management is confident that the cash will be available to carry on the various programs.

Preparing the Cash Budget

One way of preparing a cash budget is to estimate directly each expected source and use for the given time period. An illustration will best point out this method:

A cash budget for the month of June, 19—, is to be prepared. The only source of cash is from sales, and all sales are on account. Ninety-eight percent of the accounts are collected in the following manner (2 percent are considered uncollectible):

20% in month of sale
50% in month following sale
20% in second month following sale
10% in third month following sale

> Budgeted sales for June.................$1,000,000
> Actual sales:
> March........................... 900,000
> April............................ 1,200,000
> May............................. 1,300,000

Accounts payable are paid in the month following purchase since purchase discounts are not available in this industry.

> May purchases.........................$400,000
> June purchases......................... 700,000

Wages and salaries expense of $600,000 includes $40,000 accrued at the end of June to be paid in July. Wages of $30,000 were accrued at the end of May and were paid in June.

Other cash payments to be made in June:

> Semiannual interest payment..............$60,000
> Dividends............................. 80,000
> Tax payment, covers 6 months........... 70,000

The cash budget for the month is given in Illustration 16–18.

Illustration 16–18

ABC MANUFACTURERS

CASH BUDGET

For Month of June, 19—

Estimated cash balance, June 1.....................................		$ 360,000
Estimated cash receipts:		
From June sales, 20% × (98% of $1,000,000).....................$196,000		
From May sales, 50% × (98% of $1,300,000)..................... 637,000		
From April sales, 20% × (98% of $1,200,000)..................... 235,200		
From March sales, 10% × (98% of $900,000)...................... 88,200		
Total cash receipts...	1,156,400	
Cash available..	$1,516,400	
Estimated cash payments:		
On accounts payable...		$ 400,000
Wages and salaries:		
Expense..$600,000		
To be paid in July..................................... 40,000		
	$560,000	
May expense, paid in June.................................... 30,000		590,000
Interest..		60,000
Dividends...		80,000
Taxes..		70,000
Total estimated cash payments................................		$1,200,000
Cash Balance, June 30...		$ 316,400

Another method of cash budgeting, the adjusted net income method, begins with the budgeted net income figure and adjusts this figure to reflect cash transactions. It is a method similar to the one used to prepare a statement of sources and applications of funds. Costs and expenses such as depreciation and amortization which do not require cash outlays are added back to the projected net income. Cash outlays that are not reflected in the income statement are subtracted. Examples would be cash dividends or sums to be spent on the purchase of equipment. Expected excesses of collections over sales are added. Any excess of accounts receivable over sales is subtracted. Any decrease in payables is also subtracted. The resultant figure is the expected increase or decrease in cash.

The Capital Expenditure Budget A company's comprehensive budget should include not only an operating budget and a cash budget but also a capital expenditure budget. The capital expenditure budget may be the most difficult to prepare. Expenditures involve large sums of money, and commitments once made bind a company for many years.

What kinds of items are included in the capital expenditure budget? Generally, any expenditure which is not in payment of an obligation arising out of routine operations is a capital expenditure and includes:

1. Replacement of facilities.
2. Expansion of facilities.
3. Expansion of products, services, and sales territories.
4. Improvements in products and processes.

A businessman may or may not have a choice in deciding whether or not he will invest in a given item. For example, if the steam boiler at Plant No. 1 is judged unsafe by insurance inspectors, a replacement must be made if the plant is to continue in operation and if the old boiler cannot be repaired. On the other hand, the manager may have a choice in situations such as should the old stamping machine be used or should a new one be purchased? This discussion will assume a choice exists, and thus the manager needs a rational method to aid him in deciding whether or not he should invest in a particular item. The company's funds available for capital expenditures are often limited, and only the more profitable opportunities commensurate with the desired risk can be considered. The potential investment opportunities must be evaluated.

Criteria to Use in Evaluating Proposals The businessman will invest in a given project if the likelihood exists that he will earn the desired return on his investment. The return on the investment may be in the form of a cost saving resulting from replacing an old machine with a new one or it may be in the form of additional profit resulting from the adoption of a new product. This cost saving or additional profit is often referred to as the *operating advantage*.

The *investment* is the amount that must be expended, generally once, because of the proposal. It may involve the cost of a machine (plus shipping, and installation costs) in an equipment replacement decision or it may involve the allocation of additional funds to inventories in a new product situation, etc.

Estimates of the *operating advantage* and the *investment* are necessary in evaluating capital expenditure proposals. Funds are spent NOW with the expectation that some benefit will be derived in the FUTURE. On the one hand is the "one-shot" investment, that which is given up. On the other hand is the operating advantage, a *stream* of expected benefits. After the proposed investment and the operating advantage are analyzed, the businessman finds himself in a better position to judge whether or not to invest. The methods of analysis that will be used in this chapter are the payback, the simple rate of return, and the time adjusted rate of return.

Payback Evaluation   The *payback* method measures the length of time necessary to recoup the investment. It is primarily a method used to measure the return *of* the investment. An illustration will be of help. Management of the ABC Plating Company has the opportunity to purchase a new machine for $19,000 plus $1,000 of installation, etc., costs. A cost study has shown that the operating advantage is expected to amount to $2,000 per year over the life of the new machine. The new machine's estimated life is 10 years, and the combined federal and state tax rate is 50 percent.

The payback period is computed as follows:

$$\frac{\text{Net investment}}{\text{Operating advantage} + \text{Depreciation} - \text{Income tax}} = \text{Payback period.}$$

$$\frac{\$20,000}{\$2,000 + \$2,000 - \$1,000} = 6.67 \text{ years.}$$

Note that depreciation is added back to the operating advantage. This is necessary because this method measures the full amount that flows into the business, i.e., the cash flow. Each year $3,000 of new cash is generated, and at that rate, 6.67 years are necessary to recoup the $20,000 new investment. The fact that the depreciation and the savings each amount to $2,000 is coincidental but a possibility as shown here.

Most businessmen have at some time relied on the payback method as it discloses how fast one will get his money back and thus has some use in evaluating risk, especially if it is possible that the new machine may become obsolete before the end of the 10 years estimated as the useful life. Payback computations also are of help in determining the liquidity of the company as the new cash generated is determinable. However, the method does not show how much will be earned; profitability is not shown.

Simple Rate of Return Evaluation   The simple or accounting rate of return method measures the profitability of the investment proposal; the return *on* the investment is computed. The calculation is made as follows:

$$\frac{\text{Operating advantage (after tax)}}{\text{New initial investment}} = \text{Rate of return on investment.}$$

If the same data are used as in the preceding illustration, the simple rate of return is:

$$\frac{\$1,000}{\$20,000} = 5 \text{ percent.}$$

Of the $3,000 of new cash generated each year, $1,000 is profit and $2,000 is the return *of* the investment, i.e., depreciation. Since $2,000 of the investment is recouped each year via depreciation, the *average* investment is $10,000. Some analysts thus use the average investment rather than the initial investment:

$$\frac{\$1,000}{\$10,000} = 10 \text{ percent.}$$

Not only does a difficulty arise in determining whether to use initial investment or average investment but the simple rate of return treats each year's savings the same as any other year's savings. Also, a comparison is made between savings to be received in the future with an investment to be made now; the two are not comparable. The time adjusted rate of return method solves the problems created by the simple rate of return method.

Time Adjusted Rate of Return Method   The time adjusted rate of return method brings in the time element, and the investment is evaluated on a comparable basis with the stream of future payments. A dollar to be received sometime in the future is worth less that $1 today. For example, if one wants

$1 a year from now and the going rate of interest is 4 percent (compounded annually), the present value table on page 505 shows that $0.962 invested now will yield $1 a year from now. That $1 is worth only $0.962 today. Similarly, if an investor wants $1 per year for 10 years and the going rate of interest is 4 percent, the investor would need $8.111 now as per the table on page 504. Note the difference between the two tables. The one on page 505 measures the present value of $1, and the one on page 504 measures the present value of $1 *per year* for N years, i.e., a flow.

The table on page 504 is useful in determining the time adjusted rate of return. The stream of future payments must be discounted to present value and compared to the investment. Using the data from the illustration, the net investment was $20,000 with an operating advantage of $2,000 less taxes of $1,000. Depreciation was $2,000. The $20,000 of investment is compared with the stream of $3,000 which is the saving plus depreciation minus taxes. If $20,000 is expected to yield $3,000 per year for 10 years, $20,000/$3,000 or $6.667 of investment is needed to produce $1 per year for 10 years. (The tables are in the form of $1.) If $6.667 is the present value of the future stream of $1 payments to be received in each of the next 10 years, what is the rate of return? The table on page 504 shows the following under 10 years in searching for 6.667:

$$8\% = 6.710$$
$$10\% = 6.145$$

Interpolating yields the following results:

$$\frac{0.043}{0.565}\ (2\%) = 0.0152 + 8\%, \text{ or } 8.015\%.$$

The 8 percent return is what the investor expects to receive on his investment when the element of time is considered. The time adjusted rate of return incorporates both the return *of* the investment and the return *on* the investment. The use of this method has resulted in the various investment proposals being placed on comparable bases. Today, many companies use the time adjusted rate of return method in evaluating investment opportunities.

Applications of Capital
Expenditure Analysis
The type of analysis presented earlier pertaining to the purchase of a new machine may be used to evaluate other types of proposals; any type of investment opportunity may be evaluated. For example, the analysis may be of help in a situation where the replace-

Present Value of $1 Received Annually for N Years

Years (N)	1%	2%	4%	6%	8%	10%	12%	14%	15%	16%	18%	20%	22%	24%	25%	26%	28%	30%	35%	40%	45%	50%
1	0.990	0.980	0.962	0.943	0.926	0.909	0.893	0.877	0.870	0.862	0.847	0.833	0.820	0.806	0.800	0.794	0.781	0.769	0.741	0.714	0.690	0.667
2	1.970	1.942	1.886	1.833	1.783	1.736	1.690	1.647	1.626	1.605	1.566	1.528	1.492	1.457	1.440	1.424	1.392	1.361	1.289	1.224	1.165	1.111
3	2.941	2.884	2.775	2.673	2.577	2.487	2.402	2.322	2.283	2.246	2.174	2.106	2.042	1.981	1.952	1.923	1.868	1.816	1.696	1.589	1.493	1.407
4	3.902	3.808	3.630	3.465	3.312	3.170	3.037	2.914	2.855	2.798	2.690	2.589	2.494	2.404	2.362	2.320	2.241	2.166	1.997	1.849	1.720	1.605
5	4.853	4.713	4.452	4.212	3.993	3.791	3.605	3.433	3.352	3.274	3.127	2.991	2.864	2.745	2.689	2.635	2.532	2.436	2.220	2.035	1.876	1.737
6	5.795	5.601	5.242	4.917	4.623	4.355	4.111	3.889	3.784	3.685	3.498	3.326	3.167	3.020	2.951	2.885	2.759	2.643	2.385	2.168	1.983	1.824
7	6.728	6.472	6.002	5.582	5.206	4.868	4.564	4.288	4.160	4.039	3.812	3.605	3.416	3.242	3.161	3.083	2.937	2.802	2.508	2.263	2.057	1.883
8	7.652	7.325	6.733	6.210	5.747	5.335	4.968	4.639	4.487	4.344	4.078	3.837	3.619	3.421	3.329	3.241	3.076	2.925	2.598	2.331	2.108	1.922
9	8.566	8.162	7.435	6.802	6.247	5.759	5.328	4.946	4.772	4.607	4.303	4.031	3.786	3.566	3.463	3.366	3.184	3.019	2.665	2.379	2.144	1.948
10	9.471	8.983	8.111	7.360	6.710	6.145	5.650	5.216	5.019	4.833	4.494	4.192	3.923	3.682	3.571	3.465	3.269	3.092	2.715	2.414	2.168	1.965
11	10.368	9.787	8.760	7.887	7.139	6.495	5.937	5.453	5.234	5.029	4.656	4.327	4.035	3.776	3.656	3.544	3.335	3.147	2.752	2.438	2.185	1.977
12	11.255	10.575	9.385	8.384	7.536	6.814	6.194	5.660	5.421	5.197	4.793	4.439	4.127	3.851	3.725	3.606	3.387	3.190	2.779	2.456	2.196	1.985
13	12.134	11.343	9.986	8.853	7.904	7.103	6.424	5.842	5.583	5.342	4.910	4.533	4.203	3.912	3.780	3.656	3.427	3.223	2.799	2.468	2.204	1.990
14	13.004	12.106	10.563	9.295	8.244	7.367	6.628	6.002	5.724	5.468	5.008	4.611	4.265	3.962	3.824	3.695	3.459	3.249	2.814	2.477	2.210	1.993
15	13.865	12.849	11.118	9.712	8.559	7.606	6.811	6.142	5.847	5.575	5.092	4.675	4.315	4.001	3.859	3.726	3.483	3.268	2.825	2.484	2.214	1.995
16	14.718	13.578	11.652	10.106	8.851	7.824	6.974	6.265	5.954	5.669	5.162	4.730	4.357	4.033	3.887	3.751	3.503	3.283	2.834	2.489	2.216	1.997
17	15.562	14.292	12.166	10.477	9.122	8.022	7.120	6.373	6.047	5.749	5.222	4.775	4.391	4.059	3.910	3.771	3.518	3.295	2.840	2.492	2.218	1.998
18	16.398	14.992	12.659	10.828	9.372	8.201	7.250	6.467	6.128	5.818	5.273	4.812	4.419	4.080	3.928	3.786	3.529	3.304	2.844	2.494	2.219	1.999
19	17.226	15.678	13.134	11.158	9.604	8.365	7.366	6.550	6.198	5.877	5.316	4.844	4.442	4.097	3.942	3.799	3.539	3.311	2.848	2.496	2.220	1.999
20	18.046	16.351	13.590	11.470	9.818	8.514	7.469	6.623	6.259	5.929	5.353	4.870	4.460	4.110	3.954	3.808	3.546	3.316	2.850	2.497	2.221	1.999
21	18.857	17.011	14.029	11.764	10.017	8.649	7.562	6.687	6.312	5.973	5.384	4.891	4.476	4.121	3.963	3.816	3.551	3.320	2.852	2.498	2.221	2.000
22	19.660	17.658	14.451	12.042	10.201	8.772	7.645	6.743	6.359	6.011	5.410	4.909	4.488	4.130	3.970	3.822	3.556	3.323	2.853	2.498	2.222	2.000
23	20.456	18.292	14.857	12.303	10.371	8.883	7.718	6.792	6.399	6.044	5.432	4.925	4.499	4.137	3.976	3.827	3.559	3.325	2.854	2.499	2.222	2.000
24	21.243	18.914	15.247	12.550	10.529	8.985	7.784	6.835	6.434	6.073	5.451	4.937	4.507	4.143	3.981	3.831	3.562	3.327	2.855	2.499	2.222	2.000
25	22.023	19.523	15.622	12.783	10.675	9.077	7.843	6.873	6.464	6.097	5.467	4.948	4.514	4.147	3.985	3.834	3.564	3.329	2.856	2.499	2.222	2.000
26	22.795	20.121	15.983	13.003	10.810	9.161	7.896	6.906	6.491	6.118	5.480	4.956	4.520	4.151	3.988	3.837	3.566	3.330	2.856	2.500	2.222	2.000
27	23.560	20.707	16.330	13.211	10.935	9.237	7.943	6.935	6.514	6.136	5.492	4.964	4.524	4.154	3.990	3.839	3.567	3.331	2.856	2.500	2.222	2.000
28	24.316	21.281	16.663	13.406	11.051	9.307	7.984	6.961	6.534	6.152	5.502	4.970	4.528	4.157	3.992	3.840	3.568	3.331	2.857	2.500	2.222	2.000
29	25.066	21.844	16.984	13.591	11.158	9.370	8.022	6.983	6.551	6.166	5.510	4.975	4.531	4.159	3.994	3.841	3.569	3.332	2.857	2.500	2.222	2.000
30	25.808	22.396	17.292	13.765	11.258	9.427	8.055	7.003	6.566	6.177	5.517	4.979	4.534	4.160	3.995	3.842	3.569	3.332	2.857	2.500	2.222	2.000
40	32.835	27.355	19.793	15.046	11.925	9.779	8.244	7.105	6.642	6.234	5.548	4.997	4.544	4.166	3.999	3.846	3.571	3.333	2.857	2.500	2.222	2.000
50	39.196	31.424	21.482	15.762	12.234	9.915	8.304	7.133	6.661	6.246	5.554	4.999	4.545	4.167	4.000	3.846	3.571	3.333	2.857	2.500	2.222	2.000

Present Value of $1

Years Hence	1%	2%	4%	6%	8%	10%	12%	14%	15%	16%	18%	20%	22%	24%	25%	26%	28%	30%	35%	40%	45%	50%
1	0.990	0.980	0.962	0.943	0.926	0.909	0.893	0.877	0.870	0.862	0.847	0.833	0.820	0.806	0.800	0.794	0.781	0.769	0.741	0.714	0.690	0.667
2	0.980	0.961	0.925	0.890	0.857	0.826	0.797	0.769	0.756	0.743	0.718	0.694	0.672	0.650	0.640	0.630	0.610	0.592	0.549	0.510	0.476	0.444
3	0.971	0.942	0.889	0.840	0.794	0.751	0.712	0.675	0.658	0.641	0.609	0.579	0.551	0.524	0.512	0.500	0.477	0.455	0.406	0.364	0.328	0.296
4	0.961	0.924	0.855	0.792	0.735	0.683	0.636	0.592	0.572	0.552	0.516	0.482	0.451	0.423	0.410	0.397	0.373	0.350	0.301	0.260	0.226	0.198
5	0.951	0.906	0.822	0.747	0.681	0.621	0.567	0.519	0.497	0.476	0.437	0.402	0.370	0.341	0.328	0.315	0.291	0.269	0.223	0.186	0.156	0.132
6	0.942	0.888	0.790	0.705	0.630	0.564	0.507	0.456	0.432	0.410	0.370	0.335	0.303	0.275	0.262	0.250	0.227	0.207	0.165	0.133	0.108	0.088
7	0.933	0.871	0.760	0.665	0.583	0.513	0.452	0.400	0.376	0.354	0.314	0.279	0.249	0.222	0.210	0.198	0.178	0.159	0.122	0.095	0.074	0.059
8	0.923	0.853	0.731	0.627	0.540	0.467	0.404	0.351	0.327	0.305	0.266	0.233	0.204	0.179	0.168	0.157	0.139	0.123	0.091	0.068	0.051	0.039
9	0.914	0.837	0.703	0.592	0.500	0.424	0.361	0.308	0.284	0.263	0.225	0.194	0.167	0.144	0.134	0.125	0.108	0.094	0.067	0.048	0.035	0.026
10	0.905	0.820	0.676	0.558	0.463	0.386	0.322	0.270	0.247	0.227	0.191	0.162	0.137	0.116	0.107	0.099	0.085	0.073	0.050	0.035	0.024	0.017
11	0.896	0.804	0.650	0.527	0.429	0.350	0.287	0.237	0.215	0.195	0.162	0.135	0.112	0.094	0.086	0.079	0.066	0.056	0.037	0.025	0.017	0.012
12	0.887	0.788	0.625	0.497	0.397	0.319	0.257	0.208	0.187	0.168	0.137	0.112	0.092	0.076	0.069	0.062	0.052	0.043	0.027	0.018	0.012	0.008
13	0.879	0.773	0.601	0.469	0.368	0.290	0.229	0.182	0.163	0.145	0.116	0.093	0.075	0.061	0.055	0.050	0.040	0.033	0.020	0.013	0.008	0.005
14	0.870	0.758	0.577	0.442	0.340	0.263	0.205	0.160	0.141	0.125	0.099	0.078	0.062	0.049	0.044	0.039	0.032	0.025	0.015	0.009	0.006	0.003
15	0.861	0.743	0.555	0.417	0.315	0.239	0.183	0.140	0.123	0.108	0.084	0.065	0.051	0.040	0.035	0.031	0.025	0.020	0.011	0.006	0.004	0.002
16	0.853	0.728	0.534	0.394	0.292	0.218	0.163	0.123	0.107	0.093	0.071	0.054	0.042	0.032	0.028	0.025	0.019	0.015	0.008	0.005	0.003	0.002
17	0.844	0.714	0.513	0.371	0.270	0.198	0.146	0.108	0.093	0.080	0.060	0.045	0.034	0.026	0.023	0.020	0.015	0.012	0.006	0.003	0.002	0.001
18	0.836	0.700	0.494	0.350	0.250	0.180	0.130	0.095	0.081	0.069	0.051	0.038	0.028	0.021	0.018	0.016	0.012	0.009	0.005	0.002	0.001	0.001
19	0.828	0.686	0.475	0.331	0.232	0.164	0.116	0.083	0.070	0.060	0.043	0.031	0.023	0.017	0.014	0.012	0.009	0.007	0.003	0.002	0.001	0.001
20	0.820	0.673	0.456	0.312	0.215	0.149	0.104	0.073	0.061	0.051	0.037	0.026	0.019	0.014	0.012	0.010	0.007	0.005	0.002	0.001	0.001	0.001
21	0.811	0.660	0.439	0.294	0.199	0.135	0.093	0.064	0.053	0.044	0.031	0.022	0.015	0.011	0.009	0.008	0.006	0.004	0.002	0.001		
22	0.803	0.647	0.422	0.278	0.184	0.123	0.083	0.056	0.046	0.038	0.026	0.018	0.013	0.009	0.007	0.006	0.004	0.003	0.001	0.001		
23	0.795	0.634	0.406	0.262	0.170	0.112	0.074	0.049	0.040	0.033	0.022	0.015	0.010	0.007	0.006	0.005	0.003	0.002	0.001			
24	0.788	0.622	0.390	0.247	0.158	0.102	0.066	0.043	0.035	0.028	0.019	0.013	0.008	0.006	0.005	0.004	0.003	0.002	0.001			
25	0.780	0.610	0.375	0.233	0.146	0.092	0.059	0.038	0.030	0.024	0.016	0.010	0.007	0.005	0.004	0.003	0.002	0.001	0.001			
26	0.772	0.598	0.361	0.220	0.135	0.084	0.053	0.033	0.026	0.021	0.014	0.009	0.006	0.004	0.003	0.002	0.002	0.001				
27	0.764	0.586	0.347	0.207	0.125	0.076	0.047	0.029	0.023	0.018	0.011	0.007	0.005	0.003	0.002	0.002	0.001	0.001				
28	0.757	0.574	0.333	0.196	0.116	0.069	0.042	0.026	0.020	0.016	0.010	0.006	0.004	0.002	0.002	0.002	0.001	0.001				
29	0.749	0.563	0.321	0.185	0.107	0.063	0.037	0.022	0.017	0.014	0.008	0.005	0.003	0.002	0.002	0.001	0.001					
30	0.742	0.552	0.308	0.174	0.099	0.057	0.033	0.020	0.015	0.012	0.007	0.004	0.003	0.002	0.001	0.001	0.001					
40	0.672	0.453	0.208	0.097	0.046	0.022	0.011	0.005	0.004	0.003	0.001	0.001										
50	0.608	0.372	0.141	0.054	0.021	0.009	0.003	0.001	0.001	0.001												

ment of facilities is being contemplated. An illustration will be of help.

Assume a situation where operating expenses before depreciation are expected to amount to $2,900 per year if manufacturing is continued with the present machine. For an investment of $6,000 in a new machine lasting 10 years, the operating expenses before depreciation can be cut to $1,500. The dismantling cost of the old would about equal any revenue realized from its sale. The tax rate is 50 percent.

Should the company buy the new one or keep the old? Computation of the payback and time adjusted rate of return will be of help:

	Annual Cost of New	Annual Cost of Old
Operating expenses..................	$1,500	$2,900
Depreciation........................	600	0
	$2,100	$2,900

Saving, $800 (before tax)
Tax, $400
Net saving, $400

$$\text{Payback} = \frac{\$6,000}{\$600 + \$400} = 6 \text{ years}$$

The time adjusted rate of return method shows that for the $6,000 investment, $1,000 is returned each year, or $1 for each $6 of investment. The table on page 505 discloses a rate of return of approximately 11 percent.

Note that in the above computation, depreciation on the old machine was ignored. The decision whether or not to replace the machine should be based on *future* costs and not on past costs. The cost of the old machine is a *sunk cost,* and whether the amount is written off over one day, one year, or several years is not relevant for the decision of whether or not to buy the new one. What is relevant is any future cost. If the old machine had a resale value, that amount would be depreciated over its remaining life. The reason is that if the company kept the old machine, it gave up the opportunity to receive the proceeds from its sale.

The Preparation of the Capital Expenditure Budget   Capital expenditure proposals in a modern company originate at all levels, but the evaluation of the proposals is made by the staff of the chief financial executive with the data supplied by the originating units. Once the proposals are evaluated and ranked, preferably with the use of the time adjusted rate of return method, it is up to management to make the decisions as to which, if any, of the investment opportunities to accept. The level of management making the decision might depend on the amount of the expenditure. To illustrate, in one company, expenditures of $2,000 or less may be made at the plant level, expenditure decisions involving $2,000 to $10,000 are made at division, $10,000 to $50,000 decisions are made by the president, and any expenditure over $50,000 needs authorization by the board of directors.

Once management selects the desired proposals, these are incorporated into the master budget of the company. The capital expenditure budget would show the detail for the various expenditures. The budget has to be constructed by time period and by project as a given project such as construction of a plant may cover more than one accounting period.

Cost Control of Capital Expenditures The capital expenditure budget should be used in a manner similar to the other budgets, and cost control should be exercised by using the budget as a basis of comparison with the actual data. The most effective cost control is achieved when actual costs and budgeted costs are compared by *project.*

Post-completion audits should also be conducted to see whether or not the project actually developed in a manner similar to what was forecast, i.e., is the operating advantage that which was expected and is the rate of return comparable to what was estimated, etc.? Did the investment produce the results that were expected?

QUESTIONS FOR REVIEW

1. Why should flexibility be desirable since the budget is supposed to set forth the one best program for the business to follow?

2. What are two ways in which an overhead flexible budget might be stated?

3. Distinguish among *theoretical capacity, normal capacity,* and *practical capacity.* Why is it important to distinguish among these concepts?

4. "The plant and equipment budget is one of the most important parts of the budget program." Do you agree? Explain.

5. "A profitable business need not worry about cash as cash will always be available." Do you agree? Explain.

6. Briefly describe the following methods and the advantages, if any, and disadvantages, if any, of using each in deciding among alternatives while in the process of capital budgeting:
   a) Payback method.
   b) Simple rate of return.
   c) Time adjusted rate of return.

7. Distinguish between the two methods of cash budgeting. Which do you prefer? State your reasons.

8. Explain how you would isolate the fixed and variable components in a

semivariable cost. What assumption or assumptions did you make when you isolated the fixed and variable components?

9. How often should actual and budgeted data be compared?

10. How can a capital expenditure budget be used as a cost control device?

PROBLEMS—GROUP A

Problem 16–1.   Purpose: *Flexible Budgets for Overhead*

Following is a summary of the flexible overhead budget for the Baker Manufacturing Company:

TOTAL COSTS

Type of Cost	60%	70%	80%	90%	100%
Total variable:					
Variable........................	$ 675.00	$ 787.50	$ 900.00	$1,012.50	$1,125.00
Semivariable portion..............	375.00	437.50	500.00	562.50	625.00
	$1,050.00	$1,225.00	$1,400.00	$1,575.00	$1,750.00
Total fixed:					
Semivariable portion..............	$ 125.00	$ 125.00	$ 125.00	$ 125.00	$ 125.00
Fixed...........................	525.00	525.00	525.00	525.00	525.00
	$ 650.00	$ 650.00	$ 650.00	$ 650.00	$ 650.00
Total Costs....................	$1,700.00	$1,875.00	$2,050.00	$2,225.00	$2,400.00

Budgeted labor hours at 100 percent of capacity are 2,500.

Required:

a) Assume that the overhead rate is established on the basis of labor hours. Compute the rate at each of the above levels of production.

b) Indicate the reason or reasons for the differences in rates.

c) Assume that the overhead rate is established at 100 percent of capacity. Also assume actual production reached 95 percent of capacity and that $2,350 of costs were incurred. Account for the differences, if any, between budget and actual.

Problem 16–2.   Purpose: *Budgeting Capital Expenditures*

The ABC Company is considering the purchase of a new boring machine to replace the two boring machines presently in use. The new machine would cost $50,000 and have an estimated useful life of 10 years. This machine would have almost no residual value at the end of the 10 years. The new machine would have a "practical" capacity three times as great as each of the present boring machines; it would be run by one man receiving $3 per hour.

The present machines have a combined book value of $11,000, a sound value of $8,500, and a remaining useful life of five years. The engineers estimate that the machines could be sold for a total of $1,000 at the present time; scrap value five years from now would be negligible. Each of the present machines requires one operator receiving $2 per hour and can produce 60 per hour.

Potential production is based on an eight-hour day, five-day week, 50-week year.

If the production forecasts for the next 10 years indicate that an average of

252,000 work units will be required each year, should the ABC Company purchase the new boring machine? (Assume 50 percent income tax rate.)

Problem 16–3.   Purpose: *Budgeting Overhead Costs*

The Adams Machine Company estimated the following for the year 1968:

Dept.	Floor Space	Value of Machinery	Horsepower Hours	Number of Employees	Indirect Material Cost	Direct Labor Cost	Indirect Labor Cost
1............1,500		$10,000	2,500	15	$1,250	$25,000	$ 2,000
2............4,500		10,000	2,500	25	1,150	45,000	1,500
3............3,000		20,000	5,000	25	500	30,000	1,500
Service X....1,000		10,000	2,000	10	500		10,000

Estimated general manufacturing expenses not listed above were:

```
Rent................................$ 2,000
Repairs to building....................  10,000
Depreciation of machinery..............  5% of investment
Superintendence.......................$ 7,500
Power.................................  3,600
Insurance on machinery................  1,000
```

Service Department X was distributed as follows: Dept. No. 1, 1/7; Dept. No. 2, 4/7; and Dept. No. 3, 2/7.

Required:

a) Prepare a budget for each of the departments.

b) Determine the applied manufacturing expense rate for each producing department on the basis of direct labor cost.

c) Suppose the Adams Machine Company would have had three service departments. Discuss the problems that might arise in allocating service department costs to producing departments. How would you solve these problems?

Problem 16–4.   Purpose: *Cash Budgeting*

The Byrnes Mercantile Corporation is a wholesaler and ends its fiscal year on December 31. You have been requested in early January, 1968, to assist in the preparation of a cash forecast. The following information is available regarding the company's operations:

1. Management believes the 1967 sales pattern is a reasonable estimate of 1968 sales. Sales in 1967 were as follows:

```
January.............................$ 360,000
February............................  420,000
March...............................  600,000
April...............................  540,000
May.................................  480,000
June................................  400,000
July................................  350,000
August..............................  550,000
September...........................  500,000
October.............................  400,000
November............................  600,000
December............................  800,000
    Total...........................$6,000,000
```

2. The accounts receivable at December 31 total $380,000. Sales collections are generally made as follows:

> During month of sale........60%
> In first subsequent month....30
> In second subsequent month.. 9
> Uncollectible.............. 1

3. The purchase cost of goods averages 60 percent of selling price. The cost of the inventory on hand at December 31 is $840,000 of which $30,000 is obsolete. Arrangements have been made to sell the obsolete inventory in January at half of the normal selling price on a C.O.D. basis.

  The company wishes to maintain the inventory as of the first of each month at a level of three months' sales as determined by the sales forecast for the next three months. All purchases are paid for on the tenth of the following month. Accounts payable for purchases at December 31 total $370,000.

4. Recurring fixed expenses amount to $120,000 per month including depreciation of $20,000. For accounting purposes the company apportions the recurring fixed expenses to the various months in the same proportion as that month's estimated sales bears to the estimated total annual sales. Variable expenses amount to 10 percent of sales.

  Payments for expenses are made as follows:

	During Month Incurred	Following Month
Fixed expenses	55%	45%
Variable expenses	70	30

5. Annual property taxes amount to $50,000 and are paid in equal installments on December 31 and March 31. The property taxes are in addition to the expense in item "4" above.
6. It is anticipated that cash dividends of $20,000 will be paid each quarter on the 15th day of the third month of the quarter.
7. During the winter unusual advertising costs will be incurred which will require cash payments of $10,000 in February and $15,000 in March. The advertising costs are in addition to the expenses in item "4" above.
8. Equipment replacements are made at the rate of $3,000 per month. The equipment has an average estimated life of six years.
9. The company's income tax for 1967 is $230,000. A Declaration of Estimated Income Tax was filed for 1967. The Declaration estimated the company's total 1967 tax as $210,000 and payments were made as prescribed by income tax regulations. The balance of the tax due will be paid in equal installments.

  For 1968 the company will file a Declaration estimating the total tax as $220,000.

10. At December 31, 1967, the company had a bank loan with an unpaid balance of $280,000. The loan requires a principal payment of $20,000 on the last day of each month plus interest at $\frac{1}{2}$ percent per month on the unpaid balance at the first of the month. The entire balance is due on March 31, 1968.

11. The cash balance at December 31, 1967, is $100,000.

12. The client understands that the ethical considerations involved in preparing the following statement will be taken care of by your letter accompanying the statement. (Do not prepare the letter.)

Required:

Prepare a cash forecast statement by months for the first three months of 1968 for The Byrnes Mercantile Corporation. The statement should show the amount of cash on hand (or deficiency of cash) at the end of each month. All computations and supporting schedules should be presented in good form.

(Adapted from an AICPA Uniform Examination)

Problem 16–5. Purpose: *Budgeting Capital Expenditures*

Five alternate investment opportunities were presented to the president of the Barnhart Manufacturing Company. They are listed below:

Investment	Outlay	Annual Proceeds	Expected Life
1.	$ 62,500	$ 9,000	16 years
2.	76,820	21,000	21
3.	380,000	41,000	19
4.	18,000	6,000	10
5.	5,400	3,000	4

Required:

a) Compute the payback period for each of the above.

b) Compute the simple rate of return for each of the above.

c) Compute the time adjusted rate of return for each of the above.

d) Which of the above proposals is most desirable? The least desirable? Why?

Problem 16–6. Purpose: *Flexible Budgeting*

You have been designated as the chief budget officer of the Brenline Manufacturing Company. You have decided to employ flexible budgets in the manufacturing expense area. A study of the repairs and maintenance costs for a group of machines has disclosed the following:

	Machine-Hours	Repairs and Maintenance
January	3,000	$ 900
February	3,500	930
March	4,000	980
April	5,000	1,050
May	2,700	840
June	2,900	870
July	4,200	1,210
August	2,600	830
September	3,100	910
October	3,000	905
November	2,400	810
December	2,600	830

Required:

a) Determine the fixed and variable portion of the repairs and maintenance expense.

b) Prepare a budget for each of the following months of the coming year:

	Month	*Estimated Machine-Hours*
January		2,800
February		3,700
March		4,200

c) What could be the reason for the sudden increase from June to July? Should this have any effect on budget construction? Explain.

Problem 16–7. Purpose: *Comparison of Budgeted and Actual Overhead*

The Kent Company, engaged in production of heavy equipment, has applied factory overhead to its product on the basis of an average rate of 115 percent of direct labor cost. This rate, at the time it was established, was based on the following information as to expected operations:

Direct labor hours	136,000
Direct labor cost	$163,200
Average rate per hour	$1.20
Fixed overhead	$ 57,936
Variable overhead	129,744
Total overhead	$187,680

At December 31, 1968, the end of the first accounting period, the records disclosed the following information:

Direct labor hours	130,000
Direct labor cost	$183,040
Average rate per hour	$1.408
Fixed overhead	$ 75,400
Variable overhead	145,600
Total overhead (actual expense)	$221,000
Underabsorbed overhead	10,504

The management is concerned with the fact that it failed to absorb overhead of $10,504 in the year's operations.

Required:

a) You are to prepare an explanation for management showing why the $10,504 underabsorption existed. You are to compute and show the effect of variation in direct labor rates and direct labor hours on the absorption of both fixed and variable overhead. Support your conclusions with computations and explanatory comments setting forth the significance of each item in the analysis. (Computations should be corrected to the nearest dollar.)

b) Criticize the system currently being used to absorb overhead.

(Adapted from an AICPA Uniform Examination)

PROBLEMS—GROUP B

Problem 16–8. Purpose: *Flexible Budgeting for Overhead*

The flexible budget of the assembly department of the Lyle Manufacturing Company is shown below:

	0%	20%	40%	60%	80%	100%	120%
Supervision	$200	$200	$ 200	$ 200	$ 200	$ 200	$ 200
Powerhouse labor	140	172	204	236	268	300	332
Fuel	240	292	344	396	448	500	552
Tools	60	76	92	108	124	140	156
Supplies	20	35	50	65	80	95	110
Maintenance	25	60	95	130	165	200	235
Depreciation	50	50	50	50	50	50	50
Taxes	15	15	15	15	15	15	15
	$750	$900	$1,050	$1,200	$1,350	$1,500	$1,650

Operations are expected to be at 80 percent of capacity during the coming period. Actual activity was, however, at 75 percent of capacity with the following costs:

Supervision	$ 220
Labor	295
Fuel	450
Tools	125
Supplies	75
Maintenance	140
Depreciation	50
Taxes	15
	$1,370

Required:

a) By how much do the actual costs differ from the budgeted variable costs, in total? Show computations.

b) Prepare an analysis comparing budgeted and actual costs.

c) What is the usefulness to management of the analysis made in (b)?

Problem 16–9. Purpose: *Capital Expenditures Budgeting*

The Liverpool Production Company currently is using a machine which cost $40,000. The machine has a present net book value of $18,000; is being depreciated at the rate of $1,500 per year; has a remaining useful life of 10 years; will have an estimated salvage of $3,000 at the end of its estimated useful life; and has a current salvage value of $12,000. The machine currently produces profit before taxes or depreciation of $6,000 per year, but in order for this to continue for the next 10 years, the company will need to make extensive repairs during the coming year in the amount of $6,000.

As an alternative to continuing under present conditions, the company is considering the acquisition of a new machine. The purchase price of the new machine is $35,000. Shipping charges to be paid by the purchaser will amount to $1,500, and installation costs are estimated at $800. As with the old machine, depreciation of the new machine will be taken on a straight-line basis over a period of 10 years, with an allowance being made for no residual salvage value at the end of the 10 years. The new machine will produce profit before taxes or depreciation of $12,000.

If the new machine is purchased, the old machine will be sold for $12,000.

The company's income tax rate is 50 percent.

Required:

a) Determine the net cost of the new machinery for investment analysis.

b) Compute (1) simple accounting rate of return; (2) simple payback; and (3) time adjusted rate of return.

c) Should the company dispose of the old machine and acquire the new machine? Why?

Problem 16–10.   Purpose: *Cash Budgeting (CPA Problem)*

The Loading Company is planning to construct a two-unit facility for the loading of iron ore into ships. On or before January 1, 1968, the stockholders will invest $100,000 in the company's capital stock to provide its initial working capital. To finance the construction program (the total planned cost of which is $1,800,000), the company will obtain a commitment from a lending organization for a loan of $1,800,000. This loan is to be secured by a 10-year mortgage note bearing interest at 5 percent per year on the unpaid balance. The principal amount of the loan is to be repaid in equal semiannual installments of $100,000 beginning June 30, 1969.

Inasmuch as the proceeds of the loan will only be required as construction work progresses, the company has agreed to pay a commitment fee beginning January 1, 1968, equal to 1 percent per year on the unused portion of the loan commitment. This fee is payable at the time amounts are "drawn-down," except at the time of the first "draw-down."

Work on the construction of the facility will commence in the fall of 1967. The first payment to the contractor will be due on January 1, 1968, at which time the commitment and loan agreement will become effective and the company will make its first "draw-down," for payment to the contractor, in the amount of $800,000. As construction progresses, additional payments will be made to the contractors by "drawing-down" the remaining loan proceeds as follows (it is assumed that payment to the contractors will be made on the same dates as the loan proceeds are "drawn-down"):

April 1, 1968.	$500,000
July 1, 1968.	300,000
December 31, 1968.	100,000
April 1, 1969.	100,000

Because of weather conditions, the facility can operate only from April 1 through November 30 of each year. The construction program will permit the completion of the first of the two plant units (capable of handling 5,000,000 tons) in time for its use during the 1968 shipping season. The second unit (capable of handling an additional 3,000,000 tons) will be completed in time for the 1969 season. It is expected that 5,000,000 tons will be handled by the facility during the 1968 season; thereafter, the tonnage handled is expected to increase in each subsequent year by 300,000 tons until a level of 6,500,000 tons is reached.

The company's revenues will be derived by charging the consignees of the ore for its services at a fixed rate per ton loaded. Billing terms will be net, 10 days. Based upon past experience with similar facilities elsewhere, it is expected that the Loading Company's operating profit should average $0.04 per ton before charges for interest, finance charges, and depreciation of $0.03 per ton.

Required:

A cash forecast for each of three calendar years starting with 1968 to demonstrate the sufficiency of cash, to be obtained from (*a*) the sale of capital stock, (*b*) "draw-downs" on the loan, and (*c*) amount to be produced by operating facility, to cover payments to the contractor and on the debt principal and interest.

Problem 16–11.   Purpose: *Flexible Budgeting*

The controller of the Lakeville Company has asked you to aid in the construction of flexible budgets. A study of the delivery expense has disclosed the following over a period of time and there is no indication that past trends will change in the future:

Sales Volume	Delivery Expense
$ 9,000,000	$2,700
10,500,000	2,790
12,000,000	2,960
15,000,000	5,190
8,100,000	2,520
8,700,000	2,620
12,600,000	3,750
13,500,000	3,800
8,800,000	2,590
9,300,000	2,900

Required:

a) Determine the fixed and variable portions of the delivery expense.

b) Prepare a delivery expense budget assuming sales of $9,600,000; $10,200,000; $11,300,000.

c) Should the fact that one period of $15,000,000 sales have any effect on budget construction? Explain fully.

Problem 16–12.   Purpose: *Budgeting Capital Expenditures*

Top management of the Livernois Manufacturing Company realized that although cash was "tight," the company needed to make certain capital expenditures. You were asked to aid in the preparation of alternate proposals to management and you determined that the following four alternatives deserved special consideration:

Investment Opportunity	Economic Life	Cost	Annual Proceeds
I	12 years	$54,000	$19,000
II	22	70,000	22,000
III	10	58,000	14,000
IV	16	58,000	13,000

Required:

a) For each of the above:
(1) Compute the payback period.
(2) Compute the simple rate of return.
(3) Compute the time adjusted rate of return.

b) On the basis of your recommendations management will choose among alternatives. Which of the alternative proposals do you favor? Why?

CHAPTER

17 Standard Costs—
Materials and Labor

The Nature of Standard Costs

In general, cost data may be divided into two major categories: *historical costs* and *predetermined costs*. Historical costs are computed upon the completion of the manufacturing process, or at a later date. Data thus determined have value in providing information for *future* use to correct or improve practices followed in the past, but the inefficiencies and errors of production are not revealed until after the damage has occurred. This undesirable feature encouraged the development of a more satisfactory costing approach. Management's desire to have data that provide not only cost experience needed in forecasting future costs but also methods of measurement of current production led to the outgrowth of *predetermined costs*. Predetermined cost estimates permit management to know *before* production starts what the costs should be so that inefficiency and waste may be detected at the source.

Predetermined cost figures that are made on a scientific basis result in a *standard* cost with which the actual costs may be compared to determine the extent of variation. These variations or differences between the predetermined standard and actual costs form the basis of management review to ascertain the causes of such differences so that inefficiency and waste may be eliminated insofar as possible. This analytical approach is not confined to any one type of cost system; standards may be used when the costing basis is a process or department, as well as where specific order accounting is used. *A standard cost system is not a system separate and apart from specific order or process costing;* it represents one or the other type of cost system, with the added feature of cost analysis incorporated therein.

517

Standard costs are widely used because they serve as an effective tool for managerial control. Through a standard cost system, management is able to analyze the variations in material costs and labor costs both on a *quantity* or *efficiency* basis as well as on a *cost* basis. Variations of the actual costs from the standard costs may be further analyzed on the basis of idle plant or machinery, idle direct labor, excessive spoilage or reworkings, excessive inspection costs, or, simply, insufficient factory production volume. It should not be overlooked that standards and standard costs apply to process cost industries as well as to job order plants.

Advantages of Standard Cost Systems

There are several reasons for using standard costs. The first of these has already been mentioned, namely, the effective analysis of cost data. Through the use of standards, it can be determined why costs are not what they should have been because the standard serves as a measuring device focusing attention on cost variations. Suppose an accountant reports that 10 model X machines shipped to the Granite Motor Company cost $250 each. The executive does not know whether this total cost or the individual costs for material, labor, and overhead represent efficient or inefficient operation. If, on the other hand, this executive has a detailed report of material, labor, and overhead costs which indicates that the standard cost should have been $240 per machine, then he knows that the producing department is not so efficient as was expected. He may then proceed to uncover the causes for this difference. Thus, the moving, changing nature of cost figures is brought clearly into view and the fluctuations of cost can be more easily controlled.

A second reason for using standard costs is that the use of standards reduces bookkeeping costs which have for years been important factors restricting the use of cost accounting by businessmen. A complete standard cost system is usually accompanied by standardization of productive operations in that a standard production order calling for a standard quantity of product is prepared in advance of actual production. All production orders for a given product involve identical components so that material requisitions, labor time tickets, cost sheets, and operating instructions can be prepared on standard forms. Whenever an order is placed in the factory to manufacture a certain product, a standard cost sheet already complete with the standard amounts for materials, labor, and overhead is processed. The requisitions are sent to the storeroom for the standard amount of materials, and the job time tickets for the standard labor charges are forwarded to the factory. The historical costing procedure is reversed, since it will not be necessary to sort and tabulate the many material requisitions and job time tickets because the *standard* amounts are already recorded on the summary cost sheets. When an order is completed, credit slips are issued for unused materials or unused labor time tickets. Should additional material or labor be required, a special colored requisition or job time ticket is prepared. This means that when an order is completed, entries on the standard job sheets are necessary only for the amount of material or labor *above* or *below* standard; this notation takes but a few moments

Illustration 17–1

Excess Labor Cost Report				
Clock Number & Name	Excess minutes	Excess cost	Total	Explanation
Total Cost—Failure to Make Standard				
Departmental Lost Time				
701—Waiting for setup or adjustment				
702—Machine breakdown				
703—Waiting for material				
704—Waiting for order or assignment				
705—Reworking				
706—Nonstandard operation				
707—Nonstandard material				
708—Salvage nonstandard material				
710—Other				
Total Departmental Lost Time				
Unaccounted for Time				
Cost of Overtime Premium				
Total Excess Labor Cost for the Day				

SOURCE: *N.A.A. Accounting Practice Report No. 9, Reports Which Managements Find Most Useful.*

after the last manufacturing operation. Both job sheet and manufacturing operation are completed almost simultaneously.

Other important advantages may be claimed for standard cost systems. Because of the emphasis on cost variations, the entire organization can be made cost-conscious; foremen and workmen can readily see the importance of efficient operations, and costs can be reduced by concerted effort. The use of standard costs places emphasis upon budgetary control because of the close relationship between budgets and standards. The use of standard costs and the attempt to apply them to factory operations necessitates close cooperation between the engineering and costing departments in developing and improving the standardization of product design, quality, and methods of manufacture. These advantages inherent in standard cost systems represent but one type of benefit being derived from the general standardization movement throughout industry.

Presented in Illustration 17–1 is a daily excess labor cost report used by one company to ascertain the reasons for labor inefficiency and to emphasize to accountable management their responsibility to "realign manpower or adjust production schedules to produce the best efficiency possible." This report is distributed to foremen within four hours after the current shift starts and covers operations of the preceding day. Illustration 17–2 shows and explains the use of a "scoreboard" of labor efficiency.

Illustration 17–2

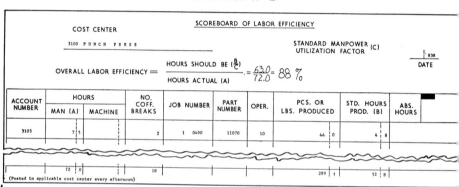

Daily departmental report detailed by operation is tied in to budgeted hours which have bee related to budgeted labor dollars. The efficiency ratio of 88% at the top is the result of dividing actual hours (72) into the quotient of standard hours produced (528) divided by a "manpower utilization factor" for the particular cost center (.838). The factor reflects the relationship of budgeted direct hours to budgeted total hours. Review of operation detail shown may disclose the cause of the "score" or outcome.

SOURCE: *N.A.A. Accounting Practice Report No. 9, Reports Which Managements Find Most Useful.*

Different Types of Standards

The two principal considerations affecting the classification of standards are: (1) *attainability* of standard—that is, the ease with which it is possible to achieve the standards set—and (2) the *frequency* with which the standards are revised. On the basis of these two factors, it is possible to classify standards as *ideal, normal, expected actual,* and *basic.*

Ideal Standards. These represent the level of performance which would be achieved under the best possible combination of factors—the most favorable prices for materials and labor, highest output with best equipment and layout, and maximum efficiency in the utilization of the manufacturing resources—in other words, maximum output at minimum cost. Such standards are engineering standards in the strictest sense. Once set, they are rarely changed unless radical changes are made in the product or the manufacturing processes.

Normal Standards. Costs predicated upon normal operating conditions for a company *over the period of a complete business cycle* are called *normal standards.* While these are more likely to be attainable, they are difficult to compute because of the probable errors in predicting the extent and duration of cyclical effects. They are also troublesome in that cyclical economic effects may cause *large variations from standard* at certain periods in the cycle. Many of these variations are, for the most part, beyond the control of the individual firm, and are, therefore, of little significance in controlling cost variations. Normal standards are based upon an attainable goal and serve to isolate the effects of the business cycle on costs.

Current or Expected Actual Standards. These standards are based on *current business conditions* and represent the achievement level at which management aims for the ensuing accounting period. The standards that are set are attainable. Any deviation from this standard represents inefficiency in the manufacturing operations, unless due to uncontrollable factors. If the factors are not controllable, it must be assumed that the standards are not correct and must be revised accordingly. These current standards represent a *short-run* point of view and are prepared with the understanding that they will be revised when necessary. These current standards are easily understood and have proved most useful in managerial control.

Basic or "Bogey" Standards. These represent a special class of standards of a statistical nature, prepared for some base year, and used in much the same way as the statistician uses commodity price indices. These standards merely serve as a yardstick with which to compare actual performance and are not revised unless the products or the manufacturing operations or processes are changed.

To illustrate this method, the year 1950 is assumed to be the basis for comparison and calculation. The raw material used by this firm is copper sheeting, the price of which during most of that year was 18 cents a pound. This figure is then used to represent the 100 percent figure. In the year 1966, the average price of copper is 36 cents a pound. The *basic standards* for the copper material to be used must first be adjusted by 200 percent before a comparison with the actual costs can be made. Similarly, standard labor costs and manufacturing overhead charges must first be adjusted for their relationship to the basic standard before making comparisons with the actual costs. The main advantage of the basic standard is that it minimizes the number of revisions which would be required because of changes in cost of materials or labor. When *expected actual standards* are used, revisions must be made whenever conditions or costs change. When *basic standards are used*, no change is required other than a computation of the cost relationships between the basic period and the current period. This computation is used in adjusting the standard costs before making comparisons with the actual costs. In view of the statistical nature of the basic or "bogey" standards, they are not recorded in the regular accounting records but they may be recorded in memoranda columns to facilitate the computation of the percentage relationships between standard and actual. The use of basic standards is usually confined to the study of cost variations by statistical rather than accounting methods. Basic standards are less commonly used than *expected actual* or *current standards*.

Comparative Illustration of Ideal, Normal, and Current Standards. In the illustration that follows, an assumption is made that under ideal conditions the maximum operating capacity will permit a larger volume of purchases, resulting in a price reduction of 10 percent under the regular price. Labor costs per unit will not change with increased volume of production, but idle time costs are eliminated from the manufacturing overhead charges. On the basis of these assumptions, the comparative standard costs might be as follows:

PRODUCT: *Steel Cabinets—Per Unit Standard Cost*

Type of Standard	Material Cost	Labor Cost	Overhead Cost	Total Cost
Ideal standard	$18.00	$10.00	$7.00	$35.00
Normal standard	19.00	11.60	8.50	39.10
Current standard	20.00	12.20	9.20	41.40

In selecting the type of standards to be used, management must consider these two basic questions:

1. Which type of standard will be most effective for control purposes?
2. Should the standard cost accounting information be incorporated into the records or treated as statistical data?

While all of the methods have found some application in industry, the method most widely used by firms having a complete standard cost accounting system is that of *expected actual standard costs*.

Responsibility for Setting Standards   For standard costs to be used successfully, definite authority and responsibility must be placed with some person or group of persons. To be effective, the authority so assigned must be at least commensurate to the level of authority delegated to those who are responsible for variations from standards. This is frequently accomplished by means of a *standards committee* or the organization of a *standards division*. The *product engineering department* must be represented on the *standards committee* or *division,* since this department designs the product and determines what materials to use. The *purchasing department* must be represented in this group, since the purchasing agent must be able to indicate the standard cost of the materials to be used during the period. The production management people who are responsible for the routing and scheduling of the manufacturing operations must be represented in the setting of standards. The personnel manager must be represented since he is responsible (adhering to union contracts) for the labor rates. The cost accounting personnel are interested in the work of this committee because they must tie all the standard cost figures together. Because so many different persons and departments are interested in setting standards, there must be one person who coordinates, summarizes, and interprets the results of standard cost accounting. He is usually the *controller.* He is responsible for the preparation of the statement of variations, and he is responsible for suggestions regarding revision of the standards.

Methods of Determining Standards

The success of a standard cost system depends upon the reliability and accuracy of the physical standards as well as the standard costs. But the problem of determining what an item should cost is not easily solved. In many cases, averages of past experience taken from costs of previous periods are used as standards. Unfortunately, relying exclusively upon past experience may have the effect of perpetuating inefficiencies. What has happened in the past should not be indicative of what should have happened in the past. It is better to take the "grass-roots" approach where standards will be set on the basis of each aspect of the production process. The process of determining standards is one of the more important aspects of standard cost accounting as the benefits to be derived will vary in direct proportion with the care with which standards have been established.

Standards are usually computed for use over a 12-month period. Some firms use the same standards year after year until some drastic change in the price or nature of the product occurs. Some of the more progressive firms are constantly reviewing their standards and standard costs and view this function as a continuing process.

Partial Use of Standards

Many accountants believe that standard costs, if used, must be adapted to the complete manufacturing cycle. Although desirable, this is not necessary. In one concern it was extremely difficult to allocate the labor in the cutting and shearing department to the various jobs. The amount of work in handling the job time tickets was so great that this department always held up the cost work of all the other departments. And, what was more important, the volume was so great as to cause all kinds of inaccuracies in the labor cost allocations. It was suggested that in this department standards for labor costs be set up and each job charged with the standard cost of work done. At the end of each month the difference between the standard charges and the actual labor costs was the variation from standard. This amount was then prorated to all the jobs worked on during the month on the basis of the value of materials used on the jobs. By this partial use of standards it was possible to reduce by more than 80 percent the volume of clerical work connected with labor costs and still have reasonably accurate and acceptable costs.

Similarly, in some instances, the partial use of standards can be applied to materials. Some accountants study the variations of only the most important materials used in the manufacturing operations. In other instances, a firm may desire to study the labor cost variations only in some of the departments. The partial use of standards will help reduce the volume of cost accounting work and at the same time permit a study of cost variations of the most important components of the costs of manufacturing.

Standards for materials are more tangible and may be easier to establish than the so-called "operating" standards of labor and manufacturing overhead. Methods of determining the various standards will be discussed separately under the headings of the respective elements of cost.

**Direct Material
Quantity Standards**   In setting standards for the direct material costs of manufacturing a certain product, two factors must be considered·

1. The *quantity* of material to be used.
2. The *price* or *cost* of this material.

It is comparatively simple to ascertain the *quantity of material* to be used in a given unit of manufacture. These standards may be established from records of past experience; from test runs; from mathematical or scientific computations; or through the use of standard bills of material. Current material quantity requirements and their costs are subject to constant examination and revision if necessary—both as to the *kind* of material and the *quantity*. An important factor that must be considered in some industries in setting material quantity standards is the standard allowance for waste, shrinkage, and scrap. This spoilage and shrinkage allowance is more important in firms using a raw material which must pass through one or more converting stages than when a firm is merely using a number of purchased parts in assembling a finished product.

In determining *material quantity standards,* past records may be analyzed and an average quantity of materials used may be selected as the standard. The average may be computed in several ways: (1) using an *average* of all similar jobs for a given period such as a month or three months, or (2) using an *average* of the best and poorest performance in the period preceding the setting of the standards, or (3) using the *best* previous performance with reference to material used quantities.

If the product to be manufactured is new, or if the past records are not considered a reliable basis on which to predicate future costs, quantity standards may be set by the engineering department after due consideration has been given to the most economical size, shape, and quality of the article and the results to be expected from the use of various kinds and grades of materials. These standards may be established by either of two methods: *test runs* or *mathematical and technological analysis.* Where the test-run method is used, a quantity of material or units are put into process and the results carefully noted and studied. Results obtained in this manner are usually somewhat artificial because workmen tend to focus undue attention upon the test lots and use greater than ordinary care in using materials. These factors result in better performance on tests than can be expected in actual future operations. With union supervision of test runs, the reverse may also be true.

In some cases the processing is of such nature as to make possible fairly exact predictions of material consumption. Chemical processes are of this kind. One concern engaged in chromium plating metal containers placed a measured quantity of chromium salts in an electrolytic solution and then found out how many containers could be plated with this quantity of the chemical. This number could be checked scientifically by measuring the thickness and area of the plating; quantitative chemistry would indicate the theoretically perfect result. Such computations are often used to check standards set by other methods.

In some industries the materials issued from the stock room for the various manufacturing operations are fairly well standardized. This is particularly true in firms assembling a finished product, such as a television set, a sewing machine, a typewriter, or some such product. In some departments it is possible to use a single requisition for all the necessary material. It can be adapted to many concerns which use a variety of raw materials for manufacturing operations, such as foundries and plastic manufacturers. Such a form adapted to standard cost accounting procedures is known as the *standard bill of materials*. On it are listed the *standard quantities* and detail of all materials that should be used in various departments on various jobs or in various processes. Most good standard cost accounting systems will sooner or later attempt to use a standard bill of materials to save time in issuing materials to the factory, to reduce the clerical work in handling but a single requisition form, and to have better *quantity control* over materials used. There are no special forms for these standard bills of materials because each firm prepares a form adapted to its business. It is simply a composite requisition standardized in the same way that the production is standardized. The standard bill of materials may be on a deck of punched cards or on magnetic tape. The form of the document does not alter its purpose. For foundries, bakeries, and similar types of manufacturing, there are *standard metal mixture sheets* which indicate the quantity of each kind of material necessary to make the various products. These formula sheets are similar to standard bills of materials.

Material Price Standards

Setting *material price* standards involves quite a different problem. The type of material price standards to be used is determined by the type of standard costs to be used. Three types of standards for material prices or costs are in use:

1. *Current or expected price standards* are the most desirable and effective. When these are used, the purchasing department must determine in advance either by long-term commitments or forecasting what the expected actual costs are to be during the ensuing accounting period. The accuracy of these price standards is a measure of the efficiency of the purchasing department. One well-known manufacturer sets these standards in November of each year for the following year. The price standards are not changed, once they are set, until the following year when they may again be revised. The purchasing department is held accountable for any variations.

2. *Normal price standards* are more in the line of statistical or average price standards for materials. Usually these are not recorded on the books because the prices cover a period of years, allowing for seasonal variations and long-term trends. Under such conditions inventories of materials, work-in-process, and finished goods must be based upon the actual, not standard, costs for materials.

3. *Fixed price standards* are usually part of a system which uses basic or bogey standards. Once the prices have been set for materials, these are used as the standards as long as that product is being manufactured. Here again, inventories of materials, work-in-process, and finished goods must be based upon the actual cost, not the standard cost, of the material, since the variations are not indicative of current practices but of a trend over a relatively long period of time.

When *current or expected price standards* are in use, standard costs for materials may be set by the purchasing or stores department as follows:

1. Through prices agreed upon in *long-term purchase* contracts, usually sufficient to take care of the manufacturing requirements for three to six months in the future.
2. Through the use of a *statistical forecasting* group either within or without the business organization. This group will attempt to forecast probable prices during the coming period.
3. Through the computation of the *weighted average* of purchase prices on the most recent purchase orders, or
4. Through the use of the *median price* paid on recent orders.
5. Through the use of *arbitrary estimates* based upon knowledge and experience in this type of business.

It should not be overlooked in setting these price standards that the best standards should take into consideration the price advantages to be obtained by determining the most economical quantity to buy, the best methods of delivery and storage at the lowest cost, and the credit terms which will result in cost or price savings.

Illustrations of Material Cost Standards   To illustrate more specifically the nature of material cost standards, the standard material costs for two manufacturers are shown, namely, (1) a candy manufacturer, operating on a formula cost basis, producing 100 pounds of any one type of candy on each job (Illustration 17–3); and (2) a clothing manufacturer, producing a standard quantity of one dozen articles of each style (Illustration 17–4). On both of these illustrations, both the *standard quantities* and

Illustration 17–3. Standard Material Costs for Candy Manufacturer

STANDARD COST SHEET PRODUCT: *Coconut BonBons, Formula 42*			
	Quantity	Price	Total
Materials:			
Corn Syrup	50 lbs.	$0.13	$ 6.50
Sugar	30	0.08	2.40
Chocolate	10	0.30	3.00
Coconut	20	0.60	12.00
Flavoring and Coloring	1	1.00	1.00
Total Material	111 lbs.	$2.11	$24.90
Percentage of Waste, 10%	11	0.38	......
Total Material	100 lbs.	$2.49	$24.90

Illustration 17–4. Standard Material Costs for Clothing Manufacturer

STANDARD COST RECORD					
Product: Hunting Coat *Manufacturing Unit:* 1 Dozen				*Date* 3/4/— *Size Scale:* 37–49	
Direct Materials:				Standard Cost per Dozen	
Code	Description	Width	Quantity	Price	Extension
23	*Body Materials* 11 oz. Army Duck............	40 in.	40 yds.	$0.65	$26.00
	Total......................				$26.00
	Trim Thread.....................	*Unit*			$ 0.93
610	Size Tickets.................	M	12	$0.80	0.01
420	36/E Br. Buttons.............	G	108	0.60	0.45
	Total.....................				$ 4.00
	Total Materials..............				$30.00

the *standard costs* of the materials to be used are shown. These two illustrations represent the *material sections* of the standard cost sheets.

Direct Material Variations

Differences between the *standard cost* of material as shown on the standard cost sheets for the various products being manufactured and the *actual cost* of materials used are known as *variations* or *variances*. The two basic types of such variations may be described as follows:

1. *Material cost or material price variations* which result from paying more or less for the materials purchased than was anticipated when the standard cost sheets were prepared. The causes of these variations or differences include:

   a) Unfavorable or favorable purchasing contracts and terms.
   b) Unforeseen changes in market prices.
   c) Higher or lower delivery costs than were expected.
   d) Miscalculation of amount of purchase discounts expected.
   e) Proper or improper timing of purchases.

2. *Material quantity or material usage variations* which result from using more or less material on the various jobs or in the various operations than was estimated on the standard cost sheets. These variations may be attributable to—

   a) Using a different grade or a substitute material.
   b) Better control or lack of control of waste or spoilage.

c) Efficient or inefficient plant operations which result from supervision of type of tools used and the workers' capabilities.

d) Variations in the yield of materials used.

Material price variations may be computed and recorded either (1) at the *time of the purchase* of the materials, or (2) at the *time that the material is used.* In the first procedure, the Stores account is kept on the books at the *standard price* of the materials. The *total cost or price variation* is recorded on the books *before* the materials are used. Unless there is an adjustment at the end of the accounting period for that portion of the material price variation related to the unused portion of the materials purchased, there may be a distortion in the cost of the final stores inventory. This distortion may be eliminated by recording the material price variation only at the time when the material is used. This method meets with the approval of the income tax authorities who are interested in the more accurate costing of inventories. However, recording the price variation only at the time of the usage of the material involves additional expense. Even more important an item to consider is the control feature. Isolating the material price variance at the time of purchase highlights the variance early. Management becomes aware of the differences between actual and standard costs.

Illustration of Material Cost Variations

To compute the material cost variations, four items of information are necessary:

1. The *standard quantity* of material required to produce a given unit or number of units. This will appear on the standard cost sheet.
2. The *standard cost* of the material required in production. This also appears on the standard cost sheet.
3. The *actual quantity* of material used as shown by the requisitions.
4. The *actual cost* of the materials used as shown on the accounting records or purchase invoices.

To illustrate the computation of the material cost variations, the following facts are assumed:

> To manufacture 100 units of Product X on one job, 200 pounds of Material A are required, as shown on the standard cost sheet, at a standard cost of $2 per pound. During the month, 10 jobs were completed. The *actual* material used, as shown by the requisitions, was 2,250 pounds. Latest invoices indicated that this material cost $2.10 per pound.

The procedure followed in computing the material variations is as follows:

Quantity or usage variation:

Actual quantity of material used...................................... 2,250 lbs.
Standard quantity of material used (10 jobs × 200 pounds).............. 2,000
Excess quantity of material used, resulting in an unfavorable quantity
variation... 250 lbs.
250 pounds × $2 (standard cost of material)..........................$ 500

Material cost or price variation:

Actual cost of materials used (actual quantity × actual price) 2,250
pounds × $2.10..$4,725
Standard cost of materials used (actual quantity × standard price) 2,250
pounds × $2... 4,500
Difference represents material price variation, which is unfavorable.......$ 225

Proof or total material cost variation:

Actual costs: 2,250 pounds × $2.10...................................$4,725
Standard costs: 2,000 pounds × $2.................................... 4,000
Total material variation...$ 725

Material quantity or usage variation..................................$ 500
Material price variation... 225
Total Variations (All Unfavorable)...............................$ 725

Sometimes a further refinement is made. The material cost or price variation is made up of two components: (1) the price change due to the standard quantity used; and (2) the price change due to the additional quantity used.

To illustrate, the total material price variation of $225 resulted from a price rise of 10 cents per pound times the 2,250 pounds used. Of the 2,250 pounds used, 2,000 pounds represented the standard quantity. If there had been no quantity variation, the price variation of the materials used would have been 2,000 pounds times 10 cents, or $200. Since 250 additional pounds were used, 250 times 10 cents or $25 of the price variation was due to the increased quantity used. This is often referred to as the *price-quantity* variation.

Although the *price-quantity* variation is of interest to management and should be computed, it is rarely stated separately in a standard cost accounting system. The remainder of the discussion in the text will assume that the *price-quantity* variation is incorporated in the *price* variation.

Nature of Labor Standards

As in the case of direct materials, labor standards are established for both *cost* and *quantity* (efficiency). These may be computed in the same manner used for direct materials. For standard cost purposes, *direct labor* is treated separately from *indirect labor,* which is included in the manufacturing overhead cost. Conditions under which labor standards must be set vary from firm to firm. Each company requires a detailed study of the payroll procedures, payroll rates, and the labor supervision conditions under which the standards are to be used. The same basic approach should be taken for labor as was taken for materials.

This discussion is primarily concerned with the basic principles and practices which are used in setting labor standards.

Labor Efficiency Standards   The determination of how much time workers should use in performing the various manufacturing operations represents one of the most important phases of managerial control. Therefore, the *labor efficiency or quantity or time standards* are an important phase of any standard cost accounting system. Through the careful preparation of time standards, management is able to *measure and control the productivity* of labor, a significant cost element. Great care must be exercised in setting these standards so that their comparison with the actual results will be realistic and meaningful.

Preceding the determination of direct labor time standards must come the standardization of *conditions of work,* in addition to the standardization of the *products* and the *quantity to be manufactured* on each manufacturing order. Specific prerequisites to effective labor time standards include:

1. Efficient plant layout with modern equipment to provide maximum production at minimum cost.
2. Development of a planning, routing, scheduling, and dispatching staff to provide a smooth flow of production without undue delay and confusion.
3. Provision for the careful purchase of materials to flow into production at the proper time, when workmen and machines are available.
4. Standardization of labor operations and methods, with adequate instructions to and training of workers so that the manufacturing will be performed under the best possible conditions.

Labor *time* or *quantity* or *efficiency standards* may be developed by:

1. Averaging past performance records as shown on the cost sheets for the preceding periods. Care must be exercised so that no existing inefficiencies are perpetuated.
2. Making experimental test runs of the manufacturing operations under expected normal conditions.
3. Making time and motion studies of the various labor operations under expected actual conditions. As a result of these the engineering department prepares routing sheets indicating the standard amount of time to be used for each labor operation.

4. Making a reasonable estimate based upon experience and knowledge of the manufacturing operations and the product.

To illustrate the forms used in setting these labor time standards, a *route sheet* (Illustration 17–5), a *time-study observation sheet* (Illustration 17–6), and the Labor Cost section of the standard cost sheet (Illustration 17–7) are shown.

Illustration 17–5. Simple Route Sheet

ROUTE SHEET				
Part Name: _Motor Shaft_			Part No.: _1255_	
Material: _SAE 2315_				
Approve: _J. B. Corkin_			Date: _2/12/_	
No.	Operation Description	Hours per C	Pieces per Hr.	Tools Needed
5	Pick up piece and place in jig	0.47	213	Jig #1255
10	Drill ¼" hole	0.95	105	H.S. Drill ¼"
15	Remove piece from jig	0.20	500	
20	Blow out chips	0.19	526	
	Total base time	1.81	55	
	Allowance for personal and unavoidable delay	0.36		
	Total standard	2.17	46	

Illustration 17–7. Part of Standard Cost Sheet, Showing Labor Costs for Manufacturing of Motor Shaft*

STANDARD FACTORY COST PER 100					
Part Name: *Motor Shaft*				Part No.: *1255*	
LABOR COSTS					
	Operation Number	Operation Description	Standard Hours	Rate	Standard Labor Cost
	1	*Place in jig*	0.56	$1.50	$0.84
	2	*Drill ¼" hole*	1.14	1.50	1.71
	3	*Remove from jig*	0.24	1.50	0.36
	4	*Blow out chips*	0.23	1.50	0.345
		Total labor cost	2.17	1.50	$3.255

* Prepared from routing sheet and time-study observation sheet.

Illustration 11–6. Time-Study Observation Sheet

STUDY NO. 275

OPERATION Drill 1/4" holes PART NAME Motor Shaft PART NO. 1255
SHEET 1 OF 1 SHEET

TIME STUDY OBSERVATION SHEET

NO.	DESCRIPTION	1 T	1 R	2 T	2 R	3 T	3 R	4 T	4 R	5 T	5 R	6 T	6 R	7 T	7 R	8 T	8 R	9 T	9 R	10 T	10 R
1	Pick up piece and place in jig	19	19	16	216	19	398	18	681	20	765	19	849	19	1027	20	1108	21	1293	19	1477
2	Tighten set screw	(23)	42	20	236	20	418	20	701	19	84	19	66	18	46	28	28	21	1312	19	96
3	Advance drill to work	50	50	9	245	10	28	9	10	10	94	9	75	10	56	30	38	19	21	19	1505
4	Drill 1/4" hole	144	144	89	334	90	518	92	802	90	884	89	964	88	1144	90	1228	92	1413	90	85
5	Raise drill from hole	(11)	155	5	339	6	24	5	07	6	89	5	70	5	49	5	33	5	18	5	1600
6	Loosen set screw	9	164	10	349	9	33	9	16	9	99	9	79	9	58	8	41	9	27	9	09
7	Remove piece	14	178	11	360	12	45	10	26	11	810	10	89	11	69	11	52	12	39	10	19
8	Blow out chips	22	200	19	379	18	63	19	45	18	28	19	1008	19	88	20	72	19	58	19	38

FOREIGN ELEMENTS

	T	R	DESCRIPTION
A			
B			
C			
D			
E			
F			
G			
H			
I			
J			
K			
L			
M			
N			

Summary

ELEMENT NUMBER →	1	2	3	4	5	6	7	8
	174	93	904	47	9	91	112	192
TOTAL "T"	190							
No. OBS	10	9	10	9	5	10	10	10
AVER. "T"	19	19	90	9	5	9	11	19
MIN. "T"	16	8	88	5	8	8	10	18
MAX. "T"	21	20	94	6	10	14	14	22
RATING								
LEVELING FACTOR	0	0	0	0	0	0	0	0
SELECTED TIME	19	9	90	5	9	11	19	
% ALLOWANCE								
NORMAL TIME								

SKILL

SUPER	+15		KILLING	+15
EXCELL.	+10		EXCELL.	+10
GOOD	+6		GOOD	+6
✓ AVERAGE	0		✓ AVERAGE	0
FAIR	−7		FAIR	−7
✓ POOR	−15		POOR	−15

EFFORT

CONDITIONS / CONSISTENCY

EXCELL.	+6		EXCELL.	+6
GOOD	+4		GOOD	+4
✓ AVERAGE	0		✓ AVERAGE	0
FAIR	−4		FAIR	−2
POOR	−7		POOR	−4

COMB. RATING FOR STUDY	SKILL	EFFORT	COND.	CONSCY.
STUDY STARTED	STUDY FINISHED	OVERALL TIME		

**Labor Cost or Rate
Standards**

Standard cost *rates* for direct labor may be
determined on the basis of:

1. Union contracts.
2. Past experience data. The average, weighted average, or median labor cost for the preceding period might be used as standard.
3. Computations involving *normal operating conditions.*
4. Arbitrary or estimated rates. The person setting the standard costs uses his experience or judgment.

The type of wage system in use also influences the standard cost *rates.* The basic types are: (1) day or hourly wage systems, (2) straight piece rates, and (3) multiple piece rates or bonus systems.

Daily or Hourly Wage Systems. When daily or hourly wage systems are used, the standard costs may be affected by the union contracts. Frequently this simplifies matters, especially if it is a long-term contract, because there will be little variation in the rate during this period. On the other hand, the volume of production of hourly wage employees may be controlled by the speed of the automatic machines in use. Changing the rate of speed of the machine will affect the standard labor cost per unit of production.

Straight Piece Rates. These result in the payment of a flat amount per unit of production. Subject to correction for the effect of the minimum wage and hour regulations applicable to these employees, when straight piece rates are used the direct labor cost of manufacturing a unit or number of units is fixed and will not be subject to any variation. Theoretically it is ideal for standard costs, but from a practical viewpoint, this type of wage payment is frequently opposed by labor unions.

Multiple Piece Rates or Bonus Systems. These usually involve several wage rates depending upon the volume of the worker's production. Among such plans are the Halsey, Gantt, Bedaux, and the "differential" piece-rate systems. When this type of wage system is in use, the cost accountant must ascertain from management answers to questions such as:

> Is the premium or bonus to be considered as part of the direct labor cost? Will the standard used in computing the bonuses be the same as the standard used on the cost sheets? If not, what differences or adjustments must be considered?

In studying material standards, it was pointed out that variations were of two kinds: those involving the *quantity* of materials used, and those involving the *price* or *cost* of the materials used. Similarly, in studying labor standards, two types of variation must be considered: those involving the *quantity* of labor to be used in producing a certain quantity, thus indicating the *efficiency of labor;* and those involving the *cost* of the labor to be used, thus indicating the *labor cost variation.* The *labor efficiency variation* is computed as follows:

Difference between the *standard* hours and the *actual* hours multiplied by the standard labor rate. If the standard hours are more than the actual hours, the variation is considered favorable; if less, it is unfavorable.

The *labor cost or rate variation* is computed in one of two ways:

1. The difference between the *standard wage rate* and the *actual wage rate* multiplied by the number of direct labor hours used in production.
2. The difference between the *actual costs of direct labor incurred* and the product of the *actual number of direct labor hours* and the *standard labor cost rate.*

Illustration of the Computation of Labor Variations

As in the case of material variations, four types of information are required to compute labor variations. These are obtained from the standard cost sheets, job time tickets, and payroll records. The data required are:

1. The *standard time or hours* allowed for each operation.
2. The *standard labor cost rate* per hour or per piece.
3. The *actual time or hours* spent in the manufacturing operations.
4. The *actual labor costs* paid for the work.

Continuing the illustration used in computing the material cost variations, the following operating and standard cost data are used:

On the standard cost sheet for manufacturing 100 units of Product X on a single job, 35 hours of direct labor at a standard cost of $2.40 per hour are required. During the month 10 jobs were completed, on which 360 direct labor hours were used at an average cost of $2.25 per hour.

To compute the two labor cost variations, namely, *efficiency,* based upon the time used, and the *cost or rate variation,* based upon the rate of pay used, the procedure would be:

Standard number of hours (10 jobs × 35 hours).............350 hours
Actual number of hours...................................360
Excess hours (time or inefficiency variation)................ 10 hours (unfavorable)
10 hours × standard rate of $2.40 shows that the *time or inefficiency* variation cost................................$ 24 (unfavorable)
Actual cost of labor, 360 hours × $2.25...................$810
Standard cost of labor, 360 hours × $2.40................. 864
Savings or favorable cost variation is 15¢ per hour (or 360
 hours × 15¢)...$ 54 (favorable)
     Net Favorable Labor *Cost* Variation ($54 − $24)......$ 30

Proof or total labor cost variation:

Standard cost to complete ten jobs (35 hours × 10 jobs ×
   $2.40)...$840
Actual cost to complete 10 jobs (360 hours × $2.25)........ 810
      Net Labor Cost Variation..........................$ 30

A *cost-efficiency* variation for labor may be computed in a manner similar to the *price-quantity* variation for materials.

To illustrate, the $54 savings indicated by the cost variation was due to a 15 cents an hour savings over the 360 actual hours used. Had there been no difference between the actual and standard hours worked, the savings would have been 15 cents times 350 hours, or $52.50. The additional 10 hours times the 15 cents or $1.50 was due to the additional hours worked times the savings. Had there not been a 15 cents an hour saving, the additional hours used would have cost $1.50 more.

As in the case of the *price-quantity* variation for materials, the *cost-efficiency* variation for labor is important to management and should be computed. The variation, however, is rarely stated separately in the accounts. The remainder of the discussion in the text will assume that the *cost-efficiency* variation is incorporated in the *cost* variation.

Illustration of Standard Costs and Variations

To illustrate the general nature of standard costs as they affect direct material and direct labor, a hypothetical situation is presented so that variations from standard

Illustration 17–8

COMPARATIVE COST RECORD July 26, 19—		Article: A Standard Quantity: 100		
Cost Components	Standard Cost	Actual Cost	Variation
Materials:			
50 lbs. @ $0.32.....................	$ 16.00		
52 lbs. @ $0.30.....................		$ 15.60	$ 0.40*
Labor:			
Operation No. 1:			
18 hrs. @ $2.50.....................	45.00		
16 hrs. @ $2.45.....................		39.20	5.80*
Operation No. 2:			
20 hrs. @ $2.40.....................	48.00		
24 hrs. @ $2.42.....................		58.08	10.08†
Operation No. 3:			
10 hrs. @ $2.60.....................	26.00		
15 hrs. @ $2.55.....................		38.25	12.25†
Manufacturing overhead:			
48 hrs. @ $0.70...................	33.60		
55 hrs. @ $0.70...................		38.50	4.90†
Total........................	$168.60	$189.63	$21.03†

* Under standard.   † Over standard.

can be computed and so that it is possible to discuss how responsibility for these variations might be placed within a manufacturing organization.

In the first illustration, the standard and actual costs are shown in comparative form (Illustration 17–8), so that in a second illustration (Illustration 17–9) the quantity and cost (price) variations might be indicated. Since the manufacturing overhead is applied on the basis of direct labor hours, any variation due to labor inefficiency will be

Illustration 17–9

SUMMARY OF VARIANCES

Article A

Per 100 Units

July 26, 19—

| Variance Factor | Amount of Variations | | | |
| | *Variance over Standard | †Variance under Standard | Net Variation | |
			*Over Standard	†Under Standard
Materials:				
Quantity 2 lbs. more @ 32¢.............	$ 0.64			
Price 2¢ per lb. less for 52 lbs.........		$1.04		
Net Variation......................				$0.40
Labor:				
Quantity 2 hrs. less @ $2.50.............		$5.00		
Price 5¢ less for 16 hrs..............		0.80		
Net Variation......................				5.80
Quantity 4 hrs. more @ $2.40............	$ 9.60			
Price 2¢ more for 24 hrs.............	0.48			
Net Variation......................			$10.08	
Quantity 5 hrs. more @ $2.60............	$13.00			
Price 5¢ less for 15 hrs.............		$0.75		
Net Variation......................			12.25	
Manufacturing Overhead:				
Quantity 7 hrs. more @ 70¢.............			4.90	
			$27.23	$6.20
Final Net Variation.................			$21.03	
($27.23 − $6.20)				

* Unfavorable variations if the standards are properly set.
† Favorable variations if standards are properly set.

reflected in a single variation figure for overhead. A more detailed analysis of manufacturing overhead variations will be discussed in the following chapter.

An examination of the comparative cost statement indicates that the variations are due either to *price (cost)* or *quantity (efficiency)* factors. Some variations are due to the fact that the actual costs were higher than the standard, in which case they are *unfavorable;* or less than standard, in which case they are *favorable.*

A detailed statement of the variations is shown in Illustration 17–9.

Placing Managerial Responsibility for Variations. One purpose of standard costs is to permit a comparison of the actual costs with those predetermined so that managerial or supervisory personnel may be held accountable for unfavorable results and credit may be given for favorable performance. Just how this responsibility might be placed will be explained in the following paragraphs. It must always be remembered, however, that the standards may have been incorrectly or improperly computed.

Material. Responsibility for material cost variations lies in either the *purchasing department* or the *manufacturing department.* The purchasing department may have experimented by buying a different grade or kind of material at a lower price, and because of this it was necessary to use more material. But, nevertheless, even though more material was used, the saving in price might be greater than the cost of the additional quantity.

However, it is also possible that the purchasing department was able to purchase the standard grade of material at less than standard prices, although through waste or spoilage in the manufacturing department the effect of the savings was somewhat nullified, since more than the standard quantity was used in production.

Labor. Responsibility for labor cost variations belongs to either the *personnel department* or the *manufacturing department.*

The fact that fewer hours were used in manufacturing may be attributable to more careful supervision, better machine arrangement, or to the fact that the personnel department selected more efficient workmen and is perhaps paying a higher wage to some of them.

The increased cost of labor may be due to labor market conditions or to a sudden increase in production volume, necessitating higher wages or the employment of poorly trained workers. Improper supervision or machine setup might also cause labor cost variations by requiring the use of more than the standard number of hours. An inferior grade of material might have required more labor for proper processing. The exact reasons can usually be found with a little careful investigation. In many large concerns there will be no cost variation for labor due to wage rates since they have long-time contracts with labor unions fixing the hourly rates of pay for a definite period of production. In other firms the union contracts fix the labor piece rates, and this also eliminates the labor cost variation. The variations will be due primarily to inefficiency resulting from poor supervision, poor tools, or poor materials.

Manufacturing Overhead. Since manufacturing overhead costs in this illustration are computed on the basis of labor hours, the amount of manufacturing overhead charged to the order is affected directly by the number of direct labor hours. Therefore, the overhead variation shown for the order is only a quantity variation. The price variation of manufacturing overhead does not appear on specific orders but is part of the over- or underapplied manufacturing overhead at the end of the period, which must be separately analyzed.

Again it must be emphasized that this illustration was used to bring out the nature of variations and does not clearly indicate the clerical routine of standard cost accounting.

Statistics and Variance Analysis   In order to effectively study variances from standard costs, it is necessary for a company to accumulate experience. The cost accountant must have accumulated variances for extended periods of time or from a large number of jobs. Only after some experience has

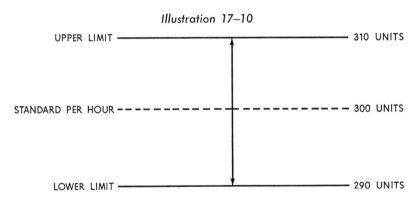

Illustration 17–10

UPPER LIMIT ——————————————————— 310 UNITS

STANDARD PER HOUR — — — — — — — — — — — — — — — — — 300 UNITS

LOWER LIMIT ——————————————————— 290 UNITS

been obtained can the standards and standard costs become defensible and the variances meaningful as quite often the cost accountant will find that a particular standard cost is not realistic and therefore needs adjustment.

Statistical methods may be used by the cost accountant in the area of variance analysis. A problem that comes up again and again in industry is that of determining which variances should be investigated by management. Earlier discussions have shown that even though scientifically determined, a standard is an average and that in any one period, actual performance may vary from the average. Since the standard represents an average, it might be said that variations that occur within the *range* of where the standard was set need not be investigated. For example, if stamping 300 units per hour is standard and the normal range goes from 290 to 310, then only variances above 310 and below 290 need to be investigated, i.e., only those above or below the limits as shown in Illustration 17–10.

QUESTIONS FOR REVIEW

1. Distinguish between *standards* and *standard costs*.
2. What are the differences, if any, between *budgeted costs* and *standard costs?*
3. "Standard costs are widely used because they serve as an effective tool for managerial control." Explain briefly.
4. If a firm uses standard costs for control purposes, etc., can it still report its inventories at "actual cost" on the balance sheet? Explain how this might be accomplished.
5. Explain what material variances might be isolated. Include in your discussion comments on whom you would hold responsible for the variances you isolate.
6. The materials price variance might be isolated when materials are *purchased* or when materials are *used*. Give the pros and cons of each of the two possibilities. Which of the possibilities do you prefer? Why?
7. What kinds of labor variances might occur? Explain these and also indicate where you would fix responsibility for the variances.
8. How might statistics be used in variance analysis?
9. How often should standards and standard costs be revised? How would you go about revising the standard cost of items that are in inventory at the old standard cost if a new cost is to be substituted?
10. Does standard cost accounting lend itself for adaptation to computerized operations? Why or why not?

PROBLEMS—GROUP A

Problem 17–1. Purpose: *Determination of Materials and Labor Variances*

Product ZNQ is manufactured in standard batches of 200 units by the Calvin Company. The company uses a standard cost system.

Production for the month of August, 1968, amounted to 210 batches. The relevant statistics are:

Overhead cost	$41,184.00
Average overhead rate per hour	$2.60
Standard output per month	48,000 units
Raw materials used	26,000 lbs.
Cost of raw materials used	$12,300.00
Direct labor cost	$34,280.20

The standard costs for producing a batch of ZNQ are:

```
Raw materials................120 lbs. @ $0.45 per lb...............$ 54.00
Direct labor................. 72 hrs. @  2.15 per hr...............  154.80
Overhead.................... 72 hrs. @  2.75 per hr...............  198.00
                                                                   $406.80
```

Required:

Prepare a variance report for raw materials and direct labor. Be sure you show all computations.

Problem 17–2.   Purpose: *Determining Actual Costs from Standard Costs*

The Casper Manufacturing Company opened a new plant in early January of 1968 for the purpose of producing "Casp," a new product used by the electronics industry. The Casper Manufacturing Company uses a standard cost system in which all inventories are maintained at standard cost. The company does, however, prepare financial statements showing actual costs.

The inventory accounts at standard cost show the following balances on December 31, 1968:

Materials	Materials-in-Process	Finished Goods—Matl.	Labor-in-Process
15,000	60,000	30,000	40,000

	Cost of Sales—Matl.	Cost of Sales—Labor	Finished Goods—Labor
	420,000	250,000	20,000

The following other accounts also appeared in the ledger:

Material Price Variance	Material Usage Variance	Labor Rate Variance	Labor Time Variance
25,000	25,000	15,000	5,000

Required:

a) Compute the actual cost of the materials portion of cost of goods manufactured. Do the same for cost of goods sold.

b) Compute the actual cost of the materials portion of the ending inventory.

c) Do the same for labor as was done for materials in (a) and (b) above.

Problem 17–3.   Purpose: *Preparation of Standard Cost Sheet; Variance Analysis*

A new product of Elise Toiletries, Inc., is Lano-Lov Skin Lotion, to be sold in 4-ounce bottles at a suggested retail price of $1. Cost and production studies show the following costs:

CONTAINER

Item No.	Description	Cost	Comments
2147	4-oz. bottle	$5.50 per gross	Allow for waste and breakage—2%
315	Label	3.30 per 1,000	Allow for waste and breakage—3%
	(Product will be reshipped in bottle cases)		

RAW MATERIALS

Item No.	Description	Cost	Quantity Used per 125-Gallon Batch
4247	Compound 34A	$40 per 100 lbs.	70.0 lbs.
3126	Alcohol and glycerin	40 per 100 lbs.	76.0 lbs.
4136B	Perfume oil*		3.5 lbs.

*Perfume oil is mixed by the company according to its secret formula.

Standard costs of a 90-pound batch of perfume oil are as follows:

Ingredients $2,169.95
Direct labor—4.4 hours @ $2.28 per hour 10.03
Manufacturing overhead—$7.50 per batch plus $1.95 per standard
    labor hour.
(Note: A gallon contains 128 oz.)

ALLOWANCE FOR LOST MATERIAL

Overfilling, waste, and breakage—allow 4% of standard material cost.

DIRECT LABOR PER GROSS

Compounding . . . . 0.12 hours at $1.90
Filling and packing . . . . 1.00 hours at $1.60

MANUFACTURING OVERHEAD

Compounding . . . . $3.00 per standard labor hour
Filling and packing . . . . 1.50 per standard labor hour
                                                            plus $0.90 per gross

Required:

a) You are to prepare a standard cost sheet for one gross bottles of this product, arranging the data under the five subheadings listed above. Calculations should be made to the nearest cent per gross.

b) The company expected to produce 1,000 gross of Lano-Lov Lotion in its first week of production, but actually produced only 800 gross. Its direct labor cost of filling and packing was:

Filling and packing, 780 hours—$1,263.60

Prepare an analysis of the labor cost variance from standard showing the causes of the variance.

(Adapted from an AICPA Uniform Examination)

Problem 17–4. Purpose: *Determination of Variances from Standard*

Following is a standard cost sheet for Item 941-J manufactured by the Cook Company:

STANDARD COST FOR:		Item: #941-J Quantity: 200	
			Total Cost
MATERIAL		X—150 lbs. @ $4.50...................	$ 675.00
		Y—100 lbs. @ 3.00...................	300.00
		Z— 60 lbs. @ 1.50...................	90.00
		Total Material Costs..................	$1,065.00
LABOR		Dept. I —100 hrs. @ $2.40	$ 240.00
		Dept. II —100 hrs. @ 2.00	200.00
		Dept. III— 50 hrs. @ 3.00	150.00
		Total Labor Costs....................	$ 590.00
MANUFACTURING OVERHEAD		250 hrs. @ $4.00.....................	$1,000.00
TOTAL STANDARD COST FOR 200			$2,655.00

Data applicable to the manufacturing operations for the first month:

Material	Quantity Purchased	Purchase Price	Quantity Used on Ten Production Orders of 200 Units Each
X..................	900 lbs.	$4.20	900 lbs.
X.................1,000		4.65	700
Y.................1,200		3.20	980
Z................. 800		1.80	650

Labor costs incurred on these jobs:

Department	Hours	Pay Rate
I.................800		$2.50
I.................300		2.25
II.................750		2.00
III.................400		3.10
III.................130		3.00

You are asked to prepare a comparative report or statement showing the standard costs, the actual costs, the variations separately listed for quantity (efficiency) and cost (price), and whether favorable or unfavorable for total production. Also, supplement this statement with a report describing the possible causes and responsibility for each variation.

PROBLEMS—GROUP B

Problem 17–5.   Purpose: *Determination of Materials and Labor Variances*

The Milden Corporation manufactures a product which it nationally advertises as "Brand 'X.'" The production line turns Brand X out in standard bundles of 1,000 units. A standard cost system is in use. Upon examination of the operations of the company for a recent operating period, you find the following:

1. Standard cost for a bundle (of 1,000 units):

```
Direct material............60 lbs. @ $0.45 per lb...........$ 27.00
Direct labor...............36 hrs. @  2.15 per hr...........  77.40
Mfg. overhead..............36 hrs. @  2.75 per hr...........  99.00
    Total Standard Cost........................................$203.40
```

2. Operating budget:

```
240,000 units—240 bundles
Direct materials—14,400 lbs. @ $0.45.....................$ 6,480.00
Direct labor    — 8,640 hrs. @  2.15.....................  18,576.00
Mfg. overhead   — 8,640 hrs. @  2.75.....................  23,760.00
    Total Budgeted Manufacturing Costs....................$48,816.00
```

3. Data from actual operations:

```
210,000 units—210 bundles
Direct materials used—13,000 lbs. @ $0.47................$ 6,110.00
Direct labor        — 7,920 hrs. @  2.12................  16,790.40
Overhead................................................  20,592.00
    Total Actual Manufacturing Costs......................$43,492.40
```

Required:

Prepare a variance report for *direct material* and *direct labor*. In addition to computing the variances, be sure you state whom you would hold responsible for the variances.

Problem 17–6.   Purpose: *Determination of Variances from Standard*

The following represents the standard costs of the Melton Company for the production of 500 units of OMH:

Element of Cost	Total Cost
Material costs:	
200 gals. Material H @ $2.10.....................$ 420	
100 lbs. Material M @ 2.10..................... 210	
50 lbs. Material O @ 2.00..................... 100	
	$ 730
Labor costs:	
80 hrs. in Dept. I @ $2.00.....................$ 160	
50 hrs. in Dept. II @ 3.00..................... 150	
100 hrs. in Dept. III @ 4.00..................... 400	
	$ 710
Manufacturing overhead costs:	
230 hrs. @ $5.00.....................................$1,150	
Total Standard Cost of 500 Articles...................$2,590	

The actual costs of 10 jobs of 500 units each during the past six months were as follows:

Element of Cost	Total Cost
Material costs:	
1,600 gals. Material H @ $2.10	$ 3,360
600 gals. Material H @ 2.00	1,200
900 lbs. Material M @ 2.20	1,980
150 lbs. Material M @ 2.30	345
500 lbs. Material O @ 1.60	800
	$ 7,685
Labor costs:	
900 hrs. Dept. I @ $2.10	$ 1,890
300 hrs. Dept. II @ 3.05	915
300 hrs. Dept. II @ 3.10	930
600 hrs. Dept. III @ 3.90	2,340
300 hrs. Dept. III @ 4.20	1,260
	$ 7,335
Manufacturing overhead costs:	
2,400 hrs. @ $5.00	$12,000
Total Actual Cost of 5,000 Articles	$27,020

You are asked to prepare a statement or comparative table showing the standard costs, the actual costs, and the variations listed separately for quantity and efficiency, and grouped into favorable and unfavorable columns.

Problem 17–7. Purpose: *Determination of Actual Costs from Standard Costs*

The Made-Rite Corporation was established in 1968 and manufactures a single product which passes through several departments. The company has a standard cost system.

The company's inventories at standard cost are as follows:

	December 31, 1968
Raw material	0
Work-in-process:	
Material	$ 75,000
Labor	7,500
Overhead	15,000
Total	$ 97,500
Finished goods:	
Material	$ 60,000
Labor	20,000
Overhead	40,000
Total	$120,000
Total Inventories	$217,500

The company's preliminary income statement for the year ended December 31, 1968, prior to any year-end inventory adjustments, follows:

Sales..		$900,000
Cost of goods sold:		
Standard cost of goods sold:		
Material.....................................	$300,000	
Labor.......................................	100,000	
Overhead...................................	200,000	
Total.....................................	$600,000	
Variances:		
Material.....................................	$ 25,400	
Labor.......................................	25,500	
Overabsorbed overhead........................	(16,500)	
Total.....................................	$ 34,400	634,400
Gross profit......................................		$265,600
Selling expenses:		
Salaries.....................................	$ 28,000	
Commissions.................................	72,000	
Shipping expense.............................	18,000	
Other.......................................	7,000	
Total.....................................	$125,000	
General and administrative expenses.................	50,000	175,000
Profit from operations.............................		$ 90,600
Other income:		
Purchases discount............................	$ 8,000	
Scrap sales..................................	9,000	17,000
Net Income before taxes...........................		$107,600

All purchase discounts were earned on the purchase of raw materials. The company has included a scrap allowance in the cost standards; the scrap sold cannot be traced to any particular operation or department.

Required:

a) Prepare a schedule computing the actual cost of goods manufactured. The schedule should provide for a separation of costs into material, labor, and overhead costs.

b) Prepare a schedule comparing the computation of ending inventories at standard cost and at actual cost. The schedule should provide for a separation of costs into material, labor, and overhead costs.

(Adapted from an AICPA Uniform Examination)

Problem 17–8. **Purpose:** *Preparation of Comparative Standard Cost Sheets for Ideal, Normal, and Expected Actual Conditions*

The Martinsville Company produces a single product in lots of 1,000. To manufacture each unit of this product, 20 pounds of Material X and 30 pounds of Material Y are the standard quantities required. The per unit labor cost at standard is as follows:

Dept. I	Dept. II	Dept. III
2 hrs. @ $2.70	3 hrs. @ $2.25	5 hrs. @ $3.00

The manufacturing overhead cost budget for the year indicated the following data:

	100%	90%	80%	70%	60%	50%
Plant operating capacity....	100%	90%	80%	70%	60%	50%
Direct labor hours..........	520,000	468,000	416,000	364,000	355,200	319,000
Budgeted mfg. overhead....	$780,000	$753,800	$749,000	$728,000	$710,400	$559,000

At the present time, the plant is operating at 60 percent capacity, and it is expected that this rate will continue for the coming year. The maximum capacity of the plant is 52,000 units per year.

Materials purchased are contracted for on a three-month basis, but are delivered monthly as needed. Special prices and discounts are offered for purchases in larger quantities, as indicated in the following schedule:

Material X		Material Y	
Quantity contracted for:	*Price per lb.*	*Quantity contracted for:*	*Price*
Less than 150,000 lbs	$1.20	Less than 200,000 lbs.	$2.00 per lb.
150,000–200,000 lbs.	1.00	200,000–300,000 lbs.	Less discounts of 20% and 20%
200,000–1,000,000 lbs	0.80	300,000–1,200,000 lbs.	Less discounts of 30% and 30%
Over 1,000,000 lbs.	0.60	Over 1,200,000 lbs.	$0.80 per lb.

From the above information, prepare a standard cost sheet for 1,000 units with parallel columns so that the standard costs may be shown in comparative form under each of the following conditions:

a) *Ideal* standards at 100 percent operating capacity.
b) *Normal* standards at 80 percent operating capacity.
c) *Expected* actual standards.

CHAPTER

18 : Standard Costs—

Manufacturing Overhead

Nature of Manufacturing Overhead in Standard Costs

Manufacturing overhead cost standards are much more complex than those of direct material and direct labor. The standard cost of materials and the standard cost of labor for each article produced are much more definite in that these costs do not vary greatly with changes in the capacity of the plant, nor with the volume of production. In fact, direct material and direct labor costs are generally assumed to be variable costs. Manufacturing overhead costs, however, while applied to specific jobs or departments, and as such are standard costs for the article produced, are nevertheless also affected by certain *plant* factors rather than *job* factors. The *total plant volume* of production must be a consideration in computing overhead standards. Manufacturing overhead costs include many definite items, but all of these do not follow the same pattern. Some are closely related to the manufacturing operations. Power, indirect materials, supplies, and compensation insurance vary in the same manner as the volume of production, i.e., the *variable overhead* costs. Other manufacturing overhead costs have no direct relation to the volume of the manufacturing operations but are incurred for the *period* whether there is a large or small volume of production. These are classified as *fixed* charges and relate specifically to the overall plant rather than to specific jobs. *Period costs* or *fixed costs* include such items as rent, taxes on building, fire insurance of building, and the superintendent's salary. Between these two groups of overhead costs are a number of indirect costs which are neither definitely fixed nor completely variable, but the amounts incurred will increase less than in

548

proportion to volume increases, or at irregular intervals as the volume of production increases. This group includes such items as indirect labor and inspection costs. This complexity in the makeup of the total manufacturing overhead must be taken into consideration when setting standard costs.

The Predetermined Nature of Overhead Costs

Long before many firms used standard costs for materials and labor, they were using a predetermined rate for manufacturing overhead. This form of standard was the forerunner of a broader application of standards to materials and labor. The analysis of the over- and underapplied overhead into detailed factors is one of the managerial advantages of a more complete system of standard costs.

The predetermined manufacturing overhead rate is primarily related either to the overall plant or to the various departments within the plant rather than to specific jobs. It is only after the plant or departmental rate has been first determined that it is possible to compute an applied cost for overhead for a specific product. In other words, setting a predetermined overhead rate which subsequently becomes the basis for the standard overhead cost for each product involves certain plant factors. These factors are the *budgeted capacity* of production expressed in terms of direct labor hours or machine-hours or some other base and the overall standard *indirect costs* of operating the plant at this budgeted capacity or volume of production.

The *budgeted capacity* used in setting overhead standard costs for managerial control involves agreement on what is to be considered *normal output* for setting standards, and then developing a *flexible budget* to show the effect on costs for fixed, variable, and semivariable items at varying operating capacities. In other words, setting standard overhead costs requires the determination of (1) *standard capacity* and (2) *standard overhead costs* for this capacity.

Standard or Predetermined Overhead Rates

Predetermined overhead rates, previously discussed in Chapter 8, related to historical costs, but the concept of predetermining overhead costs started the development of standard costs for managerial control. There is an increasing tendency to use *separate* predetermined overhead rates for fixed overhead and for variable overhead. The purpose of this breakdown is to permit a more effective analysis and control of variations by function.

To compute a standard or predetermined overhead rate, the formula used is:

$$\frac{\text{Budgeted manufacturing overhead}^1}{\text{Budgeted production}} = \text{Predetermined rate.}$$

The budgeted production in a plant may be measured in various ways. For some firms in which there are a few uniform products, this production may be expressed in terms of *units*. Where there are many different products requiring different amounts of material and productive time, production may be expressed in terms of *hours,* either *direct labor* or *machine.* Sometimes, either due to the uniformity of the wage payment per hour or the difficulty in computing the labor or machine-hours, the production may be measured in terms of *direct labor wage payments* or *labor costs.*

Predetermined *standard* overhead rates may be set in various ways depending on the circumstances in a given company as one company-wide rate may not be enough. If operations are carried on in various departments with a heterogeneous group of products passing through the departments, a predetermined rate for each department is necessary. Production may be expressed in labor hours in some departments and in machine-hours in others. In some companies, the departmental rates are further divided between fixed and variable.

In addition to these, if a firm has a large number of factories scattered throughout the country, all or part of the general administrative overhead from the central main office may be allocated to each plant as an element of manufacturing overhead costs. This may also require a separate predetermined overhead rate.

Controlling Standard Overhead Costs   Because *comparison* is a necessary element of control, a standard cost system is a good control technique. Because certain costs tend to vary with changes of activity while others ordinarily do not, *volume* is an important consideration in attempting to control manufacturing overhead costs.

To determine proper standards for the comparison of predetermined estimated costs with actual costs at various volume levels, manufacturing overhead must be accumulated in such fashion that the relationship of cost to volume of activity may be readily ascertained. Therefore, in addition to classification by *department* or function or cost center, costs

---

[1] The budgeted manufacturing overhead is calculated upon the *normal operating capacity,* whether this is at theoretical, average, or expected actual capacity.

must be further classified as to *behavior*. *Cost behavior* is determined through the process of distinguishing between *fixed* and *variable* costs. Understanding *cost behavior* is an important phase of managerial control.

Manufacturing overhead costs, grouped first by department and then by behavior, fixed or variable, are further reduced to a predetermined or standard basis for each unit of production—either units of product, per labor hour, per machine-hour, or per labor cost dollar. Since the *per unit* fixed overhead cost will increase as the volume of production decreases, and vice versa, adequate control of the overhead costs can best be established by using a *flexible* or *sliding* budget instead of one based on an arbitrarily selected "normal" volume.

The development and application of *flexible budgets* (discussed in Chapter 16) facilitates more effective cost control and improved management planning by:

1. Recognizing the elements of *cost behavior at varying levels of production,* thus providing the total estimated overhead costs at each output level so that throughout a given period, proper standard overhead rates which will most nearly represent the anticipated volume of production can be used, and
2. Providing data for management's extension of *cost behavior relationships* to the overall planning of the company.

Timely analysis and interpretation of the *effect of volume on costs* have done much in aiding progressive management to institute better techniques of cost control to maintain and improve profits.

Illustration 18–1 shows the flexible budget for overhead costs for Machine Department No. 1. It is assumed that these figures represent hypothetically a period of one year. In studying this illustration it should be noted:

1. A standard rate should be used for an entire year. The flexible budget is used for comparative purposes if the volume of production or the cost of the overhead items do not equal those used in computing the standard overhead rate.
2. The various manufacturing overhead costs are grouped functionally. Within each group there may be fixed or variable costs. This grouping aids in managerial control of the costs.
3. The effect of the volume of production on these various overhead cost items and groups is shown for plant operating capacities of 50, 60, 70, 80, 90, and 100 percent.
4. Total overhead costs are shown for each operating capacity so that a predetermined standard overhead cost rate may be computed for each.
5. The various predetermined overhead cost rates determined for the different operating capacities, based upon direct labor hours (approximate computations), are:

Illustration 18–1. Manufacturing Overhead Costs at Various Operating Capacities

MANUFACTURING OVERHEAD COSTS
AT VARIOUS OPERATING CAPACITIES

Machine Dept. No. 1
E. J. Fuller, Foreman

Direct Labor Hours		4,000	4,800	5,600	6,400	7,200	8,000
Per Cent of Capacity		50	60	70	80	90	100
Code No.	**Overhead Cost Items**						
	Supervision and Clerical Expense:						
01	Foreman	$ 360.00	$ 360.00	$ 360.00	$ 400.00	$ 500.00	$ 500.00
02	Inspectors	....	....	....	....	....	....
03	Clerical	196.00	196.00	196.00	196.00	220.00	220.00
	Total Supervision and Clerical Expense	$ 556.00	$ 556.00	$ 556.00	$ 596.00	$ 720.00	$ 720.00
	Indirect Labor:						
10	Oilers, Sweepers, and Cleaners	$ 140.00	$ 148.00	$ 156.00	$ 164.00	$ 172.00	$ 180.00
11	Internal Transportation	28.00	28.00	28.00	36.00	36.00	36.00
12	Idle or Lost Time	....	....	....	....	....	....
13	Other Indirect Labor	240.00	264.00	288.00	312.00	336.00	360.00
	Total Indirect Labor	$ 408.00	$ 440.00	$ 472.00	$ 512.00	$ 544.00	$ 576.00
	Operating Supplies:						
20	Fuel	....	....	....	....	....	....
21	Nails, Rods, and Wire	....	....	....	....	....	....
22	Grinding and Polishing Wheels	$ 116.00	$ 120.00	$ 124.00	$ 128.00	$ 132.00	$ 136.00
23	Paints, Lubricants, and Waste	120.00	120.00	124.00	128.00	128.00	132.00
24	Stationery and Office Supplies	14.00	14.00	14.00	18.00	18.00	18.00
25	Miscellaneous Supplies	20.00	20.00	20.00	20.00	24.00	24.00
	Total Operating Supplies	$ 270.00	$ 274.00	$ 282.00	$ 294.00	$ 302.00	$ 310.00
	Maintenance and Repairs:						
40	Machinery	$ 120.00	$ 144.00	$ 168.00	$ 192.00	$ 216.00	$ 240.00
41	Motors	24.00	28.00	32.00	36.00	40.00	44.00
42	Tools	360.00	432.00	504.00	568.00	648.00	720.00
43	Miscellaneous Equipment	16.00	16.00	16.00	16.00	16.00	18.00
	Total Maintenance and Repairs	$ 520.00	$ 620.00	$ 720.00	$ 812.00	$ 920.00	$1,022.00
	Miscellaneous:						
50	Machinery Setup	$ 11.00	$ 14.00	$ 18.00	$ 20.00	$ 23.00	$ 30.00
51	Telephone	5.00	5.00	5.00	5.00	5.00	5.00
52	Inventory Adjustment	....	....	....	....	....	....
53	Employee Welfare	8.00	8.00	12.00	12.00	12.00	12.00
54	Liability Insurance	20.00	24.00	28.00	32.00	36.00	40.00
59	Miscellaneous Expense	16.00	16.00	16.00	16.00	20.00	20.00
	Total Miscellaneous	$ 60.00	$ 67.00	$ 79.00	$ 85.00	$ 96.00	$ 107.00
	General Charges:						
70	Depreciation	$ 100.00	$ 100.00	$ 100.00	$ 100.00	$ 100.00	$ 100.00
71	Insurance	9.00	9.00	9.00	9.00	9.00	9.00
72	Taxes	14.00	14.00	14.00	14.00	14.00	14.00
	Total General Charges	$ 123.00	$ 123.00	$ 123.00	$ 123.00	$ 123.00	$ 123.00
	Total All Overhead Costs	$1,937.00	$2,080.00	$2,232.00	$2,422.00	$2,705.00	$2,858.00

At 50% capacity, $1,937 ÷ 4,000 hours = $0.48 per direct labor hour
At 60% capacity, $2,080 ÷ 4,800 hours = $0.43 per direct labor hour
At 70% capacity, $2,232 ÷ 5,600 hours = $0.40 per direct labor hour
At 80% capacity, $2,422 ÷ 6,400 hours = $0.38 per direct labor hour
At 90% capacity, $2,705 ÷ 7,200 hours = $0.37 per direct labor hour
At 100% capacity, $2,858 ÷ 8,000 hours = $0.36 per direct labor hour

As a general rule, the rates should be lower at each successive level of increased volume, since the fixed costs are allocated over more units.

6. Some of these budgeted overhead costs are fixed, such as telephone, depreciation, insurance, and taxes. Others are variable, but even part of the variable is fixed—that is, would be incurred if there were no production at all. Among such we have the wages of oilers, sweepers, cleaners, and supervisors. Analyzing a few of the fixed or semivariable overhead items into their fixed and variable elements, the following table might be prepared for the 90 percent capacity rate:

	Fixed Portion	Variable Portion
Supervision and clerical expense	$556	$164
Internal transportation	28	8
Employee welfare	8	4
Miscellaneous expense	16	4

To be most effective, the changes in the fixed and semivariable overhead costs must be studied to determine whether or not they are controllable items.

7. This illustration indicates the overhead costs for Department No. 1. Although it is possible to prepare such a budget on a plantwide basis, for most effective managerial control it is desirable to compute predetermined overhead cost rates and variations for each group of costs on a *departmental* basis.

8. Although in this illustration a single composite rate for the department is computed for the total of the fixed, variable, and semivariable overhead costs, many firms prefer a more detailed control by establishing separate rates for the fixed, variable, or semivariable overhead items, or by having separate rates for each group within the department, such as supervision, indirect labor, operating supplies, maintenance and repairs, general charges, and miscellaneous. This procedure is much more costly than having a single departmental rate, and therefore can be justified only if the managerial control and economies effected through the use of many rates results in higher profits.

Variations in Overhead Costs

Variations from standard costs for manufacturing overhead fall into two general classifications:

1. Those that have to do with the *level of operations.*
2. Those that have to do with the *level of performance.*

The variations from standard costs may be computed by using the three-variance or the two-variance method. The method that is chosen will depend on the data available and the information desired. The three-variance method is based upon a budget for *actual* hours while the two-variance method is based upon a budget for *standard* hours for the production attained. Both methods will be illustrated in the following paragraphs.

Manufacturing Overhead Variations with a Flexible Budget   Manufacturing overhead variations become *more meaningful* as control devices when flexible budgeting techniques are used. The budget may be adjusted to the level of operations that existed during the period. A three-variance system and a two-variance system may be utilized. Both will be illustrated.

The three-variation system utilizing a flexible budget is similar to the three-variation system where a fixed budget is being used. The difference is that the budget is adjusted for the actual hours worked. The variations computed under this method are:

1. *Budget* or *spending* variation.
2. *Capacity* or *plant volume* variation.
3. *Efficiency* variation.

In lieu of the three-variation system, a two-variation system may be utilized. Under this system, the following two variations are isolated:

1. *Plant Volume Variation.* This variation is the difference between what was applied to production and the budget adjusted to standard production.

2. *Controllable or Spending Variation.* This variation is the difference between actual manufacturing overhead and the budget adjusted to the standard production. This is an important variation for control purposes as the difference between what costs were and what costs should have been is highlighted.

Illustrations of both the three- and two-variation methods follow using the same basic data:

The following cost data affecting the manufacturing overhead costs are obtained from the records of the Efandee Manufacturing Company for the period under study. This firm expects to operate at 100 percent capacity and is using a flexible budget, separating the overhead costs into the fixed and variable.

Budgeted manufacturing overhead costs for the period at the 100 percent capacity were:

Fixed.......................................	$150,000
Variable....................................	100,000 $250,000

Budgeted volume of production at 100 percent capacity, in terms of direct labor

hours..125,000 hours

Standard overhead rate for period:

   $0.80 variable cost rate

   1.20 fixed cost rate $2.00 per hour

Standard direct labor hours for production for period......................126,000 hours

Actual hours worked on production for period............................126,710 hours

Actual manufacturing overhead costs for period:

Fixed.......................................	$150,000
Variable....................................	103,200 $253,200

Three Variations—Flexible Budget. The budget or spending variation is determined as follows:

Actual manufacturing overhead.............		$253,200
Budget adjusted to *actual* hours:		
Variable costs 126,710 × $0.80..........$101,368		
Fixed costs........................... 150,000		251,368
Budget or Spending Variation..........		$ 1,832 unfavorable

The $1,832 is the difference between actual factory overhead costs and budgeted costs. Note that the budget has been *adjusted* to the actual hours worked.

The *capacity* or *volume* variation is computed in the following manner:

Budget @ actual hours.........................$251,368
Actual hours @ standard rate (126,710 × $2)......... 253,420
Capacity or Volume Variation..................$ 2,052 favorable

The capacity or volume variation has the same meaning as in the case of the static budget except that the budgeted figure has been adjusted for actual hours worked. The plant worked 1,710 hours above the budgeted volume that was used in setting the standard rate. The plant worked 126,710 hours instead of the 125,000 hours that was used in setting the budget. The difference of 1,710 hours multiplied by a rate of $1.20 which is the fixed expense rate equals $2,052, the amount of the capacity variance.

The *efficiency* variation is determined in the following manner:

Actual hours @ standard rate....................$253,420
Standard hours @ standard rate (Applied to work-	
in-process) (126,000 × $2)..................... 252,000
Efficiency Variation........................$ 1,420 unfavorable

The efficiency variation indicates that 710 hours in excess of standard was necessary to complete the production.

Summary of the three variations:

Budget variation.................................$1,832 unfavorable
Capacity variation............................... 2,052 favorable
Efficiency variation............................. 1,420 unfavorable
Net Variation.............................$1,200 unfavorable

Two Variations—Flexible Budget. The *controllable* or *spending* variation is computed as follows:

Actual manufacturing overhead.............		$253,200
Budget adjusted to the *standard* hours:		
Variable costs, 126,000 × $0.80.........$100,800		
Fixed costs........................... 150,000		250,800
Controllable or Spending Variation.....		$ 2,400 unfavorable

The $2,400 is the difference between actual cost and what was allowed for the budget based on standard production. It represents the difference between what was incurred and what should have been incurred for the production that was made. This is the variation that can be used to measure operating management especially if the controllable variation is further analyzed into price and volume variations. The $2,400 may be due to changes in volume and changes in cost of overhead items.

The *volume* variation is computed as follows:

```
Budget adjusted to standard hours..................$250,800
Standard hours × standard rate (applied to work-in-
    process: 126,000 × $2).........................  252,000
        Volume Variation...........................$  1,200 favorable
```

The $1,200 arose because the company operated at more than 100 percent of capacity. In fact, the volume variance under the two-variation method arises because of the behavior of fixed costs. The standard rate of $2 per hour included $1.20 of fixed costs and $0.80 of variable costs. The $1.20 rate was established at a level of 125,000 hours. Since the company worked 126,000 standard hours, 1,000 hours more × $1.20 was applied than had been budgeted resulting in the favorable volume variation of $1,200.

The two variations are summarized:

```
Controllable variation............................$2,400 unfavorable
Volume variation..................................  1,200 favorable
        Net Variation (Underapplied)...............$1,200 unfavorable
```

The two-variation system has been becoming more popular since it is the one that the businessman can understand; variations are isolated for changes in performance and for changes in volume. Until a company adopts flexible budgeting techniques, however, it is precluded from using the two-variation method. Furthermore, the two-variance method results in tighter control because it measures performance against a budget for completed production and not just for putting in time.

Illustration of Departmental Overhead Variations

Having observed the general methods and principles of computing manufacturing overhead variations on a plantwide basis, it is desirable to show this on a departmental basis. The departmental unit is considered best for effective managerial control. In the following illustration the data shown for the flexible budget for *Machine Department No. 1* are used in computing the two manufacturing overhead variations:

1. Manufacturing overhead budget for Department 1 for the period at the expected operating capacity of 100 percent, or 10,000 direct labor hours:

	Fixed Amount	Variable Amount*	Total
Supervision...............	$ 556	$150	$ 706
Indirect labor............	408	200	608
Operating supplies........	270	50	320
Maintenance and repairs...	520	300	820
Miscellaneous costs.......	60	50	110
Depreciation.............	100	...	100
Insurance................	9	...	9
Taxes....................	14	...	14
Total...............	$1,937	$750	$2,687

* Variation due to increased volume over 50 percent capacity.

2. Budgeted hours for Machine Department 1 for month................10,000 hours
3. Standard predetermined overhead rate for department for month at operating capacity of 100 percent:

Fixed overhead costs: $1,937 ÷ 10,000 hours = $0.1937
Variable overhead costs: $ 750 ÷ 10,000 hours = 0.0750
Total departmental overhead rate, per labor hour...$0.2687

4. Actual hours worked during month in Department 1.................. 9,200 hours
5. Standard hours called for by the *actual production* in Department 1 during the month... 9,000 hours
6. Budgetary report showing actual and budgeted overhead costs for the month for Department 1:

Dept. *Machine Department No. 1 (E. J. Fuller, Foreman)*			
Planning Budgeted Hours	10,000		
Actual Hours	9,200		
For Month of June 19— Standard Hours	9,000		

Overhead Cost Items	Adjusted Budget (9,000 Hours)	Actual	Controllable Variation
Supervision...........................	$ 691.00	$ 730.00	+$39.00
Indirect labor........................	588.00	680.00	+$92.00
Operating supplies....................	315.00	290.00	−$25.00
Maintenance and supplies..............	790.00	850.00	+60.00
Miscellaneous factory expense..........	105.00	90.00	−15.00
Depreciation.........................	100.00	100.00	0
Insurance............................	9.00	9.00	0
Taxes................................	14.00	14.00	0
Total.........................	$2,612.00	$2,763.00	+$151.00
Applied to production for month (9,000 hours × $0.2687)....................		2,418.30	
Underapplied.........................		$ 344.70	

The two manufacturing overhead cost variations computed on a departmental basis from these data are:

Controllable variation:

Actual manufacturing overhead		$2,763.00
Budget adjusted to 9,000 hours ($750 × 90% + $1,937)		2,612.00
Unfavorable		$ 151.00

Volume variation:

Budget adjusted to 9,000 hours		$2,612.00
Applied: Standard hours × standard rate (9,000 hours × $0.2687)		2,418.30
Unfavorable		$ 193.70

Summary:

Controllable variation—unfavorable		$ 151.00
Volume variation—unfavorable		193.70
Net Variation (Underapplied)		$ 344.70

The determination of the variances on a departmental basis is a common procedure in practice as better managerial control is achieved than if the variances had been determined for the company as a whole. The departmentalization of the variances permits the pinpointing of responsibility for the variances. For example, in the above illustration, E. J. Fuller, foreman, should be asked why the indirect labor expense was $92 more than anticipated, etc.

Manufacturing Overhead Variations with a Fixed or Static Budget

If a company uses a fixed or static budget for overhead instead of a flexible budget, the *three-variation system* is the only one that may be used. These are:

1. *Budget or Spending Variations.* These are overhead *cost* variations and are due primarily to the fact that the overhead costs were higher or lower than the estimate as shown in the budget. They indicate that the various items of overhead for the plant cost more or less than anticipated. The causes may be due to change in volume of production or to improperly estimating the cost of the various items which make up the overhead. It is computed by taking the difference between the *estimated* or *budgeted* overhead costs and the *actual* overhead costs.

2. *Capacity or Volume Variations.* These represent *volume* variations for the plant as a unit. Volume may be measured in terms of units produced, direct labor hours, machine-hours, or some other base. This variation arises because the estimated volume of production in the plant as a unit differs from the actual. For example, if the estimated volume of production for a given period was 100,000 direct labor hours on the

basis of the standards set for the various products, and the firm worked 106,000 hours, then the firm worked 6,000 hours more than the anticipated capacity. Ordinarily this would be a favorable condition, unless this increase in capacity was due to the inefficiency of the workers on the jobs. In other words, increased capacity to be considered favorable must result in increased production; otherwise it merely offsets the inefficiency due to excess labor hours. This variation is computed by multiplying the excess hours (6,000) by the predetermined standard rate for overhead.

3. *Efficiency Variations.* These variations arise because more or less time or effort was expended on the production than should have been expended.

The sum of these three manufacturing overhead variations is equal to the over- or underapplied manufacturing overhead. Hence, these variations represent an analysis of over- or underapplied manufacturing overhead into variations due to changes in costs and variations due to changes in the volume of production.

An illustration that will aid in the computation of the variations follows:

The following cost data affecting the manufacturing overhead costs are obtained from the records of the Milden Manufacturing Company. This firm uses a fixed budget.

```
Budgeted manufacturing overhead costs for the period.......$250,000
Budgeted volume of production........................  125,000 hours
Standard overhead rate (based upon the budget)...........  $2 per hour
Standard direct labor hours for production...............  126,000 hours
Actual hours worked on production.....................  126,710 hours
Actual manufacturing overhead costs for period...........$253,200
```

The *budget* or *spending* variation is determined as follows:

```
Actual manufacturing overhead...............$253,200
Budgeted manufacturing overhead............. 250,000
     Budget or Spending Variation............$  3,200 unfavorable
```

The $3,200 is the difference between what was budgeted and what was incurred. Since actual costs were greater than anticipated costs, the variation is considered unfavorable.

A weakness in the usefulness of this budget variation is that no recognition is given to changes in production volume. The budget was 125,000 hours, and the actual hours worked were 126,710. The use of flexible budgeting techniques will help solve the problem as a budget adjusted for actual production will be prepared. This is illustrated in the next section.

The *capacity* or *volume* variation is determined as follows:

```
Budgeted manufacturing overhead...............$250,000
Actual hours @ standard rate (126,710 × $2)...... 253,420
      Capacity or Volume Variation..............$  3,420 favorable
```

The $3,420 indicates that more hours were worked than had been anticipated and that the $250,000 had been allocated over too few hours. The standard rate of $2 had been determined by dividing $250,000 by 125,000. The $250,000 should have been divided by the 126,710. The $3,420 is considered favorable as more work had been done in the plant than had been planned.

The *efficiency* variation is determined as follows:

```
Actual hours @ standard rate (126,710 × $2)...... $253,420
Standard hours @ standard rate (this is the amount
   applied to work-in-process under a standard cost
   system) (126,000 × $2)........................ 252,000
         Efficiency Variation...................... 1,420 unfavorable
```

The $1,420 indicates that more hours were used to complete the units than the standard called for. Seven hundred and ten more hours were used than should have been used; the efficiency variation in this illustration was unfavorable. It measures the production efficiency of the work done.

The three variations are summarized as follows:

```
Budget variation.................................$3,200 unfavorable
Capacity variation............................... 3,420 favorable
Efficiency variation............................. 1,420 unfavorable
      Net Variation (Underapplied).................$1,200 unfavorable
```

The net variance of $1,200 may also be computed by subtracting the amount applied to production ($252,000) from the actual ($253,200). Since $1,200 less was applied to production than should have been, the amount is underapplied. The causes of the underapplied are explained by the three variations.

Illustrations of Standard Cost Sheets

Illustration 1. In the manufacture of ice cream, candy, cereals, and similar process cost products, it is possible to have *test runs* to determine the standard costs of definite quantities, lots, or batches, and to determine the *allowable or standard* amount of waste or spoilage. The products indicated are representative of *continuous process* or of operation costs, as contrasted with job order or job lot costs.

Illustration 18–2

February 14, 19—

STANDARD COST SHEET
(HARD CANDIES AND BULK PACKAGES)
PRODUCT: *Coconut Bonbons, Formula 42*

	Quantity	Price	Amount
Material:			
Corn Syrup	50 lbs.	$0.13	$ 6.50
Sugar	30	0.08	2.40
Chocolate	10	0.30	3.00
Fruits and Nuts	20	0.60	12.00
Flavoring and Coloring	1	1.00	1.00
Total Material	111 lbs.		$24.90
Percentage of Waste, 10%	11		.....
Total Material	100 lbs.	$0.249	$24.90

	Labor			Manufacturing Overhead	
	Hours @	Amount		Rate	Amount
Labor and Manufacturing Overhead:					
Heating and Boiling		$18.00		50%	$ 9.00
Whipping and Mixing		3.00			1.50
Coating		1.50			0.75
Mix Coating		2.10			1.05
Hand Dipping		15.40			7.70
Hand Packing		.....			.....
Machine Dipping		.....			.....
Machine Packing		.....			.....
Subtotal		$40.00			$20.00
Percentage of Waste		.....			.....
Cartoning		2.00			1.00
Total Labor and Manufacturing Overhead		$42.00			$21.00
Boxes and Labels		$ 3.00			$.....
Cases and Cartons		1.10			.....
Material as Above		24.90			.....
Total Material Cost		$29.00			$.....
Total Factory Cost		$92.00			$.....
Commercial Expense		30.00			.....
Interest and Discounts		.....			.....
Total Cost per Pound		$ 1.22			$.....
Total Cost per Unit		$ 1.22			$.....
Selling Price		2.00			.....
Profit		$ 0.78			$.....

* Adapted with permission from *Cost Accounting for Hattie Hicks Sweets Co.* by C. W. Bennett and W. P. Fiske *N.A.A. Bulletin.*

Once the standards of such a test run have been set up, it will not be necessary to change the standards unless wide variations result in the manufacturing operations, at which time new standards and new test runs will be necessary. This type of standard cost sheet (see Illustration 18–2) is characteristic of the ease and simplicity of setting continuous process standards.

Illustration 2. This represents the standard cost sheet of a company

Illustration 18–3. Standard Cost Record*

STANDARD COST RECORD											
DESCRIPTION					DATE		CUSTOMER		STYLE NO.		
Hunting Coat–1 dozen					SIZE SCALE *37–49*		SIMILAR TO		CODE NO.		
DIRECT MATERIALS					STANDARD COST PER DOZEN		ESTIMATED		ESTIMATED		
CODE	DESCRIPTION	WIDTH	QUANTITY	PRICE	PRICE	EXTENSION	PRICE	EXTENSION	PRICE	EXTENSION	
	BODY MATERIALS			$	$		$	$	$	$	
23	*11 oz. Army Duck*	*40"*	*40*	*.65*	*26.00*						
	TOTAL				*26.00*						
	TRIM	UNIT									
	Thread				*.93*						
610	*Size Ticket*	*m*	*12*	*.80*	*.01*						
420	*36/E Br Buttons*	*G*	*108*	*.60*	*.45*						
	TOTAL				*4.00*						
	TOTAL MATERIALS				*30 00*						
	TRANSPORTATION IN			%			%		%		
LABOR AND EXPENSE		COST CENTER	RATE	SAH	EXTENSION		SAH	EXTENSION	SAH	EXTENSION	
CUTTING		*5¢*	*2.00*	$*1.00*	$ *2.00*		$	$	$	$	
SEWING		*5¢*	*1.50*	*12.00*	*18 00*						
INSPECTION		*5¢*	*1.50*	*.50*	*.75*						
TOTAL LABOR AND EXPENSE					*20.75*						
STANDARD MANUFACTURING COST					*50.75*						
ADMINISTRATION											
SELLING–CHAIN–JOBBER–RETAIL											
PROFIT AND LOSS					*9.00*						
TOTAL STANDARD COST					*59.75*						
COMMISSION %											
DISCOUNT %											
MARK-UP %					*5.30*						
STANDARD SELLING PRICE					*65.05*						

* With permission, from *N.A.A. Bulletin.*

which manufactures a variety of trousers, coats, and vests used in hunting or as work clothes. The products manufactured by this firm are divided equally between those for stock and those made to the order of the customer. The company uses a job-lot plan of manufacturing because of the constantly changing design of a diversified line of more than 200 to 250 separate items. The standard cost sheet shown in Illustration 18–3 is used to record the cost of producing *one dozen* garments and is a rather simple form of standard cost sheet.

Illustration 3. In some firms, a large number of small parts must first be manufactured before the main product can be assembled. In the production of sewing machines, vacuum cleaners, pianos, washing machines, and various motors, a separate standard cost sheet must be used for each part manufactured, and finally an assembly standard cost sheet for the final product. The cost control of the individual parts manufactured is often more important than the cost control of the final assembly because the latter may not offer much variation from the standard. This is emphasized even more when one considers the manufacturing process of a piano, which requires more than *four hundred*

Illustration 18–4. Standard Cost Sheet Prepared from Routing Sheet and Time-Study Observation Sheet

STANDARD FACTORY COST PER 100					
Part Name: *Motor Shaft*				Part No.: *1255*	
LABOR COSTS					
	Operation Number	Operation Description	Standard Hours	Rate	Standard Labor Cost
	1	*Place in jig*	*0.56*	*$1.50*	*$ 0.84*
	2	*Drill ¼" hole*	*1.14*	*1.50*	*1.71*
	3	*Remove from jig*	*0.24*	*1.50*	*0.36*
	4	*Blow out chips*	*0.23*	*1.50*	*0.345*
		Total labor cost	*2.17*	*$1.50*	*$ 3.255*
MATERIAL COSTS					
	Entry Point	Description	Gross Quantity	Standard Price	Standard Cost
	Oper. 1	*SAE 2313*	*250#*	*$0.10*	*$25.00*
		Total material cost			*$25.00*
STANDARD COST SUMMARY					
		8/1/—			
	Material	*$25.00*			
	Labor	*3.255*			
	Mfg. overhead 160% D.L.	*5.208*			
	Total	*$33.463*			

different parts, and for each part there is a standard cost sheet for control of production costs.

The illustration of the standard cost sheet for this type of procedure is based upon the manufacture of 100 motor shafts. (See Illustration 18–4.) The material costs used in this work can be ascertained fairly easily, either by measurement, test runs, or past experience. The computation of the standard costs for labor is not so simple. Management must first standardize the *flow of work* in the factory to create the most efficient work. This is done by preparing a *job routing sheet.* Industrial engineers and the production manager usually are responsible for this phase of the work. Once the job routing sheets have been completed, it becomes necessary to set *job time or operation standards.* This is done most effectively by having time and motion studies made of each operation.

Factors Interfering with the Successful Use of Standards

Some of the factors which tend to interfere in the successful use of standards as reported in the *N.A.A. Research Series No. 12* ("Standards to Aid Control of Manufacturing Costs") are:

1. *Lack of interest or understanding of the usefulness of standard costs by management.* Some companies have well-developed standard cost plans for product costing but make little use of the standard costs for managerial control purposes. One glaring and almost unbelievable example is that of an important valve manufacturing concern that had been collecting labor cost variations by departments for several years and yet did not know what to do with them. When a discussion of these variations with the foreman in the department in which they occurred was suggested, the cost accountant could not believe that he had overlooked such obvious procedure for managerial control.

2. Some standards are out of date or unreliable and are therefore not taken seriously.

3. Some standards are designed to give product, rather than operation, costs. This prevents management from making effective use of the standards, since it is difficult to determine the source of the variances. And when these sources are eventually discovered, so much time has elapsed since they occurred that the managerial effectiveness of control is lost.

4. Reports are not prepared in terms which management understands. Using technical accounting terminology will not help executives having a production or sales background.

5. Changing conditions make it necessary to revise standards more often. Many firms do not do this.

QUESTIONS FOR REVIEW

1. "Manufacturing overhead cost standards are much more complex than those of direct material and direct labor." Do you agree? Why or why not?

2. Why might the manufacturing overhead area be a logical area in which a firm might begin working toward a standard cost system if one had never been used before?

3. How might a company establish predetermined standard overhead rates?

4. Why are the variances isolated in the case of overhead basically different from those isolated for labor and materials?

5. Distinguish between the two- and three-variance systems.

6. Why can't a two-variance system be used when a fixed overhead budget is used?

7. Distinguish among *fixed, variable, controllable, noncontrollable* costs.

8. "If this standard costs business is as good as you claim it is, why haven't all companies adopted standard costs?" Comment.

9. Distinguish between *semivariable* and *semifixed* costs.

10. "The determination of the variances on a departmental basis is a common procedure in practice as better managerial control is achieved than if the variances had been determined for the company as a whole." Comment.

PROBLEMS—GROUP A

Problem 18–1. Purpose: *Computation of Two and Three Variances for Overhead*

The management of the Dietermee Manufacturing Company installed a standard cost system. They learned of the possibility of computing overhead variances under both two- and three-variance systems. They provide you with the following data for overhead:

Flexible budget:

	100%	90%	80%
Fixed costs	$1,160	$1,160	$1,160
Variable costs	1,340	1,206	1,072
Total	$2,500	$2,366	$2,232

Budget hours (100%)	2,000
Actual hours	1,950
Standard hours	1,900
Actual costs:	
Fixed costs	$1,160
Variable costs	1,345

Required:

a) Prepare an overhead expense variance report isolating two variances.

b) Prepare an overhead expense variance report isolating three variances.

Problem 18–2. Purpose: *Computation of Variances*

The Dura Furniture Company uses a standard cost system in accounting for its production costs.

The standard cost of a unit of furniture follows:

Lumber, 100 feet @ $150 per 1,000 feet......................		$15
Direct labor, 4 hours @ $2.50 per hour......................		10
Manufacturing overhead:		
Fixed (30% of direct labor)..............................$3		
Variable (60% of direct labor).......................... 6		9
Total Unit Cost.......................................		$34

The following flexible monthly overhead budget is in effect:

Direct Labor Hours	Estimated Overhead
5,200...	$10,800
4,800...	10,200
4,400...	9,600
4,000 (normal capacity)..............................	9,000
3,600...	8,400

The actual unit costs for the month of December were as follows:

Lumber used (110 feet @ $120 per 1,000 feet)....................	$13.20
Direct labor (4¼ hours @ $2.60 per hour)......................	11.05
Manufacturing overhead ($10,560 ÷ 1,200 units)................	8.80
Total Actual Unit Cost................................	$33.05

Required:

a) Prepare a schedule analyzing material, labor, and manufacturing overhead variances. Use a three-variance system for manufacturing overhead.

b) Recompute the manufacturing overhead variances using a two-variance system.

(Adapted from an AICPA Uniform Examination)

Problem 18–3. Purpose: *Variances from Standard*

The Ditmar Manufacturing Company uses a standard cost system. It has three separate plants, widely distributed, but maintains a central cost system for the entire organization. Each plant specializes in and manufactures a single product. The statistics for a given accounting period are as follows (it is assumed that all materials purchased were used in the manufacturing operations):

	Plant No. 1	Plant No. 2	Plant No. 3
Budgeted units...............................	6,000	7,200	8,000
Budgeted labor hours.........................	7,200	10,800	16,000
Budgeted manufacturing overhead costs,			
based on labor hours.....................	$4,320	$ 8,640	$16,000
Actual units produced........................	6,500	7,000	8,000
Materials bought at actual (all used)..........$14,000		$19,500	$29,400
Materials bought at standard (all used)........$13,000		$21,000	$28,000
Materials quantity required at standard........$13,650		$19,600	$29,000
Labor costs at actual.....................$2.20 per hr.		$2.30	$2.00
Actual labor hours...........................	8,000 hrs.	9,000 hrs.	17,000 hrs.
Labor costs at standard......................$13,000		$21,000	$34,500
Actual manufacturing overhead costs.........$ 5,000		$ 7,800	$18,250

From this information you are asked to prepare a schedule showing the variations from standard for each plant using seven variations—two for materials and for labor and three for manufacturing overhead.

Problem 18–4. Purpose: *Revision of Standard Costs*

Following is the previously computed standard cost of Product X manufactured by the Dalton Manufacturing Company.

	Prime Cost	Manu- facturing Burden—50%	Total
Material A	$10.00		$10.00
Material B	5.00		5.00
Material C	2.00		2.00
Direct labor—cutting	8.00	$4.00	12.00
Direct labor—shaping	4.00	2.00	6.00
Direct labor—assembling	2.00	1.00	3.00
Direct labor—boxing	1.00	0.50	1.50
Total	$32.00	$7.50	$39.50

The budget called for the manufacture of 10,000 of Product X at a total cost of $395,000 for the period under review.

The following variance accounts relating to Product X appear on the books for the period:

	Debit	Credit
Material price variance— Due to a favorable purchase of total requirements of Material A....		$19,500
Material usage variance— Excessive waste during period	$ 3,000	
Labor rate variance— 5% wage increase to direct workers	7,500	
Labor productivity variance— Due to shutdown caused by strike	15,000	
Burden variance—fixed overhead— Due to shutdown caused by strike	6,000	
Burden variance—variable overhead— Due to permanent savings in costs of certain services		12,000
Total	$31,500	$31,500

The inventory at the end of the period is as follows:

100 units Material A	@ $10.00	$ 1,000
100 units Material B	@ 5.00	500
100 units Material C	@ 2.00	200
200 units Product X in process—cut	@ 29.00	5,800
200 units Product X in process—shaped	@ 35.00	7,000
200 units Product X in process—assembled	@ 38.00	7,600
200 units Product X finished and boxed	@ 39.50	7,900
Total		$30,000

Required:

a) A schedule of revised standard cost which will clearly indicate the cumulative standard for each successive operation.

b) A schedule applying the revised standard to the ending inventory.

(Adapted from an AICPA Uniform Examination)

Problem 18–5.   Purpose: *Variance Computation*

The Dulin Company manufacturers "dully," a product used in the production of computers. Dulin utilizes a standard cost system, and the standard cost per unit of "dully" is as follows:

Materials:

"a" 40 lbs...................@ $0.50 per lb...................$ 20.00
"b" 20 oz...................@ 0.60 per oz................... 12.00
"c" 3......................@ 0.55 ea......................   1.65

Labor:

12 hrs......................@ $3.50......................... 42.00

Overhead:

12 hrs......................@ $5.00......................... 60.00
                                                            _____
                                                             $135.65

Production for the month of February amounted to 4,000 units. Other data follow:

Budgeted output for February.........................4,500 units
Actual overhead...................................... $263,000
Actual labor cost 50,000 hrs......................... $180,000
Materials purchased and used:

  164,000 lbs. @ 51¢
    7,900 oz. @ 63¢
   12,050   @ 52¢

Required:

Compute as many variances as possible.

PROBLEMS—GROUP B

Problem 18–6.   Purpose: *Computation of Two and Three Variances for Overhead*

Following is the flexible overhead budget for the Noone Company:

	Percent of Capacity				
	70%	80%	90%	100%	110%
Variable costs.................$2,625		$3,000	$3,375	$3,750	$4,125
Fixed costs.................... 5,100		5,100	5,100	5,100	5,100

Actual costs for the period amounted to $9,258 of which $5,330 were for fixed costs. The actual number of hours worked were 3,040. The budget was established on the basis of 100 percent of capacity or 3,000 hours. The standard hours for the period were 2,900.

Required:

a) Prepare an overhead expense variance report isolating two variances.

b) Prepare an overhead expense variance report isolating three variances.

Problem 18–7.   Purpose: *Variances from Standard*

The Nashville Manufacturing Company has three plants producing a single product. The standard cost records are maintained in a central computer. Following are some data prepared by the computer:

Plant No.	Units	Labor Hours	Manufacturing Overhead (Based on Labor Hours)
1............10,000		60,000	$45,000
2............12,000		60,000	30,000
3............50,000		50,000	75,000

Other pertinent data for this accounting period:

	Plant No. 1	Plant No. 2	Plant No. 3
Standard:			
Cost of materials purchased (all used)..........$ 38,700		$ 33,600	$ 90,000
Quantity of material required by jobs, at			
standard cost............................ 37,200		35,400	88,000
Cost of labor............................ 189,000		139,200	104,000
Actual:			
Units produced............................ 12,000		9,600	50,000
Material costs (all used)....................$ 36,900		$ 30,000	$ 96,000
Labor costs, per hour......................$ 2.50		$ 2.80	$ 2.20
Labor hours.............................. 70,000		49,000	52,000
Manufacturing overhead....................$ 48,000		$ 31,250	$ 72,000

Required:

Prepare a schedule showing the variances from standard for each plant. Use the three-variance system for manufacturing overhead.

Problem 18–8.   Purpose: *Computation of Variances*

The Ness Metal Company uses a standard costs system in its productive process. The standard cost of a unit of product is:

Metal...................300 lbs. @ $60 per ton...................$ 9.00
Labor...................2 hrs. @   3 per hour................ 6.00
Overhead.................2 hrs. @   4 per hour................ 8.00
		$23.00

Actual unit costs for July were as follows:

Metal used—310 lbs. @ $70 per ton................................	$10.85
Labor—2.2 hrs. @ $3.10...	6.82
Overhead—$17,850/2,100 units..................................	8.50
Actual Unit Cost...	$26.17

Budgeted production was at normal capacity of 2,000 units. Fixed overhead is $8,000; variable overhead is $2 per hour.

Required:

a) Prepare a schedule analyzing material, labor, and manufacturing overhead variances. Use a two-variance system for manufacturing overhead.

b) Recompute the manufacturing overhead variances using a three-variance system.

Problem 18–9. Purpose: *Computation of Variances*

The Deauville Company manufactures product MMJ in standard batches of 100 units. A standard cost system is in use. The standard costs for a batch are as follows:

Materials...................30 lbs. @ $0.45 per lb................	$ 13.50
Direct labor...............18 hrs. @ 2.15 per hr................	38.70
Overhead.................18 hrs. @ 2.75 per hr................	49.50
	$101.70

Production for August amounted to 210 batches. The relevant statistics follow:

Standard output per month.................................24,000 units
Materials used... 6,500 lbs.
Cost of materials used...................................... $3,110.00
Direct labor cost.. $8,432.40
Overhead cost.. $11,070.00
Average overhead rate per hour............................ $2.70

The management has noted that actual costs per batch deviate somewhat from standard costs per batch.

Required:

Prepare a statement which will contain a detailed explanation of the difference between actual costs and standard costs.

(Adapted from an AICPA Uniform Examination)

Problem 18–10. Purpose: *Preparation of Statement of Variances and Causes Therefor*

The Dee Supply Company uses a standard cost system in accounting for its single product. The standard costs were set as follows:

Budgeted production for month, 12,000 units
Standard direct material per unit:
  Material X—10 lbs. @ $4.50 per pound
  Material Y— 5 lbs. @ 0.90 per pound
Standard direct labor per unit: 10 hrs. @ $2.40 per hour
Total standard cost per unit including overhead on a
  direct labor hour basis, $88.50.

Operating data taken from the records for the month of November:
1. In process, November 1, none.
2. Completed during month, 6,000 units.
3. In process, November 30, 3,000 units, as follows: one-third direct labor, all of Material X, and one fifth of Material Y.
4. Direct labor was for 72,000 hours at an average hourly rate of $2.55.
5. Materials issued to production:
   88,000 pounds of Material X @ $4.40.
   35,000 pounds of Material Y @   1.08.
6. Overhead costs for the month were $100,700, of which $63,000 was for fixed costs, the balance variable.

Prepare a schedule showing the variations of actual costs from standard costs and an analysis of variances for labor, material, and overhead, separating each into the volume (quantity or efficiency) and the price (cost) factors which caused them. Show computations supporting your schedule.

(Adapted from an AICPA Uniform Examination)

CHAPTER

19 | Accounting Procedures
for Standard Costs

Introduction In the great majority of companies using standard costs, it will be found that the standard costs are integrated into the regular accounting records. Exceptions are occasionally encountered where standards are used only as an analytical measuring device to provide statistical data without incorporating the standard costs in any way in the books of account.

There are three possibilities of recording standard costs:

1. Standard costs may be recorded as *statistical* data, without appearing in the books of account at all.
2. Standard costs may be recorded as *operating* data, with the work-in-process accounts at standard—both debits and credits. This is the most common method and the one discussed in this chapter.
3. Standard costs may be recorded as *memoranda* data—the work-in-process accounts will show both the standard and actual costs, but the standard costs are merely memoranda figures.

Recording the Standard When standard costs are treated as sta-
Costs as Statistical tistical data, the actual costs are recorded
Data in the same manner as was discussed in the sections on job order and continuous process costs. The standard costs are developed as statistical data for comparison with the actual costs thus computed. The comparisons and analyses would be similar to those discussed in the previous chapter with reference to the statement of variations.

Recording the Standard Costs as Operating Data   This method of recording standard costs is usually restricted to those firms whose standards are *expected actual.* This is true because the budget and standard cost variations can be related more closely and because it focuses attention on the *controllable* cost variations.

Two procedures may be followed in recording standard costs as operating data, viz:

Procedure 1. Two separate variations are recorded for materials—one for the *price* or *cost variation,* recorded at the time materials are purchased, and one for *quantity variation* recorded when the materials are used.

An ideal time to isolate the material price variation is at the time of purchase if maximum control is desired. Considerable time may elapse before materials that have been purchased are used, and if the price variation is not isolated until the materials are used, it may be too late to correct any undesirable situation.

Two variances are recorded for labor—one for *cost* variations and one for *efficiency* or *quantity.*

Three separate variations may be recorded for manufacturing overhead: one for *manufacturing overhead—efficiency variation,* computed and recorded at the time jobs are completed; the *budget* or *cost* variation; and the *volume* or *capacity* variation. Both the budget and volume variations are computed at the end of the accounting period. If the two-variation method is used, the *volume* variation is recorded at the end of the accounting period. The *controllable* variation may be computed whenever a job is finished, or periodically in the case of a process type of operation.

Procedure 2. One combined *price and quantity* variation is recorded for the materials when the materials are used. When materials are purchased, they are recorded at *actual* cost. However, when materials are used, the difference between the actual and standard cost of materials used is recorded as the variation. It represents a combined price and quantity variation.

A similar combined variation account for *labor cost* and *labor efficiency* may be set up for labor, but it is permissible to have a single variation for materials and two variations for labor.

Under this method, as well as under the first method described, the same three variations are recorded for manufacturing overhead—*efficiency, capacity,* and *budget.*

Combining the cost and quantity variations for materials and/or the cost and efficiency variations for labor is not so effective for managerial cost control as when separate variations are recorded. Therefore, Procedure 1 should be used whenever possible. If the cost or price variation is not computed at the time purchases are recorded, it is still possible to compute a *price* variation when the materials are used. This is done simply by comparing the actual with the standard price for the materials. Subtracting this price variation figure from the total material cost variation will indicate the variation arising from the material usage.

Procedure 1 is illustrated on the following pages.

A recent study of 62 companies by N.A.A. shows the following number using material price standards under various conditions:

No. of Companies

Materials costed at standard price at receipt.......................36
Materials costed at standard price at issue........................12
Materials costed at standard price on completion of manufacturing
process... 3
                                                                  ——
                                                                  51
                                                                  ≡≡

The frequency at which material price variations are reported often indicates the importance placed on this type of variance for managerial control. Most companies prepare material price variation reports monthly, as indicated by the following survey of 62 companies by the N.A.A. showing the frequency of *material price* variation reports:

Quarterly.. 3
Monthly...43
Weekly.. 2
Irregularly... 2
Not showing price variations..............................12
                                                          ——
                                                          62
                                                          ≡≡

The survey of 62 firms by the N.A.A. indicated that *labor variances* were reported as follows:

Reporting variances monthly................................25
Reporting variances weekly.................................21
Reporting variances daily.................................. 7
Not reporting regularly.................................... 9
                                                           ——
                                                           62
                                                           ≡≡

Recording Material Price Variations at Time of Purchase

When this method is used, the *Stores* account is maintained at standard cost. The Work-in-Process—Materials account is also maintained at standard cost. The procedure is summarized as follows:

1. When materials are purchased, the Stores account is debited at the *standard cost* of the materials and the difference between the standard and actual cost is debited or credited to a *Material Price Variation account*.

2. When materials are used, the *standard quantity* at the *standard price* is charged to the Work-in-Process—Materials account and the difference between the *standard quantity* and the *actual quantity used* at standard cost is debited or credited to the *Material Quantity Variation account*.

To illustrate these two material variations, the following data are assumed and must be recorded:

Standard cost price of material budgeted by the purchasing department and recorded on cost card, per unit.............. $ 3.00

Purchases for the month: 3,000 units at $3.15............... 9,450.00

2,000 units at $3.225.............. 6,450.00

Requisitions: 3,000 @ $3.15............................$9,450.00

1,200 @ 3.225............................. 3,870.00 13,320.00

Standard number of units allowed for the job orders put into production... 4,000 units

Material price variations recorded at time of purchase are computed as follows:

Purchases: 3,000 @ $3.15...........................$9,450.00

2,000 @ 3.225........................... 6,450.00

Total cost at actual............................... $15,900.00

Purchases at standard cost:

5,000 units @ $3................................ 15,000.00

Unfavorable Purchase Price Variation.............. $ 900.00 (debit)

Material quantity variation shows that 4,200 units were used when the standard quantity called for on the job sheets was 4,000, making an unfavorable quantity variation of 200 units at the standard price of $3 each, or $600.

Entries in journal form to record this information would be as follows:

Stores.......................................15,000.00

Material Price Variation.................................... 900.00

Accounts Payable.. 15,900.00

To record purchase of 3,000 units at $3.15 and 2,000 units at $3.225.

The entry made to summarize the issuance of materials to the factory would be as follows:

Work-in-Process—Materials...............................12,000.00

Material Quantity Variation................................. 600.00

Stores.. 12,600.00

To record the requisitions for the month.

The Work-in-Process account is kept at the standard cost—that is, the *standard quantity* of material at the *standard price*.

Recording Labor Variations

The variations for labor are similar in nature to those just recorded for materials and involve both *cost* and *efficiency* (quantity or number of labor hours).

To obtain the *labor cost variation,* the difference is computed as follows:

Actual quantity of labor (hours worked) × Standard labor rate per hour.
Actual quantity of labor (hours worked) × Actual labor rate or cost.

This difference will be recorded in the *Labor Cost Variation account*. If the actual labor cost *rate* is higher than the standard set, it is unfavorable and is recorded as a debit. If the actual is less, then it is favorable and is recorded as a credit in the variation account.

The Work-in-Process account is maintained at the standard cost— that is, the standard hours for labor × the standard labor rate. To obtain the *labor efficiency variation*, the difference is computed as follows:

Actual quantity of labor (hours worked) × Standard labor rate per hour.
Standard quantity of labor (hours allowed) × Standard labor rate per hour.

If the actual *hours* used are greater than the standard hours allowed, then the variation is *unfavorable* and is recorded as a debit. If the actual hours used are less, then the variation is *favorable* and is recorded as a credit.

To illustrate the computation and recording of these two labor variations, the following data are assumed:

```
Actual hours worked.................4,250 hours
Actual payroll costs.................$8,925
Actual rate per hour.................$2.10
Standard hours allowed..............4,000 hours
Standard rate per hour..............$2.25
```

The labor cost or rate variation computed on the basis of the foregoing data and instructions is as follows:

```
4,250 actual hours × $2.25 (standard labor rate)...................$9,562.50
4,250 actual hours × $2.10 (actual labor rate)..................... 8,925.00
    Favorable Cost (Rate) Variation for Labor....................$  637.50 (credit)
```

The labor efficiency or quantity variation is computed as follows:

```
4,250 actual hours × standard rate of $2.25........................$9,562.50
4,000 standard hours × standard rate of $2.25..................... 9,000.00
    Unfavorable Labor Efficiency (Quantity) Variation..............$  562.50 (debit)
```

When the F.I.C.A. tax rate is assumed to be 4.4 percent, the entries in journal form to record these two labor variations would be as follows:

```
Payroll......................................................8,925.00
    F.I.C.A. Taxes Payable......................................        392.70
    Withholding Taxes Payable...................................        981.75
    Accounts Payable............................................      7,550.55
        To record actual payroll costs in voucher register.
```

```
Work-in-Process—Labor.........................................9,000.00
Labor Efficiency Variation.....................................  562.50
     Labor Cost Variation.......................................                 637.50
     Payroll....................................................                 8,925.00
     To distribute the payroll and to record labor variations.
```

It is also possible but not always *practical* to record the *labor cost variation* directly in the payroll book or voucher register, in which case the two variations will appear in separate records, viz:

```
Payroll (actual hours × standard rate)..........................9,562.50
     F.I.C.A. Taxes Payable.....................................                 392.70
     Withholding Taxes Payable..................................                 981.75
     Labor Cost Variation.......................................                 637.50
     Payroll Accrued............................................                 7,550.55
     To record payroll in payroll book at standard.

Payroll Accrued.................................................7,550.55
     Accounts Payable...........................................                 7,550.55
     To record the preparation of the voucher for payroll.

Work-in-Process—Labor..........................................9,000.00
Labor Efficiency Variation.....................................  562.50
     Payroll....................................................                 9,562.50
     To record labor efficiency variation when distributing the payroll
     charges.
```

Recording Manufacturing Overhead Variations

Under the three-variation system, the manufacturing overhead variations fall into two separate groups: those determined *when the job is completed,* and those determined at the *end of the accounting period.* The former relate to the *job;* the latter to the *plant.* The job variation is called *manufacturing overhead—efficiency variation;* the plant variations are known as *manufacturing overhead—budget variation* if they are cost variations and *manufacturing overhead—capacity variation* if they are volume variations. The computation of these has been indicated previously on page 555.

To illustrate the manufacturing overhead variations, the following data will be used:

```
Normal capacity, budgeted hours.................................15,000 hours
Budgeted manufacturing overhead at this capacity:
     Fixed costs................................................$15,000
     Variable costs............................................. 15,000
                                                                 $30,000

Standard overhead rate per labor hour...........................$2.00
Standard hours for actual production for period.................11,600 hours
Actual hours used for actual production.........................14,000 hours
Actual manufacturing overhead costs incurred....................$32,500
```

To compute and record the *three manufacturing overhead variations* from these data, the following procedure is used:

1. *Manufacturing overhead—efficiency variation* (difference between standard hours and actual hours × predetermined or standard rate):

Actual hours × standard rate (14,000 × $2)........................$28,000
Standard hours × standard rate (11,600 × $2)...................... 23,200
    Manufacturing Overhead Efficiency Variation, Unfavorable (2,400
    hours × $2)...$ 4,800 (debit)

Entries in journal form to record this variation:

Manufacturing Overhead Control............................32,500.00
    Sundry Credits.......................................   32,500.00
    To record actual manufacturing overhead incurred.

Work-in-Process—Manufacturing Overhead....................23,200.00
Manufacturing Overhead—Efficiency Variation................. 4,800.00
    Applied Manufacturing Overhead.......................   28,000.00
    To record applied manufacturing overhead and the efficiency
    variation.

2. *Manufacturing overhead—budget variation* (difference between the budgeted and actual manufacturing overhead costs):

Actual manufacturing overhead costs................$32,500
Budgeted manufacturing overhead costs.............. 30,000
    Budget or Cost Variation, Unfavorable..........$ 2,500 (debit)

3. *Manufacturing overhead—capacity variation* (difference between budgeted hours and actual hours times the predetermined rate):

Budgeted hours, 15,000 × $2.00...................$30,000
Actual hours, 14,000 × predetermined rate $2.00....... 28,000
    Capacity Variation, Unfavorable (1,000 Hours × $2).$ 2,000 (debit)

Summary of variations equaling over- or underapplied overhead:

Budget variation............................$2,500 unfavorable
Capacity variation........................... 2,000 unfavorable
Efficiency variation......................... 4,800 unfavorable
    Net Variation (Underapplied)..............$9,300 unfavorable

The journal entry to record the budget and capacity variations is:

Applied Manufacturing Overhead............................28,000.00
Manufacturing Overhead—Budget Variation................... 2,500.00
Manufacturing Overhead—Capacity Variation................. 2,000.00
    Manufacturing Overhead Control.......................   32,500.00
    To close out applied and actual overhead accounts and to record
    the budget and capacity variations.

If the two-variance system is used, the budget is adjusted to the *standard hours* of production. A *volume* variance and a *controllable* or *spending* variance are computed. To compute and record the two manufacturing overhead variations from these data, the following procedure is used:

1. Manufacturing overhead—controllable variation:

Actual manufacturing overhead costs...........		$32,500
Budget adjusted to standard hours:		
Variable costs, 11,600 hours × $1............	$11,600	
Fixed costs...............................	15,000	
		26,600
Controllable variation...................		$ 5,900 unfavorable

2. Manufacturing overhead—volume variation:

Adjusted budget..	$26,600
Applied (standard @ standard) 11,600 hours × $2.........	23,200
Volume variation...............................	$ 3,400 unfavorable

Entries to record the data are:

Manufacturing Overhead Control............................	32,500.00	
Sundry Credits..		32,500.00
Work-in-Process—Manufacturing Overhead....................	23,200.00	
Controllable Variation.......................................	5,900.00	
Volume Variation...	3,400.00	
Manufacturing Overhead Control........................		32,500.00

Illustration of Entries for Standard Costs   To present a comprehensive illustration of standard cost accounting, the following data are assumed:

1. Balances, June 1, 19—, were:

	Standard Cost
Materials...	$2,800
Work-in-process—materials....................................	1,500
Work-in-process—direct labor.................................	1,000
Work-in-process—overhead....................................	1,000
Finished goods..	1,500

2. Purchases for the month were:

	Actual Cost	Standard Cost
Purchase order No. 869 (900 units).........................	$ 750	$ 720
Purchase order No. 870 (5,000 units).......................	3,700	4,000

3. Materials issued to production department, at standard cost:

Standard quantity (4,000 units)...............................	$3,200
Additional materials (100 units)...............................	80

4. Materials returned to stores, 30 units at standard cost, $24.
5. Direct labor time tickets:

Standard for orders actually put into production......................9,600 hours
Excess time.. 30
  Total..9,630 hours

6. Actual wages for direct labor (standard wage rate, $1.90 per hour):

3,420 hours, at $1.92...$ 6,566.40
5,860 hours, at $1.88... 11,016.80
  350 hours, at $1.80... 630.00
9,630 hours $18,213.20

7. Manufacturing overhead (a fixed budget is used):

Total of manufacturing overhead budget.............................$12,250
Budgeted direct labor hours.. 9,800
Standard rate per direct labor hour

$$\frac{\$12,250}{9,800} = \$1.25$$

7a. Actual manufacturing overhead, $12,670.
8. Cost of goods completed during the month at standard cost:

Material costs..........................$ 4,000
Direct labor costs...................... 19,000
Manufacturing overhead costs............ 12,500
                                       $35,500

9. Cost of sales at standard cost amounted to $30,000.

The entries for these data would appear, in journal form, as follows:

(1)
Stores... 720.00
Material Price Variation.. 30.00
  Accounts Payable.. 750.00
  To record invoice on purchase order No. 869.

(2)
Stores... 4,000.00
  Material Price Variation.. 300.00
  Accounts Payable.. 3,700.00
  To record invoice on purchase order No. 870.

(3)
Work-in-Process—Materials... 3,200.00
Material Quantity Variation... 80.00
  Stores.. 3,280.00
  To record materials issued during the month.

(4)

Stores...	24.00	
Material Quantity Variation.............................		24.00
To record materials returned to stores.		

(5a)

Payroll...	21,013.20	
Withholding Taxes Payable..............................		2,311.45
F.I.C.A. Taxes Payable (4.4%)..........................		924.58
Accounts Payable......................................		17,777.17
To record wages earned.		

(5b)

Direct Labor..	18,213.20	
Indirect Labor..	2,800.00	
Payroll..		21,013.20
To record and analyze factory payroll.		

(5c)

Accounts Payable......................................	17,777.17	
Cash...		17,777.17

(5d)

Work-in-Process—Direct Labor..........................	18,240.00	
Direct Labor Efficiency Variation.......................	57.00	
Direct Labor Cost Variation...........................		83.80
Direct Labor...		18,213.20
To close out Direct Labor account.		

(6)

Work-in-Process—Manufacturing Overhead................	12,000.00	
Manufacturing Overhead—Efficiency Variation............	37.50	
Manufacturing Overhead Applied.......................		12,037.50
To record manufacturing overhead applied to production and efficiency variation for the month.		

(7)

Manufacturing Overhead Summary........................	12,670.00	
Taxes..		900.00
Supplies...		680.00
Repairs..		820.00
Depreciation of Machinery and Building.................		3,400.00
Indirect Labor.......................................		2,800.00
Power..		3,700.00
Superintendence......................................		300.00
Miscellaneous Manufacturing Overhead..................		70.00
To close manufacturing overhead accounts.		

(7a)

Manufacturing Overhead Applied.........................	12,037.50	
Manufacturing Overhead—Capacity Variation..............	212.50	
Manufacturing Overhead—Budget Variation...............	420.00	
Manufacturing Overhead Summary......................		12,670.00
To close the Manufacturing Overhead and the Manufacturing Overhead Applied accounts and record idle capacity and budget excess variations.		

The idle capacity variation is 170 hours (9,800 — 9,630) at $1.25 per hour; the budget excess variation is the difference between actual and budgeted manufacturing overhead costs ($12,670 — $12,250).

(8)

Finished Goods..	35,500.00	
Work-in-Process—Materials............................		4,000.00
Work-in-Process—Labor................................		19,000.00
Work-in-Process—Manufacturing Overhead................		12,500.00
To record the cost of goods completed at standard cost.		

(9)

Cost of Sales..	30,000.00	
Finished Goods..		30,000.00
To record the cost of goods sold at standard cost.		

When these entries have been posted, the general ledger accounts will appear as follows:

Stores

June 1	Inventory	S*	2,800.00	June 30	S	3,280.00
30	Purchases	S	720.00			
30	Purchases	S	4,000.00			
30	Return to stores	S	24.00			

* S indicates at *standard* cost; A indicates at *actual* cost.

Material Price Variation

June 30		S	30.00	June 30	S	300.00

Accounts Payable

June 30		A 17,777.17	June 30	A	750.00
			30		3,700.00
			30		17,777.17

Work-in-Process—Materials

June 1	Inventory	S	1,500.00	June 30	S	4,000.00
30		S	3,200.00			

Material Quantity Variation

June 30 (Act. Qty.—Std. Qty.)	S	80.00	June 30	S	24.00

Direct Labor

June 30		A 18,213.20	June 30		A 18,213.20

Direct Labor Cost Variation

		June 30	83.80

Payroll

June 30		A 21,013.20	June 30		A 21,013.20

Work-in-Process—Labor

June 1	Inventory	S 1,000.00	June 30		S 19,000.00
30		S 18,240.00			

Labor Efficiency Variation

June 30		57.00	

Manufacturing Overhead Summary

June 30		A 12,670.00	June 30		A 12,670.00

Work-in-Process—Manufacturing Overhead

June 1	Inventory	S 1,000.00	June 30		S 12,500.00
30		S 12,000.00			

Manufacturing Overhead—Efficiency Variation

June 30		37.50	

Manufacturing Overhead Applied

June 30		12,037.50	June 30		S 12,037.50

Manufacturing Overhead—Capacity Variation

June 30	212.50	

Manufacturing Overhead—Budget Variation

June 30	420.00	

Finished Goods

June 1	S 1,500.00	June 30	S 30,000.00
30	S 35,500.00		

Cost of Sales

June 30	S 30,000.00	

On the books of this firm there are now seven variation accounts, with debit balances of $783 and credit balances of $353.80. These balances serve to point out what costs in total were different from the expected standard cost, and they may be summarized as follows:

Material costs were less than expected by.................................$270.00
Labor costs were less than expected by.................................... 83.80
   Total Variations under Standard.......................................$353.80

The quantity of materials used was greater than expected by.................$ 56.00
The quantity of labor required was greater than was expected by............ 57.00
Because of the inefficiency of labor, and the use of more than the standard hours,
   manufacturing overhead costs were excessively used by.................... 37.50
Facilities, measured by 170 hours, were not utilized, and this wasted capacity
   cost in manufacturing overhead.. 212.50
The cost of the manufacturing overhead exceeded the budget by............. 420.00
   Total Variations Over Standard...$783.00

If a *flexible budget* had been used for manufacturing overhead and two variances isolated, the following would have been changed in the preceding illustration (all data and entries not shown below remain the same):

7. Manufacturing overhead (a flexible budget is used).

Variable overhead is $0.60 per direct labor hour.
Fixed overhead is $6,370
9,800 direct labor hours are budgeted @ $0.60 + $6,370 = $12,250
The standard rate per direct labor hour is:

$$\frac{\$12,250}{9,800} = \$1.25.$$

The following entries are made in lieu of those made in the preceding illustration:

(6)

Work-in-Process—Manufacturing Overhead.....................12,000.00		
Manufacturing Overhead Applied.........................		12,000.00
To record overhead applied to production.		

(7a)

Manufacturing Overhead Applied............................12,000.00		
Manufacturing Overhead—Controllable Variance...............	540.00	
Manufacturing Overhead—Volume Variance....................	130.00	
Manufacturing Overhead Summary.......................		12,670.00
To close the Manufacturing Overhead and Manufacturing Overhead Applied accounts and to record the controllable and volume variations.		

The total number of variations appearing on the books would be six since the controllable and volume variances were determined in lieu of the capacity, efficiency, and budget variances.

The Disposition of Variation Accounts

The disposition of variation account balances is an area in which accountants are not entirely in agreement. There seem to be two general points of view.

One group of accountants maintains that standard cost is not the *actual* cost and that, therefore, the variation should be prorated over the cost of sales, finished goods inventory, and work-in-process inventories. For example, if the labor variance amounted to $600 for the 6,000 equivalent units that were put into production, 1,000 were still not finished, 2,000 were finished and on hand, and 3,000 were sold, $100 of the variance should be added to work-in-process, $200 to finished goods, and $300 to cost of goods sold.

This prorating process, if accurately computed, would result in a sufficient amount being added or subtracted from the various inventory accounts and Cost of Sales account to bring these figures to an approximation of *actual* cost. This procedure has the advantage of meeting the requirements of federal income tax regulations.

The other group of cost accountants takes the position that if standards are carefully determined and revised when necessary, the variation accounts will reflect losses and gains due to efficiency factors; such losses and gains are not normal items in manufacturing cost. Therefore, variation accounts should be closed to the Cost of Sales or the Revenue and Expense accounts and shown on the statements accordingly. Inventories valued at standard cost are, to this group of accountants, properly valued, since efficiency and inefficiency are not values to be recorded on balance sheets in inventories but are income-determining factors.

From a theoretical point of view, at least, there is much to be said for the second method. Income tax regulations need not determine the general accounting methods, and suitable adjustments can serve effectively to meet the legal stipulations. The argument for prorating variations over the inventories and cost of sales accounts is theoretically wrong, for there is a distinction between *cost* and *loss,* however difficult it may be to make such a distinction in practice. If standards are carefully established and their adequacy is maintained by making revisions where uncontrollable factors upset the initial estimates, *and* if management *uses* the variation data as a basis for improvement of methods, the variation balances should be small indeed. The question of the disposition of variation account balances may thus resolve itself into another and more significant one: "How well-planned and administered is this particular business?"

In the case of the extended illustration found on pages 579–84, the entry to close the variation accounts into the Cost of Sales or Profit and Loss account would be:

Cost of Sales (Revenue and Expense).............................429.20		
Material Price Variation..270.00		
Direct Labor Cost Variation..................................... 83.80		
Material Quantity Variation....................................	56.00	
Labor Efficiency Variation.....................................	57.00	
Manufacturing Overhead—Efficiency Variation....................	37.50	
Manufacturing Overhead—Budget Variation......................	420.00	
Manufacturing Overhead—Capacity Variation..................	212.50	
To close variation accounts into the Cost of Sales account.		

Shown on the income statement, these variations tell management in a broad way why the cost of sales was not the standard cost of $30,000, and in so doing call attention to the need for improved methods and procedures to eliminate inefficiencies.

Operating Statements under Standard Cost Accounting   Examples of statements of cost to manufacture prepared from a standard cost system are shown in Illustration 19–1 or as arranged in Illustration 19–2.

For many companies, interim as well as annual income statements are prepared. The question of what to do with the variations from

Illustration 19-1

POWERS MANUFACTURING COMPANY

Cost of Goods Manufactured
For the year, 19—

Standard cost:	
Materials used..	$ 7,500
Direct labor..	15,000
Variable manufacturing overhead..............................	3,000
Fixed manufacturing overhead.................................	2,000
Cost of production at standard...............................	$27,500
Deduct:	
Increase in work-in-process inventory at standard................	7,200
Cost of goods finished at standard............................	$20,300
Deduct: Variations under standard costs:*	
Labor quantity variation......................................$2,000	
Material price variation...................................... 3,400	
Idle capacity variation....................................... 2,600	8,000
Total..	$12,300
Add: Variations over standard costs:	
Labor cost variation...$1,750	
Material quantity variation................................... 2,300	
Manufacturing overhead—efficiency variation.................... 2,650	
Manufacturing overhead—budget excess variation................ 1,400	8,100
Total Cost of Goods Manufactured.........................	$20,400

*Variations may also be added or subtracted from cost of goods sold.

Illustration 19-2

POWERS MANUFACTURING COMPANY

Cost of Goods Manufactured
For the year, 19—

	Standard Cost	Variation from Standard	Actual Cost
Costs of production:			
Materials used....................................$ 7,500			
Material quantity variation......................		+$2,300	
Material price variation........................		− 3,400	$ 6,400
Labor costs....................................	15,000		
Labor cost variation...........................		+ 1,750	
Labor efficiency variation......................		− 2,000	14,750
Manufacturing overhead.........................	5,000		
Manufacturing overhead—efficiency variation......		+ 2,650	
Manufacturing overhead—budget excess variation		+ 1,400	
Manufacturing overhead—capacity variation......		− 2,600	6,450
Total..$27,500		+$ 100	$27,600
Less: Increase in work-in-process inventory, at standard	7,200		7,200
Cost of Goods Manufactured......................$20,300		+$ 100	$20,400

standard on these statements must receive attention, even though the procedures used by the various firms are not uniform. One suggested procedure relating to the interim—monthly or quarterly—statements would be:

1. Those variations which are an indication of managerial or supervisory inefficiency should be charged to the cost of goods sold for the period. These are losses and should be charged in the period when realized. These include labor efficiency, manufacturing overhead budget, and manufacturing overhead efficiency variations. Material price variation might better be prorated over the inventories of work-in-process, finished goods, and stores.
2. When the variations are favorable (credit balances), they should first be used to offset the negative or debit variations. Any unused balance should be used to reduce the inventory balances in some pro rata manner.
3. To meet the requirements of the Internal Revenue Service, material price variations should be prorated over the work-in-process, finished goods, and cost of sales in proportion to the amount of purchased materials used for each during the current period.

At the end of the fiscal period, all variations should be closed into the cost of goods sold, except that proportion of the material cost variation which relates to the unused inventory of purchases for the period.

However, it should be remembered that since uniformity is not practiced by managements, decisions on how to treat the variations in the interim as well as fiscal statements should give consideration to the following: (1) nature of variation, (2) amount involved, (3) regularity of occurrence in the manufacturing cycle, (4) cause of variation, (5) effect of method used on the income statement and balance sheet, (6) reasonableness of such treatment—what does management want to indicate to its employees?

QUESTIONS FOR REVIEW

1. What are the three possibilities of recording standard costs? Which do you prefer? Why?
2. "The manufacturing overhead variations fall into two separate groups: those determined when the job is completed, and those determined at the end of the accounting period. The former relate to the job; the latter to the plant." Explain.
3. Discuss two general points of view as far as disposition of variation accounts is concerned.
4. Describe how you would compute overhead variances under the two-variance method. Indicate whom you would hold responsible for the variances.
5. What should be the role of the cost accountant in variance analysis?
6. How often should the direct labor variances be isolated? Defend the time period you have chosen with a clear and concise discussion.
7. "We cannot use standard costs in our firm because we are afraid that the standard costs would complicate our accounting system." Explain.
8. "The argument for prorating variations over the inventories and the cost of

sales account is theoretically wrong." Do you agree? Why or why not? Discuss.

9. Part of the standard cost sheet for the Lynch Company's only product shows:

Overhead: 10 labor hours @ $3........$30

The flexible budget for November shows:

Labor Hours	Overhead Costs
20,000	$ 80,000
30,000	100,000
40,000	120,000
50,000	140,000

During the month of November, 3,500 units of product were produced. Thirty-eight thousand labor hours were used, and the actual overhead for the month amounted to $122,000.

Compute the overhead variances for November using the two-variance system.

10. Refer to the data in (9) above and compute the overhead variances for November using the three-variance system.

PROBLEMS—GROUP A

Problem 19–1.   Purpose: *The Standard Cost Accounting Cycle: Journalizing*

The relevant data of the Edwards Electrical Engineering Company, manufacturers of "elec," follow:

Normal capacity of plant—40,000 machine-hours.
Flexible budget (overhead): Variable cost—30¢ per machine-hour
                            Fixed cost—$8,000
Standard cost: Material—5 pounds at 60¢............$3.00
              Labor—2 hours @ $2................. 4.00
              Overhead—4 machine-hours @ 50¢..... 2.00
              Standard cost per product unit.........$9.00

If normal capacity is 40,000 machine-hours and standard machine-hours per unit are 4, then normal production is 10,000. Budgeted overhead at normal production of 10,000 units would then be $20,000 (10,000 × $2).

Data for period: Budgeted production—10,000 units (normal capacity).

Put into process 9,700 units, 9,300 of which were completed and transferred to finished goods. The remaining 400 were left in process, complete as to material and one-half complete as to labor and overhead. Actual machine-hours utilized—38,200.

Transactions:

1. Purchased 50,000 lbs. material at 61¢ per lb.—$30,500.
2. Used 48,000 lbs. of material in production.
3. Payroll for period—$41,000.
4. Direct labor amounted to 18,800 hours at an average wage of $2.10. The balance of the payroll account is indirect labor.

5. Miscellaneous expenses (in addition to the above indirect labor) were $17,080 for the period.
6. Expenses were applied during the period.
7. 9,300 units were completed and transferred to finished goods.
8. 9,000 units were sold at a price of $12 per unit.
9. Selling and administrative expenses were $15,620 for the period.
10. The books were closed for the period.

Required:

Journalize the transactions for the period. The company uses the three-variance system for overhead.

Problem 19–2. Purpose: *Journalize Transactions; Prepare an Income Statement*

The Elite Company uses a standard cost system. The standards are based on a budget for operations at the rate of production anticipated for the current period. The company records in its general ledger variations in material prices and usage, wage rates and labor efficiency. The accounts for manufacturing expenses reflect variations in activity from the projected rate of operations, variations of actual expenses from amounts budgeted, and variations in the efficiency of production.

Current standards are as follows:

Materials:
Material A.....................................$1.20 per unit
Material B..................................... 2.60 per unit
Direct labor..................................... 2.05 per hour

	Special Widgets	Deluxe Widgets
Finished products (content of each unit):		
Material A.	12 units	12 units
Material B.	6 units	8 units
Direct labor.	14 hours	20 hours

The general ledger does not include a finished goods inventory account; costs are transferred directly from work in process to cost of sales at the time finished products are sold.

The budget and operating data for the month of August are summarized as follows:

Budget:
Projected direct labor hours........................ 9,000 hours
Fixed manufacturing expense........................ $ 4,500
Variable manufacturing expenses.................... 13,500
Selling expenses....................................... 4,000
Administrative expenses.............................. 7,500

Operating data:
Sales:
500 special widgets............................. 52,700
100 deluxe widgets............................. 16,400

Purchases:
Material A....................................... 8,500 units   9,725
Material B....................................... 1,800 units   5,635

Material requisitions:		*Material A*	*Material B*
Issued from stores:			
Standard quantity		8,400 units	3,200 units
Over standard		400 units	150 units
Returned to stores		75 units	

Direct labor hours:	
Standard	9,600 hours
Actual	10,000 hours

Wages paid:	
500 hours at	$2.10
8,000 hours at	2.00
1,500 hours at	1.90

Expenses:	
Manufacturing	$20,125
Selling	3,250
Administrative	6,460

Required:

a) Prepare journal entries to record operations for the month of August. Show computations of the amounts used in each journal entry. Raw material purchases are recorded at standard.

b) Prepare an income statement for the month supported by an analysis of variations.

Problem 19–3. Purpose: *Journal Entries; Analysis of Variances*

The Evans Company manufactures "helio" in its Indianapolis plant. A standard cost system has been employed, and the cost sheet per unit of "helio" follows:

Material	100 lbs. @ $1.50	$150
Labor	50 hrs. @ 3.00	150
Overhead:		
Variable	50 hrs. @ $2.00	
Fixed	50 hrs. @ 2.00	200
		$500

Budgeted production at normal capacity is 2,000 units or 100,000 hours. The overhead standard costs were set at normal capacity.

The following transactions took place during April:
1. Purchased, 2,500,000 lbs. @ $1.48.
2. Used, 198,000 lbs.
3. Direct labor, 91,000 hours @ $3.05.
4. Overhead incurred, $362,598.
5. Units produced:

Transferred to finished goods	1,700 units
In process—complete as to materials; 50% complete as to conversion cost	200 units

There were no goods in process at the beginning of the period.

Required:

a) Journalize the above transactions. Assume the company utilizes the two-variance system for overhead.

b) Prepare a report analyzing the variances from standard cost.

Problem 19-4.   Purpose: *Preparation of Journal Entries from Incomplete Data*

Edwina Manufacturers, Inc., produce a single product that has the following standard cost:

Materials (5 pieces)....................	$ 5.50
Labor (1 hour)........................	3.50
Overhead (1 hour).....................	3.00
	$12.00

The units put into production were 100,000; 80,000 were completed and transferred to finished goods; 20,000 units were complete as to materials but 25 percent complete as to labor and overhead.

The following variances were isolated during the period:

Labor rate variance..	$15,850 cr.
Labor quantity or efficiency variance.........................	7,000 dr.
Overhead volume variance....................................	4,000 dr.
Overhead efficiency variance.................................	6,000 dr.
Overhead budget variance....................................	12,432 dr.
Material price variance (520,000 pieces were purchased).........	5,200 dr.
Material quantity variance....................................	6,600 cr.

Required:

Construct the journal entries that were made to create the above variances.

Problem 19-5.   Purpose: *Computation and Analysis of Standard Cost Variations*

The Ernest Company uses a standard cost system in accounting for the cost of one of its products.

The standard is based on budgeted monthly production of 100 units per day for the usual 22 workdays per month. Standard cost per unit for direct labor is 16 hours at $1.50 per hour. Standard cost for overhead was set as follows:

Fixed overhead per month.............................	$29,040
Variable overhead per month..........................	39,600
Total Budgeted Overhead.........................	$68,640
Expected direct labor cost............................	$52,800
Overhead rate per dollar of labor.....................	$ 1.30
Standard overhead per unit...........................	$ 13.20

During the month of September the plant operated only 20 days. Cost for the 2,080 units produced were:

Direct labor, 32,860 hrs. @ $1.52 =	$49,947.20
Fixed overhead..................	29,300.00
Variable overhead...............	39,065.00

From this information you are asked to—

a) Compute the variance from standard in September for—

(1) Direct labor costs.

(2) Manufacturing overhead costs.

b) Analyze the variations from standard into identifiable causes for—

(1) Direct labor.

(2) Fixed and variable overhead.

(Adapted from an AICPA Uniform Examination)

PROBLEMS—GROUP B

Problem 19–6. Purpose: *Determination of Standard Costs; Journalizing Transactions*

The Olden Corporation manufactures two simple parts which are stamped from sheet steel.

Standard specifications are as follows:

Part A

Material: Each sheet of steel weighing 100 lbs. and costing $60 per ton should yield 50 pieces.

Labor: Each stamping machine is operated by a team of two men, to receive $2.25 and $1.75 per hour respectively. Each team should produce 100 pieces per hour.

Burden: Rate, $3 per standard machine-hour.

Part B

Material: Steel as used for A should yield 100 pieces per sheet.

Labor: Each machine (one operator per machine) should produce 150 pieces per hour. Labor is paid 2¢ per piece.

Burden: Rate, $3 per standard machine-hour.

Budgeted burden at practical capacity (per month):

Fixed expenses..........................$24,000
Variable expense......................... 12,000
Total.............................$36,000

Practical capacity is figured as 12,000 machine-hours per month (60 machines × 8 hours per day × 25 working days per month).

Actual Operating Data, November

Output: Part A, 400,000 pieces.
Part B, 1,200,000 pieces.
(Work-in-process, none.)

Material: Inventory of sheet steel at November 1, 300 tons which had been purchased at $59. Purchased during November, 600 tons @ $61 and 600 tons @ $60. Used during November, 1,050 tons.

Labor: Total direct labor cost, $40,610, as follows:

Part A, 8,200 hours, $16,610
Part B, above output @ 2¢, $24,000
(actual working time, 7,700 hours)

Burden: Total actual burden incurred, $36,300.

Required:

a) Compute unit standard costs for Parts A and B.

b) Prepare the following summary entries, including all variance accounts:

(1) Material purchased.
(2) Materials issued into process.
(3) Labor costs incurred and charged into process.
(4) Burden applied; include separate breakdown to show burden variances. Use two-variance system.
(5) Transfer of work completed into finished goods.

Problem 19–7. Purpose: *Adjusting Inventories to Actual Cost*

The Johnson Company began operations on January 1, 1968. It manufactures a single product. The company installed a standard cost system but will adjust all inventories to actual cost for financial statement purposes at the end of the year.

Under the cost system, raw material inventory is maintained at actual cost. Charges to work-in-process are all made at standard prices. Variance accounts are used into which all variances are entered as they are identified.

One half of the cost of raw material for each unit is put into production at the beginning of the process and the balance when the processing is about one-third completed.

Standard cost was based on 256,000 direct labor hours with a production of 1,600 units. The standard costs were as follows:

```
Materials (100 lbs. @ $2)...........................................$200
Direct labor (160 hrs. @ $1.25)......................................  200
Manufacturing expense (based on direct labor hours) (160 @ $0.25).....   40
    Total standard cost per unit.....................................$440
```

A summary of the transactions for the year ended December 31, 1968, shows the following:

```
Material purchased (180,000 lbs. @ $2.20)....................$396,000.00
Direct labor (247,925 hrs. @ $1.30)..........................  322,302.50
Manufacturing overhead.......................................   49,585.00
Material issued to production................................  177,600 lbs.
Units processed:
    Units completed..........................................    1,500
    Units one-half complete..................................      150
    Units one-fourth complete................................       30
```

Required:

a) Record the transactions in appropriate ledger accounts for the year. In each account give an indication of the nature of each item recorded.

b) Make the entries needed to adjust finished goods to actual cost for material. Give identifiable supporting computations showing clearly the method of arriving at each adjustment. You need not adjust for labor or manufacturing expense.

c) Prepare a statement showing details of the material cost included in work-in-process inventory as adjusted to actual cost.

Problem 19–8. Purpose: *Journal Entries; Analysis of Variances*

The Oldham Company has been using a standard cost system in its operations. Plant No. 43 located at Shelbyville manufactures "shelly," a product used in roofing operations. The standard cost per batch of "shelly" is:

```
Material................200 lbs. @ $0.60..............$120
Labor................... 10 hrs. @  3.50.............. 35
Overhead............... 10 hrs. @  3.00.............. 30
     (50% of the overhead cost represents variable costs; 50%
     fixed costs)
                                                     ─────
                                                     $185
                                                     ═════
```

The overhead standard costs are set at normal capacity of 5,000 batches or 50,000 hours.

An examination of the records yielded the following data:

1. Purchased 1,500,000 lbs. materials @ 59¢ lb.
2. Produced the following:
   4,700 batches started, of which 4,000 were completed; 700 complete as to materials; 50 percent complete as to conversion.
3. Used 950,000 lbs. of materials.
4. Direct labor—44,200 hours @ $3.54.
5. Actual overhead— $128,452.

Required:

a) Journalize the above transactions. Assume the company utilizes the three-variance system for overhead.

b) Prepare a report analyzing the variances from standard cost.

Problem 19–9.   Purpose: *Preparation of Journal Entries from Incomplete Data*

Oliver Suppliers manufactures a single product with the following standard cost:

```
Materials (10 gallons).....................$ 7.50
Labor (2 hours)........................... 6.00
Overhead (2 hours)....................... 5.00
                                          ──────
                                          $18.50
                                          ══════
```

During the month of November, 80,000 units were started; 50,000 were completed and transferred to the finished goods storeroom; 30,000 were complete as to materials and 33⅓ percent complete as to labor and overhead.

During the period 780,000 gallons of material were purchased.

The ledger contained the following balances in the variance accounts:

Material Price Variance	Material Quantity Variance	Labor Rate Variance
7,800.00	9,000.00	1,200.00

Labor Efficiency Variance	Overhead Budget Variance	Overhead Capacity Variance
13,200.00	9,200.00	15,000.00

Overhead Efficiency Variance
11,000.00

Required:

Construct the journal entries that were made to create the above variances.

Problem 19–10.   Purpose: *Journal Entries for Standard Cost System; Statements*

From the information following, prepare an income statement showing therein appropriate manufacturing cost variances of Olson Company for January, 19—, supported by journal entries of transactions for the month.

The Olson Company makes unit M. The manufacturing of unit M is based on three successive and continuous operations, namely, operations M-10 to M-12, inclusive, in which the manufacturing cost of such unit is developed as shown by the following tabulation of percentages of cost of manufacture.

PERCENTAGES OF COST OF MANUFACTURE OF UNIT M

Operation	Material	Labor	Overhead
M-10	20%	20%	40%
M-11		35	40
M-12	80	45	20
Total	100%	100%	100%

(The company does not record the actual labor charges applicable to each operation.)

The Olson Company operates a cost accounting system based on standard costs which are incorporated in the manufacturing cost accounts. The differences between standard costs and actual costs are reflected in appropriate variance accounts, namely, material price, material usage, direct labor rate, direct labor time, and overall manufacturing overhead. The material price variance is assumed to be realized at the time of purchase, irrespective of time of usage.

The standard manufacturing costs used for unit M (based on a planned monthly production ranging between 8,000 and 12,000 units M) are as follows:

	Per Unit M Quantity or Hours	Amount
Material:		
Item M-a (Issued in Operation M-10)	1	$0.50
Item M-b (Issued in Operation M-12)	1	2.00
Direct labor (total for all operations at uniform rate of $5 per hour)	¼ hr.	1.25
Overhead (applicable to operations as a whole):		
Variable expenses		0.60
Fixed expenses		0.90
		$5.25

The inventories applicable to unit M as at December 31, 19—, stated in accordance with the foregoing schedule of standard costs, are as follows:

Material: item M-a—100 units; item M-b—100 units.
Work-in-process: 50 units complete through operation M-10.
Finished goods: none.

Transactions during January, 19—, are submitted as follows:
The voucher register reflects applicable transactions incurred and paid as follows:

Amount

Material purchases:
Item M-a—12,000 units @ $0.45 per unit.........................$ 5,400
Item M-b—12,000 units @ 2.10 per unit......................... 25,200
Payroll for all operations:
Direct labor—3,100 hours @ $1.2625 per ¼ hr................... 15,655
Indirect labor.. 1,500
Manufacturing overhead, other than indirect labor............... 15,000
Selling, administrative, and general expenses.................... 25,000

Other facts are:

During January, 19—, 11,000 units M were transferred to the finished goods warehouse and 10,500 units were sold at $9.00 per unit M.

As at January 31, 19—, 100 units of work-in-process are complete through operation M-11.

Stores requisitions indicate issuances of material items M-a and M-b in the quantities required for the production carried through the respective operations. A supplementary stores requisition, however, indicates that item M-a actually used was 2 percent in excess of standard quantity required.

(Adapted from an AICPA Uniform Examination)

CHAPTER

20 The Installation of the Cost Accounting System and Managerial Reports

Administrative and Managerial Direction in the Installation of a System

The cost accounting system may be installed by the firm's public accounting firm, or by a firm of management engineers, or by the chief cost accountant under the direction of the controller. Regardless of who has the responsibility for installing the system, it is necessary first of all to obtain the approval and direction of top management of the objectives to be achieved through the cost accounting system.

This direction and control from top management should include the following:

1. What products are or will be produced?
2. The estimated profitability of these products.
3. The relative product mix of the production and sales.
4. The type of costing to be used—historical or predetermined standard; job order or departmental process.
5. The approximate cost of operating the system.
6. The reports to be issued and the use to be made of these reports—responsibility accounting and control.
7. The acceptable accounting procedures to be used in such matters as—
   a) Inventory control and pricing methods.
   b) Depreciation methods of plant and equipment.

Having obtained appropriate direction from top management, the second step requires the survey of the plant and manufacturing procedures.

Preliminary Surveys to Be Completed

Surveys must be made at the outset of what is being done and what should be done in the matter of planning, operating, and accounting. These surveys are guides for planning the cost accounting system. It has already been determined what type of system will be installed—job order, process, historical, or standard.

In planning a new or revising the current cost accounting system, the *first* survey will involve:

   a) A study of the plant layout and the flow of work.
   b) Preparation of flow charts of the operations in each department, and should cover
        receipt, movement, and transfer of production;
        the working personnel involved;
        the forms used or suggested to be used;
        controlling the operations.
   c) Survey of the production and service departments in the matter of floor area, equipment investment, number of employees, equipment horsepower ratings.

A *second* survey should develop a chart of accounts for the general and subsidiary ledgers. These accounts must be properly coded and would cover the—

   a) General ledger chart and code.
   b) Factory ledger and code.
   c) Subsidiary ledger accounts for the factory overhead on a cost center basis.

A *third* survey will cover the compilation of the present or contemplated forms to be used in completing the cost accounting cycle. This survey may have to include the mechanical devices such as punched card or electronic computers which are to be used with the forms.

A *fourth* survey will indicate the present and proposed personnel required for the general and factory accounting work with a clear definition or description of the duties and routines to be followed.

On the basis of these preliminary surveys, the firm is now ready to proceed with the installation of the cost accounting system.

Designing the Cost Accounting System   The preliminary work has resulted in the determination of the kind of cost accounting system that will be used—job order or departmental (process); historical or predetermined. Modern cost accounting thinking seems to favor the use of a predetermined standard cost accounting system as the most effective for managerial control. On this latter acceptance, it now becomes necessary to agree on how the standards are to be determined. What type of standards will be used—past experience, test runs, or scientifically set standards? If the latter, then the firm must organize a standards department. Will it be a full-time or part-time organization, and who will be on it? The larger the firm, the greater the need for a separate group of industrial engineers, properly directed by a senior official of the firm, to operate this department. A flexible budget should be set up for the manufacturing overhead costs at different operating levels. This flexible budget could very well be reviewed monthly or quarterly in order to have the most responsible costs and control.

With these preliminary matters settled, the design of the cost system will proceed with the planning of the paper work to be instituted.

First on this will be the design of the job order cost sheet or the cost of production report. These will be necessary to summarize the job or periodic costs. The design will be influenced by the nature of the manufacturing operations and departmentalization of the labor and overhead costs.

Second will be the design of the forms to be used for the materials acquisitions and usage, with due consideration of the internal control. Where possible, preprinted standard bills of materials should be used for controlling the materials used. Inventory records should be maintained for all important materials. Mechanical methods for computing, recording, and summarizing these forms should be carefully studied, especially if punched-card accounting equipment is available.

Third, the forms for compiling labor costs by jobs or by departments should be planned and simplified. Using a Calculagraph to expedite payroll cost computations for the job order system, as well as telephone or telegraph or teletypewriter methods of transferring labor costs to a central department, should be considered.

Fourth, manufacturing overhead forms should be designed and routines planned for their use. These would include:

a) Survey of plant facilities by departments or work centers as a basis for allocating the overhead costs.

b) Separating the overhead into its fixed and variable items both for the budgeted as well as the actual costs should be developed if such managerial control is desirable.

c) Flexible budgeting procedures should be outlined—both the preparation as well as the use and revision.

d) Determining the bases to be used in applying the manufacturing overhead to production or to departments. Questions of whether to use more than one rate for each department, whether to use a separate rate for materials handling, and whether to use a rate for central administration must all be considered when planning the forms and procedures to be instituted for this phase of costing.

Special Managerial Decisions before Installing the Cost System

Is it planned to have the cost accounting integrated with the regular financial accounting records or merely treated as a statistical compilation? If only partial cost accounting is to be used—that is costing and control only of the major products or the activities of the most important departments, then it will not be possible to integrate the cost accounting records with the financial records. And this means that some of the internal control of accounting which results from an integrated accounting system will be lost.

Pricing the materials used will have an effect on the unit costs of production. Should FIFO, LIFO, average, or standard costs be used in such pricing? From the management viewpoint, which represents the more accurate costing method? This also will revert back to the first point mentioned—namely, integration of the cost accounting with the regular accounting records—because the income tax effects of the various inventory pricing methods must also be considered.

In a few concerns at present, management must also decide whether in the matter of accountability, it feels that *direct costing* should be used. If so, because of the Internal Revenue Service's disallowance of inventories on the direct costing basis, the cost systems must be maintained independently of the financial accounting records.

Management Reports   Along with the variety of managerial decisions which will require special studies such as break-even point, variable product mix of sales, to buy or to manufacture, and to modernize the equipment or to use present equipment, management must be supplied a series of periodic reports which will measure the supervisory and employee accountability. These reports should be planned when the accounting system is first installed; should be checked upon when later used to determine their usefulness; and should be revised or eliminated if necessary.

The basic reports to be considered relate to the elements of materials, payroll, manufacturing overhead, and overall profitability of the manufacturing operations.

For *material cost control,* the following reports might be considered as useful when installing a cost accounting system:

1. *Material cost variations from the standards set up.* This report should indicate the material price and the material quantity variations, and the causes therefore. Whether this report should be prepared monthly, quarterly, or at less frequent intervals will be determined by the nature of the manufacturing operations and the customary fluctuations in the kind of materials used.

2. *Spoiled materials reports* may be necessary where spoilage affects the output and sales of the firm. This spoilage report may be part of the previous report on material variations from standard.

The use of these two types of reports is one form of managerial measurement of the accountability of the supervisory personnel in the various departments.

For *payroll cost control* the following might be considered:

1. *Efficiency* reports by workers or departments—a measurement of the variations of the actual payroll costs from the standard costs.
2. *Idle time reports* or machine *setup cost reports* may be necessary if not already a part of the efficiency report in (1).
3. Ratio of indirect labor to total labor costs or the ratio of the payroll costs to total cost of production may also be an important index of operating efficiency.

However, it must be remembered both in the case of material cost accounting and payroll cost accounting, reports and analyses should only be made in those instances where the material costs or the labor costs are an important phase dollarwise of the total cost of production, and if the material or labor costs are subject to fluctuation without justification. In the matter of increased automation, reports on labor costs or efficiency become unnecessary or meaningless.

Manufacturing overhead cost reports should be concerned with the analysis into the fixed and variable items, since the latter are controllable. It should further be concerned with arranging these overhead costs on a departmental basis. After meeting these two prerequisites, the cost accountant can now determine what reports should be prepared. Presumably the control center is the department, and therefore the reports should be prepared departmentally. If the material and labor reports are prepared monthly or quarterly, then the manufacturing overhead reports must follow a similar time pattern. The reports for manufacturing overhead will show the actual and applied for each department and the amount of the difference. Departmentally, the causes of the over- or underapplied manufacturing overhead should be ascertained. They may be due to faulty cost estimates or improper estimate of the volume of production. Furthermore, the variation of the applied overhead from the standard job or departmental overhead (efficiency variation) must also be shown. These reports measure the effectiveness of the production supervisory staff.

Organization Chart of Cost Accounting Function

Having planned the accounting records for the cost system, it is well also to plan the personnel and functional organization of the various segments of this system—materials control, payroll costs, overhead costs, statements, reports, standards, and budgets. Both the divisions and the staff should be diagrammed.

First of these charts would be the place of the cost accounting department within the framework of the accounting (controller's) department. This might be as shown in Illustration 20–1.

Although surveys have indicated that the number of clerks engaged in the compilation of the costs of production as compared with the

Illustration 20–1

ORGANIZATION OF THE ACCOUNTING (CONTROLLER'S) OFFICE
FUNCTIONS

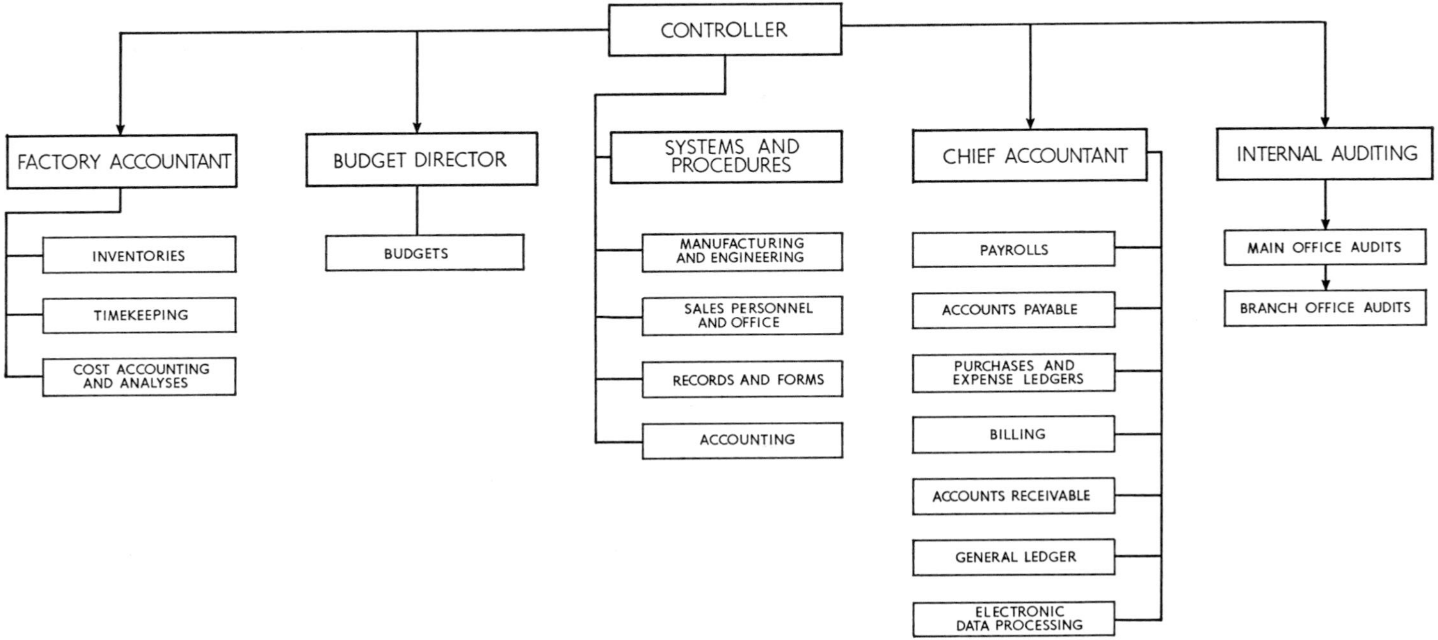

Illustration 20-1—(Continued)

ORGANIZATION OF THE FACTORY COST ACCOUNTING STAFF

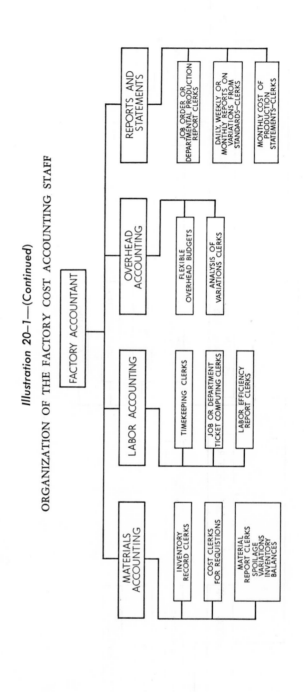

number of factory employees decreased as the size of the company increased, it is still desirable to have some criterion by which to gauge the maximum size of the clerical force required in cost accounting. Automation in the plant and automation in compiling cost accounting data no doubt seriously alter these figures. The following is given as a guide subject to adjustment for automation or special factors.

In smaller companies employing up to 600 factory workers, one cost clerk for each 80 employees was the average, whereas in larger firms the average was one cost clerk for each 150 employees. When this ratio is reconciled with the ratio of the total cost of operating the cost accounting function in business (approximately one fourth of 1 percent of sales), management should have a definite idea of the maximum cost of operating the cost accounting department.

Evaluating the Cost Accounting System   Either before or after the cost accounting system has been installed, management will probably want to evaluate the job. Before doing so, it might be necessary to outline the personnel, forms, and routines to be used in completing the work and the cost of its operation. This will answer the first question: "How much does it cost to operate the system?" Some years ago a study was made of the cost of all accounting work related to the sales income of the firms. It was found that the cost of operating an accounting system was 0.82 percent of the sales— less than 1 percent of sales. In this same study, the cost of operating a cost accounting system was 0.27 percent of sales, a little more than one quarter of 1 percent of sales. Times and conditions have changed, but these percentages are an average of 11 types of manufacturing firms covering 59 plants having sales of $346 million. This cost ratio might be suggestive of how to evaluate a cost accounting system.

A second method of evaluating a cost accounting system is "Does it work?" This means does it produce usable cost accounting information in time for proper managerial action. Does it indicate not only what the costs are but what they should be and the causes for the differences? Finally, the evaluation must answer the question: "Does it pinpoint responsibility?" Has or will it permit cost reduction through increased efficiency?

And as part of this evaluation, are the cost reports such that they will be used by top management to direct supervisory management to do a better job?

Importance of Managerial Reports   As a company grows and expands its activities, proper reports must be made available to all levels of management. The reports must be accurate, useful, and timely as many a decision regarding the

Illustration 20-2. Administrative Organization Chart of a Manufacturing Company (with Detail of Controller's and Production Departments)

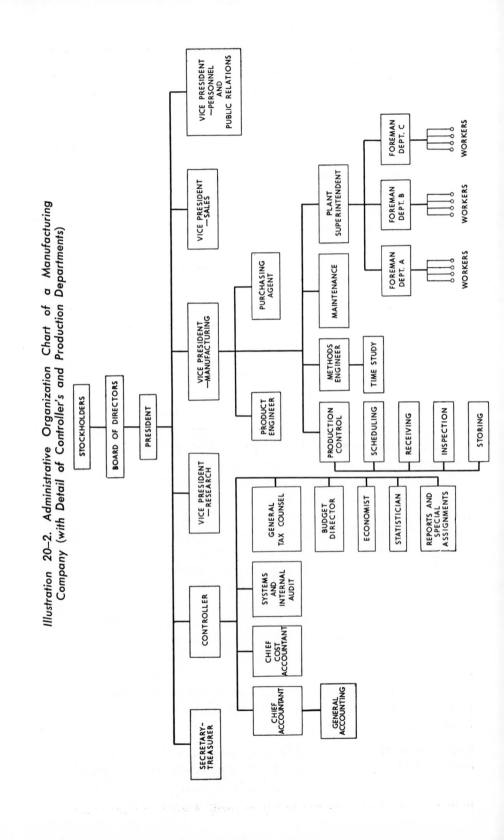

firm's future will be made based on the reports. The report is generally the only means of communicating financial information within the business firm.

In a dynamic economy containing a large number of industries, no one system of reports will be applicable to every business. Much ingenuity, research, planning, and judgment must be exercised in developing an integrated report system which will be of greatest benefit to an individual company. Obviously, the selection of proper reports is a continuing task so that obsolete reports will be dropped.

If the report system is to be effective, a clear understanding of the definite lines of authority and responsibility is a prerequisite to determining the specific reports required in a company. Illustration 20–2 presents in condensed form an administrative organization chart indicating the lines of authority followed by one corporation.

In addition to understanding the functional and supervisory organization, the *duties* of the executives must be clearly set forth so that proper reports may be given to the right people. Illustration 20–3 describes

Illustration 20–3

Executive	*Typical Duties*
President, vice president, treasurer, and corporate secretary	General administrative and supervisory, by establishing policy and providing means of checking on adherence to these policies.
Controller	Organization of detailed and summary accounting procedure, supervisor of semisenior executives, such as chief accountant and cost accountant.
Budget director	Preparation and control of budget.
Chief engineer	Engineering and technical supervisor.
Production manager	Organization and coordination of those activities relating to planning and scheduling, purchasing, factory personnel, and inspection.
Sales manager	Organization and supervision of sales force.
Chief accountant	Under the controller; responsible for general accounting work.
Cost accountant	Responsible to controller for cost data to be used in preparing some of the reports; assist controller in installing cost system.
Purchasing agent	Under supervision of manufacturing vice president; responsible for receipt and storage of materials.
Factory superintendent	Responsible to manufacturing vice president for the use of materials, men, and factory facilities in efficient production of the finished products.
Foremen	Line deputies assisting the superintendent in creating efficient production.

some of the typical duties of various executives in a manufacturing company.

This chapter considers primarily those reports which deal with cost and efficiency that serve as the basis for better cost control. Chapter 21 deals with the direct costing method of facilitating cost control and planning. Chapter 22 examines analytical and graphic methods of portraying the probable effect on profits of future policies of manufacturing and distribution which management has under consideration. Chapter 23 deals with specific managerial problems which require cost data for solution and discusses the manner in which the cost accountant selects the type of cost data appropriate to the solution of a specific problem.

Objectives of Reports A primary objective of a report is to communicate desired information to management. The various reports summarize, in understandable and usable form, essential facts of the functional areas of production and distribution, as found in the details of cost accounting systems, so that management may:

1. Study the trend of operating costs of material, labor, and overhead costs.
2. Measure the effectiveness of the various manufacturing and distribution functions.
3. Measure the efficiency of supervisory personnel held accountable for control of specific costs.
4. Plan future production and distribution policies for the entire firm.
5. Make specific price, production, financial, and labor policy decisions based on adequate cost information appropriate to the particular problem.

A basic objective of reports is the CONTROL of operations. For example, management is put into a position where manufacturing operations may be controlled when actual cost figures are compared with predetermined costs and the variances explained.

Cost accounting should furnish the necessary details of production and efficiency through the medium of reports. The number of these reports and their arrangement and content vary with the individual concern.

If the system of cost and efficiency reports is adequate, management should be able to answer questions such as:

Are the variations in material costs due to changes in the quantity used or to a change in the price of the material?
Are variations in labor costs due to a change in the number of workers, rate of wages, or efficiency?

Are increases in factory expenses due to idle time, waste, inaccurate budget estimates, or poor supervision?
Where does spoilage occur and why?
What department has inefficient workers and why?

Reports should be prepared for the three levels of management: the *proximate*—the foremen; the *intermediate*—the plant superintendent; and the *remote*—the president and board of directors. A different type of information may be required for each level. The closer the recipient is to the activity, the greater the amount of detail that must be provided. The top level of management should receive information that has been greatly condensed and summarized.

Scope of Reports Although there are many kinds of reports that are supplied to management, this discussion will concern itself with a coordinated system of cost reports whose basic purpose is to provide data necessary for control. A coordinated system of accounting reports to management provides historical data indicating the results of *past operations,* measures the degree of management control of *current operations,* and anticipates the estimated results of *future operations.* Reports are an aid to management, never a substitute for it. The accountant must not only determine and interpret significant information accurately but he must also translate the information in the best possible manner for users. Specialists in the fields of engineering, production, and sales do not usually have an extensive background in accounting principles and procedures. The unimportant should be deleted, repetitive data should be consolidated, and appropriate comments should be included emphasizing the significance of the report figures.

The effective report serves an *immediate purpose* and is a composite of many ingredients, including visual attractiveness; language that is simple, clear, and "to the point"; and a format that is neither overdetailed nor too brief. Reports should be comparative in form whenever possible, and adequate data should be presented in support of suggestions as to possible courses of action. Developments in the area of electronic computers and integrated data processing provide countless techniques that tend to improve and simplify the job of reporting financial data to management, but the lack of a carefully conceived plan of presentation may create considerable confusion which results in costly inefficiency.

As mentioned earlier, cost accounting reports and statements must be prepared for and distributed to three different levels of management. Each type of management—the *general executives,* the *departmental executives,* and the *foremen*—comes within a special sphere of influence, and the reports sent to a man should deal with matters falling within his sphere, thus providing him an effective tool for facilitating his particular management tasks. Primarily, the foreman is interested in the performance of his workers; the department head desires knowledge of the progress of a section; and the general executive requires information concerning all departments. The scope of a report, therefore, is determined by its expected use.

Cost accounting reports may be classified as *financial* or *efficiency.* Financial reports include cost statements of material, labor, and expenses; summary costs of production; and budgeted statements. Efficiency reports include those relating to idle machines, machine repairs, spoiled goods, employee productivity, plant productivity, or consumable tool expense.

Cost reports may be further classified as to *frequency*—i.e., daily, weekly, monthly, semiannual, or annual. The greater the degree of control required, the shorter the period of time covered in the report.

A list of the reports intended to provide adequate data for effective control customarily includes:

For *top management* (*board of directors and corporate officers*):
Comparative monthly, quarterly, and annual income statements.
Master budget covering the entire company.
Summaries of as many of the more detailed cost and efficiency reports listed below as may be desirable or necessary in a particular company.

For *senior departmental executives* (*controller, production manager, sales manager, etc.*):
Comparative income statements.
Master budget and detailed departmental budgets.
Weekly, monthly, and cumulative comparisons of budgeted and actual figures by department.
Weekly and/or monthly reports on purchases, inventories, labor costs, idleness, repairs, spoilage, expenses, and production.
Sales—actual versus budgeted.

For *semisenior departmental executives* (*including the factory superintendent, chief accountant, purchasing agent, etc., who are the liaison or connecting links between the senior executives, on the one hand, and the foremen or department managers, on the other*):
Material reports showing receipts, issuances, and balances on hand.
Material reports showing budgeted and actual figures.
Labor reports showing budgeted and actual figures.
Indirect labor costs, both budgeted and actual.
Indirect material and small tool expenses on a budgeted and actual basis.
Budgeted and actual figures of controllable expenses.
Spoilage reports.
Idle labor and idle machine reports.
Reports on variation from standard costs of materials, labor, and overhead.

Machine repair cost reports.

Monthly production reports.

For foremen:

Comparisons of budgeted with actual costs of their section(s).

Various efficiency reports, limited in scope.

Summaries of other controllable conditions within their departments or within related or comparative departments.

Many of the cost and operating reports are prepared through the cooperation of the semisenior executives and the cost accountant. The chief accountant will participate in preparing the financial and cost statements; the purchasing agent in preparing material reports and budgets; and the factory superintendent in preparing efficiency reports on labor, machines, and expenses.

Whether or not a report will be used in a given company is determined by the degree of control desired and whether its use justifies the expense of preparation.

Type of Reports   A report may include a *financial statement* or statements as for example an interim income statement. Illustration 20–4 presents a comparative income statement.

A report often used is the *product activity* report, an example of which is shown in Illustration 20–5. Related to the product activity report is the group of reports disclosing *labor efficiency.* The labor efficiency report needs to be more detailed for the foreman than for the factory manager. Illustrations 20–6 and 20–7 are labor efficiency reports; Illustration 20–6 is for the factory manager while Illustration 20–7 is for the foreman.

Analyses of manufacturing overhead represent another category which may be used. Illustration 20–8 is an example of the type of report that might be prepared under this category.

Quite often, selected items need to be reported to a particular level of management. Obviously, the items to be included will vary among the companies. Illustrations 20–9, 20–10, and 20–11 are examples of this type of report. Cost and usefulness are the only limits as to the type of information that could be reported under this category.

Importance of Graphic   Graphic illustrations should possibly sup-
Presentation   plement the reports of cost data. The graphic illustrations are not a substitute for the report but a simple, more emphatic and perhaps more easily understood presentation, and hence, more usable. For this reason, perhaps, graphs and charts arouse the interest of executives.

Illustration 20-4

COMPARATIVE STATEMENT OF INCOME

FOR MONTH ENDED MARCH 31, 19—

(Thousands of Dollars and Pounds)

	Current Period			Year to Date		
	Budget	Actual	% of Budget	Budget	Actual	% of Budget
Net sales—pounds: Product A..	100	110	110%	400	300	75%
Product B....	150	150	100	300	350	117
Total.................	250	260	104%	700	650	93%
Net sales: Product A............	$200	$220	110%	$ 800	$600	75%
Product B...........	ⅰ 150	150	100	300	350	117
Total.................	$350	$370	106%	$1,100	$950	86%
Less: Variable cost of sales.....	$190	$200	105%	$470	$450	96%
Freight on sales..........	10	20	200	30	30	100
Total variable cost.......	$200	$220	110%	$ 500	$480	96%
Contribution margin: Product A..	$ 60	$ 60	100%	$ 180	$ 50	28%
Product B..	40	55	138	120	100	83
Contribution margin—total.....	$100	$115	115%	$ 300	$150	50%
Less: Fixed costs:						
Plant operations............	$ 10	$ 10	100%	$ 30	$ 30	100%
Corporate management.......	30	30	100	30	30	100
Research..................	10	20	200	90	100	111
Selling....................	10	10	100	30	40	133
Administration.............	10	10	100	30	30	100
Depreciation..............	30	30	100	90	90	100
Total fixed costs........	$100	$110	110%	$ 300	$320	107%
Income before Taxes...........	$100	$110	110%	$ 300	150	50%

Graphic presentation is most effective in showing comparisons, whether they are historical, current, or prognostic. The pictorial display of graphic presentation appeals to the different types of minds among the various grades of employees, from the unskilled factory worker to the trained corporate executive.

Types of Graphic Presentation   Many different types of graphic presentation exist, but not all are suitable for industrial use. The following will be described and illustrated in this section: bar graphs, curve charts, strata

Illustration 20-5

Analysis of Orders Received and Shipments

	Week Includes 8/7-8/13						Cumulative to Date			
	Unfilled Orders Beginning of Week	Weekly Orders Received	Weekly Capacity	Per Cent Activity	Weekly Shipments	Unfilled Orders End of Week	Unfilled Orders Beginning of Year	Cum. Orders Received	Cum. Shipments	Unfilled Orders End of Week
A Division										
X Product	4,000	2,000	2,500	80	1,800	4,200	4,500	59,700	60,000	4,200
Y Product	3,000	1,000	1,000	100	950	3,050	3,200	29,850	30,000	3,050
Z Product	2,000	500	750	67	600	1,900	2,500	14,400	15,000	1,900
Total A Division	9,000	3,500	4,250	82	3,350	9,150	10,200	103,950	105,000	9,150
E Division										
X Product	2,000	500	550	91	500	2,000	2,400	24,600	25,000	2,000
Y Product	3,000	1,000	1,200	83	800	3,200	3,600	29,600	30,000	3,200
Total E Division	5,000	1,500	1,750	86	1,300	5,200	6,000	54,200	55,000	5,200
Grand Total	28,000	11,000	12,500	88	9,750	29,250	33,400	316,850	321,000	29,250
Wkly. Avg. (32 Wks. This Yr.)		9,901			10,031			9,901	10,031	
Wkly. Avg. (32 Wks. Last Yr.)		9,500			9,800			9,500	9,800	

Adapted from *N.A.A. Accounting Practice Report No. 9, Reports Which Managements Find Most Useful.*

Illustration 20–6

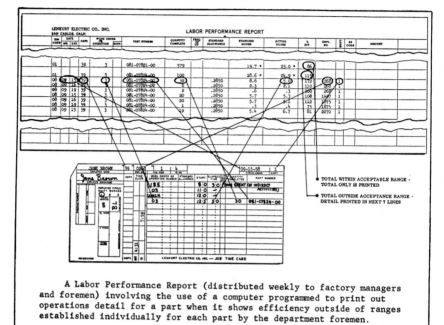

A Labor Performance Report (distributed weekly to factory managers and foremen) involving the use of a computer programmed to print out operations detail for a part when it shows efficiency outside of ranges established individually for each part by the department foremen.

SOURCE: *N.A.A. Accounting Practice Report No. 9, Reports Which Managements Find Most Useful.*

Illustration 20–7

DEPARTMENTAL EFFICIENCY REPORT

Department No. 78

Week Ending April 12, 19—

Ford A. Waters, Foreman

No.	Name	This Week	Last Week	Previous Month	Remarks
401	J. Columbus	96%	98%	95%	O.K.
402	R. Donlon	99%	100%	100%	O.K.
403	C. Cohen	90%	92%	95%	O.K.
404	R. Burton	100%	100%	102%	Exceptional Worker
405	F. George	100%	96%	98%	O.K.
406	A. Flint	70%	76%	80%	New Worker Not Familiar with Machine
407	M. Barb	80%	85%	90%	Machine Repairs
408	S. Chensi	80%	82%	80%	Delayed Waiting For Work
	Average	89.3%	91%	92.5%	

90% to 100% operating efficiency considered good. Above or below this figure some comment should be made by foreman in "remarks" column.

Illustration 20-8

DEPARTMENTAL COST STATEMENT

Unit of measure: Machine hours
Actual: 1,118
Normal: 980
% of normal: 114.1

Dept.: 942
Period: 3-19XX

EXPENSE	NORMAL STANDARD	PERCENTAGE Variability	PERCENTAGE Revision	REVISED STANDARD	ACTUAL EXPENSE	VARIANCE—GAIN OR (LOSS) Controllable	Volume Per Cent of Normal Standard	Volume Amount	Controllable Year to Date
.01 Direct labor—applied	$3,575	100	114.1	$4,079	$4,296	($217)	......	......	($605)
.02 Direct labor—unapplied	160	100	114.4	183	150	33	......	......	(4)
.03 Indirect labor	1,642	60	108.5	1,782	1,805	(23)	5.6	$ 92	(97)
.04 Supervision and clerical	735	20	102.9	756	740	16	11.3	83	90
Total wages and salaries	$6,112			$6,800	$6,991	($191)		$175	($616)
.11 Belting	133	90	112.8	150	158	(8)	1.4	2	(28)
.12 Machine parts	445	90	112.8	502	453	49	1.4	5	(10)
.13 Chemicals	496	90	112.7	559	516	43	1.4	7	159
.14 Miscellaneous supplies	164	75	110.4	181	205	(24)	3.5	6	(5)
.21 Maintenance department charges	265	70	109.8	291	405	(114)	4.2	11	33
.22 Power and light	470	60	108.5	510	530	(20)	5.6	26	19
.31 Spoiled work	530	100	114.1	605	502	103			196
Total direct costs	$8,615			$9,598	$9,760	($162)		$232	($252)
.61 Fixed charges	646			646	646				
Total expense	$9,261				$10,406				

PROOF

Variance above:
Volume............. 232
Controllable........ (162)
Total.......... 70

Direct expense absorbed:
8,615 × 114.1% = 9,830
Actual direct expense 9,760
70

Source: David R. Anderson and Leo A. Schmidt, *Practical Controllership* (Homewood, Ill.: Richard D. Irwin, Inc.)

Illustration 20–9

MONTHLY REPORT TO TOP MANAGEMENT
INCOME STATEMENT
For the Two Months Ended February 28, 19—
(In Thousands of Dollars)

	This Month Actual	This Month Budget	This Year to Date Actual	This Year to Date Budget	Last Year Actual
Net trade sales:					
Dollars......................	$100	$120	$180	$250	$170
Number of cases..............	50	60	90	125	85
Cost of trade sales:					
Standard cost.................	$ 60	$ 70	$110	$150	$100
Manufacturing variances........	5	...	7	...	6
Purchase price variances........	2	...	3	...	2
Other costs...................	3	4	6	8	7
Research costs................	2	2	4	4	5
Engineering..................	2	4	4	8	5
Total cost of trade sales.......	$ 74	$ 80	$134	$170	$125
Gross profit on trade sales.........	$ 26	$ 40	$ 46	$ 80	$ 45
Operating expenses:					
Selling......................	$ 5	$ 8	$ 10	$ 16	$ 10
Advertising—budget basis......	2	2	4	4	5
Stock and shipping............	2	3	4	6	4
Transportation................	2	2	4	4	4
Administrative................	3	3	6	6	6
Corporate and legal...........	1	2	1	4	1
Total operating expenses....	$ 15	$ 20	$ 29	$ 40	$ 30
Operating profit.................	$ 11	$ 20	$ 17	$ 40	$ 15
Other income...................	2	3	4	6	2
Other expenses.................	1	1	2	2	1
Income before taxes.............	$ 12	$ 22	$ 19	$ 44	$ 16
Tax provision...................	4	5	5	10	8
Net Income....................	$ 8	$ 17	$ 14	$ 34	$ 8
Percentages to trade sales:					
Gross profit....................	26%	33%	26%	32%	26%
Operating expenses.............	15	17	16	16	18
Income before taxes...........	12	18	11	18	9

SUMMARY OF FINANCIAL CONDITION
As at February 28, 19—

	This Month	Last Month	Beginning of This Year
Cash.................................	$60	$50	$65
% of total current liabilities..............	30%	27%	25%
Due from customers......................	$80	$80	$70
Number of days sales....................	20	20	18
Current ratio...........................	2½:1	2½:1	2:1

```
                        STATISTICAL DATA
                    As at February 28, 19—

                                        This      Last    February,
                                        Month     Month   Last Year
NUMBER OF EMPLOYEES:
  Salaried:
    New York
    Chicago
    Dallas

  Salaried Employees with Base Salary
    of $9,000 a Year or More

  Employed at Straight Time Hourly Wage Rates:
    New York
    Chicago
    Dallas

NUMBER OF CASES SHIPPED (000's omitted):
  New York
  Chicago
  Dallas
    Total

UNSHIPPED ORDERS AT SALES VALUE  (000's omitted):
  New York
  Chicago
  Dallas
    Total

BACK ORDERS AT SALES VALUE (000's omitted):
  New York
  Chicago
  Dallas
    Total

PRICES PAID FOR PRINCIPAL COMMODITIES:
  Cotton, strict middling   1b.
  Crude Rubber              1b.
  Talc                      1b.
```

Source: Adapted from *N.A.A. Bulletin*, Volume 36, No. 4.

charts, semilogarithmic charts, area or volume charts, and special graphs.

Bar graphs (see Illustrations 20–12 and 20–13) use *horizontal* columns to present values, the length of the bar indicating the value. Bars arranged *vertically* are known as *column* graphs. If these bar graphs present but a single fact, they are known as *simple* bar charts; if several facts are presented in each bar, by means of coloring or cross-hatching, the graph is known as a *composite* bar graph. If two or more bars are used for a single accounting period, the chart is known as a *grouped* bar graph. Bar graphs are most useful in presenting simple facts but are not so satisfactory as other graphic forms in presenting comparative data. Bar graphs have been used in cost accounting to:

a) Show the elements of cost for a unit or a period.

b) Show inventory figures for each kind of material, that is, the amount on hand and the amount used during a month.

Illustration 20–11

Comparison of Significant Figures

	BASE PERIOD	JANUARY	FEBRUARY	DECEMBE
DIRECT LABOR PERFORMANCE	00%	00%	00%	00%
Machining Division	00%	00%	00%	00%
Welding Division	00%	00%	00%	00%
Total Manufacturing Department				
RATIO OF INDIRECT TO DIRECT LABOR HOURS				
Machining Division	00%	00%	00%	00%
Welding Division	00%	00%	00%	00%
Total	00%	00%	00%	00%
VOLUME (in 000's)				
Actual Direct Labor Hours	000	000	000	000
Standard Direct Labor Hours	000	000	00	000
Total Standard Dollars of:				
Prime Products Produced	0000	0000	0000	0000
Transfers to Other Plants	000	000	000	000
DEPARTMENT CONTROLLABLE COST/STD. DIR. LABOR HR.	$ .00	$ .00	$ .00	$ .00
Accounting	0.00	0.00	0.00	0.00
Manufacturing	$ 0.00	$ 0.00	$ 0.00	$ 0.00
Total				
OTHER COST INDEXES				
Spoilage Due to Defective Labor (in 000's)	$ .00	$ .00	$ .00	$ .00
Per Std. Direct Labor Hour	.00	.00	.00	0,000
Purchases of Materials & Supplies	0,000	0,000	0,000	$ 000
Material Variance (in 000's)	---	$ 000	$ 000	00.0%
Material Variance Percent	---	0.0%	0.0%	
EMPLOYMENT AND HOURS				
Hires	00	0	0	000
Separations	00	000	00	00
Employment By Department				
Accounting	000	000	000	000
Manufacturing	0000	0000	0000	0000
Total	0000	0000	0000	0000
Actual Hours Worked (in 000's)				
Hourly Roll—Direct	000	000	000	000
Hourly Roll—Indirect All Departments	000	000	000	000
Hourly Roll—Total	000	000	000	000
Weekly Roll	00	00	00	00
Total Hourly and Weekly Rolls	000	000	000	000
Overtime Hours Worked (in 000's)				
Hourly Roll	0.0	0.0	0.0	0.0
Weekly Roll	0.0	.0	.0	.0
Total	00.0	0.0	0.0	0.0
INVENTORIES AT STANDARD COST (in 000's)				
Production Stores	$ 0,000	$ 0,000	$ 0,000	$ 0,000
Indirect Inventories and Supplies	000	000	000	000
Prime Product Inventories	0,000	0,000	0,000	0,000
Total	$ 0,000	$00,000	$00,000	$00,000

SOURCE: *N.A.A. Accounting Practice Report No. 9, Reports Which Managements Find Most Useful.*

c) Show the relationship between the sales price and the cost of sales for a unit or a given period.

Illustrations 20–12 and 20–13 show but two of the many applications of the bar graph. Illustration 20–12 reflects the total costs for a given period, and Illustration 20–13 shows the comparative costs by products. These graphs may be prepared on the basis of either unit costs or total costs.

Curve graphs are used to present data in a continuous line, joining the various points on cross-section paper. These points usually indicate

Illustration 20–12. Simple and Composite Bar Graphs Showing the Amount of the Various Elements of Cost at a Given Date*

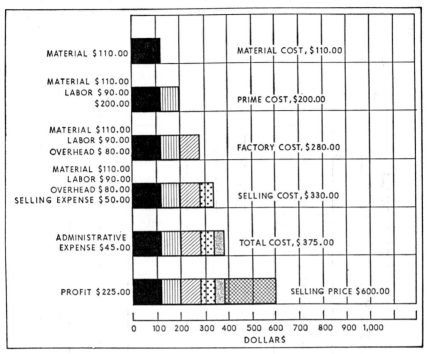

* SOURCE OF DATA: A manufacturing, income, and profit and loss statement at a given date.

Illustration 20–13. Simple Bar Graphs Showing Cost Elements on a Percentage Basis*

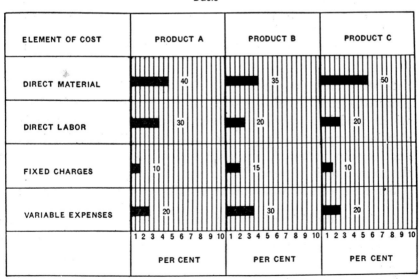

* SOURCE OF DATA: Detailed comparative statement on percentage basis of unit of total costs for each product.

the time factor of a series of comparative data and, in this particular instance, cost data. If but one curve appears on the chart, the chart is known as a *single curve chart;* if two or more appear on the same chart, it is a *multiple curve chart* (see Illustration 20–14). By cumulating the

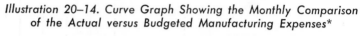

Illustration 20–14. Curve Graph Showing the Monthly Comparison of the Actual versus Budgeted Manufacturing Expenses*

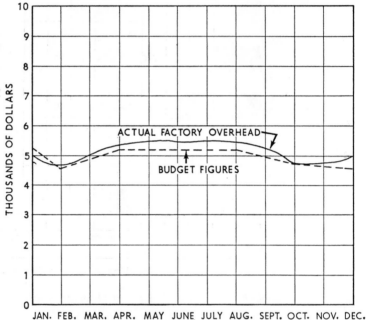

* This chart may also be prepared by plotting the percentages of variation. In that case the center horizontal line would be 0 percent, and the plus variations above the line and minus below the line.

SOURCE: Monthly statements showing the relationship of budgeted versus actual manufacturing expenses.

data before preparing the curve graph, a *cumulative* curve chart can be prepared (see Illustration 20–15). Curve graphs are by far the most widely used in submitting business statistics and are most useful in showing comparative data, at the same time indicating historical data and long-time trends. Almost every type of cost data can be plotted in this form. The time interval may consist of weeks, months, or years.

Some purposes for which this type of display may be used include:

1. Plotting the high and low cost of direct labor per unit of manufacture.
2. Plotting the actual and budgeted manufacturing expenses for each depart-ment and for the factory as a whole on a monthly basis.
3. Showing the trend of the cost of manufacture for various articles.
4. Showing the relationship between the sales and the cost of sales of individual articles on a monthly or yearly basis.

5. Showing relationship between total sales and total cost of sales on a monthly or yearly basis.
6. Showing on a monthly basis the inventory of direct materials, finished goods, and work-in-process.

*Illustration 20–15. Curve Graph Showing the Relationship between the Budgeted Manufacturing Expenses on an Accumulated Basis**

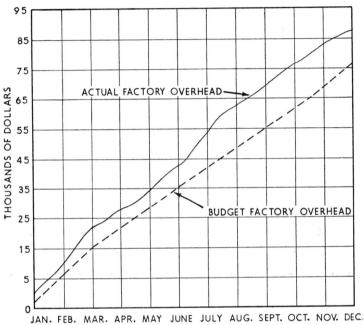

* SOURCE: The cumulative figures in the monthly statement of actual versus budgeted manufacturing expenses.

Strata graphs are combinations of curve and area charts, the area being variously colored or shaded to show the component parts. They are most useful in showing comparisons over a long period of time, since the shading or coloring is more effective than the use of simple cumulative line curves. In cost accounting they are most practical in showing the component parts of certain figures over a relatively long period of time, such as the elements of cost of the cost of goods manufactured for each month of the year or an analysis of the various items on the monthly balance sheets. Illustration 20–16 is an example of this type of graph.

The *semilogarithmic curve* chart is sometimes called a *ratio graph*. It is most useful when rates of change, rather than absolute changes, are desired or when the data of two or more related graphs, the quantitative units of which are different, are to be shown. For example, the amount of manufacturing expense incurred and the number of units manufac-

Illustration 20–16. Strata Chart Showing the Elements of Cost
over a Period of Years*

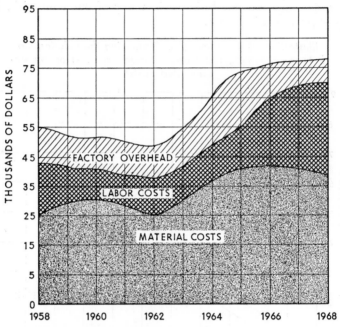

* SOURCE: Annual cost of manufacturing statements.

tured during a given month have a direct relationship, but one item is expressed in dollars and the other in units. The logarithmic graph shows not the direct effect of the absolute figures but the ratio relationship of these figures.

The semilogarithmic curve chart is useful in presenting graphically the comparative relationship of all cost accounting data which involve a time or trend period, whether or not the data are expressed in terms of the same unit.

It must be kept in mind that the horizontal lines are drawn on a percentage scale. The distance from 5 to 10 represents a 100 percent increase over 5; the distance from 10 to 20, or 20 to 40, also represents a 100 percent increase and therefore must be equal to the distance from 5 to 10.

The scale figures on such a graph may represent 1,000,000 to 100,000,000 bushels or $1 to $100 and, when plotted, actually indicate the percentage relationship of the figures in a given series.

Illustration 20–17 shows the semilogarithmic curve chart. The figures are cumulative.

Area or volume charts present data on a two-dimensional scale. Because of the illusory optical effects created, most of these displays

*Illustration 20–17. Semilogarithmic Curve Chart Showing the
Cumulative Figures for the Various Elements of Cost**

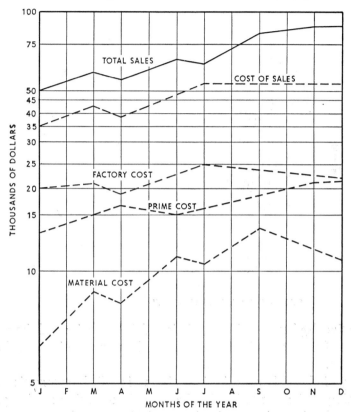

* Each line is related to the one immediately above and to the total sales.
For example, in April, although the price of materials used dropped, as did the
sales and cost of sales, the prime cost increased because of higher labor costs.
The decrease in factory expenses more than offset the increase in labor.

have been discarded in the presentation of business and accounting data.
A circle could be used to show the amount of each element of cost—the
entire circle representing the selling price and the various segments,
proportionately divided, showing the material cost, labor cost, factory
expense, administrative expense, selling expense, and profit. Similarly,
trees, people, cars, and other characters have been used to portray
quantities or values.

The circle or pie chart shows the analysis of a manufacturer's
monthly cost of sales. See Illustration 20–18.

**Automation and
Management Reports**   Two unfortunate obstacles that formerly
caused much concern in connection with
report preparation have been greatly mini-
mized by office automation. The *high cost of preparation* and the *unde-*

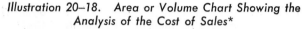

*Illustration 20–18.   Area or Volume Chart Showing the
Analysis of the Cost of Sales**

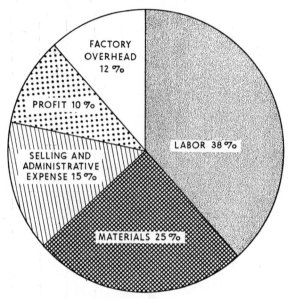

* Also called "circle or pie chart."

sirable time lag between the completion of the operation and the reporting thereof to personnel affected can now be overcome in a number of companies.

Many industrial organizations have installed automatic data-processing equipment to handle the normal accounting routine procedures, and this equipment is also available to produce cost control reports for management at little or no added expense. Even more important is the fact that these reports are now made available for distribution within a few *hours,* rather than the days or weeks previously required. Illustration 20–19 describes, in a general way, how an electronic data-processing system functions. Illustration 20–20 presents the detailed steps of automatically processed budgetary control statements and analyses.

In an adequate integrated data-processing system, available instant reference to accounting data required for proper control permits the automatic presentation of data in the form of unit, product, department, individual plant, and/or companywide operating results and, if desired, in comparative form. Inventory control of stores and finished products are available immediately. No substantial delay is necessary in receiving from or distributing to distantly located plants any required information.

Reports that were formerly considered too expensive to prepare,

Illustration 20–19

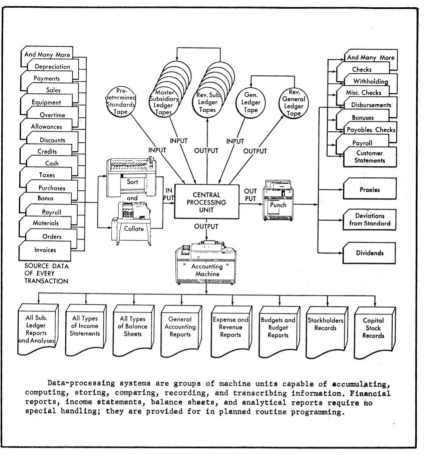

Data-processing systems are groups of machine units capable of accumulating, computing, storing, comparing, recording, and transcribing information. Financial reports, income statements, balance sheets, and analytical reports require no special handling; they are provided for in planned routine programming.

Courtesy: International Business Machines Corporation.

reports that lost their effectiveness because they arrived too late to permit corrective action, and reporting problems created by the distance factor of multiplant locations might soon be considerations of the past. Automatic data processing can permit the expeditious preparation and distribution of timely, comparative reports at a minimum of additional expense.

Report Review   Periodically, accounting reports should be reviewed to determine their continued usefulness. The number of reports issued has a habit of increasing, and diligence must be exercised to see that only useful reports are prepared; a useful report two years ago may not be necessary today.

Those receiving reports should be asked whether or not they are still considered necessary, and if the answer is in the affirmative, to suggest

Illustration 20–20

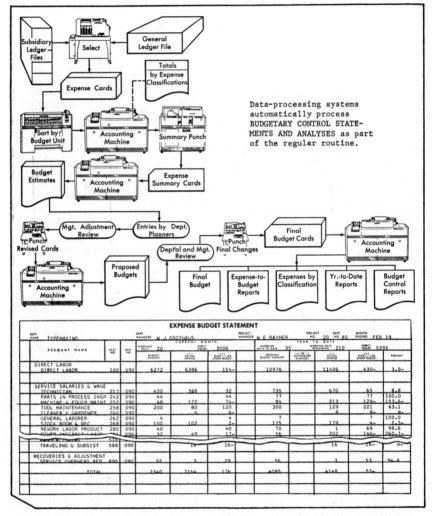

how the form(s) might be revised to provide greater benefit. The controller's department frequently initiates accounting report changes, but to assure the effectiveness of any reporting program it is of utmost importance that both accounting and nonaccounting managerial personnel participate actively in proposed revisions.

An Income and Cost Control Report Program

A large textile manufacturing concern has developed a program of control through a series of 11 income and cost reports under the direction of the controller. These reports are properly calendarized and scheduled, and the executives who are to receive and study these file them in an executive's handbook for constant reference.

This report program included the following:

1. Monthly operating statement, supported by—
   a) Sales analysis both in dollars and in percents.
   b) Sales returns and allowances.
   c) Gross profit analysis by types of outlet and by products.
   d) Selling expenses analysis, budgeted and actual.
2. Manufacturing operating reports
   a) Material price variations.
   b) Material usage variations.
   c) Analysis of cost variations by cost centers, both service and productive.
   d) Budget comparison of yarn preparation cost center.
   e) Spoiled or damaged finished products.
   f) Idle machine report.

These reports are illustrated in Appendix C. They are distributed to the following executives:

1 and 1(a) to the vice president in charge of sales.

1 (b) to the vice president in charge of mill operations, who writes a letter of comment and sends a copy to the mill foreman.

1 (c) to the vice president in charge of sales and vice president in charge of manufacturing.

1 (d) to the vice president in charge of sales and to the branch managers.

2 (a) to the mill vice president and the purchasing agent.

2 (b) to the vice president in charge of mill operations, to the superintendent of the weaving room, and to the department supervisors handling the material.

2 (c) to the vice president of the mill operations and to the supervisors of the various production and service centers.

2 (d) to the vice president of the mill operations and to the foreman of the particular center (yarn preparation).

2 (e) to the vice president in charge of mill operations and the foremen of the finishing and weaving departments.

QUESTIONS FOR REVIEW

1. "As a company grows and expands its activities, proper reports must be made available to all levels of management." Discuss.

2. Who should be responsible for determining what reports are necessary?

3. "A basic objective of reports is the control of operations." What role should the cost accountant play in achieving this objective?

4. What are the essential criteria for a good report?

5. "Cost reports may be classified as *financial* or *efficiency*." Distinguish between the two.

6. "Graphic illustrations should possibly supplement the reports of cost data." What, if anything, can be accomplished by graphic illustrations?

7. How often should the system of reports and reporting be reviewed? For what purpose or purposes should the review be made? Who should be responsible for the report review?

8. "Automatic data processing can permit the expeditious preparation and distribution of timely, comparative reports at a minimum of additional expense." Do you agree? Explain fully.

9. Does a cost report always have to be stated in dollars? Discuss.

10. Who should be responsible for the establishment of a cost accounting system? What are the criteria for a good cost accounting system?

PROBLEMS—GROUP A

Problem 20–1. Purpose: *Preparation of Statements for Management*

The Fine Gravel Company mines and processes rock and gravel. It started in business on January 1, 1967, when it purchased the assets of another company. You have examined its financial statements at December 31, 1967, and have been requested to assist in planning and projecting operations for 1968. The company also wants to know the maximum amount by which notes payable to officers can be reduced at December 31, 1968.

The adjusted trial balance follows:

THE FINE GRAVEL COMPANY

ADJUSTED TRIAL BALANCE

December 31, 1967

Cash	$ 17,000	
Accounts receivable	24,000	
Mining properties	60,000	
Accumulated depletion		$ 3,000
Equipment	150,000	
Accumulated depreciation		10,000
Organization expense	5,000	
Accumulated amortization		1,000
Accounts payable		12,000
Federal income taxes payable		22,000
Notes payable to officers		40,000
Capital stock		100,000
Premium on capital stock		34,000
Sales		300,000
Production costs (including depreciation and depletion)	184,000	
Administrative expense (including amortization and interest)	60,000	
Provision for federal income taxes	22,000	
	$522,000	$522,000

You are able to develop the following information:

1. The total yards of material sold is expected to increase 10 percent in 1968, and the average sales price per cubic yard will be increased from $1.50 to $1.60.

2. The estimated recoverable reserves of rock and gravel were 4,000,000 cubic yards when the properties were purchased.

3. Production costs include direct labor of $110,000 of which $10,000

was attributed to inefficiencies in the early stages of operation. The union contract calls for 5 percent increases in hourly rates effective January 1, 1968. Production costs, other than depreciation, depletion, and direct labor, will increase 4 percent in 1968.

4. Administrative expense, other than amortization and interest, will increase $8,000 in 1968.

5. The company has contracted for additional movable equipment costing $60,000 to be in production on July 1, 1968. This equipment will result in a direct labor hour savings of 8 percent as compared with the last half of 1967. The new equipment will have a life of 20 years. All depreciation is computed on the straight-line method. The old equipment will continue in use.

6. The new equipment will be financed by a 20 percent down payment and a 6 percent three-year chattel mortgage. Interest and principal payments are due semiannually on June 30 and December 31, beginning December 31, 1968. The notes payable to officers are demand notes dated January 1, 1967, on which 6 percent interest is provided for and was paid on December 31, 1967.

7. Accounts receivable will increase in proportion to sales. No bad debts are anticipated. Accounts payable will remain substantially the same.

8. Percentage depletion allowable on rock and gravel is to be computed at 5 percent of gross income and is limited to 50 percent of net income before depletion.

9. It is customary in the rock and gravel business not to place any value on stockpiles of processed material which are awaiting sale.

10. Assume an income tax rate of 50 percent.

11. The company has decided to maintain a minimum cash balance of $20,000.

12. The client understands that the ethical considerations involved in preparing the following statements will be taken care of by your letter accompanying the statements. (Do not prepare the letter.)

Required:

a) Prepare a statement showing the net income projection for 1968.

b) Prepare a statement which will show cash flow projection for 1968 and will indicate the amount that notes payable to officers can be reduced at December 31, 1968.

Note: Round all amounts to the nearest $100. If the amount to be rounded is exactly $50, round to the next highest $100.

(Adapted from AICPA Uniform Examination)

Problem 20–2.   Purpose: *Projected Operations Report for Management*

The Fuller Company, Inc., is engaged in manufacturing and wholesaling two principal products. As their accountant, you have been asked to advise management on sales policy for the coming year.

Two different plans are being considered by management, either of which, they believe, will (1) increase the volume of sales, (2) reduce the ratio of selling expense to sales, and (3) decrease unit production costs. These proposals are as follows:

Plan 1—Premium Stamp Books:

It is proposed that each package of Product A will contain eight premium stamps and each package of Product B will contain four premium stamps. Premium stamp books will be distributed to consumers, and when a book is filled with stamps (100 stamps) it will be redeemed by the award of a cash prize in an amount indicated under an unbroken seal attached to the book at the time of distribution. Every 10,000 books distributed will provide for prizes in accordance with the following schedule:

Number of Books	Prize for Each	Total Prizes
1	$150.00	$ 150
5	50.00	250
14	20.00	280
50	10.00	500
160	5.00	800
1,020	1.00	1,020
8,750	0.40	3,500
10,000		$6,500

This schedule is fixed and not subject to alteration or modification. The cost of this plan will be as follows:

Books, including distribution cost.....................$ 15 per 1,000 books
Stamps...$ 1 per 1,000 stamps
Prizes..$650 per 1,000 books

The premium stamp book plan will take the place of all previous advertising, and previously established selling prices will be maintained.

Plan 2—Reduced Selling Prices:

It is proposed that the selling price of Product A will be reduced by 8⅓ percent and of Product B by 5 percent and to increase the advertising expenditures over those of the prior year. This plan is an alternative to Plan 1, and only one will be adopted.

Management has provided you with the following information as to the previous year's operations and as to anticipated changes:

Prior Year's Operations	Product A	Product B
Quantity sold..............................	200,000 units	600,000 units
Production cost per unit..................	$0.40	$0.30
Selling price per unit....................	0.60	0.40

Selling expenses were 18 percent of sales, of which one third was for advertising.

Administrative expenses were 5 percent of sales.

Expected changes:
Increase in unit sales volume:
Plan 1....................................	.50%	50%
Plan 2....................................	.40%	25%

Decrease in unit production cost:
Plan 1....................................	5%	10%
Plan 2....................................	7½%	6⅔%

Advertising:
Plan 1....................................	None	None
Plan 2....................................	8% of sales	7% of sales

Other selling expenses:
Plan 1....................................	.15% of sales	12% of sales
Plan 2....................................	.12% of sales	12% of sales

Premium book expenses:
Plan 1....................................	As indicated	
Plan 2....................................	None	None

Administrative expenses:
Plan 1....................................	4% of sales	4% of sales
Plan 2....................................	Same dollar amount as prior year	

Required:

Prepare a report for submission to management comparing operations of the previous year with those under both proposed plans.

(Adapted from AICPA Uniform Examination)

Problem 20–3.   Purpose: *Report Correcting Inventories, Overhead, etc.*

You are engaged in an audit of the French Mfg. Company for the year ended December 31, 1968. To reduce the work load at year-end the company took its annual physical inventory under your observation on November 30, 1968. The company's inventory account, which includes raw material and work-in-process, is on a perpetual basis and the first-in, first-out method of pricing is used. There is no finished goods inventory. The company's physical inventory revealed that the book inventory of $60,570 was understated by $3,000. To avoid distorting the interim financial statements the company decided not to adjust the book inventory until year-end except for obsolete inventory items.

Your audit revealed the following information regarding the November 30 inventory:

1. Pricing tests showed that the physical inventory was overpriced by $2,200.
2. Footing and extension errors resulted in a $150 understatement of the physical inventory.
3. Direct labor included in the physical inventory amounted to $10,000. Overhead was included at the rate of 200 percent of direct labor. You determined that the amount of direct labor was correct and the overhead rate was proper.
4. The physical inventory included obsolete materials recorded at $250. During December these obsolete materials were removed from the inventory account by a charge to Cost of Sales.

Your audit also disclosed the following information about the December 31 inventory:

1. Total debits to certain accounts during December are listed below:

December

Purchases...$24,700
Direct labor... 12,100
Manufacturing expense....................................... 25,200
Cost of sales.. 68,600

2. The cost of sales of $68,600 included direct labor of $13,800.

3. Normal scrap loss on established product lines is negligible. However, a special order started and completed during December had excessive scrap loss of $800 which was charged to Manufacturing Expense.

Required:

a) Compute the correct amount of the physical inventory at November 30, 1968.

b) Without prejudice to your solution to part (*a*), assume that the correct amount of the physical inventory at November 30, 1968, was $57,700. Compute the amount of the inventory at December 31, 1968.

c) Compute the amount of the over- or underabsorbed overhead at December 31, 1968.

(Adapted from AICPA Uniform Examination)

Problem 20–4. Purpose: *Reports to Management: Inventory Loss*

The president of The Felton Company asks for your assistance because he believes a former employee has stolen a large quantity of finished goods. The employee, who disappeared on May 1, 1968, was the production manager and had access to all production and inventory records. The president requires the information to file a claim with the insurance company.

The Felton Company manufactures two types of kitchen chairs, All Steel and Open Seat. The legs and frames of the chairs are made of ⅞″ metal tubing which is purchased in both random mill lengths and precut 72″ lengths. Each chair has four 24″ legs. The All Steel chair frame is made from a 72″ length of tubing; the Open Seat chair frame requires a 36″ length of tubing. The scrap loss in cutting random mill lengths has averaged 3 percent. Other fabrication losses are negligible.

Under your observation a physical inventory is taken promptly, and by applying cutoff techniques, you determine the following physical inventory at May 1, 1968. Other chair components are not subject to verification. Your audit working papers for the 1967 audit reveal the inventory quantities at December 31, 1967.

	5/1/68	12/31/67
Raw materials:		
72″ lengths of tubing.................................... 8,500		13,500
Random mill lengths....................................34,800 feet		9,800 feet
Work-in-process:		
Individual legs... 9,700		2,900
All Steel chair frames.................................. 800		1,300
Open Seat chair frames................................. 100		300
Finished goods:		
All Steel chairs.. 5,500		10,700
Open Seat chairs....................................... 1,300		900

Your examination reveals metal tubing purchases during 1968 amounted to 202,000 pieces of 72″ lengths and 125,000 feet of random mill lengths. You determine that 100,000 chairs were shipped to customers during 1968. Of this number, 10,000 were Open Seat chairs selling for $3.75 each. The All Steel chair sells for $5 each. Your audit work papers show that The Felton Company has generally added 25 percent to its manufacturing cost to arrive at selling prices.

Required:

Prepare a report for management computing the amount of the dollar loss sustained by The Felton Company assuming that the types of chairs missing were in the same ratio as the sales.

(Adapted from AICPA Uniform Examination)

Problem 20–5.   Purpose: *Reports to Management: Inventories*

Bisto Corporation manufactures valves and pumps for liquids. On December 1, 1968, Bisto paid $25,000 to the Poplen Company for the patent for its Watertite Valve. Bisto planned to carry on Poplen's procedure of having the valve casing and parts cast by an independent foundry and doing the grinding and assembling in its own plant.

Bisto also purchased Poplen's inventory of the valves at 80 percent of its cost to Poplen. The purchased inventory was comprised of the following:

	Units
Raw material (unfinished casings and parts)	1,100
Work-in-process:	
Grinding (25% complete)	800
Assembling (40% complete)	600
Finished valves	900

Poplen's cost accounting system provided the following unit costs:

	Cost per Unit
Raw material (unfinished casings and parts)	$2.00
Grinding costs	1.00
Assembling costs	2.50

Bisto's cost accounting system accumulated the following costs for the month of December which do not include cost of the inventory purchased from Poplen:

Raw material purchases (casings and parts for 5,000 units)	$10,500
Grinding costs	2,430
Assembling costs	5,664

Bisto's inventory of Watertite Valves at December 31, 1968, follows:

Raw material (unfinished casings and parts)	2,700
Work-in-process:	
Grinding (35% complete)	2,000
Assembling (33⅓% complete)	300
Finished valves	2,250

No valves were spoiled or lost during the manufacturing process.

Required: (Bisto uses the process costing method in its accounting system.)

a) Prepare a schedule to compute the equivalent units produced and costs incurred per unit for the month of December, 1968.

b) Prepare a schedule of inventories on the FIFO basis as at December 1 and 31, 1968, setting forth by layers the number of units, unit costs, and amounts. Show all supporting schedules in good form.

(Adapted from AICPA Uniform Examination)

PROBLEMS—GROUP B

Problem 20–6. Purpose: *Reports to Management: Inventories*

On December 31, 1967, Awon Company was organized and purchased the fixed assets and inventories of Drain Company at 66⅔ percent of the value reported on the books of the seller. Operations consist of producing iron hardware castings in a foundry and finishing them in a machine shop. Certain finished parts are purchased and installed in the finished castings to meet customer specifications.

Following is the inventory as shown on the records of the seller on December 31, 1967:

	Pounds
Raw materials	2,200,000
Work-in-process (machine shop operations 50% complete)	540,000
Finished goods	2,460,000

The inventories were priced by the seller in accordance with the following schedule:

	Per Pound
Material cost	3¢
Foundry conversion cost	9¢
Machine shop conversion cost	6¢

In addition, purchased finished parts were carried at a cost of $180,000.

At December 31, 1968, the books of Awon Company show the following information:

Raw material purchases during the year (10,480,000 lbs.)	$335,360
Foundry conversion costs	$1,140,000
Machine shop conversion costs	$822,500
Raw material inventory	680,000 lbs.
Work-in-process inventory:	
Rough castings (not machined)	300,000 lbs.
In machining process (50% complete)	440,000 lbs.
Finished goods inventory	2,660,000 lbs.
Purchased parts inventory	$210,000

The purchased parts inventory was priced at December 31, 1968, current costs. The average prices for purchased parts at December 31, 1968, were 105 percent of the price level prevailing at December 31, 1967.

Intending to avoid taking into operating income any portion of the discount received on the bargain purchase of the inventories, Awon Company has adopted the last-in, first-out method for pricing inventories.

The LIFO costs for inventory layers are to be determined on a unit-value method except that the purchased parts inventory is to be determined on a dollar-value method. Increments are to be priced at average costs for the year.

Required:

Prepare a report showing inventories on LIFO basis as at December 31, 1967, and December 31, 1968, setting forth by layers the number of units, unit costs, and amounts. Show all supporting computations in good form.

(Adapted from AICPA Uniform Examination)

Problem 20–7.   Purpose: *Reports to Management: Variances from Standard Costs*

The Products Company employs departmental budgets and performance reports in planning and controlling its process costing operations. Department A's budget for January was for the production of 1,000 units of equivalent production, a normal month's volume.

The following performance report was prepared for January by the company's accountant:

	Budget	Actual	Variance	
Variable costs:				
Direct material	$20,000	$23,100	$3,100	(unfavorable)
Direct labor	10,000	10,500	500	(unfavorable)
Indirect labor	1,650	1,790	140	(unfavorable)
Power	210	220	10	(unfavorable)
Supplies	320	330	10	(unfavorable)
Total	$32,180	$35,940	$3,760	
Fixed costs:				
Rent	$ 400	$ 400	......	
Supervision	1,000	1,000	......	
Depreciation	500	500	......	
Other	100	100	......	
Total	2,000	2,000	......	
Grand Total	$34,180	$37,940	$3,760	

Direct material is introduced at various stages of the process. All conversion costs are incurred uniformly throughout the process. Because production fluctuates from month to month, the fixed overhead is applied at the rate of $2 per equivalent unit of direct labor.

Variable costs are applied monthly as incurred.

There was no opening inventory at January 1. Of the 1,100 new units started during January, 900 were completed and shipped. There was no finished goods inventory. The units in process at January 31 were estimated to be 75 percent complete as to direct materials and 80 percent complete as to conversion costs. There is no shrinkage, spoilage, or waste of materials.

Required:

a) Prepare a schedule of equivalent production for January.

b) Prepare a schedule computing the amount of under- or overapplied overhead at January 31.

c) Prepare a schedule computing the cost of goods shipped and the cost of the work-in-process inventory at January 31 at actual cost.

d) Comment on the performance report in 150 words or less. What specific conclusions, if any, can be drawn from the report?

(Adapted from AICPA Uniform Examination)

Problem 20–8. Purpose: *Manufacturing Reports*

The Processing Company produces a chemical compound, Supergro, that is sold for $4.60 per gallon. The manufacturing process is divided into the following departments:

1. Mixing department. The raw materials are measured and mixed in this department.

2. Cooking department. The mixed materials are cooked for a specified period in this department. In the cooking process there is a 10 percent evaporation loss in materials.

3. Cooling department. After the cooked materials are cooled in this department under controlled conditions, the top 80 percent in the cooling tank is siphoned off and pumped to the packing department. The 20 percent residue, which contains impurities, is sold in bulk as a by-product, Groex, for $2 per gallon.

4. Packing department. In this department special one-gallon tin cans costing 60 cents each are filled with Supergro and shipped to customers.

The company's research and development department recently discovered a new use for the by-product if it is further processed in a new boiling department. The new by-product, Fasgro, would sell in bulk for $5 per gallon.

In processing Fasgro the top 70 percent in the cooling tank would be siphoned off as Supergro. The residue would be pumped to the boiling department where one-half gallon of raw material, SK, would be added for each gallon of residue. In the boiling department process there would be a 40 percent evaporation loss. In processing Fasgro the following additional costs would be incurred:

Material SK.................................$1.10 per gallon
Boiling department variable processing costs........$1.00 per gallon of input
Boiling department fixed processing costs..........$2,000 per month

In recent months, because of heavy demand, the company has shipped Supergro and Groex on the same day that their processing was completed. Fasgro would probably be subject to the same heavy demand.

During the month of July, which was considered a typical month, the following raw materials were put into process in the mixing department:

Material FE —10,000 gallons @ $0.90 per gallon
Material QT— 4,000 gallons @ $1.50 per gallon

July processing costs per gallon of departmental input were:

Mixing department...$0.40
Cooking department.. 0.50
Cooling department.. 0.30
Packing department.. 0.10

For accounting purposes the company assigns costs to its by-products equal to their net realizable value.

Required:

Prepare a statement computing total manufacturing costs and gross profit for the month of July that compares (*a*) actual results for July, and (*b*) estimated results if Fasgro had been the by-product.

(Adapted from AICPA Uniform Examination)

Problem 20–9. Purpose: *Cost Reports in a Nonprofit Institution*

You have been requested by the Prentice Blood Bank, a nonprofit organization, to assist in developing certain information from the Bank's operations. You determine the following:

1. Blood is furnished to the blood bank by volunteers and when necessary by professional donors. During the year 2,568 pints of blood were taken from volunteers and professional blood donors.
2. Volunteer donors who give blood to the bank can draw against their account when needed. An individual who requires a blood transfusion has the option of paying for the blood used at $25 per pint or replacing it at the blood bank. Hospitals purchase blood at $8 per pint.
3. The Prentice Blood Bank has a reciprocal arrangement with a number of other banks that permits a member who requires a transfusion in a different locality to draw blood from the local bank against his account in Prentice. The issuing blood bank charges a set fee of $14 per pint to the home blood bank.
4. If blood is issued to hospitals but is not used and is returned to the blood bank, there is a handling charge of $1 per pint. Only hospitals are permitted to return blood. During the year 402 pints were returned. The blood being returned must be in usable condition.
5. Blood can be stored for only 21 days and then must be discarded. During the year 343 pints were outdated. This is a normal rate of loss.
6. The blood bank sells serum and supplies at cost to doctors and laboratories. These items are used in processing blood and are sold at the same price that they are billed to the blood bank. No blood bank operating expenses are allocated to the cost of sales of these items.
7. Inventories of blood are valued at the sales price to hospitals. The sales price to hospitals was increased on July 1, 1967. The inventories are as follows:

	Pints	Sales Price	Total
June 30, 1967.	80	$6	$480
June 30, 1968.	80	8	640

8. The following financial statements are available:

PRENTICE BLOOD BANK

BALANCE SHEET

ASSETS	June 30, 1967	June 30, 1968
Cash	$ 2,712	$ 2,093
U.S. Treasury bonds	15,000	16,000
Accounts receivable—sales of blood:		
Hospitals	1,302	1,448
Individuals	425	550

	June 30, 1967	*June 30, 1968*
Inventories:		
⸹ Blood......................................	$ 480	$ 640
Supplies and serum...........................	250	315
Furniture and equipment, less		
depreciation..............................	4,400	4,050
Total Assets..............................	$24,569	$25,096

LIABILITIES AND SURPLUS

Accounts payable—supplies.....................	$ 325	$ 275
Surplus......................................	24,244	24,821
Total Liabilities and Surplus................	$24,569	$25,096

PRENTICE BLOOD BANK

STATEMENT OF CASH RECEIPTS AND DISBURSEMENTS
For the Year Ended June 30, 1968

Balance, July 1, 1967:			
Cash in bank..............................			$ 2,712
U.S. Treasury bonds.........................			15,000
			$17,712
Receipts:			
From hospitals:			
Prentice Hospital..........................	$7,702		
Good Samaritan Hospital...................	3,818	$11,520	
Individuals.................................		6,675	
From other blood banks......................		602	
From sales of serum and supplies...............		2,260	
Interest on bonds............................		525	
Gifts and bequests...........................		4,928	
Total Receipts...........................			$26,510
Total to Be Accounted for.....................			$44,222
Disbursements:			
Laboratory expense:			
Serum...................................	$3,098		
Salaries.................................	3,392		
Supplies.................................	3,533		
Laundry and miscellaneous..................	277	$10,300	
Other expenses and disbursements:			
Salaries.................................	$5,774		
Dues and subscriptions......................	204		
Rent and utilities..........................	1,404		
Blood testing.............................	2,378		
Payments to other blood banks for blood given			
to members away from home...............	854		
Payments to professional blood donors.........	2,410		
Other expenses............................	1,805		
Purchase of U.S. Treasury bond...............	1,000	$15,829	
Total Disbursements......................			26,129
Balance, June 30, 1968........................			$18,093
Composed of:			
Cash in bank..............................			$ 2,093
U.S. Treasury bonds.........................			16,000
Total.................................			$18,093

Required:

a) Prepare a statement on the accrual basis of the total expense of taking and processing blood.

b) Prepare a report computing (1) the number of pints of blood sold and (2) the number of pints withdrawn by members.

c) Prepare a report computing the expense per pint of taking and processing the blood that was used.

(Adapted from AICPA Uniform Examination)

Problem 20–10. Purpose: *Reports to Management: Pricing*

Primrose Electronics Corporation's sole activity in 1968 was a federal government fixed-price incentive contract awarded in January, 1968. The corporation's prior government contracts were cost-plus-fixed-fee or firm fixed-price contracts which were completed by December, 1967.

Provisions of the fixed-price incentive contract include the following:

1. Primrose is to construct eight identical digital computers, deliveries to be made between July, 1968, and June, 1969.
2. The total contract target price is $780,000, which includes a target cost of $700,000. The total adjusted price cannot exceed a ceiling of $810,000.
3. The incentive clause states:

The total adjusted price (final contract price) shall be established by adding to the total adjusted cost (final negotiated cost) an allowance for profit determined as follows:

When the total adjusted cost is: | *The allowance for profit is:*
Equal to the total target cost.............Total target profit.
Greater than the total target cost.........Total target profit less 20% of the amount by which the total adjusted cost exceeds the total target cost.
Less than the total target cost............Total target profit plus 20% of the amount by which the total adjusted cost is less than the total target cost.

The following information is available at December 31, 1968:
1. Costs accumulated on the contract:

Direct materials	$170,000
Direct labor	192,000
Overhead	240,000
Total	$602,000

2. The estimated costs to complete the contract:

Direct materials	$ 30,000
Direct labor	48,000
Overhead	60,000
Total	$138,000

3. Past experience indicates that 1 percent of the gross amount of accumulated overhead charges will be disallowed by government auditors as contract costs. No provision has been made for this disallowance.

4. In addition to the estimated 1 percent disallowance in (3), the following 1968 costs will probably be disallowed:
   a) Depreciation on excess equipment, $1,000. The equipment was sold in January, 1969.
   b) Special nonrecurring recruiting costs, $4,000.
5. The corporation failed to take cash discounts totaling $2,000 in 1968. Lost discounts are credited to costs when found by government auditors. The corporation treats cash discounts, when taken, as a reduction of costs.
6. All costs that will probably be disallowed have been treated consistently as period costs by the corporation. Estimated allowable costs have been consistently allocated equally to identical units being manufactured under a contract.
7. Five computers were delivered in 1968 and billed at the target price. Progress payments of $75,000 were received for each computer delivered.

Required:

a) Prepare a schedule computing the estimated total adjusted price (estimated final contract price) for the fixed-price incentive contract.

b) Prepare a schedule computing the work-in-process inventory at estimated cost at December 31, 1968.

c) Assume that the estimated total adjusted price determined in (a) was $800,000. Prepare a schedule computing the estimated total amount receivable from the federal government at December 31, 1968, for the computers that were delivered.

(Adapted from AICPA Uniform Examination)

CHAPTER

21 | Profit Planning—Direct Costing

Need for
Profit Planning
The industrial scene has recently undergone numerous changes in markets, materials, labor requirements, and methods of production and distribution, and accompanying these changes there have been many developments of importance in cost accounting. Cost accounting methods have been improved in the traditional areas of usefulness—measurement of performance, cost control, statement preparation—and have been extended to facilitate management planning and policy decisions involving pricing, labor, plant expansion, and finance. Today, business—both small and large—requires coordinated management effort in which the services of each individual specialist and technician and each functional operating division are integrated with the aims of the business as a whole. Working closely with all other members of the team, the cost accountant must determine and analyze the facts which will assist in timely current operating control and form the basis for proper planning and sound business judgments.

In previous chapters the use of flexible budgets and standard costs were discussed as effective methods for assisting management in current operating control. The engineering study, operating experience, and knowledge of cost behavior which are necessary to develop a flexible budget and to set material, labor, and overhead standards, also make their contributions in the development of direct costing presentations, cost-profit-volume studies, and special cost analyses and comparisons. These additional methods of guidance and control are necessary tools which enable management to anticipate and measure the effect of internal changes in methods and policies, and external changes in prices,

641

wage rates, and in the volume and composition of demand for its products.

Nature of Profit Planning Profit planning is a management function requiring a thorough knowledge of the interplay of prices, fixed costs, variable costs, and sales volume as these factors affect earnings. It is the deviation from the profit plan due to variations in one or more of these factors that must receive immediate attention and such corrective action as may be deemed necessary. All profit planning and the interrelationship of the four factors are based upon practical budgeting and budgetary control, both short and long term. Budgetary planning and control, as they concern a manufacturing enterprise, have already been discussed. The purpose of this and the following chapters is to indicate how management may use budget and cost accounting information to plan and control the various profit aspects. This discussion will consider the following topics:

1. Profit planning through direct costing procedures.
2. Profit planning through cost-volume-profit studies.
3. Profit planning through comparative cost analyses.

In this chapter, the emphasis is on direct costing as a tool of management since its principles affect the discussion of the other topics listed.

Background of Direct Costing Direct costing, as a cost accounting technique, has gradually been increasing in popularity with the most rapid extension of its use occurring since World War II. However, the basic understanding of different patterns of cost behavior upon which direct costing is based has long been recognized. While "direct costing" is the popular designation of this concept, it is not an accurate descriptive title for the underlying method. A more nearly accurate designation might be "variable costing," since those costs identified as direct costs are the company's "variable costs"—costs that tend to vary directly with volume of production.

Individual firms and industries go through successive stages of growth and contraction and are affected by changes in the level of general business activity. This was as true a hundred years ago as it is today. Since the primary use of costs was as a guide to pricing, the pricing viewpoint was important in the early development of cost accounting. At first, the costing of product was done on an actual cost basis with the manufacturing overhead being spread over the production of the period after all the actual costs and actual production volume were known. This type of total unit cost was found to be inadequate and arrived too late for management purposes, especially for bidding on new work. Moreover, this type of total cost per unit was subject to the influence of changes in volume. It was recognized that many of the overhead costs tended to vary less as volume changed than did direct material and labor, the prime costs. Increased mechanization tended to increase the percentage of overhead cost to total cost. As a result, unit costs varied inversely with changes in volume, with highest unit costs shown in periods of low demand. Obviously, such total costs per unit of product were not satisfactory as the basis for quoting prices.

About the turn of the century some cost writers recommended the use of a "preliminary rate" which could be used in making estimates for bids and which could be added to the direct labor and material costs of a job as it progressed through the factory. This preliminary rate was the forerunner of our modern predetermined burden or overhead rates. Along with the preliminary rate, a supplementary rate was used to adjust the preliminary costs to the amount which would have been developed by actual cost methods.

About 1920, the next development in overhead costing introduced the use of a "normal" burden rate. Such rates are still widely used. The first step in setting this rate was to determine an activity measure (in units of product, labor hours, or machine-hours) which represented the normal or average level of activity which the firm was expected to maintain over a period of years. The next step was to estimate the overhead costs for the coming year at this normal volume level. The final step was to divide the overhead estimate by the normal volume in order to obtain the normal burden rate.

While the adoption of this concept was a slight improvement for some pricing and control purposes, it caused distortions in income determination when the volume of sales and production deviated substantially from the normal level. At the end of the fiscal year and when interim statements were prepared, substantial balances of over- or underabsorbed overhead would frequently appear. The disposition of these balances would cause substantial deductions from, or additions to, profit. As likely as not, as sales increased, costs remained approximately the same, but profits would drop. The absorption of overhead in product costs on a normal activity basis has not provided a fully satisfactory solution to the problem of the interaction of cost, volume, and profit.

The next development of importance in dealing with overhead costs was the introduction of the flexible budget. This device was developed primarily to facilitate cost control and was only secondarily concerned with pricing. It also provided a partial solution to the appearance of unusually large over- and underabsorbed overhead balances. Such budgets have been discussed previously in Chapter 16. Note that the costs are budgeted only at the levels of productive capacity at which the firm is likely to be operating. This flexible budget takes into account the various kinds of fluctuations (patterns of cost behavior) in each type of overhead cost item at the various levels of productive activity. This procedure has the advantage of segregating the variable from the fixed costs and the variable components of certain costs from the fixed components of those costs. When actual activity begins to vary considerably from the expected plant activity, revised costs can be readily prepared for consideration along with market factors in revising pricing policy. Also, the costs that should have been incurred at the actual level of operations can be compared with each type of actual cost incurred to reveal phases of the work in which cost control action is needed.

Some companies use the flexible budget as an analytical device to assist in cost control without incorporating it in any way in the accounting records. Some use the flexible budget procedure to derive predetermined standard overhead rates for specific departments or cost centers. These predetermined overhead rates may be expected capacity rates, normal capacity rates, or practical[1] capacity rates.

Flexible budgets, however, still include fixed expenses, and their application to product through overhead rates may produce unusual variations in profit determination when the quantity of production and the quantity of sales are at substantially different levels. While the flexible budget and related overhead rates are quite helpful in promoting cost control and in deriving costs for certain uses, they may not represent the answer to problems relating to cost-volume-profit relationships.

Nature and Purposes of Direct Costing   In matching cost and revenue to determine periodic income, conventional cost systems distinguish between manufacturing and nonmanufacturing costs. These systems, commonly referred to as "absorption costing," because the product "absorbs" manufacturing overhead costs, use predetermined overhead rates which apply both fixed and variable costs to production without recognition of the amount of the fixed application or the amount of the variable application.

In contrast, "direct costing" systems, in matching cost and revenue to

---

[1] Practical capacity for a department or cost center represents the productive level (in labor hours, machine-hours, or product units) at which the department is equipped to operate, taking into account minimal normal operating interruptions as the only obstacle to attaining ideal capacity. Practical capacity is ideal capacity less an allowance for minimal operating interruptions.

determine periodic income, recognize the distinction between direct (variable) and period (fixed) costs. It is this distinction between direct and period costs that is the basis of the direct costing concept. "Direct costs" (or "variable costs") tend to vary directly with the volume of production; "period costs" are incurred to keep facilities ready for manufacturing and marketing.

Period costs include not only costs customarily associated with plant and equipment but also research costs, some advertising costs, and costs required to maintain a basic organization. They are the costs—both manufacturing and nonmanufacturing—that must generally be incurred once facilities are being operated whether these facilities are functioning at 60 percent or 90 percent of capacity. Because they represent the fixed costs *of the period in which they are incurred,* period costs are charged against income of the period. *Direct costs* include the *additional* costs required only if specific products are manufactured and sold.

Under direct costing, fixed costs are distinguished from variable costs not only in the budget statements but also in the ledger accounts. Costs of direct materials and direct labor are handled in exactly the same manner under both absorption costing and direct costing. It is the manufacturing overhead that is treated differently.

Management of companies successfully employing direct costing techniques are able to offer several reasons for their use of this method. A company that pioneered the cause of direct costing and developed one of the first effective systems over 30 years ago did so in response to objections from its president that the income statements continued to show profits even though sales had declined considerably—a result he could not comprehend.

Even in companies having limited experience with direct costing, it is felt that management decisions have been expedited and improved since the accounting department has been able to supply timely information regarding the relationship of cost, volume, sales prices, and profit. If management is to benefit from the data furnished by cost accounting analyses, the information not only must be as complete and as nearly accurate as possible but also it must be prompt and presented in such a fashion that members of the management team who have not been schooled in the basic fundamentals of accounting can readily interpret the significance of the operating results. The major benefit, proponents of direct costing contend, is the prompt availability of cost data in an uncomplicated, usable form suitable for sound profit planning.

Direct costing procedures permit the presentation of data that is useful to various levels of management in current cost control; in the establishment of sound pricing policy if the market conditions for the firm's products are such as to give the company some degree of control over price; in guiding management in the making of specific decisions relating to materials, labor, equipment, and financial policy. This is particularly true where *physical* production and sales volume do not coincide.

Matching of Cost and Revenue

A basic goal of accounting is to bring about a proper matching of income and expense in order to arrive at a clear determination of net income. The process of matching cost and revenue under direct costing may be outlined as:

```
Revenue from products sold this period.............................xxxx
Less: Variable costs of manufacturing and selling these products.........xxxx
Marginal income or contribution margin............................xxxx
Less: Fixed costs.................................................xxxx
Net Income......................................................xxxx
```

Careful analysis of the above-described "matching process" reveals this fact: Within any volume range in which period costs are constant (i.e., *not* variable), marginal income per unit also tends to remain constant; and, therefore, if the marginal income rate is determined, it is possible to forecast with a reasonable degree of accuracy the increase in net income which will result from any specified increase in volume. This is accomplished by multiplying the estimated volume increase by the applicable rate of marginal income.

The marginal income ratio may also be used in determining other significant answers such as the volume of sales necessary to "break even," the volume of sales required to yield a desired rate of return on investment, or a product selling price to yield a desired rate of return.

"Marginal income" is sometimes called "contribution margin" on the theory that this figure represents the *contribution* provided by the "revenue from products sold this period" to meet the "period costs" of providing manufacturing and marketing capacity.

Direct costing may be used to provide information to management on the profitability of products. A direct costing income statement may be prepared analyzing operations by product or product line. Illustration 21–1 is an example of a direct costing income statement by products.

The statement points out the profitability of each of the products in dollar and percentage terms. Arbitrary decisions having to do with the allocation of fixed costs are eliminated and only the variable costs are assigned to the products. The statement highlights the *contribution margin* of each of the products. In Illustration 21–1, if excess capacity exists and if the demand is present, the company might do well to push

Illustration 21–1

XYZ COMPANY

INCOME STATEMENT—DIRECT COSTING

For Month of August 19—

	Total	Product A	B	C
Sales...	$1,000,000	$500,000	$300,000	$200,000
Variable cost of sales..........................	600,000	400,000	100,000	100,000
Variable selling and administrative..............	100,000	50,000	20,000	30,000
Contribution margin..........................	$ 300,000	$ 50,000	$180,000	$ 70,000
		10%	60%	35%
Period costs:				
Manufacturing............................	100,000			
Selling and administrative...................	50,000			
Net Income...............................	$ 150,000			

Product B, as $0.60 from each sales dollar contributes toward fixed costs and profit. The illustration also points out that *all* of the products are profitable as they contribute to fixed costs and profit.

The same type of analysis as was done by product may be done by sales territory, plants, distribution areas, etc. Direct costing procedures permit the determination of the most profitable territory, plant, etc.

It is not only helpful to have *actual* cost and income information presented with variable costs treated separately from fixed costs, it is also helpful in portraying probable *future* cost and income. The direct costing approach is helpful in deriving and presenting future cost information which management can use in the following ways:

1. In considering the costs of changing production requirements and alternative production methods.
2. In grasping the probable effect on production and distribution costs of the anticipated changes in prices and wage rates.
3. In understanding the effect by product lines and for the total firm of changes in the volume and composition of demand.
4. In formulating marketing plans related to:
   a) Price setting on individual products and the revision of the firm's total pricing structure.
   b) The discontinuance of unprofitable items or the addition of new ones.
   c) The selection of improved methods of promotion and distribution.

In the next two chapters there will be presented in some detail the use of information available from a direct costing system, or from a system including flexible budgets and standards, in developing profit plans for the entire firm and in making cost studies to aid management in making specific planning decisions.

Some cost accountants and businessmen contend that direct costing has its limitations and doesn't provide all the answers or necessarily the best answer in certain business situations or problems. For instance, improper management action might be taken when sales substantially exceed current production and inventories are being reduced. Under such conditions direct costing profits will be substantially higher than under conventional absorption cost accounting. During the early stages of a business reaction when sales lag behind production the direct profit will be minimized or the direct loss aggravated. This may unduly impress management as to the severity of the reaction and cause them to take actions which may mean missing profit opportunities in the near future or which may have the effect of depressing the market even more.

In some situations the full cost of a product or a more complete cost of a function must be determined to provide management with proper information. In working out pricing policy, management in certain instances needs variable cost and marginal income information and at other times needs full cost information. How these costs are used depends upon the operating conditions of individual firms and the management need for information involved. Using variable costs alone would be improper when additional volume or new projects are being considered which may require the use of existing equipment during overtime or extra shift periods or the expansion of facilities. For long-run pricing policy, management should endeavor to set prices which will recover full cost and provide a profit on those products which constitute the bulk of the firm's volume. In certain special contract situations management will want to determine either full cost or full cost less certain commercial promotional expenses.

Sometimes questions are raised as to the future usefulness of direct costing with increased automation and the spread of guaranteed annual wage contracts. With such changes the portion of costs which are fixed to the firm will increase and those that are variable will decrease. An increased dollar portion of the overhead costs related to plant and equipment will tend to be fixed and more of the labor costs will tend to be fixed. Such a shift in the cost characteristics of the firm will obviously reduce the scope of usefulness of direct costing for current cost control since fewer costs will be controllable at the plant operating level. However, since more dollars of investment in machinery and plant will be at stake and the firm will have less flexibility in incurring direct labor cost, it will become more imperative that management understand the impact of fixed costs and make plans for the most effective utilization of the available high-speed machinery and the available labor force. This will mean that management will have to deliberate more carefully over the expansion of productive facilities and labor force. It will require more adequate information as to the size and stability of additional demand for its various products over an extended future period and as to the expected cost of securing that demand and producing to meet it.

Comparison of Direct and Absorption Costing Methods When Standard Costs Are Used

So that a proper comparison can be made between direct costing and absorption costing procedures when standard costs are used, Illustration 21–2 is provided, based on the following standard cost data for the months of May and June:

STANDARD COST

	Per Unit
Direct materials...	$1.00
Direct labor...	1.50
Variable manufacturing overhead..................................	0.50
Total direct (or variable) manufacturing costs....................	$3.00
Variable selling expenses (salesmen's commissions)...............	0.25
Fixed overhead costs (period costs)...............................	0.90

Standard volume of production for year........................	1,200,000 units
Fixed overhead costs for year..................................	$1,080,000
Fixed overhead costs per unit..................................	$0.90
Sales price per unit..	$6.25

PRODUCTION STATISTICS

	May	June
Units sold..	80,000	120,000
Units produced......................................	120,000	84,000
Fixed overhead assigned each month.................	$ 90,000	$ 90,000
Fixed overhead applied to production...............	108,000	75,600
Overapplied (volume variance)......................	18,000	....
Underapplied (volume variance).....................	....	14,400
Fixed selling expenses..............................	25,000	25,000
Fixed administrative expenses.......................	20,000	20,000
Fixed research and development expenses............	4,000	4,000

In studying Illustration 21–2, observe these important points:

1. Under direct costing, the ending inventory is costed at a smaller figure because only variable costs are charged to the product.
2. Net income in May under direct costing is $36,000 lower than under absorption costing because none of the fixed (period) costs have been included in the ending inventory.
3. Under the direct costing concept, cost of sales (direct costs) and marginal income vary directly with sales volume if fixed and variable costs are stable. Hence, an increase in sales volume (without a change in sales price) will result in a corresponding increase in profits. In the illustration, sales increased 50 percent in June. Note that total direct costs (cost of sales) were $260,000 in May and $390,000 in June—an increase of 50

Illustration 21-2

COMPARISON OF DIRECT AND ABSORPTION COSTING METHODS WHEN STANDARD COSTS ARE USED

INCOME STATEMENT FOR THE MONTHS OF MAY AND JUNE
(Direct Costing Method)

	May	May	June	June
Sales: 80,000 Units @ $6.25		$500,000.00		
120,000 Units @ 6.25				$750,000.00
Direct Costs:				
Manufacturing:				
Inventory at Beginning of Month	0		$120,000.00	
Direct Materials	$120,000.00		84,000.00	
Direct Labor	180,000.00		126,000.00	
Variable Overhead	60,000.00		42,000.00	
Total	$360,000.00		$372,000.00	
Less: Inventory, 40,000 Units @ $3.00	120,000.00			
Inventory, 4,000 Units @ $3.00			12,000.00	
	$240,000.00		$360,000.00	
Selling:				
Salesmen's Commissions	20,000.00		30,000.00	
Total Variable Costs		260,000.00		390,000.00
Contribution Margin		$240,000.00		$360,000.00
Period Costs:				
Fixed Manufacturing Overhead	$ 90,000.00		$ 90,000.00	
Fixed Selling Expenses	25,000.00		25,000.00	
Fixed Administrative Expenses	20,000.00		20,000.00	
Research and Development Expenses	4,000.00		4,000.00	
Total Period Costs		139,000.00		139,000.00
Net Income		$101,000.00		$221,000.00

INCOME STATEMENT FOR THE MONTHS OF MAY AND JUNE
(Absorption Costing Method)

	May	May	June	June
Sales: 80,000 Units @ $6.25		$500,000.00		
120,000 Units @ 6.25				$750,000.00
Cost of Sales:				
Inventory at Beginning of Month	0		$156,000.00	
Direct Materials	$120,000.00		84,000.00	
Direct Labor	180,000.00		126,000.00	
Direct Manufacturing Overhead	60,000.00		42,000.00	
Applied Fixed Overhead	108,000.00		75,600.00	
Total	$468,000.00		$483,600.00	
Less: Inventory, 40,000 Units	156,000.00			
Inventory, 4,000 Units			15,600.00	
Cost of Sales at Normal	$312,000.00		$468,000.00	
Less: Overapplied Fixed Overhead			14,400.00	
Add: Underapplied Fixed Overhead	18,000.00			
Cost of Sales at Actual Costs		294,000.00		482,400.00
Gross Profit on Sales		$206,000.00		$267,600.00
Operating Expenses:				
Salesmen's Commissions	$ 20,000.00		$ 30,000.00	
Other Selling Expenses	25,000.00		25,000.00	
Administrative Expenses	20,000.00		20,000.00	
Research and Development Expenses	4,000.00		4,000.00	
Total		69,000.00		79,000.00
Net Income		$137,000.00		$188,600.00

	May	June
Sales in relation to normal of 100,000 units	80%	120%
Production in relation to normal of 100,000 units	120%	84%

percent. Note further that marginal income was $240,000 in May and $360,000 in June—an increase of 50 percent.

4. Under absorption costing, even though sales increased 50 percent in June, gross profit on sales increased only 30 percent (approximately)—leading to the criticism of absorption costing that this result appears most unrealistic and confuses management in its attempt to understand and use accounting statement data. Profits are not created by production alone; it is only when the production has been converted into sales income that a realistic picture is presented.

5. In abbreviated form, an alternative form of income statement setup under direct costing would be:

May

Net sales..	$500,000
Less: Variable manufacturing cost of sales.................	240,000
Manufacturing margin.....................................	$260,000
Less: Variable selling expenses...........................	20,000
Marginal Income (or Merchandising Margin)..............	$240,000

Separation of Variable and Fixed Costs

Direct costing procedures were developed to provide better cost control for the guidance of enlightened industrial management through a more reliable system of assigning and fixing responsibility for controllable costs, pricing, planning, and related decisions.

The primary difference in the accounting techniques of direct costing, as distinguished from other costing methods, is that direct (variable) costs must be separated from the period (fixed) costs. Therefore, successful application of direct costing is dependent upon an adequate knowledge of *cost behavior* so that *cost responsibility* may be properly assigned.

Four typical patterns of cost behavior are found. These are: fixed, semifixed, semivariable, and variable. It is a common contention that any cost may be separated as direct or period (variable or fixed), depending upon the department involved and the purpose for which such cost was incurred. However, it can be a task far from simple to distinguish between every variable and fixed cost, and occasionally certain parts of the separation process will be decided on the basis of practicability or expediency rather than on the basis of strict adherence to an established accounting principle. Whatever the decision may be, it should be adhered to consistently. The fixing of accounting policies is necessary in order that the net income be determined on a basis that is consistent from period to period, thereby making comparisons between periods truly valid. Of course, this does not mean that a change is precluded if conditions warrant or justify a change.

Sound departmentalization is a prerequisite for the control of costs because it permits the separation of direct and period costs so that supervisory effort may be properly directed and rated. Proper departmentalization facilitates the achievement of the objectives of cost accounting in the following ways:

1. By following more closely the specific functional productive and service efforts of the firm, more reasonable and accurate bases for tracing and assigning costs to functions become evident and can be used.
2. By obtaining more accurate costing of each function or operation, more accurate assignment of costs to any product or products passing through each function can be achieved.
3. Cost control is aided by localizing the cost performance of the various individuals who are responsible for initiating actions for spending the firm's money through their functions. The performance of each function tends to be free from influence by the performance of other functions so that responsibility can be pinned down.
4. The breaking down of the effort to the level of just one particular type of activity means that costs will tend to fluctuate if they are affected by changes in volume of productive effort in some discernible relationship to this one activity variable. This permits more valid study of cost behavior which will aid cost control and various types of planning.
5. With the productive effort subdivided into a number of operational steps, there will be smaller in-process inventories at any stage of production, and their degree of completion can be more accurately evaluated. This leads to more accurate and easier costing of inventories which gives better support for statement figures.

Accounting Procedures When Direct Costing Is Used

Because they are entirely variable (varying with volume of production), direct materials and direct labor costs are handled in exactly the same manner under direct costing as under absorption costing. The segregation between period (or fixed) and direct (or variable) costs, however, necessitates a change in overhead accounting technique.

Conventional cost systems separate manufacturing and nonmanufacturing costs but do not distinguish between fixed and variable, and a predetermined overhead rate is used to charge *both* fixed and variable costs to production. Under direct costing, fixed overhead costs and expenses are charged directly against income when incurred, and, therefore, separate accounts must be maintained to account for variable overhead.

When direct costing is to be incorporated in the accounting records, the following control accounts, supported by adequate subsidiary records, may be used:

┌─────────────────Account─────────────────┐	┌─────Income Statement Presentation─────┐
Variable Manufacturing Overhead Costs Control	Part of cost of manufacturing.
Variable Selling Overhead Control ⎫ ⎬ Variable Administrative Overhead Control ⎭	Combine with other variable costs to arrive at marginal income (or, deduct from manufacturing margin to arrive at marginal income).
Fixed Manufacturing Overhead Costs Control ⎫ ⎪ Fixed Selling Overhead Control ⎬ ⎪ Fixed Administrative Overhead Control ⎭	Combine and deduct from marginal income to arrive at net income.

In the above account titles, the term "direct" might well be substituted for "variable" and "period" used instead of "fixed." Each of the above accounts functions as follows:

Actual costs incurred (supporting detail accumulated on subsidiary cost analysis records)	Closed to Revenue and Expense account (Profit and Loss account)

If standard costs are used, variable overhead is accounted for by using:

Variable Manufacturing Overhead Control		Applied Variable Manufacturing Overhead	
Actual costs incurred	Close against Applied Variable Manufacturing Overhead and record variance, if any	Close against Variable Manufacturing Overhead Control, recording variance, if any	Predetermined manufacturing overhead rate X production (debit: Work-in-Process)

The variance(s) between the control, representing actual expenditures, and the applied, representing standard, must be further analyzed as to cause. The variance adjustment is periodically charged to Cost of Sales, as in other costing methods, but because under direct costing fixed expenses are considered a cost of the accounting period rather than a cost of the manufactured product, over- or underapplied manufacturing overhead is normally minimized.

For each production department a monthly manufacturing variance statement may be prepared showing for each class of cost the actual costs incurred and the variance from standard. In addition, for each nonproduction department, a statement may be prepared comparing actual expenses with budgeted expenses. In one company, it is a monthly requirement that foremen and plant managers explain the manufacturing variances, that sales managers attempt to account for volume variances, and that staff department heads analyze their budget variances.

Illustration 21–3, presented in *N.A.A. Research Report 37* described earlier, indicates how an operating statement may be prepared showing an analysis of period expenses by functional responsibilities.

Illustration 21–3

Operating Statement Showing Period Expenses
by Functional Responsibilities

Details	Actual	Budget	Variance Favorable or (Unfavorable)	Responsibility of Name	Title
Sales	$3,100,000.00	$3,400,000.00			
Cost of sales (at standard)	1,922,000.00	2,040,000.00			
MARGINAL INCOME (at std.)	$1,178,000.00	$1,360,000.00	($ 182,000.00)	J. Smith	V.P. of Sales
Variations from standard:					
On purchasing materials	5,000.00	--------	5,000.00	T. Brown	V.P. of Pur.
On processing materials	(28,950.00)	--------	(28,950.00)	W. Lowe	V.P. of Mfg.
MARGINAL INCOME (Actual)	$1,154,050.00	$1,360,000.00	($ 205,950.00)		
Period expenses:					
Manufacturing	$ 185,400.00	$ 182,000.00	($ 3,400.00)	W. Lowe	V.P. of Mfg.
Personnel	125,400.00	124,500.00	(900.00)	C. Downs	V.P. of Per.
Accounting	89,100.00	84,000.00	(5,100.00)	B. Brown	Controller
Marketing	90,175.00	82,000.00	(8,175.00)	J. Smith	Mgr. of Mkt.
Purchasing	67,800.00	62,900.00	(4,900.00)	T. Brown	V.P. of Pur.
Plant engineering . . .	38,225.00	40,500.00	2,275.00	R. Roy	Dir. of Eng.
Legal	43,290.00	38,750.00	(4,540.00)	A. Wiley	Secretary
Treasury	35,410.00	37,200.00	1,790.00	W. Cash	Treasurer
Public relations	25,200.00	26,800.00	1,600.00	D. Cole	Dir. of P.R.
Research and development	21,850.00	18,300.00	(3,550.00)	A. Mack	V.P. of Res.
Total period costs .	$ 721,850.00	$ 696,950.00	($ 24,900.00)		
PROFIT BEFORE TAXES . .	$ 432,200.00	$ 663,050.00	($ 230,850.00)		

If a company wishes to report operating results in published statements and tax returns on an absorption costing basis, conforming to generally accepted accounting principles, direct costing statements may be converted to more conventional accounting results by charging part of the period, or fixed, manufacturing overhead costs to the work-in-process and finished goods inventories. The principles involved are demonstrated in Illustration 21–4.

Illustration 21-4

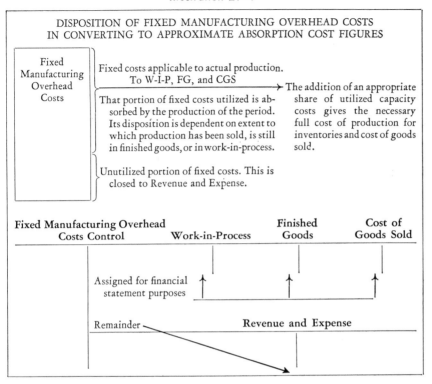

DISPOSITION OF FIXED MANUFACTURING OVERHEAD COSTS
IN CONVERTING TO APPROXIMATE ABSORPTION COST FIGURES

Fixed Manufacturing Overhead Costs

Fixed costs applicable to actual production.
To W-I-P, FG, and CGS → The addition of an appropriate

That portion of fixed costs utilized is absorbed by the production of the period. Its disposition is dependent on extent to which production has been sold, is still in finished goods, or in work-in-process.

share of utilized capacity costs gives the necessary full cost of production for inventories and cost of goods sold.

Unutilized portion of fixed costs. This is closed to Revenue and Expense.

Fixed Manufacturing Overhead Costs Control   Work-in-Process   Finished Goods   Cost of Goods Sold

Assigned for financial statement purposes

Remainder   Revenue and Expense

Effect of Different Costing Methods on Net Income

The difference between the amount of net income of any accounting period computed by absorption costing and the net income under direct costing will be equal to the change in the amount of period costs deferred in inventory under the different methods. Both methods, of course, will result in identical amounts of *total* net income over a complete cycle of inventory buildup and liquidation.

If *inventory* of manufactured goods:

1. DOES NOT FLUCTUATE from period to period,
   net income under "absorption costing" is identical to net income under "direct costing."

2. DOES FLUCTUATE from period to period,
   net income will differ somewhat under the two methods because the absorption costing theory requires that part of the period costs be deferred in inventory, whereas direct costing defers no period costs, therefore:

   a) When inventory is *increased*,
      net income will be higher under absorption costing because inventory includes a portion of the period costs, while under

direct costing all period costs are charged against current revenues.

b) When inventory is *decreased,*

net income will be lower under absorption costing because the period costs previously included in inventory are now being charged against current revenues, whereas under direct costing only *current* period costs are being charged against current revenues.

A reconciliation of net income determined under direct costing procedures with net income under conventional absorption costing is demonstrated in Illustration 21–5 using the following basic standard cost data:

Normal capacity.........100,000 units Production this period.... 90,000 units Sales this period......... 95,000 units	Selling price per unit...........$10.00

Standard variable costs per unit:
  Material and labor............$4.00
  Factory overhead............. 1.00
  Selling expense............... 0.50
	Fixed costs for period:
	  Production*............$200,000.00
	  Selling................. 75,000.00
	  Administration.......... 50,000.00
	  Others................. 25,000.00
	  * Equal to $2.00 per unit if spread over
	  normal capacity of 100,000 units.

Operating variances:
  Representing excessive in-
  currence of variable costs $4,500.00	

Illustration 21–5

INCOME STATEMENT—ABSORPTION COSTING

Net sales..		$950,000
Less: Standard cost of sales (95,000 × $7)......................		665,000
Standard gross profit...		$285,000
Less: Variances:		
Operating variances.....................................$ 4,500		
Volume variances (10,000 × $2)........................... 20,000		
Total variances...		24,500
Gross profit...		$260,500
Less: Selling expenses ($47,500 + $75,000)....................$122,500		
Administrative expenses.................................... 50,000		
Other expenses.. 25,000		
Total expenses...		197,500
Net Income..		$ 63,000

INCOME STATEMENT—DIRECT COSTING

Net sales..	$950,000
Less: Standard variable cost of sales (95,000 × $5)..............	475,000
Manufacturing margin...	$475,000
Less: Variable selling expenses (95,000 × $0.50).................	47,500
Distribution margin..	$427,500
Less: Operating variances...................................	4,500
Contribution margin..	$423,000

Illustration 21–5—Continued

Less: Fixed costs:

Production..	$200,000	
Selling expenses...................................	75,000	
Administrative expenses............................	50,000	
Other expenses....................................	25,000	
Total fixed costs................................		350,000
Net Income......................................		$ 73,000

Reconciliation of Direct Costing Income to Absorption Costing Income

Direct costing net income..	$73,000
Less: Reduction of fixed costs in inventory*...............................	10,000
Absorption Costing Net Income..	$63,000

* More units were sold than produced. This caused a 5,000-unit reduction in inventory. Each of these units sold resulted in a charge to standard cost of sales this period of $2 per unit, fixed production cost, which was carried forward from last period in the absorption cost method.

General Acceptance of Direct Costing

The National Association of Accountants does not issue judgments on accounting practices, but in 1961 it published *Research Report No. 37* entitled: *Current Application of Direct Costing* in which is summarized the experience of 50 companies that participated in the study by contributing information about their applications of direct costing. These companies indicated that their experience with direct costing has been quite favorable.

Critics of direct costing charge that oversimplification of operating results to aid management in making decisions is illogical because we are dealing with relationships that, of necessity, are complicated. Others argue that the problem of distinguishing between direct and period costs can become very involved and that it is not necessary to include direct costing procedures in the accounting records to obtain data. With flexible budgets and standards incorporated into an absorption cost system, the same basic information is available that a direct costing system provides.

The American Accounting Association in releases of its Committee on Accounting Concepts and Standards holds that: ". . . the cost of a manufactured product is the sum of the acquisition costs reasonably traceable to that product and should include both direct and indirect factors. The omission of any element of manufacturing cost is not acceptable." Because direct costing requires the omission of all fixed manufacturing costs from inventory, it is not considered an "acceptable" concept.

Neither the American Institute of Certified Public Accountants nor the Internal Revenue Service has recognized direct costing as *generally acceptable* for inventory valuation. While not specifically mentioning direct costing, the use of the term "indirectly incurred" would seem to include items of period cost which must be utilized in order to obtain production.

The Internal Revenue Service in its regulations defines inventory cost to include (*a*) raw materials and supplies entering into or consumed in connection with the product, (*b*) expenditures for direct labor, and (*c*) indirect expenses incident to and necessary for the production of the particular item. Here again, the inclusion of "indirect expenses necessary for production" would seem to include many items of capacity or period cost which are excluded from inventory in the direct costing method. Court decisions have not provided a definite answer as to the acceptability of direct costing for tax purposes because the decisions have been based on issues other than direct costing. For example, in Geometric Stamping Company (26 TC 301), the Commissioner of Internal Revenue did not contest the propriety of the direct costing method used by the taxpayer, and the court specifically excluded the question of acceptability of direct costing in its decision. In Frank G. Wikstrom & Sons, Inc. (20 TC 45), the court upheld the Commissioner's objection to the taxpayer including in inventory only direct labor and material applicable to specific jobs and deducting all other expenses from income in the year incurred. In Montreal Mining Company (2 TC 688), exclusion of certain overhead expense from inventory was advocated by the Commissioner and upheld by the court. It would appear that if it is to the government's advantage to disallow the use of direct costing as applied by the taxpayer that the Commissioner might well challenge the acceptability of the method.

The fact that statements prepared under the concept of direct costing may not be acceptable by the Internal Revenue Service or for published reports by some public accountants does not mean that these statements are not useful. A company may prepare *both* direct costing and absorption costing income statements. Each has its use.

Conclusions   In our present complex economic system which is constantly undergoing changes in markets, materials, labor requirements, and methods of production and distribution, it is important that management be supplied with information that will guide them in carrying out their cost control and planning responsibilities. Flexible budgets, standards, and direct costing can be used as separate or complementary devices in the attainment of these objectives. Most cost systems, either through the use of flexible budgets or flexible budgets and standards, can provide information for cost control and planning purposes. The chief advantage of the direct costing method seems to lie in the fact that presentations to management for internal use can be more readily prepared and are more readily understood and used by management in taking action or in making plans.

Current control of costs requires that costs within functional areas of responsibility be identified as to their fixed and variable characteristics in the short run. This separation is a prerequisite and is reflected in all direct costing statements prepared for management. This identification of costs aids the individual immediately responsible for controlling those costs to detect excesses and take corrective action. It also aids higher level supervisory personnel in evaluating the performance of men responsible to them. The impact of fixed costs in specific functions and in the firm as a whole is conveyed to management in a more forcible manner. Through successive reports management gradually achieves a better understanding of the effect of certain functional fixed costs and the firm's combined fixed costs upon the income result. This leads to management proposals to achieve better utilization of existing facilities and personnel.

The direct costing method strives to compile both manufacturing and nonmanufacturing costs in such a way as to determine the variable costs of each product or product line and the fixed costs by cost center, division, or the entire plant, whichever classifications are appropriate to the particular industrial situation. This provides the basis for furnishing management with timely information as to each product's contribution to combined marginal profit, that is, dollar sales of product less its variable costs.

QUESTIONS FOR REVIEW

1. Define "profit planning."

The following statement refers to questions 2, 3, and 4: Supporters of direct costing have contended that it provides management with more useful accounting information. Critics of direct costing believe that its negative features outweigh its contributions.

2. Describe direct costing. How does it differ from conventional absorption costing?
3. List the arguments for and against the use of direct costing.
4. Indicate how each of the following conditions would affect the amounts of net profit under conventional absorption costing and direct costing:
   a) Sales and production are in balance at standard volume.
   b) Sales exceed production.
   c) Production exceeds sales.
   (Adapted from an AICPA Uniform Examination)
5. Explain the concept "period cost."

6. "There is no volume variance when direct costing is used in conjunction with a standard cost accounting system." Do you agree? Explain.

7. "Successful application of direct costing is dependent upon an adequate knowledge of cost behavior so that cost responsibility may be properly assigned." Do you agree? Explain.

8. "Under absorption costing, profits are tied to production, while under direct costing, profits are tied to sales." Explain.

9. "Direct costing may be more useful as a managerial tool in a multiproduct company than in a single-product company." Comment.

10. Why have accountants been reluctant to accept direct costing as "generally accepted" for inventory valuation?

PROBLEMS—GROUP A

Problem 21–1.   Purpose: *Preparation of Direct Cost Income Statement*

The trial balance of the Garrison Company contained the following balances on April 30, the end of the fiscal year:

Materials purchased	$ 60,000
Selling expense—variable	10,000
Selling expense—fixed	30,000
Sales	300,000
Direct labor	40,000
General and administrative expense—variable	10,000
General and administrative expense—fixed	30,000
Factory expense—variable	20,000
Factory expense—fixed	45,000
Beginning inventory:	
Materials	25,000
Direct labor	20,000
Factory expense—variable	10,000
Ending inventory:	
Materials	20,000
Direct labor	15,000
Factory expense—variable	8,000
Material price variance	2,000 dr.
Material quantity variance	1,500 cr.
Labor rate variance	1,000 dr.
Labor efficiency variance	2,000 dr.
Overhead variances	1,000 dr.

Required:

a) Prepare an income statement for the year under the direct cost method.

b) What use, or uses, might be made of the statement prepared in (*a*)?

Problem 21–2.   Purpose: *Preparation of Direct Costing Statements and Absorption Costing Statements*

The Groff Manufacturing Company manufactures one product called "gro." Budgeted sales for the Groff Manufacturing Company are estimated at 100,000 units per year for 1968 and 1969. Estimated sales price is $10 per unit.

Budgeted costs for each of the two years follow:

Materials...$2.50 per unit
Labor..$2.00 per unit
Variable manufacturing overhead.........................$1.00 per unit
Fixed manufacturing overhead.............................. $50,000
Variable selling and administrative costs..................$1.00 per unit sold
Fixed selling and administrative costs..................... $60,000

There is no beginning inventory at January 1, 1968 (estimated). Current production plans call for the manufacture of 125,000 units in 1968 and 80,000 units in 1969.

Required:

a) Prepare a budgeted income statement under direct costing for 1968.

b) Prepare a budgeted income statement under absorption costing for 1968.

c) Explain the difference, if any, of the net incomes as between (*a*) and (*b*) above.

d) Repeat steps (*a*), (*b*), and (*c*) for 1969.

Problem 21-3. Purpose: *Direct Costing and Absorption Costing Compared*

Relevant production, cost, and sales data for the Grant Company follow:

Direct labor.. $1.00 per unit
Materials... 2.00 per unit
Overhead:
    Variable... 1.50 per unit
    Fixed...$75,000 per month
Selling expenses.....................................$60,000 per month
General and administrative expenses....................$50,000 per month
Sales price... $8.00 per unit

During January and February the company experienced the following:

	January	February
Production (units)...................................	190,000	205,000
Beginning inventory (units)...........................	0	10,000
Sales (units).......................................	180,000	210,000

Normal capacity—200,000 units.

Required:

Prepare income statements for each month:

a) Using the direct cost method.

b) Using the absorption cost method.

c) Reconcile (*a*) and (*b*) in each month.

Problem 21-4. Purpose: *Preparation of Direct Costing and Absorption Costing Statements*

The following data were derived from the Garfield Manufacturing Company's records:

Annual data:

Maximum capacity....................................400,000 units
Normal capacity......................................360,000 units
Factory overhead—fixed............................... $1,080,000
Selling and General Expenses—Fixed...................   425,000
Selling price per unit of product....................   65
Variable manufacturing cost per unit.................   32
Variable selling cost per unit.......................   6

1968 results of operations:

Budgeted production..................................360,000 units
Actual production....................................330,000 units
Sales..310,000 units
Beginning inventory.................................. 10,000 units
Unfavorable variance from standard variable manufacturing
cost... $60,000

Required:

Prepare income statements for 1968 under:

a) Absorption costing.

b) Direct costing.

Problem 21–5. Purpose: *Comparison of Inventory and Units Costs; Direct and Absorption Costing*

Gordon Manufacturers opened its Smithville operation in early January. One product was manufactured during the year. The relevant data follow:

Units

Sales (at $10 per unit)...........................50,000
Production (no spoilage incurred)................60,000

	Per Unit	Total	Fixed
Costs and expenses:			
Direct materials...........................	$1.00	$60,000	
Direct labor...............................	1.50	90,000	
Maintenance labor..........................	0.25	15,000	$ 9,000
Packaging cost.............................	0.10	6,000	
Production supervision.....................			30,000
Depreciation:			
Production department.....................			45,000
Other departments........................			5,000
Insurance on Equipment:			
Production department.....................			3,000
Other departments........................			2,000
Miscellaneous manufacturing overhead..........	0.20	12,000	15,000
Selling and administrative expenses...........	0.75	45,000	60,000

Required:

Compute the following:

a) The ending inventory under direct costing.

b) The ending inventory under absorption costing.

c) Difference in net income under the two costing methods.

PROBLEMS—GROUP B

Problem 21–6. Purpose: *Preparation of Direct and Absorption Costing Statements*

The Quick Company produces a chemical compound that is sold by the gallon. Management estimates that 2,000,000 gallons per year will be sold in 1968 and 1969 at a sales price of $2.50 per gallon.

The expectation is that there will be no beginning inventory at January 1, 1968. Management plans to produce 2,200,000 gallons in 1968 and 1,950,000 gallons in 1969.

Estimated variable costs are:
Materials...................................$0.80 per gallon
Labor.......................................$0.70 per gallon
Overhead....................................$0.30 per gallon
Selling and general expenses................$0.20 per gallon sold
Estimated fixed expenses are:
Overhead.................................... $200,000
Selling and general......................... $100,000

Required:

a) Prepare a budgeted income statement under direct costing for 1968 and for 1969.

b) Prepare a budgeted income statement under absorption costing for 1968 and for 1969.

c) Explain the differences, if any, of the net incomes in each of the years.

Problem 21–7. Purpose: *Preparation of Direct Cost Income Statement*

The following account balances appeared in the ledger of the Queens Company at December 31: (The company closes its books on December 31 each year.)

Material quantity variance.................................$ 1,700 dr.
Material price variance.................................... 2,000 dr.
Labor rate variance.. 2,000 dr.
Labor efficiency variance.................................. 3,000 cr.
Overhead variances... 2,200 dr.
Purchases—materials.. 73,000
Selling expense—variable................................... 22,000
Selling expense—fixed...................................... 29,000
Direct labor... 63,000
General and administrative expense—variable................ 21,000
General and administrative expense—fixed................... 19,000
Variable overhead—factory.................................. 29,000
Fixed overhead—factory..................................... 77,000
Ending inventory:
Materials.. 7,000
Direct labor... 5,000
Variable overhead—factory.................................. 6,000
Beginning inventory:
Materials.. 10,000
Labor.. 7,000
Variable overhead—factory.................................. 8,000
Sales.. 425,000

Required:

    a) Prepare an income statement for the year under the direct cost method.

    b) What uses, if any, might be made of the statement prepared in (*a*)?

Problem 21–8. Purpose: *Preparation of Direct Costing and Absorption Costing Statements*

The Quite-Big Manufacturing Company makes a product called "quib," and in 1968 had the following experience:

Sales	21,000 units
Budgeted production	25,000
Actual production	23,000
Beginning inventory	4,000

The company uses a standard cost system, and in 1968 the unfavorable variance from standard variable manufacturing cost amounted to $11,000.

    Other data that were obtainable showed:

Maximum capacity	27,000 units
Normal capacity	25,000 units
Sales price per unit	$105 per unit
Fixed manufacturing expenses	$67,000
Variable manufacturing cost per unit	$67
Variable selling cost per unit	$15
Fixed selling and general expenses	$35,000

Required:

Prepare income statements for 1968 under:

    a) Absorption costing.

    b) Direct costing.

Problem 21–9. Purpose: *Direct Costing and Absorption Costing Compared*

Quantos Suppliers, Inc., reported the following during the early part of the third quarter of the year:

	First Quarter	Second Quarter
Sales in dozens	20,000	28,000
Production in dozens	27,000	22,000
Beginning inventory in dozens	...	7,000

The company incurred the following costs:

Materials	$16 per dozen
Labor	$16 per dozen
Variable factory overhead	$32 per dozen
Fixed factory overhead	$90,000 per quarter
Other fixed costs:	
Selling	$35,000 per quarter
General	$55,000 per quarter
Normal capacity—30,000 dozen produced.	
Sales price $110 per dozen.	

Required:

Prepare income statements for each month using:

    a) The direct cost method.

b) The absorption cost method.

c) Reconcile (*a*) and (*b*) in each month.

Problem 21–10. Purpose: *Comparison of Inventory and Unit Costs; Direct and Absorption Costing*

The following costs and expenses were incurred by the Quentin Manufacturing Company during January, the first month of the new model year. (No inventory was carried over from the last model year.)

	Fixed	Variable
Materials...		$280,000
Labor..		210,000
Maintenance..$23,000		14,000
Supervision...	43,000	35,000
Depreciation:		
Factory..	24,000	
Other...	6,000	
Insurance:		
Factory..	5,000	2,100
Other...	4,000	
Other manufacturing overhead items.......................	35,000	35,000
Selling and administrative items..........................	28,000	25,000

Sales—50,000 units @ $150 per batch of 10 units.
Production—70,000 units.

Required:

Compute the following:

a) The ending inventory under direct costing.

b) The ending inventory under absorption costing.

c) Difference in net income under the two costing methods.

CHAPTER

22 | Cost-Volume-Profit Analyses

Introduction The success of a business is generally attributable in great measure to the ability of its management personnel to cope with probable conditions of the future. Short-range as well as long-term plans must be made *today* for the business operations of *tomorrow,* and this is accomplished by sound management evaluation of not only the potentials of tomorrow but also its pitfalls.

The success of a business is most frequently measured in terms of *profit.* Profit is dependent on three basic factors—the selling price of the product, the costs of manufacturing and distributing the product, and the volume of sales. No one profit factor is independent of the others because cost determines the selling price to arrive at a desired rate of profit; the selling price affects the volume of sales; the volume of sales directly influences the volume of production; and the volume of production influences the cost. This relationship of COST-VOLUME-PROFIT, frequently abbreviated to C-V-P, means that accounting must play a vital role in the planning function because management must have adequate data to properly appraise the probable effects of tomorrow's profit opportunities.

The direct costing procedures, as discussed in Chapter 21, are most conducive to the simplification of C-V-P analysis. A popular starting point in C-V-P analysis which has been used for many years is the *break-even chart.* Its practical applications have gone beyond just the determination of the break-even point—the volume level at which the income from sales is just sufficient to cover all costs.

Cost-volume-profit analyses are helpful to management in appraising

Illustration 22–1

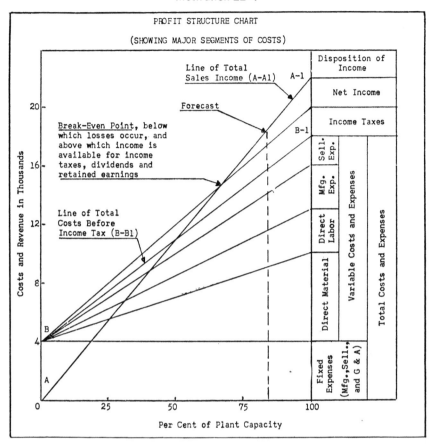

PROFIT STRUCTURE CHART

(SHOWING MAJOR SEGMENTS OF COSTS)

SOURCE: J. D. Willson, Controller of Tidewater Oil Company, *Practical Applications of Cost-Volume-Profit Analysis*, N.A.A. Bulletin.

the effect of changes in selling prices, fixed costs, and variable costs upon the earnings. (See Illustration 22–1.) The break-even chart constitutes a useful starting point for these analyses. The determination of a firm's break-even point supported by related volume, selling price, and cost analyses is an important aid in anticipating and meeting current problems. It involves techniques of assembling, coordinating, and interpreting quantitative production and distribution data to assist management in arriving at informed decisions. It is frequently the responsibility of the top financial executive to derive and summarize such data.

In any study looking toward the determination of the break-even point and other cost and profit facts or probabilities, the starting point is the estimation of costs at various levels of output. Thus, in order to tackle any phase of profit planning, it is necessary to provide for separation between fixed and variable costs through all of the firm's functions.

If flexible budget information is derived periodically and a standard cost or direct cost system is used, such separation has been the basis of these devices; therefore, they serve as a most satisfactory point of departure in developing the current cost information necessary for profit planning. While the controller coordinates and assembles cost and market data, in a large firm the measurement and prediction of probable prices and sales volumes for the firm's products is the primary responsibility of a marketing research department, the sales manager, staff economists, or some combination of these.

Costs, volume, profit, and the break-even point may be expressed graphically and mathematically. Either of these devices may be helpful in communicating the underlying data to management and in explaining the probable effects of alternative proposals. By presenting this information in chart or graphic form, its effectiveness is increased since management is more readily able to grasp the significance of the related quantitative data.

Illustration 22–2

ANY MANUFACTURING COMPANY			
BUDGETED INCOME STATEMENT			
For Year Ended December 31, 19—			
Sales (100,000 @ $20)................................			$2,000,000
Costs:	*Fixed*	*Variable*	
Direct material.................................	0	$ 450,000	
Direct labor.....................................	0	750,000	
Manufacturing overhead........................	$100,000	160,000	
Administrative expenses........................	28,000	73,200	
Selling expenses................................	108,000	90,000	
Total.......................................	$236,000	$1,523,200	1,759,200
Budgeted Net Income............................			$ 240,800
(Capacity production, 140,000 units)			

To illustrate a simple break-even chart, it is assumed that management is budgeting its sales and production costs for the year on an estimated sales volume of 100,000 units of one product. With the related budgetary and unit information as it is given in Illustration 22–2, the break-even point and income at various volume levels are presented.

This information is shown graphically in the charts given in Illustrations 22–3 and 22–4. In these charts, the following procedures are used:

1. The *vertical* scale is expressed in dollars and indicates the fixed and variable costs and revenue.

2. The *horizontal* scale is used to indicate the volume and may be expressed

in terms of dollar volume, volume in units, percentages of capacity, direct labor hours, or some other suitable index of volume.

3. On these two charts, three lines are drawn—one for the *fixed costs,* one for the *variable* costs, and one for the *sales income,* showing these elements for the different volumes. The sequence of these items on the chart may vary. On the *first* chart, the base area is representative of fixed costs and indicated by drawing a line parallel to the base scale, since *fixed* costs are the same regardless of the volume. The *cumulative* effect of adding the *variable* costs to the fixed cost area is now drawn. Finally the *sales income* line must be drawn from the point where there are no sales (zero intersection of horizontal and vertical scales) to the point where there are $2,000,000 in sales. Where the *total cost* (cumulative effect of the fixed and variable costs) and the *sales income* lines intersect, that is the *break-even point* (the volume of sales at which there is neither a profit nor a loss).

On the second chart, the *variable costs* are *first* plotted on the base or horizontal line and then the *fixed costs* are recorded. Since the fixed costs are the same for all volumes of production, this line will be parallel to the variable cost line and will represent the *cumulative total of variable plus fixed costs.*

Illustration 22–3

BREAK-EVEN CHART WITH SALES VOLUME AS BASE

(Fixed Costs Plotted on Base or Horizontal Line)

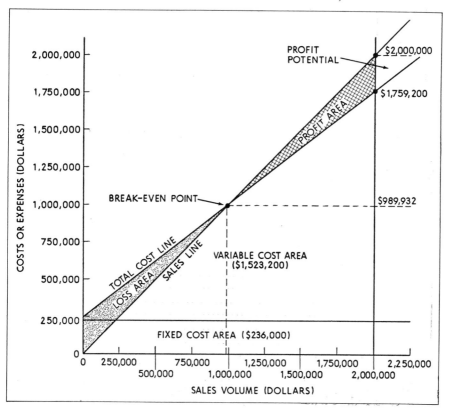

Illustration 22–4

BREAK-EVEN CHART WITH SALES VOLUME AS BASE

(Variable Costs Plotted on Base or Horizontal Line)

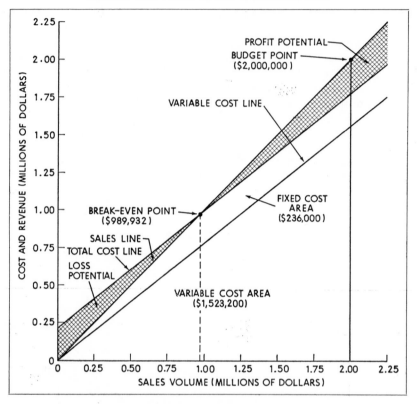

In studying and analyzing the statements and charts, it should be noted that it is necessary to have costs and expenses grouped into *fixed and variable*. If an expense is semivariable, it is separated into its fixed and variable components as previously indicated in this text.

To illustrate the computation of the break-even point on the basis of sales volume, the statement previously used is presented in condensed form, viz:

Sales income (100,000 at $20).................................	$2,000,000	100.00%
Variable costs total...	1,523,200	76.16
Contribution margin...	$ 476,800	23.84%
Fixed costs..	236,000	11.80
Net Income..	$ 240,800	12.04%

Interpreting this information, it is observed that:

1. Out of every $100 of sales, $76.16 is required for variable expenses or costs. If there is no production, these costs will not be incurred.

2. Out of every $100 of sales, $23.84 is left to meet the fixed expenses or costs.

Therefore, to compute the dollar volume of sales necessary to meet the fixed charges, that is, just break even, the fixed charges of $236,000 must be divided by the 23.84 percent, viz: $236,000/0.2384 = $989,932.

This amount, $989,932, represents the amount of sales under the budgeted operating conditions which will result in just breaking even. Any amount of sales above this should produce a profit. However, these conclusions assume that:

1. Any changes in *sales volume* will not affect the price per unit.
2. That *fixed costs* will be the same in total for all volumes.
3. That *variable costs* will all vary in direct proportion to sales volume.

It is possible to construct the break-even chart with the sales line curved to indicate that the price per unit is not necessarily constant at different volume levels. It is also possible to reflect any changes in the fixed cost behavior over the wide range of volume between shutdown and 100 percent of capacity operations by showing appropriate step-up changes in the diagram. Changes in variable cost behavior can be shown by altering the slope of the variable cost line at different volume levels.

If more than one product is included in the sales analysis, then management is faced with the problem of *sales mix*, that is, the volume of each product to be included in the sales total. This problem can be solved satisfactorily by preparing several analyses and charts, assuming different sales mixes for each, thus indicating to management the effect on the break-even point and on net income of promoting or failing to promote the more profitable lines. Management usually needs more than one analysis because of the numerous possible combinations of sales volume and sales mix, the different degrees of variability of costs as the sales volume and mix changes, and the fixed costs of alternative plans are not identical. Break-even analyses and charts must be kept current and not attempt to reflect probable operating circumstances over a period longer than a year because not only the mixture of variable cost and income elements may change but also fixed costs gradually shift over extended periods of time.

A *static* break-even analysis, or one such as in the foregoing illustration that simplifies the actual production and distribution circumstances, has limitations for profit planning which many firms have not always recognized. These limitations arise from four different causes:

1. Inaccuracies in estimating cost behavior for certain costs in certain functions of the firm.

2. Oversimplification of the revenue probabilities as to volume and market price of each product in a multiproduct firm.
3. Dynamic forces outside the firm in the market for materials, supplies, and labor and in productive technology which may cause unanticipated shifts in prices, rates, and productive conditions.
4. The impossibility of anticipating certain specific production and distribution problems which will confront management as the period ahead unfolds and to which management will have to adapt its forecast policy.

Awareness of these causes of limitations in usefulness can lead to improved and extended analysis which may sharpen the interpretation and application of the resulting projections. It must be kept in mind that any single break-even analysis or cost-volume-profit study will only show profit expectations under a single set of assumed conditions— external market conditions and internal management planning.

Illustration 22–5

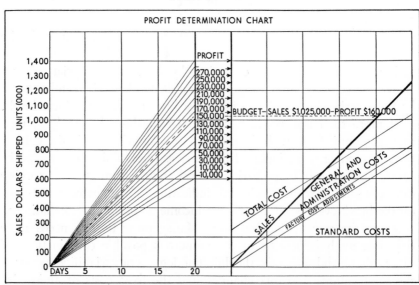

PROFIT DETERMINATION CHART

The righthand half constitutes a break-even chart and identifies budgeted volume and profits. A battery of alternative sales volume lines are plotted on the lefthand half in such a manner that the profit results for the month, implied by volume achieved to any date in the month, can be read from the chart. . .where volume and cost ratios remain relatively constant, some form of this chart can be an indication of performance before the formal reports are prepared.

SOURCE: *N.A.A. Accounting Practice Report No. 9, Reports Which Managements Find Most Useful.*

Various claims have been made concerning the managerial usefulness of break-even analysis. These claims include not only profit planning but also cost control both in the short and long run and assistance in the development of pricing policy. For these purposes, as well as for profit planning, the existence of the foregoing limitations must be taken into account.

Illustration 22–5 sets forth a simple device for within-the-month reference to probable results, a *profit determination chart.*

Deriving Data to Assist Management in Profit Planning   In order to plan effectively, the management of a firm must have some approximate profit goal or goals in mind. Is it striving for a certain rate of return on the investment in the total firm? Is it striving for certain rates of return on investment for each product division? Is it striving to get above-average profits in the coming period when volume is expected to be relatively high? The particular profit goals should be set by those top executives who are responsible for the financial management of the firm.

Management must have some ideas as to various ways to achieve the particular profit goal or goals set for the firm. Some responsible planning group, consisting of executives or representatives from each major function, must be established. Proposals from all functional sources— sales, product design and engineering, production departments, purchasing, etc.—must be considered. These proposals must be discussed by the planning group and those that seem feasible recommended for further study and development. *At this point the top financial executive has the responsibility of taking those proposals recommended for study and showing the probable effects on costs and/or income of each proposal.*

The group participation necessary to develop figures for the various proposals enlists the cooperation of at least the head of each staff and operating function involved. Much the same procedure is followed as that described previously for the development of figures for a flexible budget. If up-to-date flexible budget data are already available, many of the cost figures related to proposals can be derived directly. However, for profit planning it may be necessary to derive additional figures because some of the proposals being considered involve different assumptions as to price, labor rates, manufacturing method, etc., than those upon which the flexible budget figures are based. Through regular budgeting procedures and these special studies for profit-planning purposes, the responsibilities and problems of each function in the business become more familiar to each participant. This usually leads to the type of working relationship that will permit more thorough and more nearly accurate analyses in terms of the effect of a particular proposal upon a specific function.

A more detailed explanation of the typical procedures used in developing the probable revenue and cost effects of proposed changes is given in the following paragraphs.

**Determining
Attainable Volume
and Price Alternatives**
The first step in the development of cost-volume-profit studies and break-even analyses is the determination of the probable *volume levels* at which the firm would operate if certain recommended marketing plans were adopted. The level finally selected as the overall volume goal for the firm, or the levels selected for each individual product line, will be influenced by the general economic condition of the nation and by the characteristics of the particular business and the industry of which it is a member. For example, a business producing necessity items would expect more gradual and less drastic change in its volume than a business producing luxury items. Other basic considerations in deriving and evaluating the validity of volume figures are the degree of market maturity that has been reached for each line of product and the firm's competitive position as compared to the other firms in the industry. With respect to market maturity, it must be determined which of the following stages applies to each line of product to be offered for sale in the coming year:

1. *Low volume:* Customer acceptance of the firm's particular design and quality of product, or for this type of product throughout the industry, is not yet certain.
2. *Expanding volume:* Customer acceptance of the product has been achieved and each firm in the industry producing the product is striving to service that portion of the future potential market which seems to be consistent with sound expansion plans for production and distribution facilities.
3. *Rather stable volume:* The bulk of the customers in the potential market have made their first purchase of the product, and the total demand is now made up partly of new customers and partly of those acquiring replacement units of the product.
4. *Declining volume:* Few new customers in the market, some replacement customers, with suitable substitutes making inroads on volume.

In order to formulate a production volume and price policy, it is also necessary to consider the type of competition that will be encountered by the firm. Three general types of relative competitive position are customarily found. They are:

1. The firm is but one of many suppliers producing for a broad market where the actions of any one of the firms does not have much impact on the total market.
2. The firm is one of several large competitors each having a substantial share of the market, but it is not controlling or leading the market.
3. The firm is in a dominating position in the market where it can at least maintain its large share of the total volume and even set prices for the industry.

Even though a firm understands these basic conditioning circumstances affecting the volume of product it may sell, the task of forecasting product-volume levels for a multiproduct firm is far from simple. In a dynamic and competitive economy, the problem of determining total volume is complicated further by these factors: (1) a live firm is periodically making changes in the quality and design of existing products and the degree of acceptance of these changes varies; (2) any newly developed products are in the trial stage where demand is uncertain; and (3) in order to achieve maximum utilization (least waste) of basic materials, it is constantly seeking to expand the use of existing by-products or to develop marketable by-products. Despite these difficulties *some forecasting must be done;* otherwise, the firm will drift aimlessly without a goal.

In companies not having market research specialists, the president, sales manager, and controller ordinarily are those most frequently called upon to estimate the probable volume levels for each product and in total. In larger organizations the volume levels to be projected are developed by market research specialists and are subsequently reviewed, perhaps modified, and approved by executive management.

The planning group may adopt a final sales budget or may request information on the relative costs and relative profitability of several different volume levels and product mixes. At this point other departments in the organization and the controller begin active work to determine how they would meet the forecasts and what costs would probably be incurred in so doing. First, the production departments should compute the production and time demands on each operation in order to determine the adequacy of present facilities and needs, if any, for new equipment or plant. For the sales department, it may mean more advertising, sales promotion, increased sales personnel and facilities, and expanded territories to increase or maintain sales levels. For research and engineering, it may mean greater activity on development and improvement of new products and helping manufacturing departments improve methods to increase production, reduce down time, and reduce repairs. If new products are involved, the production engineering and purchasing departments will have to work cooperatively in preparing estimates of new material and equipment needs, their availability and cost.

Determining the Costs of Meeting Selected Volume Alternatives The costs of meeting a particular volume level will depend upon and vary with: (1) the product mix; (2) the proposed promotional and distribution plans for securing the volume of each type of product; (3) the way in which manufacturing capacity will be used; (4) the effect of concurrent plans to improve efficiency of men and machines; and (5) the effect of the changing prices of various types of material, of changing rates of various classifications of labor, and of changing costs for replacement, maintenance, and repair of machines. The probable effect of such contemplated or expected changes must be estimated for each type of fixed, semifixed, semivariable, and variable cost in each producing and distribution function of the firm.

In obtaining information on cost behavior which will serve as a point of departure for projecting costs for the coming period, a variety of methods are used. These range from the simplest interpretations of past operating results to intensive cost accounting and engineering studies similar to the methods already discussed which are used in developing each element of cost in establishing flexible budgets.

The most simple, but least exact, approach is to analyze a series of operating statements for that span of recent years which will be useful in projecting coming year experience. Each selected year's sales and corresponding costs are plotted against the sales volume. This provides points on a scatter chart to which straight lines are fitted. The result is two lines representing the basic historical relationship between sales and costs and the resultant profits in relation to volume levels experienced by the company in the past. Refer to Chapter 16 on budgetary control for a detailed illustration of the scatter graph. In order to refine such studies, the effects of price level changes must be removed by appropriate index number techniques to achieve even a fair degree of accuracy. Unfortunately, except for some small single-product concerns, price change is only one of the possible distortions present in this type of analysis. For most concerns changes in plant size and production methods are almost certain to have taken place over the period of years studied. These different conditions of production cannot appropriately be intermingled in an historical analysis without careful adjustment if the objective is to arrive at the volume-cost relationship which exists now and will probably be effective in the year ahead. In spite of these difficulties, this approach has some usefulness where changes in various productive and distributive efforts have not been substantial and when only approximate results are desired.

If the management of the firm needs more nearly accurate information but has not yet adopted the practice of preparing periodic flexible budgets, then it must engage in more detailed analysis of the type which is preliminary to the establishment of a flexible budget. While this procedure has been discussed previously, a brief review of the steps involved will be helpful. A typical starting point is the historical analysis of monthly data over the past year or so when the operating conditions of particular functions have been substantially the same. A study of each specific type of cost is made department by department (or cost center by cost center) in order to determine the existing cost behavior pattern (cost to output relationship) for that type of cost in relation to the activity measure of that department. From this a scatter chart is prepared for each cost element. A linear relationship between the measure of output (activity measure) and the cost element is derived by visual inspection of the pattern or by statistical techniques. With the pattern of each cost in each factory function identified, there has been established a satisfactory point of departure for projecting each element of future cost of production.

Selling and administrative expenses and other nonfactory expenses can likewise be related to levels of product or service activity or sales in order to get an approximate pattern of their change with different levels of volume.

The two foregoing approaches are widely used, but in those situations where up-to-date cost standards and flexible budget data are available, the task of determining costs for different volume alternatives can be done more quickly and accurately. Some of the cost elements may be derived directly from the standards or flexible budget, or these may be readily modified to take into account any changes which are expected to be effective in the period ahead.

Once the detailed quantitative data are derived, they may be used in various combinations to present to management cost-volume-profit and break-even analyses. Before management decides upon a profit plan for the coming year, it will want to know the probable profit results of the several alternatives under consideration. For example, it may want a comparison of these two alternatives:

1. The maintenance of present volume and product mix in the coming year with the effect of various price and wage rate changes on cost elements.
2. The increase of volume to certain forecast volumes for each product line. In addition to taking into account the effect of various price and wage rate changes, this analysis should reflect: (a) the effect on income of any selling price or policy changes, (b) the effect on costs of the changes in nature and extent of promotional effort and other additional distribution services planned to attain the forecast volume, and (c) the effect on costs of production of the change in operating level.

These alternatives are suggestive of just two possible sets of conditions for which management would like to see the effects on cost, volume, and profit carefully analyzed and summarized. Illustrative data and charts for various combinations of changes in selling price, volume, fixed costs, and variable costs are presented later in this chapter.

When certain proposals have been adopted and constitute the profit plan for the coming year, the standards and budgets vital to their development can be used as *control* devices to guide and coordinate management action and to measure performance as the operations of the year take place. Previous chapters on budgetary control and the use of standards have described in detail how this might be accomplished. Carefully prepared cost-volume-profit analyses thus become an indispensable management tool for *profit planning* and *control.*

The Use of Cost-Volume-Profit Analyses by Management

Cost-volume-profit relationships are influenced by five factors or a combination of them. These are the result of changes in (1) *selling prices,* (2) *volume of sales,* (3) *product mix of the sales,* (4) *variable costs per unit,* and (5) *total fixed costs.* The preliminary marketing and cost analysis work provides management personnel with an improved understanding of each of these factors. Different combinations of these factors will be involved in each alternative proposal for profit improvement being considered by management. To permit effective profit planning, management must foresee the part that each of these factors plays, or will play, in changing the net income, the break-even point, and the return on investment for the firm. Carefully developed budgetary figures for income and costs and the graphic portrayal of these in break-even charts are the most effective means of providing the necessary information to management. This enables management to anticipate the effects of proposed actions and of changes in market conditions. The responsible group of executives are then in a position to select those proposals which will contribute most to the profit pattern in the year ahead. This is profit planning.

Before proceeding to the detailed study of the various cost-volume-profit relationships, two terms frequently used in this connection must be examined. These are *marginal income* or the *contribution margin* and *margin of safety* (*M/S*) *ratio.*

The *contribution margin* or *marginal income* is the difference between the *sales income* and the total of *variable costs and expenses.* A statement showing separately the marginal income is today an important management tool used in studying the effect of *changes* in volume (income) of sales. The ratio of the marginal income to sales is known as the *marginal income ratio* or *profit-volume ratio.*

Margin of safety ratio is computed by dividing the difference between the *total sales income* and the *break-even sales point* by the *total sales.* It merely indicates what portion of the sales are available to create profits for the firm.

To illustrate these two definitions more specifically, the following data are used:

Sales (10,000 units × $125).............................	$1,250,000	100%
Variable costs and expenses................................	800,000	64
Marginal income or contribution margin......................	$ 450,000	36%
Fixed costs and expenses....................................	400,000	32
Net Income...	$ 50,000	4%

The *marginal income* is $450,000. The *marginal income ratio* (marginal income to sales) is $450,000/$1,250,000, or 36 percent.

The *margin of safety ratio* is total sales income — break-even sales ÷ total sales income, or more specifically, $1,250,000.00 — $1,111,111.11 ÷ $1,250,000.00. This results in a margin of safety ratio of 11.1 percent, which is rather low. (Break-even sales are computed by dividing 36 percent into $400,000.)

Break-Even Analyses for Changing Conditions

Break-even analysis as previously illustrated represented certain static conditions. It is possible to superimpose on such charts the effect on the break-even point of certain changing conditions which may be expected in the future such as:

1. Increase in variable costs.
2. Decline in sales.

In order to compare the existing situation with a future situation in which there will be increases in variable costs, the first step is the cost analysis necessary to derive the new variable cost figures. Then, the existing income and costs and the projected income and costs can be presented on a break-even chart or charts. It is probably easier for management to see the effect of the change in variable costs if both situations are presented on one chart, as in Illustration 22–6.

To illustrate such a comparative break-even chart when there is a *10 percent* increase in variable costs due to such items as materials, labor, etc., but no change in selling price of product, the following data are assumed:

Sales..	$2,500,000
Fixed costs..	800,000
Variable costs before increase..............................	1,600,000
Variable costs after increase...............................	1,760,000

Break-even point before increase:
  Variable costs of $1,600,000 equals 64% of sales.
  Profit margin is 36%. B.E. point is $800,000 ÷ 36%, or $2,222,222.22.

Break-even point after increase:
  Variable costs of $1,760,000 equals 70.4% of sales.
  Profit margin is 29.6%. B.E. point is $800,000 ÷ 29.6%, or $2,702,702.70.

Illustration 22–6

BREAK-EVEN CHART FOR CHANGING CONDITIONS

Increase in Variable Costs—Selling Price and Fixed Costs Do Not Change

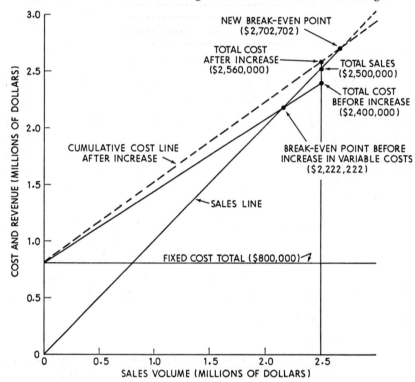

This is presented graphically in Illustration 22–6. A similar procedure may be followed in presenting the data when a decline in sales is anticipated or a change is expected in any of the other factors affecting cost, volume, and profit.

Cost-Volume-Profit Analysis for Plant Expansion

If a plant is operating at full capacity and management is confronted with the problem of meeting a substantial increase in demand for the product, a choice must be made between overtime, extra shift operation, and plant expansion. This may involve the entire plant or only those departments in which production bottlenecks are serious.

Overtime and extra shift operation will result in better utilization of existing plant and equipment facilities and some reduction in fixed overhead costs per unit of production. Offsetting this saving there will be certain increases in labor costs on overtime and extra shift operation. Because of time and a half and shift differential premiums on wages, the out-of-pocket unit costs for direct labor will be higher. This effect is far-reaching and includes the indirect labor involved in the job or process being operated and the various types of service and maintenance labor supporting the operation, to the extent that overtime or extra shift work is required in these areas. In addition, certain factors tending to lower efficiency may be involved, such as worker fatigue on overtime work or the lower productive skill of the employees added for extra shifts. If all of the departmental equipment is not operated and less than a full staff of direct labor is used, such additional time operation may involve disproportionate supervision, materials handling, timekeeping, and other types of indirect labor costs both within and without the departments operating additional time. The advisability of using these methods of producing additional volume will depend on the relationship of the reduction in fixed cost per unit to the extra cost per unit incurred for certain labor and service costs.

Plant expansion is an alternative means of obtaining the increased volume to meet a demand which is taxing plant facilities. It involves long-term investments in additions to building and equipment and additional periodic outlays for maintenance, taxes, and insurance that are of a fixed nature. It will be considered by management if the outlook is for rising demand over an extended future period with little possibility of severe demand cutbacks to below the present level. Only with sustained utilization of the additional facilities will it be possible to maintain or improve production efficiency and to match or reduce production cost per unit.

To illustrate the effect of plant expansion, the following data are used:

Present plant facilities (assumed to be 100 percent capacity) result in—

Sales	$2,500,000
Fixed costs	400,000
Variable costs	1,600,000

Proposed increase of plant facilities will increase production 25 percent and fixed charges by $150,000.

Using this information it is possible to compute the break-even points before and after expansion and then plot them in the graph.

At 100% plant capacity:
Variable costs are $1,600,000, or 64% of sales.
Profit margin is 36%.
Break-even sales point is $400,000 ÷ 36%, or $1,111,111.11.
When present plant facilities are increased 25%:
It is assumed that variable costs will remain at same ratio to sales, namely, 64%.
Profit margin is still 36%.
Break-even sales point is $550,000 ÷ 36%, or $1,527,777.77.

Illustration 22–7

BREAK-EVEN CHART WHEN PLANT FACILITIES ARE INCREASED

(Fixed Charges Are Increased; Other Costs and Income Do Not Change)

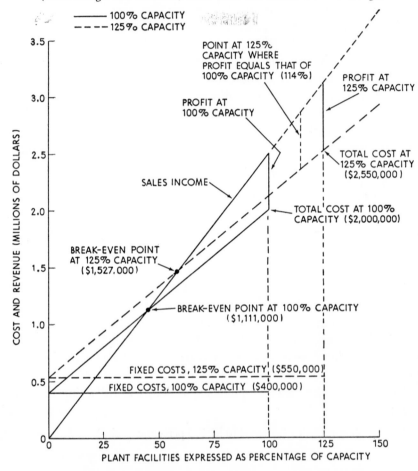

On the respective graphs (Illustration 22–7) it is possible to compute, by measuring the vertical distance between the total cost line and the sales line in the profit area, the sales volume that will produce a certain desired profit.

In developing this graph, the same procedure was followed as in the previous illustrations, with the fixed costs forming the base to which the variable costs are added to obtain the line showing the total costs. The dotted line represents the break-even data for the increase in plant and equipment. To determine at what point the new plant capacity will create the same amount of profit as is presently being produced, the sales line and the total cost lines for the proposed 125 percent plant facility operations must be extended until the vertical distance between them on the graph equals $500,000. This point will be approximately at 114 percent.

In the illustration presented, it was assumed that the variable costs would continue at the same rate of variability as in the original plant and that the rate of gross profit and sales mix would also continue uniformly as before. This may not be so. The added plant facilities might permit increased labor efficiency so that the variable cost per unit would change for the added production. Other modifications might also result from the added facilities. However, this should not change the importance of the break-even analysis to management. It merely means additional cost analysis and the preparation of two separate, almost independent, charts on the same sheet of graph paper, or separately, taking into account the changed conditions at the two different operating levels. It must be remembered and emphasized that since conditions in manufacturing and distribution are not static in a particular business for any length of time, break-even charts should only be used to project operating results for a short period of time, usually not exceeding one year.

Cost-Volume-Profit Analysis in Evaluating Selling Price Changes

In the next two illustrations, the following basic information is assumed as having been budgeted for the next 12 months and is used in projecting the probable cost-volume-profit relationships should certain changes in prices, volume of sales, variable costs, and/or fixed costs take place:

Estimated sales volume, 1,000,000 units @ $8.00	$8,000,000
Less: Variable costs, 1,000,000 units @ 4.80	4,800,000
Marginal income or contribution margin	$3,200,000
Less: Fixed costs	2,500,000
Net Income	$ 700,000

On the basis of these figures, the following ratios and figures may be computed:

Marginal income ratio ($700,000 + $2,500,000) ÷ $8,000,000 = 40%.
Net income ratio ($700,000 ÷ $8,000,000) 8.75%
Break-even sales point ($2,500,000 ÷ 40%) $6,250,000

In order to present the effect of selling price changes on net income and the break-even point, it is assumed that management wishes to examine the probable effect of the various price and volume conditions raised in the following questions:

1. If prices were increased 15 percent and there was no change in the physical volume of sales, what would be the effect on profit and the break-even point?

Illustration 22–8

COST-VOLUME-PROFIT ANALYSIS FOR CERTAIN VOLUME AND SALES PRICE CHANGES

	On Chart, See Line Indicated	Budgeted Figures Sales of 1,000,000 Units @ $8.00	No Change in Volume		Prices Decreased 25% Volume Increased 20%	Prices Increased 15% Volume Decreased 10%
			Prices Increased 15%	Prices Decreased 20%		
Sales:						
1,000,000 units @ $8.00..........	A	$8,000,000				
1,000,000 units @ 9.20..........	B		$9,200,000			
1,000,000 units @ 6.40..........	C			$ 6,400,000		
1,200,000 units @ 6.00..........	D				$ 7,200,000	
900,000 units @ 9.20..........	E					$8,280,000
Sales as projected.........		$8,000,000	$9,200,000	$ 6,400,000	$ 7,200,000	$8,280,000
Variable costs:						
1,000,000 units @ $4.80.........		4,800,000	4,800,000	4,800,000		
1,200,000 units @ 4.80.........					5,760,000	
900,000 units @ 4.80.........						4,320,000
Marginal income or contribution margin.......		$3,200,000	$4,400,000	$ 1,600,000	$ 1,440,000	$3,960,000
Fixed costs.......		2,500,000	2,500,000	2,500,000	2,500,000	2,500,000
Net Income.......		$ 700,000	$1,900,000			$1,460,000
Net Loss.......				($ 900,000)	($ 1,060,000)	
Management's analysis:						
Net income ratio (net income ÷ sales)...........		8.75%	20.65%	(14.06%)	(14.72%)	17.63%
Percentage change in net income (budgeted figures equals 100%)...........		.....	+271%	−229%	−251%	+209%
Marginal income ratio (marginal income ÷ sales)......		40%	47.8%	25%	20%	47.8%
Break-even sales point (fixed costs ÷ P/V ratio)........		$6,250,000	$5,230,000*	$10,000,000	$12,500,000	$5,230,000*

* Approximate computation.

( ) loss.

2. If prices were increased 15 percent and the volume of sales decreased 10 percent, what would be the effect on profit and the break-even point?
3. If prices were decreased 20 percent and there was no change in the physical volume of sales, what would be the effect on income and the break-even point?
4. If prices were decreased 25 percent and the volume of sales increased 20 percent, what would be the effect on income and the break-even point?

The comparative analysis presented in statement form in Illustration 22–8 and graphically in Illustration 22–9 shows the results of the several volume and price alternatives.

Illustration 22–9

PROFIT/VOLUME RELATIONSHIPS IF VOLUME AND SALES PRICES CHANGE

(Statement on Page 684)

Intersection of Sales Line with Horizontal (Zero) Line Is the Break-Even Point of Sales

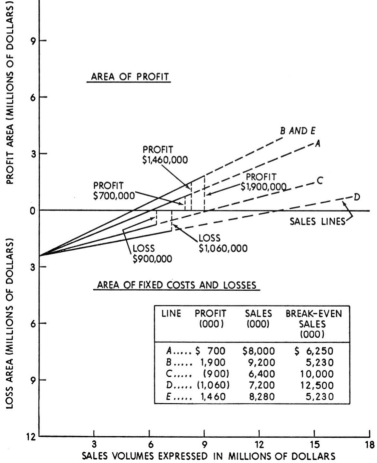

LINE	PROFIT (000)	SALES (000)	BREAK-EVEN SALES (000)
A.....	$ 700	$8,000	$ 6,250
B.....	1,900	9,200	5,230
C.....	(900)	6,400	10,000
D.....	(1,060)	7,200	12,500
E.....	1,460	8,280	5,230

SALES VOLUMES EXPRESSED IN MILLIONS OF DOLLARS

The analysis assumes that variable cost per unit remains constant, that total fixed costs will not change, and that there is no change in the sales mix. Should any of these assumptions have to be modified to conform more closely to expected conditions, then different analyses would have to be prepared. Should any of these assumed conditions not remain the same, then further adjustments of the figures will be necessary. Interpreting this statement on the basis of the foregoing assumptions, it should be noted that:

1. *Increasing* prices 15 percent, with no change in volume, will result in a 271 percent increase in the total amount of profit, with a return of 20.65 percent net profit on the sales instead of the budgeted figure of 8.75 percent. On the other hand, if it is necessary to *reduce* prices 20 percent to meet competition and still maintain the present sales volume, then the firm will suffer a loss of 14.06 percent on sales. To *break even* when prices are increased 15 percent, sales total will have to be only $5,230,000. But if prices are decreased 20 percent, the firm will not break even unless the total sales equal $10,000,000.
2. As the marginal income ratio increases, the break-even point of sales decreases, and vice versa.

Cost-Volume-Profit Analysis in Evaluating a Combination of Changes

Increases in variable cost per unit may be anticipated because of new wage agreements or because the price of materials is increasing; decreases in variable costs may occur because of expected gains in labor efficiency or lower unit prices of materials. Gains in labor efficiency may be expected due to methods study and improvement, increased mechanization, employee training programs, or the effect of incentive systems. Lower material prices may be made possible by changing market conditions or purchasing in more economical lots. Selling price reductions may be initiated by a firm when decreased variable costs per unit permit such an adjustment or to secure additional volume which will utilize available capacity more effectively. Also, selling price reductions may be forced by competitors, even though the variable costs of an individual firm may be rising. Substantial decreases in selling price will usually result in expanded sales both for the individual firm and throughout the particular industry in which the firm is operating.

The effect on income and the break-even point of a firm of various combinations of the foregoing conditions may be shown in statement and chart form. The comparative analysis statement (Illustration 22–10) and the related chart (Illustration 22–11) depict the results if the following sets of conditions are anticipated:

1. Variable costs decrease 10 percent, selling price per unit remains the same, and volume increases 20 percent;

Illustration 22-10

COST-VOLUME-PROFIT RELATIONSHIPS RESULTING IF VOLUMES, SALES PRICES, AND VARIABLE COSTS ARE CHANGED

	Budgeted Figures of Sales of 1,000,000 Units @ $8.00	SALES VOLUME INCREASES OF 20% — Variable Costs Decreased 10% — No Change in Sales Price per Unit	SALES VOLUME INCREASES OF 20% — Variable Costs Decreased 10% — Sales Price per Unit Decreased 8%	SALES VOLUME INCREASES OF 20% — Variable Costs Increased 5% — No Change in Sales Price per Unit	SALES VOLUME INCREASES OF 20% — Variable Costs Increased 5% — Sales Price per Unit Decreased 15%	VOLUME DOWN 25% — Variable Costs Increased 5% — Sales Price per Unit Increased 10%
Sales:						
1,000,000 @ $8.00	$8,000,000					
1,200,000 @ 8.00		$9,600,000		$9,600,000		
1,200,000 @ 7.36			$8,832,000			
1,200,000 @ 6.80					$8,160,000	
750,000 @ 8.80						$6,600,000
Sales income as projected	$8,000,000	$9,600,000	$8,832,000	$9,600,000	$8,160,000	$6,600,000
Variable costs:						
1,000,000 @ $4.80	4,800,000					
1,200,000 @ 4.32		5,184,000	5,184,000			
1,200,000 @ 5.04				6,048,000	6,048,000	
750,000 @ 5.28						3,960,000
Marginal income or contribution margin	$3,200,000	$4,416,000	$3,648,000	$3,552,000	$2,112,000	$2,640,000
Fixed Costs	2,500,000	2,500,000	2,500,000	2,500,000	2,500,000	2,500,000
Net Income	$ 700,000	$1,916,000	$1,148,000	$1,052,000	($ 388,000)	$ 140,000
Management's analysis:						
Net income ratio (net income ÷ sales)	8.75%	19.96%	13.00%	10.96%	(4.75%)	2.1%
Percentage change in net income (budgeted figure equals 100%)	......	+274%	+164%	+150%	−155%	−80%
Marginal income ratio (marginal income ÷ sales)	40%	46%	41.3%	37%	25.9%	40%
Break-even sales amount (fixed cost ÷ P/V ratio)	$6,250,000	$5,435,000*	$6,053,000*	$6,756,000*	$9,652,000*	$6,250,000

* Approximate computation.

( )Loss.

Illustration 22–11

COST-VOLUME-PROFIT RELATIONSHIPS SHOWN GRAPHICALLY WITH
VARIOUS COMBINATIONS OF VOLUME, SELLING PRICES, AND
VARIABLE COSTS

Intersection of the Sales Line with the Horizontal (Zero) Line
Is the Break-Even Point of Sales

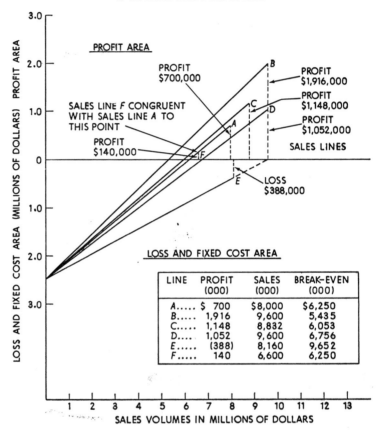

LINE	PROFIT (000)	SALES (000)	BREAK-EVEN (000)
A.....	$ 700	$8,000	$6,250
B.....	1,916	9,600	5,435
C.....	1,148	8,832	6,053
D.....	1,052	9,600	6,756
E.....	(388)	8,160	9,652
F.....	140	6,600	6,250

SALES VOLUMES IN MILLIONS OF DOLLARS

2. Variable costs decrease 10 percent, selling price reduced 8 percent, and
volume increases 20 percent;

3. Variable costs increase 5 percent, selling price remains the same, and
volume increases 20 percent;

4. Variable costs increase 5 percent, selling price reduced 15 percent, and
volume increases 20 percent; and

5. Variable costs increase 5 percent, selling price raised 10 percent per
unit with a volume decrease of 25 percent.

The results of these various sets of conditions may be summarized as
follows:

1. (See Sales Line B.) If it is possible to decrease variable unit costs by 10
percent and volume will expand 20 percent without added marketing
effort or price concessions, the net profit rate will jump to 19.96 percent

on sales. The decrease in variable costs combines with better utilization of existing facilities to make this possible.

2. (See Sales Line C.) A decrease in variable unit costs of 10 percent makes possible a price reduction of 8 percent. With this price reduction the firm will be able to secure more readily a volume increase of 20 percent. This will produce a profit of $1,148,000, at a rate of 13 percent on sales.

3. If it is possible to increase sales volume 20 percent without any change in selling price or shifts in promotional effort, it will be possible to increase the rate of net profit to 10.96 percent despite a variable cost increase perhaps due to overtime or other causes.

4. If competitive pressures are likely to force a decline in unit selling price of 15 percent, the additional volume will result in a net loss. This firm with its present cost structure needs to secure a price of about $7.20 to cover variable cost per unit and the approximate fixed cost per unit at the anticipated level. Certain increases in variable costs incurred to produce the additional volume cause the loss to be $388,000.

5. If variable costs per unit will increase 5 percent due to new wage agreements or rising material prices, management may consider a price increase. If study shows that this will reduce volume by 25 percent, a profit of only $140,000, 2.1 percent of sales, will result.

If substantial changes in fixed costs are involved in any alternatives, then additional cost analysis would be necessary and separate charts would have to be prepared.

The trend of sales for individual products or the review of marketing plans by management may make a change in product mix likely. With cost of production data classified by types of product and shown on a direct costing basis, it is possible to determine those products which contribute most to the recovery of overhead and to the total profit of the business. Additional analyses and charts can be prepared to show the effect of planned shifts in product mix and volume with the related changes in variable unit costs and some fixed costs.

C-V-P Analysis in Evaluating Feasible Profit Plans

In order to present an analysis involving a large number of changes, the following basic facts and circumstances are assumed for a hypothetical firm:

Estimated sales volume, 800,000 units at $10	$8,000,000	100%
Less: Variable costs, 800,000 units at 4	3,200,000	40
Marginal income	$4,800,000	60%
Less: Fixed costs	3,800,000	47½
Net Income	$1,000,000	12½%

The firm has been experiencing a gradual increase in sales and is now operating at almost full capacity. The trend in sales volume is expected to continue. Management also recognizes the fact that the total demand for the type of product being sold is only partially satisfied and that several of its competitors also have substantial shares of the market. Management is trying to decide whether to continue its present policy of gradual growth and maintenance of its share of the market or to take a course involving more risk, that is, try to seize competitive leadership in price and volume.

In determining its objective for the coming year, the basic budget is used to assist in projecting the two plans which seem most feasible.

Alternative No. 1: This involves the following modifications of the budgeted facts:

Volume would increase 5 percent as it has in recent years with prices maintained at present levels.

Variable costs per unit would increase 5 percent.

Fixed costs would increase 2 percent.

In order to meet the normal growth in demand, the company expects to operate a half-day overtime on Saturday during part of the year. This will cause certain increases in variable labor and service costs and a slight increase in fixed costs.

Alternative No. 2: This involves the following modifications of the budgeted facts:

Prices would be decreased 10 percent.

Volume would increase 20 percent.

Variable costs per unit would decrease 5 percent.

Fixed costs would increase 8 percent.

In order to seize competitive leadership, the company would decrease prices 10 percent. The expectation is that this will result primarily in expanding total demand for the type of product, since competitors will probably react with their own price concessions. Yet management also expects to achieve good customer relations by initiating the price reductions and to obtain a small share of volume from its competitors by being the first to reduce prices. Some improvements to existing facilities and some additions of modern equipment are planned to meet the substantial increase in volume. These changes will increase fixed costs. Small savings from larger purchases of materials and from increased processing efficiency are expected to decrease variable costs per unit.

The cost-volume-profit analysis comparing the probable results of these two alternatives is shown in Illustration 22–12.

From a cost and income standpoint the first alternative produces more favorable results for the year ahead. Since its assumed conditions involve less departure from experienced sales trends and from known cost patterns, the projected figures should be very reliable. The second alternative, involving some expansion, raises the break-even point, but with the assumed volume still provides a fairly good profit. However, if there should be only a 10 percent increase in volume, instead of the 20 percent shown in the analysis, the firm would find its profits reduced almost one half, to $472,000.

Illustration 22-12

COST-VOLUME-PROFIT RELATIONSHIPS RESULTING FROM POSSIBLE CHANGES IN
SALES VOLUMES, SALES PRICES, VARIABLE COSTS, AND FIXED COSTS

	Budgeted Figures	Situation No. 1	Situation No. 2
Sales:			
800,000 @ $10.00	$8,000,000		
960,000 @ 9.00			$8,640,000
840,000 @ 10.00		$8,400,000	
Variable costs:			
800,000 @ $4.00	3,200,000		
960,000 @ 3.80			3,648,000
840,000 @ 4.20		3,528,000	
Marginal income	$4,800,000	$4,872,000	$4,992,000
Fixed costs	3,800,000		
Plus 8%			4,104,000
Plus 2%		3,876,000	
Net Income	$1,000,000	$ 996,000	$ 888,000
Net income ratio (sales ÷ profit)	12½%	11.9%	10.3%
Percentage change in net income (budget equals 100%)		−0.4%	−11.2%
Marginal income ratio (marginal income ÷ sales)	60%	58.0%	57.8%
Break-even sales (fixed costs ÷ P/V ratio)	$6,333,000	$6,683,000	$7,100,000

Before accepting the first alternative as the basis for its profit plan for the coming year, management needs to examine all relevant circumstances. This is especially important since the firm and industry expect substantial steady growth. Questions such as the following need to be studied and their answers evaluated:

1. How soon would expansion be advisable if it is not undertaken this year?
2. Could a small amount of expansion for the coming year be done economically and be coordinated with the basic long-range plans for expansion?
3. Can competitive leadership be maintained, or will the reactions of competitors leave the firm in approximately the same relative position?
4. Are there any indications that competitors are making plans to grab the initiative?

When these and possibly other significant noncost factors have been reviewed, then management must make the decision which it believes will produce satisfactory profits in the year ahead and be most beneficial in the long run.

QUESTIONS FOR REVIEW

1. "This relationship of COST-VOLUME-PROFIT, frequently abbreviated to C-V-P, means that accounting must play a vital role in the planning function

because management must have adequate data to properly appraise the probable effects of tomorrow's profit opportunities." Explain.

2. What relationship exists, if any, between an income statement prepared under the concept of direct costing and a break-even chart?

3. What assumptions are made when a break-even chart is constructed?

4. "Various claims have been made concerning the managerial usefulness of break-even analysis." What are some of these?

5. What is a "scatter chart"? How can this chart be useful in cost-volume-profit analysis?

6. What is the "margin of safety ratio"? How is this ratio useful to management?

7. What is the effect on the break-even point when there is an increase in fixed costs? In variable costs?

8. "Knowing the break-even point is the most useful piece of information that I as a manager can have. . . ." Discuss.

(Questions 9 and 10 have been adapted from an AICPA Uniform Examination:)

9. After reading an article you recommended on cost behavior, your client asks you to explain the following excerpts from it:

(1) *"Fixed costs* are variable per unit of output and *variable costs* are fixed per unit of output (though in the long run all costs are variable)."

(2) *"Depreciation* may be either a fixed cost or a variable cost, depending on the method used to compute it."

Required: For each excerpt:

a) Define the *italicized* terms. Give examples where appropriate.

b) Explain the meaning of the excerpt to your client.

10. A break-even chart, as illustrated below, is a useful technique for showing relationships between costs, volume, and profits.

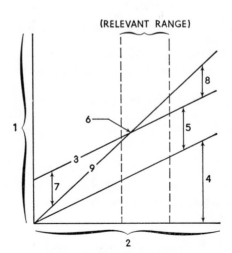

(RELEVANT RANGE)

Required: Identify the numbered components of the break-even chart. Discuss the significance of the concept *relevant range* to break-even analysis.

PROBLEMS—GROUP A

Problem 22–1.   Purpose: *Break-Even Analysis*

A cost analysis was performed by the Harold Vending Machine Company with the following results:

1. For each $10 sales, variable costs of goods amounted to $6.
2. Fixed costs averaged about $80,000 per year.
3. The average investment amounted to $200,000.

Required:

a) Compute the break-even point.

b) What must sales be if the company wants to earn 10 percent return on its investment?

c) Suppose fixed costs increase 10 percent. What is the new break-even point? What must sales be if the company wants to earn 10 percent on its investment?

d) Suppose variable costs rise from $6 per $10 sales to $8. What is the new break-even point? What must sales be if the company wants to earn 10 percent in its investment? (Disregard [*c*].)

e) Suppose total fixed costs increase $10. By how much do sales have to rise so that there is no change in net profit? Disregard (*b*), (*c*), and (*d*).

f) Suppose total variable costs increase $10. By how much do sales have to rise so that there is no change in total profit? Disregard (*b*), (*c*), (*d*), and (*e*).

Problem 22–2.   Purpose: *Cost-Volume-Profit Relationships*

The following information has been made available by management of the Hendrix Manufacturing Company:

	1967	1968	1969
Sales..	$420,000	$460,000	$520,000
Cost of sales..................................	300,000	320,000	350,000
Gross margin.................................	$120,000	$140,000	$170,000
Selling and general expenses..................	50,000	58,000	70,000
Operating margin.............................	$ 70,000	$ 82,000	$100,000

There were no increases or decreases in prices or unit costs.

Required:

a) Compute the fixed costs for Hendrix.

b) Compute the break-even point for the company.

c) Suppose federal and state income taxes amount to 50 percent. What sales volume must be realized to earn $80,000 after taxes?

d) Compute the break-even point under the assumption that sales prices increase 5 percent.

Problem 22–3.   Purpose: *Cost-Volume-Profit Relationships and Direct Costing*

Flear Company has a maximum productive capacity of 210,000 units per year. Normal capacity is regarded as 180,000 units per year. Standard variable manufacturing costs are $11 per unit. Fixed factory overhead is $360,000 per year. Variable selling expenses are $3 per unit, and fixed selling expenses are $252,000 per year. The unit sales price is $20.

The operating results for 1968 are: sales, 150,000 units; production, 160,000 units; beginning inventory, 10,000 units; and net unfavorable variance for standard variable manufacturing costs, $40,000. All variances are written off as additions to (or deductions from) standard cost of sales.

Required:

(For items [a], [b], and [c] assume no variances from standards for manufacturing costs.)

a) What is the break-even point expressed in dollar sales?

b) How many units must be sold to earn a net income of $60,000 per year?

c) How many units must be sold to earn a net income of 10 percent on sales?

d) Prepare formal income statements for 1968 under:

(1) Conventional costing.

(2) Direct costing.

e) Briefly account for the difference in net income between the two income statements.

(Adapted from an AICPA Uniform Examination)

Problem 22–4. Purpose: *Computation of Profit-Volume Relationships if Prices Increase or Decrease and the Volume Is Affected; Computation of Break-Even Points*

The *normal operations* of the Hinoflex Supply Company were as follows for the current year:

HINOFLEX SUPPLY COMPANY

INCOME STATEMENT

For Year Ended December 31, 19—

Sales: 200,000 units @ $2.50	$500,000
Variable costs of sales: $1.25 each for 200,000 units	250,000
Marginal income	$250,000
Fixed costs of sales	160,000
Net Income for Year	$ 90,000

Management is desirous of learning the effect on profit of a change in volume due to price changes. It is estimated that the following conditions might arise and cause the following changes in volumes and profits:

1. A 10 percent decrease in price will result in a 15 percent increase in volume of sales.

2. A 10 percent increase in price will result in a 20 percent decrease in volume of sales.

3. A 20 percent decrease in price will result in a 30 percent increase in volume of sales.

4. A 20 percent increase in price will result in a 50 percent decrease in volume of sales.

The plant is presently operating at 60 percent capacity so that it could use an increase in volume of production. If plant operations were to increase 20,000 units, fixed costs might be increased $12,000; if plant operations were increased 40,000 units, fixed costs might increase $15,000; if plant operations were increased 60,000 units, fixed costs might increase $21,000.

Prepare a comparative statement showing the effect on the net profit for each of the four situations described above. Indicate in each case the break-even sales point, percentage of change in net profit, and profit-volume ratio.

Problem 22–5.   Purpose: *Decisions Based on Cost-Volume-Profit Relationships*

The management of the Hay Cottonseed Company has engaged you to assist in the development of information to be used for managerial decisions.

The company has the capacity to process 20,000 tons of cottonseed per year. The yield of a ton of cottonseed is as follows:

	Average Yield per Ton of Cottonseed	Average Selling Price per Trade Unit
Oil	300 lbs.	$ 0.15 per lb.
Meal	600	50.00 per ton
Hulls	800	20.00 per ton
Lint	100	3.00 per cwt.
Waste	200	

A special marketing study revealed that the company can expect to sell its entire output for the coming year at the listed average selling prices.

You have determined the company's costs to be as follows:

Processing costs:
  Variable: $9 per ton of cottonseed put into process.
  Fixed: $108,000 per year.
Marketing costs:
  All variable: $20 per ton sold.
Administrative costs:
  All fixed: $90,000 per year.

From the above information, you prepared and submitted to management a detailed report on the company's break-even point. In view of conditions in the cottonseed market, management told you that they would also like to know the average maximum amount that the company can afford to pay for a ton of cottonseed.

Management has defined the average maximum amount that the company can afford to pay for a ton of cottonseed as the amount that would result in the company's having losses no greater when operating than when closed down under the existing cost and revenue structure. Management states that you are to assume that the fixed costs shown in your break-even point report will continue unchanged even when the operations are shut down.

Required:

a) Compute the average maximum amount that the company can afford to pay for a ton of cottonseed.

b) You also plan to mention to management the factors, other than the costs that entered into your computation, that they should consider in deciding whether to shut down the plant. Discuss these additional factors.

c) The stockholders consider the minimum satisfactory return on their investment in the business to be 25 percent before corporate income taxes. The stockholders' equity in the company is $968,000. Compute the maximum average amount that the company can pay for a ton of cottonseed to realize the minimum satisfactory return on the stockholders' investment in the business.

(Adapted from an AICPA Uniform Examination)

PROBLEMS—GROUP B

Problem 22–6. Purpose: *Break-Even Analysis*

The Richardson Company manufactures and sells a product known as "rics." The following data are also available:

> Current sales volume, 500,000 units per month.
> Sales price, $1 per unit.
> Variable expenses and costs, 70 cents per unit.
> Fixed expenses and costs, $1,000,000 per year.
> Average annual investment, $3,000,000.

Required:

a) What is the present total profit for a year?

b) What is the present break-even point in units and dollars?

c) How many units must be sold if the company wants to earn 15 percent on its investment?

d) Fixed costs rise by 10 percent. What is the new break-even point? How many units must be sold if the company wants to earn 10 percent on its investment?

e) Ignore (*d*) and assume variable costs rise from 70 cents to 75 cents per unit. What is the new break-even point? How many units must be sold if the company wants to earn 10 percent on its investment?

Problem 22–7. Purpose: *Cost-Volume-Profit Relationships and Direct Costing*

The following information was derived from the records of the Reginald Manufacturing Company:

Budgeted level of production at normal capacity............	84,000 units
Factory overhead—fixed................................	$144,000
Fixed selling and administrative expenses.................	$108,000
Selling price per unit....................................	$8.00
Variable production cost per unit........................	$4.00
Variable selling costs per unit..........................	$1.00
Actual production for the year..........................	64,000 units
Sales...	60,000 units
Beginning inventory.....................................	4,000 units
Net variances from standard variable manufacturing costs....$16,000	unfavorable

Required:

(For [*a*], [*b*], and [*c*] assume no variances from standards for manufacturing costs.)

a) What is the break-even point expressed in dollars and units?

b) What must the sales volume be to earn $24,000 per year?

c) How many units must be sold to earn a net income of 15 percent on sales?

d) Prepare income statements for the year under direct costing and under absorption costing.

Problem 22–8. Purpose: *Cost-Volume Relationships*

The Rich Mining Company mines selum, a commonly used mineral. Following is the company's report of operations:

THE RICH MINING COMPANY

Report of Operations

For the Years Ended December 31, 1969, and 1968

	1969	1968	Increase (Decrease)
Net sales...............................	$891,000	$ 840,000	$ 51,000
Cost of goods sold............................	688,500	945,000	(256,500)
Gross profit (loss)............................	$202,500	$(105,000)	$ 307,500

The following information pertains to the company's operations:
1. The sales price of selum was increased from $8 per ton to $11 per ton on January 1, 1969.
2. New mining machinery was placed in operation on January 1, 1969, which reduced the cost of mining from $9 per ton to $8.50 per ton.
3. There was no change in ending inventories which were valued on the LIFO basis.

Required:

Prepare an analysis accounting for the change in the gross profit of The Rich Mining Company. The analysis should account for the effects of the changes in price, volume, and volume-price factors upon (1) sales and (2) cost of goods sold.

(Adapted from an AICPA Uniform Examination)

Problem 22–9. Purpose: *Computation of the Profit-Volume Relationships if Prices Decrease and the Volume Increases; Computation of Break-Even Points*

The Rhone Manufacturing and Supply Company is presently operating at 60 percent capacity and thus producing 120,000 units of the single product it sells, at a unit price of $6 each.

For the current year, the results have been as follows:

RHONE MANUFACTURING AND SUPPLY COMPANY

Income Statement

For Year Ended December 31, 19—

		Fixed	Variable	
Sales: 120,000 units @ $6.................................				$720,000
Cost of sales:				
Direct materials...			$120,000	
Direct labor...			240,000	
Variable overhead.......................................			60,000	
Fixed overhead...		$90,000		
Total...		$90,000	$420,000	510,000
Gross profit on sales......................................				$210,000

Selling and administrative costs:

Fixed..	$ 48,000	
Variable..	24,000	
Total...		72,000
Net Income...		$138,000

It was felt that if the prices per unit could be reduced 20 percent, the sales would increase to 185,000 units, with only a $3,000 increase in the so-called fixed overhead costs.

If prices could be reduced as much as 25 percent, sales would reach 195,000 units, with an increase in the so-called fixed overhead costs of only $4,000.

On the basis of this information you are asked to prepare comparative statements showing the net income under the new profit-volume relationships. Also indicate in each case the break-even sales point.

Problem 22–10.   Purpose: *Decisions Based on Cost-Volume-Profit Relationships*

The president of Ryan Corporation, which manufactures tape decks and sells them to producers of sound reproduction systems, anticipates a 10 percent wage increase on January 1 of next year to the manufacturing employees (variable labor). He expects no other changes in costs. Overhead will not change as a result of the wage increase. The president has asked you to assist him in developing the information he needs to formulate a reasonable product strategy for next year.

You are satisfied by regression analysis that volume is the primary factor affecting costs and have separated the semivariable costs into their fixed and variable segments by means of the least-squares criterion. You also observe that the beginning and ending inventories are never materially different.

Below are the current year data assembled for your analysis:

Current selling price per unit.........................	$ 80	
Variable cost per unit:		
Material..	$30	
Labor..	12	
Overhead......................................	6	
Total..	$ 48	
Annual volume of sales............................	5,000 units	
Fixed costs.....................................	$51,000	

Required:

Provide the following information for the president using cost-volume-profit analysis:

a) What increase in the selling price is necessary to cover the 10 percent wage increase and still maintain the current profit-volume-cost ratio?

b) How many tape decks must be sold to maintain the current net income if the sales price remains at $80 and the 10 percent wage increase goes into effect?

c) The president believes that an additional $190,000 of machinery (to be depreciated at 10 percent annually) will increase present capacity (5,300 units) by 30 percent. If all tape decks produced can be sold at the present price and the wage increase goes into effect, how would the estimated net income before capacity is increased compare with the estimated net income after capacity is increased? Prepare computations of estimated net income *before* and *after* the expansion.

(Adapted from AICPA Uniform Examination)

CHAPTER

23 : Cost Analyses for Special Purposes

Management Needs Cost Information for Different Purposes   The numerous responsibilities of management require frequent reference to detailed quantitative information, much of which can be provided by an effective cost accounting system. Thus, from the viewpoint of management, a cost system becomes one of the chief facilitating devices in the direction and control of the enterprise. It is unfortunate that much too frequently costs are designed primarily for financial statement presentation and are woefully inadequate when used as the basis for deciding alternative courses of action. Fortunately, this has been changing in recent years.

In preceding chapters it has been shown that historical cost information can provide certain types of usefulness—support for financial and operating statements, measurement of cost performance for each functional subunit of the firm, and data to assist in cost control. Through proper functionalization and detailed classification it has been shown that each type of cost can be studied in relation to a productivity measure appropriate to its function in order to derive a reasonably accurate pattern of behavior for the cost. This serves as the point of departure for establishing the probable amount of this type of cost in the year ahead, taking into account internal as well as external factors which might modify the amount of cost to be incurred. Following this type of approach, expected future or replacement costs are estimated for each cost element in order to prepare flexible budgets and standard costs. Through the use of these "should be" costs, as expressed in flexible budgets and standards, it has been possible to determine more timely and valid measurements of performance, more timely cost information to serve many purposes, and more effective cost control. In addition, the techniques have been described for deriving and presenting the probable future costs for alternative production and marketing plans for the firm as a whole. In providing the foregoing types of usefulness the preceding chapters have dealt primarily with certain classifications of past costs and their counterparts in future costs.

Assuming several general plans of action had been selected by management as feasible, Chapter 22 dealt with the derivation and presentation of costs in cost-volume-profit analyses so that management could make informed decisions as to the best profit plan for the firm in the year ahead. This chapter deals with the use of costs in making *specific* operating decisions related to production or marketing and in the preparation of special studies which will provide the type of quantitative information which will help management select, from alternative ways of accomplishing some specific production or distribution objective, the one which is most economical or makes the most satisfactory profit contribution.

In operating the modern multiple-product enterprise, the alternatives available are so varied that different concepts of cost are needed for significant comparison and evaluation. Book figures usually do not measure these alternatives correctly, but they do provide the basic data (types of cost elements involved, rough indication of magnitude, and pattern of cost behavior) for building the cost estimates to fit the management need. The better the records available, the more time can be spent by the cost accountant in constructive interpretation and projection. The ability to arrive at proper conclusions depends very much on the reliability of the source data, subject to the degree of care exercised in the establishment of cost centers and flexibility to change cost centers and costs in line with changes in activity in the cost center.

Cost information for decision making requires an understanding of some additional cost concepts and combinations of cost data. Cost has meaning only in terms of specific objectives and specific problems. Cost as a generic term has substantially different meanings in accounting and in economics. Each of these areas of knowledge deals with more than one cost concept. This means that the type of cost concept or concepts being used in facilitating the achievement of any management goal must be carefully identified by appropriate descriptive adjectives. The management use that is to be made of cost data governs the kind and combination of costs which are to be included. It is the responsibility of the cost accountant to determine clearly the use to be made of his reports. He may then proceed with the selection of the type of cost data which will be most reliable and helpful to management in making a particular decision.

Special Decision-Making Cost Analyses

Some additional concepts of cost useful for decision-making purposes are described in this chapter. How they are designed to guide management in making specific decisions is illustrated later.

Differential Costs. Differential costs can be helpful in determining the effect on profits of changing sales volume; changing product mix; in making pricing decisions; in deciding whether to make or buy equipment, parts, or materials; and in comparing production methods. The usual meaning is that these are the costs which change from one level of activity to another, or it might refer to the combined *effect* of these individual cost changes, that is, the difference in total cost at one volume and total cost at another volume. If an increase in activity is being studied, they may be referred to as incremental costs; if a decrease in activity is being studied, they may be referred to as avoidable costs. This term sometimes is used to embrace those changes in cost occurring from one point in time to another (commonly from present period to the coming year) because of the changes in prices of the firm's productive factors and with, or without, a change in volume or product mix. Another use of the term is to refer to the differences in the cost of employing one specific method as opposed to another method to accomplish some productive or distributive objective. Distributive and general administrative costs, as well as productive costs, are often involved as differential costs. Mostly variable, semivariable, and semifixed costs are included in a differential cost analysis, but fixed costs may also be involved in certain changes in activity, changes from one time to another, or one method to another.

Traceable Costs. Those costs which are traceable directly to a job or product, a cost center, department, or operating division of a firm are referred to as traceable costs. It it obviously necessary to know whether a product or an operating division is involved as the objective of the tracing since the traceable costs of product will be different from the traceable costs of an operating division. It is not necessary that *all* costs be completely traceable for this distinction to be useful to management. For accurate costing and measurement of performance on jobs, products, cost centers, departments, or divisions, the more costs that are traceable, the more valid and useful the measurement. For example, a multiproduct firm may incur some common manufacturing costs on the various products, but the costs may differ considerably from product to product in other manufacturing and marketing processes. Information on traceable costs is significant in such decisions as adding or subtracting from a product line, product pricing, or modifying product merchandising effort.

Replacement Cost. The cost which attaches here may be selected from a contemporary market or from some anticipated future market. The contemporary market concept is widely used in financial accounting through the application of the "lower of cost or market" principle to obtain the valuation of certain current assets. It may also be used in certain interpretive statements to obtain a restatement of expenses in "real cost" terms. The cost of replacement in the coming year's market is widely used in cost accounting for budget preparation and setting standards. The cost of replacement projected two or more years into the future may become important for certain management purposes, especially capital budgeting (the planning of plant and equipment improvements, additions, replacements, and retirements).

Opportunity Cost. This represents the measurable advantage (some opportunity to obtain a differential or marginal income) foregone in the past or that may be sacrificed as a result of the rejection of alternative uses of material, labor, or facilities. Opportunity cost is often included as an imputed cost in comparing certain proposals for improving profits. It is used in cost accounting systems where decentralization of operations and authority have taken place and measurement of profit performance is made by operating divisions within the company. Its use in this situation places each individual organizational unit in the same position that it would occupy if it were an independent business rather than an operating component of an integrated enterprise.

Imputed Cost. An imputed cost is the dollar amount assigned for the use of any productive service which has not been the subject of an independent transaction between supplier and user to establish a liability or cause a cash outlay. Therefore it is not precisely measurable. It can be inferred or estimated from similar situations outside the firm. Opportunity costs are often imputed in certain comparisons to give a proper presentation of the costs of alternatives.

Sunk Cost. This is the amount invested in a tangible productive asset, an intangible right, or some extended contract for service which can only be recovered by use of the asset over its service life, or the use of a service over the term of the contract. Sunk cost is an invested cost or recorded cost. Future costs are subject to the decision of management and are controllable, whether basically of a fixed or variable nature, until a firm financial investment or commitment is made.

Out-of-Pocket Cost. Those elements of cost which have required, or will require, cash disbursement in the period under consideration are designated as out-of-pocket costs. Many fixed costs, such as taxes, insurance, supervisory salaries, as well as most variable, semivariable, and semifixed costs, are out-of-pocket costs.

Planning and decision-making costs involve primarily traceable, differential costs priced on a replacement dollar basis. In addition, certain imputed costs, or opportunity costs, must often be included to make proper cost constructions for guiding management. These will be illustrated in the section entitled "Different Analyses for Different Purposes."

Importance of Defining the Problem   Before any reliable cost or income information can be developed, the several proposed courses of action which management believes are feasible must be clearly defined. A searching examination of each proposal must be made to determine its impact on the firm in terms of functions affected, time commitment, and its relationship to other management plans. For example, many firms are faced with the problem of more complete utilization of facilities when sales drop. The management alternatives in this instance probably include:

1. To work on quality and design improvement of present product and on improving the efficiency of certain operations.
2. To make, rather than buy, certain component parts for production of present product.
3. To begin the production of new product which has favorable marketing prospects.
4. To solicit special order work where the skilled labor and equipment facilities are such that they will be able to satisfy the expected custom demands.

To explore the effect of any of the foregoing proposals, a number of questions must be answered. Which departments will be affected directly and which indirectly? Will changes in cost type or cost level occur in affected departments? Even without careful definition, out-of-pocket costs such as material, labor, certain utilities, and operating supplies would be included in the cost analysis for each alternative. However, investigation may reveal other costs that need to be recognized in preparing a complete analysis. In order to clearly picture the impact of a proposal, questions such as the following should be asked: What will be the effect on material unloading and handling costs? On inspection costs? On maintenance and repair costs? On engineering costs? On setup costs? On costs of maintaining payroll and labor cost records? On production planning costs? On supervisory costs?

In order to reap cost-saving or income advantages, certain proposals may have to be adopted for a trial period. If any substantial investment in modification of existing equipment or acquisition of new equipment is contemplated, the time commitment is important and would have to be known before the analysis for that alternative could be completed. A specific trial period is frequently assigned to production of new product.

The relationship of each proposal to other management plans must be examined because it may be found that certain proposals either fit rather closely to tentative future plans or will keep the firm in a more flexible position for future change. The estimated costs of discontinuance or reconversion in certain instances may be small, while for other proposals they may be substantial enough to include in the analysis. For example, the alternative to make parts may conflict with the alternative to begin production of new product which is part of the long-range planning program. Therefore, in connection with the second alternative we may have to take into account the prospect of early discontinuance or the fact that, after a few years, facilities would have to be expanded to continue production of the parts.

When each individual proposal is thus examined and more clearly understood, it can be clearly defined. Cost and income analyses may then be properly prepared.

Different Analyses for Different Purposes It has been emphasized that there is no one concept or combination of cost data that will satisfy all the requirements of management. To determine what items should be included in a specific cost analysis, the cost accountant must be familiar with the present and probable future operating conditions of the firm and the purpose for which a particular cost measurement is to be made. Examples which illustrate typical situations in which specific managerial problems require cost data will now be discussed. These analyses will involve *comparisons* of one set of cost figures with another set of cost figures for an alternative solution, or the *comparison* of the marginal income— additional income derived less additional cost incurred in deriving that income—of one proposal with that of an alternative proposal. In comparing alternatives it is usually neither necessary nor advisable to present an analysis showing full cost for each alternative. Only those elements of cost which are expected to be different for the one alternative as compared to the other should be included, i.e., *relevant costs*. Costs which will not be affected by the decision to be made are irrelevant and are preferably excluded from the analysis so that the significant cost data may be highlighted. Consequently, *differential costs* may be the most useful in preparing suitable comparative cost analyses for management. The following illustrations describe how differential and comparative cost analyses may be prepared to assist management in selecting those proposals that will contribute most effectively to the profit plan of the firm.

Acceptance of Additional Volume   To demonstrate the nature of differential costs, several illustrations are given, and the results will be shown under both the traditional cost procedure and the differential cost procedure. In the first illustration, it is assumed that:

The plant is not operating at full capacity. In this instance, 80 percent capacity is used, and volume of production is 240,000 units. The *fixed* overhead cost is $180,000 under present operating conditions. The *variable* costs per unit are:

Direct materials	$1.50
Direct labor	2.00
Variable overhead costs	0.50
Total variable costs	$4.00
Fixed overhead per unit, ($180,000 ÷ 240,000 units)	0.75
Total Cost per Unit	$4.75

An offer is received from a foreign importer to buy 60,000 units at $4.30 per unit. Management hesitates to accept this offer because this price is less than the total cost per unit as computed under the usual costing method, and also because the current selling price is $5.25.

In solving this problem, it is assumed that the fixed overhead costs will not increase, because with this order the production of the firm will be expanded to, but not beyond, 100 percent capacity. Fixed selling and administrative costs under present scheduled production total $82,000, and this figure will not be affected by the additional production.

It is immediately apparent that if management were to make a decision based upon traditional cost accounting, the order would be rejected because the per unit cost of manufacturing is $4.75, and any sale at $4.30 would result in a *per unit loss of 45 cents*. Using differential cost analysis, an income statement in comparative form—with and without the foreign order—would be prepared as shown in Illustration 23–1.

The results in this statement indicate that under the assumed conditions the foreign order should be accepted because:

1. The differential income derived from the additional volume will increase total net income by $18,000.
2. The total average cost, including selling and administrative costs, will be reduced from $5.09 to $4.87. This permits an adeqaute profit margin since the average sales price of the entire production is $5.06.

Illustration 23–1

ANY COMPANY

COMPARATIVE INCOME STATEMENT
SHOWING DIFFERENTIAL INCOME AND DIFFERENTIAL COSTS

For Period Ended June 30, 19—

	Current Business	Additional Sales	Total
Sales:			
240,000 units @ $5.25.	$1,260,000		
60,000 units @ 4.30.		$258,000*	$1,518,000
Variable costs:			
240,000 units @ $4.00.	960,000		
60,000 units @ 4.00.		240,000†	1,200,000
Marginal income or contribution margin. . . .	$ 300,000	$ 18,000	$ 318,000
Fixed costs.	180,000		180,000
Gross profit on sales.	$ 120,000	$ 18,000	$ 138,000
Selling and administrative costs.	82,000		82,000
Net Income for Period.	$ 38,000	$ 18,000	$ 56,000

* Differential sales.
† Differential cost (considers only the variable costs).

It should be indicated at this point that the reason for the differential profit is that the *regular* sales price was not affected by the foreign order. If *all* prices had to be reduced to $4.30 per unit because of the acceptance of the foreign order, the result would be a loss of $172,000 for the firm as a whole. It is only when two separate markets exist for the product or where price discriminations can be made between buyers that the differential cost approach is important in pricing. In the long run, the total average selling price must be higher than the total average cost. Assuming acceptance of the foreign order, note that the total average selling price in the comparative income statement, $5.06, is higher than the total average cost, $4.87 ($1,462,000 divided by 300,000 units). The total average cost will be reduced by acceptance of the foreign order from $5.09 to $4.87 because of better utilization of the fixed production, selling, and administrative facilities. Where plants are operating at less than full capacity and the market is not completely and freely competitive, *differential,* not average, costs should be used to determine whether or not a particular order should be accepted.

A second type of differential cost analysis projects operating business conditions at various stepped-up production levels. The rate of change in variable costs will not remain the same as production increases or decreases. As has been stated previously, increased production may change the per unit variable costs because of lower material prices due to large-scale purchases; higher or lower direct labor costs due to incentive systems, overtime, spoilage; lower variable indirect costs such as power because of increased volume of consumption; and so on. The differential cost analysis can be projected at various levels. Many decisions can be reached by merely inspecting the variable costs and comparing them with the differential sales, assuming the rate of change for incurring variable cost does not increase or decrease substantially. However, it is possible that a substantial increase in the rate of incurring variable costs may occur when production reaches such a level that it may require overtime or it may result in greater waste and spoilage.

In this illustration the following is assumed:

A company is operating at 60 percent capacity, with production at this level of 24,000 units and fixed overhead of $12,000. Fixed selling and administrative costs amount to $14,400. Present selling prices per unit are $4.

A customer offers to purchase increasing quantities during the current year at the following prices:

> First 6,000 additional units at $3.00
> Next 6,000 additional units at 2.50
> Next 6,000 additional units at 2.00

Should the orders be accepted? The variable costs under present production schedules show a per unit cost of $2, viz:

> Direct materials. $1.00
> Direct labor. 0.60
> Variable overhead. 0.40
> $2.00

A comparison of these figures and the offered selling prices indicates that the first two lots could be accepted profitably if the anticipated sales did not interfere with the present market. For the first two lots the customer offers $3 and $2.50, respectively, while the differential unit cost is only $2. But these decisions are based upon the fact that the variable costs will not change with the increased production. Let us assume further, however, that conditions are not static and that the changes in the variable costs due to the aforementioned labor, materials, and overhead factors are as follows:

First order of 6,000, no change in rate of incurring variable costs, additional variable costs, $12,000.

Next order of 6,000, some variable costs incurred at reduced rates, additional variable costs, $10,800.

And the third order of 6,000 units involves some overtime and additional costs so that additional variable costs for this order would be $15,060.

Information on the changing pattern of differential costs as the firm approaches its 40,000-unit (100 percent) capacity will make it possible for management to see at a glance that the third lot of 6,000 would not be profitable. For the third lot the differential income is $12,000, while the differential costs have risen to $15,060.

For management consideration the relevant cost and income information could be presented effectively in a comparative and cumulative statement as shown in Illustration 23–2.

Illustration 23–2

STATEMENT OF DIFFERENTIAL COST ANALYSIS

Quantity of Output	Cost of Output		Cumulative Average Cost Per Unit	Selling Prices		Net Income	
	Total	Per Unit		Total	Per Unit	Per Lot	Cumulative
24,000.......	$60,000.00	$2.50*	$2.50	$ 96,000.00	$4.00	$36,000.00	$36,000.00
6,000.......	12,000.00	2.00†	2.40	18,000.00	3.00	6,000.00	42,000.00
6,000.......	10,800.00	1.80†	2.30	15,000.00	2.50	4,200.00	46,200.00
6,000.......	15,060.00	2.51†	2.33	12,000.00	2.00	(3,060.00)‡	43,140.00
42,000.......	$97,860.00		$2.33	$141,000.00	$3.36§		$43,140.00

* Includes variable plus fixed costs.
† Includes only variable costs.
‡ Loss.
§ Approximate figure.

STATEMENT OF DIFFERENTIAL COSTS OF ADDED PRODUCTION

Variable Costs	Volume of Production (in Units)			
	24,000	6,000 Added	12,000 Added	18,000 Added
Direct Material..............	$24,000.00	$ 6,000.00	$11,760.00	$17,600.00
Direct Labor.................	14,400.00	3,600.00	7,100.00	11,500.00
Direct Variable Overhead......	9,600.00	2,400.00	3,940.00	8,760.00
	$48,000.00	$12,000.00	$22,800.00	$37,860.00
Fixed Overhead Costs.........	12,000.00			
Totals.....................	$60,000.00	$12,000.00	$22,800.00	$37,860.00
Number of Units..............	24,000	6,000	12,000	18,000
Differential Costs per Unit......		$2.00	$1.90	$2.10

Interpreting this statement, it should be noted that:

1. If production were to be increased 6,000 over the present 24,000, any sales over the differential cost figure of $2 per unit would be profitable, but if computed on the average or traditional cost basis, it would appear that the sales price of the entire production in a competitive market would have to be above $2.40 to be profitable.

2. If production were to be increased 12,000 over the present production of 24,000, the unit sales price of this additional production would have to

be more than $1.90. On the average or traditional cost basis it would appear that the sales price would have to be above $2.30 for the entire lot to be profitable.

3. If production were to be increased 18,000 units over the present volume of 24,000 units, the unit sales price of this additional production on a *differential* cost basis would have to be above $2.10 per unit to be profitable. On the average cost basis it would appear that the entire lot would have to be sold at a price above $2.33 to be profitable.

4. On a differential cost basis, it would not be profitable to accept the order for the last 6,000 because it would result in a loss of $3,060, decreasing the cumulative profit from $46,200 to $43,140.

A serious limitation of cost analysis is that management may go overboard in using differential costing and a company could find itself in financial difficulty. Profits will be increased or losses minimized in the short run if differential costs are covered and something is left over to contribute to fixed costs. The assumption generally made is that differential costing applies to the increment only. For example, assume a company manufactures and sells one product with the following cost:

```
Materials, 1 unit @ $5.00.............................$ 5.00
Labor, 2 hours @     3.50............................  7.00
Overhead:
    Variable, 2 hours @ $2.00.........................  4.00
    Fixed,  2 hours @  1.75.........................  3.50
                                                    $19.50
```

The fixed costs for the period are expected to amount to $35,000 at a normal capacity of 10,000 units. The normal sales price is $27 and the company expects to sell 7,000 during the period. A special order for 2,000 units could be obtained at a sales price of $17. If the company accepts the order, $2,000 ($1 per unit X 2,000 units) will be the amount contributed to fixed costs and profit. However, if *all* of the business is accepted at $17 per unit, *all* of the costs would not be covered, and although a company might minimize losses in the short run, the full $19.50 must be covered in the long run. Management must be sure to keep this in mind. Differential cost analysis is useful for increments only; the thing to avoid is calling all of the sales "incremental," i.e., every salesman brings in every order at $17!

Operation versus Shutdown

Many executives might feel that a plant shutdown is better than operating continuously at a loss, but a differential cost analysis will prove that often this is not so. For example, assume that the American Sewing Machine Company for many years has had a successful product but in recent years competition with foreign products manufactured at lower labor costs has caused it to operate at a loss. The firm has been trying to diversify its manufacturing operations and is seeking new products since it foresees no change in the competitive market. The firm is now faced with the problem of shutting down completely until new products and plant facilities can be developed, or of continuing to operate at a loss, thus keeping together its skilled labor force. The primary information needed to solve this problem involves a comparison between the probable loss at the anticipated low level of operations and the loss that would be suffered if the plant shut down temporarily. Data obtained from the records and from management estimates are:

Normal capacity of plant............................	120,000 machines per year
Fixed costs when plant is operating...................	$150,000
Fixed costs when plant is shut down..................	$100,000
Variable costs per machine (direct labor, direct material, and variable overhead)............................	$40
Estimated selling price to meet foreign competition.......	$46
Estimated sales volume at new selling price.............	10,000 machines

Using this information a brief statement can be prepared to show the *differential* costs and the probable net loss if the firm continues to operate:

Fixed costs if plant is operating...........................		$150,000
Less:		
Differential income: 10,000 × $46.......................	$460,000	
Differential costs: 10,000 × $40.......................	400,000	
Differential income....................................		60,000
Loss if Plant Is Operated at 8⅓% Capacity................		$ 90,000

If the plant closed down, the loss due to fixed charges would be $100,000; whereas if it operated at a small capacity, the loss would only be $90,000. The plant operating at this small capacity would suffer a smaller loss and would be able to retain most of its skilled labor force and management personnel.

The Grand Department Store has been maintaining, among others, a silverware department and a luggage department. A well-known company which retails television sets wishes to lease space in the department store to display and sell its line. It has offered an annual rental of $3,600 for the space now occupied by the luggage and/or $4,500 for the space now used by the silverware department on a lease agreement which is to run for five years. The department store is undecided whether to accept or reject the offer in view of last year's profits, which are representative of the usual results of the two departments in question. The silverware department has shown a net income, after distributing all actual expenses, of $6,000, while the luggage department shows a net income of $4,500. Should the Grand Department Store lease the space of either of these two departments, and, if so, which one?

The profitability of these departments has been determined after proper tracing of all actual costs for which a reliable measure of assignment has been established. It would seem, at first glance, that neither of the present departments should be discontinued so as to lease the space; but in this case the "actual" costs do not reflect the alternative involved. It is necessary, in order to get a clear picture of what is involved, to "impute" charges to these two departments. First, consider the rental income which might be obtained, as against the present net income of the departments:

	Silverware	Luggage
Profits, per books	$6,000	$4,500
Imputed rent expense	4,500	3,600
Net Income	$1,500	$ 900

In addition to the rent, consider also the fact that the Grand Department Store has capital invested in the inventories and fixtures of these departments which would be available for other uses if the departments were closed. A fair estimate of current values of inventory and fixtures in the two departments reveals:

	Silverware	Luggage
Inventory (average for year)	$20,000	$6,000
Fixtures (present values)	8,500	2,000
Total Invested Capital	$28,500	$8,000

Computing imputed interest at 6 percent on the investment changes the basis of comparison to:

	Silverware	Luggage
Profits, per books	$6,000	$4,500
Imputed rent	4,500	3,600
	$1,500	$ 900
Interest on investment	1,710	480
Net	($ 210) Loss	$ 420 Profit

The Grand Department Store should, on this basis, discontinue the silverware department, for it will be better off by $210 per year to lease the space than to operate the department. The luggage department, however, should not be closed, for the potential rental income and funds released for other purposes are not sufficient by $420 to offset the present profits. The luggage department is producing $420 a year *more* income by not leasing the space.

Imputed costs may be continuously charged to cost accounts if, for purposes of efficiency measurement, it becomes advisable to do so. Such procedure need not affect the general books of account. Department charges for interest on investment may be credited to a special income account—Imputed Interest on Investment—which can be used to offset the overstatement of cost from a financial point of view.

Equipment Replacement Problems   Comparative cost analyses may also be used in connection with equipment replacement decisions. Company E has been using a machine for five years. It was estimated that the machine, purchased for $45,000, could be used for 10 years. The annual costs of operation of this machine are as follows:

Direct labor	$ 4,800
Taxes	800
Repairs	200
Supplies	550
Depreciation	4,500
Power	1,810
Apportioned charges:	
Indirect labor	520
Building expense, 100 square feet	300
Total	$13,480

A new semiautomatic machine is now on the market, priced at $45,000 and with the same potential output, 10,000 units per year. However, certain cost savings are claimed for the new machine. Its estimated operating costs are:

Direct labor	$ 500
Taxes	1,200
Repairs (estimated)	250
Supplies	600
Depreciation	4,500
Power	1,600
Apportioned charges:	
Indirect labor	430
Building expense, 150 square feet	450
Total	$9,530

Although the old machine will still function for another five years, the question arises as to whether the company should dispose of the old machine (which can be disposed of *now* for $1,500) and buy the new one.

The alternative in this situation is not adequately depicted by the foregoing cost schedules. We have the alternative not of *buying* one machine *or* the other, but rather that of *keeping* the old machine or *acquiring* the new one.

This situation is more adequately portrayed if we recognize that the value of the old machine is a "sunk" or irrecoverable cost, and consider only the "out-of-pocket" costs, i.e., the future costs of the two alternatives. A more nearly accurate comparison of relative cost is obtained by:

	Keep Old Machine	Acquire New Machine
Direct labor	$4,800	$ 500
Taxes	800	1,200
Repairs	200	250
Supplies	550	600
Depreciation	300	4,500*
Power	1,810	1,600
Indirect labor	520	430
Building expense	300	450
Total	$9,280	$9,530

* Many firms would use either a sum-of-years'-digits' method or a fixed-percent-of-diminishing-value method. This would result in a much larger charge for depreciation the first year.

These schedules of cost result in an entirely different picture. The depreciation charge on the old machine does not enter into the computations of cost in this case, except for the amortization over five years of the $1,500 sacrificed by keeping the old machine. The $300 per year is an *opportunity cost,* the cost of rejecting the opportunity to realize $1,500 on replacement.

However, the foregoing is not yet a completely accurate comparison, for there is another factor which has not yet been considered in these schedules—the investment involved in the purchase of the new machine. This would require a net outlay of $43,500 ($45,000 — $1,500, value of old machine). Regardless of where these funds are obtained, the investment of $43,500 involves an important factor. If we have the cash on hand, we can invest it in securities or other income-producing assets rather than buy the new machine; the income that might be received is *sacrificed* in purchasing the new machine. If we borrow the money to buy the new machine, we shall have to sacrifice cash to pay interest for the use of it. Therefore, we should add to the annual operating costs of the new machine an *imputed cost* for using $43,500 in this way. This cost is often imputed at the going rate, e.g., 4 percent, to recognize this aspect of the situation. This amounts to $1,740 ($43,500 × 0.04). However, if the present earning power of the firm's assets is higher, e.g., 10 percent, this rate should be used.

	4%	10%
Annual cost, new machine, including imputed interest	$11,270	$13,880
Annual cost, old machine	9,280	9,280
Annual Saving by *Keeping* Old Machine	$ 1,990	$ 4,600

Obviously, we should *not* buy the new machine under the present circumstances.

Suppose that additional alternatives were available to Company E.

The company can continue to buy its power from the local utility or it may build a power plant to manufacture its own. Each year the company spends $260,000 on light and power.

The cost of building a power plant would be $1,000,000, and engineers estimate the plant could be used for 25 years before it became obsolete. Operating costs, including interest costs on expected borrowings to finance the $1,000,000, are expected to average $100,000 per year before depreciation. The combined federal and state tax rate is 50 percent.

The acquisition of the power plant should result in the following *annual* savings:

Cost of purchased power	$260,000
Operating expenses of power plant	100,000
Depreciation of power plant	40,000
Savings before tax	$120,000
Tax	60,000
Savings after Tax (Operating Advantage)	$ 60,000

The *payback period* is Investment/Savings + Depreciation:

$$\frac{\$1,000,000}{\$60,000 + \$40,000} = 10 \text{ years.}$$

The *time adjusted rate of return* is computed with the use of the table on page 504. The $1,000,000 investment will return $100,000 in new cash ($40,000 depreciation plus $60,000 savings) in each of 25 years. To reduce to $1 so that the table may be used, $10 of investment is needed for each $1 received annually for 25 years. The table shows that 10.675 is equal to 8 percent and 9.077 is equal to 10 percent. Ten dollars would be equal to approximately 9 percent.

If management of Company E can earn more than 9 percent on alternate investments with comparable risk, the power plant should not be built. If, however, alternatives yield less, the power plant proposal might be accepted.

Another use of comparative costs is found in those firms that manufacture materials or parts which are subsequently used in the production of other products. The materials thus used to make the final finished products might profitably be purchased from other suppliers at less than it would cost to produce the materials or parts in the manufacturer's own plant. This lower cost may be due to the greater specialization or larger volume of the potential supplier of the materials to be used in manufacturing the finished salable products. The manufacturer is faced with the problem of how to determine whether to produce the materials or parts in his own plant or to buy them from outside suppliers. Again, profitability of business operations is the major determining factor.

To illustrate *one method* of solving this problem and answering the question, a woolen company is used and its procedures discussed.

The Woolen-Worsted Company buys raw wool fleeces and processes this material by washing, drying, carding, spinning, and dyeing before knitting the wool into sweaters, gloves, and other finished products. These operations (except the various knitting and finishing operations) result in a series of products which could be sold at the completion of each of several processes. Washed and carded wool, and spun yarn and dyed yarn are "products" in their own right.

The company wishes to make certain that the product of no process be allowed to cost more than the amount at which the goods could be purchased at that stage. In fact, it expects that a process justify its continued operation by showing total costs at the completion of the process less than the amount at which similar goods could be purchased. How can this control be achieved in the cost accounts?

The procedure used is known as *"opportunity" cost* procedure. Goods are charged to the first process at market price, and transfers made to the next process are valued at market price of similar goods, the difference being credited to a Departmental Profit account. It is true that for income measurement purposes such profits are not realized and therefore adjustments will have to be made; but, nevertheless, control is achieved by using this method, which is effective and inexpensive. The departmental profits or losses will have to be eliminated against inventories and cost of goods sold when financial statements are prepared for publication.

The procedure may be made clearer by exhibiting the Spinning and Dyeing Process accounts in skeleton form:

Spinning

Carded wool (at market price)	10,000.00	To Spinning Department,	
Labor costs (actual)	2,000.00	Revenue and Expense	20,000.00
Factory overhead (actual)	8,000.00	(Profit and Loss)	
	20,000.00		20,000.00

Spinning Department, Revenue and Expense

From Spinning account	20,000.00	Spun yarn transferred to Dyeing at market price	24,000.00

Dyeing

Spun yarn (at market price)	24,000.00	Transferred to Dyeing,	
Labor costs (actual)	3,000.00	Revenue and Expense	38,000.00
Factory overhead (actual)	11,000.00	(Profit and Loss)	
	38,000.00		38,000.00

Dyeing Department, Revenue and Expense

From Dyeing	38,000.00	Transferred to Between-Process	
		Inventory accounts	36,000.00

Note that the spinning department operated efficiently enough to save the company $4,000 of the "opportunity" cost of spun yarn; the dyeing department "lost" $2,000, in the sense that the product of that department could have been purchased for $2,000 *less* than it cost to produce it. Before making a decision to buy any dyed wool, this $2,000 "loss" should be further analyzed by determining how much of the accumulated cost of $38,000 represents fixed cost, that is, capacity cost which is inescapable and would not have any alternative use if spun wool was sent out to be dyed or if some dyed wool was purchased outright. There may still be a saving (or "profit") if more than $2,000 of the $11,000 of dyeing factory overhead, or of any prior factory overhead, is fixed and inescapable.

Opportunity costs have not been put to so wide a use as they might have been had standard cost techniques been less developed, but the concept is useful for some purposes even though it may not be as generally employed as are other methods. Note that the purpose of opportunity costs is to focus attention on the fact that goods might be sold at the end of a given process rather than processed to a greater degree; the sacrifice of the profit which might be made at this point is considered to be a cost of the succeeding process.

A *second* illustration of whether *to make* or *to buy* component parts used in manufacturing involves the principles of *differential costs* previously discussed. Since fixed costs are assumed not to change regardless of the production volume, they will not be considered, since *it is assumed that the present plant facilities are available* for all necessary manufacturing of parts.

A manufacturer of washing machines at the present time is purchasing a substantial quantity of parts used in assembling the finished product. He wishes to know whether he should continue to purchase these parts or attempt to manufacture them. There are five main parts involved in these machines which could be manufactured, or could still be purchased from the suppliers. Without much additional expense, the firm has facilities available to produce these parts either because they are *idle* or because the facilities are used for assembling the machines and can also be used for manufacturing. The following figures have been compiled to help you in advising management what to do:

			Estimated Costs to Make per Thousand			
Part Number	Direct Materials	Direct Labor	Additional Variable Overhead	Total Differential Costs	Cost to Buy	Difference
1..........	$1,000	$1,500	$ 500	$3,000	$2,400	$600*
2..........	600	600	200	1,400	1,600	200†
3..........	380	420	200	1,000	1,200	200†
4..........	840	160	200	1,200	960	240*
5..........	500	300	100	900	1,000	100†
Total......	$3,320	$2,980	$1,200	$7,500	$7,160	$340*

* Purchase price is lower.
† Cost to make is lower.

An examination of these figures suggests the following conclusions relating to the question of whether or not to buy or to make any or all of the parts:

1. To buy all the parts and not make any would be $340 cheaper.
2. If some of the parts were purchased and some manufactured, it would be possible to reduce the total cost of 1,000 units even further, namely, to $6,660, viz:

```
Purchase Part No. 1, cost.....................................$2,400
Purchase Part No. 4, cost.....................................   960
Manufacture Part No. 2, cost.................................. 1,400
Manufacture Part No. 3, cost.................................. 1,000
Manufacture Part No. 5, cost..................................   900
    Total Cost of 1,000 Parts of Each.........................$6,660
```

The saving by purchasing some of the parts and making others over the plan of buying all of the parts is $500 ($7,160 − $6,660). The saving by purchasing some of the parts and making others over the plan of making all the parts is $840 ($7,500 − $6,660).

Of course it should not be overlooked that there may be other factors which might influence the final decision, such as the cash required to obtain a plant large enough to carry on the manufacturing operations or the lack of skilled labor to work in the manufacturing operations.

Sell or Process Further   The problem of sell or process further is particularly prevalent in the chemical and the oil refining industries. This problem also uses *differential cost* analysis. The following data are used to illustrate this type of situation:

The Acme Chemical Company produces Product A, which is used in manufacturing Product B and Product C. It is possible to sell Product A, or to retain it in the plant to produce B and C. Presently the plant is operating at 75 percent capacity. The firm has 100,000 tons of Product A which it could sell without further processing or it could be kept and used in manufacturing Products B and C.

Product A costs $7 a ton to produce and can be sold for $9.50 a ton.

To use this 100,000 tons of Product A in the manufacture of Products B and C will result in salable production, through added materials, of 120,000 tons of Product B and 40,000 tons of Product C. Product B sells for $25 a ton, and Product C sells for $18 a ton.

The *differential costs* of processing this 100,000 tons into Products B and C, reduced to a per-ton basis, are:

	Product B	Product C
Materials: Product A	$ 7.00	$ 7.00
Other material	5.00	2.00
Direct labor	10.00	4.50
Direct overhead	2.00	2.50
Total Variable or Differential Costs per Ton	$24.00	$16.00

Differential income if 100,000 tons of Product A are sold at $9.50 per ton:

Income from sale of 100,000 tons @ $9.50	$950,000
Less: Cost of Product A, 100,000 tons @ $7.00	700,000
Differential Income	$250,000

Differential income if Products B and C are sold:

Income if Product A is used to produce B and C:

120,000 tons of Product B @ $25	$3,000,000	
40,000 tons of Product C @ 18	720,000	
Total estimated income		$3,720,000
Less: Cost per ton of Products B and C (exclusive of Product A cost):		
120,000 tons of Product B @ $17.00 ($5.00 + $10.00 + $2.00)	$2,040,000	
40,000 tons of Product C @ 9.00 ($2.00 + $4.50 + $2.50)	360,000	
100,000* tons of Product A @ 7.00	700,000	3,100,000
Differential Income		$ 620,000

* As indicated above, 100,000 of A in the manufacture of B and C will result in salable production, through added materials, of 120,000 tons of B and 40,000 tons of C.

On the basis of these figures and the assumptions made, it is apparent that if the 100,000 tons of Product A were further processed to produce Products B and C, it would be more desirable than to sell Product A at $9.50 per ton. By additional processing, there is an advantage of $370,000.

Pricing Problems

Frequently, replacement values are much more important than actual costs. It is entirely logical, for certain purposes, to consider the "cost" of materials, to be the cost of *replacing* the materials consumed at *present* prices. The *sacrifice* of materials to one particular production order may sometimes be more accurately measured by the cost of replenishing the stock in the materials storeroom than by historical cost. For this reason, cost accounting systems sometimes provide for charging costs on a replacement price basis (last-in, first-out inventory pricing).

For example, Company D has been in business for many years manufacturing a product that has no competition. Prices have been set at average cost plus 10 percent. The income statement shows a profit for last year of $20,000 (10 percent of the cost of sales), but the company's Cash account always seems to show a precariously low balance, despite the fact that the physical size of plant, inventories, etc., has not changed. Prices of materials and equipment are constantly rising, but the president thinks that since prices are set at 10 percent above cost, the price increases can be ignored.

Cost plus 10 percent may not be an adequate price if material prices have risen greatly and if material costs constitute a substantial part of the total. For example, a cost sheet may show the following (actual) costs for a given order:

Materials	$ 8,500
Direct labor	1,200
Factory expense	900
Total	$10,600

A selling price of cost plus 10 percent would, in such case, be $11,660. This amount would be collected from the buyer, resulting in an increase in cash of $11,660. But if, meanwhile, prices of materials had advanced from $85 a unit to $100 a unit, the purchase of materials to replace those used in the order just sold would mean an outlay of $10,000, instead of $8,500. Since the money profit on the sale transaction was only $1,060, the $1,500 additional outlay to replace the materials results in an *economic* loss of $440 ($1,500 — $1,060) on the order. This result may be obscured by the fact that materials inventories, valued at cost, would show the $1,500 as additional inventory value, causing the books to show a profit of $1,060; but the profit would be represented only as part of the higher valuation of an inventory of the same kind and size as the original one. Thus, profits may be swallowed up in inventory values in periods of rapidly rising prices, and the cash position of the firm become dangerously weak. The tricks which our unstable monetary unit can play upon our judgment are subtle but nonetheless real.

In order to avoid such a condition, a firm might decide to show on the cost sheets not the actual but the replacement costs of materials. This can be done by changing the pricing of requisitions, showing *replacement* costs to be charged to specific orders or cost sheets and *actual* costs to be credited to the Materials account. The difference is carried to a Variation account such as was described in the chapter on standard costs. The cost sheet for the order we have been discussing would then appear as follows:

Materials	$10,000
Direct labor	1,200
Factory expense	900
Total	$12,100

A selling price of cost plus 10 percent would be computed at $13,310, which would protect the company from the effect of price increases in materials which had occurred at the time of sale or shortly thereafter.

Similar provision might be made to handle other costs on replacement bases. Depreciation of fixed assets should, theoretically at least, be so handled if costs are used as the basis for determining selling prices. The consumption of fixed assets can be measured accurately for this purpose only by considering the depreciation charge as the expense of replacing service units consumed in production at *current* price levels. Space limitations prohibit an extended discussion of this point, but there is no justification for *setting selling prices* on the basis of costs incurred at low price levels which may have no relation to current or future considerations.

Limitations of Cost Analysis   The illustrations given in the foregoing discussion may have tended to overemphasize the importance of cost and income data in solving business problems. Cost computations and income estimates are one means of "attacking" such problems; in many cases, this information is conclusive in making the decision. Many projects and proposals have been shelved simply because the costs involved were too high or the relative income contribution was lower than that of an alternative. Perhaps this is the very reason why the cost accountant needs to be extremely careful in the translation of the data with which he works lest the use of an inappropriate cost concept preclude the adoption of a proposal which might be beneficial to the enterprise or result in losses that might have been avoided by the use of a proper concept of cost.

The cost accountant must at all times maintain the proper perspective about the usefulness of cost data. He must recognize that management must give consideration to factors other than cost to ensure the long-run progress of the firm. The pressure of competition, the maintenance of sources of supply and of certain marketing outlets, and the maintenance of existing personnel, organization, and morale may often be the real determinants of business decisions. While costs are important, they do not in themselves provide the key to the solution of all business problems; other factors must be considered and may sometimes outweigh the cost factors.

The cost of deriving information for management usefulness should not exceed the potential benefits to be obtained. Methods must be devised to accumulate and distribute timely cost information for management control and planning at the least possible expense. Efficiency in processing and analyzing cost data has not yet reached its potential maximum, and much can be done to increase the usefulness of cost data by reducing the cost of obtaining it.

Modern integrated data processing applications can provide better service to management at no extra cost and in many cases at substantial savings if there is a large volume of data to be processed to meet daily, weekly, and monthly needs for information regarding sales, production, labor, etc. In most applications, the equipment is used only a portion of the time for other needs, thus leaving some time to make special analyses. While the financial executive must still do the creative thinking that is necessary in a proper program of comparative cost analyses, certain elements of each analysis can be secured more quickly, more accurately, and at less cost. Furthermore, he will be able to devote more time to anticipating management needs for information and to preparing studies which would have been impossible under the time and cost limitations of prior methods.

QUESTIONS FOR REVIEW

1. "Cost has meaning only in terms of specific objectives and specific problems." Explain.
2. Define briefly the following terms:
   a) Differential costs.
   b) Traceable costs.
   c) Opportunity costs.
   d) Imputed costs.
3. "We can ignore fixed costs for purposes of decision making. Therefore, fixed costs are unimportant." Do you agree with this statement? Why or why not?
4. "It is possible for us to 'differential cost' our way right out of business!" Comment on the validity of this argument.
5. What is the difference between *return on investment* and *return of investment?*
6. "Many executives might feel that a plant shutdown is better than operating continuously at a loss, but a differential cost analysis will prove that often this is not so." Explain.

7. How may cost analyses be used in connection with equipment replacement analysis?

8. Define the *payback, simple rate of return,* and *time adjusted rate of return* methods. Which do you feel is the most useful?

9. What are some of the limitations of cost analysis?

10. What items should be considered as to whether a company should make or buy a component part?

PROBLEMS—GROUP A

Problem 23–1. Purpose: *Cost Analysis to Determine Whether to Make or Buy*

The Internal Company manufactures a single product known as "inter." The standard costs for one unit of product is:

Materials	15 lbs. @ $0.90 per lb.		$13.50
Labor	12 hrs. @ 3.00 per hr.		36.00
Overhead—variable	12 hrs. @ 2.00 per hr.		24.00
Overhead—fixed	12 hrs. @ 2.00 per hr.		24.00
			$97.50

The standard overhead rate is based on an output of 15,000 units per year.

The normal workweek in the industry is 36 hours, and the company employs 100 direct laborers.

Twenty-one hundred units were completed during the last eight weeks. The beginning inventory consisted of 200 units complete as to material but one-fourth complete as to conversion cost. Fifty units complete as to material and one-half complete as to conversion were in the ending inventory.

The External Company has proposed to sell this product to Internal at $87 a unit.

Required:

Should Internal buy from External or should Internal continue manufacturing "inter"? Indicate both financial and nonfinancial items that might influence a decision.

Problem 23–2. Purpose: *Using Cost Analysis in Decision Making*

The Ina Company has asked your assistance in determining an economical sales and production mix of their products for 1968. The company manufactures a line of dolls and a doll dress sewing kit.

The company's sales department provides the following data:

Doll's Name	Estimated Demand for 1968 (Units)	Established Net Price (Units)
Laurie	50,000	$5.20
Debbie	42,000	2.40
Sarah	35,000	8.50
Kathy	40,000	4.00
Sewing kit	325,000	3.00

To promote sales of the sewing kit there is a 15 percent reduction in the established net price for a kit purchased at the same time that an Ina Company doll is purchased.

From accounting records you develop the following data:

1. The production standards per unit:

Item	Material	Labor
Laurie............................	$1.40	$0.80
Debbie............................	0.70	0.50
Sarah.............................	2.69	1.40
Kathy.............................	1.00	1.00
Sewing kit.......................	0.60	0.40

2. The labor rate of $2 per hour is expected to continue without change in 1968. The plant has an effective capacity of 130,000 labor hours per year on a single-shift basis. Present equipment can produce all of the products.
3. The total fixed costs for 1968 will be $100,000. Variable costs will be equivalent to 50 percent of direct labor cost.
4. The company has a small inventory of its products that can be ignored.

Required:

a) Prepare a schedule computing the contribution to profit of a unit of each product.

b) Prepare a schedule computing the contribution to profit of a unit of each product per labor dollar expended on the product.

c) Prepare a schedule computing the total labor hours required to produce the estimated sales units for 1968. Indicate the item and number of units that you would recommend be increased (or decreased) in production to attain the company's effective productive capacity.

d) Without regard to your answer in (*c*), assume that the estimated sales units for 1968 would require 12,000 labor hours in excess of the company's effective productive capacity. Discuss the possible methods of providing the missing capacity. Include in your discussion all factors that must be taken into consideration in evaluating the methods of providing the missing capacity.

(Adapted from an AICPA Uniform Examination)

Problem 23–3. Purpose: *Equipment Replacement Analysis*

The Ibsen Corporation is contemplating the purchase of an electronic filling machine to be used in its filling department where 1,000,000 units are manufactured monthly. The operation is currently being performed by hand. Sixteen direct laborers are being used, and these people are paid at the average of $1.50 per hour. The normal annual work period is eight hours per day, five days per week, 50 weeks per year.

The proposed machine would cost $130,000 and would have a useful life of

10 years and would do the same work as the 16 laborers. Two employees would be necessary to operate the new machine. *Each* of these would receive an annual salary of $7,500.

Assume that production levels will remain the same over the 10-year period. Also, assume that excess laborers may be absorbed by the corporation's subsidiary located in the adjacent town. Assume that the corporate tax rate will average 50 percent per year over the 10-year period. No salvage value is expected for the machine at the end of its life.

Required:

What information can you provide to management to help them reach a decision whether or not to buy the machine? Be sure to include computations of the payback, simple rate of return, and time-adjusted rate of return. Make your computations clear and label all figures. Ignore FICA taxes and other fringe benefits.

Problem 23–4. Purpose: *Make or Buy Decisions*

When you have completed your audit of The International Company, management asked for your assistance in arriving at a decision to continue manufacturing a part or to buy it from an outside supplier. The part, which is named Faktron, is a component used in some of the finished products of the company.

From your audit working papers and from further investigation you develop the following data as being typical of the company's operations:

1. The annual requirement for Faktrons is 5,000 units. The lowest quotation from a supplier was $8 per unit.
2. Faktrons have been manufactured in the precision machinery department. If Faktrons are purchased from an outside supplier, certain machinery will be sold and would realize its book value.
3. Following are the total costs of the precision machinery department during the year under audit when 5,000 Faktrons were made:

Materials	$67,500
Direct labor	50,000
Indirect labor	20,000
Light and heat	5,500
Power	3,000
Depreciation	10,000
Property taxes and insurance	8,000
Payroll taxes and other benefits	9,800
Other	5,000

4. The following precision machinery department costs apply to the manufacture of Faktrons: material, $17,500; direct labor, $28,000; indirect labor, $6,000; power, $300; other, $500. The sale of the equipment used for Faktrons would reduce the following costs by the amounts indicated: depreciation, $2,000; property taxes and insurance, $1,000.
5. The following additional precision machinery department costs would be incurred if Faktrons were purchased from an outside supplier: freight, $0.50 per unit; indirect labor for receiving, materials handling, inspection, etc., $5,000. The cost of the purchased Faktrons would be considered a precision machinery department cost.

Required:

a) Prepare a schedule showing a comparison of the total costs of the precision machinery department (1) when Faktrons are made, and (2) when Faktrons are bought from an outside supplier.

b) Discuss the consideration in addition to the cost factors that you would bring to the attention of management in assisting them to arrive at a decision whether to make or buy Faktrons. Include in your discussion the considerations that might be applied to the evaluation of the outside supplier.

(Adapted from an AICPA Uniform Examination)

Problem 23–5.   Purpose: *Cost Reduction through Redesigning of Product*

The Ilax Manufacturing Company produces one principal product. The income from sales of this product for the year 1967 is expected to be $200,000. Cost of goods sold will be as follows:

Materials used	$40,000
Direct labor	60,000
Fixed overhead	20,000
Variable overhead	30,000

The company realizes that it is facing rising costs and in December is attempting to plan its operations for the year 1968. It is believed that if the product is not redesigned the following results will occur:

Material prices will average 5 percent higher; rates for direct labor will average 10 percent higher. Variable overhead will vary in proportion to direct labor costs. If sale price is increased to produce the same rate of (gross) profit as the 1967 rate, there will be a 10 percent decrease in the number of units sold in 1968.

If the product is redesigned according to suggestions offered by the sales manager, it is expected that a 10 percent increase can be obtained in the number of units sold with a 15 percent increase in the sales price per unit. However, change in the product would involve several changes in cost.

A different grade of material would be used, but 10 percent more of it would be required for each unit. The price of this proposed grade of material has averaged 5 percent below the price of the material now being used and that 5 percent difference in price is expected to continue for the year 1968. Redesign would permit a change in processing method enabling the company to use less-skilled workmen. It is believed that the average pay rate for 1968 would be 10 percent below the average for 1967 due to that change. However, about 20 percent more labor per unit would be required than was needed in 1967. Variable overhead is incurred directly in relation to production. It is expected to increase 10 percent because of price changes and to increase an additional amount in proportion to the change in labor hours.

Assuming the accuracy of these estimates, you are to prepare statements showing the prospective gross profit if:

a) The same product is continued for 1968.

b) The product is redesigned for 1968.

(Adapted from an AICPA Uniform Examination)

PROBLEMS—GROUP B

Problem 23–6. Purpose: *Cost Analysis as an Aid in Pricing*

Compute the sales price per unit at which the Sample Manufacturing Company must sell its only product in 1968 to earn a budgeted profit before tax of $60,000.

The corporation's condensed income statement for 1967 follows:

Sales (30,000 units)...		$450,000
Returns, allowances, and discounts.............................		13,500
Net sales...		$436,500
Cost of goods sold...		306,000
Gross profit...		$130,500
Selling expenses...	$60,000	
Administrative expenses..	30,000	90,000
Net Profit (before income taxes)...............................		$ 40,500

The budget committee has estimated the following changes in income and costs for 1968:

30% increase in number of units sold.
20% increase in material unit cost.
15% increase in direct labor cost per unit.
10% increase in production overhead cost per unit.
14% increase in selling expenses, arising from increased volume as well as from a higher price level.
7% increase in administrative expenses, reflecting anticipated higher wage and supply price levels. Any changes in administrative expenses caused solely by increased sales volume are considered immaterial for the purpose of this budget.

As inventory quantities remain fairly constant, the committee considered that for budget purposes any changes in inventory valuations can be ignored. The composition of the cost of a unit of finished product during 1967 for materials, direct labor, and production overhead, respectively, was in the ratio of 3 to 2 to 1. No changes in production methods or credit policies were contemplated for 1968.

(Adapted from an AICPA Uniform Examination)

Problem 23–7. Purpose: *Cost Analysis as an Aid in Decision Making*

The Smith Corporation sells computer services to its clients. The company completed a feasibility study and decided to obtain an additional computer on January 1, 1968. Information regarding the new computer follows:

1. The purchase price of the computer is $230,000. Maintenance, property taxes, and insurance will be $20,000 per year. If the computer is rented, the annual rent will be $85,000 plus 5 percent of annual billings. The rental price includes maintenance.

2. Due to competitive conditions, the company feels it will be necessary to replace the computer at the end of three years with one which is larger and more advanced. It is estimated that the computer will have a resale value of $110,000 at the end of the three years. The computer will be depreciated on a straight-line basis for both financial reporting and income tax purposes.

3. The income tax rate is 50 percent.

4. The estimated annual billing for the services of the new computer will be $220,000 during the first year and $260,000 during each of the second and third years. The estimated annual expense of operating the computer is $80,000 in addition to the expense mentioned above. An additional $10,000 of start-up expenses will be incurred during the first year.

5. If it decides to purchase the computer, the company will pay cash. If the computer is rented, the $230,000 can be otherwise invested at a 15 percent rate of return.

6. If the computer is purchased, the amount of the investment recovered during each of the three years can be reinvested immediately at a 15 percent rate of return. Each year's recovery of investment in the computer will have been reinvested for an average of six months by the end of the year.

7. The present value of $1 due at a constant rate during each year and discounted at 15 percent is:

Year	Present Value
0–1	$0.93
1–2	0.80
2–3	0.69

The present value of $1 due at the end of each year and discounted at 15 percent is:

End of Year	Present Value
1	$0.87
2	0.76
3	0.66

Required:

a) Prepare a schedule comparing the estimated annual income from the new computer under the purchase plan and under the rental plan. The comparison should include a provision for the opportunity cost of the average investment in the computer during each year.

b) Prepare a schedule showing the annual cash flows under the purchase plan and under the rental plan.

c) Prepare a schedule comparing the net present values of the cash flows under the purchase plan and under the rental plan.

d) Comment on the results obtained in parts (*a*) and (*c*). How should the computer be financed? Why?

(Adapted from an AICPA Uniform Examination)

Problem 23–8. Purpose: *Cost Analysis—Accepting a Special Order*

The State Manufacturing Company produces an item which it sells direct to consumers under its own brand. The item sells at $12.50 per unit, which is a long-established price. Due to a general decline in business activity, sales are currently being made at the rate of 5,000 units per month, which is only 40 percent of the normal productive capacity of the plant of the company.

An analysis of the costs of the company for a recent month, during which only 4,000 units were produced and 5,000 units sold, shows the following:

MANUFACTURING COSTS

Direct labor	$ 9,900.00
Superintendent's salary	1,000.00
Assistant superintendent's salary	750.00
Power purchased	560.00
Direct materials	4,000.00
Purchased parts	2,400.00
Depreciation of building	1,420.00
Maintenance of building	206.00
Heat and light	348.00
Indirect labor	2,240.00
Miscellaneous supplies	800.00
Depreciation of machinery	3,640.00
Repairs to machinery	480.00
Property taxes	600.00
Insurance (fire)	80.00
Social security taxes	456.00
Miscellaneous	1,120.00
	$30,000.00

SELLING COSTS

Manager's salary	$ 833.33
Salesmen's salaries	18,750.00
Travel	247.05
Advertising	500.00
Clerical salaries	300.00
Packing and shipping	2,108.43
Miscellaneous	1,203.79
	$23,942.60

ADMINISTRATIVE AND GENERAL COSTS

Officers' salaries	$ 1,525.00
Office salaries	975.50
Telephone and telegraph	217.73
Supplies	486.21
Bad debts	625.00
Miscellaneous	392.86
	$ 4,222.30

An offer has been received from a chain store by the treasurer of the company to purchase 5,000 units a month of the products with only immaterial modifications, to be shipped and billed to the individual stores. The items would be sold under the store's label and would be packed and shipped as directed by the chain at their expense. They offer $7 per unit unpacked on the basis of a one-year contract. The management of the State Company does not expect that there will be an improvement in the business within the next year, and there is no fear that the sale of the items to the chain would reduce the present volume of sales to consumers. The company does not believe it can afford to accept the offer as it is losing on its present price of $12.50; therefore, it appears that losses would be substantially increased by entering into the sales contract with the chain.

Required:

a) The treasurer calls you in to prepare an analysis which will show the result of accepting the order in comparison with the result if the order is not accepted. In preparing your analysis you are to assume that all items of cost are either completely fixed or completely variable depending upon the usual dominant characteristic of each item and the data given herein.

b) What is the present break-even point?

Problem 23–9. Purpose: *Cost Analysis to Determine Whether to Replace Existing Machines*

The controller of the Doane Manufacturing Company asks for your advice and assistance regarding the problem of whether or not they should replace their "A" machines with new and advanced "B" machines. "B" machines are capable of doubling the present annual capacity of the "A" machines. At the present time the annual finished production of the "A" machines is 2,500,000 good units. You are to assume that the increased production can be sold at the same profitable price.

The "A" machines are being depreciated by the Doane Manufacturing Company under the straight-line method using a salvage value of 10 percent and a useful life of eight years. The "A" machines cost the Doane Manufacturing Company $175,000 plus freight and installation of $25,000. The raw materials as they are fed into the machines are subject to heavy pressure; because of this there is a 20 percent waste factor on an annual basis. The waste materials have no value and are scrapped for nominal value. Direct labor costs are equal to 60 percent of prime costs at the present time (labor and materials are considered prime costs). The company has been purchasing its raw materials in small lots at a cost of $50 per 1,000 units. Factory overhead, exclusive of depreciation, is applied to the manufacturing process at the rate of 20 percent of direct labor costs.

If the company purchases the "B" machines, certain economies will be gained. Material costs will decrease 20 percent because the company will be able to buy in larger quantities. In addition, the new machines have been perfected to such an extent that the waste factor will be reduced by 50 percent. However, because the "B" machine is much larger than the "A" machine, direct labor cost will be expected to increase by 20 percent of itself. Direct labor will continue to be 60 percent of prime cost before the increase of 20 percent in direct labor cost is applied. In addition to this, it is expected that factory overhead rate will increase by 10 percent of itself. The life of the new machines is expected to exceed the life of the "A" machines by one fourth, and the salvage value of the "B" machines will be in the same ratio as the salvage value of the "A" machines. The cost of the "B" machines, including freight and installation of $35,000, will amount to $500,000. The company is aware of the fact that dismantling costs will be involved; however, they do not wish to consider this factor at the present time.

Required:

a) A statement of estimated cost comparisons on an annual basis. (Round to the nearest dollar.)

b) List additional factors that should be considered in deciding upon the replacement.

c) Comment briefly on the usefulness and validity of the comparisons made in (*a*) above.

(Adapted from an AICPA Uniform Examination)

Problem 23–10.   Purpose: *Using Cost Analysis in Decision Making*

You have been engaged to assist the management of the Stenger Corporation in arriving at certain decisions. The Stenger Corporation has its home office in Philadelphia and leases factory buildings in Rhode Island, Georgia, and Illinois. The same single product is manufactured in all three factories. The following information is available regarding 1968 operations:

	Total	Rhode Island	Illinois	Georgia
Sales............................	$900,000	$200,000	$400,000	$300,000
Fixed costs:				
Factory........................	$180,000	$ 50,000	$ 55,000	$ 75,000
Administration.................	59,000	16,000	21,000	22,000
Variable costs...................	500,000	100,000	220,000	180,000
Allocated home office expense.......	63,000	14,000	28,000	21,000
Total.......................	$802,000	$180,000	$324,000	$298,000
Net Profit from Operations.........	$ 98,000	$ 20,000	$ 76,000	$ 2,000

Home office expense is allocated on the basis of units sold. The sales price per unit is $10.

Management is undecided whether to renew the lease of the Georgia factory, which expires on December 31, 1969, and will require an increase in rent of $15,000 per year if renewed. If the Georgia factory is shut down, the amount expected to be realized from the sale of the equipment is greater than its book value and would cover all termination expenses.

If the Georgia factory is shut down, the company can continue to serve customers of the Georgia factory by one of the following methods:

1. Expanding the Rhode Island factory, which would increase fixed costs by 15 percent. Additional shipping expense of $2 per unit will be incurred on the increased production.

2. Entering into a long-term contract with a competitor who will serve the Georgia factory customers and who will pay the Stenger Corporation a commission of $1.60 per unit.

The Stenger Corporation is also planning to establish a subsidiary corporation in Canada to produce the same product. Based on estimated annual Canadian sales of 40,000 units, cost studies produced the following estimates for the Canadian subsidiary:

	Total Annual Costs	Percent of Total Annual Cost That Is Variable
Material............................	$193,600	100%
Labor...............................	90,000	70
Overhead...........................	80,000	64
Administration.......................	30,000	30

The Canadian production will be sold by manufacturer's representatives who will receive a commission of 8 percent of the sales price. No portion of the United States home office expense will be allocated to the Canadian subsidiary.

Required:

a) Prepare a schedule computing the Stenger Corporation's estimated net profit from United States operations under each of the following procedures:

   (1) Expansion of the Rhode Island factory.

   (2) Negotiation of long-term contract on a commission basis.

b) Management wants to price its Canadian product to realize a 10 percent profit on the sales price. Compute the sales price per unit that would result in an estimated 10 percent profit on sales.

c) Assume that your answer to part (*b*) is a sales price of $11 per unit. Compute the break-even point in sales dollars for the Canadian subsidiary.

(Adapted from an AICPA Uniform Examination)

CHAPTER

24 ┊ Distribution Cost Analyses

Definition *Distribution costs* have been defined in two ways. The more common interpretation includes all costs incurred from the time the product is manufactured and placed in the stock room until it has been converted into cash. From this definition it is apparent that the term embraces not only what are commonly known as *selling expenses* but also the *administrative* and perhaps part of the *financial management expenses.* A second, more narrow definition, sometimes used, limits the term *distribution costs* to what is customarily called *selling and marketing expenses.* In the discussions and illustrations in this chapter, the broader connotation of distribution costs is used. These *distribution costs* might include:

1. *Packing and shipping expenses*—packing materials, packing labor, apportioned building expenses, delivery equipment expenses, and clerical expense.
2. *Selling expenses*—salesmen's salaries, salesmen's travel expenses, commissions, advertising, postage, collection expenses, apportioned charges, rent, taxes, insurance, depreciation, and office expense.
3. *Administrative and financial expenses*—applicable to the conversion of manufactured goods into cash.

Distribution costs may also be grouped into two major categories:

1. *Order-getting costs* which include all cost items involved in the functions of obtaining an order. Included in this catagory would be salesmen's costs, commissions, and advertising.
2. *Order-filling costs* include costs incurred in getting the goods to the customer and collecting the cash from the customer. Included in order-filling costs are the functions of packing and shipping, billing, and collection expense.

Purposes of Distribution Cost Analyses

At the beginning, *curiosity* was the primary reason for pioneering in this area, but the recent, rapid strides made in marketing research coupled with the increasingly high costs of distribution have added new stimulus to the further study and application of distribution costs analyses as another valuable tool for management control. Furthermore, federal legislation in the matter of price fixing and marketing practices makes a knowledge of distribution costs a necessity. The Robinson-Patman Act, for example, administered by the Federal Trade Commission, is an act under which manufacturers may at any time be called upon to justify, on the basis of *cost,* quantity discounts or price concessions given to large quantity purchasers.

The development of accounting procedures for the costs of distribution has lagged somewhat compared to the progress made in industrial *production cost* accounting. One reason for this has been the difficulty in establishing uniform rules of accounting for the many possible variations of application. The cost of distributing a product, for example, will vary not only with the product distributed but also with the territory in which the sale is made, the type of customer, the method of sale, and the method of delivery. Recently, increased attention has been given to the area of distribution costs as these costs may make up a significant portion of total costs. In some industries, distribution costs are greater than production costs.

Analysis of distribution costs may lead to the implementation of responsibility accounting concepts. Cost data should be accumulated in accounts that are grouped by function so that the person in charge of the function knows his costs. For example, all costs of the billing function such as salaries, supplies, and postage should be determinable so that the manager of the billing department could be held accountable for his costs. The concepts of departmentalizing costs in the factory should be carried over to the distribution effort by functionalizing the costs under the order-getting and order-filling categories.

Classifying Distribution Costs

For the most effective managerial control, distribution costs must be classified as either *direct* or *indirect,* distinguishing between those which can be allocated directly to a product, a sale, a territory, or a method of distribution, and those which must be apportioned. There must be a further analysis of the distribution costs into those which are *fixed* and those which are *variable.* Some, such as salesmen's commissions, vary with the sales; others, such as rent of sales facilities, are fixed or period costs. As in the case of manufacturing overhead costs, distribution costs must be carefully analyzed and grouped, and become part of the computations of *marginal income, contribution margin,* and *break-even point.*

Effective distribution cost control also requires that periodically, actual expenses be compared with predetermined standards; hence, standards must be established. A flexible budget showing the fixed and variable distribution costs at various sales volumes permits ready comparison with actual to determine the causes of variations from the predetermined or standard distribution cost rates.

Accumulating and Recording Distribution Costs   The concept of distribution costs involves a threefold task which in its final analysis resolves itself into (1) *accumulating and recording the costs of distributing the product,* (2) *analyzing the costs of distribution on some acceptable basis,* and (3) *the control and interpretation of distribution costs through the use of predetermined standards and budgets.*

Distribution costs may be grouped under the following major functions and then further subdivided according to the salaries, supplies, rent, and other expenses within the group:

Order-getting costs:
1. Direct selling costs.
2. Advertising and sales promotion.

Order-filling costs:
1. Transportation and delivery.
2. Warehouse and storage expense.
3. Credit and collection expense.

Each of these five categories represents a control account with a subsidiary ledger for the detailed accounts. A section of such a Code of Accounts is shown in Illustration 24–1. This Code of Accounts is by no means complete; it is merely indicative of accounts found in the subsidiary ledger.

If no subsidiary ledgers are desired, it is possible to record the individual expenses of selling and distribution in their respective accounts and at the end of regular periods to close them out to summary accounts. The diagrammatic effect is somewhat like that shown in the illustration which follows:

SALESMEN'S SALARIES		
SALESMEN'S BONUSES		
SALESMEN'S COMMISSIONS	CLOSED INTO	DIRECT SELLING
SALESMEN'S TRAVELING EXPENSES		EXPENSE SUMMARY
SALES OFFICE EXPENSES		

Illustration 24–1

SUGGESTED CODE OF CHART OF ACCOUNTS OF THE DISTRIBUTION COSTS

Control Account		Subsidiary Ledger	
Acct. No.	Account	Acct. No.	Account
510	Direct Selling Expense Control		
		511	Salesmen's Salaries
		512	Salesmen's Commissions
		513	Salesmen's Bonuses
		514	Salesmen's Traveling Expenses
		515	Sales Office Expenses—Supplies
		516	Sales Office Salaries
		517	Sales Office Telephone
		518	Sales Office Rent
520	Advertising and Sales Promotion Control		
		521	Salaries
		522	Office Supplies
		523	Rent of Office
		524	Samples—Cost and Distribution
		525	Newspaper Advertising
		526	Magazine Advertising
		527	Direct Mail
		528	Billboard Advertising
530	Transportation Expense Control		
		531	Freight-Out
		532	Shipping Department Salaries
		533	Shipping Department Supplies
		534	Delivery Expense
		535	Depreciation Delivery Equipment
		536	Salaries of Drivers
		537	Freight-In on Returned Sales
540	Warehouse and Storage Expense Control		
		541	Supplies
		542	Salaries
		543	Rent or Taxes
		544	Repairs
		545	Depreciation of Buildings or Equipment
		546	Insurance
		547	Heat and Light
550	Credit and Collection Expense Control		
		551	Collection Department Salaries
		552	Collection Department Supplies
		553	Credit and Collection Rent
		554	Credit Services and Expense
		555	Legal Fees
		556	Heat and Light
		557	Losses from Bad and Doubtful Accounts
570	General Distribution Costs		
		571	Prorated Administrative Expenses

This procedure is similar to that used in summarizing the individual manufacturing overhead costs in a Manufacturing Overhead Summary account.

Analyzing the Costs of Distribution
The purpose of distribution cost analysis is to enable management to determine the answers to some or all of the following questions: "What *customers'* accounts are profitable?" "What *products* are most profitable to sell?" "In which *territories* are the most profitable sales made?" "What are the most profitable *methods* of distribution?" "What *salesmen* are making the most profitable sales?" These questions indicate to a certain degree the nature of the analyses which are required. Management must decide under which bases it desires to have distribution costs analyzed and whether such analysis is to be the result of a *statistical study carried on periodically* or whether the analysis is to be part of a *continuous, routine accounting function.* If it is to be a statistical study, then the accounting department will merely furnish the expense figures, and the marketing or statistical sections will analyze these data and prepare reports for management. Our discussion will be based on the assumption that the distribution cost analysis is an integral part of the accounting system.

Distribution costs may be classified to expedite the following analyses:

1. The cost of distribution *of each product.*
2. The cost of distribution *within each territory.*
3. The cost of distribution for *classes of customers,* which may be further subdivided as follows:
   a) According to *size of sale.*
   b) According to *territorial classification*—urban or rural.
   c) According to *type of customer organization*—chain stores, mail-order houses, and independents.
   d) According to *type of store*—drugstore, department store, variety store, etc.
4. The cost of distribution for each *method of sale,* which may be subdivided into—
   a) Branch offices.
   b) Salesmen.
   c) Mail.
   d) Unsolicited,
      or as an alternative classification, as—
   a) Cash sales.
   b) Credit sales.
   c) Installment sales.

The *first two* of the foregoing types of analyses are most reasonably and accurately determined because the number of variables is smaller than when the customer factor is considered. The many individual differences in types of customers cause the greatest complication in distribution cost analysis; and that is why, so frequently, most concerns leave methods 3 and 4, above, to a method of statistical analysis of accounting data rather than to a method based on recorded continuous data, such as might be used for methods 1 and 2.

Product Method of Distribution Cost Analyses
Distribution cost analyses on the basis of *products sold* may be advantageously used if the nature of the products, the selling effort, and the size of order are such as to prevent the use of a uniform basis, such as sales dollar volume, quantity of units, or weight. This method could be used by sellers of few products, each of which is produced and sold in large volume and each of which has different characteristics that prevent a uniform analysis of distribution costs. Companies selling many products might group products by *product line.* For example, a manufacturer of motor vehicles might classify his distribution costs by type of vehicle. A company that manufactures many products but has a distinctly seasonal demand for some products might well benefit from an analysis of costs *by product* to provide necessary data to determine whether or not the company should encourage off-season orders at reduced prices.

The "product" method of distribution cost analyses lends itself most readily to continuous accounting records and statements. The distribution costs can be recorded under: (1) direct selling costs; (2) advertising and sales promotion; (3) transportation; (4) warehousing and storage; (5) credit and collection; (6) general administrative expenses; and (7) all other distribution costs. A subsidiary ledger may be provided for each expense group. Periodically—weekly, semimonthly, or monthly—the expenses can be allocated to each product by the use of product expense analysis sheets, corresponding to the departmental expense analysis or standing order sheets used for manufacturing expenses.

The allocation of the various expenses requires further explanation. Expenses for allocation may be classified as: *direct,* chargeable directly to the product or territory; *semidirect,* such as advertising copy which may cover several products; and *indirect* expenses.

A suggested basis for the allocation of the various distribution costs is shown in Illustration 24–2 on page 739.

The same basis of allocation can be used if it is desired to compile distribution costs *by territories;* here, the total sales in each territory rather than the sales of each product would be the basic factor. However, when it is desirable to analyze the costs of distribution by

Illustration 24-2

Expense or Cost Functionally Grouped	Basis of Allocation
Direct selling expenses:	
Salesmen's salaries......................	Sales value of product
Salesmen's commissions..................	Sales value of product
Salesmen's bonuses......................	Sales value of product
Sales or branch office expenses, including supplies, salaries, telephone, rent or building maintenance, entertainment......	Sales value of product
Advertising and sales promotion expense:	
Salaries and office expenses................	Sales value of products
Samples................................	Specific cost of each product samples
General company advertising..............	Sales value of products
Direct product advertising, newspaper, magazine, and direct mail................	Directly to product being advertised
Transportation expenses:	
Freight-out............................	Apportioned on the basis of one of the following: (a) sales value of each product, (b) relative weight of product sales, or (c) size of product weighted by quantity sold
Shipping department salaries and supplies	
Delivery expenses......................	
Warehouse and storage:	
Supplies and salaries....................	Number of units sold and shipped or on basis of relative size of product weighted by number handled
Depreciation...........................	
Insurance..............................	Average cost value of each product on hand
Credit and collection expenses:	
Salaries................................	Sales value of each product sold
Supplies...............................	Sales value of each product sold
Rent...................................	Sales value of each product sold
Legal fees..............................	Number of accounts and products sold to each
Heat and light..........................	Sales value of each product sold
Loss on bad and doubtful accounts........	Number of accounts and the value of products sold to each
Administrative expenses:	
Salaries and expenses of bookkeeping department............................	Either number of sales invoices or lines per invoice for each product
Other administrative expenses............	Either on sales value of each product, or the number of orders received for each product

classes of customers or by method of sale, some modifications in procedure must be made for certain expenses.

To illustrate the method used to record as accounting data the distribution costs accumulated and analyzed on a product basis, the case of the Harvey Paint Manufacturing Company is used. This firm produces three main groups of products: (1) white lead and oils; (2) paints; and (3) enamels, lacquers, and varnishes. Although these are distributed to dealers and jobbers, that fact is not pertinent to our present problem. An analysis of the books and records for the past three months brings forth the following necessary information concerning business operations:

	White Lead and Oils	Paints	Enamels, Lacquers, Varnishes	Total
Sales for past three months	$150,000	$400,000	$250,000	$800,000
Number of orders received	1,500	3,800	2,200	7,500
Volume of sales in gallons	70,000	150,000	80,000	300,000
Specific product advertising	$ 10,000	$ 30,000	$ 20,000	$ 60,000

The distribution costs for the period were:

Code No.	Accounts		
510	Direct Selling Expense Control		$40,000.00
511	Salesmen's Salaries and Commissions	$32,000.00	
512	Sales Office Expenses	8,000.00	
	Total	$40,000.00	
520	Advertising and Sales Promotion Expense Control		68,200.00
521	Product Advertising	$60,000.00	
522	Company Advertising	3,200.00	
523	Samples (Paints, $3,000; Lacquers, $2,000)	5,000.00	
	Total	$68,200.00	
530	Transportation Expense Control		18,000.00
531	Freight-Out	$ 3,000.00	
532	Shipping Salaries and Supplies	9,000.00	
533	Delivery Expenses	6,000.00	
	Total	$18,000.00	
540	Warehousing and Storage Expense Control		6,600.00
541	Salaries and Supplies	$ 4,800.00	
542	Rent and Maintenance	1,800.00	
	Total	$ 6,600.00	
550	Credit and Collection Expense Control		4,200.00
551	Salaries and Supplies	$ 3,000.00	
552	Legal Fees	900.00	
553	Loss on Bad Debts	300.00	
	Total	$ 4,200.00	
560	Administrative Expense Control		5,250.00
561	Supervision of Office Work	$ 3,000.00	
562	Bookkeeping and Clerical Work	2,250.00	
	Total	$ 5,250.00	

As is evident, this list of expenses is only partially complete and is used for illustrative purposes only. In a complete distribution cost accounting system, there would be six controlling accounts, with a subsidiary expense ledger for each group. However, the controlling accounts may be dispensed with if the individual expense accounts are not too numerous. In either case, it should be noted that this illustration is one of *historical costs,* not predetermined standard costs, which will be illustrated later in the chapter. Furthermore, no matter what method is used, it will be necessary to accumulate the distribution costs by products, and the simplest method is by use of *distribution cost product analysis sheets.* Continuing the illustration, the relationship of the

Illustration 24–3. Control Accounts and Subsidiary Ledger Accounts for Distribution Costs

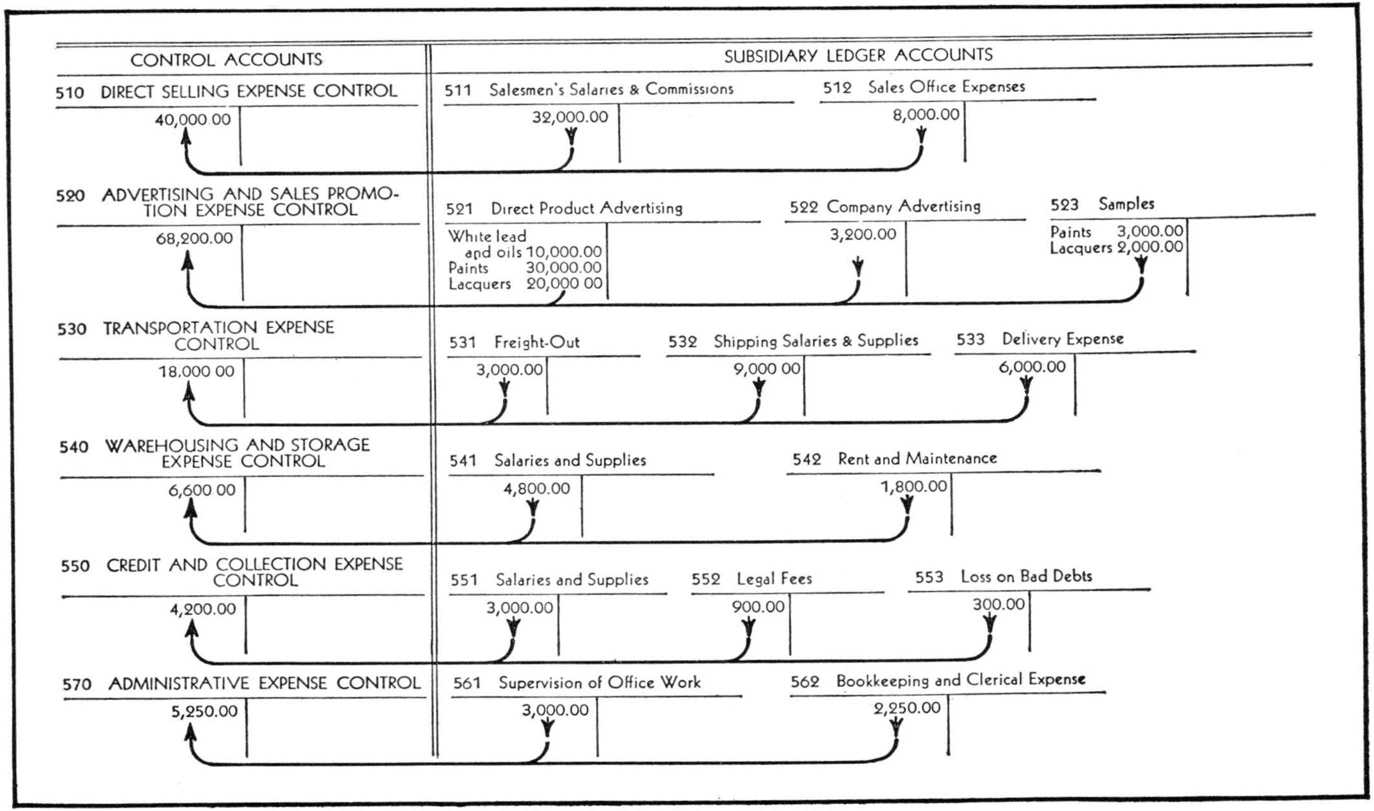

CONTROL ACCOUNTS

510 DIRECT SELLING EXPENSE CONTROL
40,000.00

590 ADVERTISING AND SALES PROMO-
TION EXPENSE CONTROL
68,200.00

530 TRANSPORTATION EXPENSE
CONTROL
18,000.00

540 WAREHOUSING AND STORAGE
EXPENSE CONTROL
6,600.00

550 CREDIT AND COLLECTION EXPENSE
CONTROL
4,200.00

570 ADMINISTRATIVE EXPENSE CONTROL
5,250.00

SUBSIDIARY LEDGER ACCOUNTS

511 Salesmen's Salaries & Commissions
32,000.00

512 Sales Office Expenses
8,000.00

521 Direct Product Advertising
White lead
and oils 10,000.00
Paints 30,000.00
Lacquers 20,000.00

522 Company Advertising
3,200.00

523 Samples
Paints 3,000.00
Lacquers 2,000.00

531 Freight-Out
3,000.00

532 Shipping Salaries & Supplies
9,000.00

533 Delivery Expense
6,000.00

541 Salaries and Supplies
4,800.00

542 Rent and Maintenance
1,800.00

551 Salaries and Supplies
3,000.00

552 Legal Fees
900.00

553 Loss on Bad Debts
300.00

561 Supervision of Office Work
3,000.00

562 Bookkeeping and Clerical Expense
2,250.00

control accounts and the subsidiary ledger are shown (see Illustration 24–3) and then the use of the standing order sheets (Illustration 24–4) and the product distribution cost analysis summary accounts (Illustration 24–5, p. 743).

Illustration 24–4. Distribution Cost Analysis Sheet by Products

DISTRIBUTION COST ANALYSIS

For Month of March, 19—

Date	Code No.	White Lead and Oils Amount	Paints Amount	Enamels, Lacquers, and Varnishes Amount	Total
3/31	511	$ 6,000.00	$16,000.00	$10,000.00	$ 32,000.00
	512	1,500.00	4,000.00	2,500.00	8,000.00
	521	10,000.00	30,000.00	20,000.00	60,000.00
	522	600.00	1,600.00	1,000.00	3,200.00
	523	. . . . .	3,000.00	2,000.00	5,000.00
	531	562.50	1,500.00	937.50	3,000.00
	532	1,687.50	4,500.00	2,812.50	9,000.00
	533	1,125.00	3,000.00	1,875.00	6,000.00
	541	1,120.00	2,400.00	1,280.00	4,800.00
	542	420.00	900.00	480.00	1,800.00
	551	600.00	1,520.00	880.00	3,000.00
	552	181.00	454.00	265.00	900.00
	553	60.00	152.00	88.00	300.00
	561	600.00	1,520.00	880.00	3,000.00
	562	450.00	1,140.00	660.00	2,250.00
		$24,906.00	$71,686.00	$45,658.00	$142,250.00

One of these standing order sheets is used each month, with sufficient columns for each group of products. It is also possible to prepare this sheet so that there would be one for each group of products, with columns for each month, so that the sheet could be used for a three-month, six-month, or one-year period.

The journal entry made from the summary of the standing order sheets, based on distribution costs analyzed and recorded by products, would be:

```
Distribution Costs—White Lead and Oils.....................24,906.00
Distribution Costs—Paints...................................71,686.00
Distribution Costs—Enamels, Lacquers, and Varnishes..........45,658.00
    Direct Selling Expense Control...........................      40,000.00
    Advertising and Sales Promotion Expense Control...........      68,200.00
    Transportation Expense Control...........................      18,000.00
    Warehousing and Storage Expense Control..................      6,600.00
    Credit and Collection Expense Control....................      4,200.00
    Administrative Expense Control...........................      5,250.00
    To close out the distribution expense control accounts to the prod-
    uct analysis summary accounts.
```

DISTRIBUTION COST ANALYSIS SHEETS

One for Each Product for Which Distribution Costs Are Being Analyzed

One of these may be used each month or quarter, or one with twelve columns can be used for an entire year. For basis of cost allocation see footnotes.

Standing Order Sheet No. 1

PRODUCT: White Lead and Oils

Date	Code No.	Amount
3/31	511	$ 6,000.00[1]
	512	1,500.00[1]
	521	10,000.00[2]
	522	600.00[1]
	531	562.50[1]
	532	1,687.50[1]
	533	1,125.00[1]
	541	1,120.00[3]
	542	420.00[3]
	551	600.00[4]
	552	181.00[4]
	553	60.00[4]
	561	600.00[4]
	562	450.00[4]
	Total	$24,906.00

Standing Order Sheet No. 2

PRODUCT: Paints

Date	Code No.	Amount
3/31	511	$16,000.00[1]
	512	4,000.00[1]
	521	30,000.00[2]
	522	1,600.00[1]
	523	3,000.00[2]
	531	1,500.00[1]
	532	4,500.00[1]
	533	3,000.00[1]
	541	2,400.00[3]
	542	900.00[3]
	551	1,520.00[4]
	552	454.00[4]
	553	152.00[4]
	561	1,520.00[4]
	562	1,140.00[4]
	Total	$71,686.00

Standing Order Sheet No. 3

PRODUCT: Enamels, Lacquers, and Varnishes

Date	Code No.	Amount
3/31	511	$10,000.00[1]
	512	2,500.00[1]
	521	20,000.00[2]
	522	1,000.00[1]
	523	2,000.00[2]
	531	937.50[1]
	532	2,812.50[1]
	533	1,875.00[1]
	541	1,280.00[3]
	542	480.00[3]
	551	880.00[4]
	552	265.00[4]
	553	88.00[4]
	561	880.00[4]
	562	660.00[4]
	Total	$45,658.00

[1] On basis of sales value. [2] Direct product charges. [3] On basis of physical volume. [4] Number of sales orders.

Distribution Costs—White Lead and Oils

March 31 24,906.00

Distribution Costs—Paints

March 31 71,686.00

Distribution Costs—Enamels, Lacquers, Varnishes

March 31 45,658.00

The same effect is realized without the use of the control accounts by crediting the expense accounts and charging the product summary distribution expense accounts. When this point has been reached in recording distribution costs on a historical cost plan, the distribution cost product summary accounts are closed out to the Profit and Loss account, to wit:

```
Profit and Loss Account.....................................142,250.00
    Distribution Costs—White Lead and Oils.................     24,906.00
    Distribution Costs—Paints.............................     71,686.00
    Distribution Costs—Enamels, Lacquers and Varnishes.......     45,658.00
    To close out the distribution cost summary accounts.
```

Analysis of Distribution Costs by Territories   The territorial analysis of distribution costs should be made as this may be desirable to control the costs of definite territorial areas. Naturally, when distribution costs are analyzed by territories, sales and costs of sales would follow the same pattern. The plan of this type of distribution costing and analysis is the same as that for product analysis. Frequently, within a given territory, the method of distribution of the products includes sales from warehouses, sales from branch offices, and sales made directly to customers. When these variations are not the same for each territory, the analysis can become complex. Computers may be of help here by providing the necessary data. The analysis of territorial distribution assumes a more or less uniform procedure in each territory. The final summary of distribution costs will show: Distribution Costs, Territory I; Distribution Costs, Territory II; and Distribution Costs, Territory III.

In allocating certain expenses to the respective territories, the following should be taken into consideration:

Expense	*Method of Allocation*
Salesmen's salaries and expenses.........	Time spent in each territory
Billing and office expenses..............	Number of billing items or direct charge
Advertising...........................	Territory covered by media
Transportation........................	Either direct, or on the basis of mileage
Credit and collection..................	Number of accounts in each territory or number of sales

Other Methods of Distribution Cost Analysis   Distribution cost analysis may be continued under the headings of *classes of customers* and *methods of sales.* As a general rule they are not recorded on the books as functional or dynamic costs. They represent studies made by the marketing department to aid management.

Distribution costs collected by *classes of customers* might be analyzed and interpreted in one of five ways:

1. The distribution costs might be analyzed or allocated to the sales according to the *size of the sale* made. Sales might be grouped: $1 to $50; $51 to $100; $101 to $200; and over $200. Such an analysis would be fundamentally useful to manufacturers who sell to both large-volume and small-volume customers and who wish to give inducements to the large buyers.
2. The distribution costs might be analyzed or allocated to the sales on the basis of the *territorial* distribution of the customers. Customers might be grouped as rural and urban, by states, or by cities. This method of collecting distribution costs would be useful in justifying different selling prices in the various territories.
3. The distribution costs might be analyzed or allocated to the sales on the basis of the *size of the community* in which sold. This method is similar to the territorial.
4. The distribution costs might be analyzed or allocated to sales on the basis of type of *customer organization.* Customers might be grouped as *chain stores, mail-order houses,* and *independents.*
5. The distribution costs are sometimes analyzed or allocated to sales on the basis of the *type of customers,* such as drugstores, department stores, grocery stores, etc.

In each of the foregoing methods, distribution cost analysis can become complex. Here again, the computer should be of help.

If the distribution costs are to be determined on the basis of customers, it is necessary to apportion or allocate the various expenses on the basis of the amount of service which each customer or class of customer receives. This type of cost analysis is important to large distributors who wish to have data to justify special price concessions or discounts to certain customers. Illustration 24–6 shows a summary of the costs, in terms of percentage of sales, of handling accounts of varying sizes. It is

Illustration 24–6

THE CHAPELA COMPANY

Cost to Handle Sales of Various Sizes

Expressed as a Percentage of Sales Prices

	Sales under $200	Sales between $201 and $500	Sales between $501 and $5,000	Total
Number of sales..........	400	150	50	600
Percent of total..........	66⅔	25	8⅓	100
Sales volume............$45,150		$61,580	$157,270	$264,000
Percent of total.......... 17.10		23.33	59.57	100
Cost to handle............$ 2,265		$ 1,875	$ 2,160	$ 6,300
Cost to handle as per- cent of sales.......... 5.02		3.04	1.37	2.39

comparatively easy to determine the number of sales in the various price classifications and the total sales for each group. The cost of handling the sales in each group must be determined by charging against each its share of the 15 previously listed marketing expenses. Expenses such as advertising may be charged directly; several of the others must be allocated. Often, detailed studies must be made to determine an equitable basis of allocation. To determine the portion of sales office expense applicable to each group it is necessary to make a detailed study of the cost of taking an order, entering an order, billing and accounting for the sale, etc. Similarly, the cost of general company advertising must be apportioned on some fair basis. The total of the distribution expenses for each group of sales is known as the total *cost to handle.* This figure is also shown as a percentage of sales.

Illustration 24–7

THE CHAPELA COMPANY

Cost of Distribution as a Percentage of Sales

Advertising	2.12% of sales
Salesmen's salaries	5.48
Salesmen's traveling expenses	2.41
Sales office expenses	3.79
Shipping and transportation	1.61
Warehousing	0.80
Credit and collection expense	0.40
Allowance for bad debts	0.60
General administrative expenses apportioned	4.85
Total Cost of Distribution Expressed as Percentage of Sales	22.06%

A simpler method of computing the costs of handling the sales to certain customers may be used. Instead of apportioning the expenses according to the size of the sale, the average cost of handling all the sales, expressed as a percentage of the total sales, is determined. The final result tells the manufacturer approximately what percentage to add to the selling price to cover distribution costs. However, this amount is not accurate; it does not cost as much to sell a large quantity of goods to a single buyer as it does to distribute the same quantity to 50 different customers. Furthermore, greater sales effort may be required to sell certain commodities. The result obtained by using total expenses and total sales is an average cost and, like all averages, may be misleading.

These average costs, obtained by dividing each expense by the total sales, are shown in Illustration 24–7.

A few organizations analyze their marketing costs on the basis of the *methods of distribution,* which might be either:

1. Costs of direct selling by company representatives:
   a) To wholesalers.
   b) To large retailers.
2. Costs of unsolicited or mail orders.

Sometimes the methods of distribution are based on the *credit terms* of the sales. Distribution expenses are then allocated to sales by:

1. Cash sales.
2. Credit sales.
3. Installment sales.

No matter what the basis is for allocating marketing and distribution costs, the total costs are usually expressed as a percentage of the net sales, and when so expressed, distribution cost analysis becomes useful to management in fixing selling prices, in attempting to eliminate unprofitable practices, and in determining the size of quantity or cash discounts. Total costs may also be reduced to a cost per unit of product or per sales order.

To illustrate distribution costs on the basis of *methods of distribution,* an analysis could be made of the sales of a large wholesaler. The types of sales made by a wholesale dealer in hardware might be (1) retail—cash and carry; (2) country sales—truck delivery; (3) country sales—freight delivery; and (4) mail-order sales—shipped by freight. In order to analyze cost of marketing in this manner, it is necessary to ascertain the amount of the sales in each class.

It is also necessary to compute the amount of the distribution costs applicable to each kind of sales. This procedure requires a statistical analysis similar to that made in the other methods of allocating distribution costs. Illustration 24–8 shows, in condensed form, the method of presenting this information. In analyzing the data in this illustration, the following meaningful conclusions are drawn:

1. Retail sales are responsible for 48.25 percent of the distribution costs, yet furnish only 15.7 percent of the profit.
2. Retail sales furnish 20 percent of total sales, but only 15.7 percent of the net income.
3. Country sales—truck delivery are above average in profitability. They consume 29.03 percent of the distribution costs and still produce 31.4 percent of the net income.
4. Country sales—freight delivery consume 8.62 percent of the distribution costs and produce 13.1 percent of the net income.
5. Mail-order sales required 14.1 percent of the distribution costs but supplied 39.8 percent of the income.

Illustration 24–8. Statement of Distribution Costs and Profits

	Retail Cash Sales	Country Sales, Truck Delivery	Country Sales, Freight Delivery	Mail-Order Sales	Total
THE CHAPELA COMPANY STATEMENT OF DISTRIBUTION COSTS AND RATIOS For the Month of August, 19—					
Sales volume...............	$40,000	$60,000	$30,000	$70,000	$200,000
Percent of total sales.........	20%	30%	15%	35%	100%
Distribution costs...........	$12,000	$ 7,200	$ 2,100	$ 3,500	$ 24,800
Percent of total distribution costs....................	48.39%	29.03%	8.47%	14.11%	100%
Distribution costs expressed as percent of sales.........	30%	12%	7%	5%	12.4%
Net income................	$ 3,600	$ 7,200	$ 3,000	$ 9,100	$ 22,900
Percent of total net profit	15.7%	31.4%	13.1%	39.8%	100%

Distribution Costs and the Direct Costing Concept

Companies using direct costing procedure have stated that the usefulness of a *decision-making* cost report is greatly enhanced by separating those period costs which are specifically traceable to a product from those which are shared in common with other products. See Illustration 24–8.

Reference to the statement will illustrate an important point. The period costs have been divided among those that are *specific to product lines* and those that are *allocated general period costs.* Although the allocation of general period (or fixed) costs is necessary in order to achieve a "full-cost" concept, the results of allocation may be misleading. For example, see the results of Product Line No. 3 in Illustration 24–9. This product line shows a loss of $6,014 which could lead to a conclusion by management that Product Line No. 3 is unprofitable and should be dropped. Further analysis, however, is necessary.

An examination of the sales and cost structure of Product Line No. 3 shows that the amount left to contribute to period costs is $36,000. Even after the fixed costs applicable to Product Line No. 3 are deducted, there is still $14,000 left to cover the general fixed costs. If Product Line No. 3 is discontinued, the $14,000 would disappear and the loss would be increased to $20,014 as the general period costs would go on.

The validity of allocating the general fixed expenses is thus subject to question. Of course, eventually, *all* fixed costs must be covered by the

Product Line Income Statement

Product Lines

	Total Amount	Pct.	No. 1 Amount	Pct.	No. 2 Amount	Pct.	No. 3 Amount	Pct.
Net sales	$600,000.00	100.0	$300,000.00	100.0	$200,000.00	100.0	$100,000.00	100.0
Direct costs								
Manufacturing								
Direct materials	$150,000.00	25.0	$ 75,000.00	25.0	$ 55,000.00	27.5	$ 20,000.00	20.0
Direct labor	90,000.00	15.0	30,000.00	10.0	30,000.00	15.0	30,000.00	30.0
Direct overhead	60,000.00	10.0	30,000.00	10.0	20,000.00	10.0	10,000.00	10.0
Selling								
Freight-out	12,000.00	2.0	9,000.00	3.0	3,000.00	1.5	----	----
Salesmen's commissions	24,000.00	4.0	12,000.00	4.0	8,000.00	4.0	4,000.00	4.0
Total direct costs	$336,000.00	56.0	$156,000.00	52.0	$116,000.00	58.0	$ 64,000.00	64.0
Marginal income . . . : . . .	$264,000.00	44.0	$144,000.00	48.0	$ 84,000.00	42.0	$ 36,000.00	36.0
Period costs specific to product lines								
Depreciation	$ 40,000.00		$ 20,000.00		$ 10,000.00		$ 10,000.00	
Property taxes and insurance	20,000.00		10,000.00		2,000.00		8,000.00	
Advertising	24,000.00		20,000.00		---		4,000.00	
Total	$ 84,000.00		$ 50,000.00		$ 12,000.00		$ 22,000.00	
Margin after specific period costs	$180,000.00	30.0	$ 94,000.00	31.3	$ 72,000.00	36.0	$ 14,000.00	14.0
Allocated general period costs								
Manufacturing	$ 40,000.00		$ 20,000.00		$ 13,320.00		$ 6,680.00	
Selling	30,000.00		15,000.00		10,000.00		5,000.00	
Administrative	30,000.00		15,000.00		10,000.00		5,000.00	
Research and development	20,000.00		10,000.00		6,666.00		3,334.00	
Total	$120,000.00		$ 60,000.00		$ 39,986.00		$ 20,014.00	
Income (loss) before taxes	$ 60,000.00	10.0	$ 34,000.00	11.3	$ 32,014.00	16.0	($ 6,014.00)	(6.0)

SOURCE: Adapted from *N.A.A. Research Report 37, Current Application of Direct Costing.*

company, but for managerial usefulness in the short-run, it might be desirable *not* to allocate common costs that will continue even if a product or product line is discontinued.

The Use of Standards and Budgets   Historical analysis is not sufficient for effective managerial control. As in industrial accounting, management must know what the distribution costs *should have been,* as well as *what they are.* The utilization of budgets and predetermined standard costs are as necessary for effective distribution cost control as for manufacturing cost control. If distribution costs are to be prorated and determined on the basis of *products* or on the basis of *territory,* the predetermined distribution cost rate can be based on the estimated sales value by products or by territories. Standards must be set for each function of order getting and order filling.

Standard costs make use of a single predetermined rate for each group of distribution costs, and later the individual expenses are analyzed on a statistical report. For example, an estimate of the various expenses by Products A, B, and C for a certain manufacturer resulted in the calculation of the predetermined distribution cost rates, expressed as a percentage of sales as shown in Illustration 24–10.

Illustration 24–10

PREDETERMINED RATES FOR APPLYING SELLING AND DISTRIBUTION EXPENSES TO THE COST OF GOODS SOLD

(Percentage Based upon Cost of Sales)

Expense	Product A	Product B	Product C
Direct selling expenses	4.61%	4.20%	4.15%
Advertising and sales promotion	3.41	3.14	3.60
Transportation	2.72	2.70	2.60
Warehousing and storage	.90	.90	.90
Credit and collection	2.75	2.15	2.20
General administrative expenses	8.71	8.51	7.05
Total	23.10%	21.60%	20.50%

Although these predetermined rates for selling and distribution expenses might be used in a manner similar to the predetermined rates for manufacturing overhead—that is, make entries and have accounts for both the actual expenses and the applied expenses—this is not always done. In many cases, the various selling and distribution expenses by groups are analyzed *statistically* and compared regularly in the same manner as any other budgeted figures. The statistical analysis is usually made by the marketing analysis division in cooperation with

Illustration 24–11. Schedule of Actual and Applied Direct Selling Expense

THE CHAPELA COMPANY

SCHEDULE OF ACTUAL AND APPLIED

DIRECT SELLING EXPENSES

For Month of August, 19—

Expense	Product A	Product B	Product C	Total
Salesmen's Salaries.....................	$ 600.00	$ 800.00	$1,000.00	$ 2,400.00
Salesmen's Commissions................	800.00	1,200.00	1,800.00	3,800.00
Salesmen's Bonus.......................	....	....	250.00	250.00
Salesmen's Traveling Expense...........	120.00	160.00	170.00	450.00
Sales Office Supplies....................	50.00	55.00	60.00	165.00
Sales Office Salaries....................	200.00	210.00	220.00	630.00
Sales Office Telephone.................	45.00	48.00	52.00	145.00
Sales Office Rent.......................	60.00	60.00	60.00	180.00
Direct Selling Expense Total............	$1,875.00	$2,533.00	$3,612.00	$8,020.00
Applied Direct Selling Expense..........	1,720.00	2,400.00	3,800.00	7,920.00
Underapplied Direct Selling Expense.....	$ 155.00	$ 133.00	$ 188.00*	$ 100.00

* Overapplied.

Illustration 24–12. Schedule of Actual and Applied Advertising and Sales Promotion Expense

THE CHAPELA COMPANY

SCHEDULE OF ACTUAL AND APPLIED

ADVERTISING AND SALES PROMOTION EXPENSES

For Month of August, 19—

Expense	Product A	Product B	Product C	Total
Salaries..............................	$ 150.00	$ 160.00	$ 170.00	$ 480.00
Office Supplies........................	100.00	90.00	200.00	390.00
Rent of Office........................	60.00	60.00	60.00	180.00
Samples..............................	400.00	375.00	600.00	1,375.00
Newspaper Advertising................	4,000.00	....	....	4,000.00
Magazine Advertising.................	....	....	700.00	700.00
Direct Mail Advertising...............	....	300.00	....	300.00
Billboard Advertising..................	100.00	100.00	100.00	300.00
Advertising and Sales Promotion Expense Total.............................	$4,810.00	$1,085.00	$1,830.00	$7,725.00
Applied Advertising and Sales Promotion Expense...........................	4,600.00	1,000.00	1,600.00	7,200.00
Underapplied Advertising and Sales Promotion Expense.....................	$ 210.00	$ 85.00	$ 230.00	$ 525.00

Illustration 24–13. Summary of Distribution Costs

THE CHAPELA COMPANY

SUMMARY OF DISTRIBUTION COSTS—CLASSIFIED BY PRODUCTS

For the Month of August, 19—

Expense	PRODUCT A			PRODUCT B			PRODUCT C			TOTAL FOR ALL PRODUCTS		
	Actual	Applied	Under-Applied	Actual	Applied	Under-Applied	Actual	Applied	Under-Applied	Actual	Applied	Under-Applied
Direct selling expense..	$ 1,875.00	$ 1,720.00	$155.00	$2,533.00	$2,400.00	$133.00	$ 3,612.00	$ 3,800.00	$188.00*	$ 8,020.00*	$ 7,920.00	$100.00
Advertising and sales promotion.........	4,810.00	4,600.00	210.00	1,085.00	1,000.00	85.00	1,830.00	1,600.00	230.00	7,725.00	7,200.00	525.00
Transportation.........	3,760.00	3,500.00	260.00	870.00	950.00	80.00*	1,560.00	1,710.00	150.00*	6,190.00	6,160.00	30.00
Warehouse and storage.	186.00	200.00	14.00*	245.00	200.00	45.00	353.00	300.00	53.00	784.00	700.00	84.00
Credit and collection...	433.00	400.00	33.00	544.00	600.00	56.00*	610.00	580.00	30.00	1,587.00	1,580.00	7.00
General administrative expenses...........	1,189.00	1,180.00	9.00	1,540.00	1,500.00	40.00	1,845.00	1,880.00	35.00*	4,574.00	4,560.00	14.00
Miscellaneous distribution costs.........	843.00	900.00	57.00*	1,034.00	1,000.00	34.00	1,160.00	1,030.00	130.00	3,037.00	2,930.00	107.00
Total Cost of Distribution........	$13,096.00	$12,500.00	$596.00	$7,851.00	$7,650.00	$201.00	$10,970.00	$10,900.00	$ 70.00	$31,917.00	$31,050.00	$867.00

* Overapplied expense.

the accounting department. For example, it is assumed that the distribution expenses are to be grouped under the following headings:

Order-getting costs:
1. Direct selling expenses.
2. Advertising and sales promotion.

Order-filling costs:
1. Transportation.
2. Warehousing and storage.
3. Credit and collection.
4. General administrative expenses.
5. Miscellaneous distribution expenses.

A statistical analysis can be made monthly showing the distribution of these actual expenses to the various products, territories, etc. In the illustrations which follow, these analyses are by *products*. On the basis of the sales made during the month and the predetermined rates previously calculated, the over- or underapplied expenses are computed. The preceding illustrations show:

1. The schedule of the direct selling expenses by products (Illustration 24–11).
2. The schedule of the advertising and sales promotion expenses by products (Illustration 24–12).
3. A recapitulation sheet showing the actual and the applied expenses by the seven groups for each of the three products sold (Illustration 24–13).

Analysis of Over- or Underapplied Expense   The over- or underapplied expense is analyzed further in a manner similar to what was done in the case of factory overhead. If the standard costs for the distribution effort were established with the use of flexible budgets, the *controllable* or *spending* variations and the *volume* variation are isolated. An illustration will help bear this out. Illustration 24–13 showed $1,875 as actual direct selling expense for Product A. The amount applied yielding $155 of underapplied expense was $1,720.

Suppose that the monthly flexible budget appeared as given in Illustration 24–14.

If the planning budget for the month of August anticipates $18,000 in sales of Product A, the rate of $8.60 becomes *the* standard cost rate for the period. As a result, when actual sales of Product A registered $20,000 for the month of August, $1,720 was applied for direct selling expense ($8.60 per $100 sales × $20,000 sales).

A comparison of the $1,720 applied with the actual of $1,875 shows $155 as underapplied. If the analysis is carried a step further as in

Illustration 24–14

THE CHAPELA COMPANY

FLEXIBLE BUDGET

DIRECT SELLING EXPENSE—PRODUCT A

Level of sales	$18,000	$20,000	$22,000
Expense:			
Salesmen's salaries	$ 450	$ 450	$ 450
Salesmen's commissions	720	800	880
Salesmen's traveling expenses	90	110	140
Sales office supplies	40	50	70
Sales office salaries	150	150	150
Sales office telephone	38	40	54
Sales office rent	60	60	60
Total Expense	$ 1,548	$ 1,660	$ 1,804
Standard rate per $100 sales	$8.60	$8.30	$8.20

Illustration 24–15, comparisons are made between what the *budget should have been* at the $20,000 sales level with the actual expense. In addition, the budget and applied are compared.

The difference between the adjusted or allowable budget and the amount applied is the *volume* variance. In the illustration, the favorable volume variance of $60 resulted from the fact that more units of Product A were sold than had been planned. The planning budget called for $18,000 of sales with a resulting $8.60 rate. If the level of sales had been estimated correctly at $20,000, the standard cost rate would have been $8.30. The $0.30 difference in rate multiplied by the $2,000 increase in sales accounts for the $60 volume variance.

The difference between the adjusted budget and the actual expense denotes the *controllable* or *spending* variance. This variance has important control implications since it is the resultant of a comparison between what was spent and what should have been spent. In the

Illustration 24–15

THE CHAPELA COMPANY

VARIANCE REPORT—MONTH OF AUGUST, 19—

DIRECT SELLING EXPENSE—PRODUCT A

Expense	Budget Adjusted to $20,000 Sales	Applied	Actual	Net Variance	Volume Variance	Controllable Variance
Salesmen's salaries	$ 450		$ 600			$150
Salesmen's commissions	800		800			0
Salesmen's traveling expenses	110		120			10
Sales office supplies	50		50			0
Sales office salaries	150		200			50
Sales office telephone	40		45			5
Sales office rent	60		60			0
	$1,660	$1,720	$1,875	$155	$60	$215
				unfavorable	favorable	unfavorable

Chapela Company illustration, $1,875 was incurred as expense compared to the $1,660 allowable when the budget is adjusted to the actual sales level of $20,000. The result of the comparison is a $215 unfavorable controllable variance. Further analysis discloses excesses were incurred as follows:

Salesmen's salaries.........................	$150
Salesmen's traveling expenses...............	10
Sales office salaries.........................	50
Sales office telephone.......................	5
	$215

Investigation should then be undertaken to determine *why* the variances arose with the result that steps may be taken to see that they are eliminated or reduced in the future.

Distribution Costs and the Robinson-Patman Act   The general purposes of the Robinson-Patman Act are: (1) to prohibit discrimination in price or in terms of sale between competitive purchasers of commodities of like grade and quality, (2) to prohibit the payment of brokerage or commissions under dummy brokerage firms, (3) to suppress pseudo-advertising allowances, and (4) to provide a presumptive measure of damages in certain cases.

Price discrimination in price or in terms of sale between purchasers of commodities of like grade and quality implies that a businessman must first *classify his products or commodities* into groups. Identical products with different brand labels may frequently be considered as different products because of the imputed value interpreted as a return on an investment in the brand name. Price discrimination further implies competition between purchasers within a given area or market. Therefore, the manufacturer must define his competitive markets. A manufacturer who sells women's handbags to retailers in Syracuse and in New York City would not have to consider these cities as being in the same market area. The sales prices to retailers in New York City need not be identical to prices to retailers in Syracuse.

Within a given area or market, in handling the same product, there can be no price discrimination. (*Differentials* are permitted, but not *discrimination.*) Variations in price are allowed for variances arising in the cost of manufacturing different quantities, the cost of sale, or cost of delivering certain quantities. A large cheese manufacturer had the following price differentials, based upon varying distribution costs in selling quantities of five-pound boxes of cheese for a single delivery.

1 to 30 lbs................	list price
30 to 150 lbs.............	1¢ off list
150 to 750 lbs............	2¢ off list
Over 750 lbs.............	2½¢ off list

The Robinson-Patman Act does not define the meaning of *cost.* The businessman presumably does not have specific costs for each article or quantity produced; for the most part, his costs are average costs. In one case the Federal Trade Commission held that the Goodyear Rubber Company had to average its overhead items, such as credit department expenses and general company advertising, over the entire production whether or not it related to the Goodyear–Sears, Roebuck & Company business. The foregoing case implies that, in compliance with the act, costs of manufacturing and distribution must be analyzed on a *product* and on an *area* or *market* basis.

Advertising allowances, either in the form of services or facilities furnished to the buyer by the seller or in payment for such services when undertaken by the buyer, except when made to all buyers on *proportionately equal terms,* are prohibited under this act.

But the meaning of *proportionately equal terms* is debatable and has not yet been finally settled by the courts. It might mean:

1. The manufacturer will pay 50 percent or any other percentage of the advertising cost to any customer who advertises his product—if he does the same for everyone else.
2. The manufacturer might pay the advertising allowance in proportion to the value of the sales of the products.
3. The manufacturer may agree to pay a definite amount based upon the circulation of the advertising media used, the area and location of window displays, or the number of people passing the windows each day.

Whatever the final interpretation, the accountant, for distribution costs must now find some way of controlling and accounting for a previously unchecked advertising expense.

Quantity discounts are allowed to mass buyers, but the same discounts must be given to all customers buying the same quantity. This law permits *differentials* but not *discrimination.* For example, if a firm sold the same product to Customer A on orders each for 10 carload lots and to Customer B on a standing order of one carload each month and to 10 other customers each on a single order for one carload, it should not be difficult to justify quantity discounts on the basis of cost of distribution.

In the Federal Trade Commission case against Bird & Sons and Montgomery Ward & Company for violation of the Robinson-Patman Act, the manufacturer (Bird & Sons) was able to submit comparative selling costs on mail-order sales of $65,000 and direct-to-retailer sales

Illustration 24–16

	Mail Order		Retailer	
	Dollars	Percent of Sales	Dollars	Percent of Sales
Advertising...............	$ 443.41	0.68	$ 2,769.20	4.02
Warehousing..............	229.98	0.35	10,311.35	14.96
Freight..................	3,111.61	4.75	7,036.88	10.21
Administration...........	1,934.76	2.96	5,247.97	7.62
	$5,719.76	8.74	$25,365.40	36.81

of $68,000, as shown in Illustration 24–16. The differential that could have been allowed to mail-order sales was a discount of 28.07 percent (36.81 percent minus 8.74 percent).

The classification of these expenses should be noted. Higher warehousing costs were due to the discontinuance by Bird & Sons of direct-to-retailer sales, and hence the existence of unusual expenses in adjusting warehousing contracts. The use of a special trade name on the Montgomery Ward product reduced considerably the amount of specific product or general company advertising allocable to the mail-order sales. The difference in freight costs was due to quantity shipments by cheaper water routes. Administration costs of the accounting and credit departments were determined on a per invoice basis.

Where only a few buyers are able to purchase certain large quantities that are available to them but not to others and such practice tends to give the preferred buyer a monopolistic advantage, the Federal Trade Commission is permitted to fix the quantity limits of the purchases.

Exceptions under the act are permitted in the case of perishable products, obsolete or seasonable goods, distress sales in good faith, or goods sold under court order.

The burden of proof under this act is on the seller; and at the initiation of a case by a competitor or customer who alleges injury through unfair competition, the seller may be required to present publicly before the Federal Trade Commission his cost figures for production and distribution. As has been indicated throughout this chapter, the cost of selling goods in varying quantities must be regularly and carefully accounted for and verified.

QUESTIONS FOR REVIEW

1. What are the two major categories of distribution costs? What possible items are included in each?
2. "Analysis of distribution costs may lead to the implementation of responsibility accounting concepts." Explain.
3. What is meant by functionalizing distribution costs?

4. Can standards and standard costs be used in the distribution cost area? Explain.

5. How can computers be of help in distribution cost analysis?

6. "Flexible budgets may be useful in the factory, but there is no place for them in the distribution cost area." Do you agree? Why or why not?

7. What relationship exists between the Robinson-Patman Act and distribution costs?

8. "Distribution cost analysis may aid in selecting proper channels of distribution." Comment.

9. "It is impossible to achieve adequate control over distribution costs." Do you agree? Why or why not?

10. Are the techniques for separating fixed and variable components from a semivariable cost the same for distribution costs as they were for production costs? Explain.

PROBLEMS—GROUP A

Problem 24-1. Purpose: *Comparisons of Sales Territories*

The Jordan Supply Company sells an electronic component nationwide. The sales territories are divided into Eastern, Midwestern, and Western. Sales of the components are made in each of the territories as shipping costs are such that it is not practical to ship from a central location.

Actual results for 1968 were as follows:

	Eastern Territory	Midwestern Territory	Western Territory
Sales @ $10 per unit	$980,000	$650,000	$850,000
Cost of sales	784,000	552,500	637,500
Selling expenses	92,000	72,000	91,000
General expenses	20,000	20,000	20,000

Required:

Prepare an analysis for management. Show as much detail as you can in accounting for the differences in sales and costs.

Problem 24-2. Purpose: *Distribution Costs—Analysis by Products, Districts, Jobbers, and Dealers*

The Jack Diamond Drill Company manufactures hand drills, light electric drills, and heavy-duty electric drills which are sold by its own sales force to customers in various lines of business. Sales activities are departmentalized on a territorial basis into two divisions, the Eastern and Western Territories.

The firm's net income from operations, after $5,423 general administrative expense, was only $9,315 during the last fiscal year, which was only about 1½ percent on net sales and a negligible return on invested capital. The firm gets a fairly large volume of business, as compared with the rest of the industry, and maintains a one-price policy, pricing all its goods at a uniform markup of 25 percent on factory cost.

The officers of the firm hand you the following schedules, drawn up by the treasurer of the firm, which are to be taken as correct in every detail.

Schedule of Distribution Expense   *Year Ended 19—*

Packing and shipping	$ 8,100
Warehouse operation	8,400
Cartage (hauling to railroad)	6,720
Credit investigation	1,980
Bookkeeping and billing	2,640
Advertising	32,200
Traveling	7,782
Salesmen—commissions	37,440
Total distribution expense	$105,262

MISCELLANEOUS COST DATA, BY LINES OF PRODUCT
Year Ended 19—

	Hand Drills	Light Electrics	Heavy Duty
Unit factory cost	$1.60	$16.80	$48.00
Shipping weight, each	2 lb.	16 lb.	40 lb.
Unit packing and shipping cost	$0.04	$ 0.21	$ 0.93
Sales commission rates	6%	5%	10%
Warehouse space used	273,000 cu. ft.	455,000 cu. ft.	182,000 cu. ft.

DISTRIBUTION STATISTICS, SALES, ADVERTISING, AND TRAVEL—
BY TERRITORIES
For Year Ended 19—

	Eastern Territory	Western Territory
Unit sales:		
Hand drills	60,000	12,000
Light electrics	4,000	12,000
Heavy duty	1,600	400
Orders received from new customers:		
Hand drills	200	300
Light electrics	100	400
Heavy duty	700	100
Total new customer orders	1,000	800
Repeat orders:		
Hand drills	4,300	500
Light electrics	900	1,600
Heavy duty	800	100
Total repeat orders	6,000	2,200
Total New and Repeat Orders	7,000	3,000
Advertising expenditures:		
Featuring hand drills only	$ 6,000	$ 3,000
Featuring light electrics only	4,000	5,000
Featuring heavy duty only	3,000	4,000
General "firm-name" advertising, total, both territories		7,200
Total Advertising Expenditures		$32,200

The firm pays its salesmen, as travel expense, a flat rate of 6 cents per mile for the use of their own automobiles. In the Eastern Territory, salesmen reported 58,400 miles; in the Western Territory, 71,300 miles. The salesmen were paid the amounts which their mileage indicated.

Required:

a) A columnar comparative statement showing sales revenue, gross margins, and detailed distribution cost allocations for each line of product in each territory. In making cost allocations to products and territories, indicate on your statement the basis used for each distribution. Do not distribute general administrative expenses.

b) What, in your opinion, are the important facts brought out by your statement? Interpret your analysis by summarizing and explaining the effects of such factors as you think the management might consider significant.

Problem 24–3. Purpose: *Analysis of Distribution Costs*

The Johnson Meat Packing Company desires to study its distribution costs (selling, administrative, and general expenses), which in the aggregate constitute 65 percent of the total cost of doing business. From the following information, prepare an exhibit showing the allocation of total distribution cost per hundredweight of meat products for each size-class of order (expressed in pounds per order). Carry out unit costs to hundredths of a cent.

An analysis made to determine basic causes of cost variation in selling, administrative, and general expense items discloses that each element of expense varies according to one of the following three bases: (1) number of orders; (2) number of items or invoice lines per order; and (3) weight of order expressed in hundredweight. Expenses varying according to these three factors account for the total distribution cost of a given order.

The analysis of each class of distribution expense discloses that these expenses are attributable to each of these three factors, as follows:

Distribution Cost Controls	No. of Orders	No. of Items	No. of Cwt.	Total
Selling expense control	$2,310	$1,080	$ 210	$3,600
Packing and delivery expense control	260	320	620	1,200
Administrative and general expense control	1,170	580	340	2,090
Total Distribution Costs	$3,740	$1,980	$1,170	$6,890

Expenses Based on— spans the three middle columns above (No. of Orders, No. of Items, No. of Cwt.)

Data by order-size classes follow:

Order-Size Class	No. of Orders	Total No. of Items	Total Cwt.
Under 50 pounds	2,800	4,090	700
50–199 pounds	2,900	8,410	2,610
200–499 pounds	600	2,280	1,860
500–999 pounds	400	2,400	2,800
1,000 pounds and over	100	820	1,030
All Orders	6,800	18,000	9,000

(Uniform Examination of AICPA)

Problem 24–4. Purpose: *Decision Making among Alternatives*

The Triangle Company makes and sells towel dispensers nationally to wholesalers and retailers. The sales price for the dispensers is $36 per dozen. The company expects to sell 20,000 dozen in 1968 at the following costs:

Variable manufacturing costs...........................$400,000
Fixed manufacturing costs.............................. 50,000
Variable selling expense................................. 40,000
Fixed selling expense.................................... 20,000
General and administrative expense—fixed................ 30,000

After the above projection was developed, the sales manager from Territory No. 2 notified the company that he could get an order for 10,000 dozen dispensers in addition to the amount already budgeted. The 10,000 dozen could be delivered in bulk to a mail-order discount house. The bid price by the discount house was $21 per dozen.

Required:

Should the Triangle Company accept the order at $21 per dozen? Present a complete analysis covering both financial and nonfinancial items.

PROBLEMS—GROUP B

Problem 24–5. Purpose: *Cost Control over Distribution Costs*

The following data were determined from the records of the Thrasher Company for the second quarter of 1968:

	Budget		Actual	
Function	*Units*	*$*	*Units*	*$*
Credits and collections—accts..............3,000		$ 6,000	3,250	$ 6,500
Salesmen's calls—no. calls.................5,000		25,000	4,500	24,000
Bookkeeping—no. orders..................4,000		5,000	4,200	5,500
Shipping—no. orders....................4,000		4,000	4,200	4,100

Required:

a) If the average gross profit is 25 percent of sales, what is the "break-even" order?

b) Analyze the differences between budget and actual. Give as much detail as possible.

Problem 24–6. Purpose: *Distribution Cost Analysis on Basis of Sales Prices*

The Thomas Stove Company wishes to analyze the distribution costs of its insulated electric ranges sold under trade name of Vulcan. These are produced in three sizes—namely, Apartment, Home, and Industrial.

The distribution expenses for the past year were:

Expense	Amount	Basis for Apportionment
Salesmen's salaries................................$ 30,000		Direct charge
Salesmen's commissions and bonuses.......... 18,000		Amount of sales
Sales office expenses......................... 6,400		Number of orders
Advertising and sales promotion:		
Direct product........................... 65,000		Direct charge
General.................................. 15,000		Amount of sales
Packing and shipping...................... 7,500		Size of product
Transportation and delivery expenses.......... 12,000		Size of product
Warehouse and storage..................... 3,000		Size of product
Credit and collection expenses................ 4,000		Number of orders
Total.............................. $160,900		

The statistics ascertained from the books of the company relating to the sales of the three sizes showed:

	Apartment	Home	Industrial	Total
Number of salesmen, all paid same salary............................	4	5	1	10
Number of orders...................	700	800	100	1,600
Percentage of direct advertising budget..	30%	45%	25%	100%
Space in cubic feet occupied per $100 of sales value.....................	5 cu. ft.	8 cu. ft.	17 cu. ft.	30 cu. ft.
Sales value........................	$175,000	$240,000	$185,000	$600,000
Average price per order..............	$ 250	$ 300	$ 1,850	

From the foregoing, prepare a schedule showing in detail the cost of distributing each product per $100 of sales.

Problem 24–7. Purpose: *Distribution Cost Analysis on Territorial Basis; Also on Sales Basis*

The Thomas Stove Company mentioned in Problem 24–6 presents the following statement at the end of the second year's operations:

STATEMENT OF INCOME

For the Year Ended October, 19—

Sales..		$950,000
Cost of sales..		585,000
Gross profit...		$365,000
Distribution costs:		
Salesmen's salaries.......................................	$ 30,000	
Salesmen's commissions...................................	47,500	
Advertising..	100,000	
Warehouse and storage....................................	4,284	
Transportation and delivery...............................	17,136	
Credit and collection.....................................	5,160	
Packing and shipping.....................................	8,568	
Sales office expenses.....................................	5,700	218,348
Net selling profit...		$146,652
General and administrative expenses.........................		60,000
Net Income for the Period.................................		$ 86,652

There are now 15 salesmen on the sales force of this company, and they cover the entire eastern part of the United States. For the purpose of analyzing the distribution costs, this territory is divided into districts, as follows: New England territory, covering the New England states and New York; the Pennsylvania district, which includes New Jersey, Pennsylvania, Maryland, and Delaware; and the Virginia district, which includes Washington, D.C., Virginia, West Virginia, North and South Carolina, and Florida. Five salesmen are allotted to each district; and each one is paid a basic salary, plus 5 percent commission on all sales.

The analysis of the sales and cost of sales for the year is presented in the following table:

District	Apartment Ranges		Home Ranges		Industrial Ranges	
	Cost of Sales	Sales	Cost of Sales	Sales	Cost of Sales	Sales
New England...........	$ 82,500	$125,000	$119,250	$180,000	$130,000	$250,000
Pennsylvania...........	47,500	75,000	50,750	70,000	57,000	100,000
Virginia...............	30,000	40,000	30,000	40,000	38,000	70,000
	$160,000	$240,000	$200,000	$290,000	$225,000	$420,000

An analysis of the district product advertising for the year showed:

	Apartment	Home	Industrial
New England district:			
Newspaper advertising......................$	2,500	$ 4,000	......
Magazine advertising..........................	3,000	4,000	$13,000
Pennsylvania district:			
Newspaper advertising..........................	2,500	5,000	3,000
Magazine advertising..........................	2,000	3,000	10,000
Virginia district:			
Newspaper advertising..........................	2,000	3,000	1,000
Magazine advertising..........................	2,800	4,200	7,000
Direct-mail advertising..........................	3,200	4,800	......
Total..........................	$18,000	$28,000	$34,000

Transportation and shipping expenses cannot be analyzed. However, a sample investigation indicates that Apartment ranges would take up about 5 cubic feet of space, Home ranges, about 8 cubic feet, and Industrial ranges, about 17 cubic feet of space per $100 sales value, and that the weight of each type of product was in the same proportion as the size or amount of space occupied.

Prepare an analysis of distribution costs.

CHAPTER

25 | Nonmanufacturing Costs Analyses

Introduction
In the preceding chapter, one increasingly important phase of nonmanufacturing cost accounting was discussed, namely, distribution costs. In recent years, the principles of cost accounting and control have been extended to other fields. The use of computers has made it possible for additional data to become available with the result that applications of cost accounting techniques to nonmanufacturing situations have become more feasible. In addition, managers of nonmanufacturing activities have become more cost conscious and thus desire more cost data to aid them in the decision-making process. The following nonmanufacturing costs should be considered:

1. Costs for retail and department stores.
2. Costs for financial institutions.
3. Costs of office work as applicable to some of the larger service establishments, such as insurance companies and public utilities.
4. Costs for governmental bodies and other entities not organized for profit.
5. Research and development expenditures.

Costs for Retail and Department Stores
The objective of cost accounting in a retail or department store is to present to management *an analysis of the cost of selling certain classes of goods,* either on a total basis or on some unit basis, such as per dollar of sales or per ton of material. A department store is, in reality, an aggregate of a number of units corresponding to retail outlets. Therefore the problem of the department store is that of segregating for each department its sales and its direct costs and of

securing an equitable apportionment of the general and administrative expenses of the entire store among the several departments. Since each department usually specializes in a single type of merchandise, costs can

Illustration 25–1

Functional Cost Element	Basis of Distribution to Departments
Administration:	
Executive office expense...................	Sales in each department
Accounts receivable......................	No. of charge sales
Credit department expense.................	No. of charge sales
Accounts payable........................	No. of invoices
Auditing................................	No. of transactions
Adjustment office........................	No. of adjustments
Training, welfare, and employee relationship................................	No. of employees weighted by number of days' service
Insurance on merchandise.................	Average merchandise inventory
Occupancy:	
Alterations and repairs to building..........	To department in which made (direct) or on area basis
Rent and taxes...........................	Area or investment basis
Insurance on building and fixtures..........	Area or investment basis
Light, heat, and power....................	Area
Depreciation on building..................	Area
Depreciation and repairs on fixtures........	Investment in fixtures
Sales promotion and advertising:	
Departmental promotion and advertising....	Direct charge to department
Direct mail and circularization..............	Direct or on basis of sales
Window displays.........................	Direct
Administration of sales promotion.........	Sales basis
Purchasing:	
Management and supervision..............	Sales
Departmental buyers, etc..................	Direct
Receiving and checking...................	Direct, or on basis of volume or number of items
Inventory control........................	Average investment in inventory or number of items
Selling:	
Salaries.................................	Direct
Wrapping and packing....................	Direct or number of packages
Supplies................................	Direct
Compensation insurance..................	Direct on salaries
Delivery................................	No. of packages, perhaps weighted according to size

then be reduced for that department to a percentage of sales. In the retail organization where such segregation of costs and expenses by departments is not always practical because of small size, an analysis can be made of sales and costs by products or groups of products.

Cost analysis in a department store or retail organization may be grouped under the following six headings:

1. Administration.
2. Occupancy.
3. Sales promotion and advertising.
4. Purchasing.
5. Selling.
6. Delivery.

Under each of these headings there is a group of expenses which must be allocated to the various departments, such as (1) men's clothing, (2) women's coats and dresses, (3) sporting goods, (4) furniture, and others. The basis of allocation, together with the expenses, might be tabulated as shown in Illustration 25–1.

Items such as bad debts and losses from theft are generally treated as financial items and kept separate from the departmental cost analysis; or they may be placed in the administrative expense section and then prorated.

The tremendous number of transactions involved in some of the department stores sales activities made cost analysis on a detailed statistical basis well-nigh impractical until the computer came along. Today, many stores have, in addition to summary entries, main office accounting records kept by departments and departmental records kept by lines of merchandise and by salesmen. The latter records are statistical, while the former are accounting records entered in the books.

Entries for sales, purchases, and direct expenses are placed in accounts for each department. The entries would be equivalent to:

(1)

Purchases—Men's Clothing Department	20,000.00	
Purchases—Women's Coats and Dresses	40,000.00	
Purchases—Sporting Goods	10,000.00	
Purchases—Furniture	90,000.00	
Accounts Payable		160,000.00
To record purchases by departments for the period.		

(2)

Cash or Accounts Receivable	220,000.00	
Sales—Men's Clothing Department		50,000.00
Sales—Women's Coats and Dresses		75,000.00
Sales—Sporting Goods		15,000.00
Sales—Furniture		80,000.00
To record sales by departments for the period.		

Under this method of accounting and control, it will be necessary to maintain an inventory for each department; it is then possible to determine from the foregoing entries the *gross* profit for each department and for the store as a whole.

In working toward a net profit for each department the expenses may in part be entered in departmental expense accounts, such as Salaries—Men's Clothing Department, etc. Not all of them, however, can be thus

Illustration 25–2

DEPARTMENTAL APPORTIONMENT OF EXPENSES FOR THE PERIOD

Expenses	Total	Men's Clothing	Women's Coats and Dresses	Sporting Goods	Furniture
Administrative					
Executive Offices......	$ 2,200.00	$ 500.00	$ 750.00	$ 150.00	$ 800.00
Accounts Receivable....	1,200.00	300.00	450.00	225.00	225.00
Credit Dept. Expenses...	800.00	200.00	300.00	150.00	150.00
Adjustment Office......	500.00	100.00	250.00	50.00	100.00
Personnel............	2,000.00	400.00	800.00	300.00	500.00
	$ 6,700.00	$ 1,500.00	$ 2,550.00	$ 875.00	$ 1,775.00
Occupancy					
Alterations (Specific)....	$ 800.00	$ 300.00	$ 500.00	....	....
Rent................	2,400.00	500.00	800.00	$ 100.00	$ 1,000.00
Light, Heat and Power..	600.00	125.00	200.00	25.00	250.00
	$ 3,800.00	$ 925.00	$ 1,500.00	$ 125.00	$ 1,250.00
Sales Promotion and					
Advertising					
Direct Advertising......	$ 1,000.00	$ 200.00	$ 450.00	$ 50.00	$ 300.00
Window Displays, direct	500.00	100.00	300.00	....	100.00
Administration........	1,100.00	250.00	375.00	75.00	400.00
	$ 2,600.00	$ 550.00	$ 1,125.00	$ 125.00	$ 800.00
Purchasing					
Supervision...........	$ 640.00	$ 80.00	$ 160.00	$ 40.00	$ 360.00
Departmental Buyers....	6,000.00	1,500.00	3,000.00	500.00	1,000.00
Receiving............	480.00	60.00	120.00	30.00	270.00
Inventory Control......	600.00	100.00	40.00	60.00	400.00
	$ 7,720.00	$ 1,740.00	$ 3,320.00	$ 630.00	$ 2,030.00
Selling					
Salaries..............	$ 20,000.00	$ 5,000.00	$ 6,500.00	$ 1,500.00	$ 7,000.00
Wrapping............	220.00	50.00	75.00	15.00	80.00
Insurance, Compensation	200.00	50.00	65.00	15.00	70.00
	$ 20,420.00	$ 5,100.00	$ 6,640.00	$ 1,530.00	$ 7,150.00
Delivery					
Departmental Expense...	$ 5,000.00	$ 1,250.00	$ 1,625.00	$ 375.00	$ 1,750.00
Total..........	$ 46,240.00	$11,065.00	$16,760.00	$ 3,660.00	$14,755.00
Sales.................	$220,000.00	$50,000.00	$75,000.00	$15,000.00	$80,000.00
Number of Charge Sales...	24,000	6,000	9,000	4,500	4,500
Adjustments............	500	100	250	50	100
Area, square feet........	240,000	50,000	80,000	10,000	100,000
Employees.	20	4	8	3	5
Inventory..............	$ 30,000.00	$ 5,000.00	$ 2,000.00	$ 3,000.00	$20,000.00

Illustration 25-3

VICTORY DEPARTMENT STORE

INCOME STATEMENT BY DEPARTMENTS

For Period Ending March 31, 19—

	TOTAL	%	Men's Clothing	%	Women's Coats and Dresses	%	Sporting Goods	%	Furniture	%
Sales.........	$220,000.00	100	$50,000.00	100	$75,000.00	100	$15,000.00	100	$80,000.00	100
Cost of Sales.....	130,000.00	59.09	15,000.00	30	38,000.00	50.67	7,000.00	46.67	70,000.00	87.5
Gross Profit on Sales.....	$ 90,000.00	40.91	$35,000.00	70	$37,000.00	49.33	$ 8,000.00	53.33	$10,000.00	12.5
Expenses:										
Administrative.........	6,700.00	3.05	1,500.00	3.00	2,550.00	3.40	875.00	5.83	1,775.00	2.22
Occupancy...........	3,800.00	1.73	925.00	1.85	1,500.00	2.00	125.00	0.83	1,250.00	1.56
Sales Promotion.......	2,600.00	1.18	550.00	1.10	1,125.00	1.50	125.00	0.83	800.00	1.00
Purchasing...........	7,720.00	3.51	1,740.00	3.48	3,320.00	4.42	630.00	4.20	2,030.00	2.54
Selling...........	20,420.00	9.28	5,100.00	10.20	6,640.00	8.85	1,530.00	10.20	7,150.00	8.94
Delivery...........	5,000.00	2.27	1,250.00	2.50	1,625.00	2.17	375.00	2.50	1,750.00	2.18
Total Expenses......	$ 46,240.00	21.02	$11,065.00	22.13	$16,760.00	22.34	$ 3,660.00	24.39	$14,755.00	18.44
Net Operating Profit.....	$ 43,760.00	19.89	$23,935.00	47.87	$20,240.00	26.99	$ 4,340.00	28.94	$ 4,755.00 (loss)*	5,944 (loss)*

recorded; some must be apportioned on appropriate bases. It will therefore be necessary to prepare a schedule of the departmental expenses, both direct and apportioned; then a departmentalized income statement can be prepared, using percentages to indicate the relation between sales and each class of expense and between the net profit and sales. These ratios or percentages are used in marketing cost analysis and also in cost analysis for department stores and retail stores. To illustrate this type of expense analysis, the following schedules are prepared, using the bases for distribution indicated in Illustration 25–1.

This tabulation of expenses, as given in Illustration 25–2, may be analyzed on a *percentage of sales* basis for each expense, but in Illustration 25–3 such costs are shown only for *groups* of expenses. In smaller retail organizations this comparative income statement by departments is prepared on the basis of sales groups, since functional departmentalization is not always so clear cut as in the larger organizations.

Cost Analyses for Commercial Banks   As indicative of the method, results, and procedure followed in cost analyses for financial institutions, the application to commercial banks is used. In recent years, greater emphasis has been placed by banks upon the cost of the various services rendered. In most banking organizations today, management knows approximately how much net income is realized on the checking accounts, on the loan service, and on trust work. Charges no longer have to be a guess or a matter of "what the traffic will bear," but can be based upon the cost of performing the services.

The functional organization of a bank must be studied in the same manner as the departments in a large store. Bank functions usually include: (1) a commercial deposit division; (2) a savings deposit division; (3) a trust division; (4) a safe deposit vaults division; (5) a foreign exchange division; (6) a capital funds (capital stock, etc.) division; (7) a loans and investments division; (8) service departments—accounting, duplication, auditing, correspondence, filing, credit, mailing, messenger, personnel, photostat, stenographic, telephone, translation, and wires and cables; and (9) indirect expenses—advertising, administration officers' expenses, directors' fees, library, new business, and pensions.

The bank derives its income from investment of funds and from rendering services such as safe deposit, trust, etc. By far the greater income comes from the loan and investment of funds. These funds cannot be segregated in their investments but are usually grouped. It therefore becomes necessary to allocate a certain amount of the investment income to each type of fund. This allocation can be made quite accurately by observing a definite pattern of analysis. The funds are all merged into one large reservoir of funds, since there is no way to pick specific investments for each. This fund is called a *conversion fund*.

The following illustration indicates how these funds, with the necessary deductions, are merged into the conversion fund to compute the income for each by an appropriate allocation.[1] These total funds are then analyzed by types of investments and the income received therefrom during the past six months. This income is reduced to an average annual rate. This rate is used in computing the allocation of the income to each type of fund.

ANALYSIS OF FUNDS AVAILABLE FOR CONVERSION

		Six-Month Averages	
Capital fund:			
Capital		$ 250,000	
Surplus		750,000	
Undivided profits		178,000	
Surplus reserves		192,000	
Total		$1,370,000	
Disposition of funds:			
Bank building	$ 174,000		
Furniture and equipment	27,000		
Accounts receivable, etc.	2,000	203,000	
Capital funds available for conversion			$1,167,000
Commercial deposits—demand:			
Due to banks		$ 863,000	
Cashier's and certified checks		52,000	
Individual deposits		7,394,000	
Demand certificates of deposit		11,000	
United States deposits		126,000	
Total		$8,446,000	
Disposition of deposits—demand:			
Customers' deposits uncollected	$ 375,000		
Federal Reserve requirement	1,211,000		
Cash requirement	404,000	1,990,000	
Commercial deposits—demand, available for conversion			6,456,000
Commercial deposits—time:			
Time deposits		$ 165,000	
Time certificates of deposit		140,000	
Total		$ 305,000	
Disposition of deposits—time:			
Federal Reserve Bank requirement	$ 15,000		
Cash requirement	5,000	20,000	
Commercial deposits—time available for conversion			285,000
Savings deposits:			
Savings		$1,055,000	
Employees' savings		2,000	
Total		$1,057,000	

(*Continued on next page*)

---

[1] Adapted, with permission, from the article "Cost Accounting in Commercial Banks," by Harold Randall, in the *National Association of Accountants Bulletin*.

Disposition of deposit:

Federal Reserve requirement..................$	53,000	
Cash requirement.........................	16,000	$ 69,000
Savings deposits available for conversion.............		$ 988,000

Foreign division deposits:

Individual accounts...................................$	3,000
Foreign bank accounts..............................	169,000
Sundry dollar accounts.............................	8,000
Other accounts......................................	12,000
Total..$	192,000

Disposition of foreign deposits:

Federal Reserve requirement.................$	26,000	
Cash requirement.........................	10,000	36,000
Foreign funds available for conversion...............		156,000
Total Funds Available for Conversion................		$9,052,000

Allocation of Expenses

In calculating the *departmental* costs, it is usually necessary to allocate expenses. The matter of proration is similar to that found in factories and department stores. Those expenses which can be charged directly to a department, such as salaries, compensation insurance, or depreciation on equipment, can be computed from the records. The building expenses are apportioned on the basis of floor space or area. The service department costs must be redistributed over the income-producing functions on appropriate bases. A list of the expenses and the methods of allocation that might be used follows:

Service Department	Method of Reallocation
Accounting	Survey of work done for each income department. May be reduced to percentage basis
Auditing	Same as accounting—by survey
Filing	Survey of work done for each department
Credit	Number of applications and investigations
Mailing	Volume of mail handled
Messengers	Survey of use or number of calls
Personnel	Number of employees
Photostat	Per page of copy
Stenographic	Survey or per page of production
Telephone	Number of telephones in each department plus direct charge for toll calls
Translation	Direct charge
Indirect expenses	These may be known as *general bank overhead* and apportioned on basis of income produced or in proportion to total expenses for each department
Legal	Survey of work actually done

To this point the bank management has been able to ascertain the income and expenses for each department. To reduce this to cost accounting requires the establishment and compilation of a *unit*. The units are of two kinds: (1) the cost unit for the type of work to be done; and (2) the charge unit—the combination of several cost units. The former might be illustrated by the computation of the cost of handling a number of cash deposits, check deposits, payrolls, and handling sight drafts, documentary drafts, or security drafts; and by machine posting in bookkeeping departments. These are really *work cost units*. Compiling statistics for these work units may be quite an

Illustration 25–4

MONTHLY COST OR SERVICE CHARGE ANALYSIS FOR A CHECKING ACCOUNT

Balance:
1. Average daily ledger balance....................................$600.00
2. Less uncollected funds.. 120.00
3. Average daily collected balance...............................$480.00

Income:
4. Earnings at $\frac{1}{3}$% (4% a year)...................................$ 1.60

Expense:
5. Checks paid and debit items handled....................$1.50
6. Deposits received....................................... 0.10
7. Deposited items... 0.30
8. Collections handled..................................... 0.30
9. Checks certified.. 0.30
10. Other expenses and charges incurred..................... 0.10
11. Account cost (per account)............................. 0.50
       Total expense... 3.10
Loss on Account for Month (Service Charge)........................$ 1.50

elaborate job, but with an accurate system of internal check and audit they can be secured with little extra effort. Translating these work units or standards into the analysis of an account or charge unit is another problem. However, sufficient progress has been made toward its solution that the cost and profitableness of handling an account can be readily computed. The formula used for a checking account is shown in Illustration 25–4.

A similar analysis can be worked out for computing the cost of trust work or for the foreign deposits. The extent to which a bank may wish to make such an analysis depends upon its general business operating results. Some banks study their accounts continuously. Others accept the standards arrived at by other banks and use them. In any event, every bank organization should make an effort to study statistically the costs of rendering the service.

Banks should develop standards and standard costs in a manner similar to what has been done in the case of manufacturing operations.

Once established and instituted, proper comparisons between actual and standard costs become possible. Variances may be isolated and appropriate action taken to correct the reasons for the variances. Banks may thus achieve the same degree of control over costs as found in manufacturing situations.

Cost Analyses for General and Administrative Office Functions
Cost analysis of office work in the organization of a manufacturer or a department store or bank has already been treated either under the heading of "Distribution Costs" or under special headings of "Department Store Accounting" or "Bank Cost Accounting." The cost analysis referred to in this section, while following the same pattern of procedure as the others, refers to those concerns whose main activity is rendering a service, such as an insurance company or a public utility.

The problem resolves itself into three parts: (1) determination of units for computing the costs of the various office activities; (2) determination of bases for allocation of the office costs, which are really a form of service, to the other departments of the firm; and (3) achieving control over the costs.

To determine the units for computing costs in office work, it is necessary to indicate the types of work that take place in the office. These and the corresponding units for allocation of costs are:

Type of Office Work	*Cost Analysis Units*
Correspondence work	Per letter or per page of letter
Dictation and transcription	Per line, per page, per stroke
Filing	Per hundred names, or papers handled
Mailing	Number of pieces
Billing	Per invoice or per item
Duplication	Number of copies
Personnel	Number of employees

One of the first tasks facing the office manager is the determination and, if possible, the reduction of the unit costs for each of the departments listed above. An examination of these departments should indicate that they are primarily service departments. In a life insurance company, they render service to the policy division, the claim division, or the investment division. Once the unit costs have been determined, then it becomes a simple job to allocate the costs of these departments to the operating divisions of the firm. To illustrate this more specifically, the costs in the life insurance company would follow the analysis pattern shown in Illustration 25–5. Thereafter, the policy division will reduce its total costs to a *per policy basis;* the investment division to a cost of *per dollar of net income;* and the claim division to the cost *per claim handled.* The functional operating departments really "absorb" the service department expenses, much in the same manner that the producing departments absorb the costs of the service departments in a manufacturing business.

As was the case with banks, standards and standard costs should be established whenever possible so that adequate cost control may be

Illustration 25–5

Service Department	Costs	Functional Operating Division		
		Policy Division	Investment Division	Claim Division
Correspondence...........	$ 5,000.00	$ 2,000.00	$ 800.00	$ 2,200.00
Dictation and Transcription....	4,000.00	1,500.00	1,000.00	1,500.00
Filing....................	2,000.00	650.00	500.00	850.00
Mailing..................	1,000.00	400.00	300.00	300.00
Billing...................	200.00	200.00	....	....
Duplication..............	3,000.00	1,800.00	200.00	1,000.00
Personnel................	3,500.00	2,000.00	500.00	1,000.00
Total Service..........	$18,700.00	$ 8,550.00	$ 3,300.00	$ 6,850.00
Building Maintenance........	$ 8,000.00	3,500.00	1,500.00	3,000.00
Direct Functional Dept. Charges	10,000.00	5,000.00	2,000.00	3,000.00
Total Costs for Period....	$36,700.00	$17,050.00	$ 6,800.00	$12,850.00

achieved. The standards that are established should be built around a series of work steps. The definition of the work step is important as the beginning and the conclusion of the step must be easily determinable. For example, the billing operation would make up a series of work steps and standards could be set for the performance of this function.

Cost Analyses for Governmental Agencies   There are about 176,000 governmental units in the United States engaged in rendering some kind of public service as well as thousands of hospitals, schools, and colleges. Sometimes there is only one type of service, as in the case of a small school district; or there may be multiple services, as in the case of a large city or state. This government service is distinctive in that in most instances it is supported by taxation. The ever-increasing tax burdens have emphasized the need for a more efficient method of studying and recording the costs of governmental services.

In industry and commerce, the use of a cost accounting system should result in greater efficiency, reflected in increased profits. Therefore, the businessman will compute the material, labor, and manufacturing overhead costs for each unit manufactured. He will then study these unit costs continuously, so that, if possible, they may be reduced. He may also use these data to set up standards so that future results can be compared regularly with the standards of operating efficiency. But behind all such cost analysis is the profit objective.

In a governmental unit the use of the cost accounting system is stimulated not by the profit motive but by the need for greater efficiency, so that the taxpayers' or donors' burdens will be less. More specifically, the purposes to which governmental cost accounting may be applied are:

1. To provide data that indicate whether or not certain activities are being performed efficiently.
2. To provide a basis for determining whether certain work should be performed by a governmental unit or by a private contractor.
3. To provide data to be used in preparing the budget.
4. To compute the cost of fixed assets which have been constructed by the government unit.
5. To provide the best service for the lowest cost.

It should be understood, of course, that *all* accounting *tends* toward these objectives. However, it is only when the data are carefully studied and analyzed by means of what is termed *cost accounting* that the *maximum* results can be obtained, since cost accounting breaks down the total figures into detailed operations, thus localizing discrepancies or high costs.

Governmental costs may be computed on either a *specific job basis* or on a *continuous basis*. Where a certain nonrecurring task is to be performed, such as the construction of a bridge or school, the use of a specific job cost system is necessary. In computing the costs of education, police, and fire protection and the other services rendered continuously from year to year, the use of the continuous cost method is necessary. Under this continuous method the total cost of a particular service is computed and then divided by the number of units of that service rendered, to obtain the unit costs.

Certain nonprofit activities are more readily adaptable to cost accounting than others. Cost accounting may be most readily used (1) in those activities where there is some physical output, such as in the construction of a building or of a highway or in the rebuilding of a street; and (2) in those services in which the use of time, materials, and equipment is fairly constant and uniform throughout successive operations. In many instances, it will not be possible to compute the departmental unit cost because there are so many different types of work being performed under one administrative head that there is no common unit. For example, the department of public works in a large city covers the following activities, many of which must be measured with different units:

Activity	Unit of Cost Analysis
Maintenance of sewers	Per mile
Maintenance of incinerator	Per ton of refuse
Collection of ashes and garbage	Per ton
Maintenance of highways and lighting	Per mile
Maintenance of garages and vehicles	Per garage and per vehicle
Bureau of parks	Per acre

It is because cost accounting necessitates the analysis of expenditures for various types of work within a large department that it is most effective in administrative control. In addition to the activities of the department of public works, the following is a list of governmental activities which can be measured by means of cost accounting:

Activity	Unit of Cost Analysis
Police	Per capita
Education	Per pupil
Welfare and relief	Per case
Trucking	Per ton-mile
Garage service	Per vehicle, or per capita
Recreation	Per capita
Hospital care	Per patient, or per capita
Electric light plant	Per kilowatt-hour[2]
Water plant	Per thousand gallons[2]
Street-cleaning	Per mile
Construction of streets	Per mile
Repair of streets	Per square yard
Library	Per capita

But the foregoing activities and units refer to the departments as a whole. That is probably the best that can be expected in *small* units. In the larger units, however, it becomes necessary to subdivide the activity

---

[2] Cost accounting for activities such as the water department and the light plant is very similar to that for a private enterprise except that some expenses, such as taxes and insurance, may not be included; frequently a sinking fund cost is included instead of depreciation.

expenses within a department and to select more accurate units for some of these activities. To use the police and fire departments and the departments of health and hospitals as illustrations, the accompanying tables[3] (see Illustrations 25–6 to 25–8) indicate how a more detailed analysis of costs may be made.

Illustration 25–6

TABLE OF ACCOUNTS FOR
COST ACCOUNTING FOR POLICE AND FIRE DEPARTMENTS

General Classification (For All Accounting)	Activity or Service (For Cost Accounting)	Performance Units (For Work Measurement)
Police departments are sometimes classified as to squads; detective, vice, morals, control, foot patrol, motorcycle, auto patrol, and so forth	Administrative and auxiliary services	(An indirect cost which must be prorated over other services)
	Traffic regulation	Intersectional—hours patrolled; curb-mile-hours patrolled (parking), Cars examined (traffic lanes) Man-hours (on duty, not reporting to calls)
	Crime prevention	Calls answered (squad cars) Active cases (detective)
	Criminal apprehension	Man-days (custody of prisoner)
	Special police services	Examinations made (laboratories) Missing persons reported Man-hours special duties (parades) $1,000 property value (recovery of property)
Fire-fighting forces may also be classified according to squads: engine companies, hook and ladder, salvage squads, rescue squads, fireboats, and so forth	Fire prevention	Inspections made Investigations made
	Fire protection	Drills supervised Talks given, etc. Man-hours (on duty, not answering calls)
	Fire fighting	Fire alarms answered
	Other fire department services	Resuscitation cases Man-hours special duty (parades), etc.

Methods of Recording and Computing Governmental Costs

Costs for governmental units may be computed on two bases: (1) statistical, and (2) accounting. In many places, governmental officers are content to have some statistical analyses made of the costs of various activities whenever time permits. This method has two vital weaknesses: (1) there is no compulsion in the

---

[3] Taken, with special permission, from *Governmental Cost Accounting*, by the Municipal Finance Officers' Association of United States and Canada (Chicago, Illinois), pp. 46, 56, and 59.

Illustration 25–7

TABLE OF ACCOUNTS FOR COST ACCOUNTING FOR A HEALTH DEPARTMENT

General Classification (For All Accounting)	Activity or Service (For Cost Accounting)	Performance Units (For Work Measurement)
According to subfunction	Administrative and auxiliary services	An indirect cost
Vital statistics	Recording and registration	Births and deaths registered Morbidity cases recorded
Control of communicable diseases	Field professional services	Nursing visits Physicians' visits
Maternity and child health service	Clinical services	Patient visits
Adult health service	Laboratories	Examinations made
Crippled children service	Distribution of drugs	Ampoules distributed
Food and milk control Sanitation	Instruction and education Inspectional services	Pamphlets, talks, etc. License applications received Inspections made Orders issued Arrests made Violations prosecuted

Illustration 25–8

TABLE OF ACCOUNTS FOR COST ACCOUNTING FOR HOSPITALS

General Classification (For All Accounting)	Activity or Service (For Cost Accounting)	Performance Units* (For Work Measurement)
Separate records for each hospital	Administrative and auxiliary services	(An indirect cost)
	Dietary services	Meals served
	Activities dealing with home and property	Pounds of laundry washed Sq. feet of plant maintained and operated Ambulance miles driven (repairs according to job orders)
	Professional services	Patient days (medical, surgical, and nursing services) X-rays taken Laboratory examinations made Pharmaceutical orders filled, etc.
	Other services	Pupil days (nursing education) Patient hours (recreational services), etc.

* "Patient days" for measurement of total hospital services.

matter of ascertaining costs; and (2) there is no method of verifying the accuracy of the figures. In business concerns, at least some relation can be established between the results of statistical cost accounting and the results shown on the financial statements. But such a condition does not exist in governmental units. The recording of governmental costs on the books as supplementary to the general accounting but integrated with it seems to be the more desirable method. The general ledger accounts will control the subsidiary cost accounts and thus ensure accurate cost data. Furthermore, the general accounts will be supported by detailed information so necessary for proper understanding and control. An integrated system of general and cost accounts with a minimum of duplication of records and entries can be accomplished by the use of controlling accounts on the general ledger and cost accounts as subsidiary records. Where it is not possible to integrate the cost accounts with the general accounts, it should be possible *periodically* to reconcile the cost accounts with the figures shown on the general accounting records.

Where cost and general accounts are to be integrated, the original installation of the system should be simple, and, as its use becomes recognized, greater detail may be added. The system should be prepared so that the costs will be accurate and will be available promptly. The method of handling funds and expenditures and the allocation between departments and within departments should be fairly consistent from year to year. In order to arrive at such a plan, it might be wise to have the cost accounting concentrated in a central finance office, instead of having each department take care of its own cost accounting with or without outside supervision.

Accounting Records and Procedures for Governmental Costs
Activities may be broadly grouped into (1) administration, (2) construction, (3) equipment service, (4) education, (5) protection, (6) health, (7) law, (8) libraries, (9) parks and recreation, and (10) public enterprises. A careful analysis of these will indicate that certain activities are similar to those performed by profit seeking enterprises—such as construction, operating public utilities—and therefore their costs usually include the use of materials, labor, and a group of expenses. The other services are in themselves rather exclusively social and public. The costs for this group will cover primarily salaries or wages, supplies (as contrasted with materials used in construction projects or a public utility), and some expenses. To explain the cost accounting for each of these activi-

ties would involve an amount of needless repetition. Therefore, only certain types of activity will be discussed.

Cost accounting requires adequate records, which for a governmental unit will include:

1. *Original documents*—evidence of work performed, such as work orders, performance reports, time reports, stores requisitions, equipment reports, and charge tickets.

2. *Registers or journals*—used as an intermediate record for the summation of the original documents. Included here are a material requisition journal, a register of work orders, and others. These journals and original documents are usually supported by subsidiary ledgers. The two most frequently found are: (*a*) the stores ledger or perpetual inventory, on which is recorded the kinds and quantities of materials on hand, received, and issued; and (*b*) the equipment ledger, in which is maintained a detailed record for each piece of equipment owned and used.

3. *Work and cost ledger*—the final basic record in any integrated cost system. In this are recorded the accounts pertaining to each work order issued.

The cost accounting procedure for governmental units must include reference to the accounting for labor, materials, indirect costs, standard costs, and cost reports. In accounting for *labor,* several factors must be considered. If the labor is on several public works jobs in the course of a day, labor reports should be made daily by the workman and checked by his supervisor. In other activities, where the same work is performed more or less continuously, such reports need not be made so frequently. In such cases, however, it might be desirable to divide the labor costs into (1) *effective,* which represents the time actually at work, and (2) *noneffective,* which includes the time spent on vacations and sick leave. Noneffective work is not included in computing the labor costs of a particular work order but will be included with the indirect expenses. Supervisory costs which apply to several activities should be prorated. Bonuses paid for overtime should be included in the expenses to be apportioned to all jobs rather than to the jobs on which they were paid, thus permitting the comparison of costs of one job with those of another. This procedure is similar to that used in industrial cost accounting.

In accounting for *materials,* there are a few principles not already discussed in the early part of this text. Adequate stores control and inventory records must be set up either on a departmental basis or on a *centralized* basis. All issues and receipts must be properly evidenced by vouchers. Pricing may be either on the first-in, first-out method or on the moving-average method.

In accounting for *indirect* costs, there are three types of expenses which require attention. One of the first relates to *equipment* used on a work order. The cost of equipment can be most effectively controlled by the use of a centralized equipment department and an individual perpetual record for each piece of equipment. Thus it becomes easier to charge each job with the proper cost for the use of equipment. This cost may be on the hourly basis or on the per mile of use basis. The cost of equipment is made up of the (1) acquisition cost and (2) the maintenance cost—repairs and operations. Usually in governmental accounting, except in the case of enterprises such as the utilities and waterworks, it is not customary to record depreciation as an expense. However, in computing rental charges for equipment, it is desirable to consider depreciation, since the equipment will wear out in the course of time and must be replaced. Other than governmental units should consider depreciation as an item of cost.

The other two types of indirect costs are (1) expenses of administration and supervision and (2) nonadministrative expenses which cannot practically be charged directly to specific activities or jobs when they are incurred. Such items as travel, telephone, and postage come under the heading of nonadministrative expenses. The use of a *predetermined* indirect cost rate, calculated on estimated direct labor cost, is an accepted procedure. The actual expenses and indirect costs are collected in the Overhead Cost account, and the charges made to various departments are credited regularly to the Overhead Applied account.

Merely to compile costs for a certain activity is not to control it or measure its effectiveness. There must be some measuring base or *standard*. The ideal standard and the one commonly used is the *minimum unit cost* at which the services or work should be done. Such standards may be computed either (1) by comparison with past experience of the governmental unit under consideration, (2) by comparison with other units of similar size and location, or (3) by engineering studies. Usually standards are not used until the cost system has been in operation for a few years, because comparisons with costs in the past are probably the most satisfactory unless the greatest care is used in comparing costs with other communities to be sure that the conditions in each case are comparable. A good illustration of such faulty comparisons is evident in the per capita educational costs in cities of similar sizes. Costs vary widely, but little consideration is given to costs of living, varied types of curricula, and quality of equipment, all of which make for variations.

To complete the picture of cost accounting for nonprofit entities, it is necessary to discuss the proper use of the system installed and the standards set. Cost summaries and reports are the essential link between the cost accounting and the managerial use of the data. To be most effective, these reports should be prepared periodically. Unless this is done, much of the effort and expense incurred in the cost accounting will be wasted. The reports most commonly presented would include the following:

1. *Monthly summary of unit costs,* showing for each activity the total costs, the units of work accomplished or completed, and the resulting unit cost.
2. *Monthly summary of labor costs,* indicating for each activity the various processes involved, the kinds of work performed, the man-hours of work, labor costs, and work units.
3. *Summary of equipment rentals,* showing for each class of equipment and for each piece of equipment, the place of use, the activities involved, the rentals charged, and the costs associated with them.
4. *Summary of materials used,* showing for each activity the type, the quantity, and the cost of materials used.

In addition to the regular reports indicated, it is possible to prepare, from time to time, special reports. Reports on idle and noneffective labor costs, reports on variations from standard costs, and departmental efficiency reports are only a few of those which might be used to study out-of-line conditions. Adequate use of graphic presentation of data is desirable.

Cost Accounting for Research and Development Activities

Substantial increases in expenditures for research and development activities in recent years has resulted in managements becoming more interested in the costs of these activities. No longer is research and development an unimportant function in many firms. In fact, many an enterprise would be out of business before very long if it were not for the constant development of new products or processes that grow out of the research activities.

Although companies distinguish between research and development activities, the financial executive usually considers the two-in-one category as they are similar for cost accounting purposes.

An important consideration facing management in companies engaged in research and development activities is how much to spend on these activities. For most items other than research and development, the amount allotted by management for costs and expenses varies with the level of operations, i.e., with expected benefits. In fact, flexible budgets based on levels of activity are often established and these point out that expenditures rise as activities rise. In the case of research and development, however, there is a special problem. A given sum may be spent on a project with the result being a new product of substantial value or the project may result in failure. Thus, although it is possible that people working on a project may be *efficient* and even cost conscious, the *benefits* from the project may be *nil*. To make things more difficult, benefits from a project may not be known until costs have been incurred.

Control over the effectiveness of research and development activities may become a serious problem. A competent manager should head this activity. He should be an individual who might be able to select projects with high probabilities of success. He should also be an individual who is cost conscious and control minded, but he should not be afraid to spend more if he feels adequate results may be obtained.

The research and development activities of a company may be carried on in a centralized research center or the activities may be carried on by each division at a number of locations. Obviously, cost data need to be accumulated for each location and for the research and development activity as a whole. More important, however, is the necessity for accumulating cost data, both actual and budget, by *project*. In this way management may compare the cost of a project with its expected cost.

The techniques of cost accumulation by projects is similar to accumulating costs by jobs in the factory. A cost sheet is prepared for each project showing actual and budgeted costs. For projects-in-process, status reports should be prepared periodically comparing expenditures and commitments to date with the budgeted amount. A status report is shown in Illustration 25–9.

Illustration 25–9

ABC MANUFACTURING COMPANY

RESEARCH AND DEVELOPMENT ACTIVITY—STATUS REPORT

August 31, 19—

Project No. 843 Date Started January 15, 19—
Purpose Improve liquifying process Expected Completion Date October 15, 19—
In Charge G. T. Jasper

Expenses	Budget	Expenditures to Date	Commitments to Date	Total Expenditures and Commitments	Unexpended
Personnel costs...............	$48,500	$32,000		$32,000	$16,500
Supplies....................	6,000	4,000	$ 500	4,500	1,500
Consultants and consulting services...................	15,000	8,000	3,000	11,000	4,000
Traveling expenses...........	6,000	4,000		4,000	2,000
Administrative..............	7,000	3,000		3,000	4,000
	$82,500	$51,000	$ 3,500	$54,500	$28,000

After a project has been completed, total expenditures should be compared with the budget. In addition, follow-up audits should be conducted to determine whether or not the project was *effective,* i.e., did it accomplish that which was desired?

QUESTIONS FOR REVIEW

1. What are some major areas outside the factory and the selling effort where cost accounting should be used?
2. Where might cost accounting techniques be of help in a department store?
3. "The use of cost accounting is all right for private enterprise, but there is no room for cost accounting in a municipal accounting situation." Comment on this statement.
4. The enactment of the law providing medicare has resulted in increased interest on behalf of hospitals in cost accounting. Why?
5. How might cost accounting become a cost control device in a commercial bank?
6. Is it necessary to use a standard cost system in a hospital in order to obtain control over costs? Explain.
7. How would you compute the cost of typing a letter?
8. How might cost accounting help in the case of a savings and loan association desiring information as to whether or not to open a new branch?
9. "There is no way in which research and development costs may be controlled." Comment.
10. What problems are encountered when an attempt is made to measure the profit of each department in a department store?

PROBLEMS—GROUP A

Problem 25–1. Purpose: *Control of Administrative Costs*

The Ulithi Company prepares a comprehensive budget to use as a guide in its operations. The sales budget for 1969 disclosed that sales are expected to increase 15 percent over 1968. Sales for 1968 totaled $2,000,000.

The office manager was asked to prepare the first draft of the 1969 budget for the accounting function of the general and administrative expense. The 1968 cost of the accounting function was estimated to amount to $40,000. Since sales were expected to increase 15 percent, the office manager budgeted a $46,000 amount for the accounting function.

The president was not satisfied with the figure determined by the office manager and has asked you for advice.

Required:

a) Do you agree with the amount determined by the office manager and the manner in which he determined the amount?

b) How would you have prepared the budget for the accounting function?

c) How would you achieve control over the cost of the accounting function? Be specific in your answer.

Problem 25–2.   Purpose: *Cost Analysis in a School District*
The Board of Education of the Victoria School District is developing a budget for the school year ending June 30, 1967. The budgeted expenditures follow:

VICTORIA SCHOOL DISTRICT
BUDGETED EXPENDITURES
For the Year Ending June 30, 1967

Current operating expenditures:			
Instruction:			
General..	$1,401,600		
Vocational training............................	112,000	$1,513,600	
Pupil service:			
Bus transportation............................	36,300		
School lunches................................	51,700	88,000	
Attendance and health service......................		14,000	
Administration..................................		46,000	
Operation and maintenance of school................		208,000	
Pensions, insurance, etc...........................		154,000	
Total current operating expenditures..............			$2,023,600
Other expenditures:			
Capital outlays from revenues......................		75,000	
Debt service (annual installment and interest on long-term debt).......................................		150,000	
Total other expenditures.......................			225,000
Total Budgeted Expenditures........................			$2,248,600

The following data are available:
1. The estimated average daily school enrollment of the school district is 5,000 pupils including 200 pupils enrolled in a vocational training program.
2. Estimated revenues include equalizing grants-in-aid from the state of $150 per pupil. The grants were established by state law under a plan intended to encourage raising the level of education.
3. The federal government matches 60 percent of state grants-in-aid for pupils enrolled in a vocational training program. In addition the federal government contributes toward the cost of bus transportation and school lunches a maximum of $12 per pupil based on total enrollment within the school district but not to exceed $6\frac{2}{3}$ percent of the state per-pupil equalization grants-in-aid.
4. Interest on temporary investment of school tax receipts and rents of school facilities are expected to be $75,000 and are earmarked for special equipment acquisitions listed as "Capital outlays from revenues" in the budgeted expenditures. Cost of the special equipment acquisitions will be limited to the amount derived from these miscellaneous receipts.
5. The remaining funds needed to finance the budgeted expenditures of the school district are to be raised from local taxation. An allowance of 9 percent of the local tax levy is necessary for possible tax abatements and losses. The assessed valuation of the property located within the school district is $80,000,000.

Required:

a) Prepare a schedule computing the estimated total funds to be obtained from local taxation for the ensuing school year ending June 30, 1967, for the Victoria School District.

b) Prepare a schedule computing the estimated current operating cost per regular pupil and per vocational pupil to be met by local tax funds. Assume that costs other than instructional costs are assignable on a per capita basis to regular and vocational students.

c) Without prejudice to your solution to part (*a*), assume that the estimated total tax levy for the ensuing school year ending June 30, 1967, is $1,092,000. Prepare a schedule computing the estimated tax rate per $100 of assessed valuation of the property within the Victoria School District.

Problem 25–3. Purpose: *Computation of Royalty Cost*

The Underground Mining Company started mining in the current year on certain land leased from T. Realty Company.

The royalty provisions in the lease are as follows:

1. Minimum annual royalty—$6,000 with minimum of $1,500 payable quarterly. Unearned minimum royalties may be recovered in any subsequent period from earned royalties in excess of minimum royalties. Minimum royalties of $18,000 were paid for the three years prior to the current year.
2. Earned royalty—$0.10 per ton shipped from the mine plus a per ton amount equal to 2 percent of the amount that the market value of the ore at the mine exceeds $4 per ton.

Operations in the current year were as follows:

		Per Ton	
Periods	Tons Shipped	Market Value at Destination	Freight from Mine to Destination
First quarter......................	None	...	...
Second quarter...................	100,000	$10.50	$3.10
Third quarter....................	200,000	10.00	3.20
Fourth quarter...................	None	...	...
	300,000		

Required:

Compute the amount of royalty to be paid to T. Realty Company for the current year and the amount of unearned minimum royalty at the end of the year.

(Adapted from an AICPA Uniform Examination)

Problem 25–4. Purpose: *Municipal Cost Accounting; Analysis of Centralized Trucking Department Costs*

Ultramodern City has organized a centralized trucking service department to service all city departments except those which have their own trucks, such as

788 COST ACCOUNTING: PRINCIPLES AND PRACTICE

garbage and street-cleaning. The latter may occasionally make use of this trucking service.

The cost of operating this service for the six months ending June 30, 19—, was:

January 1, investment in three trucks, new, costing $15,000; estimated life, five years; scrap value, $1,500. Tools cost, new, $500; estimated life, five years; no scrap value. A garage was used which is a municipally owned building, on which there is no rental or taxes.

The costs of operating this service for six months were:

Gas and oil	$1,200
Insurance	120
Repairs, outside	300
Salaries of drivers	2,250
Telephone and telegraph	30
Miscellaneous	60
	$3,960

At the beginning of the six-month period it is estimated that the expenses of this trucking department would be $4,800, and the estimated ton-miles would be 60,000.

The trucking service was rendered to the various departments, which were charged according to the predetermined rate, as follows:

School and education department	8,000 ton-miles
Health department	4,000 ton-miles
Printing department	10,000 ton-miles
Road and engineering service	6,000 ton-miles
Street-cleaning department, extra	5,000 ton-miles
Garbage and sewer service, extra	10,000 ton-miles
Relief service	12,000 ton-miles
Total Service Rendered	55,000 ton-miles

Required:

Prepare:

a) Schedule showing the per ton-mile rate, estimated.

b) Schedule of per ton-mile, actual.

c) Charges to various departments.

PROBLEMS—GROUP B

Problem 25–5. Purpose: *Control over Research and Development Costs*

The Kingman Pharmaceutical Company develops, manufactures, and sells drugs and related items. Research and development costs constitute a major expenditure for Kingman. Last year when sales were $20,000,000; $3,000,000 was spent for research and development. Currently, estimates are that sales will increase to approximately $28,000,000 this year because of the development of "kur," a new miracle drug.

Required:

a) Should research and development costs be budgeted at $4,200,000 for the current year? Explain.

b) How should research and development costs be budgeted?

c) What types of control systems should be established for research and development costs?

Problem 25–6. Purpose: *Municipal Cost Accounting; Cost Accounting for Water Company*

Prepare a statement showing the computation of the unit cost per million gallons of water delivered that would be fair to both municipalities.

The Krisp Water Company furnishes water to A municipality. The adjoining municipality, X, is anxious to obtain a supplementary supply of water and opens negotiations for a long-term contract at a fixed price per million gallons.

The costs of operating the waterworks for the year 1968 were as follows:

Water collecting system expenses	$ 12,000
Water purification expenses	24,000
Water pumping expenses	36,000
Maintenance of distribution system	24,000
Commercial office expenses	24,000
General administration expenses	10,000
Debt service requirements	150,000
	$280,000

The income for 1968 was as follows:

Metered water revenues	$240,000
Fire hydrant rentals	60,000
	$300,000

The proposed contract calls for the installation of meters for the purpose of measuring the water delivered to X municipality, and the contract is to be for not less than 20 years.

The engineering department furnishes you with the following data:

Water pumped during year 1968	1,000,000,000 gal.
Water billed to consumers	800,000,000 gal.
Water used for fire service	100,000,000 gal.
Water not accounted for—presumably leakage through mains, etc.	100,000,000 gal.
Estimated water to be delivered to X municipality per year	225,000,000 gal.

Additional facilities and costs to be incurred for the proposed contract are:

New pumping equipment, $50,000, to be acquired through issuance of 20-year, 3 percent bonds.

The water collecting system expenses and the maintenance of distribution system will be increased 10 percent each.

The purification and pumping expenses will be increased in direct proportion to the water pumped.

It is not expected that the commercial office and general administration expenses will be increased.

The present plant facilities are being used to about 60 percent of capacity.

Problem 25–7. Purpose: *Cost-Volume-Profit Relationships in a Utility*

You are preparing your long-form report in connection with the examination of State Gas Utility at December 31, 1969. The report will include an explanation of the 1969 increase in operating revenues.

The following information is available from the company records:

	1968	1969	Increase (Decrease)
Average number of customers........	27,000	26,000	(1,000)
MCF sales.......................	486,000	520,000	34,000
Revenue.........................	$1,215,000	$1,274,000	$59,000

Required:

To explain the 1969 increase in operating revenues, prepare an analysis accounting for the effect of changes in:

1. Average number of customers.
2. Average gas consumption per customer.
3. Average rate per MCF sold (MCF = thousand cubic feet).

Problem 25–8. Purpose: *Analysis of Bank Costs*

The Knowlton National Bank of Chicago, Illinois, has an organization of five income-producing departments and five service departments. These income departments are: savings, commercial, safe deposit, trust and estate, and taxation. The service departments are: accounting, advertising, legal, stenographic, and building maintenance.

The trial balance for the month of June, 19—, showed the following account balances:

TRIAL BALANCE

June 30, 19—

Account	Dr.	Cr.
Cash..	$ 500,000	
Bonds and investments....................................	850,000	
Loans receivable...	718,000	
Overdrafts...	500	
Stock in Federal Reserve Bank............................	6,000	
Building (depreciated on 20-year basis).....................	50,000	
Allowance for depreciation—building......................		$ 20,000*
Safe deposit vault and fixtures (20 years)..................	5,000	
Allowance for depreciation—vault.........................		2,000*
Deposits...		1,600,000
Capital stock...		100,000
Paid-in surplus...		100,000
Undistributed profits.....................................		300,000
Interest earned..		15,000
Service charges on checking accounts.......................		1,000
Safe deposit box rentals...................................		1,500
Trustees' fees and commissions............................		1,500
Taxation service income...................................		300
Taxes on real estate......................................	300	
Interest paid...	1,200	
Officers' salaries...	3,000	
Salaries of office workers..................................	5,000	
Salaries of other employees (building maintenance)...........	200	
Office supplies..	500	
Insurance expense..	600	
Telephone and telegraph...................................	100	
Repairs to building and maintenance.......................	200	
Traveling expenses..	300	
Advertising..	400	
	$2,141,300	$2,141,300

* Depreciation has not yet been recorded for June.

The various expenses are allocated to the income and service departments as follows:

Department	Travel Expenses and Officers' Salaries	Office Supplies and Office Salaries	Building Maintenance	Interest Earned	Interest Expense	Insurance
Accounting.................	4%	4%	500 sq. ft.			
Advertising...............	3	3	200			
Legal......................	3	3	300			
Stenographic..............	3	5	2,000			
Building maintenance.......	2	...	...			80%
Savings...................	20	20	20,000	⅓	100%	...
Commercial...............	40	45	25,000	⅔	...	...
Safe deposit..............	10	5	12,000	...	...	20
Trust.....................	10	12	10,000	...	...	...
Taxation..................	5	3	5,000	...	...	...
	100%	100%	75,000 sq. ft.			

Department	Telephone & Telegraph	Advertising	Accounting	Legal	Stenographic
Accounting..............	$ 8			5%	5%
Advertising.............	5			5	5
Legal..................	15	On basis		...	10
Stenographic...........	5	of gross		...	...
Building maintenance......	5	income		...	...
Savings................	5	in each	15%	10	15
Commercial.............	25	department	70	45	50
Safe deposit...........	5		3	5	2
Trust..................	12		10	20	10
Taxation...............	15		2	10	3
	$100		100%	100%	100%

On the basis of the foregoing data prepare:

a) A comparative income and expense statement for the month of June, by departments.

b) Compute the unit costs in the commercial department on the basis of the following data:

There were 3,750 checks deposited, of which one third are on the Knowlton National Bank, one third are on other banks in the city, and one third are on out-of-town banks. There is no charge for checks on this bank; and double the charge for out-of-town checks, as compared with checks on local banks.

There were 91,005 checks drawn on this bank by depositors of the commercial department. These are three times as costly to handle as checks deposited in this bank but drawn on local banks.

Drafts and cashier checks cost five times as much to handle as the checks drawn on this bank by depositors. There were 5,000 of these.

Problem 25-9. Purpose: *Municipal Cost Analysis*

In Knightstown, a careful study of the cost of municipal services is made. One service which loomed rather large in the 1969 budget was sewer maintenance. The work of this department consists of cleaning and repairing sanitary sewers and storm drains, excavating channels, and operating pumping, treatment, and ventilating plants. Unit costs are computed in two ways: (1) the cost per mile of sewers in service, and (2) unit cost of work performed.

There were 2,824 miles of sewers in service during the year. During the year, 88 sewer stoppages had to be corrected, at a labor cost of $966; 14,461 manholes had to be cleaned, costing $6,246.42; 166,974 manholes were inspected, along with other work, but no separate cost was allocated for these inspections; 232 miles of sewers were cleaned, at a cost of $17,278.62; 145 miles were flushed, at a cost of $1,907.68. Since the city has its own water supply system, no charge was made for the 2,122 water-hours used from fire hydrants. Although there were only 2,824 miles of sewers in operation during the year, inspection mileage was 8,249, since some sections had to be inspected several times; the cost of this inspection was $21,271.40. As a result of these inspections, the repairs were: 490 sewer manholes repaired, at a cost of $6,499.77; 482 feet of sewer manholes raised, at a cost of $5,780.07; and 2,080 feet of sewers repaired, at a cost of $4,842.03. There were numerous complaints about house connections to the sewers; the costs of the investigations were $1,458.35.

From these data, prepare a schedule showing:

a) Total cost of sewer maintenance.

b) Cost per mile of service.

c) Unit cost of work performed where such units are evident.

APPENDIXES

A—Applied Process Cost
   Accounting Procedures

B—Applied Standard Cost
   Accounting Procedures

C—Program of Cost Accounting
   Reports

APPENDIX

A | Applied Process Cost Accounting Procedures

Introduction   Process cost accounting may be a very simple and easy-to-determine statistical or accounting procedure, or it may become very complex and involved. The basic principles, nevertheless, are the same. The complexity is due to the nature of the manufacturing operations or to some inherent problem of shrinkage, waste, spoilage, or apportionment of costs. In order to show the application of process cost accounting, this appendix will present a brief statement of the methods and problems of process cost accounting of the following:

1. Cement manufacturers	4. Lumber mills
2. Brick manufacturers	5. Flour mills
3. Foundries	

Cost Procedure for Cement Manufacturers[1]   Cement is usually made from such materials as limestone, clay, shale, or blast-furnace slag. The manufacture of cement usually involves taking definite proportions of such raw materials, grinding them to extreme fineness, burning them at a high temperature, and then regrinding the resulting clinker. It is a continuous operation. There are two methods of manufacturing cement—the dry process and the wet process. In the dry process the materials are kept dry throughout the entire operations, but in the wet process water is added to the raw materials. Since the latter will cover all phases of the former, the wet process will be described in this section. As an illustration, it is assumed that

---

[1] Adapted, with permission, from "Accounting in the Cement Industry," by Leon E. Smith, in *N.A.A. Bulletin*, Vol. XXIII, No. 3.

limestone and shale are used as raw materials and are obtained from the firm's own quarries. Natural gas is used as fuel (although coal or fuel oil could also be used).

The manufacturing operations cover the following:

A. *Quarrying* of limestone and shale, which covers:
   1. *Stripping*—removing top refuse material.
   2. *Production*—loading material into quarry cars.
   3. *Crushing* and storing of limestone and shale.
B. *Clinker department,* which covers:
   1. *Raw grinding* of limestone and shale.
   2. *Slurring*—adding water to mixture (only in wet process).
   3. *Blending*—mixing proper proportions of materials (this is done in large tanks of 1,000- or 2,000-barrel capacity).
   4. *Burning* in kilns, to which slurry mixture is passed.
   5. *Clinker grinding*—of the material cooled and stored.
C. *Packing and loading,* which refers to taking the cement from the large silos. The cement is not packed until it is to be shipped either in barrels, cloth bags, paper bags, or in bulk.

The operating accounts represent the cost centers or departments. These departments or centers, as will be shown in cost of production report which follows, are: (1) Raw Material No. 1 (limestone); (2) Raw Material No. 2 (shale); (3) Clinker; and (4) Cement. Incidental or auxiliary departments, such as machine shop, carpenter shop, hospital, hotel, and clubhouse, are included under the general heading of Mill Overhead. The mill overhead may be allocated to the various producing departments or, as is more commonly the case, applied to production as one lump sum in the last—the cement department.

Illustration A–1 represents the cost summary which may be prepared from the departmental cost of production reports or analyses. A more condensed summary or statement may also be prepared. For an example of such a statement, see Illustration A–2 (p. 798).

There are a few special problems in the costing of cement. One refers to *containers*. Materials are shipped principally in cloth sacks, paper bags, and in bulk. Each bag or sack contains 94 pounds, and four sacks make one barrel of cement. Cement is sold on a delivered basis—f.o.b. destination. A charge of 10 cents per cloth sack and 15 cents per barrel is made to the customer. This charge is refundable to the customer if the containers are returned within 90 days. (There is no charge or refund for paper bags.) The company must therefore set up an account for returnable containers in the hands of customers. A second problem refers to *depletion* and *depreciation*. Depletion and depreciation are the same as for most mining companies. However, to have comparable costs from month to month, the unit or production method should be used.

Illustration A-1

THE BEST CEMENT COMPANY
COST SUMMARY
For the Month Ending March 19—

	Rock Costs	Shale Costs	Raw Grinding	Clinker Burning	Clinker Grinding	Power, Light, and Water	Machine Shop	Packing and Loading	Mill Overhead	Coal Costs	Total
Supplies	3,000.00	450.00	1,300.00	1,800.00	1,200.00	1,500.00	150.00	100.00	100.00	1,200.00	10,800.00
Payroll for Labor	5,000.00	2,000.00	8,700.00	5,200.00	2,400.00	3,000.00	7,850.00	900.00	800.00	800.00	36,650.00
Fuel	1,200.00	950.00	400.00			11,500.00	200.00			16,000.00	30,250.00
Depreciation:											
Machinery	100.00	50.00	1,500.00	2,500.00	2,400.00					180.00	6,730.00
Buildings			300.00	500.00	200.00					20.00	1,020.00
Taxes	300.00	100.00									400.00
Depletion	50.00	20.00									70.00
Insurance	250.00	80.00	300.00	100.00	200.00	150.00	120.00		50.00	20.00	1,270.00
Total	9,900.00	3,650.00	12,500.00	10,100.00	6,400.00	16,150.00	8,320.00	1,000.00	950.00	18,220.00	87,190.00
Machine Shop	2,000.00	200.00	2,000.00	2,000.00	1,000.00	720.00	8,320.00			400.00	8,320.00
Power, Light, and Water	100.00		6,000.00	4,100.00	4,600.00	16,870.00				2,070.00	16,870.00
Coal Costs				20,690.00						20,690.00	20,690.00
Total	12,000.00	3,850.00	20,500.00	36,890.00	12,000.00			1,000.00	950.00		87,190.00
Production	30,000 tons	19,250 tons	64,050 bbls.	64,050 bbls.	60,000 bbls.						
Unit Cost	0.40	0.20	0.32	0.5759	0.20						
Transfers:											
Rock, 22,000 Tons			8,800.00								
Shale, 13,200 Tons			2,640.00								
Raw Grinding, 64,050 Bbls				31,940.00							
Clinker Burning, 60,000 Bbls					64,477.20						
Gypsum Added					4,132.80						
Mill Overhead to Finished Cement Only					950.00				950.00		
Cumulative Cost Grinding			31,940.00								
Cumulative Cost Burning				68,830.00 (1.07462)							
Cumulative Cost Cement					81,560.00 (1.3593)			81,560.00			
Packing, Loading								1,000.00			
Final Cost Ready for Shipment								82,560.00			

Illustration A–2

COST OF PRODUCTION REPORT

For Month Ending March 31, 19—

	Tons or Barrels	Amount	Average per Ton or Barrel
RAW MATERIAL NO. 1—ROCK:			
Production (Tons).....................	30,000		
Stripping.............................		$ 3,000.00	
Production............................		7,000.00	
Crushing, Receiving, and Storing........		2,000.00	
Total Cost of Raw Material No. 1....		$12,000.00	
Add: Inventory at Beginning of Period.....		0	
Total...........................		$12,000.00	$0.40
Less: Inventory at End of Period..........	8,000	3,200.00	
Less: Used in Stone Dust Operations......		0	
Used in Manufacture..............	22,000	$ 8,800.00	$0.40
RAW MATERIAL NO. 2—SHALE:			
Production (Tons).....................	19,250	$ 3,850.00	$0.20
Stripping.............................		$ 1,000.00	
Production............................		2,350.00	
Crushing, Receiving, and Storing........		500.00	
Total Cost of Raw Material No. 2....		$ 3,850.00	
Add: Inventory at Beginning of Period.....		0	
Total...........................		$ 3,850.00	
Less: Inventory at End of Period..........	6,050	1,210.00	
Used in Manufacture..............	13,200	$ 2,640.00	$0.20
CLINKER:			
Production (Barrels)...................	64,050	$68,830.00	$1.07462
Raw Material No. 1—Rock.............		$ 8,800.00	
Raw Material No. 2—Shale............		2,640.00	
Grinding, Mixing, and Storing..........		20,500.00	
Burning, Cooling, and Storing..........		36,890.00	
Total Cost of Clinker..............		$68,830.00	
Add: Inventory at Beginning of Period.....		0	
Total...........................		$68,830.00	
Less: Inventory at End of Period..........	4,050	4,352.80	
Used in Manufacture..............	60,000	$64,477.20	$1.07462
CEMENT:			
Production (Barrels)...................	60,000	$81,560.00	$1.3593
Cost of Clinker.......................		$64,477.20	
Clinker Grinding......................		12,000.00	
Mill Overhead........................		4,132.80	
Reserves.............................		950.00	
Total Cost of Cement..............		$81,560.00	1.3593
Add: Inventory at Beginning of Period.....		0	
	60,000	$81,560.00	$1.3593
Less: Inventory at End of Period..........	0	0	
Less: Cement Used....................	0	0	
Bin Cost of Cement Shipped........	60,000	$81,560.00	$1.3593

A third problem should be noted. The unit of costing is per ton for raw material, and this is changed to per barrel in the burning department. This transition is accomplished merely by dividing the new quantity unit into the total cumulative cost up to that stage of production.

Cost Procedure for Brick Manufacturers   The manufacture of bricks is similar to that of cement. The variety of bricks which one manufacturer can produce is fairly large, the principal difference being in the materials used. In the main, there are usually six operating departments or cost centers, and these represent the work-in-process accounts. That is, the work-in-process is kept by cost centers, which are:

1. *Quarrying*—in which clay and sand are dug.
2. *Pans and machines*—in which the mixture of raw materials is prepared and placed in the pans. The resulting product is known as *wet bricks*.
3. *Drying*—in which the bricks are allowed to dry, making green bricks.
4. *Setting*—in which the green bricks are placed in the kilns for firing and burning.
5. *Burning*—baking the bricks in kilns.
6. *Unloading*—removing the bricks, which have been burned, from the kilns.

Before examining a pro forma cost of production statement, it is necessary to discuss various problems of cost accounting for the brick industry. These are: (1) the handling of spoiled bricks in the pans and machine center, in the process of drying, and in the kilns; (2) the equivalent production of the bricks in the kilns; and (3) plant overhead.

In most problems in the manufacture of bricks the principle laid down is that *no spoilage costs* are to be charged against the bricks still in the process of manufacture in the driers or in the kilns. This means that the bricks spoiled in drier or in the kilns should be included in the equivalent production; that is, the equivalent production represents both good and spoiled bricks produced. This results in a lower unit cost for the work-in-process, but the total cumulative costs that are transferred from department to department include the cost of the spoiled bricks. In other words, the spoiled bricks are used to compute unit costs for valuing the work-in-process; but this unit cost is a departmental figure only, since for each succeeding department a new unit cost is computed, based on the total cumulative costs divided by the good production (without the spoiled bricks).

The second problem refers to the work-in-process inventory in the kilns. This is usually divided into *fully burned bricks* (completed for that department); *half-burned bricks* (estimated to be one-half

Illustration A–3

QUANTITY STATEMENT OF BRICKS MANUFACTURED

For the Year 19—

Wet bricks placed in pans during year............................		17,450,000
Less: Bricks spoiled in pans and machines.........................		350,000
Good bricks carried to driers during year............................		17,100,000
Add: Inventory of bricks in driers at beginning of year..................		100,000
Total bricks in driers during year..................................		17,200,000
Less: Bricks spoiled in drying.......................................		700,000
Good bricks dried and in process of drying..........................		16,500,000
Less: Inventory of bricks in driers at end of year......................		600,000
Bricks set in the kilns..		15,900,000
Add: Bricks in kilns at start of year:		
Burned...	180,000	
Half-burned...	100,000	
Green...	80,000	360,000
Total bricks in kilns during year..................................		16,260,000
Less: Bricks spoiled in burning......................................		660,000
Total bricks—green, half-burned, and burned in kiln during the year.....		15,600,000
Less: Inventory of bricks in kilns at end of year:		
Burned...	150,000	
Half-burned...	100,000	
Green...	90,000	340,000
Good bricks taken from kilns during year............................		15,260,000
Add: Burned bricks in yard at beginning of year.......................		40,000
Total Bricks Available for Sale......................................		15,300,000

complete); and *green bricks,* which are costed at the unit cost of all work up to the kiln.

The third problem is one of *plant overhead.* As in the case of cement production, the plant overhead is added to production primarily in the final (unloading) department. A portion of this overhead, however, may be allocated to those bricks still in the kilns which have been completed but not unloaded.

Illustration A–3 demonstrates the computation of the quantities of bricks placed in production in the various departments, and the resulting good production.

Illustration A–4

COST OF PRODUCTION STATEMENT

Expenses	Quarrying	Pans and Machines	Drying	Setting	Burning	Unloading
Materials and supplies....$ 2,800		$14,800	$ 1,208	$ 630	$ 3,562	$ 4,000
Labor................. 12,200		35,200	7,800	26,400	64,000	26,000
Coal.................... 1,800		...	6,000	...	60,000	...
Powerhouse costs........ ...		15,000	...	...	2,000	...
Depreciation............ 1,200		5,000	800	...	21,000	...
Total Costs........$18,000		$70,000	$15,808	$27,030	$150,562	$30,000

Illustration A–5

COST OF PRODUCTION REPORT
NATIONAL BRICK COMPANY
For the Year Ended December 31, 19—

	Quantity in Thousands	Total Costs	Unit Cost per Thousand
QUARRYING COSTS:			
Material, Labor, Coal, etc............................	17,450	$ 18,000.00	$ 1.032
PANS AND MACHINES:			
Costs of Pans and Machines...........................		$ 70,000.00	
Quantity Placed in Pans and Machines.................	17,450		
Deduct: Spoiled in Pans and Machines................	350		
Good Production in Pans and Machines...............	17,100		
Total Cumulative Cost........................	17,100	$ 88,000.00	$ 5.1462
DRYING COSTS:			
Costs of Drying...................................		$ 15,808.00	
Inventory of Bricks in Driers at Beginning of Year (½ Complete)................................	100	520.00	
Total Cumulative Costs...........................	17,200	$104,328.00	
Deduct: Bricks Spoiled in Drying....................	700	....	
Total................................	16,500	$104,328.00	
Less: Cost of Bricks in Drier at End of Year (½ Complete)*	600	3,369.18	
Total Transferred.............................	15,900	$100,958.82	$ 6.3496
SETTING COSTS:			
Costs of Setting Bricks............................	15,900	$ 27,030.00	
Total Cost of Bricks Set in Kilns.....................	15,900	$127,988.82	$ 8.0496
BURNING COSTS:			
Cost of Bricks Burned during Year..................		$150,562.00	
Inventory in Kilns at Beginning of Year:			
Burned (@ $18.00)............................	180	3,240.00	
Half-Burned.................................	100	1,300.00	
Green (@ $8.00)................................	80	640.00	
Total Bricks Set in Kilns.........................	16,260	$283,730.82	
Deduct: Bricks Spoiled in Burning...................	660		
Total Bricks to Be Accounted for.....................	15,600	$283,730.82	
Deduct: Bricks in Kilns at End of Year:*			
Burned (150×$17.5249)........................	150	2,628.74	
Half-Burned...................................	100	1,278.73	
Green (90×$8.0496).............................	90	724.46	
Cumulative Cost of Burned Bricks....................	15,260	$279,098.89	$18.2896
UNLOADING COSTS:			
Cost of Bricks Unloaded............................		$279,098.89	
Unloading Costs....................................		30,000.00	
Overhead for Entire Plant...........................		2,305.11	
Total Cost of Good Bricks Produced..............	15,260	$311,404.00	$20.4066

*Computation of inventory:

Bricks in Drier at End of Year:
Transfer Cost (600 @ $5.1462).. $3,087.72
Unit within the Department Cost:
Effective Production..16,850M
Unit Cost ($15,808.00 ÷ 16,850M)................................ $0.9382
Cost in Ending Inventory (600 × ½ × $0.9382) 281.46
Inventory of Bricks in Driers.. $3,369.18

Bricks in Kilns at End of Year:
Green Bricks (90 @ $8.0496).. $ 724.46
Half-Burned Bricks:
Transfer Cost (100 @ $8.0496).................................... $804.96
Effective Production...15,890M
Unit within the Department Cost ($150,562.00 ÷ 15,890M)...........$9.4753
Cost in Ending Inventory (100 × ½ × $9.4753)........................... 473.77 ... 1,278.73
Burned Bricks [150 × ($8.0496 + $9.4753)] 2,628.74
Total Inventory of Bricks in Kilns.................................... $4,631.93

The cost of production for the year, taken from the cost production reports of the various departments, is shown in Illustration A–4.

Cost Accounting Procedure for Foundries

Castings of gray iron, steel, brass, aluminum, or other metals constitute the basic materials for numerous products manufactured by such companies as the automobile manufacturers, machine manufacturers, engine producers, and many others. Some of the larger companies operate their own foundries; others have this work done by independent foundries. Except for very small foundries manufacturing expensive castings on special order, most of this work is costed on a process basis; that is, *the costs are averaged by departments even though several different orders are involved.* The unit of costing is the pound. (See Illustration A–5.) The fact that foundry operations are required in so many industries makes it imperative that the student of industrial accounting be familiar with the *nature of the operations* and the cost procedures that can be followed.

From the accounting manual of one manufacturer of a variety of engines the following nontechnical description of foundry operations is quoted:

The first step in the manufacture of a casting is the making of a *pattern,* usually of wood, from a drawing of the part required. The pattern must be the exact shape as the part to be made and slightly larger to allow for the metal shrinkage. Patterns are made from a variety of woods, some of which are the harder woods, such as mahogany. An accurate record and careful storage is made of each pattern so that it is available for use on subsequent orders for the part.

The *molding operation* is the next step in making the casting. The pattern is placed in a box called a flask, and sand rammed tightly around it. The pattern is then withdrawn, leaving a hollow space in the sand which will shape the molten metal to be poured into it. There are a great variety of shapes and sizes of parts so that different methods of molding have been developed. Some molds are made by hand while machines are used for others. The art of molding includes the selection of the proper sand, which must be fine enough to give a smooth finish to the casting, porous enough to allow gases to escape and capable of standing up under extreme heat. Provision must be made in the mold for the inpouring of metal and for the escape of gases.

Molds can only control the outer surface of the casting. Inner surfaces such as in holes or hollows are formed by *cores.* These are made of a special sand and baked. Placed in the mold, the metal flows around them, so that when they are cleaned out the desired cavity is left in the casting. It is by the use of cores that an intricate casting can be made. The placing of the cores, called coring-up, is in itself a difficult operation.

Iron is melted in a *cupola,* which consists of a vertical cylindrical steel shell, lined with fire brick. Into this pig iron, scrap and coke are charged in alternate layers. When air is blown into the cupola the coke burns at high temperature and the iron, steel and other ingredients melt. The melt is taken off at the bottom of the cupola into ladles, and thence poured into the waiting molds.

After solidification the casting is taken out of the mold and cleaned. The cleaning, which may be chipping, grinding or sand-blasting, removes the projections and irregularities left on the casting. After cleaning the casting is weighed and reported complete.[2]

As previously indicated, the entire foundry operations may be operated on a process cost procedure. However, for independent jobbing foundries the procedure may be varied, if desired, as follows:

Melting department—process cost accounting procedure
Molding department—job order cost procedure
Core-making department—job order costing
Cleaning department—process cost accounting procedure
Special treatment of castings such as annealing—process cost procedure

The American Foundrymen's Association has prepared a manual on accounting for foundries. For detailed procedure, reference may be made to *Accounting for Foundries.* However, a few outstanding characteristics may be pointed out here.

The control accounts for manufacturing operations may be set up in either of two ways. There may be *one* work-in-process account, known as the *Foundry Work-in-Process account;* or there may be set up work-in-process accounts on a departmental basis, one for each department, such as the *Melting Department, Molding Department, Core-Making Department, Cleaning and Chipping Department,* etc.

There are certain accessory departments, the costs of which must be allocated or charged directly to the four operating departments listed in the preceding paragraph. These departments are the pattern shop, where the patterns are made for the molds; the carpenter shop; and the blacksmith shop.

The forms sometimes used are: (1) the *daily melting or cupola report,* on which is recorded the costs of materials, supplies, and labor used in the melting department; (2) the *flask card,* on which is recorded the time or labor used in molding the casting; (3) *core tickets,* on which is recorded the time and labor costs and the material costs for making the cores; and (4) a *summary cost report* showing the costs of the melting, molding, core-making, and finishing departments applicable to the various jobs or orders completed.

There are three bases on which costs are assembled in the foundry: *tonnage costs, class costs,* or *individual job order costs. Tonnage costs*

---

[2] Taken, with permission, from *Accounting and Control Manual of Cooper Bessemer Corporation, Mount Vernon, Ohio,* prepared by James E. Brown, Plant Accountant.

are determined by dividing the various expenses, both direct and indirect, by the entire output of the foundry during a given accounting period. Unless the product is quite uniform in size and complexity, this method is of little use for costing or control, since not all castings have uniform costs per pound because they vary not only in size but in the nature and number of cores. Therefore, the cost per pound, per hundred pounds, or per ton, as determined by dividing the total costs by the total weight of the good castings produced, may be erroneous.

Under *class costs,* castings are grouped (1) by *size* (weight of castings, such as 1–10 pounds, 11–25 pounds, 26–50 pounds, and on up to 401–500 pounds); and (2) by *shape* and *complexity* arising from use of cores. By weighting the size of the castings by the complexity factor (based upon the estimated additional labor required because of size or use of cores), and thus obtaining a weighted average cost per pound, a more reliable cost figure is obtained for control purposes than under the tonnage method. This method has a greater acceptance today than the tonnage method.

The *individual job order cost method* can be used by those foundries manufacturing on order only. For higher-priced castings, such as those of brass, aluminum, or other alloys, this method should be used, even though it involves greater clerical expense than either of the other two methods.

It should be noted that in most foundries not more than 25 percent of the costs are direct costs that can be charged directly to a job; the rest are indirect and must be prorated. This proration is usually done on an estimated basis. This estimated basis depends upon the yield from the tonnage of melted metal poured, which sometimes may be as low as 30 percent and may be as high as 70 percent. Such variables make costing quite difficult except on an estimated basis predicted upon experience with various types of castings.

Cost Procedure for Lumber Mills

The operations of the average lumber mill are divided for cost accounting purposes into (1) cost of logging operations and (2) cost of sawmill operations.

Logging and Lumbering Operations.[3] *Logging operations* costs are made up of three major items plus a share of the general administrative expenses. Logging costs are joint costs covering all kinds of timber,

---

[3] Adapted, with permission, from *Pathfinder Bulletin* (Charles R. Hadley Co.), No. 137 (by Burton N. Smith), and from *N.A.A. Bulletin,* Vol. XXIII, No. 9 (by Edward S. Rittler).

since it is quite impossible to cut separately each kind of standing trees. The three cost items are:

1. *Stumpage costs,* which represent the cost of the standing timber. Stumpage costs correspond to the material costs of the average manufacturer. These costs may be computed in several ways, depending upon the method of acquiring the standing timber. These methods are: (1) the ownership of the land and the timber, in which case the value of the land and the standing timber must be amortized over the quantity produced, as compared with the estimated footage in the property; (2) the purchase of the standing timber only, in which case the purchase price will be apportioned over the production on the basis of the estimated footage; and (3) the acquisition of the lumber on a royalty basis, in which case the royalty paid becomes the cost of the stumpage.

Stumpage costs may be considered as part of the logging costs or may be included only in the statement of the cost of sales.

2, 3. *Cutting and transportation costs,* which represent the labor and material costs of felling the trees and removing them to the sawmills. The labor costs thus incurred are termed "swamping"—removing the underbrush; "felling and bucking," which refers to the cutting of the trees; "skidding and loading," which refers to the removal of the logs to the transporting medium either by floating the logs, removing by sleds or tractors, or just dragging by horsepower to railroad cars. In large operations the cost of the railroad equipment and spurs are considered as part of the transportation costs. For this work, materials and supplies, such as saws, wire rope, and cutting tools, are required. Charges for depreciation of equipment, repairs to equipment, fire insurance, fire loss, maintenance of transportation equipment, amortization of rail and spur equipment costs, and operating supplies must also be added to the cost of the labor for cutting and transporting the logs.

A share of the administrative salaries, fire-patrol costs, and taxes, including the severance tax imposed by most states, should be included, together with the costs of operating camps where the workmen live during the cutting and transportation operations.

In the logging operations, the quantity of production is measured in feet according to *log scale* measurements. These measurements and expressions of quantity are not accurate, since good timber will overrun the log measurements and defective timber will fall below this quantity when finally put through the sawmill. As lumber comes from the saws, it is *tallied* according to actual measurements. The log scale measurements are then corrected to the lumber tally sheets by adding or deducting the difference. The resulting costs of the production from the saws is expressed on the basis of the board feet units.

Sawmill Operations.

Sawmill operations follow a similar pattern in cost finding. The logs may be cut into *boards,* which are pieces of lumber 1 inch in thickness; *dimensions,* which are 2 inches thick; *planks,* which are 3 inches thick; and *timbers,* which are 4 inches or more in thickness. The operating costs of the sawmill are composed essentially of the following: labor costs, supplies, maintenance charges, power costs, and amortization of the sawmill. The work of the sawmill is grouped under four headings: sawmill, yards, dry kilns, and planing mills. If the operations are not too extensive, the costs of the logging and transportation and the sawmill may be combined into a single statement.

The main cost accounting problem in this division is one of computing the costs of the inventories and of the quantity produced. At the sawmill there will usually be a supply of logs on hand. The number of logs and their footage are usually based on an *estimate.* The margin of error in this estimate is usually too small to affect the accuracy of the figures to any extent. The log inventory is generally valued at average logging cost, plus the stumpage cost if it has not already been included in the logging cost. In computing the quantity of production at the sawmill, the inventory method may be used, as shown in Illustration A–6.

Illustration A–6

	Grades of Lumber (M Board Feet)				
	A	B	C	D	Total
Inventory at end of month....................	400	500	300	100	1,300
Sales.......................................	400	100	300	200	1,000
Used by mill................................	1,000	800	700	1,500	4,000
Total....................................	1,800	1,400	1,300	1,800	6,300
Less: Inventory at beginning of month...........	500	300	200	300	1,300
Monthly Production......................	1,300	1,100	1,100	1,500	5,000

Shown herewith are: a pro forma statement of the cost of logging operations (Illustration A–7); a pro forma statement of the cost of sawmill operations (Illustration A–8); and a summary statement of operations (Illustration A–9).

Cost Procedure for Flour Mills

Nature of Operations. The operations of a flour mill consist essentially of converting wheat into flour. A bushel of wheat weighs 60 pounds, and a barrel of flour weighs 196 pounds. Flour is the main product of the mill; but there are several grades of flour, some of which are considered in the nature of by-products. Also as a result of milling, a by-product called *offal* is produced, which is sold as feed. Under the cost procedure usually followed, the total cost of manufacturing (milling) is charged to the high-grade flour produced, from which is deducted the sales value of the lower grades and the offal. The lower grades of flour are known as *first clear* and *second clear.* Daily production statements are prepared for each grade of flour, based upon

Illustration A–7

NORTHWESTERN LUMBER MILLS, INC.
STATEMENT OF LOGGING OPERATIONS
For the Month of October, 19—

	Amount	Per Thousand
STUMPAGE COSTS.................................	$ 2,000.00	$0.40
LOGGING COSTS:		
Rigging Ahead....................................	$ 200.00	
Felling and Bucking...............................	5,000.00	
Skidding and Loading.............................	2,000.00	
Equipment Repairs................................	300.00	
Supplies (Saws, Wire Rope, etc.)...................	300.00	
Depreciation.....................................	200.00	
Total Logging Costs..........................	$ 8,000.00	$1.60
TRANSPORTATION COSTS:		
Operating Labor..................................	$ 1,100.00	
Track and Road Maintenance.......................	300.00	
Operating Repairs................................	400.00	
Operating Supplies...............................	500.00	
Depreciation of Equipment........................	300.00	
Amortization of Tracks and Spurs..................	400.00	
Total Transportation Costs.....................	$ 3,000.00	$0.60
OTHER CHARGES:		
Camp Expenses...................................	$ 800.00	
Cruising Expenses for Surveying Stumpage..............	100.00	
Fire Patrol.......................................	100.00	
Taxes, Including Severance Tax......................	300.00	
Insurance..	350.00	
Salaries, Direct and Apportioned....................	2,350.00	
Total Other Expenses.........................	$ 4,000.00	$0.80
Total Cost of Logs Produced..........................	$17,000.00	$3.40
Accounted for as Follows:		
Logs Sold, F.O.B. Log Pond........................	$ 3,400.00	
Logs Kept for the Sawmills.........................	13,600.00	
Total Cost of Logs Produced....................	$17,000.00	
QUANTITY STATEMENT PER LOG SCALE		
Total Logs Produced.................................	5,000,000	
Quantity of Logs Sold to Paper Mills, etc	1,000,000	
Quantity of Logs Kept for Sawmills.....................	4,000,000	
Total Production for Month......................	5,000,000	

Illustration A–8

NORTHWESTERN LUMBER MILLS, INC.
STATEMENT OF SAWMILL OPERATIONS
For the Month of October, 19—

	Amount	Per Thousand*
SAWMILL:		
Mill Labor..	$ 6,200.00	
Power...	800.00	
Supplies..	1,050.00	
Repairs...	900.00	
General Expense.................................	1,000.00	
Depreciation, and/or Amortization..................	1,100.00	
Total......................................	$11,050.00	$2.60
YARDS:		
Labor...	$ 3,000.00	
Repairs...	475.00	
General Expense.................................	500.00	
Depreciation....................................	700.00	
Total......................................	$ 4,675.00	$1.10
DRY KILNS:		
Labor...	$ 5,000.00	
Power...	1,000.00	
Repairs...	500.00	
General Expense.................................	850.00	
Depreciation....................................	2,000.00	
Total......................................	$ 9,350.00	$2.20
PLANING MILL:		
Labor...	$ 7,200.00	
Power...	3,000.00	
Repairs...	800.00	
General Expense.................................	750.00	
Depreciation....................................	1,000.00	
Total......................................	$12,750.00	$3.00
GENERAL OPERATING EXPENSES:		
Salaries..	$ 3,000.00	
Taxes...	1,200.00	
Miscellaneous...................................	50.00	
Total......................................	$ 4,250.00	$1.00
Total Sawmill Costs.............................	**$42,075.00**	**$9.90**

*This statement assumes the averaging of the costs for all types of lumber. If costs are desired by grades, the use of additional columns for each grade may be used. A quantity of production statement is prepared from the sawmill tally sheets. These costs are based upon 4,250,000 board feet production.

Illustration A–9

NORTHWESTERN LUMBER MILLS, INC.
SUMMARY OF OPERATIONS
For the Month of October, 19—

	Scale	Amount	Per Thousand
LOGS:			
Sales...................................	1,000	$ 8,000.00	$ 8.00
Cost of Sales per Schedule................	1,000	3,400.00	3.40
Gross Profit on Sale of Logs...........		$ 4,600.00	$ 4.60
Logs at Mill at Beginning.................	1,000	$ 3,200.00	
Received from Woods per Statement of Logging Costs........................	4,000	13,600.00	
Total..............................	5,000	$16,800.00	$ 3.36
Inventory at End of Month...............	750	2,520.00	
Cost of Logs........................	4,250	$14,280.00	
Log Pond Labor and Expenses.............		4,420.00	
Cost of Logs Sent to Sawmill..........	4,250	$18,700.00	$ 4.40

	Board Feet per Thousand	Amount	Per Thousand
LUMBER PRODUCTION:			
Sales................................	4,500	$99,000.00	$22.00
Cost of Sales:			
Inventory at Beginning of Month..........	350	$ 4,729.00	
Logs Used Above.....................	4,250	18,700.00	
Sawmill Costs per Statement.............		42,075.00	
Total............................	4,600	$65,504.00	
Inventory at End of Month..............	100	1,424.00	
Cost of Sales........................	4,500	$64,080.00	$14.24
Gross Profit on Lumber.............		$34,920.00	$ 7.76

	Units (Cords)	Amount	Per Unit
FUEL PRODUCTION:			
Sales................................	2,000	$10,000.00	$ 5.00
Cost of Sales:			
Inventory at Beginning of Month..........	250	$ 1,000.00	
Labor................................	} 2,100	3,000.00	
Expenses............................		2,000.00	
Total............................	2,350	$ 6,000.00	
Inventory at End of Month..............	350	500.00	
Cost of Sales.....................	2,000	$ 5,500.00	$ 2.75
Gross Profit on Fuel*...............		$ 4,500.00	$ 2.25

* The gross profit on each type of production is carried forward to an income statement.

the market price of wheat and upon the market value of offal and the lower grades of flour.

Cost Accounting Procedure.[4]   Cost cards showing the gross recovery from milling operations are prepared daily for the various grades of flour and are based upon the market value of offal and of clear and low-grade flour and upon the market price of wheat.

To illustrate the method of preparing cost cards for the various grades of flour, the following information is assumed:

Market value of wheat..$ 0.70 per bu.
Market value of offal—average run................................ 11.00 per ton
Market value of first clear....................................... 2.20 per bbl.
Market value of second clear..................................... 1.70 per bbl.
  (4.5 bu. of grain mixture will produce 1 bbl. of flour of all grades and
  74 lbs. of offal.)
Primary grades of flour are..............................100% straight grade
                                                        85% short patent grade
                                                        10% first clear
                                                        5% second clear
Average total expense per barrel is...............................$ 1.00

To compute the cost of 85 percent short patent flour with the foregoing information, the following outline is given:

4.5 bu. of wheat at $0.70...$3.15
Add: Expense, including selling expenses................................. 1.00
    Total wheat expense..$4.15
Deduct: Feed at market: 74 lbs. of offal at $9 ($11 − $2 discount)............. 0.333
Cost of barrel of 100% straight flour....................................$3.817
Deduct: Clears (lower grade) at market:
    10% first clear at $2.00 ($2.20 − $0.20).........................$0.20
    5% clear at $1.50 ($1.70 − $0.20)............................. 0.075   0.275
85% of 1 bbl. of short patent flour......................................$3.542

As indicated, the value of the clears has been discounted 20 cents per barrel in computing the cost of patents.

If 85 percent of a barrel of short patent flour costs $3.542, the cost of producing a full barrel of 85 percent short patent flour will be $4.167 ($3.542 ÷ 85 percent). A cost card is then prepared to get an analysis of the items entering into the material cost of a barrel of flour (see Illustration A–10). Similar formulas and cost cards are prepared for other primary grades of flour.

Cost of Secondary Grades.   Secondary grades of flour are those made of a combination of parts from primary grades. First, it must be determined which of the primary grades are to be used in making the secondary grades. Then apply the percentage of the cost of the primary grades to be used. Assume that Grade C flour is to be made by combin-

---

[4] Taken, with permission from "Flour Milling Costs," by Robert R. McCreight, *N.A.A. Bulletin,* Vol. XXIII, No. 3.

Illustration A–10. Cost Card

	Pounds	Market Price Less Discount	Price	Amount
5.294 bu. of wheat (4.5 bu. ÷ 85% = 5.294)..	317.64		$0.70	$3.7058
Deduct: Low grades and offal:				
10% first clear..........	23.05*	$2.00 bbl.	$1.02 cwt. $0.2351	
5% second clear........	11.52	1.50 bbl.	0.7653 cwt. 0.0882	
27.41% offal...........	87.07	9.00 ton	0.45 cwt. 0.3918	
Total deductions.....	121.64			0.7151

1 bbl. of short patent, 196 lbs..$2.9907
Expense per barrel ($1.00 ÷ 85).. 1.1764

Cost per barrel of 85% flour..$4.1671

*(317.64 × 27.41%) = 87.07 lbs.   (317.64 − 87.07) = 230.57 × 10% = 23.05.

ing 80 percent of Grade A flour and 20 percent of Grade X—first clear flour. The costs of each of these component parts are:

Material cost of Grade A flour.....................................$2.82 bulk
Market value of Grade X flour..................................... 2.20 bulk

The computation for the Grade C would be as follows:

80% of $2.817 equals ($3.817 − $1.00 selling expense)..................$2.2536
20% of $2.20 equals....................................... 0.4400
Total (the material cost of 1 bbl. of Grade C flour)...............$2.6936

In order to get the details of this cost, the percentage of the quantities is calculated as follows:

80% of 4.5 bu. equals 3.6 bu. of wheat at $0.70........................$2.52
Plus: 20% of Grade X equals 39.2 lbs. of flour at $2.20 bbl.............. 0.44
Total..$2.9600
Less: 80% of 74 lbs. offal equals 59.2 lbs. wheat at $0.45 cwt............ 0.2664
Material cost of 1 bbl. of Grade C flour............................$2.6936

Part of a good cost system in the milling business involves a budget of manufacturing costs for the year, which should be controlled for variations on a monthly basis. Some of these variations are due to incorrect estimates of the costs, and some are due to value of production. Part of this budget relates to the manufacturing overhead and to the over- or underabsorbed overhead.

Special Items of Cost. Because of errors in estimated income or discount, or due to certain manufacturing operations, the cost figures shown on the cost cards are not always realized. Since the differences involved are not too great, most of these items appear on the income statement as adjustments to the net profit or loss on flour. These items are: (1) offal sales in excess of the cost card values; (2) realization of discount on offal sales due to rise or fall of offal values between dates of booking the order and actual milling dates; (3) realization of discount on clear flour sales, which is similar to the offal sales discount realization; (4) temper gains due to increase of weight by added moisture used to temper or heat the wheat to improve the milling operations; and (5) variances in freight costs, package costs, and ingredient costs.

APPENDIX

B ⋮ Applied Standard Cost
⋮ Accounting Procedures

Illustrations of Standard Costs Used as Operating Data To indicate how the principles of standard costs used as operating data can be applied by business firms to their accounting work, four illustrations have been given. These have been prepared by the cost accountants in the respective firms and describe the procedures used by these firms.

Illustration 1. The standard cost accounting procedure used by a prominent manufacturer of filing supplies is as follows:

There is carried in stock at all times about 5,500 different finished articles. This comprises about 60 percent of our business; the other 40 percent being made special-to-order.

It is necessary to have a complete stores system to handle all of these products, otherwise it would be easy to lose many thousands of dollars in inventory differences.

We use the order cost system for so-called "special work" where products are made to customers' specifications. Standard costs are used for standard products made for our own warehouse. This means that the standard cost is established for the finished product and for each part used in the finished product and any differences between the standard and actual costs are analyzed and recorded according to the cause of this difference.

Standard costs are established for each kind of raw material purchased, and when material is received it is charged to inventory at the standard cost and any difference between this amount and actual purchase price is charged or credited to Loss or Gain on Purchase Variance. From this point on all movements of raw material are handled at standard cost.

Before a product is released for production the engineering department prepares an operation sheet which shows complete description of the article to be made, kind and quantity of material used, a list of each operation to be performed according to departments and operation numbers, together with machine and tool numbers required to perform the work. The operation sheet also shows time allowance for each operation and standard costs per hundred are computed according to material, labor, and manufacturing burden. The operation sheets are typed on ditto master paper so that copies can be duplicated. Ditto copies of the operation sheets are used for production orders, stores issues, cost sheets, etc. This eliminates the necessity of preparing production orders and stores issues by hand or on a typewriter each time an order is issued to the factory.

Raw material withdrawn from stores against production orders is charged to the Process account at standard costs for the quantity actually issued. At the time the order is closed, material costs as charged to the order are compared with standard for the quantity completed and any difference written off to Loss or Gain on Materials Used.

At the same time that the production department releases the order to the factory they also release prewritten timecards for each operation which are prepared from the ditto master copy of the operation sheet. Timecards are sent to the factory and used by operators for reporting their time and production. Operators are unable to report time against stock production orders without these prewritten timecards. Differences between the standard labor cost and actual earnings of the operator are picked up through payroll distribution of timecards and charged or credited to Loss or Gain on Labor.

All indirect expenses which cannot be applied directly to a production order are charged to a Manufacturing Burden account. The standard hours worked in each department as reported on the timecards are accumulated on the payroll distribution, and at the end of the month an entry is made charging Process account and crediting Manufacturing Burden with the number of standard hours multiplied by standard burden rates for each department. The difference remaining in the Manufacturing Burden account is written off to Loss or Gain on Manufacturing Burden. The standard manufacturing burden rate is established at the beginning of each fiscal year and continued throughout the year unless some radical change occurs which would make it necessary to revise the rate.

Illustration 2.   Standard costs as used by a prominent manufacturer of tags and crepe paper:

We have several main products—that is, Tags, Crepe, Gummed Paper, etc., each requiring a slightly different method of accounting. I will, however, give you a brief description of some of the features of our system.

1. RAW MATERIALS:

We carry all of our book inventories of materials at a standard cost. These costs are made up in October or November for the following year. When the material is received, we charge the inventory accounts at the standard cost and charge or credit any variation between this standard and the actual cost to a Price Variation account. This Price Variation account shows the efficiency of our purchasing department in purchasing materials at or near the standard which they forecast.

2. MATERIALS IN PROCESS:

When these materials are requisitioned by the producing departments, we charge a Commodity-in-Process account at standard. Wherever possible, we set up standards of quantity necessary for any given job. We then measure the materials and deliver only that quantity. Should departments need more materials, the additional amount is charged to their Loss or Gain account. If the department is able to produce more from this quantity, we credit any overrun to this Loss or Gain account. This Loss or Gain account represents the operating efficiency of the department in utilizing materials.

Whenever it is impractical to measure materials precisely, we use a statistical checking basis of determining variations between actual and standard usage. Detailed studies are made at regular intervals by waste study men, which studies are used as a basis for accounting entries as well as a basis for a material usage improvement program.

3. LABOR AND MANUFACTURING EXPENSE:

In common with most other standard cost systems, we make up a standard manufacturing expense rate for each of our operating centers. This manufacturing expense rate is based on the budgeted expenses for the year. Each department is charged with its actual expenses. These expense accounts are credited at the budget. The difference between the charge and the credit represents a loss or gain due to the efficiency of utilizing indirect labor or indirect materials. The offsetting charge to the budget credit is to a Manufacturing Expense Variation account. We credit this Manufacturing Expense Variation account with the earned burden. This earned manufacturing expense is obtained by multiplying the predetermined manufacturing expense rate by the number of hours each center operates. The difference between the charge and the credit in this case represents a loss or gain due to volume. The offsetting charge to the credit to the Manufacturing Expense Variation account is made to a Labor-in-Process-and-Overhead account. This Labor-and-Overhead account is likewise charged with the direct labor payroll. The Labor-and-Overhead account is credited at standard. This credit is obtained by multiplying a predetermined standard rate by the number of pieces produced. The offsetting charge is against the Commodity-in-Process account.

4. MANUFACTURING EXPENSE DEVELOPMENT:

We classify our expenses into two general headings:
a) General Service Expenses.
b) Producing Departmental Expenses.

We list under General Expenses those general administrative and plant maintenance charges which cannot definitely be allocated to any individual producing department foreman. These expenses are outlined on a chart which shows the bases that we use in distributing these expenses to our operating centers. Producing department expenses are those expenses which are directly controlled by a foreman. They will include such things as sweeping, shipping, moving, repairs, experimental, etc.

5. METHOD OF PAYMENT:

Our company has a modified form of piecework payment. We use a punched card system in accumulating our payroll and our statistics for cost control.

Illustration 3. Standard cost accounting procedure used by a prominent shoe manufacturer:

At the beginning of each season or six-month period we prepare a cost catalog of standard costs which is to be used on all shoes made during that season. As these catalogs include hundreds of different prices for the upper leather items, sole leather items, lining and finding items, used on the many styles and types of shoes, we make well over 150,000 different piece rates.

The cost catalog is made up as follows—a standard price per foot for each kind of leather we plan to use during the season is established by the purchasing department. The standard cutting allowance in feet for each style of shoe on each type of leather is determined from analysis of the various patterns to be cut and from past experience. From these figures, the cost of each of the items of upper stock is determined for the catalog. The same general plan is used in determining the cost of various items of linings, trimmings, bottom stock and findings special.

Labor piece rates are determined from time studies and from negotiations with the Shoe Workers' Union, and from these the piece labor allowance for each style of shoe made from the various leathers and on the various lasts is computed.

A small percentage of daywork for each shoe is determined by analysis and from previous experience.

A variable manufacturing expense or overhead budget is determined from past experience and from adjustments in these expenses which we have made or propose to make. The total budget for the season is compared with a moving average of shipments for the previous five years, and a per pair cost for variable manufacturing expense determined for the cost catalog. All of the styles within each grade of shoes are assigned the same variable manufacturing expense charge, but the charge per pair varies between the grades of shoes in approximately the same ratio as the average labor per pair within each grade. In other words, grades of shoes calling for a higher labor cost are assigned a higher overhead.

The factory costs for production purposes are determined as outlined above. For pricing purposes, an allowance for fixed overheads is then calculated with the higher priced lines being assigned a larger amount of fixed overhead.

At the end of each month, the total of the standard costs for the pairs produced that month is compared with the actual material used and payroll spent. Variations from the standards are then shown on the monthly financial statements.

Most of our labor is paid by the piece. Each operator as he completes the work on a case of shoes, clips off a small coupon, and at the end of the week's work, he places all the coupons he has clipped off for the week in an envelope, which he drops in a box at the pay office. Most of our shoes are made in 12-pair cases, but if a case contains a greater or smaller number than the 12 pairs, this change is indicated by a different color coupon, one color for each different number of pairs.

Dayworkers are paid by the hour on timecards. All of our operators are paid by check, and at the end of each week the earnings are determined by the addition of the piecework coupons turned in during the week, or in the case of dayworkers by the number of days worked as indicated by the timecards. The pay checks for each department are written at one time, and carboned through on to journal sheets for that department. At the end of the month, the necessary journal entries are prepared and delivered to the accounting department for posting to the proper accounts.

Application of Basic
Standard Costs in
a Steel Mill

Illustration 4. The dual or memorandum standard cost procedure used by a large steel manufacturer is described below. Because this procedure represents in detail and in excellent form the dual or memorandum method of recording standard costs, a more complete description of the procedure is given.[1]

The strip mill in which this system (standard costs) has been applied receives steel in the form of billets, which are generally rectangular in cross section and are of various lengths, weighing from 150 pounds to 2,000 pounds each. These billets are first hot rolled into hot rolled strips in any of three hot mills, depending upon the size of the finished product.

The next operation on all material that is to be further processed is a pickling or cleaning operation. The steel is then successively cold rolled, annealed, and finally slit into a finished size. It may also be leveled, or flattened, and it may be copper plated in this particular plant.

The product of the mill is sold in various stages of manufacture, such as rolled, hot rolled pickled and oiled, cold rolled, and polished. The steel itself may be of any of approximately 125 individual analyses, falling within the following general classifications:

Carbon Steels	*Electrical (Silicon) Steels*
Low carbon	Field Grade
High carbon	Armature Grade
Stainless Steels	Dynamo
Chrome	Transformer
Chrome Nickel	*Magnetic and Other Special Alloys*

PREPARING THE STANDARD COST PLAN

As the first step in the installation of the plan, the important sales-billed classes were determined, and finally about twenty-five product groups or lines were chosen as being sufficiently important for separate treatment in the inventory accounts.

Next the departmentalization of the plant was studied, and finally some twenty-nine direct production centers were established and some twenty-six indirect or nonproductive centers.

The distribution of overhead was carefully analyzed, and new bases were determined wherever this was thought advisable. Then after a satisfactory distribution to production centers had been arranged, and after extended study of activity in these centers, in consultation with the management, normal activity of each center was agreed upon and a normal burden [manufacturing expense] rate in terms of dollars per hour of operation was established. . . .

Production records for several years were reviewed and time standards were established for any size and any type of product in each center, based upon statistics. The standard times so determined were then extended at the average earned rate for the crew and factored for the normal burden rate to determine,

---

[1] Taken, with permission, from a report by E. J. Hanley, Secretary and Treasurer, Allegheny Ludlum Steel Corporation, printed in the *N.A.A. Bulletin,* Vol. XXII, No. 21.

finally, a dollar standard for any size or grade of material in each operation. In only one operation, slitting, was any allowance for losses included in the standard. The raw materials in use were also analyzed and standard costs established for each of them. All mill routines were thoroughly studied and checked, and a scrap routine was devised to make sure that all scrap would be properly classified and carefully weighed.

When the job was completed, there had been established about 50,000 standards for labor and burden and about 2,000 standards for material.

OPERATION OF THE STANDARD COST PROCEDURE

When an order is received at the mill, it is scheduled and routed. The order is then passed on to the cost clerk, who really "job costs" it—that is to say, he calculates a standard cost based on the route previously established. A copy of a typical cost card is shown in Exhibit 1 [see Illustration B–1]. This card is placed in the active standard file and is used daily to cost the production reports and finally to cost sales for the particular order.

Actual expenditures for a given product line or inventory account, including overhead at normal rates, are charged to the proper inventory accounts. In the illustrated case Account No. 281, high carbon, cold rolled annealed material is used. These inventory accounts are further subdivided between labor and burden on the one hand, and material on the other. Similar accounts are maintained at standard and are charged for the actual quantities involved at the standard costs appearing on the cost card, Exhibit 1.

When material is scrapped in any operation, the labor and burden cost to that point, known as "prior labor and burden," is removed from the standard labor and burden account, a contra entry being made to the standard cost control. (The standard cost books carry a standard cost control account, to which contra entries are made in order that these accounts may be self-balancing.) Simultaneously, the standard cost of material is removed from the standard material inventory with appropriate contra entries to the control account. Only the scrap value of material scrapped is removed from the actual inventory account, however, and as a consequence at the end of any period when the ratio to be applied to the standard cost of sales is determined, this ratio picks up the material loss. As an example, assume that the actual cost of material on a particular order to a certain point is $100.00. Assume also that the standard cost of this material is $100.00. At this point there is a $100.00 debit balance in both the standard material and in the actual material account. Assume further that 20 percent of the material is scrapped and that the scrap value is $5.00. The standard value of the material scrapped would be $20.00, which would be removed from the standard inventory account, leaving a balance of $80.00. The scrap value of the material is $5.00 and that removed from the actual inventory account leaves a balance of $95.00. When the material is shipped, there is a ratio of $95.00 to $80.00, or 118 percent plus. The cost of sales of $80.00 is factored by this percentage so that the actual account would be relieved of the amount $95.00. This illustrates how losses are picked up by the variance percentages.

THE PLAN AT WORK

Now for an actual example of the workings of the cost plan. Exhibit 1 is a cost card of 75,000 pounds of copper plated material for the Blank Company—our order 64321Z. The symbol 12C440 notifies the cost department

Illustration B–1

ALLEGHENY LUDLUM STEEL CORPORATION
Standard Cost per Thousand Pounds

Exhibit 1

Customer __The Blank Company__ Order No. __64321 Z__
__Dead Soft Setting Pass Sheared Coils__ Prod. Class __281—12C440__

H.R. Width __6"__ H.R. Ga. __.078__ Fin. Width __1.4385__ Fin. Ga. __.014__ Weight __75000#__
Date __10/31/__

Steel __Carbon__ Weight __1000#__ Kind __6 x 3 x 20'__

Memo	Center	Size	Mtl.	L. & Br.	P. L. & Br.	Repl.
	6110	078	$14 10	$ 3 92	$	
	6150'			2 01	3 92	
Acid	42		14 52			
	6303	014		7 20	5 93	
	6241			5 20	13 13	
($3.52)	22#Cu		17 65		12 84	
	6180			1 41	18 04	
Total						

Memo	Center	Size	Mtl.	L. & Br.	P. L. & Br.	Repl.
	6242		$	3 01	19 45	
	6212			4 10	22 46	
	Shear Loss	15#	17 92		22 80	
	6250			1 01	26 90	
					27 91	
Total			$17 92		$27 91	

of the schedule that is to be followed in processing this order. Material falls into product class No. 281; widths and gauges are indicated, and also the kind of material and the size of billet. In this instance, we have a compound material, of which the steel accounts for 978 pounds, and plating material 22 pounds. (All figures on this card are fictitious and are shown for illustrative purposes only.)

The operations involved on this order are:

Code	Operation	Department	Code	Operation	Department
6110	Hot rolling	12″ Mill	6180	Annealing	Box Anneal
6150	Pickling	12″ Pickle	6242	Wiping	Wipers
6303	Cold rolling	7½″ Steckel Mill	6212	Slitting	Slitters
6241	Plating	Plating Dept.	6250	Wholesale and shipping	

From our file of standards the cost clerk prepares this cost card showing (1) the material cost at each operation during which the material cost changes, (2) the cumulative material cost, (3) the labor and burden for each operation, and (4) the labor and burden accumulated to the prior operation, called "prior labor and burden." It is to be noted that up to center 6241 the cost is based on 1,000 pounds of steel. At center 6241 the material is combined with plating material, and from there on the cost is based upon 978 pounds of steel and 22 pounds of plating material. At center 6212 where material is slit, a definite allowance is included for the loss, and as a result the standard cost per 1,000 pounds of both material and labor and burden are increased from there on to compensate for this allowance.

In Exhibit 2 [Illustration B–2] the whole plan is outlined and tied in with the cost card appearing as Figure A. Figure I shows two parallel accounts, in one of which appears the actual cost of material purchased and in the other the standard cost of the same material. As material is purchased and the account "Billets and Bands Purchased" debited at standard, a corresponding entry is made to Standard Cost Control—Figure K, entry N. Then, as material is transferred into process, the weight so transferred is shown on production reports and an entry is made to the proper work-in-process account, No. 281—Figure F, for actual pounds at standard cost. Simultaneously, the actual cost of material is transferred from the raw material accounts to the actual work-in-process account, Figure F, the raw material account being relieved on the basis of the standard cost of material transferred factored by the ratio obtained at the close of the period between the balance in the actual raw material account and the balance in the standard raw material account. For whatever actual material may be scrapped an appropriate credit is made to the proper work-in-process material account, Figure F, at scrap value.

Actual payroll, Figure H, is reported separately as direct labor and indirect labor. Further direct labor is also reported directly against major product groups departmentally and is allocated to product lines departmentally on the basis of relative standard labor costs for the individual lines within the product group. It is then accumulated by lines for all departments, Figure D, and is thereafter charged to the proper work-in-process account, Figure F. Expenditures for indirect labor, together with other items of expense, are collected departmentally and summarized as burden, Figure G. Burden absorbed, Figure J, is then determined by multiplying actual man or machine hours by the normal burden rate and the burden absorbed is accumulated by product classes in each production center, Figure C. It is then summarized by material classes from all departments, Figure D, and is charged to the appropriate work-in-process account, Figure F.

The difference between the normal burden or burden absorbed, Figure J, and actual burden, Figure G, is transferred directly to profit and loss and does not enter the cost picture further.

All entries to the standard cost accounts, except the entry to account "Billets and Bands Purchased," originate with the production reports from the mill. Each department reports by order number, beginning and ending weights of material, Figure B, and reference is made to cost cards to price these reports at standard.

On operations where material is introduced into process, actual material weight is extended at standard, and likewise the weight of acid and copper, as has already been mentioned. The standard labor and burden information developed from the order is summarized within the departments for the product class, Figure C, and then further summarized by product classes from all departments, Figure D. The weight loss on each item is extended at the standard material cost and also at the prior labor and burden loss. Standard slit loss, where involved. is calculated, and variations from standard slit loss in dollars determined. Appropriate entries are then made to the standard work-in-process account, Figure F. A corresponding credit for the standard labor and burden charge is made to the standard cost control. A credit is made to standard material for the standard value of the material loss and another credit to standard labor and burden for the prior labor and burden loss at standard, with a corresponding entry in each case to standard cost control. Variation from standard slit loss is treated similarly. All this information, except standard labor and burden, is summarized directly by product lines, Figure D, and is entered into work-in-process account, Figure F.

The work-in-process accounts now consist of total actual cost, including burden at normal, while the standard cost accounts include only the standard cost of material and standard labor and burden covering the material actually in the inventory with no allowance for loss material, with the exception of the slitting loss referred to heretofore. The ratios of the balances in the actual accounts and in the standard accounts represent variations for all reasons, that is to say, on account of performance and on account of material scrapped or removed from process for any reason.

During the accounting period, in this case a month, invoices have been priced at standard material cost and standard labor and burden cost, as summarized on the cost cards, and in this manner the standard cost of sales has been determined. At the close of the month "actual versus standard" ratios are computed, based on the beginning balance plus the various charges in the work-in-process accounts, Figure F. Actual cost of sales accounts are then charged on the basis of standard cost factored by these ratios with appropriate credits to actual work-in-process accounts. The corresponding standard entries are again made to standard cost control.

Perhaps the matter of parallel accounts has been unduly emphasized in this paper in order to make clear the mechanics of this cost plan. The facts are that control accounts only are duplicated and the accounting for dual values does not involve duplication of accounting computations. In any standard cost plan, the detail work involves the accumulation of standard cost information. The accumu-

Illustration B-3

A   Exhibit 3

ALLEGHENY LUDLUM STEEL CORPORATION
West Leechburg Division
PRODUCTIVE LABOR REPORT   Period: Nov. 17–30, 19—

Center	Department and Product Group	Actual	Standard	Ratio	Variation Total	Variation Time	Variation Rates
6100	9" Hot Mill						
	Carbon	$0,000	$0,000	000	$ 000	$000	$ 000
6110	12" Hot Mill						
	Carbon	0,000	0,000	00	0,000	000	0,000
	Silicon	0,000	0,000	000	00	00	0
	Chrome	0,000	0,000	000	000	00	000
		0,000		000	000	000	00

B

ALLEGHENY LUDLUM STEEL CORPORATION
West Leechburg Division
MATERIAL LOSSES   Month of November, 19—

Center	Department and Product Group	Pounds Lost	Yield %	Losses in Dollars Material	Losses in Dollars Prior Labor & Burden	Losses in Dollars Total	Losses in Dollars Recovered	Losses in Dollars Net Loss
6100	9" Hot Mill							
	Carbon Steel	00,000	00.00	$0,000	—	$0,000	$0,000	$0,000
6110	12" Hot Mill							
	Carbon Steel	0,000	00.00	000	—	000	000	000
	Silicon Steel	000	00.00		—	000	000	000

C

ALLEGHENY LUDLUM STEEL CORPORATION
West Leechburg Division
GROSS PROFIT—BY CLASSES OF PRODUCT   Month of November, 19—

Class	Product	Net Sales Pounds	Net Sales Dollars	$ Price per 1,000#	Gross Profit Dollars	Gross Profit % to S.B.
231	Plain H.R.—Low Car. Strip	0,000,000	000,000	00.00	00,000	00
232	Plain H.R.—High Car. Strip	0,000,000	000,000	00.00	0,000	00
241		000,000	00,000	00.00	0,000	00
242	P & O—Low Car. Strip	00,000	0,000	00.00	000	00
243	P & O—High Car. Strip					00

lation of so-called "actuals" in this particular application is extremely simple, as the units for which such costs are accumulated are not jobs, as in job costs, but rather some larger unit, such as the product line.

Available Reports

With respect to the reports that are available, Exhibit 3 [Illustration B–3] indicates the three that are regularly issued. Figure A, a report of productive labor, is issued at the close of each pay period, in this case every two weeks. It compares actual labor with standard labor by major product lines in each department. The ratio of actual to standard is shown, the dollar variance occasioned by more time being used than the standard contemplated or higher than standard rates per hour being paid. The calculation of the variance analysis is made as follows: Actual labor cost and actual man-hours are obtained from the payroll by departments for major product classes; standard labor and burden combined are similarly summarized from the standard cost detail; standard labor cost is then obtained by departments by factoring standard labor and burden to remove burden. Actual hours, then, times the dfifference between actual labor rates per hour and standard labor rates per hour is the variation due to rates. The difference between total variance and this amount is the variance due to time.

Figure B on Exhibit 3 shows the report of material losses by departments and by major product lines. This report is made monthly and is really a summary of all losses at standard and is obtained from the standard cost detail. Figure C of Exhibit 3 is a classified income statement showing the gross profit for each product.

APPENDIX

C Program of Cost Accounting Reports

The following pages illustrate the reports used by a large textile manufacturing company and supplement the discussion given in the chapter on managerial reports (pages 598–627). This plan is so comprehensive and practical that it is given in detail for its instructional value.

THE A. B. C. MANUFACTURING COMPANY
OPERATING REPORTS—MAY, 19—

Report No. 1

STATEMENT OF OPERATIONS

SALES DIVISION		
	Amounts	Detailed Rept. No.
Sales:		
Gross sales......................................	$334,326.00	2
Less: Returns and allowances	2,275.00*	3
Net sales......................................	$332,051.00	
Cost of sales:		
Standard cost of net sales.........................	289,237.00*	
Gross profit	$ 42,814.00	4
Selling expenses.................................	32,044.00*	5 and 6
Trading profit..................................	$ 10,770.00	

MANUFACTURING DIVISION		
Variations from standard costs:		
Price variations:		
Raw materials......................$6,859.00		
Manufacturing materials.............. 1,384.00	$ 8,243.00	7
Usage variations—raw materials.........$1,408.00*	1,408.00*	8
Cost variations:		
Labor.............................$ 981.00		
Manufacturing materials.............. 1,331.00*		
Burden 6,415.00	6,065.00	9 and 10
Damages:		
Finished damages produced $8,654.00*		
Less: Damages sold.................. 5,909.00	2,745.00*	11
Operating profit..................................	$ 20,925.00	

*Denotes red figures.

THE A. B. C. MANUFACTURING COMPANY
OPERATING REPORTS—MAY, 19—

Report No. 2

SALES ANALYSIS

Product No.	Quota	Sales	Per Cent of Quota
1.............................	$ 60,000.00	$ 67,324.00	112
2.............................	30,000.00	25,833.00	86
3.............................	30,000.00	36,325.00	121
4.............................	40,000.00	39,823.00	99½
5.............................	10,000.00	7,039.00	70
6.............................	120,000.00	144,012.00	120
7.............................	10,000.00	13,970.00	140
Total.....................	$300,000.00	$334,326.00	111 (av.)

Report No. 3

RETURNS AND ALLOWANCES ANALYSIS

Reason	No. of Credits	Amount
Damaged..................................	97	$ 273.00
Mismated.................................	3	37.00
Off color.................................	18	339.00
Short Length	7	229.00
Error in shipping..........................	8	394.00
Order duplicated	2	167.00
Returned by permission.....................	8	162.00
Error in billing............................	3	64.00
Freight allowances.........................	13	98.00
Price allowances	8	27.00
C.O.D.'s returned..........................	2	125.00
Late delivery	9	360.00
Total................................	178	$2,275.00

THE A. B. C. MANUFACTURING COMPANY
OPERATING REPORTS—MAY, 19—

GROSS PROFIT ANALYSIS

	Net Sales		Gross Profit	
	Amount	% of Total	Amount	% of Sales
Retail:				
Product No. 1	$ 30,090.00	9.1	$ 5,872.00	19.5
Product No. 2	11,546.00	3.5	2,364.00	20.4
Product No. 3	16,235.00	4.9	2,967.00	18.3
Product No. 4	17,798.00	5.4	3,298.00	18.5
Product No. 5	3,146.00	0.9	600.00	19.1
Product No. 6	64,365.00	19.4	12,167.00	18.9
Product No. 7	6,244.00	1.9	525.00	8.4
	$149,424.00	45.1	$27,793.00	18.6
Wholesale:				
Product No. 1	23,403.00	7.0	2,162.00	9.2
Product No. 2	8,980.00	2.7	843.00	9.4
Product No. 3	12,627.00	3.8	1,205.00	9.5
Product No. 4	13,843.00	4.2	1,162.00	8.4
Product No. 5	2,447.00	0.7	264.00	10.8
Product No. 6	50,062.00	15.1	4,867.00	9.7
Product No. 7	4,856.00	1.5	305.00	6.3
	$116,218.00	35.0	$10,808.00	9.3
Catalogue and chain stores:				
Product No. 1	13,373.00	4.0	864.00	6.5
Product No. 2	5,130.00	1.5	303.00	5.9
Product No. 3	7,216.00	2.2	450.00	6.2
Product No. 4	7,910.00	2.4	488.00	6.2
Product No. 5	1,398.00	0.4	118.00	8.4
Product No. 6	28,607.00	8.6	1,843.00	6.4
Product No. 7	2,775.00	0.8	147.00	5.3
	$ 66,409.00	19.9	$ 4,213.00	6.3
Total	$332,051.00	100.0 (av.)	$42,814.00	12.9 (av.)

THE A. B. C. MANUFACTURING COMPANY
OPERATING REPORTS—MAY, 19—

Report No. 5

SELLING EXPENSE ANALYSIS

Item	Summary			
	Budget	Actual	Over	Under
Salesmen:				
Travel expenses............	$ 5,000.00	$ 4,664.00		$ 336.00
Salaries and commissions.....	10,843.00	10,557.00		286.00
Social security tax..........	284.00	278.00		6.00
Sales offices:				
New York*	2,367.00	2,451.00	$ 84.00	
Chicago..................	308.00	278.00		30.00
Los Angeles..............	1,173.00	1,263.00	90.00	
General:				
Advertising..............	5,000.00	5,000.00		
Samples..................	973.00	1,065.00	92.00	
Conventions..............	2,373.00	1,992.00		381.00
Management:				
Travel expenses...........	300.00	282.00		18.00
Salaries..................	4,167.00	4,214.00	47.00	
Total..............	$32,788.00	$32,044.00	$313.00	$1,057.00

*See sample departmental report No. 6.

Report No. 6

SELLING EXPENSE ANALYSIS—NEW YORK OFFICE

Item	Budget	Actual	Over	Under
Salaries:				
Floor salesmen............	$ 605.00	$ 600.00		$ 5.00
Office....................	750.00	750.00		
Social security tax.........	39.00	37.00		2.00
Rent......................	677.00	677.00		
Light.....................	55.00	50.00		5.00
Repairs...................	25.00	36.00	$11.00	
Stationery................	20.00	15.00		5.00
Entertaining..............	100.00	190.00	90.00	
Depreciation..............	80.00	80.00		
Insurance.................	10.00	10.00		
Taxes.....................	6.00	6.00		
Total..................	$2,367.00	$2,451.00	$101.00	$17.00

THE A. B. C. MANUFACTURING COMPANY

OPERATING REPORTS—MAY, 19—

Report No. 7

PRICE VARIATIONS—MATERIALS

	Standard Price	Actual Price	Quantity Purchased	Total Value at Standard	Total Value at Actual	Price Variations
Raw Material:						
Warp yarn:						
10/2 carded............	$0.28	$0.248	54,136	$15,158.00	$13,426.00	$1,732.00
20/2 carded............	0.31	0.30	10,051	3,116.00	3,015.00	101.00
30/2 carded............	0.36	0.355	25,628	9,226.00	9,098.00	128.00
40/2 combed...........	0.50	0.41	2,107	1,054.00	864.00	190.00
Spool yarn:						
20/2 carded............	0.31	0.245	39,371	12,205.00	9,646.00	2,559.00
30/2 carded............	0.36	0.355	60,033	21,612.00	21,312.00	300.00
40/2 combed...........	0.50	0.41	5,003	2,502.00	2,051.00	451.00
50/2 combed...........	0.55	0.46	3,531	1,942.00	1,624.00	318.00
60/2 combed...........	0.60	0.52	5,362	3,217.00	2,788.00	429.00
70/2 combed...........	0.72	0.64	893	621.00	572.00	49.00
Bobbin yarn:						
80/2 combed...........	0.95	0.92	14,780	14,041.00	13,598.00	443.00
90/2 combed...........	1.06	1.03	1,891	2,004.00	1,948.00	56.00
100/2 combed..........	1.19	1.16	1,849	2,200.00	2,145.00	55.00
110/2 combed..........	1.45	1.40	974	1,412.00	1,364.00	48.00
Manufacturing materials:						
Boxes.................	0.039	0.033	38,901	1,551.00	1,284.00	267.00
Cartons...............	0.203	0.181	4,927	1,001.00	891.00	110.00
Cellophane............	0.01	0.0077	16,000	160.00	123.00	37.00
Cord and twine.........	0.38	0.305	205	78.00	63.00	15.00
Dyes..................	0.20	0.167	14,445	2,889.00	2,412.00	477.00
Envelopes.............	0.0056	0.0052	171,200	959.00	890.00	69.00
Paper.................	0.091	0.043	208	19.00	9.00	10.00
Soap..................	0.08	0.056	13,320	1,066.00	746.00	320.00
Tape..................	1.64	1.48	118	193.00	175.00	18.00
Thread................	0.565	0.501	953	539.00	478.00	61.00
Total...............	....	....	....	$98,765.00	$90,522.00	$8,243.00

THE A. B. C. MANUFACTURING COMPANY
OPERATING REPORTS—MAY, 19—

Report No. 8

USAGE VARIATIONS—RAW MATERIALS

Loom No.	Standard Cost Allowance, Including Waste	Actual Usage at Standard Prices	Usage Variation	Per Cent of Standard
1............	$ 4,006.00	$ 3,993.00	$ 13.00	99.7
2............	4,137.00	4,298.00	161.00*	103.9
3............	4,692.00	4,623.00	69.00	98.5
4............	3,675.00	3,856.00	181.00*	104.9
5............	4,322.00	4,592.00	270.00*	106.2
6............	3,684.00	3,713.00	29.00*	100.7
7............	5,003.00	4,967.00	36.00	99.3
8............	4,751.00	4,683.00	68.00	98.5
9............	3,573.00	3,693.00	120.00*	103.4
10............	3,798.00	3,903.00	105.00*	102.8
11............	3,674.00	3,715.00	41.00*	101.1
12............	3,916.00	4,003.00	87.00*	102.2
13............	4,875.00	4,822.00	53.00	98.9
14............	5,163.00	5,101.00	62.00	98.8
15............	4,572.00	4,730.00	158.00*	103.5
16............	4,564.00	4,673.00	109.00*	102.3
17............	5,003.00	5,180.00	177.00*	103.5
18............	4,738.00	4,862.00	124.00*	102.6
19............	3,786.00	3,973.00	187.00*	104.9
20............	4,803.00	4,763.00	40.00	99.1
Total.....	$86,735.00	$88,143.00	$1,408.00*	101.6 (av.)

*Denotes red figures.

Report No. 9

ANALYSIS OF COST VARIATIONS BY COST CENTERS

	Standard Cost	Actual Cost	Cause of Variations				Foremen's Budget	
			Cost Variations	Level of Operations	Management Changes	Foremen's Efficiency	Budget Allowance	% of Actual of Budget
Service cost centers:								
Boiler	$ 6,196.00	$ 5,550.00	$ 646.00	$ 302.00	$ 60.00*	$ 404.00	$ 5,954.00	93.2
Power	2,343.00	2,144.00	199.00	152.00	40.00*	87.00	2,231.00	96.1
Plant and building	2,649.00	2,231.00	418.00	164.00	47.00*	301.00	2,532.00	88.1
Machine	2,097.00	1,326.00	771.00	132.00	52.00*	691.00	2,017.00	65.7
Trucking	587.00	687.00	100.00*	40.00		140.00*	547.00	125.6
Design	5,260.00	5,099.00	161.00	203.00	123.00*	81.00	5,180.00	98.4
Pattern	4,660.00	3,958.00	702.00	286.00	140.00*	556.00	4,514.00	87.7
General administration	28,305.00	27,206.00	1,099.00	447.00	240.00*	892.00	28,098.00	96.8
Total	$ 52,097.00	$ 48,201.00	$3,896.00	$1,726.00	$ 702.00*	$2,872.00	$ 51,073.00	94.4 (av.)
Transferred to productive cost centers	52,097.00*	48,201.00*	3,896.00*					
Productive cost centers:								
Yarn preparation†	4,440.00	4,250.00	190.00	220.00	64.00*	34.00	4,284.00	99.2
Bobbin	7,760.00	7,409.00	351.00	308.00	101.00*	144.00	7,553.00	98.1
Warp	1,594.00	1,395.00	199.00	137.00	45.00*	107.00	1,502.00	92.9
Weaving	55,509.00	50,875.00	4,634.00	2,300.00	300.00*	2,634.00	53,509.00	95.1
Mending	3,375.00	3,331.00	44.00	228.00	15.00*	169.00*	3,162.00	105.3
Bleach	4,733.00	4,541.00	192.00	270.00		78.00*	4,463.00	101.7
Dress	16,876.00	17,546.00	670.00*	320.00	200.00*	790.00*	16,756.00	104.7
Cutting and splitting	17,056.00	16,891.00	165.00	350.00	226.00*	41.00	16,932.00	99.8
Finishing	17,835.00	17,597.00	238.00	393.00	37.00*	118.00*	17,479.00	100.7
Wrap and label	9,675.00	9,594.00	81.00	364.00	122.00*	161.00*	9,433.00	101.7
Stockroom	6,011.00	5,370.00	641.00	260.00		381.00	5,751.00	93.3
Grand total	$144,864.00	$138,799.00	$6,065.00	$5,150.00	$1,110.00*	$2,025.00	$140,824.00	98.6 (av.)

*Denotes red figures.
†See departmental report No. 10.

THE A. B. C. MANUFACTURING COMPANY
OPERATING REPORTS—MAY, 19—

FOREMEN'S BUDGET
Report No. 10   YARN PREPARATION COST CENTER

	Budget Allowance	Actual Cost	Over Budget	Under Budget
Labor:				
Winding spool yarn.............	$1,307.00	$1,241.00		$ 66.00
Winding warp yarn.............	172.00	139.00		33.00
Winding bobbin yarn............	125.00	125.00		
Backwinding...................	85.00	85.00		
Stripping......................	50.00	50.00		
Materials:				
Paper.........................	4.00	2.00		2.00
Sizing.........................	35.00	40.00	$ 5.00	
Burden:				
Supervision....................	290.00	364.00	74.00	
Handling......................	331.00	229.00		102.00
Repairs........................	42.00	21.00		21.00
Depreciation...................	470.00	429.00		41.00
Insurance......................	25.00	23˙00		2.00
Taxes.........................	228.00	229.00	1.00	
Share of boiler.................	132.00	124.00		8.00
Share of power.................	117.00	116.00		1.00
Share of plant and building.......	209.00	186.00		23.00
Share of general administration	818.00	847.00	29.00	
Total.....................	$4,440.00	$4,250.00	$109.00	$299.00

A. B. C. MANUFACTURING COMPANY
OPERATING REPORTS—MAY, 19—

Report No. 11

ANALYSIS OF FINISHED PRODUCTS
DAMAGED IN COURSE OF MANUFACTURING OPERATIONS

Loom No.	Standard Cost Value of Production	Weaving Damages		Finish Damages		Total Damages
		Value	% of Production	Value	% of Production	% of Production
1......	$ 13,700.00	$ 300.00*	2.2	....	....	2.2
2......	13,963.00	315.00*	2.3	....	....	2.3
3......	14,573.00	573.00*	3.9	$ 200.00*	1.4	5.3
4......	13,273.00	402.00*	3.0	168.00*	1.3	4.3
5......	14,007.00	296.00*	2.1	28.00*	0.2	2.3
6......	13,566.00	250.00*	1.8	96.00*	0.7	2.5
7......	14,500.00	266.00*	1.8	....	....	1.8
8......	14,473.00	403.00*	2.8	....	....	2.8
9......	13,109.00	294.00*	2.2	72.00*	0.5	2.7
10......	13,342.00	180.00*	1.3	156.00*	1.2	2.5
11......	12,973.00	216.00*	1.7	307.00*	2.4	4.1
12......	13,496.00	223.00*	1.7	62.00*	0.5	2.2
13......	14,750.00	329.00*	2.2	218.00*	1.5	3.7
14......	14,896.00	287.00*	1.9	162.00*	1.1	3.0
15......	13,921.00	104.00*	0.7	107.00*	0.7	1.4
16......	14,377.00	502.00*	3.5	204.00*	1.4	4.9
17......	14,502.00	490.00*	3.4	152.00*	1.0	4.4
18......	14,042.00	360.00*	2.6	117.00*	0.8	3.4
19......	13,462.00	200.00*	1.5	....	....	1.5
20......	13,723.00	510.00*	3.7	105.00*	0.8	4.5
Total..	$278,648.00	$6,500.00*	2.3 (av.)	$2,154.00*	0.8 (av.)	3.1 (av.)
Total damages..						$8,654.00

*Denotes red figures.

Report No. 12

IDLE MACHINE REPORT
DEPARTMENT #106 CUTTING

For month ending July 31, 19—
Foreman: A. B. Howard

Machine No.	Standard Hours	Actual Hours			Idle Hours							% of Standard	Burden Rate for Idle Time	Cost of Idle Time	Remarks
		Regular	Over-time	Total	No Operator	No Materials	Repairs	Awaiting Setup	Awaiting Tools	Awaiting Instructions	Total				
C-102	160	160		160											O.K.
C-103	160	150		150		10					10	6.25	$3.10	$31.00	Material held up in drilling dept.
C-104	160	160		160											
F-110	160	140		140				20			20	12.5	1.80	36.00	Improper scheduling.
F-111	130	160	15	175									1.80	27.00*	To make up loss of Mach. #110.
F-112	130	125		130					3	2	5	3.85	1.80	9.00	Job instructions not on hand.
Total	900	895	15	915		10		20	3	2	35	2.77		49.00	

* Credit for overtime.

INDEX

Index

This book has been set on the Linotype in 12 and 10 point Garamond No. 3, leaded 1 point. Chapter numbers and titles and section titles are in 18 point Lydian Bold italics; section numbers are in 18 point Lydian. The size of the type page is 27 by 47 picas.